Scottish Church Attitudes to Sex, Marriage and the Family

Scottish Church Attitudes to Sex, Marriage and the Family

1850-1914

KENNETH M. BOYD

JOHN DONALD PUBLISHERS LTD

EDINBURGH

To Pat

ISBN 0 85976 056 1

Printed in Great Britain by Bell & Bain Ltd., Glasgow

Preface

WHAT was the nineteenth-century Scottish church's attitude to sex, marriage and the family? This book tries to provide part of the answer by examining what was said on the subject by the four Presbyterian denominations whose members and adherents comprised the great majority of churchgoing people in Scotland between 1850 and 1914.

The largest and still probably the most influential of these denominations was the Established *Church of Scotland*, the national church since the Reformation of 1560 and unquestionably Presbyterian since the Revolution Settlement of 1690. During the eighteenth century, leadership of the Established church had passed to the Moderates, a party with Enlightenment ideals but not over-sensitive to their more Evangelical and democratic colleagues. Under the Moderates the Church of Scotland lost the allegiance of a substantial minority of its members, and a number of dissenting Presbyterian churches were set up.

The last denomination to secede from the Established church and also the largest, was the *Free Church of Scotland*. This energetic and vociferous body was constituted at the Disruption of 1843, partly as a result of Evangelical revival, but in particular over the question of the people's right to elect their own ministers. Despite the Enlightenment attitudes of the Moderates (by now a declining band) the Disruption involved no significant disagreement about Calvinist theology, and many of those who 'came out' in 1843 (including their leader, Thomas Chalmers) continued to believe in the principle of an Established church. During the later nineteenth century Free Church adherence to this principle grew weaker and the church as a whole became less Calvinist. In the Highlands however, where the Free Church was supreme, traditional beliefs persisted; and this led, in 1892, to a further small secession, this time from the Free Church by the Free Presbyterians.

The third major Presbyterian denomination of the period was much more unequivocally opposed to the Establishment principle and was thus, in Scottish ecclesiastical parlance, a Voluntary church. The *United Presbyterian Church* had been constituted in 1847 as a result of union between bodies which had seceded from the Establishment and from one another during the eighteenth century, for various reasons including patronage. (Lay patronage of church appointments dated from the Middle Ages, was twice abolished in the seventeenth century, but was restored in 1712 after the union of the Scottish and English parliaments: Established church congregations did not gain the right to elect their own ministers until 1874). Although some of these eighteenth-century bodies had been very Calvinist indeed, the nineteenth-century United Presbyterians were the first of the churches openly to liberalise their Calvinist heritage, a fact which hindered union between them and the Free Church.

In 1900 the Free Church and the United Presbyterians eventually merged to form the *United Free Church*. Despite formal differences, particularly on the church-state connection, majority opinion in both denominations was too close to keep them apart, and opposition to union was largely confined to the Highlands. The opposition nevertheless was sufficiently strong to maintain a small continuing Free Church (popularly known as the 'Wee Frees'), to which the House of Lords in 1904 awarded the entire property of the former Free Church. This manifestly unfair judgement, based on the majority body's departure from Calvinist, Establishment and Disruption principles, had to be reversed by Act of Parliament in the following year, but the Wee Frees continued to be a significant church in the twentieth-century Highlands, where the Free Presbyterians also survived. In 1929 the United Free Church (but again with a dissenting minority continuing) was to unite with the Church of Scotland. By this time the latter had not only got rid of patronage, but had also taken over responsibility for its own endowment, thus shedding those aspects of Establishment previously objected to.

These were not, of course, the only churches in nineteenth and early twentieth-century Scotland, and not even the only indigenous ones. The latter included other Presbyterian denominations, such as the Original Secession and Reformed Presbyterian churches and also the more substantial Roman Catholics and Scottish Episcopalians. But these other Presbyterian churches were small; and the Catholics and Episcopalians were different, both in terms of doctrine and church government and in terms of social composition. Outside a few special geographical areas traditionally loyal to them, the Catholics were to be found mainly among the large numbers of Irish working-class immigrants, the Episcopalians among the smaller numbers of the upper classes. The other churches therefore, while not without influence, were much less central to the social life of Scotland than were the major Presbyterian ones.

Each of the major Presbyterian churches was governed by a supreme court: a *General Assembly* in the case of the Church of Scotland, the Free Church and the United Free Church, a national *Synod* in that of the United Presbyterians. In Presbyterian theory, General Assemblies were intermediate governing bodies between the inferior courts (parochial *kirk sessions*, area *presbyteries* and provincial *synods*) and ecumenical councils: but because the latter no longer met in a form which the Reformed churches were prepared to recognise, General Assemblies (and the United Presbyterian Synod) were now the final arbiters of religion, doctrine, discipline and church government. In the nineteenth century these bodies were often preoccupied with the latter and in particular with the problems of church and state which divided them. Assembly discussion of matters which might involve any of these churches in conflict with one another or with the civil power thus often took place in an emotionally charged atmosphere which owed more to the peculiarities of Scottish Presbyterianism than to the merits and demerits of the matter under discussion.

The composition of General Assemblies and the way in which their business was conducted also influences what they said on various topics. The Assemblies were in one sense representative of the churches they governed: the majority of commissioners to them were ministers and elders elected by the inferior courts, and thus in touch with the grass roots and back woods; and Assembly committees also contained representatives of the silent majority. But in the Assembly the majority often *was* silent, and business dominated by a limited number of academics, church bureaucrats, city ministers, influential laymen and charismatic individuals. Assembly reports and debates, moreover, were often oriented to the national concerns of the churches, or to the particular interests of specialist committees. The average commissioner, visiting Edinburgh for about a fortnight in May (or perhaps for a day or two at some other time for the Assembly's Commission) was thus confronted with the need to make decisions about a wide range of issues which, probably, he had only very recently become aware of. In the heightened atmosphere of a large and historic gathering, he might well have felt under pressure to say something, or at least to approve of something said, which was not at all the sort of thing he would have said, or perhaps even approved of, in his local high street, churchyard or even kirk session.

What the average commissioner occasionally, and leading churchmen more frequently, said in the reports to and debates of these national ecclesiastical gatherings, provides much of the information on which this book is based. The issues to be discussed fall into one broad and two rather more circumscribed areas. Part One deals with pronouncements on the sexual behaviour, marriage customs and family life and religion of the Scottish people and of the rural working-class population in particular. Parts Two and Three are concerned with more specific controversies occasioned respectively by the Contagious Diseases Acts of 1864-69 and the repeated parliamentary attempts to legalise marriage with a deceased wife's sister.

This book is based on a Ph.D. thesis submitted at the University of Edinburgh in 1972. I have attempted to bring the material up to date and have excised a considerable amount of rather tedious moralising. I hope that this would have pleased my supervisor, the late Professor James Blackie. I certainly owe him a lasting debt, not only in this connection, but also for friendship and encouragement over almost two decades. I hope, too, that the book will please Donald Macfarlane, who taught me to enjoy both language and history, and also the not entirely forgotten art of précis. I want to thank, in addition, Professor John McIntyre, who originally suggested that I should undertake this study and Professor Roger Short, who prodded me towards publication. Others to whom I am particularly grateful are Professors G.F.A. Best, A.C. Cheyne and T.C. Smout and the Revd W. Fergus Harris, who made valuable suggestions about sources, the staff of New College Library, and Mr John Tuckwell of John Donald. My friends among the staff and students of the Student Christian Movement, the University of Edinburgh and the Edinburgh Medical Group are too many to mention, but I owe a great deal to their stimulating company and to the support of my own family in Edinburgh, Easter Ross and Cumbria. None of these people, needless to say, are responsible for this book's shortcomings: but all of them have helped me and I am grateful to them.

Kenneth Boyd
Edinburgh 1980

Abbreviations

C. of S.G.A.R.	Reports of the General Assembly of the Church of Scotland
F.C.G.A.P. & D.	Proceedings and Debates (including Reports) of the General Assembly of the Free Church
U.P.S.P.	United Presbyterian Synod Papers
U.F.C.G.A.P. & D.	Proceedings and Debates (including Reports) of the General Assembly of the United Free Church
R.C. of P.	Religious Condition of the People (Reports of the Church of Scotland Committee on that subject)
R. & M.R.	Religion and Morals Reports (Reports of the Free Church Committee on that subject)
C.D.A.	Contagious Diseases Acts
MDWS	Marriage with a Deceased Wife's Sister

Contents

PART ONE

The Cotter Complex

IN 1850, few would have denied that the Presbyterian churches still exercised considerable social influence in Scotland. Two hundred years earlier that influence had been political as well as social. Religious questions, if not always religious motives, dominated the politics of the sixteenth and seventeenth centuries; and when the King of Scotland left for London in 1603, its religious leaders were more than ready to step into the political vacuum. During the Covenanting period churchmen were never far from the corridors of power or the camp-fires of the Scots, while on a humbler and more domestic level the pulpit and kirk session overshadowed the social life of the country. Although the church's ascendancy was always held in check by the power of the nobility, and although its writ frequently failed to run up beyond the Highland line or down into the world of the vagrant poor, it remained a force to be reckoned with by politician and peasant alike.

After the Scottish Members of Parliament left for London in 1707 the Scottish church lost much of its political significance. Junior partner to the Church of England, but without bishops professionally committed to representing its views in parliament, it grew increasingly remote from the day-to-day realities of national politics. Its residual influence with government now lay in the private negotiations of its more astute leaders rather than in the public pronouncements of its more fiery rhetoricians. In the new age of political management, totalitarian claims had to give place to trimming and compromise.

But if the Scottish church had lost much of its political significance, politics had not lost their significance for the Scottish church; and if the substance of the church's relationship with the state now meant little in London, in Edinburgh the form of that relationship had become all-important. Increasingly this question, raised by the restoration of lay patronage in 1712, lay at the heart of the church's internal politics. It was not a question which Scottish churchmen were prepared to settle peaceably. As a consequence the Scottish church split, split and split again. By the early years of the nineteenth century Scottish Presbyterianism had many voices, few of which were on speaking terms.

Despite all this, the Scottish church continued to exercise considerable social and cultural influence. Although its wishes were no longer enforced by the civil power, much of what it said remained plausible to the middle classes and even to many of the lower orders. There was, after all, no very plausible and coherent alternative to the church's definitions of reality. Christian culture, it is true, overlay an older pagan culture which was still expressed in superstitions and folkways (many of which, as we shall see, affected marriage customs). But this older culture, while in some ways plausible, was not coherent; and although the Enlightenment had begun to create an alternative post-Christian culture, that newer culture, while in some ways coherent, was too new to be very plausible. During the nineteenth century neither of these alternatives to Christian culture was able to take over its role. The older culture, under the disintegrating forces of urban, industrial and agrarian change, was becoming so incoherent that it is doubtful whether it could be called a culture at all, while Enlightenment culture, under its own momentum, was being broken down into a plurality of precariously enlightened sub-cultures. In this context the nineteenth-century church, enthused by the energy of resurgent Evangelicalism and heady with the success of the middle classes who supported it, continued to influence Scottish society and culture.

The nineteenth century, however, in the end failed to halt the church's loss of influence. During it the church's position continued to be undermined, on the one hand among the urban masses, who now represented an increasing proportion of the population, and on the other by its failure to carry intellectual conviction among those who were influenced by the Enlightenment's late fruits of biblical criticism, comparative anthropology and scientific progress. Reviewing the church's position in 1870, one of its more disgruntled ministers concluded that if things went on as they were doing,

> the intelligence of the country may depart from the churches, leaving an artificial and lifeless orthodoxy, with which they cannot sympathise, to be taught to stolid peasants or superstitious women.[1]

Five years earlier much the same situation had been described by one of the church's most independent and outstanding thinkers in the following terms:

> The Church of Scotland has for very long concentrated within itself most of that power which is now exerted by various separate and distinct agencies — as by the press, by public meetings, by poor's boards, by town councils, by Parliament, no less than by the Church courts. The unhappy splitting up of our Church by controversies into many denominations has without doubt immensely and perhaps unduly weakened the ecclesiastical power of each denomination, and even of them all combined; but if the Church had remained intact, if there had never been such a thing as dissent from it, the direct power of Church over the nation would, notwithstanding, have diminished. The progress of the people in civilization, their growing activity and energy, the application of other organs and agencies for the expression of their thoughts and purposes, would of themselves have, infallibly, in process of time, brought about the result which we now witness. The warfare of sects has only hastened what was inevitable, although we may safely say it was the very last thing any of the sects desired.[2]

This writer, more perceptive and prophetic than many of his colleagues and contemporaries, was not unduly disheartened by what was happening however; and his further comment upon this is worth quoting if only to draw a contrast with the many contrary assessments of the situation which will be cited in subsequent chapters:

> Seeing that the Church has lost its authority over these things for ever and her loss has been the world's gain, are we to conclude that all these things have become atheistical, irreligious, unchristian, because they have separated themselves from the Church, asserted rights of their own, and jealously guarded these rights? . . . Assuredly no, for the Church is not the kingdom of God . . . These elements of social life in separating themselves from the Church have not separated themselves from the kingdom of God. Nay, by the very act of rejecting the control of the Church they set aside the mediation of the Church between them and the kingdom of God and secured for themselves as a portion of their independence the right of standing in immediate contact with the word and kingdom of God. Before their independence they were related to the Kingdom of God only through their connection with the Church; now since their independence they may justly claim to be portions of the kingdom of God, each one of them as much a portion of it as the Church itself.[3]

This view, unfortunately, was all too rarely heard from churchmen during this period. Their continued sectarianism and authoritarian tone prevented them from seizing the opportunity implied in this analysis of their situation, and as a consequence their residual authority continued to decline. Yet even at this stage no other single agency was able to take over the church's role in Scottish society. It was still to the church, however unsatisfactory it might have been, that the majority of the people continued to turn for the celebration of their rites of passage, and in search of meaningful symbols.

The subject of the Scottish church's social and cultural influence is, then, a problematic one; and many questions about its extent and depth, throughout the four centuries of its existence, remain unanswered. To answer these questions, much more would have to be known both about how the Scottish people themselves secretly regarded it, and about what lay behind pronouncements of the church concerning their life and religion. The first part of this book is concerned with the latter, and in particular with those church pronouncements of the second half of the nineteenth century which dealt with two aspects of Scottish society, sensitive not only in themselves, but also because of the church's previous involvement in them: the social control of sexual behaviour through ecclesiastical discipline and the regulation of marriage, and family religion. We begin with the first of these.

CHAPTER ONE

The Social Control of Sexual Behaviour in Scotland

Discipline in the Early Nineteenth Century

IN his report to the Board of Agriculture in 1811, the Ayrshire lawyer William Aiton wrote that agriculture and society in Scotland were alike making progress 'from barbarism to refinement'.[1] Even Scottish religion was losing 'that gloominess of aspect, that bitterness of spirit' and that 'noisy virtue'[2] which had characterised it since the Reformation. It was unfortunate, however, that amid these scenes of improvement,

> Too many of the clergymen of Ayrshire, still keep up the ridiculous farce of public repentance, for breaches of the seventh commandment; though that stool has been the cause of so many children being murdered. Some of them render themselves unhappy, and disturb the peace of their parishioners, by hunting after scandal themselves and employing ten or a dozen of officious elders to assist them in that ridiculous research.[3]

That Aiton could make this criticism was a sign of the times. The clergymen he criticised were exceptional. In many parishes public repentance was now a rare if not an unknown event. With an eye on the improvement of their churches many ministers were getting rid of the redundant stool of repentance.[4] Others, taking Aiton's hint 'that the labours of an officious eldership might well be dispensed with',[5] were getting rid of them as well.[6] Of course this was too blatant an example of ministerial management for the Presbyterian Church of Scotland to sanction; but the church did commend the abandonment of traditional disciplinary practices. As early as 1804 the Presbytery of Strathbogie decided that its ministers and sessions might give up the practice of reproving offenders in public on the grounds that this was not 'conducive to edification'.[7] In the rapidly changing society of the early nineteenth century many moderate ministers must have thought that this was only common sense, while those who were not so moderate must have felt that they were the last remnant of the church remaining faithful to Reformation principles. But what in fact was the tradition these ministers were faithful to? And how had their church managed to produce their careless colleagues?

In the Sixteenth and Seventeenth Centuries

The Scottish Reformers of the sixteenth century had attempted to exercise control over the sexual behaviour of the people in two ways. They had insisted that the celebration of marriage should be a public event. And they had insisted that sexual intercourse outside marriage should be punished. In principle there was nothing essentially new in this; in practice the Reformers' Catholic predecessors also had attempted to exercise such controls.[8] But in principle and practice alike the Reformers were more radical than those who had gone before them.

For the moment we shall leave aside the question of the public character of marriage, which will be dealt with in a subsequent chapter.[9] As far as sexual behaviour was concerned the Reformers were determined to sweep away the double standard. The practice of priestly celibacy, they believed, had been a mistake. Promoted by 'superstitious little fellows who dream up something new to win admiration for themselves', as Calvin put it, priestly reliance upon celibacy had made them 'callous to all crimes', while 'fornication prevails among them unpunished'.[10] Most men were not, in the Reformers' view, capable of celibacy: they should marry rather than burn — or worse. The Reformers were thus committed to the establishment of a single standard of sexual behaviour. With great confidence, they believed that it was possible to sweep away not only the practice of celibacy but also the complexities of casuistry, and so return to the plain teaching of Scripture, which everyone — once they were taught to read — could understand.

This single standard had to be not only established, but enforced. The Reformers therefore mounted a fierce attack on fornicators and adulterers, whom they were determined to suppress. In their attempt to do this they gained official support. After 1560 the Privy Council, Parliament, the General Assembly and town councils all passed Acts with this end in view, and in towns where the reforming party was well established, sexual offenders were sought out and punished. An Act of 1564, passed by the Privy Council, ordered what should be done with fornicators. If it was their first offence they were to be fined, imprisoned and pilloried; if it was their second, they were to be fined more heavily, imprisoned longer and pilloried with their heads shaved; and if even this did not deter them they were, for a third or subsequent offence, to suffer larger fines, longer imprisonment, ducking 'in the foulest pool of water in the town or parish', and finally, banishment. These punishments were to be exacted of both persons involved, for the Privy Council was no respecter of sex. Equally zealous was the town council of Edinburgh where, as in some other towns, similar policies to these were being pursued even before the 1564 Act had been passed. The Edinburgh bailies three years earlier had prepared a hole in the malodorous North Loch specially for the ducking of fornicators, who, together with adulterers, had been assigned a special prison. Adultery was particularly severely punished: although the statutory capital punishment of this sin seems rarely if ever to have been exacted, adulterers were variously imprisoned, 'scourged at the cart's end through the streets', banished and punished in a number of other ways.[11]

It is difficult today to justify activities of this kind by reference to Scripture. The Reformers' warrant for the punishment of fornicators can scarcely be found in the teaching of Jesus, and although fornication is clearly condemned in Pauline teaching, the New Testament does not provide a model for the legislation of the Privy Council or the activities of the Edinburgh bailies. Even the Old Testament does not prohibit simple fornication as such: for the sexual sins prohibited there are intercourse with foreign women and ritual prostitution; and these are seen as sinful primarily because they were acts of religious apostasy. It was only at a late date that Judaism reinterpreted the Seventh Commandment to include simple fornication between Jews.

These difficulties, however, seem not to have troubled the Reformers. Calvin, for example, aware that the Commandment referred only to adultery, commented that:

> it is sufficiently plain, from the principle laid down, that believers are generally exhorted to chastity; for, if the Law be a perfect rule of holy living, it would be more than absurd to give a licence for fornication, adultery alone being excepted. Furthermore it is incontrovertible that God will by no means approve or excuse before His tribunal, what the common sense of mankind declares to be obscene; for, although lewdness had everywhere been rampant in every age, still the opinion could never be utterly extinguished that fornication is a scandal and a sin.[12]

Some people might argue, he continued, that 'the crime of idolatry was mixed up with it', but Paul's remark 'that we should not "commit fornication as some of them committed, and fell in one day three-and-twenty thousand" (Numb.xxv.9; I Cor.x.8)', showed 'that God was the avenger of fornication in this infliction of punishment, which would not accord, unless it were a transgression of the Law'.[13]

The confident anthropological and exegetical speculation which thus lay behind the Reformers' attitude to fornication also informed the view — which Knox shared with Calvin[14] — that adultery deserved the death penalty. In his commentary on Genesis, Calvin explained:

> The Law of God commands adulterers to be stoned. Before punishment was sanctioned by a written law, the adulterous woman was, by the consent of all, committed to the flames. This seems to have been done by a divine instinct, that, under the direction and authority of nature, the sanctity of marriage might be fortified, as by a firm guard: and although man is not the lord of his own body, but there is a mutual obligation between himself and his wife, yet husbands who have had illicit intercourse with unmarried women have not been subject to capital punishment; because that punishment was awarded to women, not only on account of their immodesty, but also of the disgrace which the woman brings upon her husband, and of the confusion caused by the clandestine admixture of seeds. For what else will remain safe in human society, if licence be given to bring in by stealth the offspring of a stranger? to steal a name which may be given to spurious offspring? and to transfer to them property taken away from the lawful heirs? It is no wonder, then, that formerly the fidelity of marriage was so sternly asserted on this point.[15]

It was not, however, a point which Calvin was altogether successful in establishing in his own city. Much to his disgust, he went on to complain:

How much more vile, and how much less excusable, is our negligence at this day, which cherishes adulterers, by allowing them to pass with impunity. Capital punishment, indeed, is deemed too severe for the measure of their offence. Why then do we punish lighter faults with greater rigour? Truly the world was beguiled by the wiles of Satan, when it suffered the law, engraven on all by nature, to become obsolete. Meanwhile, a pretext has been found for this gross madness, in that Christ dismissed the adulteress in safety, (John viii. 11), as if, truly, he had undertaken to inflict punishment on thieves, homicides, liars and sorcerers. In vain, therefore, is a rule sought to be established by an act of Christ, who purposely abstained from the office of an earthly judge.[16]

But by whatever covert casuistry of their own the Reformers appealed to Scripture, it is clear that they introduced a new element into the Scottish scene. Thereafter, the principle that adulterers and fornicators alike were sinners and should suffer was built into Scottish life. The agency by which this was to be ensured was not in the long run, however, the Privy Council or the town council, but the kirk session. The institution of session discipline marked a break with mediaeval tradition as significant as that with celibacy and overt casuistry, and its most significant aspect was the role it gave to the laity in the administration of discipline. Since the exercise of discipline was in origin envisaged as the granting of a privilege to the sinner by his fellow-sinners, not only the session but the whole congregation had a part to play in it. And although in practice the support given by the state to the totalitarian claims of the church undermined this ideal, the system appears to have been reasonably free from corruption. None was exempt from discipline, at least in theory, and in practice only a limited number of influential people would have been able to escape a determined session, each of whom, including the minister, was subject to the discipline not only of his colleagues on the session but also of the visiting presbytery. Initially, the system of session discipline was — up to a point — democratic, and its strength must have derived to some extent from its popularity. In a society where godliness was one of the main grounds for esteem, the system by which minimal godliness was enforced would itself have seemed estimable.

The system of session discipline instituted and organised by the Reformers and their successors was not however solely concerned with sexual behaviour. In the sixteenth and seventeenth centuries Scottish society was relatively undifferentiated, and the lines of distinction between the civil and the ecclesiastical jurisdictions were blurred. In towns the burgh council and the kirk session were frequently hand in glove, and sometimes it was the same hand, since some men were members of both. Under this system kirk sessions at first exercised remarkably wide powers over everyday life; and although they seem to have spent a good deal of their time dealing with sexual offences, they also dealt not only with other obvious and physical sins such as fighting, drunkenness and Sabbath-breaking, but also with such things as sharp business practice and the subtler physical sins of pride and avarice.[17] Making allowance for the violence of the age, this period can be seen as one in which an attempt was made to produce a society which disciplined itself on the basis of a set of commonly held values.

The basis of this society was however too narrow and its values were held by too small a proportion of the total population for it to enjoy long term success. The Reformers were moreover too dependent upon the co-operation of the aristocracy, who were by no means always in agreement with their ideals; and from the first they had to fight for what they wanted against those who considered that their ideals were either impracticable or undesirable. This conflict arose from a tension inherent in Calvinism with its ideal of the church as:

> both national and free . . . a voluntary and a compulsory organisation . . . based on the assumption that all the elect, if they are sufficiently well taught, will open their minds to the Truth, while . . . all the non-elect must be suppressed, to the glory of God and for the protection of the elect, and must be prevented from expressing both their unbelief and their non-morality in public.[18]

To put this Calvinist ideal into practice the support of the civil sword was absolutely necessary, and this tended to make Calvinism less of a democratic and popular movement than it might have become had the struggles of the mid-sixteenth century resulted in a more radical political solution. As it was, despite the popular element in the Reformers' campaign to suppress sexual offences, opposition was present from the beginning, even among those classes from whom the Reformers drew support. It was, for example, only after the town council of Edinburgh had called in the help of the Privy Council that they were, in 1560, able to carry through the punishment of the fleshers' deacon for adultery: the deacons of the other crafts had refused to co-operate in carting him through the town and banishing him, on the grounds that 'they would not allow such extreme punishment to be inflicted upon any honest craftsman'.[19] If opposition of this kind was encountered among respectable inhabitants of the towns, it was even more likely to be found among the ruling aristocracy, many although not all of whom co-operated with the church because it suited their immediate political purposes and not because they were bowled over by the obvious truths of Calvinism. Under such circumstances the Calvinist programme could have been carried through only if it had been backed by a considerable weight of popular public opinion.

The instinctive Calvinist reaction of calling upon the state for help was not however the only aspect of their policy which prevented the growth of sufficient pro-ecclesiastical public opinion to maintain the Calvinist programme at full steam after the withdrawal of the civil sword from the scene. The structure of Presbyterian government itself did this, insofar as the eldership, which had originally been elected popularly and for a limited period, was, according to the Second Book of Discipline of 1578, to be for life, and elders were to be nominated by the existing session through a process in which the people as a whole were largely passive. Although elders were laymen, and in many ways indistinguishable from other laymen, this system formalised church government in a manner which made it less sensitive to shifts in public opinion and less flexible in times of change, so that session discipline became, for many, less a form of social self-discipline than a form of oligarchy.

During the seventeenth century, however, the church's discipline was probably prevented from becoming altogether oligarchic by the way in which the church's struggles became for many Scots a matter of national identity. Religious and national or party ideals were inextricably interwoven and in the resulting ideological confusion the ministers were often able to wield great and sometimes catastrophic influence. Power went to the heads of some and while it is a serious charge to say that they became as corrupt as the Scottish aristocracy, much of the mud and blood of the seventeenth century certainly clung to their clothing. Partly as a consequence of this, the Old Testament ideals of Scottish churchmen were by the end of the century becoming less attractive to their aristocratic supporters (as well as to the long-suffering common people of Scotland) and their eyes were beginning to turn in the direction of the fleshpots of England. The Jews on their Exodus had after all wandered in the wilderness for only forty years. But the final establishment of the Presbyterian promised land looked as if it was going to be delayed for ever.

In the Eighteenth Century

Presbyterianism, however, was established in 1690 and the Union with England came seventeen years later. The Union of 1707 preserved Presbyterianism in Scotland in principle, and thereby deprived the church of much of its potential political influence.[20] But this perspective was not available at the time, nor in the early eighteenth century was any real diminution in the church's social and cultural influence immediately obvious. During the eighteenth century, apart from Jacobite interludes, Scotland was to be in for a quieter time. Even the leaders of the church were to quieten down, especially after 1750 when the Moderates came to power.

Session discipline, as exercised in the seventeenth century, had kept many of the features already described. It had lost something of its comprehensive character however, and eventually the church adopted a new system of disciplinary procedure which altered its approach to the control of sexual behaviour. In the seventeenth century disciplinary practice had varied from parish to parish, and in an attempt to standardise it the church adopted, in 1707, *The Form of Process in the Judicatories of the Church of Scotland with relation to Scandals and Censures. The Form of Process*, as its name suggests, was more legalistic than the standards hitherto provided by the Books of Discipline, and it narrowed the range of offences with which sessions might deal to those of an outward, obvious and physical nature. Since this form was adopted at a time when the state was becoming less willing to enforce the church's discipline, it is difficult to escape the conclusion that the church, lacking the ingenuity or perhaps the integrity to discipline the sins of the spirit, had decided to make do with the sins of the flesh, which were all that was left now that most political and commercial offences had been removed from its jurisdiction. During the eighteenth century, sessions dealt with cases of petty theft, fighting and swearing sometimes, intemperance and Sabbath-breaking frequently, and fornication incessantly.[21]

An important aspect of this system was the stress it laid upon proving that offences had in fact taken place, when they were not confessed to voluntarily — and in the early eighteenth century few were.[22] In cases of sexual offences the session was warned 'to be very cautious . . . where there is not a child in the case',[23] and in practice the existence of an illegitimate child 'eventually became the *sine qua non* in cases of this nature'.[24] This need for evidence explains why Aiton's clergymen were described as 'hunting after scandal', and the fact that an illegitimate child was taken as evidence goes some way towards explaining his reference to infanticide. How far 'the dread of facing the disgrace and terrible ordeals of the Church', as H. G. Graham[25] put it, led to infanticide becoming 'a crime of terrible frequency' is a disputed point. Certainly there seems to have been a good deal of infanticide in seventeenth-century Scotland, but how great the incidence of it was by comparison with that of other countries at the same time, and how far it can be connected with session discipline, is not clear.[26] A variety of social and psychological pressures may be operative in a situation which produces infanticide and abortion. Most societies have felt threatened by these acts and have tried to deter or at least limit them by the exercise of social sanctions.[27] Such sanctions do not need to be embodied in anything as concrete as session discipline for them to drive a woman to remedies of this kind. Nor are such pressures in any case necessarily the only or even the major cause of them. Economic and psychological factors also play a part, so that although the connection with session discipline was no doubt one factor in this situation, it was only one among others. The fact that women suffered more than men is, equally, a criticism of the age, rather than of Scotland or Calvinism in particular. Calvinism indeed stressed the element of companionship in marriage and thereby at least implied some recognition of women as persons. (The myth of multitudes of petty Knoxes getting rid of their sexual frustrations by persecuting regiments of uncrowned but deflowered Marys is too dear to the hearts of the popular critics of Presbyterianism to fade away, but the truth was probably much less melodramatic. More interesting, however, is why the myth is still perpetuated.)

The Form of Process could not have been easy to operate. And since, during the seventeenth century, the presbyteries' strict supervision of kirk sessions had been relaxed, uniformity of practice, even if the Assembly desired it, could not readily be enforced. Here too the removal of external controls left session discipline dependent on popular support, and although during the eighteenth century there were still no doubt many Scots besides ministers and elders who believed that session discipline was a useful way of keeping young people, the lower orders and their sexual behaviour in order (there is after all nothing old-fashioned about the cry for law and order even today), doubts began to arise about whether it was the most useful and appropriate way of doing this. Even some sessions thought that too frequent discipline might harden offenders, and that, because it was so common, discipline might not be taken very seriously.[28] An unsympathetic visitor to Scotland in the early eighteenth century remarked, with this in view, that 'it serves for a direction where to find a loving girl on occasion'.[29]

The effectiveness of session discipline as a method of exercising control over the sexual behaviour of seventeenth and eighteenth-century Scots, even within the pale of respectable society, thus remains a subject about which it is difficult to generalise. The wide variety of disciplinary practice in seventeenth and, despite the *Form of Process*, in eighteenth-century Scotland complicates this question farther. In some parishes the stool of repentance was never vacant, in others cases were less frequent, and in some, even in the seventeenth century, there were offenders who refused to submit quietly.[30] The fact that the 'greater excommunication', which made the offender a virtual outcast in his community, was rarely pronounced,[31] suggests not only that sessions were unwilling to impose it, but also that the people may have been unwilling to enforce it, and this too implies that there were limits to the effectiveness of discipline. On the other hand some congregations criticised their sessions for not being strict enough.[32] The overall picture thus is far from clear, and of course beyond all these other doubts there is the consideration that, even without effective contraception, by no means all acts of sexual intercourse result in conception. There must then have been many inhabitants of that sparsely populated country who could, if they wished, have eluded the eyes of even the most vigilant searchers. What we cannot know is how many did, or in doing so how many worried sufficiently about the eyes of God to exercise continence; and perhaps it is advisable not to push this fruitless question farther.

Whatever the effectiveness of session discipline in these matters during the seventeenth and early eighteenth centuries, by the middle of the latter century the character of the Church of Scotland was changing, and although the Moderate party which came to power around 1750 was neither as large nor as powerful as its critics were to claim,[33] it represented a new mood in the church, and a ministry not dedicated to the zealous prosecution of discipline.

Perhaps the most important factor affecting the exercise of discipline at this time however was the simultaneous growth of population and dissent. Between 1750 and 1800 the population grew by about a quarter, the urban population of the West of Scotland more than doubling. At the same time the number of Presbyterian sects outside the Establishment, of which there had been only two or three in 1700, rose from about five in 1750 to about nine in 1800. Other non-Presbyterian bodies, additional to the native Catholics and Episcopalians, were also emerging, and although neither they nor the Presbyterian seceders had the faintest hope of challenging the nationwide and massive numerical predominance of the Established Church, the existence of one or two of them in a parish made it easier for offenders to avoid the discipline of any church. Given the growth in, and mobility of, the population, avoidance was made even easier, especially as the Church of Scotland had failed to extend its parish system on any comparable scale and with any comparable speed. By 1850 the population of Scotland was almost, and by 1870 was more than, twice that of 1800. By 1850 the population of Lanarkshire was nearer four than three times what it had been in 1800, and by 1870 it was over five times the 1800 figure. The number of Presbyterian bodies outside the Established Church did not rise significantly in the nineteenth century thanks to ecclesiastical mergers, notably that which resulted in the creation of the

United Presbyterian Church in 1847: the Disruption of 1843 however meant that Presbyterian dissent was now more serious. In 1870 there were only 1,254 Church of Scotland churches in the country compared with a combined total of 1,473 Free Church and United Presbyterian congregations, even though the Establishment still claimed 460,464 members as against a combined total for the other two of 444,315.[34]

Nineteenth-Century Evangelicalism

By the time that Aiton was writing, then, the traditional machinery of ecclesiastical social control was breaking down. Understandably, therefore, those ministers who believed in it and who tried to keep it going were unhappy. These ministers, it has been suggested, were the spiritual survivors of the early eighteenth century. But in another sense they were the precursors of the nineteenth. Moderatism of a sort lingered on well after 1800, but in Scotland as elsewhere, as a result of revivals and awakenings in the late eighteenth and early nineteenth centuries the initiative passed to Evangelicalism; and because the Scottish Evangelical tradition had not died out during the eighteenth century thc form Evangelicalism took was Presbyterian, and, initially at any rate, it did not lead to the formation of a major new denomination, such as Methodism in England. It did however lead to a re-writing of church history, and the Evangelicals, erasing the Moderate picture of John Knox the barbarian, rehabilitated both the Reformers and the Covenanters.

These new Evangelicals were to talk a good deal about the glories of their Reformed and Covenanting inheritance: but at the same time they were aware that they were not living in the seventeenth century. When the crunch came and Evangelicalism led to the Disruption of 1843, the whole affair was managed in a most un-Covenanting fashion. There was plenty of cheering and weeping and waving of handkerchiefs; and the Established Presbytery of Tain nervously petitioned the government to keep its gunboat in the Cromarty Firth 'till after the present excitement shall have subsided',[35] but it was all a very pale reflection of the good old days. The God-fearing bark of the nineteenth-century North-West could not be compared with the bloodthirsty bite of the seventeenth-century South-West. Neither government nor people were willing to let the castrated Calvinism of the Evangelicals regain its old virility, least of all in the exercise of session discipline, and the Evangelicals for their part were not very willing to try, for all their rhetoric.

Yet at the same time the Evangelicals were not entirely happy about relinquishing control over the morals, especially the sexual morals, of the Scottish people. If they could not be moulded into morality by discipline, other methods would have to be found. Aiton, although they probably knew nothing about it, was suggesting the way they might and to some extent would follow.

In his report Aiton had discussed, among many other things, the condition of farm buildings, and turning to farmhouses in particular had remarked that it was common in Ayrshire 'to place beds in the kitchen, part of which are occupied by the men, and part by the maid servants'. Apart from creating 'an unwholesome effluvia' in the kitchen, and giving those who slept there 'rheumatisms, deafness and other diseases' due to ground floor dampness, there could, wrote Aiton, certainly

> be nothing more indelicate and indecorous, than for groups of people of both sexes to sleep in the same apartment; and to put off and on their clothes together.[36]

In his view it surely would be better 'for the health and morals of the lower orders' if farmhouses were constructed with smaller kitchens, and if the building materials saved were then used to build an attic story 'so as to have bed rooms (or barracks if that be too refined)' for each of the sexes.

What really surprised Aiton about these arrangements was:

> that the men and women servants in farm houses, sleeping in the same apartments, had not roused the indignation of the ministers and elders, the guardians of chastity and decorum. From the zeal which many of them have shown in prying into matters of scandal, and bringing delinquents to their *stool of repentance*, one might have expected that every pulpit would have been made to ring with remonstrances, against practices so indecent. So far from this, the servants and children of the greatest part of the elders sleep every night in this promiscuous and indelicate manner.[37]

Had Aiton been writing at the end rather than the beginning of the nineteenth century he would have found it difficult to complain that the church had ignored questions of this kind. Although pulpits failed to ring with remonstrances sufficiently frequent or forthright to satisfy some of those who directed the strategy of the churches, Assemblies pursued the question of the socio-sexual state of farm servants with an obsessive interest. Aiton indeed might well have thought that this, too, was 'ridiculous research', and that it would have been better to leave the subject to the new breed of secular sanitary reformers, rather than to the old experts in moral hygiene.

But moral hygiene was hardly a seventeenth-century term: and however much the Evangelicals might repudiate Moderatism, their social thinking was inevitably influenced by that of the previous century, as well as by the new problems which that century bequeathed to them and to their contemporaries. If it was impossible to see contemporary society simply in terms of its irrationality, it became equally impossible to see it simply in terms of its sinfulness. The social problems of the nineteenth century were too serious simply to be solved either by fervent preaching or by reasonable behaviour. A combination of passion and planning was required, although few hit on the right combination. The churches, caught in the toils of the sin thesis and the problem antithesis, found it particularly difficult to create an adequate synthesis. Their rhetoric showed this up very clearly. Popular preachers and theologians, searching for ways of describing God's activity, turned from traditional dogmatics to such fields as medicine, making God out to be a Great Doctor, and then to railways, turning him into a Divine Engineer (sin could be equated with a dislocated joint and a derailment in the same breath),[38] and in practical terms 'the visitation of the minister' could be described, in an Assembly Report, as an opportunity 'when practical advice can be given as to ventilating, drains, etc.',[39] as well as for more traditional pastoral activities.

If the new Evangelicals brought Puritanism back, then, it was a new kind of Puritanism; and the admission that there were social problems as well as sins to be dealt with (although the admission was limited, and although many social problems — perhaps many of the most important — were overlooked) pointed to a change in the churches' strategy as far as moulding the morals of the people was concerned. It was now to involve an attempt to raise the moral tone, as it was called, of society, partly through the kind of legislation temperance and Sabbath enthusiasts pressed for, and partly by the preaching of the Evangelical Gospel and morality. The aim was to change public opinion by any means possible: speeches, preaching, tracts, revivals, meetings, causes, movements. The problem lay not so much in finding respectable persons to organise all this, but in getting to the non-respectable audience. Before looking more closely at the Scottish churches' pronouncements on sexual questions it may therefore be useful to consider first of all some aspects of their relation to this larger society which Evangelicals wished to make respectable.

CHAPTER TWO

The Church and Scottish Society in the Nineteenth Century

The Breakdown of the Urban Parish

EVEN before the Disruption it was clear that it was going to be almost impossible to mould the morals of the non-churchgoing urban population. In Glasgow during the early 'twenties Thomas Chalmers had made a brave effort to operate the traditional parish system in his St. John's experiment. But, as one of them commented, Chalmers' followers simply did not know 'what to do with immorality and drunkenness'.[1] In Edinburgh, in the late 'thirties, Thomas Guthrie had come with similar ideals from a rural parish, only three of whose thousand inhabitants did not attend church,[2] to Greyfriars Church. Although Greyfriars had a large and fashionable congregation, the first hundred and fifty parishioners Guthrie visited yielded only five who attended any church. He therefore followed Chalmers' principles and was soon minister of a new church extension parish carved out of Greyfriars in an attempt to make the parish system manageable. But his new church was not built until 1840, and the Disruption three years later effectively destroyed all hope of fulfilling his and Chalmers' dream of an adequate territorial ministry.

Chalmers and Guthrie, however, were exceptions and although two hundred new churches were erected in the pre-Disruption church extension scheme, the church had awakened to its responsibilities too late and its response was too little. When in the two years after the Disruption the Free Church built 500 churches, this only served to point up what might have been done by an undivided Church. In 1867 Guthrie still hoped that the situation could be put right, and wrote:

> Let the ministers or representatives of the different denominations within the city — Episcopalian, Baptist and Independent, United Presbyterian, Free Church and Established Church — meet, and form themselves into a real working Evangelical Alliance. Agreeing to regard all old divisions of parishes with an ecclesiastical right over their inhabitants as nowadays a nullity — and, so far as these are preventing Christian co-operation, and the salvation of the people, as worse than a nullity — let them map out the dark and destitute districts of the city, assigning a district to each congregation. Let each congregation then go to work upon their own part of the field, and giving each some five hundred souls to care for, you would thus cover 'the nakedness of the land'.[3]

But it was a vain hope. The wasted effort was on a massive scale. It was estimated in 1870[4] that if every churchgoing individual in the total population (that is, the total population less one-sixth to represent the lapsed masses and one third of the remainder to represent children under twelve) 'were to worship at one time, which never is or can be done, there would still be a church for every 524 of them'. Robert Wallace, who made this estimate, considered this was

> a fact which, in view of the much larger accommodation actually provided, indicates a very considerable waste of clerical power, and justifies, on the ground of economy at least, the efforts of those who seek to promote ecclesiastical unity.[5]

The Missionary Alternative

The churches, then, as the founder of the Glasgow City Mission remarked, were 'not doing their duty'.[6] If they had been, he continued, there would be no need for City Missions. In the absence of an adequate territorial ministry, therefore, such missions sought to do something for the lapsed masses of the cities.

The home missionary movement was helped by the example of modern foreign missions, which had begun at about the same time, were flourishing by the 'fifties and provided inspiring examples with which to fill out the missionary metaphor. Foreign and home missions also had two other aspects in common: an acceptance of fundamental class distinctions, racial in the one case, social in the other, by many of their agents and those who supported them; and a tendency to operate through a great variety of agencies and societies, some of them only loosely connected with the churches. In the case of home missions these two aspects of their operations led to difficulties.

The acceptance of social class distinctions in urban missionary activity was recognised, by the eighteen-nineties, as a major blunder. The Commission on the Religious Condition of the People, reporting to the General Assembly of the Church of Scotland in 1896, wrote that the cities were divided into wealthy, middle-class and working-class zones and that 'between the first and the last of these divisions there is a great gulf fixed'.[7] Although (with perhaps an unconscious reference to the part played by the P. & O. in foreign missions) the Commission wrote that 'many boats of Christian compassion are ever plying in that gulf', it complained that

> the house of God, which ought to be the meeting-place for rich and poor — the house in which all are equal — is in the city too often the sign of the distance by which they are apart. More and more the richer are worshipping by themselves and the poorer by themselves — an unspeakable loss to both and to the Church of Christ.[8]

The missionary strategy of the churches at home, then, far from reclaiming the lapsed masses, seemed to be reinforcing those social barriers which made such reclamation so difficult.

The tendency of home missions to operate through a great variety of agencies and societies also created problems. The missionary situation in cities was confused, because in addition to the congregations and parishes of the more respectable denominations which might be found in the city centre (in Edinburgh, after the Disruption, Chalmers and Guthrie were both trying to operate their Free churches — in the West Port and on Castle Hill — as if they were parish churches), and in addition to missionary activities organised by them, there were increasing numbers of strange sectarian bodies; and as well as these there were many missionary, charitable and philanthropic societies, working independently and not co-operating. Every observation of a new area of need, it seemed, created the need for a new agency. Some efforts at co-operation between religious denominations in home missionary activity were of course successful. The Temperance Movement, although not all ministers, especially at first, were agreed about total abstinence, was able to bring Free Churchmen and Church of Scotland ministers back under the same umbrella; and an 'Association for the Suppression of Drunkenness' formed by these and others in Edinburgh in 1850 helped bring about the Forbes Mackenzie Act of 1853, which closed public houses on Sundays and limited drinking time during the week.[9] This, and stricter enforcement later in the century of laws against street-walking by prostitutes,[10] helped to clean up the streets, but did not get to the roots of the problem. Attempts to do something more radical — such as Guthrie's Ragged Schools — were hampered, despite the participation of most non-Roman Catholic denominations in their work, partly by controversy with Catholics and partly by the Government's unwillingness to subsidise and supplement the education of vagrant as well as criminal children.[11] There were many children of both classes in the cities during the middle of the century, begging, stealing, wandering about and spending the night in police offices; and while Guthrie's Ragged School movement helped some of them to become respectable citizens, a much larger degree of caring, protective and preventive activity was needed.

This situation was desperate enough in many people's eyes even to justify such schemes as that organised by the Free Church Professor W.G. Blaikie and his wife, who sent children from the Edinburgh slums to Canada, to be adopted or employed by settlers. Between 1870 and 1890 the Blaikies were emigrating up to 809 children a year: orphans, deserted children, or those whose parents were 'drunken and ill-doing', were sent, and inevitably there was criticism. A drunk woman turned up at the Caledonian Railway station denouncing Mrs. Blaikie 'for stealing the children of honest folk and selling them to foreigners',[12] and tried to get her daughter off the train. Blaikie tried to talk her out of it and 'a report was circulated that I had bribed her to be quiet'.[13] There was also some press criticism, and while the scheme was vindicated by an official Canadian Government enquiry, Blaikie admitted that they did not apply pressure on parents to let their children go (consent had to be in writing, and the parents had the right to withdraw it),

> without a certain qualm that we were interfering with the law of nature. We could but fall back on the principle, that extreme evils require extreme remedies.[14]

And, as has already been noted, these extreme remedies were applied by a great variety of agencies. When the Blaikies first thought of this scheme they tried to persuade existing agencies to take it on because, as Blaikie put it, Edinburgh was 'already overrun with a whole legion of charitable societies'.[15] They all refused. And some argued that by emigration they 'might produce a scarcity of home labour that would embarrass employers'.[16]

The confusion of missionary and philanthropic work in the cities seems to have become worse rather than better as the century went on. Certainly, twenty years later, the Commission on the Religious Condition of the People found that things had not improved. Visiting central Edinburgh in the winter of 1892 they discovered that in the Grassmarket, Mothers Meetings, each organised by a different agency, gave away tea, bread, butter, rugs and blankets on Mondays, old clothes, boots and shoes 'at nominal prices' on Tuesdays, and cups of tea, bread and butter and jugs of milk for the children on Wednesdays. There were at least three other such meetings in the Grassmarket (whose peculiar bounty and day of meeting were not recorded in the report), and many of the women who lived in the area also went to other meetings in other parts of the city. The same pattern, according to the Commission, characterised other cities, and they complained that 'well-meant benevolence fails to accomplish the good it should accomplish' because its methods were indiscriminate and 'inadequate to reach the seats of social evil'.[17]

Missionary activity among the unchurched urban working classes and the poor, then, did not provide the churches with ways of exercising social control over them: the desire to do so was frustrated by the scale of the problems involved and by the nature and multiplicity of the methods employed by the churches and other agencies. The feeling that they were missionary-explorers confronted by a new, threatening, and incomprehensible Scotland was graphically expressed in the metaphors used by those involved. Guthrie, contrasting the Cowgate with his rural parish, compared his experience of the former with going down into a coal-pit, and in 1838 declared, after visiting in that area, that

> I have come up the College Wynd with the idea that I might as well have gone to be a missionary among the Hindoos on the banks of the Ganges.[18]

To a Glasgow minister, writing in 1867, the slums

> seemed like a great marsh, the lowest level physically and morally in the city. It was impossible to drain and dress it, so long as the higher levels around it on all sides continued to overflow and empty themselves here.[19]

This minister, Mr. McColl, was afraid lest

> the black seething bog might burst upon the green fruitful borders that were still with difficulty retained;[20]

and he longed for 'detailed husbandry' and 'large engineering schemes' so that 'those waste areas might be reclaimed'. But, although in the event this was what happened, it happened literally rather than metaphorically. The worst slums were demolished to make room for a railway station and the problem moved elsewhere.

In one sense, of course, those who were engaged in missionary work in the cities were going into foreign territory, since these inner-city areas had a large population of Irish Catholics, whose priests did not attend to them as faithfully earlier in the century as they would later. The presence of Catholics in the slums did little to help the situation, since anti-Catholicism brought out the worst in many Presbyterians. Vitriolic as some anti-Catholic propaganda — particularly that of the Free Church — was, not all Free Churchmen were equally culpable: the Glasgow minister just quoted, faced during the 'sixties with rioting Catholics at his open-air services (aggravated no doubt, as he admitted, by his inflammatory choice of psalms), rejected the assistance of Orangemen who wanted a fight, telling them that the gospel 'was not meant to break men's heads, but hearts'.[21] The fault seems to have been on both sides, only it was no doubt worse for the Catholics because there were so many Presbyterians.

The Respectable Working Class

The churches could not, then, exercise any effective social control over the morals of many of the working class who lived in the centres of large cities. What influence they had over working men and women in more respectable parts of cities and large towns, or in mining and other industrial areas, is harder to say. Clearly, during the second half of the century there were some working people in the churches of the urban and industrial areas: a report from five Glasgow congregations of the Free Church in 1881 states that 'the office-bearers are almost all labourers, trades people or otherwise employed daily for long hours',[22] and even given that not everyone in these categories might have been working-class (it could have included shopkeepers, for example), the statement suggests that members of the working classes could reach the eldership,[23] so that there must have been some of them in the congregations. During the last thirty years of the century Free Church congregations in the towns also took pride in reporting the numbers of domestic servants who attended regularly and regularly subscribed to the funds of the church.[24] But there may have been an element of coercion in the attendance of domestic servants; and the Free Church's view of working-class attendance in general was not very sanguine, especially as Howie, their statistician, showed a growth in the overall number of those who did not attend any church during this period from 16.97 per cent. in 1876 to 26.54 per cent. in 1881, to 37.72 per cent. in 1891.[25] On the distribution of non-attenders, a report from the Synod of Fife in 1870 to the Free Church's Committee on Religion and Morals expressed the opinion that, in the towns, while atheism and open opposition to the churches (which had been evident there earlier in the century) was dying out, there were many 'nominal' Christians, and many more who had no connection with any church; that, in the mining areas, while most miners professed to belong to a church and wanted baptism for their children, only about a fifth were churchgoers; that the fishing population were much affected by revivals (other reports of this committee suggest that this led, too often for the Free Church to be happy with it, to fishermen joining revivalist and other sects rather than the Free Church — although this was more evident farther north); and that shepherds and cattle-feeders found it hard to get away from work to church (other reports suggest that it would be the Establishment rather than the Free Church which they would attend in any case). The synod was more reticent about the churchgoing habits of factory workers and handloom weavers, although it acknowledged that both classes were highly intelligent![26]

Reports of this kind are not however sufficiently informative about the churchgoing or non-churchgoing habits of the urban and industrial working classes outside the slum districts of the large cities to provide a comprehensive picture of the country as a whole during the second half of the nineteenth century. What was true of Fife in 1870, or at least how things seemed in Fife through Free Church eyes, might well not have been true of other parts of Scotland. (Fife was not, for example, a place where the Free Church was very strong, at least not around 1880 when there were more United Presbyterian than Free Church members in most of its Presbyteries, and the Establishment had about half as many members again as the combined Free Church and United Presbyterian total.[27] A different picture would be presented, for example, by the Presbytery of Greenock, which would also have had a sizeable urban working-class population, but where, again around 1880, there were about 2,000 more Free Church members than United Presbyterians; and Establishment members were about 2,000 less than the combined total of Free Church and United Presbyterians. Again, the total number of Establishment, Free and United Presbyterian members in Greenock Presbytery represented about one-fifth of the total population within the Presbytery's bounds, compared with between one-third and a quarter in, for example, the Fife Presbytery of Dunfermline.)[28] At present, then, we are not in a position to assess the overall influence of the church over the more respectable members of the working class during this period. But before turning from this subject, two further reports may be mentioned which shed a little more light on late nineteenth and early twentieth-century Scottish working-class attitudes to the churches.

During the eighteen-nineties the Church of Scotland Commission on the Religious Condition of the People went round Scotland gathering information of various kinds about church and society. The Commission made the most comprehensive enquiry of its kind into such subjects to be attempted by the churches during the second half of the century. Other committees had been gathering information about similar subjects during this period: the Free Church's Committee on Religion and Morals had been investigating the religious condition of the country since the early 'sixties, when it was established as a follow-up to the Revivals of 1859-1861, and the Church of Scotland's Committee on Christian Life and Work, which was appointed in 1869, again to some extent as a result of revival movements (but more out of anxiety about the loss in membership they caused the Establishment than was the case in the Free Church, although it too was concerned about the growth of sects) also sent out queries and deputations. These committees helped the churches to devise new structures for their work and to extend the amount of control exercised by the central bureaucracy over congregations. The Commission, then, was in this tradition, but also represented a greater degree of concern about thc growing numbers who were lapsing from (it might more accurately be said, the growing numbers who were not joining) the churches.

The Commission, although suspicious of statistics and any interpretation which might be put upon them, divided Scotland into four types of district: fishing villages, rural districts, mining districts and the larger towns and cities, and reported that non-churchgoing was greatest in the last two types.[29] In the mining districts of Lanarkshire it amounted to more than a quarter of the Protestant population and in Fife to the majority. Estimates for the cities were vaguer. The Presbytery of Edinburgh had estimated non-churchgoing within its bounds in 1890 as between 3 and 33 per cent., an estimate the Commission, comparing it with more detailed estimates from Glasgow and Aberdeen, considered to be too low. It had, after all, been calculated that in Glasgow 'a very large proportion, if not half, of the young men of the city, have no special relation to the Christian Church'.[30] The population of the fishing villages, by contrast, were much more religious, although, as has already been noted, this led them away from regular denominations to revivalist sects, especially in the North-East, while in the country

> the answer almost invariably given by kirk-sessions of purely rural parishes was, that indifference to the ordinances of the Church does not prevail to any great extent.[31]

Church attendance in rural areas, then, even though it was not ideal — for there were complaints about irregularity of attendance — was much more satisfactory than in the urban and industrial areas. In analysing the causes of non-churchgoing the Commission made clear, by implication, that it was primarily concerned with the working classes. Sunday labour was examined and was considered to be less of a deterrent to churchgoing than the effect of long hours of weekday, and especially Saturday, employment. Sports too were scrutinised, especially attendance at football matches on Saturdays. These and Sunday bicycling and excursions were thought to be more serious deterrents. How far pew rents deterred potential worshippers was also a controversial subject, about which there were conflicting opinions in the church. Since these deterrents primarily affected the less affluent members of the population, it seems that it was this class whose lapsing worried the Church of Scotland most. This, however, was denied by the Commission, which stated that

> The 'lapsed masses' — to use the objectionable phrase so often repeated — do not belong exclusively to any order, lower or higher. An Edinburgh clergyman, as the result of his experience, stated 'that the amount of non-churchgoing among the

> working classes has been exaggerated, and that too little account is taken of it among the upper and professional classes'. Whatever may be said as to the former part of this statement, a timely word is spoken in the latter. It may be doubted whether the lapse is not as great and is not more on the increase, in the wealthier or more cultured portions of the community. The West Ends need their missions and missioners no less than the East Ends.[32]

This may well have been true, since the significant decline in working-class church attendance probably took place well before 1890, and since middle-class lapsing probably only became significant at around that time. But since working-class lapsing was on a greater scale, and since, as has already been noted, the church was beginning to criticise itself for its acceptance of class distinctions, comments of this kind do not remove the impression that it was working-class lapsing which the church was most interested in. The lapsed middle classes were, after all, less likely to become unrespectable than the lapsed working classes.

A final point to be noted here in connection with the Commission's report is that, like the Free Synod of Fife a quarter of a century earlier, it did not believe that the problem of non-attendance was rooted in what it called 'theoretical and deliberate unbelief'. It lay rather in 'the general free-thinking tendency of our time' and in 'the absence of the right kind of control, and in the right atmosphere in the family'.[33] And among the causative factors it listed

> The pressure of material interests, the excitement caused by questions peculiarly urgent in a transitional period such as the present, the play of new social forces and the opening up of new realms of thought to all through the diffusion of cheap popular literature — these and other circumstances give additional force to the trend which bears away from the spiritual and the eternal.[34]

The churches' influence over the working classes, then, obviously was giving rise to a good deal of concern during the second half of the nineteenth century. But when the Great War lifted a few stones the overall picture appeared much worse than had been thought. An ecumenical enquiry[35] into a number of issues raised by the war contrasted the official statistics of the membership of all the Scottish churches, given as 63 per cent. of the population, with the findings of research among Scottish soldiers. Its categories were not the most easily measurable, as those who conducted it admitted. What they attempted to estimate was the number of men in and out of 'vital relationship' with the churches. The suggested criteria of 'vital relationship' were:

> Does the man *love* his Church or congregation, does it *mean* anything to him as a fellowship and school of knowledge and virtue? Has he a living sympathy with its aims?[36]

Using these criteria, the enquiry found that while among Scottish soldiers the number outside vital relationship with the churches was, at about 70 per cent., 10 per cent. lower than that of English soldiers, the number of Scottish soldiers in this category who came from cities was about 80 per cent., compared with English city soldiers at about 89 per cent.[37] In the light of nineteenth-century estimates this might not have been entirely unexpected, but it nevertheless represented a very large degree of alienation from the churches. Part of the reason for the great difference between these and the official ecclesiastical statistics was attributed to the fact that the latter included women and 'in Scotland, as elsewhere, the proportion of women members and adherents very considerably exceeds that of men';[38] but the 'aloofness' of the men from the church was very disturbing.

Seeking reasons for this aloofness, those who conducted the enquiry were told that the men were highly critical of the churches, primarily because they were 'out of touch with reality'.[39] Intellectually the churches, with their 'contending creeds' and their 'unnatural' services, failed to convince the men of the truth of their profession, especially since there was so great a distinction between their profession and their practice. The churches' 'lack of love' was also criticised, and was seen in the 'lack of fellowship' and class distinctions within congregations, in the churches' 'want of sympathy with workers' efforts for social reform' and in 'the confusing and humiliating spectacle of ecclesiastical divisions'[40] which the men found baffling and unnecessary, especially since this made so little sense to 'plain' or 'ordinary' people. The churches were criticised, thirdly, for their 'lack of life', their deadness and bondage to tradition: they were 'too official and "safe"'.[41] And, as far as his men were concerned, an officer of a regiment from the North-East of Scotland remarked, the churches were 'the embodiment of cant'.[42]

The churches, then, came out of this enquiry very badly, and although wartime conditions allowed these criticisms to come into the open, it cannot be supposed that they were new. The existence of lapsed masses was in itself already an indication that many Scots were either not concerned about salvation or, more probably, that they thought it perfectly possible 'extra ecclesiam'; and the accusation of class consciousness had, as we have seen, already been admitted by the churches. It also seems likely that the internecine feuds of nineteenth-century Presbyterianism, and the principles upon which they were conducted, were much less important to the average Scot, even to the average churchgoer, than to those church leaders who spent so much of their time arguing about them. Perhaps indeed there was an undercurrent of scepticism, or even cynicism, about the whole business. Robert Wallace, the minister of Greyfriars, who later became editor of the *Scotsman* and an M.P., recorded in his autobiography that his father, a Fife gardener and a tolerably religious member of the Church of Scotland, had frequently remarked that the Disruption was 'just the ministers wantin' mair poo'er';[43] and in his essay in *Recess Studies* he commented that the average Scotchman

> is practical and cautious, and does not willingly take up an extreme and singular position, especially upon speculative questions. In his secret heart he may, and in very many questions does, rebel against his clergyman if he seems to dogmatise too confidently on the mysteries of theology, but he is disinclined to make any public stand in the matter, and prefers waiting to see what other people will do.[44]

On these grounds, rather than on any theological ones, Wallace believed, the majority of Scots acquiesced in Presbyterianism:

> The average Presbyterian has no belief in the divine right of Presbytery. He approves of it because it suits him. He assents to it just as he assents to a locomotive engine or a reaping machine; it answers its purpose . . . God, he conceives, cannot have spoken miraculously on a mere matter of detail and convenience like church government.[45]

If this picture of the average Presbyterian was near the truth — and the wartime findings which have been quoted suggest that it probably was — there are grounds for suspecting a considerable credibility gap between the leadership of the later nineteenth-century churches, with its official version of Christianity, and the people who continued to attend church, with their folk-Presbyterianism. There was of course nothing new in this. The institutional preoccupations of church leaders have by no means always been the preoccupations of the people. But the institutional preoccupations of nineteenth-century Presbyterian church leaders, apart perhaps from a few years round about the Disruption, seem to have been singularly out of touch with the preoccupations of many of those whom they led. As far as social control was concerned, then, it seems likely that provided the church leadership did not attempt anything too extreme, in practice anything much beyond the osmosis of respectability, then the average Presbyterian would put up with it, and probably even approve of it. As for those who had lapsed, especially those who lived in the industrial and urban areas and were members of the working classes, much of what the church said and did must have seemed a matter of indifference. In times of crisis no doubt the church had its uses — if it knew that the crisis was taking place. It also had its uses for the rites of passage of many working-class Scots. But as far as its disciplinary functions were concerned, it seems likely that the inhabitants of these areas regarded the representatives of the churches as moral policemen who had mislaid their truncheons, blowing their whistles for help that never came.

The Rural Scene

The churches, then, were in no position to mould the morals of the majority of the urban and industrial working classes. But what of the rural areas, where, as has already been noted, church attendance and church membership were from the churches' point of view much more satisfactory? This question is of particular relevance here since most of what General Assemblies said about the subject of sexual behaviour and family life during this period did in fact relate to the rural rather than to the industrial and urban population.

During the first half of the century General Assemblies said comparatively little about social issues of any kind. There is however some evidence from this period that ministers were beginning to become concerned about the connection between social conditions and sexual behaviour, and that they were beginning to take up issues similar to those mentioned by Aiton. It was perhaps only a straw in the wind, but down in Dumfriesshire, the young James Begg, beginning his ministry in 1830 at the chapel of Maxwelltown,[46] 'heard some statements in regard to the immorality of the district, which, till then, I could scarcely have believed credible'.[47] More will be said about Begg's views in due course: at this time he attributed the immorality he heard of to the influence of eighteenth-century Moderatism.

Elsewhere many ministers' concern about social conditions and sexual behaviour was connected with their view of agricultural improvement. Towards the end of the eighteenth century this was changing the pattern of rural society, enlarging the holdings of some small farmers and making others dependent on them. In the eyes of many nineteenth-century churchmen, this deprived many families of that stake in the land which was seen as an inducement to respectability. The ministers of agricultural Easter Ross, who were almost all Evangelicals, expressed concern about this in their contributions to the New Statistical Account. The minister of Nigg recorded that

> Three important events have occurred at various periods since 1694, that have had marked effects on the identity and character of the population. The first of these was the seven years famine betwixt 1694 and 1701 . . . The second event is the cruel and unchristian settlement of a minister, in the year 1756 . . . The third event is the introduction of the large farm system, about forty years ago.[48]

This third event was complained of also by a number of his colleagues, and David Carment, the well-known Evangelical minister of Rosskeen, protested that

> The depopulation of the country by large farms is a serious evil and is likely to bring along with it consequences which the landed interest seem not to have contemplated. There is no longer an independent peasantry. The morals of the people are deteriorating by the loss of independence, and their spirits embittered by what they deem oppression. The ties which united master and servant are severed; and when the time comes, to which we look forward with fearful anticipations, it will, we fear, be found that an error has been committed, by grasping too much, at the risk of sooner or later losing all.[49]

The claim that the morals of the people were deteriorating was echoed by other ministers, despite their pride in the district's high reputation among Evangelicals, and despite whatever they might say in defence of their own parishioners when it came to the point. The minister of Kiltearn (although he defended his people by saying that a magistrate was rarely needed in the parish) reported that

> there is but one opinion as to the fact, that vice and immorality are now more common than formerly. The poverty and degraded state of the lower classes appear to furnish the only rational explanation. In the former state of the parish many occupied that respectable rank which is now confined to a few. These felt an interest in maintaining a good character, and their conduct had a beneficial influence on all immediately under them.[50]

What specific forms of 'vice and immorality' the minister of Kiltearn had in mind he did not specify. Perhaps he was thinking of the four illegitimate births which had taken place in his parish during the previous three years.[51] To some Easter Ross ministers, certainly, *any* illegitimate births would have been seen as a sign of declining morals. Noble, the Free Church minister of Lairg, writing in his chronicle of *Religious Life in Ross*, in the late nineteenth century, about a 'remarkable religious awakening' in the parish of Rosskeen in 1742-1743, remarked that

> It has been said that in a wide district of the parish in which the effects of the revival were most powerfully felt, there was not for many years a single case of illegitimacy. The first instance that happened produced such a sense of shame and sorrow that the people of the locality held meetings for humiliation and confession of sin.[52]

On the other hand, however, the minister of Kiltearn may not have been thinking of anything so specific. As well as furnishing a 'rational explanation' of the declining morals of his parishioners he remarked that some of them

> are disposed to ascribe it to the gradual deterioration which this world has physically and morally undergone since men began to record their opinions of the times in which they lived,[53]

and such ascriptions probably pre-dated any actual observations.

But the opinion that there had been a decline in morals was not universal. The evidence of the ministers indeed was often either curiously ambiguous, as in the case of Dingwall, of whose people it was said that 'the tone of their morality is perhaps rather *strict* than *high*',[54] or even self-contradictory. The minister of Nigg, who believed that improvement had been carried out at the 'expense of morals', also stated that the people of his parish 'exhibit a moral character superior, perhaps, to that of any parish which can be named'.[55] And turning to examine his session records, he observed that these,

> for the thirty years succeeding 1705, while they afford abundant evidence of the zeal and faithfulness of ministers and elders in checking vice of every description, are disgusting in the extreme, as exhibiting a frequency and grossness of vice among the people which the succeeding generation would shudder to contemplate.[56]

Across the Moray Firth, the minister of the inland agricultural parish of Alvah in Banffshire was equally unimpressed by the morals of the previous century. In 1718, when the population of the parish had been smaller, the records showed that there had been more crime. 'Notwithstanding the severe discipline which the church then exercised' there had been as many illegitimate births in the early eighteenth century as there were at present. (The annual average was now 'one-thirteenth' of '32$\frac{6}{7}$', he noted, with extreme statistical caution.) And these had been 'not infrequently attended with circumstances of a revolting and aggravated description, which are now unheard of in the parish'.[57]

Other Banffshire ministers were less convinced about moral improvement. The minister of Boindie believed that the morals even of fishermen were deteriorating. In his parish, as elsewhere, they had formerly maintained a 'high reputation for purity'. There had, he claimed, 'scarcely been an illegitimate birth in the memory of man'.[58] But within the last twelve years things had begun to change. Fishermen, however, did not worry him nearly as much as farm-servants. Fishermen were still reasonably respectable: they worked steadily to buy a share in a boat and then a house and furniture (at which point they moved, together with wife and children, for they married early, out of their parents' house). Farm-servants, by contrast, did not go to church, and 'feel themselves independent of public opinion'.[59] As a class they were poorly educated and

> with wages varying from L5 to L7 in the half year, they not infrequently enter into the married state; their wives and families being left at a distance without active employment and without the benefit of parental authority and care. Not having the means even of supporting their offspring with adequate food and clothing, they cannot suitably educate them. At the earliest possible age their children are sent to earn their subsistence, when, removed from all parental oversight, and often neglected by their employers, they perhaps lose any good they have learned, and grow up to furnish new instances of the evils of which we complain.[60]

This vicious circle was made worse by their housing conditions for, while 'the labouring classes suffer generally from their want of opportunity for retirement', farm-servants were even more badly served, and many of them were,

> besides, subjected to the powerful demoralizing influence of young persons being congregated in a bothy, or out-kitchen, without either the humanizing ties, or the wholesome restraints, of the domestic institution.[61]

Much more was to be said on this subject in the years which followed.

CHAPTER THREE

Sin and Social Conditions: Housing and Morality, 1850-1870

Bothies and Bad Housing

THE minister of Boindie's concern about the demoralising effect of life in bothies and out-kitchens was not an isolated example of ecclesiastical interest in this subject. As early as 1839 the Synod of Perth and Stirling had set up a committee to enquire into conditions in bothies, and ten years later the Church of Scotland's Committee to Suppress Intemperance presented a report to the General Assembly which listed the bothy system among the causes of intemperance. This connection had also been made in Banffshire: a minister whose parish included the Glenlivet distilleries wrote in the New Statistical Account that prior to the recent decline in whisky smuggling

> the females . . . were in the habit of spending no small portion of their time, by night as well as by day, in the *bothie*, — a prey to the licentious and the immoral.[1]

The fact that this subject had reached the Assembly was in its way something of a breakthrough. Such social aspects of moral issues had not hitherto figured in Assembly business, and it was largely as a result of the success of the Temperance Movement in the 'thirties and 'forties that the breakthrough could be made. The Committee to Suppress Intemperance was set up in 1848, a year after the Free Church had appointed a similar committee. Thereafter temperance enthusiasts were rarely far away from General Assemblies, ready at all times to lay the blame for any social evil or problem at the door of drink, with a singlemindedness paralleled in our own time perhaps only by those who explain everything in terms of economics.

The more general terms in which the subject of bothies had been raised by the minister of Boindie, however — terms which related as much to housing conditions as to drinking habits — provided the context within which this subject was to be given its first full-length examination in a General Assembly; in this case not the General Assembly of the Establishment, although it would soon catch up on the subject, nor the Synod of the United Presbyterians, which did not show so much interest in it, but the General Assembly of the Free Church.

Housing conditions, then, were the context of this first extended Assembly discussion of rural sexual behaviour. Scottish housing was bad. The great majority of the Scottish people, who had never enjoyed very adequate housing, were particularly poorly housed during the first half of the nineteenth century. Houses were overcrowded,[2] and overcrowding became worse. In the cities old houses were made down[3] and cramped new tenements were built: industrial housing outside the cities was little better; even in the countryside it was unsatisfactory. In the rural areas, it was true, cottages had often been improved, but there were not enough of them, and after the Poor Law Act of 1845[4] cottages were actually demolished in order to prevent too many poor persons having a claim upon parish relief. In addition, agricultural improvement, creating large farms and greater numbers of itinerant labourers, presented peculiar problems, which have already been referred to. During this period an increasing amount of information about the quantity and quality of the housing available was gathered by means of census returns and other enquiries such as Aiton's. As a result of all this the churches began to question the connection between the quality of housing and the quality of sexual behaviour and family life.

But it was the bothy which first drew the churches' attention to this problem. The bothy was a sort of rural doss-house, and in nineteenth-century Scotland it could be found in many shapes and sizes and many degrees of comfort from the 'model bothy' downward. It was particularly useful on large farms where tenants or owners needed to house those itinerant labourers whom they were unable or unwilling to lodge in their own or in their more permanent workers' houses. Most inhabitants of bothies were unmarried men, but sometimes they were women and sometimes the accommodation was mixed.

Many contemporary writers were critical of bothies, and there are many descriptions of just how unpleasant life in them could be. But bothies seem to have varied greatly in quality, and they had their defenders. The convener of the committee which the Synod of Perth and Stirling had set up in 1839 told the Free Church Assembly nineteen years later that although the general circumstances of bothy life, even despite recent improvements, were 'highly unfavourable', the men who lived in them 'afford some of the finest specimens of our Scottish peasantry', and that as long as some farm workers were unmarried, bothies on large farms were probably unavoidable.[5]

Another member of the Free Church was also taking an interest in bothies. James Begg, the Free Church minister who might be loved or hated but never ignored, had developed an interest in housing in his rural parish of Liberton, near Edinburgh, during the 'thirties, and soon he was spending his holidays in extensive visits to city slums and a variety of experimental housing schemes. Begg believed that the housing problem in the cities could only be solved by the working classes becoming their own landlords. To achieve this end, he argued, there would have to be changes in the law, facilitating the cheap and easy purchase of sites and the development of co-operative building and investment societies. Rural housing however, he believed, was the responsibility of the landowners, although here too legal changes, especially in the law of entail, were a necessary prerequisite of progress.

During the 'fifties Begg's interest in this subject grew and by the early part of

1858, after ten years of propagandising inside and outside the church, he was still busily agitating the question both in the Synod of Lothian and Tweeddale and in the columns of the Free Church newspaper, *The Witness*, whose late editor, Hugh Miller, had also been a critic of bothies. Writing in January 1858, Begg blamed the bothy system for 'drunkenness, profligacy and crime',[6] and in May he informed the Synod that he believed there was a connection between the system and rural illegitimacy.[7]

Illegitimacy and Infanticide

In choosing to attack the bothy system on these grounds, Begg showed that he was a clever publicist, for drink,[8] infanticide and illegitimacy were all live issues at the time, and whether or not a connection between them and the bothy system could be proved, the suggestion that one existed directed public attention to the subject, at least until the connection could be disproved. The churches least of all could take lightly allegations concerning drunkenness and sexual immorality, subjects which had so often been pronounced upon by their predecessors.

Infanticide and illegitimacy in particular were controversial subjects in 1858. Some time before this there had been rumours that numerous cases of infanticide were escaping detection,[9] and in 1858 the crime was discovered and on a number of occasions brought to court with a good deal of publicity.[10] Illegitimacy also became a subject of much discussion at this time because the Registration of Births, Deaths and Marriages (Scotland) Act of 1854 had made it possible for the Registrar-General for Scotland to quantify, for the first time, its overall incidence. Statistics which he published in March 1858 'took the public mind by surprise', as a speaker reminded the Free Church Assembly in the following year, and it was perhaps characteristic of the nature of this public response, which Begg was able to make use of, that this speaker continued:

> For himself, he might say that, although a Sheriff of a county and having large opportunities of knowing a great deal of the subject, still he had been completely appalled by the extent to which the evil seemed to have reached over the whole country.[11]

The overall extent of illegitimacy in Scotland as revealed by the Registrar was nine per cent. of all births. But what was worse was that this percentage was higher than that of England and several other European countries. Equally shocking, and later statistics from the same source only confirmed this picture as they expanded it,[12] was that the illegitimacy rate[13] was substantially higher in some rural areas than in the towns. These statistics gave rise to a good deal of press criticism of the churches for falling down on their job, and according to the Sheriff, newspapers 'represented Scotland as a hypocritical country — as a country in which theology had no corresponding morality'.[14] To allege then, as Begg did, that rural illegitimacy and sexual immorality in general were connected with housing conditions, was an effective way of getting the church to think about the latter.

Not surprisingly therefore, Begg succeeded in persuading the Synod of Lothian and Tweeddale to bring an overture on 'Houses for the Working Classes and the Bothy System' to the Assembly of the Free Church in May 1858, and not surprisingly the Free Church agreed to set up a committee 'in regard to the Housing of the Working Classes' with Begg as its convener. Even *The Witness*, in an editorial three days after it had published the Registrar's statistics (and in the ongoing excitement of an infanticide trial in which the law had been lax and a 'minister and laymen were ready to bear witness' to the good character of a girl who 'had in her possession means avowedly intended to procure abortion'), had taken the church to task for its weakness:

> There was a day in Scotland when the discipline of her church was powerful to suppress that vice of unchastity which now makes her hang her head in the presence of England. Has the refinement of the age smoothed down Presbyterian discipline until it inspires no dread and produces no effect? Or do our ministers find it impossible to deal so closely in their public ministrations as to bear directly and potently on this vice? Or are our social arrangements calculated to make our country population more immoral than that of England? Or is Scotch law so loose on the subject of marriage, that certain forms of unchastity are hardly recognised, and that the cause may be almost accidental whose ultimate effect is murder? We believe that each of these questions may point out some producing cause of the fearful evils which we deplore; and the time has come when Scotland should put every weapon of law, religion and social improvement in operation in order to retain — we fear we ought to say regain — her character as a moral nation.[15]

Begg's committee was ready to deal with these questions.

Housing, Sin and Politics

This committee, later known as the Committee on 'Houses for the Working Classes in Connection with Social Morality',[16] met from 1858 until 1867 and during this period brought a great variety of subjects connected in one way or another with housing to the notice of the General Assembly.[17] Among these subjects infanticide was not included, and indeed seems, after 1858, to have dropped almost entirely out of the churches' sphere of interest. Illegitimacy, however, was discussed at length, particularly between 1859 and 1864, but in 1863 the Committee on Religion and Morals began to investigate this subject, stealing some of Begg's thunder,[18] and in 1864 the controversy surrounding illegitimacy in Scotland was somewhat deflated by the discovery that because the English Registrar-General had been failing to record up to 20,000 illegitimate births each year, the English illegitimacy rate had in fact been greater than that of Scotland.[19] The discovery that it had all been a statistical mistake could not hold back the Committee on Religion and Morals in its pursuit of information about immorality, now that it had the bit between its teeth, but its activities in this sphere took the form of a routine rural ride rather than that of a breathless chase.

After 1864 the Housing committee also had less to say about illegitimacy. It appears to have been very much a one-horse committee, and in 1865 its convener narrowly escaped death in a railway accident in March only to be made Moderator in May. There was consequently no Housing Report that year, and although reports appeared again in 1866 and 1867, they had less to say about immorality and illegitimacy. Perhaps because of this, their political content stood out in greater relief. The Housing reports had always been political, and may have contributed in some way to the change in the law of entail which in 1860 made it easier to erect cottages. But Begg's interests were always more far-reaching, and he did not hesitate to attack those, especially landowners and lawyers, who obstructed his reforming path. Begg's political enthusiasms were not, however, shared by many of his contemporaries in the Free Church, and even those who were sympathetic to some of his ideas wished that he would not drag all these secular details into the courts of the church. Their suspicion of Begg was summed up by W.G. Blaikie who, in the Free Church Assembly of 1864, after a great deal of abstract theorising on the churches' relation to secular matters, got down to brass tacks and said that he 'had the greatest pleasure in seeing and hearing Dr. Begg express his views on the details of all these topics outside the Church'.[20]

To the end, or at least until 1867, Begg rejected this view of the church and claimed that

> the social reformer and the Christian minister must not only combine in seeking to alleviate and remove the destruction of many generations, but they must be combined in the same individuals.[21]

He had, he believed, the weight of the church's history behind him, and cited Knox and Chalmers in his defence, and against the 'spiritual canker' which had

> invaded many in all parts of the Protestant church — not only the idea that the ministers of Christ have nothing to do with such so-called secular matters as the houses of the people, but that to manifest an utter indifference on the whole subject is a mark of superior sanctity.[22]

It particularly pained Begg that even Romish priests took more interest in the condition of the working classes. Despite this, however, he agreed in 1867 that 'public attention was now thoroughly alive on the subject', and recommended that the Assembly discharge the committee.[23]

Public opinion may have been aroused, but how effective this arousal was is questionable, since a Royal Commission on Housing, which Begg's committee frequently advocated and for which the Free Church Assembly petitioned Parliament in 1862, had to wait until the 1880's, and housing remained a major social problem in Scotland well into the twentieth century,[24] while bothies were still being scourged by Scottish churchmen in the years immediately before the Great War.[25] No doubt the Housing committee helped to some extent by publicising the problem. In 1867, however, Begg had other causes to press[26] and although he continued to keep a watching brief upon this subject and that of immorality, his major contribution to them had now been made.

But the history of Begg and the Housing committee has been dealt with elsewhere,[27] and it has been introduced here neither to repeat what has been said about its significance as an early and abortive example of the so-called recovery of the church's social criticism, nor in order to shed light on the character of Begg, although he undoubtedly was one of the most interesting if not the most likeable of Scottish nineteenth-century churchmen, but rather to discover what it can tell us about the attitude to sexual behaviour of the church which, as long as it owned this committee, gave tacit approval to its pronouncements.

So far then we have seen something of the circumstances in which the Free Church took up the question of housing. How far the 1858 illegitimacy statistics were responsible for this, or how far a broader interest in working-class housing was the decisive factor is impossible to say. But the way in which the level of the Assembly's interest in rural housing dropped, once illegitimacy seemed less of a threat and once that subject was being dealt with by the Religion and Morals committee, suggests that it was illegitimacy rather than housing in which the Assembly was primarily interested.[28]

The Moral Epidemic

Why was the church so concerned about illegitimacy? The accusation of hypocrisy and failure on the church's part was obviously one factor. Another was the threat of what were believed to be the consequences of illegitimacy, social, economic and even eschatological. How seriously these were taken remains a matter for speculation about the relation between public oratory and private judgement in the Free Church — a matter particularly of how many grains of salt were taken with the Housing reports and the speeches of that committee's convener.

Begg evidently believed, or purported to believe, that illegitimacy was a 'moral epidemic', and during the period from 1859 to 1864, when he had more or less cornered the Free Church market in illegitimacy, the reports and his speeches were full of variations on the theme of its magnitude and dangers. In 1860, the Housing Report, noting from the Registrar that there had been 9,606 illegitimate births in the previous year, stated:

> Now at this rate, of nearly 10,000 bastards a year, we shall in ten years have in Scotland nearly 100,000 bastards, or a population of them equal to that of one of our largest cities; a result sufficiently startling, and well fitted to alarm all classes of moral and social reformers.[29]

Not least startling was the expense of illegitimacy. Pauperism, already nearly twice as bad as in England, would certainly increase, 'as every bastard is apt to be a beggar',[30] and so, according to Begg's speech in elaboration of this report, would crime, which had already risen by 10 per cent. between 1857 and 1859. Lunacy also would increase, since the number of pauper lunatics had already grown by thirty-six per cent. between 1855 and 1859, and since 'we all know how . . . habitual immorality has the effect of unsettling the mind and plunging its victims into the dark depths of insanity'.[31] Even death, claimed Begg, quoting the Registrar-General's mortality statistics, was becoming more common.

There were, it seems, few fashionable fears which Begg could not press into service in his speeches on illegitimacy. Including the spectre of revolution. He warned the Assembly of 1859 that there was

> a yawning gulf being gradually established between the various classes of society which, if this European crisis should ever portend disaster to Scotland, may bring us to the brink of a general revolution.[32]

And in the Report of 1860 he followed this up with dark hints that 'the "illegitimates" of the large cities of France, cut loose from all ties of family, constitute to a large extent the "dangerous classes" of that country'.[33] Fortunately for his argument, Paris, the revolutionary city of respectable men's nightmares, had an illegitimacy rate of 32.5 per cent. (as opposed to 4 per cent. for France as a whole). The Report went on to declare that

> Christianity and civilization are both threatened and men are speculating upon the utter overthrow of Britain by its own internal corruptions, after the manner of the ancient nations.[34]

What made all this so alarming of course was the high rate of rural illegitimacy — the fact that illegitimacy had attained 'its most gigantic dimensions among that class who in other nations are the most virtuous and moral'.[35] Especially so, since 'until Moderatism spread like upastree over the land, Scotland presented the noblest peasantry under heaven, for intelligence, for Bible knowledge and moral character'.[36] For it indicated that the church's critics might be right, since if the church could not keep order among pious peasants, then neither the resurgence of Evangelicalism, nor the rapid growth of the Free Church, nor the current revival movements had had or were having much effect.

Moral Epidemiology

Throughout the Housing reports evangelical religion and the Free Church were defended against these charges of ineffectiveness by the suggestion that the church's failure was relative and temporary. But failure, however relative and temporary, required explanation and this Begg provided at an early stage when he produced tables of comparative statistics[37] to show that where illegitimacy was high, bothies or the old system of farm-kitchen accommodation were prevalent, cottages were difficult to find and evangelical religion was 'at a low ebb' as a consequence of Moderatism[38] or Popery;[39] whereas in counties where illegitimacy was low the opposite conditions obtained.

This equation, essentially formulated by Begg before the implications of the illegitimacy statistics could be studied, was questioned within the Free Church by those who, like the Presbytery of Dunkeld, could not,

> so far as their information goes, trace many cases of licentiousness very distinctly to the bothy system or to the want of house accommodation,[40]

as well as by those who, like Thomas Guthrie, believed that

> the fact is that the immorality was there before; and I believe that it was worse before — only the Registrar was not there before. That gentleman has but rent the veil that concealed the immorality. (Cheers.) They talk of diagnosis. Well I have a diagnosis of the affair too — (laughter) — and it is this, that the licentiousness which abounds in certain parts of our country is the spawn of an old, cold, dead, dreary Moderatism. (Loud cheers)[41].

Despite the rapture with which Guthrie's diagnosis was greeted, a monocausal theory of this kind did not satisfy Begg, much as he was at one with Guthrie in condemning Moderatism. For Begg, like many of his contemporaries, was in love with social science,[42] and the complex attitude to which this led was illustrated when, calling upon the Registrar-General to provide statistics showing all the 'connections and causes' of illegitimacy, he wrote:

> We could even construct a kind of map exhibiting these results, in a visible form, like the operations of a rain-gauge, upon which even the most obtuse of men could trace connections, which, however little understood, are as well established apart from the omnipotence of Divine grace, as the revolutions of the planetary system.[43]

The complexity of the attitude reflected here is shown by the co-existence of two languages of causation, that of theology on the one hand and that of social science on the other. For what in this context does 'Divine grace' signify if human behaviour is compared to the movement of planets? It may have been something of this creeping positivism as much as of his introduction of 'mere secular details' into the courts of the church which led Rainy to say of Begg that 'no man did more to lower the tone of the Church and to secularise it'.[44] For although Begg may have been relatively unsuccessful at the time, the churches were not in the long run cured of the addiction to social science.

Of course Begg's attitude to social science was ambivalent, and like many churchmen after him he preferred to make use of it only when it provided ammunition for the conclusions he had already reached. Further evidence of this ambivalent attitude was provided in 1861 when Begg, whose 1859 report had recommended better and more widespread education as a means of raising the conditions of and hence reducing illegitimacy among farm servants, took the Registrar-General to task for speculating 'as to the probable effect of education — mere education — in arresting immorality'.[45] The effect of education, Begg claimed, depended entirely upon that education being 'accompanied by the element of Christian principle'. On this tack Begg was continually urging the Registrar to produce statistics about the religious denomination of the mothers of illegitimate children, on the ground that in moral as well as other epidemics information should be sought from the sub-registrars about the cause of the evil. (There were, after all, Begg remarked somewhat scornfully, '1,100 or 1,200 of these men employed by Government'.[46])

But on another tack, in defence of better housing rather than in defence of the Free Church, Begg attacked the Registrar-General for underplaying the importance of bothies 'as a leading cause of our social immorality'. The Registrar had claimed that those counties where the illegitimacy rate was above average had an average size of farms 'much below' those in the counties where the rate was below average, and that since bothies were only found on large farms they could not be responsible for the high illegitimacy rate. Begg denied that large farms and bothies always went together, and in line with his earlier arguments said that the absence of adequate cottages and the farm-kitchen system of accommodation had also to be seen as causes. Taken together these factors were productive of illegitimacy.[47]

Good Men Without Houses

In support of this contention Begg quoted, among others, Dr. Gerrard, a Banffshire medical practitioner who had studied the illegitimacy problem in the North-East. In discussing the predicament of the parents of an illegitimate child, Gerrard wrote:

> The countryman cannot marry or make amends in this manner, for, no matter how anxious the parties may be to legitimize their child by their marriage, they cannot overcome impossibilities, and with no house, no home, must live apart. Their marriage perhaps is delayed in the hope that by and by some spare closet or apartment may turn up, and this state of matters continues till a second child makes its appearance. With its arrival the prospects of the parents are no better; it may be that the circumstances occur which cause an estrangement between the parties, and the prospect of their ever being in a position to marry becomes less and less, till a second or even a third child, not owned by both, destroys any chance of a marriage taking place . . . So long as a man continues in unsettled circumstances, with no prospects of acquiring a home and household of his own, so long, in too many cases, it is to be feared, will these unfortunates successively appear, draining the man's hard-earned means, and above all and more to be regretted, destroying the usefulness of the unfortunate mothers. By and by perhaps his turn comes, and he succeeds to some vacant domicile, but he has two families depending on him for support. The elder and illegitimate children have so burdened his earnings during his earlier and better years and may still be in part so dependent on him, that, as his younger family increases, he finds his means barely, or not at all adequate to meet his necessities. These multiplying demands, with his declining strength and increasing years, and it may be, interruption to labour from ill-health, so overburden him that he is compelled to seek assistance from his parish. True, his later family are bound to aid him, but they, in all likelihood, have followed in the father's footsteps and are themselves no better circumstanced. This is not a pleasant picture, and it is a matter for regret that it is a very common one. Whether or not its outline of the usual course of events be in accordance with the truth may be left to the testimony of any country clergyman or Poor-Law inspector conversant with the family history of the paupers on his roll.[48]

When Begg brought stories like this to his aid they no doubt created an impression, and Gerrard's account may have sounded plausible.[49] But, particularly in view of his own reservations about its universality, how far did a few such accounts establish a causal connection between defective house accommodation and illegitimacy; and further, how far did it establish that rural illegitimacy in the North-East and South-West generally was a product of these new agricultural conditions? For Begg seems to suggest that before Moderatism and agricultural improvement, illegitimacy in rural areas was, if not unknown, at least very much less prevalent than in the mid-nineteenth century.[50]

Bad Women in Bothies

In answer to the first of these questions it probably could not be denied that at any rate some bothies had what even those who denied the direct connection with illegitimacy called a 'demoralising and degrading' effect.[51] And opponents of the bothy system who could cite mixed bothies,[52] as could the Revd. Charles Thomson of Wick, were able to wax eloquent on the subject:

> The women — for the truth must come out — encourage the men. Deeds of shame are shamelessly committed in those dens of darkness, and gloried in . . . The sleeping place of the females is generally some off-closet or other place entering from the lad's apartment, or from very near it and between the two places there is, or may be, quite unrestricted intercourse. In some especially disgraceful instances the beds of both sexes are in the same apartment. No further particulars need to be given of so painful a description . . . the truth is that our bothy system is like the Romish confessional — its own indescribable foulness is its protection. Decency forbids the disclosure of a hundredth part of its abominations. The light of day cannot be let in on a Caithness bothy.[53]

But there were other counties than Caithness, and even in Caithness how characteristic were Thomson's examples? If, as was sometimes claimed, many ministers were not regular visitors of bothies, it might be difficult for the Assembly to form an opinion which commanded much confidence. And even if it could, the argument about the bothies did not go very far towards explaining the illegitimacy question; rather it complicated the latter since in demonstrating how demoralised and degraded were the inhabitants of bothies, it went some way towards undermining Gerrard's picture (shared by Grierson) of men and women essentially good but the victims of their environment.

Not by Houses Alone

Bothies, however, were only part of the question, and even if the Registrar's or Begg's questions could have been substantiated, a great deal would have remained uncertain. As it was, nobody seems to have had hard evidence, conclusive for the country as a whole, on the connection of illegitimacy with rural housing.[54] Clearly illegitimacy was higher among farm-servants in the North-East and the South-West than among many other sections of the population. But the habit of what Lord Dalhousie called 'gentlemen amateurs'[55] picking the worst cases and projecting a map of immorality upon them was no conclusive method. And even Begg, with his frequent appeals for more information from the sub-registrars and for a Royal Commission, had to admit this.

But if this information had been available, would it have satisfied Begg? Probably not, for Begg was essentially a social reformer rather than a social scientist, and if the map of 'connections and causes' which he wanted could have been produced, he would doubtless have been infuriated by the complexity of roads, lanes and sheep tracks which led to illegitimacy.

And what would such a map have to say about the good old days to which Begg looked back with nostalgia? Would it have suggested that Reformed Scotland was as pure as he maintained? At different points in the Assembly's deliberations on housing, hares had been started which suggested that there was more to illegitimacy than the after-effects of Moderatism and agricultural improvement. Almost at the start, in 1859, the Sheriff who had been shocked by the Registrar's revelations had expressed 'his conviction that the comparative looseness of (the marriage) law had a very material effect on producing the species of immorality already referred to',[56] and this of course had also been touched upon in *The Witness*' editorial. And again, in the 1861 Housing report, Begg himself had noted

> the perilous manner in which in Scotland it is customary for the young of both sexes to come into intimacy before marriage . . . not in open domestic society, but in secret interviews by night, even to advanced hours of the morning. The pernicious results of this usage might easily be anticipated, and are, in fact, as deplorable as they are undeniable.[57]

Begg's phrasing here suggests that not even he thought of this as an innovation; and further evidence of doubt about the good old days was furnished by a speech in which R.S. Candlish defended the church against the charge that drunkenness and licentiousness

> were just the result of attempting to draw too tightly the cords of religion; and that the present condition of the country was in fact only a reaction against spiritual tyranny. But (said Candlish) the Presbyterian Calvinistic Church, thwarted in all quarters from the first, and especially by the aristocracy, had never had fair play, or a very different result would be seen to that which now in many quarters filled them with apprehension and alarm.[58]

These questions about the causes and history of illegitimacy thus did not entirely support Begg's picture of national moral degeneracy caused by Moderatism and bad housing. But then it was not in Begg's interest to dissolve the atmosphere of crisis. He had too much insight into the irrationality of his fellow creatures, and the peculiar irrationality of Free Churchmen, to seek to persuade them by logic and statistics alone.

Calvinism and Progress

Begg's rhetoric of crisis, then, combined an appeal to the religious sensibilities of his hearers with an appeal to their social sensibilities. His religious arguments on housing were based first of all on the Westminster Confession's gloss on the eighth commandment, requiring 'an endeavour, by all just and lawful means, to procure, preserve and further the wealth and outward estate of others, as well as our own'. This, together with appeals to farmers to imitate patriarchs like Abraham and Boaz,[59] gave him a foothold in the Old Testament. Requiring Dominical authority also, he was fond of saying that when ministers told people to go into their closets to pray, 'they should first enquire if they had closets'.[60] Beyond this he frequently cited Knox, Carstares, Chalmers and other church leaders who cared for the poor.

On illegitimacy, his major religious arguments were that any social arrangements which hindered marriage were against the divine law. Marriage was a 'divine ordinance', and the family system 'one of the most beautiful institutions of Divine Providence'. 'It can never be excluded or even for any length of time interrupted without injurious consequences.'[61] 'Compulsory celibacy' (a term which combined his distaste for bothies and for Romanism) was therefore highly dangerous in the eyes of religious men.

Begg's arguments, however, were never simply religious in this narrow sense, and in attacking the supposed causes of illegitimacy and defending family life he appealed to the middle classes' sense of self-preservation, to their belief in progress, to their national pride and to their belief in Scottish democracy.[62] Expressing concern at contemporary economic and class differences, in which he saw the seeds of revolution, he insisted that

> all classes must be made to feel that their paramount interest consists in building a strong middle class ... This may justly be called the cheap and strong defence of nations.[63]

With particular reference to rural problems Begg saw this end being achieved in the following way:

> a good cottage not only prevents evils but promotes a great amount of good. A man proceeds to acquire furniture and to have something at stake. He is not so ready to flit at every term, and therefore he takes care to make himself most useful and agreeable. Farmers will very soon discover that whoever has the best cottages will get the pick of the market in choosing servants.[64]

The ideal therefore which Begg, following Thomas Chalmers, held out for the approval of his hearers was that of 'a property-owning Christian democracy',[65] and the universal extension of the middle-class family — or rather the universal extension of what he and many of his contemporaries liked to think was the middle-class family. 'The family system,' he wrote,

> is the true basis of social morality . . . All experience proves that the divine ordinance of marriage is the true remedy for many social evils and the grand foundation of social progress.[66]

To further this aim Begg could appeal, in the same breath, to 'the age of progress and the march of intellect', and to the Covenanters, for moral support;[67] and he applauded farmers who argued for raising the status of their workers 'on the ground of Christianity, patriotism, and self interest'.[68]

For Begg all these interests met in the conservative and romantic image of Burns' cotter. His vision, with its many contradictions, was summed up in the peroration of the first Housing report:

> Divine Grace is no doubt omnipotent, but such a man (who has no prospect of ever rising to respectability) is placed in circumstances of peculiar temptation, and in point of fact is generally reckless and unprincipled . . . The noblest picture of a peasant that probably was ever drawn, is that of the 'Cotter's Saturday Night', and it embraces all the elements of a pleasant home, coupled with the sweet smiles of domestic welcome and crowned with the noblest manifestations of Christian principle. Just in proportion as our men of influence know that labourers are men of like passions and feelings with themselves, and recognise it to be their duty to act in a just, enlightened and a Christian spirit towards the cultivators of the soil, seeking by every means to elevate the condition of those by whose energy their own comforts are maintained, may we expect to find those low and grovelling habits, which are at present the bane of rural life, abolished from Britain, and a noble peasantry rising under the influence of Christian teaching, as 'a wall of fire' around the land of our birth.[69]

Between 1858 and 1867, then, the General Assembly of the Free Church took notice of the possible results of bad and inadequate housing on the sexual morality and family life of the rural working classes. Whether or not the Free Church would have spent this time discussing housing had it not been for Begg's manipulation of the illegitimacy and infanticide controversies of 1858 must remain an open question. All that can be said here is that the illegitimacy statistics and the infanticide cases, together with the sense of unease about rural sexual morality which they generated, were important factors in persuading the Free Church to take up the subject, while Begg's persistence and rhetoric kept it alive. (The further question of what good the church's discussion of housing's effect on morality did is even more open: in the short run the illegitimacy rate actually rose during the period of the Housing committee from 10.1 per cent. in 1863 to 10.27 per cent. in 1866.[70] By the end of the century, however, housing conditions were getting better — there was at any rate less overcrowding. And by 1903 the illegitimacy rate was down to 6.21 per cent.[71] None of this, however, had any necessary connection with discussion of housing and illegitimacy in the General Assembly of the Free Church.) But the subject of illegitimacy was also discussed in the churches outside the context of the Housing committee's reports.

The United Presbyterian Synod

The United Presbyterian Synod's interest in illegitimacy and immorality was reflected in a report of 1864 which, on the basis of returns from its churches to a question about 'the principal causes which produce licentiousness in your district', stated that 'intemperance is all but universally assigned as the one great cause of licentiousness'. The returns also cited overcrowding, 'licentious conversation' among men and women field and mill workers, the carelessness of masters and mistresses, difficulties preventing early marriage, and the bothy system.[72] The Synod criticised the Poor Law for its 'encouragement to the sin of fornication', advocated tighter control of licences for the sale of spirits, recommended the abolition of the proclamation of banns in parish churches and the substitution of a civil system, and urged the continued exercise of faithful discipline by ministers and sessions, 'plain dealing' in sermons about immorality, and co-operation, especially in relation to discipline, with the committees of the Free Church.[73] This assortment of miscellaneous causes and remedies for immorality, produced for the most part by the Synod's Committee on Social Morality,[74] showed that while the United Presbyterians were responding to similar stimuli, their treatment of the subject lacked the single-minded devotion of the Free Church. But then United Presbyterians tended not to discuss such matters extensively in their Synod, perhaps because many of their leading members discussed them elsewhere, possibly to greater effect.[75]

The Church of Scotland

The Establishment also was not as vocal as the Free Church on this subject. In 1860, however, it set up a committee on 'The Increase of Immorality in Rural Districts', which survived into the 'seventies, and in 1861 the Assembly issued a Pastoral Address on this subject.[76]

On some aspects of the question the Pastoral Address took a line similar to Begg's. It urged all concerned 'to labour in inquiring into the particular causes from which this lamentable degeneracy has arisen', and instructed landowners and farmers to 'adopt prudent measures in regard to dwellings and accommodation of their workers'.[77] But in its analysis of the question, social science was secondary to a more traditional sin-oriented view of things. Ministers were urged

> to raise the tone of feeling and opinion on this subject, especially among the labouring population (for) there is much reason to fear that the immoralities in question are regarded as very trivial matters . . . the people . . . look upon unchastity as rather a venial weakness, or even as a misfortune, than as a sin, highly offensive to God, most derogatory to the Christian character, and most pernicious to all the true interests of society . . . The correction of this state of mind evidently lies at the root of any reformation of the manners of the people in this respect.[78]

The Established church, then, appeared to take the view that rural immorality, although on the increase, was as much the result of habit as of housing. In another respect also it diverged from the Housing committee's treatment of the subject. This was in the assumption that those who were responsible for the increase of immorality should be directly addressed, as Christians, by the General Assembly. Free churchmen were apt to allege that many farm servants who were heathens at heart usually claimed to belong to the Establishment; and in the Pastoral Address the latter, by appealing to its 'brethren' not to 'walk in the lust of uncleanness as they do "who know not God and obey not the gospel of our Lord Jesus Christ"',[79] acknowledged this spiritual paternity. Thus whatever farm servants may have made of the Address, even supposing they actually read it or heard it read, the Established church in drawing it up was marginally less 'holier than thou' than the Free Church, which even in the Housing reports betrayed its anxiety to prove that Free Church congregations were free of immoral adherents.

The Free Church: Religion and Morals

The Free Church's Committee on Religion and Morals, first appointed in 1860, was even more anxious than the Housing committee to make this point. In 1863 it reported, on the basis of returns to its questions, that in parishes where illegitimacy was prevalent it was rarely found in the Free Church congregation, with its 'faithful evangelical ministrations';[80] and it urged the Registrar-General to provide statistics which illustrated this, 'in order to help lay bare the causes of the evil and so lead to the application of efficient remedies'.[81] The same point was made again in 1866, and it was suggested that the virtual absence of illegitimacy among the members of the Free Church

> would seem to indicate that the teaching and discipline of the Free Church of Scotland have a decidedly salutary influence in keeping her people comparatively free from this disgraceful sin.[82]

Another deficiency in the Registrar's reports was also detected by the committee. The Registrar, it told the 1863 Assembly, did not account for 'antenuptial cases' (i.e. cases of premarital sexual intercourse, usually those followed by marriage after the discovery of the woman's pregnancy), as opposed to illegitimacy. The situation, in the committee's eyes, was therefore worse than it appeared to be from the illegitimacy statistics, and 'many' returns to the committee's questions

> state that in those parts of the country where it is prevalent the people hardly regard it as a sin. They seem to think that marriage covers all; and there is every reason to believe that in many cases young women yield to sin, from regarding that to be the best way to secure marriage.[83]

On the subject of premarital intercourse, then, the committee was taking a similar view to that of the Establishment: that rural immorality — which neither Assembly differentiated very clearly or consistently from rural illegitimacy — was something of an ingrained habit among the people. (An advocate, in the debate on the committee's 1865 report, remarked that he was struck by the 'levity' with which certain parents, who had appeared in a case he was concerned with, regarded the immorality of their offspring.)[84] What, the committee asked, was the point of calling for parental supervision to deal with immorality, when the parents' own marriage had begun in the same way?[85] And in its 1867 report it stated that in agricultural parts of Banff and Moray illegitimacy seemed to run in families.[86]

It was of course understandable that the Religion and Morals committee should want to emphasise this aspect of the immorality question. It was at this time involved in promoting the revival movement, and one way of doing this was by pointing out the depths of depravity to which men sank without the benefit of an evangelical ministry. The committee, therefore, although it conceded that the absence of cottages and other hindrances to early marriage played a part in the causation of rural immorality, was unwilling to lay too much of the blame on bothies or overcrowding, and described these and other material and environmental factors as secondary and subordinate:

> The real radical cure of this monster evil, which is a huge plague-spot and disgrace in the land, is the prevalence of true religion. A number of returns notice the blessed results of the recent spiritual awakening in lessening and nearly sweeping away the sin.[87]

The difference between this account of the immorality question and that of the Housing committee however lay more in emphasis than anything else. The Religion and Morals committee emphasised the dearth of true religion among immoral farm workers, believing that 'the great bulk of them consist of those who are connected with no church',[88] and emphasised that evangelism was needed; while the Housing committee emphasised the dearth of cottages. Each committee, in other words, had its own axe to grind, and each was predisposed to paint a black picture of the rural scene. To this extent the analyses provided by both committees, in their denunciations of unmeasurable immorality, and in their recognition of housing conditions or of heathen habits as the cause of this, were somewhat less than objective.

Immorality and Discipline

The question of immorality, as *The Witness* had pointed out, obviously had a bearing on the subject of ecclesiastical discipline, and the accusation that immorality was a reaction to Calvinist religious practices, mentioned by Candlish in 1862, seems to have been not uncommon at this time. Some members of the Established church (according to Free churchmen) even went so far as to suggest that the Disruption and the 1858-1861 revivals were causes of the increase of immorality, and that sinners were escaping from the discipline of the Church of Scotland by joining the Free Church.[89] The Free Church's spokesmen on Religion and Morals stoutly denied this, sometimes returned the compliment, and one Free Church minister described the Establishment as 'a cave of Adullam'.[90] But on the whole they preferred to class the immoral as heathens, whether or not they claimed to belong to the Establishment.

Discipline did however present a problem to all of the churches, and the Religion and Morals committee was given as one of its first assignments the task of finding out what the state of discipline in the church actually was.

Its report,[91] presented to the 1861 Assembly, is disappointingly vague. The majority of cases dealt with by Free Church sessions were either of intemperance or of 'violations of the Seventh Commandment'. But the committee was unable to provide figures, stating only that it believed cases of the latter, while 'far too frequent', to be less than before the Disruption. It was perhaps not surprising that there were few cases — the committee found it 'gratifying' that in some places there had been none during the previous three years — since discipline was exercised only over members; and membership of the Free Church must have implied some agreement with its values and some commitment to respectability. (Adherents could be disciplined also — but only if they 'made application for that purpose' themselves.) The committee also noted that only a few congregations kept up public appearance of penitents on one to three Sabbaths, while most cases were dealt with privately before the minister and session. But it was still the general practice at the revision of the membership roll for the minister or the elders to call privately on members of the congregation

> who seem to need advice or warning, and to have friendly and kindly dealings with them.[92]

It is some indication however of the change which had taken place in Scotland since the seventeenth century that the committee could note that there existed in some parts of the country 'a feeling against faithful and strict discipline'.[93] This is especially remarkable, since, while no doubt convention and social pressure as well as agreement with its values played some part in Free Church membership, it was by no means compulsory, and delinquents could easily escape. To deal with escapers the possibility of negotiating some sort of 'inter-ecclesiastical law' had been suggested, but the committee rejected the idea of this spiritual extradition treaty

> till greater spirituality, and respect for the authority of Jesus Christ and so greater faithfulness pervade the Churches.[94]

Obviously the Establishment was still, in Free Church eyes, the great Moderate menace, and the only remedy in the meantime was 'the elevation of the moral tone, by the faithful preaching of the gospel',[95] and by revivals.

On the subject of the practical utility of discipline the committee was pessimistic: the returns suggested that its effects varied from 'salutary' to 'negligible'; but discipline was 'an ordinance of Christ, and therefore, as such must be beneficial to his Church'.[96] The same rather ambivalent attitude was expressed in the debate on this report, and nothing fresh on the subject was expressed when the reports of the committee touched upon it in 1866 and 1867. The Free Church in fact was in something of an impasse: it might want stricter discipline, and perhaps believed that this, in some cases, might reduce the amount of immorality. To be effective, however, discipline would have to extend much wider than the Free Church membership. But if members of the Free Church themselves were beginning to question its necessity, what hope was there of this? The institutional custodians of the church's tradition were forced back on the hope of an almost magical transformation of public opinion, to which hope perhaps only the revivals lent plausibility. This hope receded however; and when in the 'seventies a new wave of revivals sang their way across the Atlantic, their approach was more popular and less Calvinist. By this time it became possible to write manuals of Pastoral Theology which contained very little about ecclesiastical discipline. Patrick Fairbairn, the Principal of the Free Church College in Glasgow, wrote one,[97] which was published posthumously in 1875, and only 20 of its 351 pages dealt with 'The Administration of Discipline'. In these Fairbairn referred to 'the mournful confounding of the civil and spiritual jurisdictions'[98] which characterised the churches of the Reformation. W.G. Blaikie also wrote a volume on 'homiletical and pastoral theology',[99] which did not mention discipline at all, although it mentioned practically everything else, from the need for Scottish ministers 'to pay more attention to the culture of the voice', to the equally important need for them to be punctual in all things, and especially 'in money matters'.[100]

CHAPTER FOUR

Law, Marriage, Discipline and Morality, 1850-1880

Opinions About the Scotch Marriage Law

THE WITNESS' editorial of 1858, which had questioned the effectiveness of session discipline in dealing with immorality, had also asked if the law of Scotland was 'so loose on the subject of marriage, that certain forms of unchastity are hardly recognised'.[1] This question was one which interested a number of nineteenth-century Scots, and although some churchmen considered that there had been 'much exaggeration in the statements of certain English journalists and lawyers on this subject',[2] other contemporaries, including such influential self-made men as William Chambers, the Lord Provost of Edinburgh, and his predecessor Duncan McLaren, later a Liberal M.P., thought that reform of the untidy Scotch Marriage Law was overdue. The Edinburgh lawyers however were divided on this subject and so, to some extent, were the Presbyterian churches. Matters came to a head in 1865 with the appointment of a Royal Commission to look into the state and practical working of the marriage laws of Scotland, England and Ireland. (The Irish laws were, if anything, more confused than the Scotch.) The Commission, it was hoped, might suggest ways of bringing these laws into closer harmony, on the basis of a few simple and clear principles.

This chapter is mainly about what the churches and others had to say to the Royal Commission on the relation between immorality and the marriage law, but it may be useful to begin by noting the different ways in which the marriage laws of England and Scotland had grown up, since this has some bearing upon what was said.

Pre-Reformation Development of the Marriage Law

The marriage customs of the early inhabitants of Scotland are obscure. Until about the eleventh century the Celts and Anglo-Saxons seem to have regarded marriageable women as a form of property. If they were not actually bought and sold, then at least their parents or guardians had to be compensated for their loss. Any safeguards attached to the deal protected the rights of the family rather than those of the woman as an individual. The question of the woman's consent to marriage thus hardly entered into consideration, at any rate in those unions where the transaction was formalised and involved the transfer of property: among the lower classes the formalities of marriage may well scarcely have existed.

Outside Scotland different marriage customs had developed. In ancient Egypt, for example, marriage had required the consent of both partners, and by the fifth century B.C., with the decline of the old family religions, this principle had also been accepted in Roman society. The church, as early as the fourth century A.D., was following Roman Law in this respect and the classical Roman statement: 'nuptias non concubitus, sed consensus facit' was echoed, in ecclesiastical talk, by 'matrimonium non facit coitus sed voluntas'. This acknowledgement of the principle of consent however did not prevent the church for many centuries from recognising civil and tribal forms of marriage in which consent had little or no place. At the same time, in practice, it attempted to ameliorate the harsher aspects of purchase. The church, also in line with its ancient teaching, urged that Christians should marry only other Christians.

About the eleventh century, things changed. For some time the church had been developing a marriage liturgy alongside the non-ecclesiastical forms of marriage: it also had been encouraging the practice of marriage in a church building. Now its growing power enabled it to assume responsibility for the celebration of marriage in society at large,[3] a function which it and its descendants would retain. It was important at this point therefore for the church to formulate its ideas about the nature of marriage, and in particular about what exactly constituted marriage.

In making its decision the church was faced with three alternatives. It could (1) follow Roman law and earlier ecclesiastical judgements by pronouncing that mutual *consent* constituted marriage, or (2) it could follow the tribal notion that what mattered was the *handing over* of the bride by her father, or (3) it could follow the widespread primitive practice of assuming that *sexual intercourse* was the decisive factor. In the event the church decided, not without a good deal of argument, that mutual consent was still the essential component. But again it did not reject local customs entirely and incorporated these into its marriage liturgy. This was as a result very different in different countries, being modified by the local traditions which had preceded it.[4] Thus elements of tribal marriage, such as 'giving away' the bride, persisted in local liturgies just as elements of primitive practice were embodied in canon law — for example on the subject of whether or not a marriage had been consummated, and could or could not be annulled. These elements however were now secondary to the principle that the exchange of consent between two persons who were capable of giving it was the *sine qua non* of marriage. Even if a marriage was clandestine, that is to say even if it took place secretly, the consent of two baptised Christians, who were not prohibited from marrying by canonical impediments, made a valid marriage.

On the practical level things were more complicated. There were still many poor people in pre-Reformation Scotland who could scarcely have been concerned with property, and it is uncertain how far, if at all, recognisable forms of marriage existed among them, especially if both parties were subject to the same superior and no question of the loss of human livestock arose.[5] Among the lower orders the primitive practice of regarding intercourse, or more probably conception, as the beginning of a marriage may well have been common, and the practice of handfasting, a form of trial marriage, certainly seems to have been prevalent in some parts of Scotland, although the church tried to control this by providing priests to tie the final knot for those who wished it. Marriage at the lower end of society was thus probably pretty haphazard. And at the other end, while the more respectable members of society may have appeared conformist, family interests and questions of property continued to be weighty factors, while women were often in no position to exercise the rights which they enjoyed in principle. The many exceptions which had to be made to canon law were further evidence of the distance between principle and practice.

This situation produced many problems, and clandestine marriages were too common for the church to be happy about them. They could lead to difficulties such as bigamy, or marriages by force, or marriage within the prohibited degrees of relationship. Since at this time there were an inordinate number of these degrees, and since the geographical mobility of the people was low, the risk of marriages of the last kind was very real. Because these and other impediments, according to ecclesiastical law, either prevented marriage from coming into existence at all, or at best made it unlawful, the church began to take steps to regularise the constitution of marriage still further, and to put down clandestine marriage with all its risks.

Measures to achieve this were finalised in 1563 when the Council of Trent decided that in all apart from exceptional cases the presence of a priest and two witnesses was a condition of the validity of a marriage. In the Roman Catholic tradition clandestine marriages henceforward became void in countries where the relevant Tridentine decree, *Tametsi*, was promulgated. But Protestant nations were not among these,[6] and in any case by this time the mainstream Scottish Church had ceased to acknowledge the authority of Rome.

After the Reformation

Although a number of radical changes were made in the Scotch marriage law at the time of the Reformation, the consensual basis of marriage, governed by the principles of canon law as they had been before Trent, was retained. Reformed Scotland thus inherited a system in which marriage could be constituted in two ways: either (1) by consent *per verba de praesenti*, that is by the present exchange of consent by the parties (under canon law this had constituted marriage, although marriage could later be dissolved if *copula carnalis* could be proved not to have followed); or (2) by consent *per verba de futuro* (under canon law this had been a form of betrothal which, if followed by *copula carnalis*, automatically became marriage: coitus was necessary to make the marriage indissoluble, even though the betrothal form was legally binding and ruled out the possibility of marriage to a third party). In this system, if there was any doubt that marriage had taken place (and this could be important when matters of inheritance were involved), marriage could be proved, either by citing witnesses to the exchange of consent, or by adducing proof that the parties, by common knowledge, had been clearly known to have treated one another as husband and wife in all respects. At the same time, however, this inherited system was transformed to some extent by the effect of the Reformers' new legislation, especially the introduction of divorcc (at first only for adultery and then in 1573 also for desertion), which removed many of the problems of casuistry associated with the question of unconsummated marriage. But the Commissary Court which dealt with marriage cases until 1830 (when they were transferred to the Court of Session) continued to be guided by canon law, at least until its outlines were dimmed and the courts came to rely more upon new legislation and, for precedents, on the court decisions of the seventeenth and eighteenth centuries.

Although the law rested upon the consensual basis of marriage, the Reformers, like the Council of Trent, attempted to add a greater element of certainty to the celebration of marriage. Here again they opted for a solution which was both simple and comprehensible. Marriage, according to the First Book of Discipline, was to take place, after due proclamation of banns, publicly, before the congregation in church, and preferably at noon on Sunday. The parties, after declaring that they knew of no impediment to their marriage, were to exchange consent in the context of a simple service of worship preceding the normal morning service. The minister led the worship and told the parties that they could be sure that God had united them; but the minister took no active part in making the marriage itself. Thus the Reformed position continued to rest on consent, but rested upon it in such a way that the question of whether consent alone was sufficient to make a marriage without publicity should not be allowed to arise. In one sense, then, there were in Scotland after the Reformation at least two definitions of marriage: a legal definition based on consent and an ecclesiastical definition based on consent and publicity. The church, in trying to impose the latter, was in conflict with the customs, superstitions and inertia of a society through which the osmosis of Christian culture had made uneven progress — a social factor which the law seems by implication to have acknowledged.

How successful the Reformers and their early seventeenth-century successors were in this conflict is difficult to assess: in the towns and the lowlands they appear to have achieved a degree of outward conformity with their standards,[7] and no doubt they were relatively successful in persuading those who were married regularly to be married in church. However, as we shall see, this success was short-lived.

During the seventeenth century further measures were introduced to extend the church's influence over marriage. Parental consent, never a legal requirement, since in law boys of 14 and girls of 12 were free to marry without it, was frequently insisted upon, and marriage was often refused until the partners' Bible knowledge was improved. In this close society, although banns were a required preliminary to marriage, they probably had only limited usefulness: whatever legal or ecclesiastical impediments existed were likely to be common knowledge already.

As a consequence of the church's influence and espionage during this period, those who did not share the views of the ruling ecclesiastical faction either resorted to irregular marriages or to clandestine marriage[8] before a priest or a minister not of or deposed by the church; or, if they were able, they took off to England or Ireland to be married there. All these alternatives were certainly legislated against by Parliament in 1641, 1649 and 1661, and this would seem to suggest that the church's control over regular marriage was tight enough to force some Scots into seeking these alternatives.

The seventeenth century thus saw the first phase of Border marriages, when Scots crossed into England for this purpose. In England, marriage was managed rather differently. After the Reformation the exchange of consent *de praesenti* was retained as, in principle, the only necessary condition of valid marriage. (Although the law in this respect was changed under Henry VIII and again during the Interregnum, the change was in each case a temporary one.) In practice, however, the great majority of marriages in sixteenth- and seventeenth-century England took place according to the Prayer Book and before a clergyman (during the Interregnum, before a J.P. and God) in a church of the partners' choice. This element of choice, together with the fact that any delay due to lengthy preliminaries such as banns (which were required by the Prayer Book) could be avoided by the immediate issue by the celebrant of a marriage licence, meant that there was no incentive for the English to be married in any other way, and although consensual marriages did take place in some parts of England they were not in the majority.

The Eighteenth and Early Nineteenth Centuries

In the mid-eighteenth century a significant change in English law reversed the direction of the Border marriage trade. In 1753 Lord Hardwicke's Act laid down that all marriages in England, apart from those of Jews, Quakers and members of the Royal Family, had to be celebrated in the parish church of one of the parties, after the proclamation of banns or the issue of a licence; and that irregular marriages were now null and void. The occasion for this Act was a wave of concern in England over the number of marriages performed by deposed or dissenting clergy (some of them even in prison) or by parties posing as clergymen. Many of these marriages were fly-by-night affairs, some of them bigamous or defying other impediments. Hardwicke's Act also insisted on parental consent where the parties were under twenty-one, and the issue of a licence was dependent on this. This Act did not apply to Scotland however, and although an attempt was made to introduce parallel legislation for Scotland, it did not succeed, partly because it looked too much like 'English interference'. One consequence of Hardwicke's Act, then, was that English couples began to travel to Scotland (particularly, but by no means only, to Gretna) in order to be married *per verba de praesenti*. A marriage business grew up on the Scottish side of the Border, where entrepreneurs read the

Prayer Book service over them, but claimed, if they were wise, that they were merely acting as witnesses.

This was not the only reason for the increase of irregular marriages in eighteenth-century Scotland. Presbyterian dissent was growing, and many dissenters were unwilling to be married by ministers of the Established church who, together with Episcopal ministers (after the Toleration Act of 1711) were alone legally able to celebrate regular marriage. In addition to this the whole state of the Scotch marriage law was so obscure that many people might not have known the difference between regular and irregular marriage, especially when the church began to relax its disciplinary supervision. It was estimated, by nineteenth-century commentators, that up to one third of Scottish marriages in the eighteenth century had been contracted irregularly. By the eighteenth century also the church had given up its insistence that marriages should be celebrated in a church building,[9] and it was normal even for regular marriages before a minister to be celebrated in a private house. (Frequently, if the parties were poor, this took place in the manse: Episcopalians, however, were normally married in their own churches.)

During the first half of the nineteenth century the number of irregular marriages seems to have dropped considerably. There is however no conclusive proof of this: the estimate that up to a third of eighteenth-century marriages had been irregular was generally accepted in the nineteenth century, but rests on no firm statistics, while the estimate of an average 20 irregular out of 20,663 marriages registered annually between 1854 and 1862 depends on the records of a system of voluntary registration of marriages, and does not include all those persons who might have been as anxious to escape registration as they had been anxious to escape regular marriage.[10]

Nineteenth-century legislation however tended to remove some of the reasons for contracting irregular marriage. An Act of 1834 allowed priests and ministers of denominations other than the Established and Episcopal to celebrate marriage, thereby removing a respectable and religious reason, while Lord Brougham's Act of 1856, by invalidating marriages unless one of the parties normally lived in or had fulfilled a 21-day residence requirement in Scotland, removed many of the less respectable advantages offered by the Border marriage brokers. Thus although irregular marriages continued to exist, all who gave evidence to the 1865 Royal Commission agreed that they were rare and were no longer considered respectable.

The 1834 Act, then, revived interest in marriage reform. One of the most compelling arguments for reform had been stated by Lord Hailes in 1772:

> All the European nations, Scotland excepted, have departed from the more ancient common law, and have required the interposition either of Church or of State to validate a marriage. Thus what was the law of all Europe, while Europe was barbarous, is now the law of Scotland only, when Europe has become civilised.[11]

These sentiments were again current in the nineteenth century, and in 1849 a reforming Bill designed to simplify the law was prepared by Lord Advocate Rutherford. So optimistic about its chances was Mr. Fox Maule, Secretary at War in Lord John Russell's Cabinet, that he undertook in a Commons committee 'to answer for the contentment of the Free Church', of which he was an elder, on the subject. But the Free Church was not to be contented,[12] and opposition to the Bill in Scotland (again the fear of English interference was voiced) was so widespread that it had to be dropped.

When the Royal Commission on the Marriage Laws of England, Scotland and Ireland was set up in 1865, those who were in favour of reform explained away the failure of sixteen years earlier: on one hand the 1834 Act had not then had time to show sufficient results; on the other, Brougham's Act had not at that time been passed. Now, they argued, with the subsequent decline in the number of irregular marriages, public opinion was ready for civilised reform.

The Arguments Against Irregular Marriage

Various reforms were under consideration. Reforming lawyers wanted to abolish one, two or even all three of the irregular forms of marriage. Some legal authorities held that the first of these, marriage *per verba de praesenti*, although it now legally constituted marriage, was a recent innovation, the antecedents of which had only continued after the Reformation as a form of pre-contract. This was a disputed historical point however. No less disputed was the second form, marriage by promise *subsequente copula*. This form was not even in accordance with the basic principle of consent, upon which the Scotch law of marriage rested, since, if it could be proved, the promise of marriage followed by sexual intercourse made marriage, whether or not those involved intended it. Or did it? It was questioned by some whether the promise followed by *copula* really did constitute marriage until it had been settled by a judicial sentence during the lifetime of both parties. In any event, to prove this form of marriage the promise had to be in writing beforehand, or sworn on oath afterwards, fine legal points which were not widely known. This uncertain form of marriage, a relic of the Middle Ages distorted by its nineteenth-century context, was widely canvassed as a candidate for abolition.

The third irregular form, marriage by cohabitation with habit and repute, had fewer legal critics. But then it was not strictly a form of marriage at all, but simply evidence of marriage. The admission of 'habit and repute' as evidence of the existence of marriage was, according to the Royal Commission, 'common to every system of enlightened jurisprudence'. What appeared peculiar to Scotland was

> the notion . . . that a man, by living for 20 years with a woman and recognising her as his wife, going to church with her and sitting at table with her, where he speaks to her and treats her as his wife . . . will thereby by these proceedings gradually slide into marriage with her.[13]

For this notion, some lawyers held, there was not 'the slightest countenance' in

Scots law. In popular practice, however, and in a number of legal cases, the notion did seem to have been countenanced, and in Scotland, where habit and repute could be involved in proving the existence of a marriage constituted secretly and without witnesses *per verba de praesenti*, legal enquiries often were concerned with whether or not marriage had been the intention of the parties. The law however was sufficiently flexible here for marriage to be proved in some cases even when the parties' intention was in doubt, and when they had begun simply by cohabiting without intending marriage. On these points there were 'copious elements of doubt and uncertainty'.[14]

The system of irregular marriages, then, raised a considerable number of legal problems, and reformers contrasted it unfavourably with the state of the law in England. There, although the strictness of Lord Harwicke's Act had produced some problems (including the Border marriage trade), more recent legislation of 1836 had created the office of Registrar of Births, Deaths and Marriages, before whom marriage could be contracted without religious ceremony, after publication of notice or on the issue of a licence by the registrar. The subsequent creation of the Scottish office of registrar in 1854 had made it possible to register the irregular marriages of persons fined for having made such marriages or of persons whose marriages had been established by a court decision; and Brougham's Act (1856) had allowed those who were irregularly married the alternative of having their marriage registered by applying within three months to the sheriff for a warrant. These innovations got rid of the need for the devious processes resorted to previously: by these an irregularly married couple who wanted to have their marriage registered had made use of the seventeenth-century legislation against clandestine marriage by confessing to a magistrate or a J.P. that they had been married irregularly and then paying a nominal fine and receiving an extract from the court books, which served as a marriage certificate.[15] Neither this older system, used collusively, nor the more recent and simpler processes were civil marriage as it was known in England however: irregular marriage had to come first, and it was this complication which reformers felt to be unnecessary and wished to see abolished.

Reformers thus wanted the law to embrace 'the maximum of simplicity with the maximum of certainty'.[16] Neither of these basic requirements notably characterised the Scotch marriage law. As we shall see, however, some lawyers and others held that the great advantage of the Scotch law was that practically nothing could undermine the existence of a Scottish marriage. If it could not be proved to exist on one ground, another could usually be found. Reformers also believed that marriage, like all other contracts, ought to be publicly ascertainable, and many of them believed that irregular marriages should therefore be abolished, and something like the English system put in their place.

The Arguments For Irregular Marriage

That the proposed reformed system was English seems, as in earlier attempts at reform, to have had a good deal to do with those objections which were raised to the reformers' arguments. Various sections of Scottish public opinion were in favour of the retention of the irregular forms of marriage, but in the present context it is what the Presbyterian churches had to say on the subject with which we are primarily concerned.

This was a subject upon which the churches were in remarkable agreement. Each church submitted evidence to the Royal Commission through, in each case, a specially appointed committee. The Church of Scotland's evidence in favour of leaving things as they were was not accompanied by any supporting arguments, unlike that of the United Presbyterians and the Free Church, but it is clear from what representatives of the Establishment said under examination by the Royal Commission that its reasons were much the same as those of the other churches.

The churches argued in favour of retaining irregular marriages, then, in the belief that

> the public opinion of Scotland is strongly in favour of regular and solemn marriages *in facie ecclesiae*, and is against clandestine marriages; but it is also in favour of allowing the latter to be established by competent and sufficient evidence.[17]

The major reason given by the churches for allowing the latter to remain was that they prevented concubinage and illegitimacy. They did this, said the Free Church, in the following ways:

> Instead of leaving a woman to dishonour and ruin who has yielded on the faith of a solemn promise of marriage, and enabling her seducer to escape, the law protects the weaker party and gives her the rights of a wife and her children the status of lawful children.
>
> In regard to marriage by habit and repute it affords the sanction of a virtuous connection to that which may have commenced in irregularity, while it is fitted to deter licentious men from indulging in concubinage under the veil of a pretended marriage.
>
> It gives effect to the mutual consent of the parties evidenced by a course of conduct more publicly and unequivocally than any one formal act or declaration before a registrar or clergyman, while the doctrine of legitimation *per subsequens matrimonium* tends to convert a relation which was injurious into one which is beneficial to society, and to give all the children of the same parents the benefit of the same status.[18]

As evidence of the beneficial effect of Scotch law the churches claimed that there was 'reason to believe' that 'there are more cases of bigamy and seduction under the more formal system of the English Law than under that of Scotland'.[19]

Now the question which the churches' evidence raised was that of whether or not what they said actually was the case. Did the existence of marriage by promise *subsequente copula* really protect defenceless women? And did the existence of habit and repute, as was claimed, really push the couple in the direction of regular marriage? And were seduction and bigamy (as well as divorce for adultery, which was also mentioned in some of the evidence) really more common under English law? The weak point in the churches' arguments about this, and a point which their representatives under pressure of questioning by the Royal Commission were unable to strengthen, was their lack of evidence sufficiently concrete to take their arguments beyond the level of theorising about the law.

The Habits of the People

The Commission, however, was provided with concrete evidence about sexual and marriage customs among at least one section of the Scottish people. But this evidence did little to substantiate the churches' arguments. The source of its information, on which it laid considerable weight, was J.M. Strahan, a doctor from Dollar who had a large midwifery practice, and who had conducted a systematic study of 'immorality among the working classes'. Although Strahan's investigations were at this time confined to five parishes in his own part of Stirlingshire, his findings, he believed, represented 'the average state of Scotland'.[20]

Strahan, whose practice included women of all classes, those from a woollen manufacturing district as well as those from agricultural areas, found on careful scrutiny of parish registers and from his own experience, that among agricultural labouring families nine out of ten women at the time of their marriage 'either had illegitimate children or were in the family-way'.[21] Only about one third of this proportion was to be found among the woollen-manufacturing families, and among those of the middle and upper classes Strahan had 'never attended a single case of childbirth where the child was not beyond the nine months after marriage', except among working ('not gentlemen') farmers, who were in this respect 'more near to the state of the working class'.[22]

Strahan attributed the high illegitimacy rate among the agricultural population to their courtship habits:

> There is a good deal of what is called courtship in Scotland, which does not mean courtship in the ordinary sense of the word, but rather flirtation. Young men and women meet together at night, when everyone else is in bed; there is no engagement to be married, but it is more like courtship with the hope of, perhaps, becoming sweethearts. This at late hours leads to familiarities, and that leads to fornication, and I believe frequently the woman is led more easily to fall in the hope thereby of securing a husband.[23]

Night courtship Strahan attributed in turn to the fact that

> the fathers and mothers will not allow their daughters to meet a young man in the daytime . . . the customs of the country are such that a young man could not be seen going in daylight to visit his sweetheart.[24]

The parents however had no objection to night courtship. Strahan, attending illegitimate births, had often remonstrated with the girls' parents, but they, who had

> done it themselves before . . cannot imagine any other way of doing it; their daughters must have husbands, and there is no other way of courting.[25]

Night courtship, according to Strahan, 'very commonly' took place once a week. In the middle of the night the young man — for example a ploughman — slipped out of the farmhouse window or, if he lived in a bothie, went out the door 'without any trouble' and made a noise or knocked at the girl's window. Then

> the girl comes to the window, and if she knows the young man, or after a little parley if she does not know him, she either comes out and goes with him to an outhouse, or he comes into her bedroom.[26]

The girl's father, said Strahan, would not interfere with this, but fully aware of it, would

> lie comfortably in his bed . . . shutting his eyes to it in the same way that a person in the higher ranks would shut his eyes to his daughter going out for a walk with a young man.[27]

In describing these customs Strahan emphasised their experimental nature. Courtship went on

> till they are in the family-way, and then if the young man is well behaved and the woman at all respectable the friends probably interfere, and the marriage is hurried on.[28]

This, 'from a vague recollection' Strahan thought, happened in about two-thirds of the cases, especially if the girl had respectable parents who interfered. But

> young men who have no particular connexions, who can go quite easily to another farm service, very often abandon the girl and leave the place.[29]

Strahan's account of night courtship clearly struck the commissioners as very strange. Their purpose, however, was to ascertain the bearing of this on the marriage law, and besides asking questions 'hardly within our inquiry but still . . . interesting to know',[30] they enquired how far irregular marriage was involved in these cases. In reply, Strahan, who could 'see no ground for retaining . . . any of the irregular forms of marriage', stated that when marriage followed night courtship and pregnancy it was almost always regular marriage. Young men, he believed, 'very often, being in the dark and so on',[31] gave a verbal promise of marriage and this led the girl on; and the young man if he was of 'good character' kept his promise. But they had only 'hazy notions' of marriage and would not draw the necessary legal distinction between a verbal and a written promise. In any case, Strahan commented,

> The woman who has coolness enough to insist upon a written promise before falling is, I think, little deserving of sympathy.[32]

One aspect of the law which Strahan did believe had 'considerable influence' however was that marriage could legitimate children born before it. This law, he thought, gave 'great encouragement to vice'.[33] By 'making an honest woman of' the woman, and by putting the children 'on a par with other children' it led 'to a laxness of feeling in regard to marriage'.[34] The law of legitimation *per subsequens matrimonium* in fact applied only to the children of the parties who married and not to children the woman may have had previously by another man; and in practice according to Strahan,

> the distinction is always kept up; very often the illegitimate child goes by his own father's name even among the other children.[35]

This however was no objection, among the agricultural working class, to marrying an unmarried mother:

> it is very frequent to marry a woman that has a child by another man; the only objection is the burden of the child; the burden of the child may be an obstacle, but the disgrace would be none.[36]

The only other connection Strahan saw between those parts of the law which reformers wanted to abolish and the customs he had enquired into, concerned habit and repute. Although irregular marriages were rare in Strahan's part of Scotland, marriage by habit and repute was 'pretty common', he thought, 'among the lowest of the working classes, the vagrant class'.[37] Among these

> parties go and live as man and wife without any ceremony . . . and there is no question about it till they become burdens on the poor funds and then it becomes an important question whether they are married or not, because if they are not married, the burden of the woman and children falls on the woman's parish, being illegitimate children, and in the other case upon the man's parish.[38]

In these cases the existence of the marriage, giving rise to a dispute between the respective poor law guardians, had to be settled at law before the guardians could assume responsibility. Another witness to the Commission stated that in cases where 'the father does not acknowledge a marriage when the facts amount in law to evidence of marriage'[39] — the witness was referring both to promise *subsequente copula* and cohabitation with habit and repute — the mother could go to the solicitor appointed (in each county solicitors performed this duty in rotation) by his society 'to look after the interests of the poor' and have an action raised without financial cost to herself.

Strahan, then, gave an account of the sexual customs and marital habits of the agricultural working classes which was far more informed and detailed than anything the lawyers[40] and ministers could give. He believed that

> the general feeling among the working classes is that if they are afterwards married there has been no sin; there is no scandal, no shame, no disgrace and consequently they feel that there has been no sin.[41]

This was, of course, what many churchmen said, but they were not in as advantageous a position as Strahan was to evaluate the situation in detail. Even so, their habit (in Assembly at any rate) of taking refuge behind broad generalisations of a denunciatory character (not that Strahan was any less critical of immorality) allowed them to give general support to the position expressed in their memoranda to the Commission; and when their representatives, who seem to have been chosen, not entirely with justification, for their knowledge of the law rather than of the people,[42] were questioned about irregular marriage they seemed woefully ignorant beside Strahan, especially as the lawyers, under questioning, kept telling the commissioners to ask the ministers for information about the true state of popular behaviour.

The Churches' Ignorance

It may have been, of course, that those who spoke were not those who knew, and those who knew were not those who wished to tell what they knew about popular sexual behaviour. Clergymen who make public pronouncements about this sort of subject, after all, are less well defended against the suspicion of voyeurism or exhibitionism than are doctors, whose professional work makes their interest acceptable and whose clinical detachment allows them (if they choose) to be descriptive rather than judgemental. Even in the pre-Freudian era, such considerations may well have contributed to clerical silence, while on the other hand Strahan's anecdotal and interpretative evidence about courtship (as opposed to his statistics) may not have told the whole story. Social scientific investigation is not the same as clinical, and those (including doctors) who conduct it into sexual subjects may well be led up the garden path by respondents who find their questions either amusing or impudent.

But even given these qualifications, the ministers of the churches still seem to have been very ignorant of, or vague about, popular sexual and marital customs. A remark of Strahan's to the Commission, in reply to questions about church discipline, hinted at why this might have been the case. Strahan claimed that it was common for the parents of an illegitimate child or a child conceived outside wedlock to tender themselves to the session for rebuke. They did this by going to the minister, when they wanted the child to be baptised, or if they wished to be admitted to the sacrament. They did it without invitation and the rebuke was administered before the session rather than before the congregation. If they were not already regularly married the minister would often insist on this before he and the session delivered the desired rebuke. (Strahan believed that in the past when irregular marriages had been more common this had not been insisted on.)

Since many of these people (if Strahan's evidence, that regular marriage normally followed the discovery of pregnancy, was correct) must have already been married before a minister, it would seem that discipline was not required before such marriages, but only before admission to the sacraments. (It would also suggest that such marriages followed very quickly on the discovery of pregnancy.)

Discipline however appears to have been a formality: Strahan doubted if it had much effect on sexual morals, but said that those involved 'like to be rebuked', since

> it cleans and restores them thoroughly in the church; a large proportion of them come to be rebuked.[43]

This procedure, Strahan claimed, 'is considered whitewashing'.[44] We shall see below how the church eventually came to deal with it. But in the present context it may be noted that, like magistrates who at an earlier date had provided *de facto* wedding certificates for irregularly married couples (by giving them a court record for a nominal fine), so in this case ministers and sessions entered into collusion with sinners. If this was in fact how discipline worked, then ministers might well not have been willing to admit to understanding the sexual behaviour and marriage customs of their parishioners — as long as the disciplinary system continued to create the appearance that the church was still in control of their behaviour. This then could have been one reason why the church representatives based their case on a state of affairs which scarcely existed.

There were also other reasons. The commissioners asked Strahan why, in his opinion, 'the clergy of the General Assembly and others, should be so attached to the system?' In reply Strahan made three points. First, he thought that there was 'a confusion when people talk of the Scotch Marriage Law':[45] regular marriage before a Presbyterian minister in a private house was often called 'a Scotch marriage' and it was thought by some people that it was this, which was popular, rather than irregular marriage, which was rare and unpopular, which was currently in question. Secondly, said Strahan,

> a number of clergymen have an idea that marriage with a written promise is a means of doing justice to the woman,[46]

but what they failed to understand was the infrequency of written promises and the lack of legal connection between whatever promises were given and the almost universal regular marriage. If Strahan was right about the infrequency of written promises,[47] these clergymen were either very ignorant of part of the law or of some of the people or perhaps of both.

The third reason, in Strahan's opinion, why the churches favoured the existing law was that 'some clergymen' were 'in favour of putting the different children of the same parents on the same footing'.[48] They were, in other words, in favour of the existing law of legitimation, *per subsequens matrimonium*, and Strahan thought that there might be something to this view.

Members of the Commission however denied that the legitimation law was in question, and the Commission did not in fact recommend changing it. But it was a point on which Scotch and English law differed,[49] and in registering his dissent from the Commission's proposal to abolish irregular marriage the Lord Justice General of Scotland[50] stated that

> if the great end of Marriage Law reform is uniformity in the laws of the different parts of the United Kingdom, it will be very difficult (after a general statute, founded on the recommendations of this report, shall become law) to resist the progress and expansion of the favourite idea of uniformity, when it comes to be suggested by-and-by, that the small remnant of disconformity, still to be found in the Scottish legitimation *per subsequens matrimonium*, should in turn be abolished.[51]

It is of course an open question whether, if what the Commission recommended had passed into law in 1869 instead of in 1939, this would have followed, but among Strahan's reasons it seems the only one which did not make the churches seem either ignorant of or confused about the subject of irregular marriage. Dealing with the churches' evidence, the Royal Commission commented that while the clergy of the Presbyterian churches 'represent, in matters concerned with religion, the sentiments of the great majority of the people of Scotland', and while 'they practically administer the system of regular marriage', the system on which their comments on irregular marriage was based *was* that of regular marriage and they were not thereby in a position to judge whether the law of irregular marriage was 'salutary or otherwise'.[52]

One further point may be made here about elements of ignorance or confusion in the churches' testimony. Their representatives had argued in favour of retaining irregular marriage on the ground that the 'more formal' system of English law gave rise to more cases of bigamy and seduction than occurred in Scotland. In making this accusation they were not alone: much the same thing was suggested by some of the legal witnesses. But again the churches and those who agreed with them were short on evidence for their statements. Seduction, the Commission found, could quite easily take place under the existing Scotch law, since so many people were unaware of the need of a written promise to make sure that marriage followed; and the Roman Catholic Vicar Apostolic of Western Scotland had complained quite specifically of bigamy among 'ill-instructed and ignorant Roman Catholics'[53] who thought that because their first irregular marriage was illicit it was also invalid. There were, it was true, proportionately more cases of seduction, bigamy and divorce for adultery before the English courts, but the Commission did not consider that this was due to the absence of irregular marriage from the English law.

In reply to further criticisms of England made by the churches and others the Commission stated that although it was suggested that the Scottish illegitimacy rate only appeared greater because the Scottish registers were more accurately kept, and because children registered as illegitimate were subsequently legitimated by the marriage of their parents, no hard evidence had been produced for this.[54] (The witnesses who had suggested this had tended to base what they said about England on hearsay.)[55] In proportion to the population no more marriages were registered in Scotland than in England, whereas the number of illegitimate births registered in Scotland was proportionately not less overall, and 'in some Scotch counties exceeds the maximum rate even of the least moral districts in England'.[56] On the claim that 'avowed concubinage' was less common in Scotland the Commission suggested that Scots did not call concubinage 'by its proper name' (that is, that it was passed off as habit and repute) and cited the evidence of the Corporation of Edinburgh and the Parochial Board of Leith, both of which had complained of the amount of urban concubinage.[57]

The Cost of Banns

In complaining of this, these bodies had also been complaining of the excessive fees charged by the Established church for the proclamation of banns. The complaint was universal, and only the Church of Scotland itself, among the churches giving evidence, had failed to mention it. The United Presbyterian and Free churches had both complained bitterly, as had the Roman Catholics, that banns, which were the only recognised preliminary to marriage, were the perquisite of the Established church. Even Dr. Stark, the Superintendent of Statistics for Scotland, who had been the convener of a Church of Scotland committee on irregular marriages in the 'fifties,[58] contributed to the criticism.

The system of proclamation of banns was criticised on two grounds. Firstly, it was said that divisions in the Reformed church made the parish church no longer a place where the community as a whole met, and thus the purpose of publicity was not achieved. Secondly, complaints were made that banns were read three times on one Sunday, rather than once on each of three Sundays, only if the parties were willing to pay a larger fee to the session clerk. (The session clerk read the banns before the service began, although in some churches the precentor might read them.) The price charged by session clerks seems to have varied from place to place. Between 7/6 and 10/6 for proclamations on three Sundays and about one guinea for all three proclamations on the same Sunday seems to have been the average fee. Since the average weekly wage of Scottish working men at this time was about 9/-[59] (and agricultural labourers were below the average), the charge that the cost of banns, which were necessary for a regular marriage, was an inducement to irregular marriage, seems to have had some foundation.[60] Even the Principal Clerk to the General Assembly of the Church of Scotland seems to have been rather uneasy when explaining the 'lax practices'[61] which involved a higher fee for three proclamations on the one Sunday; and the minister of St. Mary's parish in Edinburgh, who thought it involved 'a very objectionable principle', seemed positively relieved to inform the Commission that although the session clerk held 'a lucrative office'[62] in large parishes (his had 8,000 inhabitants), the minister received no part of the proclamation fee nor any fee in connection with performing marriages.

The Commission's Conclusions

The Royal Commission, when it reported in 1868, naturally enough recommended the abolition of banns as a necessary preliminary to marriage. They had outlived their usefulness. Instead, due notice of marriage was to be given to the minister or civil officer concerned and this was to be recorded, 'filed and preserved',[63] but not generally published. 'We look,' said the Commission, 'upon the exhibition of notices . . . as nugatory.'[64]

This was the only one of the Commission's main recommendations (it also dealt with minor matters concerning the rights of non-Anglican ministers to marry British subjects abroad — rights which the Scottish churches naturally argued for) to be accepted, and even this was accepted only in part. The Marriage Notice (Scotland) Act of 1878 introduced the system of written publication on the registrar's office door (nugatory or not) as an alternative to, but not in place of, proclamation of banns. The General Assembly of the Church of Scotland[65] did not oppose this Act, and by implication conceded that there had been abuses; it instructed its ministers to prevent the exaction 'of any fees higher than absolutely necessary to meet the expenses of making and certifying the publication'.[66] At the same time, however, the Church of Scotland was not willing to recognise the alternative system and required that banns, in addition to notice, be published before its ministers should conduct the ceremony.

The other churches were much more sympathetic to the change, as might be imagined. The United Presbyterian Synod petitioned Parliament in 1876,[67] and again in 1877,[68] to pass the Marriage Notice Act; and the Free Church, going even farther, pursued Government throughout the late 'seventies and early 'eighties with appeals for the total abolition of banns and the implementation of the Royal Commission's original proposals on this subject. The Free Church's abolitionist zeal was heightened when, in a case brought by the (Established) kirk session of Cambusnethan to interdict the minister and kirk session of the *quoad sacra* Parish of Wishaw from proclaiming banns in the latter's church, the Court of Session, supported by the House of Lords, concluded (in 1875) that the proclamation of banns was 'part of the discipline of the church, which the state simply recognised and confirmed';[69] and that banns could be proclaimed in a *quoad sacra* church, since banns were part of what was covered by the term '*sacra*'. This case (which no doubt confirmed Free Church suspicions about the avarice of the Establishment — and certainly it seems discreditable that the sessions had to resort to litigation) removed any possible doubt that the reason for proclaiming banns in the parish church was a civil one. Dissenters, as an Established minister commented (in a favourite phrase of nineteenth-century churchmen) 'had to bow like Naaman in the house of Rimmon'.[70] Understandably, therefore, Free churchmen were incensed. The session clerks of the Established church, one speaker in the Free Assembly of 1878 claimed, were 'hangers-on to the Government Establishment in Scotland', practising 'extortion'. The whole system of banns was

> a relic of the old Popish system; it was a kind of Papal aggression, worse than the hierarchy for it attacked the pockets, while the hierarchy did not.[71]

Support for the Marriage Notice Act was not however universal throughout the Free Church, for in the following year another speaker in the Assembly complained that now the celebration of marriage, 'a religious service', which had previously depended upon the proclamation of banns, which was 'an ecclesiastical function', was to be performed by ministers 'upon the sanction of a civil functionary'.[72] But this view was given short shrift. It was, the speaker of 1878 declared, Popish, and in the Free Assembly that was enough to squash any suggestion. James Begg seems not to have shared this view since he, by his own process of reasoning, remarked that there was 'something secular' about the whole idea of proclaiming banns on the Lord's Day. The Free Church however avoided getting into any deeper water on the subject by agreeing to welcome the 1878 Act and by discharging in 1881 the committee which had been watching over the subject.[73]

In doing this the Assembly described the Marriage Notice Act as 'the first instalment of a Disestablishment and Disendowment Act of Parliament',[74] and it is in this context rather than in the context of any theological reflection specifically concerning the nature of marriage that the churches' pronouncements on banns have to be understood.

The Royal Commission's recommendations about banns were part of a larger package which did not see the light of legislation. Its other recommendation included the abolition of marriage *per verba de praesenti* and marriage by promise *subsequente copula*, together with the introduction of civil marriage in the office of local registrars. But, as has already been mentioned, the Lord Justice General for Scotland had entered his dissent to the report, defending the way in which the Scottish system of irregular marriage removed any possible doubt about the validity of a marriage. This, together with the much talked about public opposition to change, had its effect and these forms of irregular marriage survived until 1939.

In fact the number of *registered* irregular marriages was rising at this time; and until 1939 they continued to increase in number and in proportion to regular marriage. At this point we can simply note, without comment, three reasons which have been advanced[75] for this increase: first, that as

> the possibility of registering irregular marriages became better known and as the population became more literate and more accustomed to the idea that an official marriage certificate was desirable a larger proportion of irregular marriages would presumably be registered.[76]

Thus all irregular marriages may not have been increasing at the same or even at as great a rate as were the number being registered; second, that towards the end of the nineteenth century 'there may have been more people who preferred a civil marriage as such',[77] and although registration was not strictly civil marriage, it was sometimes thought to be; and third, that some lawyers made a business of arranging the registration of irregular marriage for those who wanted to avoid the delay and difficulty of marriage before a minister (although the parties were, in fact, often involved in as long a delay by this as by the regular process).

Myths and Tactics

The evidence presented to the Royal Commission of 1865 helps to confirm some impressions formed in reviewing the work of the Housing committee and other contemporary church pronouncements. Before leaving the subject for the time being, then, some general comments can be made about rural sexual behaviour and the churches' response to it.

The first and most obvious comment is that the high illegitimacy rate of Scottish lowland rural areas seems to have been symptomatic of a fairly high incidence of premarital sexual intercourse among farm workers in these areas. In this respect many lowland farm workers appear to have differed not only from the middle classes, but also from fishing communities, Highlanders and the industrial working classes outside large cities. How far they differed from the urban working classes is more difficult to say, since an urban norm is not readily ascertainable.[78] But it seems reasonable to suggest that the criterion of sexual respectability among many lowland farm workers was whether or not the woman married reasonably quickly after discovering that she was pregnant. No doubt in many cases (but perhaps not all)[79] this was tied up with a traditional desire to prove the woman's fertility for economic reasons. But whatever the reasons, it seems to have been common enough, and generally accepted. As John Tulloch wrote to another parish minister in 1850, after moving from Dundee to the rural parish of Kettins near Coupar Angus:

> The gravest practical offences (immorality before marriage, for instance, which is sadly prevalent among the farm-servants) are spoken of and apparently quite sincerely regarded as very trifling things. Do you find anything of the same sort with you?[80]

A second, but more debatable comment, is that what happened in Kettins and many other parts of lowland rural Scotland may have reflected a pattern of behaviour and attitudes common throughout Europe. Generalisations on this scale are difficult, and contrary views exist,[81] but one authority on the family has described the common pattern as follows:

> The supposed high level of 'rural morality' may be only a widespread myth. In much of north and central Europe, and in rural regions of France, Holland and even Scotland, a widespread pattern of courtship during the eighteenth century included premarital sexual intercourse and, especially in south Germany, Austria and Sweden, a relatively high rate of illegitimacy (about 20 per cent). Outsiders were barred from this courtship pattern, since they were of different social status and could not be held to account. The pairing-off process was evaluated and shaped by peers as well as parents. Young men could not escape their responsibilities without leaving the region and thus abandoning their sole means of a livelihood, the family farm. Marriage often postdated the birth of a child, but the couple was eventually united legally. Both church and state denounced the pattern, but in some regions it continued until well into the nineteenth century. It permitted some sexual freedom among the young, but maintained close social control over marriage.[82]

This courtship pattern, then, was similar to what appears to have existed in those parts of Scotland of which Strahan's description was representative.[83] An important aspect of it was, as he recorded, that rural society did have methods of controlling legitimacy, even if the social definition of legitimacy did not square with the legal one. Even here, however, the gap between the two, given the legal doctrine of subsequent legitimation, was not so very great. How irregular marriage related to the control of legitimacy is far from certain. If, as was widely believed in the nineteenth century, one third of all eighteenth-century Scottish marriages were irregular, then irregular marriage must in some communities have performed a function analogous to regular marriage, as far as legitimation was concerned. But then, since it was or was believed to be legal, there is no reason why it should not have done so. Our knowledge of the incidence of irregular marriage prior to the nineteenth century is too sketchy however for any definite conclusions to be made about this. And as far as the mid-nineteenth century is concerned it appears to have been of only marginal social significance.

If the description of a European rural courtship pattern quoted above is thus in some respects consistent with what appears to have been going on in nineteenth-century Scottish society, in two other respects there are significant differences.

The courtship pattern described was one which existed in a relatively static society, and outsiders were barred from it. But by comparison with what had gone before it, nineteenth-century Scottish rural society was not static. The family farm was no longer the sole means of livelihood: on the one hand many families no longer had farms: on the other, alternative forms of employment, agricultural and industrial, now existed. Farm workers now moved about, many of them frequently and with little regard to family ties. It was therefore much more difficult to exclude outsiders, and if Strahan's estimate, that about one third of courtships ended with the departure of the father to another farm, was correct, it is clear that the safeguards attached to the old system of courtship were not able to operate in many cases because of the new conditions.

If, then, as seems likely, ecclesiastical anxiety about illegitimacy was grounded in an awareness of some such breakdown in the methods by which rural society controlled legitimacy, it was perhaps not entirely unjustified. And if the increased mobility of some farm servants did in fact lead to a larger proportion of unmarried and abandoned mothers, then the churches' representatives, pointing an accusing finger at bothies and bad housing, were not entirely on the wrong track. In isolating these factors they were probably mistaking the symptoms for the cause. But those of them who were interested were, as has already been noted, social reformers rather than social scientists; and if a social reformer was intent on arousing public opinion to desire (although perhaps not to effect) change, he was as likely to be successful by such methods as by means of a detailed and careful analysis of a situation which was in any case changing as he described it.

The existence of such social reformers and of a rudimentary form of social science was in itself the second of the significant differences between the traditional European courtship pattern and what was going on in nineteenth-century Scottish society. Before the Registrar-General published his statistics, the subject of rural sexual behaviour could be discussed either in anecdotal terms or, at best, in terms of local statistics. In either case the behaviour under discussion was that of a population of which the discussants probably had some first-hand knowledge. But as statistics assumed a greater importance this first-hand knowledge, while it continued to play a part, was subordinated to the knowledge of statistics and to analyses of the situation in less personal terms. The subordination of first-hand knowledge of the behaviour of individuals to the more general knowledge of social scientists and reformers (the distinction between these was not clear: the Registrar-General and Strahan were as interested in the practical bearing of their information as was Begg) led to statements being made about farm workers as a class, which while they may have been true of the majority, undermined the myth of rural morality. Since, in its own terms, rural society had been moral — that is to say that it had exercised its own forms of social control over sexual behaviour — prior to the upheavals of the late eighteenth century, the demytholygising of rural morality helped to harden the middle classes in the conviction that farm servants were a race apart, by exaggerating the difference between their respective patterns of sexual behaviour. Quite important differences did exist between these patterns and they were, apparently, growing at this time. And these differences would have existed quite apart from the reflex action of social scientific study upon them. But this reflex action, demonstrated in the attitudes of the middle classes, did nothing to help and may have hindered the survival of the social control of sexual behaviour in rural areas. Blanket condemnation of rural immorality falsified the situation in the eyes of the middle classes and led them to regard agricultural workers in such a way as to discourage the latter from any attempts they may have wanted to make to recover from the disintegrating effects of social change.

This was the context in which church pronouncements on the subject were made. But, as we have seen, condemnation of rural immorality was only one side of the churches' complex attitude to this question. The churches were not willing to go the whole way with the demytholygising of rural morality. They also wished to preserve the myth, and their desire to do so was discernible both in the confused opinions they appeared to hold on the subject of irregular marriage, and in the apparent hypocrisy of the way in which session discipline, as described by Strahan, was exercised.

The churches' desire to preserve the myth of rural morality led them to misunderstand the nature of traditional rural morality, which they confused with that of the middle classes. It also led them to contradict themselves in their estimates of contemporary rural sexual behaviour. Their misunderstandings and contradictions were, in part, the consequence of their ignorance: but ignorance was not the only reason for what they said or failed to say. There was method in their misunderstanding, even if it was unconscious.

The declared aim of the churches was to raise the level of public opinion among the rural working classes on the subject of sexual behaviour. In effect this implied an effort to make rural working-class behaviour approximate more closely to that of the middle classes. Much can be said in criticism of the means adopted to further this end. Begg, for example, saw clearly that for the working classes to adopt middle-class forms of behaviour it was necessary for them to have a foothold in a property-owning society. But when this point was pressed by Begg the churches became cautious, sensing in the elevation of the lower story a threat to middle-class supremacy. The churches' caution in this respect thus makes their claims appear, in historical perspective, less credible. Nevertheless, although it is no part of the present purpose to present an apologia for these nineteenth-century churchmen, it may be said in their defence that their attempt to raise the level of public opinion was a response, however inadequate, to a situation in which the traditional social controls of sexual behaviour were breaking down under the weight of contemporary social and economic conditions. It was a response moreover whose logic led to the development of what Begg proposed. Given the social changes which were taking place, rural society could not on its own exercise traditional controls over sexual behaviour and new forms of control had to be found.

In this context the churches' desire to preserve the myth of rural morality was not entirely out of place. If two thirds of the agricultural population still desired regular marriage, and if some of them were still willing to submit themselves voluntarily to session discipline, rural morality, even if misunderstood, was not yet a myth. It was possible therefore for the churches to hope that their evocation of an earlier and more moral Scotland might have some effect. The revivals of the period added some credibility to the hope that the preaching of the evangelical gospel might improve the morals of the people, as it had done in earlier centuries.

But how far it had in fact done so is highly debatable, and brings us back to the question of how far Scottish rural society can be equated with what has been described as a European pattern. It was assumed above that rural Scotland had not been very different from other rural societies. But what we do not know here is how far the courtship customs which seem to have existed in mid-nineteenth century Scotland had been suppressed by session discipline, especially in the seventeenth century — or how far, if they existed throughout this period, the concomitant controls over legitimacy were sufficiently tight to ensure that, although premarital sexual intercourse was tolerated, marriage normally preceded the birth of any children. It is difficult to form any firm conclusions about this subject, but some evidence supporting this latter possibility is provided by the contrast between the South-West, where the illegitimacy rate was high, and the North-West, where it was low. The South-West had been a Covenanting stronghold in the seventeenth century, but by the nineteenth its congregations were not markedly Evangelical, if adherence to the Free Church was any indication of this.[84] In the North-West, by contrast, Evangelical religion was a more recent and more influential social factor, and may have played an important part in the situation which inhibited illegitimacy.[85]

Returning from these speculative questions to what the churches actually said, it may be useful to conclude this chapter by summarising the tactics with which the churches responded to their situation, and by asking how they legitimated their response in theological terms. So far, in fact, we have noted a number of different forms of response. In connection with the subject of the social control of sexual behaviour we have seen how an already existent atmosphere of ecclesiastical concern over a supposed decline in working-class sexual morality was heightened by the illegitimacy controversy of the late 'fifties. This controversy threatened the idealised self-image of the churches, not least because of the high illegitimacy rate among the rural population, over whose everyday life the church might have been assumed to have had greater influence than over that of town dwellers. The churches did not respond to this situation, we have seen, by means of an overall strategy: the internal divisions of Presbyterianism, on the one hand, and on the other the absence of the desire or the ability to exercise a coercive form of social control over sexual behaviour (except in terms of general watchfulness among parents and employers), meant in effect that the Calvinist strategy was no longer viable. In its place the churches resorted to three sets of tactics. The first set of tactics was that used by the Housing committee of the Free Church, whose aim was to interest public opinion in those social conditions which encouraged the evils complained of, and who consequently emphasised the serious nature of those social conditions as much as possible. These tactics were vitiated to some extent by the difficulty of proving the causal connections which were being suggested, and by the fear of identifying the Free Church with radical political pressure groups, and thereby either secularising or dividing the church. These tactics were, however, successful to the point that the connection between social factors and morality was gradually accepted by the churches.

The second set of tactics was that used by the Religion and Morals committee of the Free Church, by Guthrie and to some extent by the Church of Scotland and the United Presbyterians. These tactics (whose validity the Housing committee also in the last resort acknowledged) were aimed at 'raising the tone of feeling and opinion on this subject, especially among the labouring population'.[86] It was difficult, in the area of sexual behaviour, however, to give expression to this in practical terms. Over the drink question it was easier: supportive legislation could be worked for, public houses could be closed or their hours limited, and temperance associations could be formed. Sex was more problematic. Associations like the White Cross League, and the Onward and Upward Association, would play a part in the near future, and towards the end of the century the churches would attempt to do more about urban prostitution, but the social phenomenon with which they were primarily concerned at this point did not readily lend itself to such direct action. It had therefore to be treated as part of a larger religious problem, and as we have seen, the Free Church viewed it as a lapse into paganism from the high religious standards of the seventeenth century, while the Church of Scotland regarded it as a form of backsliding among persons who were still basically Christians. These two approaches reflected, on the one hand the nominal adherence of large sections of the lowland rural population to the Established Church, and on the other the voluntary character, in this sense at least, of the Free Church outside the Highlands. In practice the different approaches of these two churches meant that the Free Church at this stage had a much greater investment in revivalism than had the Church of Scotland (although the latter's attitude would change). These different approaches were reflected in the churches' different disciplinary practices. The Free Church was gratified that it had so few cases to deal with, but since its jurisdiction was restricted to its membership, this was not particularly surprising. The Establishment on the other hand exercised discipline over a wider sphere, but after the fashion of a semi-superstitious folk-religion. Neither the Established church, nor the Free Church, nor for that matter the United Presbyterians, thus seem to have exercised very much control over sexual behaviour by means of their disciplinary systems as such.

The third set of tactics exercised by the churches — or at least endorsed by their Assemblies — concerned irregular marriage and provided the churches with something of a long-stop. They saw irregular marriages as minimal safeguards of sexual order and defended them on the ground that their continued existence was desired by the Scottish people. In doing this they acted without any regard for theological principles — certainly without regard for the insistence of their Reforming forbears that marriage should always be a public event. In some respects, of course, the Reformers' demands had been met: the majority of nineteenth-century marriages were public events, and although most Presbyterian marriages did not take place in church buildings, this may have had more to do with the Presbyterian churches' low view of church buildings than with the relationship between the church and marriage.[87] But given this, there seems little theological basis for what the churches said about irregular or even regular marriage at this time. They took the attitudes they did largely because they had no real alternative. Basing what they taught on scripture, they found themselves without any scriptural mandate for being marriage superintendents. This was a role which had been assumed by the church during a period which nineteenth-century Presbyterians either regarded as one of religious degeneracy or preferred not to think about. Their Reformed predecessors, still within that world, had been able to accept this role by making it part of the life of their holy community — a community whose perfect realisation would follow from their educational and disciplinary activities. In the nineteenth century this realisation remained too imperfect for the churches to enforce total regularity and publicity, but not imperfect enough for the state and public opinion to discharge the churches of their responsibility.

This was not a situation, then, in which any clear theological teaching by the churches concerning their relation to marriage might be expected. Their fundamentalist and undialectical attitude to scripture did not help, and teaching on this subject was not forthcoming in this context. The churches did however have a few theological views about family religion, and these will be considered in the next chapter.

CHAPTER FIVE

Pastoral Advice on Family Religion, 1850-1870

UP to this point we have been discussing what the churches said about sexual behaviour, discipline and the constitution of marriage. Now, in turning from these to pronouncements on family religion, it might seem reasonable to expect some shift in the churches' interest — from the things of the flesh to the things of the spirit, or from external behaviour to inward piety. The transition however is not quite so abrupt: the term 'family religion' referred as much to the supervision and discipline of children and domestics as to family worship; and even in their discussion of family worship, the churches were concerned with external behaviour as well as with inward piety. Yet at the same time, it cannot be denied that they were concerned with inwardness. And here, if anywhere, in their appeal to the religious awareness of the people, some impression may be gathered of how far the churches believed that their own understanding of piety reached into the homes of the Scots.

Family Worship and the Scottish Presbyterian Tradition

By way of a very brief introduction to these pronouncements, it may be noted that family worship, although by no means an innovation of the Reformers,[1] was important and integral to Reformed piety, providing it with a model for public worship. In the seventeenth century it was assumed that family worship was regularly practised in the Christian home. Observance of it was a condition of election to and deposition from the eldership.[2] And kirk sessions conducted investigations to see that it was kept up.[3] Since daily services of worship and lectures were held in the churches (at least in the towns), a good deal of time must have been spent in religious exercises of one kind or another. Despite, or perhaps because of this, General Assemblies condemned the neglect of family worship, in 1596, and urged its better observance in 1694, 1697 and 1711.[4]

We shall not speculate here however about how widely family worship was neglected or observed in the seventeenth century. Suffice it to say that by the nineteenth, the notion that family prayers had been universally observed in the good old days was a well-established part of Presbyterian mythology, and that, in the figure of the cotter conducting family worship, Burns gave the churches an example of domestic devotion to which ministers seeking inspiration and sermon illustrations would repeatedly turn.

Evidence that Burns' cotter was more than a myth was provided by Aiton when he wrote:

> All ranks of people in Ayrshire, devoutly ask a blessing to each meal, and a considerable part of them perform family worship daily. As these exercises are performed extemporary, and set forms rejected, the language used is homely, and often absurd. They are generally too ambitious to introduce into their graces and prayers, scripture phrases, which they do not understand and sometimes misapply, so grossly as to render their language inconsistent. Instead of retailing sentences of scripture, or those they pick up from clergymen, the meaning of which they do not comprehend, it would be much better for the clergy to compose for them a few pious prayers, in a plain and easy style, which the simplest might easily understand, and which could either be read, or committed to memory, and repeated correctly, in a decent and proper manner.[5]

Here, as before, Aiton was anticipating what was to happen in the church. The Church of Scotland issued a book of 'Prayers for Social and Family Worship' in 1859 and the Free Church, despite protests, published a book of family prayers in 1891. But before they produced these books the churches were beginning to become aware that the cotter was not so common a figure as had once been supposed; and in expressing their concern about this they did not for the most part express themselves in Aiton's cool and rational accents.

What the churches had to say on this subject, between 1850 and 1870, was expressed in a series of Pastoral Addresses: in a Pastoral Letter issued by the Church of Scotland in 1836 and re-issued in 1869, in an address by the United Presbyterian Synod, issued in 1857, and in a series of addresses issued by the Free Church in 1858, 1860 and 1862.

The Perennial Piety: the Pastoral Letter of the Church of Scotland

The Church of Scotland's 1861 Pastoral on 'the Increase of Immorality in Rural Districts' had, as we have seen, referred to family worship as a prophylactic against sexual immorality. But the letter we are concerned with here had originally been issued long before the alarums of 1858, and its re-issue in 1869 seems not to have been related to the illegitimacy question. It was one of a series of letters on the religious duties of the church's people, drafted by Dr. John Lee, Assembly Clerk and Principal of Edinburgh University, whose compositions even Chalmers praised.[6]

In issuing this Pastoral, the 1836 Assembly had disavowed 'any recent ground for apprehending' that family worship was 'likely to fall into more extensive neglect': they knew however 'too well' that it was 'by no means universally practised',[7] and desired to remind members of the Church of Scotland, whose 'faith and devotion have long been spoken of throughout the world', of their obligations, so that they might continue to be like their 'forefathers in times of clearest light'.[8] Family worship, they were reminded, was as necessary for spiritual nourishment and refreshment as eating and sleeping were to the body. Scripture, they wrote, enjoined this duty

> at sundry times and in divers manners, adding line upon line, precept upon precept, promise upon promise, and threatening upon threatening, so as to bring perpetually to remembrance both the blessings which are multiplied to them that fear the Lord, and the fury which is poured out on families which call not on His name.[9]

In the same solemn tone, and in language so permeated with quotations from and paraphrases of the Authorised Version that in some paragraphs only the conjunctions were unscriptural, the Letter went on to describe the blessings experienced by those whose participation in daily domestic devotions was not 'a mere formal ceremony'[10] but came from the heart. 'All men of sound mind and Christian experience,' its readers were reminded, had always regarded the domestic altar not as 'the imposition of an irksome yoke',[11] but as a great privilege; and the benefits of such worship were to be seen in growth in 'the graces of humility, resignation and patience'.[12]

The Assembly, however, claimed no special insight into the divine economy. In a passage which suggests that even they might have regarded prayer as something of a problem, they observed that although God had prior knowledge of men's needs, men had no reason to expect that they would receive without asking. Prayer was not magic; nor was it explicable to 'our feeble understandings'.[13] 'It is not for us,' the Letter stated, 'to unfold the laws of the spiritual world, or to demonstrate why and how it is that the communication of heavenly influence and favour are in any degree suspended on the frequency and fervour of our supplications.'[14] It was simply a matter of experience under the Old and New Covenants alike that believers received grace through prayer.

Family prayer was important also, of course, in the upbringing of children. Although it was not 'within the compass of human ability to infuse grace into the souls which are most tenderly beloved', yet, the Pastoral ventured, 'great will probably be the influence of a pious example on those who confide in your affection and have cause to revere your worth'.[15] Even if the child did not respond immediately, and even if he went wrong, he might afterwards be 'awakened to a new obedience, by recalling to his agonised mind with reverential awe the solemn image of the parental guide, in whose quiet habitation the daily exercises of prayer and praise hallowed every pursuit'.[16]

After an appeal to its hearers to pray for non-praying families, the Letter concluded by asking them to pray for times of blessing in which the household of faith might be enlarged. In making this last request the Assembly had not in mind local revivals (of which many of its members were suspicious) but 'plenteous showers of blessings, not confined to . . . any privileged community, but dropping down fertility far and wide over fields coextensive with the inhabited world'.[17]

Then, it declared, 'the ways of Sion, which have mourned because few came to the solemn feasts, shall be thronged with multitudes who keep the holy day with thanksgiving in their hearts'.[18]

The Letter, then, was an appeal for more faithful observance of family prayer, in the hope that this would help bring about more godly, and more churchgoing, times. Its general manner is reminiscent of the Old Testament and implies similarities between the Jews and the Scots. But it misuses Scripture, lacks the specific element of Old Testament prophecy, and appears strangely dissociated from the concrete situation in which those to whom it was addressed were living. Although its language — too evangelical for a product of the late eighteenth century and too humane for a product of the seventeenth — makes it very much of its own time, it could, judged by its content, equally well have been written for any age.

This was perhaps why, although issued in 1836, it was ordered 'to be read from the pulpit on the first Sabbath after they received it'[19] by ministers in 1869. Five years earlier it had been inserted by the Assembly as a preface to their manual of family prayers. This book contained different prayers for morning and evening use on each day of four weeks, plus some additional prayers for use on Sacramental Fast Days and Sundays, on the last evening and first morning of the year (not yet at Christmas or any other festivals), and at times of sickness and bereavement. The prayers themselves, 'adapted, not to any particular class, but to the general circumstances of all Christian households',[20] were not long by Presbyterian standards: accompanied by the reading of a chapter from the Bible the exercise might have lasted for fifteen minutes; and they contained the conventional elements of adoration, confession, thanksgiving, petition and intercession. The language, like that of the Pastoral, was reminiscent of the Authorised Version; and although the collect form was utilised, this was done half-heartedly, the general style being discursive. The only sources acknowledged were two prayers of Calvin's, altered and amended, and two prayers 'from' Jeremy Taylor. There were prayers for the traditional virtues of faith, hope and charity, as well as 'for grace to fill our station aright',[21] and 'for earnestness in religious duties'.[22] We shall return below to the question of how far books of this kind were used.

Spiritual Backsliding among the Faithful: the Pastoral of the United Presbyterian Synod

Like the Church of Scotland's Pastoral, that issued by the United Presbyterian Synod in 1857[23] was not concerned with immorality — it was, after all, directed to the parents and families of the United Presbyterian Church — but with spiritual backsliding among those who ought to have known better. No special circumstances seem to have surrounded the decision to issue it other than a request by a large number of United Presbyterian elders.

The Synod, taking as its ideal a twice-daily diet of domestic devotion, was not sure how many of its families neglected regular family worship. But it did express concern that in 'many' United Presbyterian homes 'the duty is only partially performed', and that, in many others, 'it is not performed at all'.[24] It was of course true that many families did live up to the ideal. Yet generally, the Synod believed, 'in this respect we have declined from "the good old ways" of our fathers'.[25] That the United Presbyterian Synod should have thought this is interesting, since its members, the majority of whom were inheritors of the Secession tradition, were the least likely of Presbyterians to abandon — insofar as it was abandoning — the tradition of family worship.[26]

Some other points made by the Synod were similar to those in the Established church's Pastoral. Prayer, both in private and in families, was a means of grace, and was commanded by God. It was important for the godly upbringing of children, and 'as necessary as are religious instruction and example'.[27] Indeed, by conducting family prayers in fulfilment of the vows taken at the baptism of their children, parents were giving instruction and example in the most influential way. Family prayer was also important for the success and prosperity of the church, which would be blessed as much by the daily prayers of its families as by their financial contributions. A further reason for it, the Synod told its people, was that God dealt with them not just as individuals but as families: family prayer was the appointed way to give thanks for family blessings, to understand 'domestic trials and afflictions',[28] and to confess family sins. But while encouraging its families in this way, and while appealing to their higher religious sensibilities, the Synod also warned them, in the same phrase used by the Establishment, that 'God "pours out his fury on families that call not on his name"'.[29]

The Pastorals of the Free Church: Commercial Crisis and Religious Revival

The Free Church also sought to put the fear of God into backsliders, but its Pastorals were more closely interwoven with the public events of the period. The Assembly of 1858, which was very interested in the American revivals as well as in housing and illegitimacy, received a request from the Presbytery of Edinburgh for a Pastoral Address 'in connection with the disclosures, during the commercial crisis, of the way in which trade and commerce was often carried on'[30] and these aspects of the commercial crisis were woven into the Pastoral Address of 1858 as one of the four social factors which were obstructing the Spirit's work and hindering that revival with which the Address was primarily concerned. The other hindrances were the state of 'social relations' in general, intemperance and illegitimacy. The attack on intemperance took in

> more than habitual drunkenness. Occasional acts of it, which some seem to regard as scarcely sins at all, are absolutely fatal to the Christian character, if thought lightly of, or repeated from time to time. And even the state of flushed excitement — the marked change in the speech and behaviour, in which compliance with the usages of society frequently land numbers, is something quite alien to the perfect sobriety and command of mind and action, which God's children are bound to maintain.[31]

This 'sobriety and command of mind and action' was fundamental to the Free Church's view of Christian character: it lay behind its criticism of commercial immoralities, insofar as it meant that you should not put yourself in a risky financial position where you might lose control of your affairs, while in matters religious it lay behind the fear, as a subsequent address[32] would put it, of 'mere excitement' during revivals. In addition, this view emphasised the dangers of the little sins which lead on to large ones, and the Address, turning to those 'immoralities through breach of the seventh commandment' which were 'grievously numerous in Scotland', warned against the 'things to which this sin can often be traced — strong drink, love of dress and such like'.[33] In its criticism the Assembly did not however analyse causes any further, nor, as was usual, did it say exactly what it had in mind because, as it put it, 'the sin is so vile and shameful, that it can hardly be spoken about'.[34] But it seems pretty clear from the context that the condemnation was the standard Calvinist one of all forms of pre-and extra-marital sexual intercourse, including the more intense forms of courtship even when intercourse did not technically take place. The authors of the Pastoral, aware that, because the sin could 'hardly be spoken about', it escaped 'that rebuke and those warnings which it so much needs',[35] described it in phrases from the Epistles,[36] and claimed that there was 'no dubiety in this language'.[37] Perhaps to their hearers there was not, since behind what they said lay a long tradition of the condemnation of sexual sins and the advocacy of continence. In this particular nineteenth-century form, however, the advocacy of sobriety and self-control was in curious contrast to the extravagant language with which it was advocated.

The final hindrance to the Spirit and to revivals mentioned in the Pastoral brought it closer to the theme of family religion. What, according to the Assembly, was wrong with 'the state of social relations among us'[38] was, first of all, that family responsibilities were not taken seriously enough:

> Parents are required to rule in their households, and that with affection and firmness . . . They are to regard themselves as charged with the spiritual as well as the temporal interests of their children . . . To this end family worship and family catechising (alas how often are these neglected!) ought to be found in every family.[39]

This, together with the proper observance of the Sabbath, was the parents' part. As for the children,

> submission, respect, love are necessary on their part . . . Where is the religion of those who fail in their duty to their parents?[40]

But the family was not simply made up of parents and children; and the address went on to point out that 'domestic servants are also a part of the family',[41] however many masters and mistresses might overlook this. Thus,

> they should be instructed, watched over, guarded from temptation, directed, encouraged in duty, led to feel that they have an interest in the religion and the religious duties of the family.[42]

The Free Church's conception of the patriarchalism of love extended even farther, however:

> Cottagers and farm workers, and farm servants, workers in factories, mines and in shops of the different trades, with shop-assistants and clerks, have a strong claim on the Christian kindness and good offices of their employers. Thou art thy brother's keeper . . . [43]

This inclusion of all employees enabled the authors to go on to remark that 'some of our most serious social evils' arose from 'the neglect of social duties',[44] and to mention specifically (and not surprisingly since Begg[45] was a member of the committee which drew it up) 'the dwellings of the working classes'. By the same token servants and employees were reminded of the 'duties required of them — faithful conscientious service — not eye-service, merely',[46] and were told that if subject to bad employers they should wait with 'patient endurance till the proper season of change comes round'.[47] (Not that they had much choice: if they did make off they could be arrested for breach of contract.)[48]

Reviving the Family

What the Pastoral of 1858 had to say on the subject of the family was taken up by the following Assembly, in response to an overture from members of the Assembly asking it to do something about the revivals and in response to another, from the Synod of Fife, asking it to devise 'such means as may seem best fitted for reviving family worship and household piety throughout the church'.[49] On the advice of R.S. Candlish — Melville to Chalmers' Knox in the Free Church — the two subjects were to be dealt with in the same Pastoral. This, Candlish believed, would provide an opportunity for applying

> the real remedy for almost all the evils under which the country groans, and especially the evil of licentiousness.[50]

What was needed, he remarked, in a now familiar phrase, 'was the raising of the standard of opinion among the people as regarded the sanctity of the family relationship'.[51]

In raising the subject, the Synod of Fife, like the United Presbyterian Synod, had expressed its concern that 'there was a great want of the family worship which used to prevail almost universally over Scotland', and the minister from Fife who introduced their overture supported this contention by remarking that

> He remembered hearing it said that, in former days, if a person passed through Kirkcaldy at a particular time of the evening, he would see every door shut, and find every family engaged, either in singing the praises of God, or reading the Word, or in prayer.[52]

Statements of this kind, based on secondhand reminiscences or upon accounts of the less reliable Presbyterian historians, were common in Assembly, especially in Free Assembly discussions of this subject, and were used to demonstrate how much things had changed for the worse. For, as the minister from Fife continued:

> He was sorry to say that at present in Fife, as well as in other parts of the country, family worship was being much neglected. Sabbath schools had increased of late years, but there had not been the increased attention to the instruction of children that used to characterise the land. (Hear, hear.) Instead of parents and children uniting together on the Sabbath evening in reading the Word of God and engaging in catechetical exercises, they found that, very generally, they went out to stroll in the fields, or wander by the sea-shore.[53]

Something, he believed, should be done by the Assembly, so that 'instead of lying down at night with as little reverence for the God that made them as was paid by the beasts of the field, the practice of family worship should be resumed'.[54] The Pastoral Address of 1860, together with suggestions about catechetical lectures on the Lord's Prayer, and the setting aside of a special Sunday for sermons on the subject, were to be the means adopted to this end.

The twofold task given to the committee charged with preparing the address (which again included Begg, and also included Candlish — there were few Free Church pies in which this pair did not each have a finger) meant, however, that the subject could not be dealt with as fully as the Assembly wanted, for in the meantime the full frontal system of revival had reached not only Ireland, but also Scotland, precipitating 'a measure, a large and unusual measure of the blessing from on high'.[55] Thus, the authors of the Pastoral stated,

> it is impossible for us to address you now upon any matter connected with the interests of Christ's Kingdom among us, in the same terms which might have been suitable a year or two ago.[56]

What they did say, however, was not so very different. In the first place the committee was none too optimistic about the behaviour even of the Free Church's own people. 'How many in all our congregations as we cannot but fear,' it declared, 'are unconverted sinners, still at ease in sin';[57] and turning specifically to family religion it remarked that although the family was a divine institution which might be a blessing, and the nursery 'of a seed for the church on earth and for the church in heaven',[58] the blessing might become a curse if families became involved in 'a course of heedless, worldly living',[59] damaging to their eternal interests. 'What,' it therefore asked, 'is going on in your families?'[60]

This solemn enquiry was illustrated by Old and New Testament texts enjoining or exemplifying family godliness, and children and servants were also warned that they might be in danger of 'poisoning by your influence those who should be dearest to you'.[61] Chiefly, however, the Free Church addressed 'the heads of every house', advising them of their special influence, and warning them against carelessness and 'your own undisguised worldliness',[62] with its fatal and fearsome results.

A specific form of carelessness against which the heads of Free Church families were warned was that of putting off 'the question of their (their families') spiritual interests to some vague future time'.[63] They should, instead, speak to them and pray with them right away, in the hope of an immediate family revival. Responsibility in this sphere, they were again informed, was not to be left to the Sabbath Schools. It was to be accepted by parents, whose family worship was to be conducted regularly and not in a 'formal' fashion. It seems likely however that some Free Church heads of families found all this far from easy: for the authors of the Pastoral felt the need to assure them that if they happened to 'find or imagine' difficulties in family worship, then they should consult

> pastors and other Christian friends, and you will generally find these difficulties disappear, if you learn to regard it not only as a duty, but as a great privilege.[64]

The Pastoral then concluded, with an exhortation to keep the Sabbath,

> the principal, and with many families . . . the only, day in which there is ample time and opportunity for every exercise of family religion,

and with a reminder that 'the heavenly rest is in a home'.[65]

The Free Church's Pastorals of 1858 and 1860 did not however exhaust the rich vein of its leaders' rhetoric. In 1862 they came back to the subject of family religion with renewed vigour, and determined to leave no doubt in their people's minds about it, they delivered themselves of no fewer than three Pastorals, addressing Parents, Children, and Masters and Servants in turn. Substantially these Pastorals said much the same as their predecessors, but some of the excitement of the revivals had died down, and in these more detailed attempts to get their teaching about the family across, the Free Church was rather more concerned with practical matters.[66]

Parents and Heads of Families

The Address to 'Parents and Heads of Families' was in two parts, the first dealing with parents' responsibilities, the second with their duties. It proceeded from the assumption that the long-term benefits of the revivals would depend upon the 'sound and healthy condition'[67] of family life. In style it was rather less hectoring than its predecessors, and it made a few, although only a few, concessions to human frailty.

The first part of the Pastoral, dealing with parental responsibilities, included a theological statement of the church's view of the family. Pre-dating by a decade the controversies which would attack its anthropological presuppositions, the Address began by pointing out that while civil governments,

> although Divine in a more ultimate and general manner, are yet more immediately 'ordinances of man' (1 Pet. ii 13), and thus are liable to endless diversities of form in

> different countries and periods, the institution of the family is so immediately Divine, as to have been from the beginning, destined no less to be to the end, absolutely *one* — a government unchanged and unchangeable, in all countries and ages of the world.[68]

The form of this government, despite revolutions and republics abroad, was monarchical. In each household

> there is a kingdom with the kingly power vested in the head of the family, of a singularly absolute character and yet very safe and salutary in its absoluteness, by reason partly of the narrowness of the sphere it extends over, and partly of the love which dwells in the parental heart.[69]

And just as the family was a kingdom, as well as a nursery for the United Kingdom, and a preparation for the heavenly kingdom, so it also was, or at least might be, 'a kind of church'.[70] In the family the ecclesiastical functions of ministry, discipline and government might be performed 'within the circle of his own household' by the parent who was 'at once a king and a priest'.[71]

This reference to the priestly function of the parent led the Pastoral naturally on to the first of the parental duties, which was that of prayer for and with children. For this purpose the parent should 'take them aside *individually*'.[72] Children also, however, should be present at family prayers, which should be held 'morning and evening with all possible regularity'.[73] Recognising that the conditions of nineteenth-century life and labour did not always allow for this, the authors of the Pastoral added the qualification, 'according to your circumstances in providence'.[74] They also qualified their injunction by advising parents

> to avoid fatiguing the young with too long prayers in the family, and to aim at rendering the whole exercise lively, interesting, palpably real and true.[75]

This concern to make religion real to children was also shown in the Pastoral's teaching on religious instruction. Parents, especially mothers, were to instruct their children, along lines laid down by the Old Testament, 'constantly',[76] so that what was taught would be 'interwoven gradually with all that is most sweet, sacred, endearing, enduring, in the associations of home'.[77] This end would be achieved if

> over and above all the parent's more formal and stated teaching of his child (in the quiet and hallowed hours of the Sabbath evening, for example), his instructions are to be largely occasional, incidental, habitual and as to the manner and spirit of them, frank, conversational, easy, affectionate.[78]

If this seemed difficult, the authors of the Pastoral met the difficulty by saying, ominously, that if their hearers were themselves 'strangers still to the fear and love of the Lord',[79] then they could not in any case hope to teach their children. However, if this was not the case, they should not be afraid to speak from the heart, provided they did it little by little. Nor should they be afraid to make use of aids in teaching, 'principally the Scriptures, with their charming histories, for example, of Samuel, and Joseph, and Moses, and Daniel and so many others'.[80] As for 'the more doctrinal portions of the Word, it were no small thing if your children only learned to commit considerable parts of these to memory'.[81] Further aids were provided by 'our incomparable catechisms, shorter and larger', as well as 'our psalms, hymns and spiritual songs'.

Aid of a different kind was provided by Sabbath-schools. But these (as the earlier Pastorals had noted) had their dangers. Thus, the authors wrote,

> there is no reason, of course, why you should not *supplement* your own instructions by those of the Sabbath-school teacher, provided you do not seek, by *devolving* the care and responsibility on another, to shake yourselves free of it.[82]

But even if this danger was avoided, Parental Instruction would seem 'a mockery and a lie together',[83] unless it was complemented by the performance of a third duty — that of Parental Example. Parents should give a good example to their children by being always honest with them, not deceiving them even 'in sport',[84] and by not 'promising what they do not intend to perform, or threatening what they do not mean to execute'.[85] Nor should parents sprinkle their conversation with exclamations such as 'God bless me, or God keep me' on every 'trifling occasion of surprise'.[86]

Naturally enough parental example also included, from the Free Church point of view, 'loving regard for Divine ordinances and institutions'[87] — especially the Sabbath. Parents should

> take care lest your own drowsy, irksome Sabbaths should seem to say in your children's hearing, What a weariness it is.[88]

Instead they should enjoy the Sabbath and churchgoing, training their children to attend church with them; and although

> it might not be so easy to show an example in *prayer*, secret prayer at least. Yet much might be done even as to this . . . by the *spirit* of your prayers in the family.[89]

What the Pastoral's authors wanted was a spirit of consistency among their hearers, which would be convincing to their children:

> For how quick of observation our children are! How ruinous, if a parent shall be found at a prayer meeting one day, and, the next, immersed in the world's most characteristic gaieties and follies.[90]

Children therefore should never 'have to witness a rude, noisy, quarrelsome temper in the intercourse of parents together',[91] and certainly not drunkenness: the sobriety of parents should be 'so perfect and palpable as to tell of a horror of it, proportioned in some measure to its fearful and murderous character'.[92]

The fourth duty enjoined in the Pastoral was that of Parental Government. Here again what was said was based on the concept of the parent as a loving, but absolute, ruler. The child owed obedience 'not so much because he approves the grounds and reasons of your will, as simply because it is your will'. But since the parent could 'lawfully enjoin only that which is just and reasonable' he should also often explain his will to the child. Thus, wrote the Pastoral's authors hopefully, 'shall their obedience be the more genial, as well as your authority more loving'.[93]

The possibility of this harmonious relationship breaking down raised the further question of 'that important branch of parental government — discipline, or the infliction of chastisement'; and parents were warned of three ways in which they might harm their children by misusing it: 'by the inflicting of punishment too frequently; or with too much severity; or in passion'.[94] Children should not be punished too often or for minor faults, but only for serious ones, such as 'deliberate falsehoods, wilful and persistent disobedience, abstraction of property, wilful injury done to the children of another household, &c.'; and the parent should even then punish 'only because you must and never because you will'.[95] This advice was based on Pauline injunctions against paternal overstrictness,[96] and although these might seem to contradict Solomon's dictum, 'He that spareth the rod, hateth the child', the authors pointed out that this had to be understood in the light of the fact that from some parents a frown was as effective as a thrashing.

The difficulty of performing these duties, the authors wrote, should send parents back to prayer. Only those who yielded themselves to God's authority could exercise authority in the family. God's government was their 'grand model'.[97] In conclusion they were reminded of the infant baptism of their children as a sign of their responsibility to God for them.[98]

Children

Infant baptism provided the authors of the Pastorals with an opening gambit for their Address 'To the Children of Families under their Care'. Beginning in somewhat avuncular tone by explaining what the Assembly was,[99] they asked their 'dear young friends' two questions concerning their baptism: had they considered God's goodness to them 'that He did not suffer you to be many weeks in the world, without bidding your parents carry you to his House, and there, by a solemn covenant, devote and consecrate you to Him?'[100] and had they 'taken up their baptism and made it their own?'[101] If they had not done this, the children were warned that their baptism would be 'a terrible witness against them'.[102] Even to do nothing was in itself a rejection; it was, in fact, 'this terrible thing — leaving the salvation of God lying at your feet neglected and despised'.[103] God, however, was still waiting, the authors pointed out, and urged their young hearers, with scriptural quotations[104] and with a verse from a hymn, to take up God's invitation — like the biblical children, Samuel, Timothy, Josiah and Jabez.

Having dealt with first things first, the Pastoral went on to give 'a few further advices or exhortations'. The children were told first of all to honour and obey their parents, even if they did 'not always see the reasons for their will' and to remember them in their old age. This piece of advice was illustrated by suitable biblical texts. The second: 'we exhort you to be very diligent in your schools — to make the very best of the education which your parents are able to give you',[105] was not. It illustrated again both the emphasis the authors placed upon the unquestioning obedience of children —

> Perhaps you may not see the full good which some of the lessons are to do to you. But you will find it out by and by.[106]

— and also their emphasis on the benefits to be gained from education bought by parental financial sacrifice:

> Often have parents a hard enough struggle of it to keep their children at school. Do not repay their struggles with negligence and folly. Remember that if you are to be honoured, happy, useful in after life, it must be by diligence at school *now*.[107]

And to show that this was not simply a materialistic ideal, they added that they hoped that 'a goodly number of you may in due time . . . be fitted and disposed to become ministers of the gospel of Christ'.[108]

The Pastoral's remaining exhortations concerned social relations and religious duties. Children were urged to be 'pleasant', 'kind', 'gentle', 'courteous', 'modest', 'cheerful' and 'seasonable' in their conversation with and behaviour towards other members of their families, and to 'cultivate *the singing* of our delightful psalms and hymns in your homes'[109] as a mark of harmonious family relations. They were also reminded of their influence over other children outside their own homes, for good or ill (if it were for ill they might be 'strengthening each other's hands in the service of sin and the devil'[110]); and of how during the revivals children had not only been brought to Jesus but had brought others. For this purpose 'little meetings for prayer have been formed among the young'.[111] The Assembly approved of these but (perhaps in order to prevent any proselytising sectarian agency getting hold of its young) the Pastoral went on to remind the children that the Free Church was their mother and that they ought gratefully and affectionately to acknowledge this, by taking an interest in all her schemes at home and abroad, by reading her *Records*, and by learning about her history.[112]

In its final exhortation the Assembly expressed the hope that 'if God shall be pleased to spare you in his good providence, you shall make early application for *admission to the table of Christ*'.[113] This remark raises the question of what age the children addressed were supposed to be, since while they were regarded as 'able to understand what it is to come to Jesus as sinners lost',[114] and were advised in the strongest terms to take up their baptism, admission to Communion, where they would 'at length solemnly and publicly take the vows of (their) baptism upon (them)',[115] was seen as lying in the future. Clearly, from what was said, they were regarded as of school age. Presumably, therefore, the authors of the Pastoral thought that they were addressing younger adolescents,[116] old enough for some sort of conversion (although this word is not used) experience, but not old enough to become communicants. The Free Church was still enough of a national church for its Assembly to lay great stress on the baptism of infants as in some sense an objective event. Its Assembly also, however, heavily emphasised the subjective aspect of coming to Jesus and drew a distinction between the real and the nominal Christians in its pews.

Masters and Servants

In the Address 'to Masters and Servants in the Families under their Care' the Free Assembly of 1862 returned to a theme already raised in the Pastoral of 1858. That address had instructed employers to take a greater interest in the spiritual and material wellbeing of their employees and particularly in that of their domestic servants, and it was this class also with which the Pastoral of 1862 was concerned.

The churches' interest in domestic servants was understandable: there were, after all, so many of them. In 1862 they amounted to 12 per cent. of the employed population of Scotland, a proportion exceeded, in terms of classes of employment, only by agricultural workers (over 20 per cent.) and those employed in manufacturing (35 per cent.).[117] Like the latter and unlike the former, they represented at this time a growing sector of the workforce,[118] and many of them were unmarried and lived in the homes of their employers. Members of the middle classes, such as the churchmen who wrote these Pastorals, thus had a much fuller opportunity of observing their daily lives, manners and morals than those of other members of the working classes. (Many of them no doubt considered themselves authorities on the subject of servants, whose behaviour formed a popular subject of conversation and complaint.[119]) The numbers and proximity of servants therefore must have predisposed the churches' representatives to be interested in them, just as the numbers of farm servants living in areas which were more thickly ministered than those in which the manufacturing population lived, predisposed the churches' representatives to be interested in that class.

The fact that most domestic servants were women, and that most of the employed women in the country were domestic servants,[120] raises the question of whether the churches had, by their own standards, any other grounds for being concerned about the behaviour — and especially the sexual behaviour — of domestic servants. Dr. Tait, the much-quoted authority on prostitution in Edinburgh, evidently thought that they had. Earlier in the century he had written that at a conservative estimate there were 300 servants in Edinburgh engaged in clandestine prostitution. These were, of course, 'the common class of servants'.[121] But prostitution among servants, Tait believed, was a 'very aggravated and unsuspected evil';[122] and there was 'good reason to suppose that some of those holding more respectable situations ... also frequent improper houses'.[123] Certainly, by the middle of the century, former domestic servants were the largest group applying for admission to the Edinburgh Magdalene Institute;[124] and at the beginning of the twentieth century Havelock Ellis claimed, after considerable research, that 'domestic service is the chief reservoir from which prostitutes are drawn'.[125]

Such claims seem plausible in the light of the limited evidence available. But if most employed women were domestic servants, Ellis's comment is something of a tautology. Even if, as Ellis also observed,[126] a remarkable number of nineteenth-century domestic servants seduced or were seduced by members of the households in which they were employed,[127] neither this nor prostitution in the period has been very reliably quantified, despite all that has been written about the subject. It would therefore be a mistake to lapse into compulsive Freudianism and find sex in every silence. For this reason the question of how far the churches might have had grounds for concern about the sexual behaviour of domestic servants as a class, as distinct from the sexual behaviour of a limited number of domestic servants, is not one to which any certain answer can be given. How far the churches were concerned about the sexual behaviour of domestic servants as a class is however another question, since the factors contributing to such concern included not only the actual behaviour of domestic servants, but also, and perhaps more important, the height to which the churches wished to 'raise the standard of public opinion' on such matters, as well as the height from which they believed such standards to have fallen.

It was not, however, simply sexual standards which some churchmen believed had fallen off. James Begg, persuading the Presbytery of Edinburgh to overture the Assembly for what became the Pastoral of 1858 remarked, in connection with master-servant relations, that the

> former state of things in Scotland, when there was a beautiful and most salutary connection between these two classes of society, had to a large extent been abolished, to the great injury both of these classes themselves and of the general community.[128]

This subject, as we have seen, was dealt with in that Pastoral, but there was another side to it, which the authors of the 1862 Pastoral alluded to by remarking that the legal and commercial aspect of the master-servant relationship was something

> in which we have reason even to glory, since with it the whole freedom of our servants is bound up, as in distinction from the slavery and serfdom of other times and other lands.[129]

Having noted this, however, they returned quickly to Begg's point, for beyond this aspect of the relationship lay its 'moral dimension', whose existence was 'proved' by the fact that servants 'form a part of our families, and stand in the closest and most influential relations to us and to our children'.[130] This dimension, too little regarded, the authors feared, was to be the subject of the Address.

The authors of the Pastoral, while they clearly identified themselves with masters, were ready to give advice to both classes (although in the case of the servants, but not of the masters, they limited themselves to advising 'such at least as are connected with us in Church fellowship'[131]). The advice given was about moral 'duties', which were to some extent reciprocal. In the order in which these were listed: (1) masters were to be interested in the 'comfort, health and well-being generally'[132] of their servants, while (3) servants were to be interested in the 'well-being, comfort and good name'[133] of their masters' families; (2) Christian masters were to pray for their servants, while (4) Christian servants were to pray for their masters' families; (3) masters were to be interested in the religious instruction of their servants, while (6) servants were to accept that interest 'gratefully and cordially';[134] (4) masters were to be kind and courteous to their servants, while (2) servants were to respond with 'a respectful, quiet and modest demeanour';[135] and (5) masters were to 'notice, encourage and commend service thoroughly and conscientiously done',[136] while (1) servants were 'to do the work of their particular place thoroughly, conscientiously and with all good fidelity'.[137]

The other duties described in the Pastoral were not so obviously reciprocal: (6) masters were 'to impose no needless restraints on the freedom'[138] of their servants, while (5) servants, especially females, were to guard themselves against sexual freedom; (7) servants were also to cultivate 'by every possible means an unbroken peace among themselves';[139] and in addition to their duties they were reminded that faithful and obedient service would, according to Scripture, 'ADORN the doctrine of God in all things'.[140] In conclusion, and reintroducing the element of reciprocity, members of each class were advised to consider prayerfully the religious character of members of the other when making engagements for service.

The Pastoral's list of duties makes its authors' view of master-servant relations very clear; and the order in which the respective duties were listed probably reflects what they consciously or unconsciously considered to be the respective order of priorities for each class. The model for masters, mentioned at the outset, was the patriarch Abraham, with the supplementary model of the New Testament centurion, caring for his servant, illustrating the point about the master's duty to be interested in his servant's wellbeing. But masters were also advised that they should not forget that they were in command, nor fail to deal with faults correctly. This, however, should not make them 'proud, distant (or) lordly',[141] nor should it make them fail to echo the words 'Well done, good and faithful servant' of one who was their Master also. Just in case these scriptural references did not convince them, they were reminded that if more modern masters were like the centurion, they would no doubt hear fewer of the 'many complaints of servants throwing up their places needlessly',[142] or of 'the ever-increasing shortness of their terms of service'.[143] They were cautioned further and with, perhaps, even more pragmatic considerations in mind, by being told that masters who lost control before their servants, and were angry or vituperative with them, 'defeat often their own ends' and 'expose themselves to secret disrespect'.[144]

In advising servants to be faithful and obedient the authors again had no shortage of scriptural quotations to fall back upon. But in remarking that some servants 'in the saving of their own time' were unfaithful, because their time was in fact 'the property of their masters',[145] they were saying something which was perhaps not entirely consistent with what they had said earlier about slavery. And when they came to discuss the question of servants' demeanour, not only was

Scripture not mentioned, but consistency also appears to have been absent. The Free Church, as we have seen in previous chapters, seems to have been trying to persuade working people to accept middle-class standards: at the same time, however, these working people were being persuaded to do this without giving up some of the very things which characterised their non-middle-class status:

> We press on you the high importance, duty, wisdom of knowing and keeping your proper place. Is there not to be seen sometimes a foolish aspiring after the *style*, and *dress*, and *manner* of superiors? Of the sinfulness of this before the Lord there can be no doubt. But it is also very foolish and weak; and far from raising, lowers the servant much, exciting only regret and pity in all right thinking minds. The place of the servant has its true and proper *dignity*, quite as much as the master's. But it is a dignity inseparably bound up with that quiet modesty of demeanour which *suits* the place.[146]

The complexities of a servant's lot were farther illustrated by the advice given to servants about taking an interest in their masters' families and advancing their good name. Servants were to avoid any 'forward officious meddling'; they should however 'identify' themselves with the family, and take advantage of the 'hundred quiet ways' in which they could advance its comfort and add to its good repute. If they took such an interest they might well find themselves prolonging their terms of service, since while bad masters were no doubt in part the cause of the 'needless . . . throwing up' of places, 'a mere restless desire of change on (servants') part, of which we can give no good account'[147] was also 'frequently and largely' the cause of this.

In advising masters against imposing 'needless restraints' on their servants' freedom the authors of the Pastoral were especially concerned that servants should have sufficient free time 'compatible with the order and well-being of the family' to attend church on Sunday. At the same time, however, they emphatically disapproved of permission being given, as it was 'often . . . even in pious families',[148] for servants to visit their friends on Sabbath evenings. Masters who allowed this were failing in their duty, and the practice was 'full of danger and mischief to servants themselves'.[149]

The anxiety shown here about Sunday evening visiting was of course an aspect of Evangelical sabbatarianism. This was by no means only a Free Church or even a Scottish phenomenon. It did however run at a particularly high pitch during this decade not only in the Free Church, but also in the Establishment.[150] But sabbatarianism did not entirely account for what was being said here about Sunday evening visiting. A hint that there was more to this can be found in some remarks made twenty years earlier by Dr. Tait. Discussing prostitution among servants he had observed:

> It is painful to reflect on the indubitable fact, that the hours of the Sabbath, which are set apart for divine service, are those generally selected for . . . immoral appointments; and what renders the crime still more detestable is that it is not unfrequently cloaked by the semblance of religion; for, while they lay aside all reserve of modesty, and manifest the utmost contempt for the sacred precepts which the Bible contains, it is carried openly in their hands.[151]

Tait's remedy for this state of affairs had been to suggest that employers should allow their servants free time 'during the week, and at such hours as they shall have no chance of going astray',[152] even if this meant that their mistresses had to suffer the inconvenience of re-arranging their domestic timetable. If servants objected to this, Tait wrote, it could be pointed out to them that they would not find suitable potential husbands by going 'in search of wooers on the evening of the Sabbath',[153] since

> no lad of sound moral and religious principles would so far neglect his duty as to waste that time in idle and frivolous conversation which ought to be set aside for more momentous obligations.[154]

Realising, however, that this in itself might not get round the original problem of Bible-bearing wooers, Tait proposed in addition that all taverns, gardens and places of entertainment and leisure should be closed on Sundays. Further, since like so many others he believed that 'an improvement in the moral and religious character of the people'[155] was required, he called for 'an increase of the means for communicating religious instruction both to the young and to those in mature life',[156] and for a better example of Christian living by the upper and middle classes, who at present too frequently took 'the tone of their manners from the irreligious'. If, by contrast, they themselves set the tone and refused to have anything to do with men who took part in prostitution, they might thereby lead the female servant away from 'those forms of pride, vanity, sloth and irritability which lead her on to certain ruin'.[157]

By the time that the Pastoral was being written many of the Sunday closing measures desired by Tait had been effected, but his desire for an adequate ecclesiastical strategy had not been fulfilled, nor, if the Free Church's fulminations were anything to go on, had employers become any better at giving a good example. Since, as a recent authority on this period has put it, 'most generalisations about the quality of middle class family life crumble at the critic's touch',[158] it is difficult to know how realistic these Free Church fulminations were. But even if they were overestimates of the extent of the evil, their representatives, like Tait, presumably had some reason to be concerned about sexual behaviour on Sunday evenings.

Unlike Tait, however, they did not say much about the sexual mores of the middle classes. But this did not prevent them from speaking to servants about theirs. Indeed, they wrote:

> we feel as if we should be unfaithful to the female servants we address, did we fail of earnestly and affectionately putting them on their guard against all *levity* of spirit and demeanour, all undue *freedoms* with persons of the other sex, every thing which is not in full keeping with the *purity* and gravity of Christian discipleship.[159]

In their concern with servants' Sunday evenings, as well as in their repeated warnings about servants' clothing,[160] the authors of the Pastoral echoed Tait. What they had to say about servants and family worship however suggested that times were changing. As an alternative to letting servants have their Sunday evening off the writers had remarked that it would be a good thing were family catechising to be 'resumed among us'. But to this they added the qualification: 'wherever it might be found practicable';[161] and this qualification was characteristic of the nervous vehemence which characterised Free Church pronouncements on family religion. That masters and servants should pray for one another was something about which the writers could be certain. (Servants were here directed to the example of Abraham's servant.)[162] And insofar as both classes were asked to pray for each other in their secret devotions they were advocating a course of action which, were it carried out, might just possibly have achieved the desired end of inducing mutual respect within the context of a shared religiosity and observance of the proprieties. But the problem was that this could not, of its very nature, be ensured or even observed. And when it came to observables, such as 'the master's duty to instruct his servants in religion',[163] the authors of the Pastoral faltered, remarking that they preferred to express themselves 'somewhat generally here' since this duty was 'less absolute'[164] than the parent's duty to instruct his children. What grounds they may have had for this statement were not given; and they backed it up with no scriptural quotations. All they could find to say was that

> Many things are liable to come in to modify and limit (this) duty, or materially change its form and shape. Oftentimes, indeed, it will be the clear duty of the master to take part in the stated religious instruction of the servant. But in other cases it may be enough to see that the instruction is given somehow.[165]

The same failure of nerve was observable in the apologetic tone adopted by the authors when they addressed servants on the same subject:

> Even should the methods adopted by masters not seem to you the very best and wisest, it is your duty to honour the intentions from which they spring, to be thankful for them, and to fall in with them as far as your sense of duty will at all permit.[166]

Part of the problem here may well have been the predicament of Free Church servants cast up in Establishment, or worse, in Episcopalian households, where religious instruction, if it was given, might well not have been to their taste. But perhaps the larger part may have been the resentment felt by servants who were being treated, in some religious households, as if they were children. The legal and commercial aspects of the master-servant relationship, which, as the authors of the Pastoral had pointed out, saved servants from being slaves, had implications which were still being worked out. Not least of these implications was the undermining of those social and economic conditions which allowed the head of a Victorian middle-class family to act as a patriarch, benevolent or otherwise.

Social Ideals and Realities

This review of Pastorals on Family Religion leaves us very little the wiser about the state of family religion during this period. All of the churches seem to have held the opinion that while there had been a falling-off in the number of families practising family worship, many families still maintained it. Since the era of inquisitorial church courts had ended, however, there was no way of knowing how far these judgements reflected what was actually going on; and although some churchmen were keen to devise thermometers for taking the nation's sexual temperature, they were on the whole content to measure its piety by their own blushes. The embryonic centralised bureaucracy which, in the form of the Religion and Morals committee, emerged in the Free Church at this time did, it is true, attempt to gather some information on the subject, but the estimates and/or guesses it presented in its 1865 report varied widely,[167] and although in the following year it was stated that family worship had become 'more general'[168] since the revivals, this impression was not based on any very observable foundations.

It is difficult, then, to assess the situation. The difficulty of generalising about the home life of the Victorians has already been alluded to, but according to the writer already quoted on this subject, the high Victorian ideal of home life

> can have been a practical possibility only above the manual labouring line, and a reality only where the father and mother were morally and intellectually capable of fulfilling so exalted a role and willing moreover to spend time enough with the children to accomplish it. The demands of fashion, towards one end of society, could be as domestically disruptive as the exigencies of poverty at the other . . . this moral and moralising ideal home was . . . likeliest to occur, where vital religion fertilised the pursuit of respectability.[169]

If this judgement is correct, then it would seem likely that family religion as advocated by the churches was something which for the most part existed only among middle-class families. The Pastorals of the Free Church certainly support this view: the family life about which their authors wrote was undoubtedly that of the middle classes, and while they spent much time criticising 'the demands of fashion', they gave little advice on how to overcome 'the exigencies of poverty'.

Churchmen were not of course unaware that the poor had problems with prayer. James Begg's obsession with closets[170] was in its way an admission of the fact that it was difficult for many members of the working classes to pray at all — let alone engage in family prayer. And W.G. Blaikie devoted a section of his *Better Days for Working People*[171] to describing how bad housing degraded its inhabitants spiritually as well as materially. Good housing, he believed, could help to improve religious habits:

> Perhaps no slight degree of that religious character by which the English middle-classes are distinguished, is the consequence of their peculiar isolation in distinct and separate houses, — thus acquiring almost of necessity, from frequent opportunities of solitude, those habits of reflexion which cannot be exercised to the entire exclusion of religious sentiments.[172]

But to a middle-of-the-road progressive liberal Evangelical like Blaikie, considerations of this kind could not be entertained in isolation from those of individual merit; and in advising working people on how to run their homes he contrasted some descriptions of drunken and careless parents[173] with the description of her childhood recorded in an essay by 'a Scottish labourer's daughter who had received scarcely any instruction but what she got from her mother'.[174] The implication of this contrast clearly was that despite poverty it was possible for members of the working classes to emulate this mother whose 'constant aim' was

> to make home a scene of comfort and enjoyment to her family; and so far did she carry this that she used to say that 'it was disagreeable and improper to be bustling about while father was within, and when he was gone out the work must be done up'.[175]

This 'excellent woman', who gave her children lessons four times a day, even at the wash-tub, and whose 'well ordered family' found the Sabbath, with its 'calm and holy exercises', a 'day of bright and peculiar enjoyment',[176] was held up by Blaikie as an example to the workers, as was the father of Alexander Somerville (the author of the *Autobiography of a Working Man*), who held family worship morning and evening.[177]

The difficulty with what Blaikie was advocating, however, was illustrated by his examples. Somerville's father, although one of those men who were disinherited by the social upheavals of the late eighteenth century, came from a family which had known 'better days' in the past: he had his roots in an older, more spiritually stable world. He did live, and suffer, under industrial conditions, but a good deal of his life was spent in the country. The scenes described by his son had, moreover, taken place half a century before Blaikie made use of them.

Blaikie's other example was even more problematic, partly because his rhapsodic description of the ideal mother let some cats out of the bag. In that domestic scene, while mother taught the lessons to one child, and while another watched the baby and a third read a book, the fourth child was 'bringing water from a pure soft spring some distance from the house', while the fifth was 'gathering sticks and keeping the fire alive' and the eldest brother 'assisted father in the garden'.[178] Where was all this taking place? Not, certainly, in the Edinburgh slum inhabited by the parents Blaikie compared these with. Nor, for that matter, was 'the pure soft spring' the Clyde, or even the Water of Leith. And where had the mother herself acquired the education she imparted to her children? Wherever it was, it was a different world from the mid-nineteenth-century city centre, different also from the one-roomed cottage, described earlier in the same book by Blaikie, where rain came in under the door and through the roof, falling in 'large drops' on the bed and the working surface in front of the window, making the young wife, who was by nature active, clean and tidy, give up her unequal struggle, and driving her husband to the 'watertight' public house.[179]

This criticism of Blaikie's morally improving tales is not made with the intention of suggesting that happy homes of the kind described by the labourer's daughter either did not exist, or that they were not commendable places. Where families did triumph over poverty and achieve some measure of comfort and order, their achievement was commendable, and their children were plainly more privileged than those of parents who had given up the attempt. But when Blaikie and others who wrote in a similar vein presented such models of perfection to the working classes they seemed to be suggesting that the achievement of such an ideal was a practical possibility for all of them. This however was a very doubtful claim. Perhaps a young working man brought up to respect the value of thrift, sobriety and industry, accepting his lot and endowed with a moderate degree of ambition, could become, by being a good employee and by marrying wisely, a respectable member of the working class and even of the Free Church. But in practice his path was strewn with accidents which at any moment might frustrate his purpose and hurtle him into a downward spiral of discouraging and dispiriting circumstances. In such circumstances, to triumph over unemployment, disease, bad housing and the many other accidents of life, the individual required resources derived from deep roots in a stable spiritual environment. Such an environment was precisely what the chaos of industrial society deprived many people of, by subjecting them to material conditions under which the individual was given no assurance of his significance and no hint that he could hope for better things. Under these circumstances the missionary agencies of the churches offered assistance to a section of the working population. Some of them accepted it and approximated to the ideal. Other working people were lucky, avoided the worst accidents and also approximated in some sense to the ideal. But while there must have been many others again whose failure to give their children the benefit of a happy home was not, although they were members of the working classes, dictated by grinding poverty, the same cannot be said of their countless compatriots who drowned in what must have seemed like a sea of indifference.

Blaikie's approach to the problems of the poor, then, was inadequate, because although he took some social factors[180] into consideration, these were submerged in his individualistic handling of the subject. The individualism of nineteenth-century Protestantism has of course often been criticised for ignoring many crucial social and economic factors, and much of the criticism is well-founded. At the same time however, it must be admitted that an emphasis on social factors to the exclusion of an individualistic appeal may produce, under the conditions of poverty, a passivity as dispiriting, in its ideal of the self as a patient or a client, as anything produced by the more individualistic and competitive method of the nineteenth century. It is of course impossible to compare these alternatives in a way which does justice to either, since very much depends on the social, psychological and spiritual circumstances of those involved. No determinate answer therefore can be given here to the question of how far teaching like that of Blaikie helped working people to orient themselves, beyond saying that some were helped and some were not, that some children benefited from happy homes created by religious parents, and that others, and their parents, never had a chance.

One thing which, for the present purpose, can be said however is that the churches had produced a version of Christianity so well integrated with and relevant to the family life of the middle classes that, by the same token they virtually disinherited many members of the working classes of their right to the means of ordering their everyday experience and their religious experience in a way which would enable them to set their lives in a meaningful religious context. The churches did this by channelling the stream of Christian orthodoxy between the banks of bourgeois respectability, a feat they were able to accomplish by reason of their capture of the means of production — in this case the ministers and leading laymen of the churches, who, since they were themselves members of the middle classes, preached and taught a middle-class Christianity. An important feature of this situation, which enabled ministers to continue to do this, was the ongoing recruitment, from the pious part of the working classes, of candidates for the ministry who quickly assimilated the presuppositions of their bourgeois fellow-students and colleagues, and were able to legitimate their appeal to middle-class family religion as normative by memories of their own homes, just as their colleagues who had always been middle-class were able to legitimate their teaching by pointing to them as the products of such homes.[181] They were particularly well able to do this during the mid-Victorian period because the homes remembered and described were those of the early years of the century, when the pressures of industrial society were only beginning to make themselves felt. And even later there continued to be areas of Scotland (especially the Highlands)[182] where these pressures had not entirely torn up the spiritual roots of the people from the soil of an older culture. When ministers based Pastoral Letters about Family Religion on assumptions of the kind we have mentioned, then, they were able to gain approval because the composition of the Assemblies which ratified what they wrote was, from whatever origin, now solidly middle-class.[183]

In their teaching on family religion therefore, as in what they said about sexual morality, the churches saw the present through the spectacles of middle-class respectability, and compared it unfavourably with their own and the nation's past, which they saw through the spectacles of Evangelical romanticism. Thus, orderly and pious habits of family life, like the sexual habits of farm servants, were regarded as having sadly declined; but since a good deal of the evidence for such a decline was provided by comparison with a romanticised past, it is difficult to know whether or not they were right, even if means could be devised whereby such a decline could be measured. The best that can be said about this is that the upheavals of the late eighteenth and early nineteenth centuries had produced a society in which the majority of those families which were most likely to be orderly and pious were to be found among the middle classes; that these middle classes were more clearly differentiated in economic and social terms from the classes below them than their historical predecessors had been; and that the majority of those families who were least likely to be orderly and pious were to be found among the lower classes. In terms of family worship as such there may have been some overall decline during the eighteenth century, following the loosening of ecclesiastical control over society, and there may also have been some increase in it during the late eighteenth and early nineteenth centuries, following the

Evangelical Revival, this increase taking place mostly among the middle classes. But even this has to be qualified by the consideration that during this period both the middle and working classes increased rapidly in numbers, so that it would have been possible to find evidence for decline and increase alike.

Whatever changes there may have been during the period under review in the pattern of family religion, the evidence of the Pastorals suggests that in one respect at least the churches themselves were beginning to encourage the growth of forms of ecclesiastical organisation, based on the differentiation of the ages and the sexes, which contributed to the real decline of family worship in the twentieth century. Family worship declined partly of course because the Victorian middle-class family, whose material circumstances and culture favoured it, itself declined. But, as the writers of Pastorals feared, it also declined because the churches themselves provided agencies for the religious instruction of children which allowed parents to believe that much of the responsibility for this was no longer theirs. Arguably, the provision of Sunday schools (which had begun at the end of the eighteenth century and was to diversify much more after about 1870) separated the home and common concerns of daily life from the special place where religious instruction was provided and gave religious instruction a greater ecclesiastical bias. Thus, however strongly the churches might protest that religious instruction was the duty of parents, they effectively weakened the force of their argument by providing these agencies; and, as the number of non-ecclesiastical counter-attractions for parents and children alike grew, many people, finding less time at their disposal, would choose either Sunday school or family worship, and usually, if either, the former. Of course this shift from home to Sunday school did not affect whatever religious instruction was given to children in their earliest and most formative years, when the responsibility remained that of the parents, and especially that of the mother, as the Pastorals recognised. (Although this may have meant that what was vital in religion took on a more infantile and less mature form.) And the idea that such a shift took place must be qualified in the light of criticism, made by some contemporary sociologists, to the effect that theories about the loss by the twentieth-century British family of traditional familial functions such as education, miss the point that many such functions were never very effectively performed by families other than those of the Victorian middle class.[184] But, given these qualifications, it can still be argued that the churches' provision of Sunday schools, and later of bible classes, young men's guilds and other such organisations represented in practice a further intensification of the church's hereditary antagonism to the claims of kinship. (This antagonism and the claims of a wider Christian family were of course rooted ultimately in the teaching of Jesus.)[185] In nineteenth-century Presbyterianism an operation of this kind involved the creation of organisations whose very relevance to their situation made them rapidly obsolete when the situation changed. This meant that when they did become obsolete the older methods of family worship and catechising had already largely disappeared.

Theological Presuppositions

A final point concerns the theological presuppositions of the Pastorals. In theory these were cohesive. The same model of absolute but loving authority could be attributed to God, emulated by statesmen and exercised in households. The family was a kingdom and could be a church, worshipping a God whose values were the same as its own, and thereby socialising each new generation into a pattern of behaviour and of attitudes whose self-evident nature was reinforced by its divine origin. In practice however things were not so cohesive. The idea of God as a Father-King was not of course questioned by churchmen, but few of the earthly applications of the model were now fitting as well as they once had done. Britain of course was still a monarchy — unlike an increasing number of foreign countries — but the Divine Right of Kings and absolute rulers even on the Dundas level had had their day. The middle and upper-class rulers of the nation were experimenting with new forms of democracy and even the working classes were trying out their political wings. The world of work also provided fewer applications for the model, since although many employers were petty monarchs, the absolute nature of their rule was being undermined by the interference of complex economic factors on the one hand and of government on the other. Nor, since business was business, were many of them benevolent in their exercise of authority. The theological model of the benevolent patriarch, which relied for its plausibility, as all theological models must, upon the familiar nature of its parabolic 'earthly story' was thus being attacked on all sides.

Curiously enough this did not undermine the model as much as might at first sight be expected. This is perhaps partly explained by the suggestion, based on contemporary literary sources admittedly, that the Victorian home

> was both a shelter *from* the anxieties of modern life, a place of peace where the longings of the soul might be realised (if not in fact, in imagination), and a shelter *for* those moral and spiritual values which the commercial spirit and the critical spirit were threatening to destroy, and therefore a sacred place, a temple.[186]

As such, the home could still be regarded as a place in which the old values of benevolent patriarchalism (and father) reigned supreme, in contrast to the chaos of the outside world. The orderly pious home thus provided a possibility for the perpetuation of those patriarchal values which were so inextricably intertwined with the Old Testament bias of Presbyterianism.

Blaikie, in *Better Days*, had claimed that the prospect of such an orderly and pious home gave the working man who had one, 'a sense of joy and freedom that may support him through the weary hours of labour'.[187] And no doubt there were working men who enjoyed this experience. But since for so many working men the conditions of labour were brutal and brutalising, and since the increasing scale of industry separated them from their families at work, depersonalising them and depriving them of any sense of significance, it is unlikely that many of them, so unused to the exercise of loving authority at work, were encouraged to exercise it at home.[188] The exercise of such authority was more likely to appeal to those who were captains of industry than to those who were cogs in the machine.

But even in the middle-class home the patriarchal model was threatened, as we have seen, by Sabbath schools without and servants within. The 'earthly story' on which one of the churches' prime theological models was based was here still familiar, but its familiarity depended upon a society whose future was precarious. When that society crumbled and was replaced by a society with more democratic — or at least less patriarchal — political, commercial-industrial and familial models, the Protestant churches which had relied so heavily upon the rational and common-sense nature of their message would find themselves in trouble.

This, however, is to anticipate matters somewhat, since in the following chapters we must consider what the churches said about the social control of sexual behaviour and about family religion during the remainder of the nineteenth century.

CHAPTER SIX

Sexuality and Piety: The Establishment View, 1870-1900

Ecclesiastical Reorganisation and Routine

BEFORE 1870, church pronouncements on sex, marriage and the family were made, as we have seen, on an occasional and *ad hoc* rather than a regular and systematic basis. Discussions of such subjects as temperance, housing and discipline, especially when stimulated by some mildly sensational extra-ecclesiastical event, provided a context for these pronouncements, as did the churches' Pastorals and a few special committees such as that on The Causes and Remedies of Social Evils (in the Free Church), and on The Increase of Immorality in Rural Districts (in the Church of Scotland). By 1872 however, when the latter made what appears to have been its last report,[1] the pattern was changing. The Religion and Morals committee of the Free Church was now systematically sending out its queries and deputies to synods and presbyteries all over Scotland, and despite the misgivings of many ministers, was collecting, and presenting annually to the Assembly, large amounts of information and opinion about the state of religion and morals in the Free Church and the nation. Various aspects of sex, marriage and the family were dealt with in these reports, sometimes simply in a sentence commenting on conditions in a single presbytery, and sometimes in a section of the report dealing with a single subject at greater length.

We shall return to the Religion and Morals committee in the next chapter. Our concern here is with a similar development in the Church of Scotland, initiated during the 'seventies when the Committee on Christian Life and Work was set up at the instigation and under the convenership of A.H. Charteris, the Professor of Biblical Criticism at Edinburgh University. Like the Religion and Morals committee, that on Life and Work provoked some initial resentment, and for much the same reason: bureaucratic and executive interference was disliked by many ministers and sessions, who preferred to run their own affairs in their own way. Yet the committee was in its own terms highly successful, and it made considerable changes in the life of the Church of Scotland. The church's schemes were overhauled, and various innovations made, including the creation of the Young Men's and Young Women's Guilds (the first never as successful as the second), the Order of Deaconesses, and special missions to agricultural labourers and herring fishermen.[2] In these ways the spirit and methods of the missionary movement were extended to fresh fields: and while this can be seen as a sign of the increasing social differentiation of the age, it also represented a concession to denominationalism by a church which until now, rightly or wrongly, had regarded itself as an aspect rather than a part of the nation. Now, as church organisations and missionary enterprises multiplied, catering for children, young men, women and the various categories of the working-class population, it began to seem as if the only people still unorganised and unevangelised were middle-aged, middle-class males. Committees of the churches might speak about the need for West End as well as East End missions, but in fact little was done about this; and the voice of the church consequently sounded more androcentric and patriarchal than ever.

With the rise of labour and feminism however, patriarchal and androcentric attitudes were becoming increasingly difficult to justify; and in due course the churches were to discover this. During the last three decades of the nineteenth century the Christian Life and Work committee and its successors provided a context in which issues relating to sex, marriage and the family could be kept under routine review; and few Assemblies passed without the church saying something on the subject. But if this served to allay, or at least to ventilate the anxieties of middle-aged, middle-class churchmen, it did not do so without opposition from some of those about whom they were most anxious.

Uncleanness and Revolution

Among other things in its first report, the Life and Work committee had turned its attention to 'the sin of uncleanness'. It declared that its 'lamentable commonness among us, in ranks high and low' was 'a disgrace to our Christian civilization and a proof that very much of our religious profession is false and hollow'.[3] This condemnation was supported by an attack on the 'false delicacy' which prevented the pulpit from dealing 'directly, pointedly and solemnly' with a subject discussed 'in every newspaper and periodical' and 'in law reports and petitions regarding acts of Parliament'.[4]

The committee however, despite its attacks on ministerial delicacy, did not spell out in detail exactly what it was concerned about or just what constituted 'the sin of uncleanness'. It was 'proved by the statistics of illegitimacy' that it prevailed 'chiefly in the North-East and South-West of Scotland'. But it was also and 'pre-eminently the sin of our cities and large towns'.[5] In saying this therefore the committee appears to have thought of illegitimacy and prostitution (the petitions regarding acts of Parliament were presumably those against the Contagious Diseases Acts)[6] as much the same thing. But since in the years which followed, this committee and indeed the Church of Scotland Assembly as a whole said very little about the latter dangerously political subject, its condemnation of false delicacy looks rather like the pot calling the kettle black.

The committee was not, however, insensitive to all of the problems of that society which its members, like so many of their contemporaries, believed to be 'in a state of transition'; and in the following year it expressed its alarm at the 'estrangement of classes and the growth of an idea of service which contains no affection or sympathy'.[7] It was particularly concerned about the 'decay of the idea that servants are members of the family, or even of the household' and with the 'bad effects of the migratory habits of the labouring classes',[8] particularly farm servants. The progression of the committee's thought was quite explicit: it was disturbing that the employer-employed relation 'in mining and manufacturing works . . . is often regarded as a contract referring to nothing but work and wages',[9] more disturbing that similar views were to be found in rural districts, and most disturbing of all that they were to be found even in households. Thus these two classes, farm labourers and domestic servants, were once again singled out by the church for special attention.

To be fair to the committee, it was also sufficiently sensitive to social problems not to heap all the blame for this on these two classes alone. Workmen were, it suggested, now more intelligent, more highly skilled, more conscious of their power, and better paid.[10] Where trouble arose the master was often to blame. Some millowners, for example, were bad employers, but among the worst were farmers. They 'generally' exhibited 'an utter indifference as to the moral character of their servants', regarding them 'as so many beasts of burden, or creatures of another race'.[11] Reports from all parts of the country testified to this, although it was thought that things had not deteriorated so badly in the outlying areas and in a few districts specially blessed with benevolent landowners such as Lord Kinnaird.[12]

What really worried the committee, as it had worried James Begg, was the spectre of revolution. Class antagonisms were building up, it believed, through lack of sympathy between employers and employed. These antagonisms were exacerbated by the efforts of those who, trying to help working men, treated them like children. Only such sympathy as the Christian church could — if it would — command might

> avert from our country the fearful revolution which not a few of the wisest and most patriotic men are contemplating as not only possible, but as inevitable, unless a better spirit rule us, and that speedily.[13]

If this was not done, the committee asked, 'Can life or liberty be safe?'[14] But then, as if becoming aware that this was a somewhat low motive for creating that brotherhood of men which was in any case part of the Gospel, it added that good should be done 'unto the brethren for the brethren's sake'. It would, surely, 'be poor work if men do it to secure their own selfish safety'.[15]

Domestics, Farm Servants and Licentiousness

Such a nervous awareness of social change and its problems was, then, the context in which the Christian Life and Work committee was to discuss sexual behaviour, and particularly that of domestic and farm servants. Its reports on

Family Life, made in 1872, and on Licentiousness, made in 1878, both concentrated upon these two classes, the first of these quite explicitly delineating the problematic areas by its division into three parts, dealing with Family Worship, Domestic Servants and Farm Labourers respectively.

These two reports contained much more about farm servants than about domestics however. The 1872 report admitted that the committee had not received as many returns about domestic servants as it would have liked; and that what it had received was not very consistent. Some ministers complained about the poor educational and religious state of domestics, but chiefly about 'their love of change, which has been increased by the plan of monthly engagements'.[16] The majority of ministers however believed that servants changed their employment much less 'than is commonly thought'.[17] The fact was, the committee stated, that the character and education of servants depended upon the social location of their employers. In wealthier parts of Edinburgh and Glasgow servants were 'a very superior portion of the community',[18] and were as religious as their masters and mistresses. In the poorer districts — although this was where servants were most likely to be 'treated as one of the family'[19] — many young girls, especially those who came up from the country, were ill-protected 'from the serious moral dangers around them'.[20] These dangers, the 1878 report observed in its list of causes of Licentiousness, were likely to be encountered especially when employers did not supervise their servants' behaviour; and here also a complaint was made about 'the frequent carelessness of heads of houses as to how and where their servants spend the "Sunday out"'.[21]

The problem of time off arose not only in connection with domestic servants. A country minister replying to the committee's questions about farm labourers wrote:

> The servants claim the alternate Sabbath as theirs, to do what and go where they like. I think it should be refused to them as a holiday if they will not keep it as a Sabbath. I also think that the farmers should be urged to allow their servants' underclothing to be washed on the farm; or if not, that they should grant the Saturday afternoon as a half-holiday, to allow the servants to visit their relatives and get a change of dress. A farmer lately told me that he made attendance at Church a condition at *feeing* time.[22]

This farmer was an exception. Most, according to the same minister, were not interested in their servants, and the few who 'were wont to expostulate with their servants on their godless and irregular lives'[23] were told by these servants that as long as they did their work their behaviour was no business of their employers. The behaviour of both classes thus plunged the committee into gloom. Reading ministers' replies to its queries was 'like hearing a succession of moans'[24] — caused not least by the fact that three-quarters of the farm-servant population were Church of Scotland adherents.

The ministers did not moan very much about the education of farm servants. This was not as good as improved teaching methods should have made it. But it was not totally bad, even if it was utilised to read newspapers rather than the Bible; and it was still much better than that of English farmworkers. What the ministers did complain of, 'most despairingly', was their 'religious condition'.[25] Most reported 'growing indifference to divine things'[26] and, specifically, unchastity. Unchastity, in striking contrast to intemperance (which had 'in general diminished within a generation') was now so serious that it 'almost forbids a pleasant thought in the Christian mind in regard to the rural districts of our country'.[27] As a 'painful' example of this, the committee quoted a minister from a 'northern' (presumably north-eastern) parish who reported that three-quarters of the children he baptised were illegitimate. According to this minister,

> most parents have themselves had one or more illegitimate children (the father by a different woman, and the mother by a different man) before marriage, and receive their daughters home with their illegitimate children as a matter of course, and keep their children for them to allow them to return to service. In this parish at present there is one woman with four illegitimate children to four different men, another three to three different men, and more than one two to different fathers.[28]

Understandably, then, he found it difficult to convince these people that their behaviour was sinful.

The committee attributed the irreligion and unchastity of farm labourers to three causes: first, the improved material circumstances of both farmers and servants, which produced 'a widening social gulf'[29] between them; second, the frequency with which ploughmen changed their masters; and third, the bothy system. The first of these was considered to be the cause of the second, since the 'migratory habit' was just as common 'where the cottage accommodation was excellent',[30] as where it was deficient. It had reached such a pitch, the committee claimed, that 'removals are more frequent (in the country parish) than in the towns'.[31] It was consequently 'very baffling' to the country minister. 'His work becomes like beating the air, which moves away when it is struck.'[32] And of course the migratory habit was intensified by bothy life. The inhabitants of bothies neglected church attendance and avoided visits by the minister. The 'kitchen-and-stable-loft system' was just as bad as the bothy. Under both, 'the men are lowered in civilization by being cut off from family life and home comforts';[33] and this of course led to unchastity and other evils.

The remedies proposed were the usual mixed bag which previous committees had called for: a Land Act to provide more cottages,[34] parish libraries, meetings, evening classes, 'bothy schools' and supremely 'a real grappling with this sin, by sympathetic, tender, faithful teaching from the pulpit'.[35] One minister who advocated this believed that it would 'bring back the lost idea of possible purity in rural parishes',[36] especially if it came from young ministers. Too much preaching at present was 'over the heads of the people'.[37]

The 1872 report, then, contained little information about the subject which would have been news to those who had followed the controversy since 1858. Nor did the report of the Committee on the Increase of Immorality in Rural Districts, presented to the same Assembly, which mentioned similar remedies. It too praised Lord Kinnaird and urged farmers to be more careful both in choosing and in superintending their servants. It stressed that supervision was especially necessary on Sunday evenings — when 'a great proportion of the deflections from morality take place',[38] and on fast days, as well as on the long winter evenings, when servants should be provided with instruction or 'rational amusement',[39] and also when males and females worked together in the fields. But perpetual supervision was only part of the price of virtue. The high proportion of illegitimate births[40] was in the last resort the result of the low tone of feeling. It was thus

> the duty of the clergy to impress upon their flocks, with as much delicacy as they can, the heinousness of the sin, and to disabuse the minds, especially of the female rustics, that a breach of chastity is not only a misfortune, but a great sin.[41]

It would help, said the committee, if 'the rural population' were to read 'two short addresses to young women and to young men of the working classes by Dr. Strachan of Dollar'.[42]

But if these committees brought forward no new information on the subject of rural immorality, the Life and Work committee at least was beginning to set the problem in a different and perhaps more illuminating context by its awareness of the deep social and economic divisions which lay behind it. What light it had generated, however, was virtually extinguished by its report of 1878, which attempted to tackle the highly unmanageable subject of Licentiousness.

The difficulty of making much sense of so wide and undefined a subject was clearly demonstrated by the nature of the many returns received to the committee's first question: 'To what extent is your parish or chapel district affected by this vice?'[43] Of the returns 200 could give no answer and a further 100 confined what they wrote to the subject of illegitimacy. The parishes whose returns were the 'most unfavourable'[44] were predictably, therefore, those in the North-East and South-West — although the committee did extract a crumb of comfort from the knowledge that some parishes in these areas reported a decreasing amount. The committee did not, however, say whether it was illegitimacy or licentiousness in general which was decreasing. Nor did it make clear just what was being described, when it reported returns from 400 parishes where 'the condition of matters is very lamentable' or from 172 parishes where 'the vice exists only to a limited extent, and is decreasing'.[45] The only clear point to emerge, and again it was predictable, was that 27 of the 38 parishes reporting 'little or no licentiousness'[46] were in the Highlands. As far as the towns were concerned, the committee was certain 'that licentiousness, in a form of which the Registrar-General's statistics can take no account, largely prevails'.[47] But it could not compare the towns with the country since 'a large proportion of town ministers express, or by silence imply, their inability to measure the extent of the evil'.[48] This last point provides confirmation of the opinion that at least one reason for the churches' obsession with rural sexual behaviour was their ignorance of the urban population.

In attempting to analyse the causes of and remedies for Licentiousness, the committee, which admittedly did not claim any 'exactness of logical method'[49] for its work, again tried to make some sense of the variety of opinions which had been offered to it on the subject. The causes, or rather, 'fostering circumstances' (since the 'vital cause' of licentiousness was 'deep in human nature itself') were: first, 'ecclesiastical'; second, 'individual'; third, 'in the home'; fourth, 'in the agricultural economy', fifth, 'connected with magisterial and police regulations'; and sixth, 'in society'.[50] The fourth of these comprised the standard and by now almost ritual complaints about sleeping arrangements, bothies, cottages, 'promiscuous' field labour and hiring fairs, with equally familiar remedies being suggested in a corresponding list. The much criticised migratory habits of farm servants were not however included under this head, but were described as fostering circumstances in the individual, along with 'ignorance, weakness of intellect, intemperance, vanity and love of dress'.[51]

The committee's returns must have indicated that farm servants enjoyed no monopoly of licentiousness — for although this class, like domestics, received the usual special attention, the committee's focus had in fact widened to include young people in general. This development would allow the committee and its successors to carry on pronouncing about sexual behaviour after they had given up discussing it in relation to these two classes. This point can be illustrated by the committee's reference, under fostering circumstances in the home, to 'bad upbringing, arising from the lack of family religion and the decline of parental authority',[52] as well as to lack of supervision of servants. But if youth was now the focus, it was still by implication working-class youth, since the remedies included advice to parents to get 'really good and not merely profitable situations for their children',[53] and to encourage 'visits at suitable hours, by respectable young men' with 'all the proper facilities for honourable courtship'.[54] That the committee was presumably primarily concerned with the working classes was again shown in its formidable catalogue of 'fostering circumstances in society', which included not only the usual low tone about immorality but also 'coarse manners' leading to 'improper advances' to females, 'dancing-saloons, songs glossing over the evil of impurity' and 'ill-conducted holiday excursions'.[55] The list of remedies was even more formidable, ranging from raising the tone to the summary injunctions:

> Provide wholesome recreations. A taste for music and for reading should be created. Outdoor games in summer, concerts, flower-shows, debating-societies, readings, lectures, social gatherings, superintended by ministers and others interested in the people's welfare.[56]

Further additions to this list included 'total abstinence and temperance societies and Good Templar Lodges . . . public houses without drink',[57] and 'young men's and women's associations on a broad Christian basis'.[58] Presumably the principle behind this was that the young should be kept occupied with these 'rational and moral' activities. They would thus be too tired to get up to mischief, and employers could more easily follow the committee's final injunction: 'Let masters enforce early hours'.[59]

If all this failed, however, there was another social remedy. 'Encourage early marriage,'[60] urged the committee, and here for once its members were not thinking solely of the workers, since among the fostering circumstances of licentiousness in society they had included 'deferred marriages among the upper classes occasioned by expensive modes of living'.[61]

In advising the upper classes to set a good example in this respect the committee were entering into what had for some time been a controversial subject.[62] What was 'the "proper" time to marry'? Was it when the man had enough money to support a wife and an annual addition to the family? But then, how much was 'enough'? And was not the postponement of marriage, pleasing enough to those Malthusians who believed that it kept down the population, in the interim one of the leading causes of prostitution? Where did true prudence lie? The problem was to become increasingly pressing as the cost of middle-class living rose, especially after about 1870.

The committee was, however, too busy to give this question any detailed examination at this point,[63] and passed on to other things. Licentiousness, after all, also included prostitution, and some reference to this had to be made. The committee therefore urged that measures should be taken by the police and magistrates to suppress brothels, which were too readily tolerated, and to remove temptation from the streets. The civil powers were also urged to do something — what was not specified — in the rural districts about 'the practice of giving outdoor aid to mothers of illegitimate children'.[64]

The church itself also had some responsibility in the matter, and among the fostering circumstances the returns had mentioned 'laxity of Church discipline' and 'sectarianism'.[65] Remedies for these were harder to find, however, none being suggested for the latter, while for the former all the committee could find to say was that 'stricter and more faithful discipline'[66] was required. Its view, and presumably that of the returns, on the church's task concentrated upon the need for 'plain speaking, both from the pulpit and in private'[67] by ministers to all concerned. The committee also emphasised the part to be played by religious education in home, school and Sunday school, where the young could be warned against sins as well as sin, and where young women in particular could receive from 'the *ladies* of the congregation ... many lessons and hints about the proprieties of life and their womanly duties'.[68] The committee quoted, apparently with approval, one minister's comment that 'I do not much believe in the modern theory of sanctifying people by amusing them'.[69] What the young needed were 'words of timely warning'.

Such warnings were obviously not going to be neglected by the Life and Work committee, and in 1881 it returned to the attack with a report on Family Religion, one section of which dealt with Chastity. This report sounded some familiar notes. It urged ministers to teach, and parents and employers to watch over, purity. It spoke of the need for better housing, in which sleeping accommodation would not 'destroy modesty'[70] and of the need for 'open and honourable'[71] courtship facilities. The bothy and farm-kitchen systems were again condemned. Mothers should teach their daughters, fathers their sons, ladies young women, and elders young men, about the sin of licentiousness. Servants' leisure should be regulated; employers and ministers should be more in control of 'the amusements of the people'.[72] And, probably with the sort of thing Strahan had described in mind, the committee urged that discipline should be more strictly exercised, so as 'to bring home to the guilty a sense of sin'.[73] To this end ministers were advised to 'visit the offender privately'[74] before the more formal stage of the proceedings was reached. In another section of the report, dealing with the Sabbath, ministers were advised to hold their Sunday evening services in schools and farmhouses, in order to 'prevent unnecessary walking, and the gathering of gossiping groups, where conversation is frequently very unseemly'.[75]

Chastity and Discipline in the 'Eighties

There, apart from a section of its 1885 report dealing in detail with farm servants but making no new observations,[76] and a note that White Cross sections were being added to branches of the Young Men's Guild,[77] the committee left things, at least for the time being.[78] As a prelude to later developments, however, some returns recorded in its 1887 report[79] mentioned, in addition to mixed Protestant-Roman Catholic marriages, the nature of Presbyterian session discipline among the causes of lapsing. Some ministers believed that many mothers of illegitimate children wanted them baptised but were unwilling (unless they were well-to-do) to go before the session. Many of them went to high church Episcopal or Roman Catholic churches instead, and in the latter case 'a very large number of children thus grow up as Roman Catholics, for that Church never loses hold of the children its priests baptise'.[80] This, and the fact that the same mothers who would not go before a session 'would go to a minister, confess and be penitent', pointed to the need for 'some change in our rules of discipline'.[81] Much the same point had been made in the 1885 report on farm servants, which had stated, on the basis of returns from Galloway and Aberdeenshire, that the majority of those who were kept away from church 'because of their dread of the Church discipline under which they must come before they can be members of the Church', were farm servants or members of the 'crofter class' who were '"under scandal" because of being guilty of the sin of impurity'.[82] This suggests either that the attitudes to discipline described by Strahan were not common in the North-East and South-West or that they had changed during the intervening twenty years.

Social Class, Geography and Prayer Books

During the twenty years from 1870 to 1890 the Life and Work committee did not say as much about family religion as about sexual behaviour. There was, however, a reference to it in its 1871 report in a discussion of 'the efforts made for Christian instruction or influence by employers of labour'.[83] Sandwiched among the complaints made in this report about the indifference of farmers to their servants were some remarks about remnants of 'the old forms of Scottish piety',[84] in some remote areas, where farmers conducted regular family worship with their servants (in one case twice daily) and catechised them on Sunday evenings. This last practice however was becoming very rare, and the forms of worship were changing, since many people 'who had lacked courage to begin family worship'[85] were now using the Assembly's 'Book of Family Prayers'. Where employers in the industrial areas took an interest in the religion of their employees it was usually on a less personal basis: a few of them provided salaries, housing and equipment for missionaries and ministers. But some helped by 'visiting and attempting to better the condition of the poorer portion of their workpeople and neighbours'.[86] The committee emphasised in particular the importance of 'providing means for the godly upbringing of the young',[87] and noted that this was in fact the form which the philanthropy of employers most commonly took.

In 1872 the committee undertook an enquiry into Family Worship, as part of its report on Family Life and found, according to its returns, that it was still 'general'[88] in the Highlands, the Northern Isles and in the more remote areas of the Lowlands. But even in these areas it was going out of fashion, although not as much as in most other Lowland and urban areas where it had been 'disused to a still greater extent, except among the more well-to-do families, who have of course more leisure'.[89] The contrast between working-class and middle- and upper-class families in this respect was emphasised in a number of returns, one for example claiming that while 'family worship 40 years ago was very general in families of the working class once a day . . . now it is comparatively rare'.[90] This point however was disputed by the minister of a 'populous and busy' Lowland parish, who wrote that he had 'reason to believe that in a large proportion of households of the labouring class, family worship is observed';[91] and the committee suggested that more experienced ministers sometimes found that family worship was 'observed in more families than they had at first thought'.[92] It might also, they pointed out, be a matter of definition: 'In many cases often it is a habit for a chapter of the Bible to be read aloud, by parent or child, as an act of worship'.[93] And this, they felt, could serve as the basis of an appeal from the minister for more elaborate forms of worship.

The minister of the populous and busy parish had also observed 'a great improvement . . . within the last 25 years'[94] in families who employed servants. Very few of these, he noted, failed to gather both their family and their servants for worship. But the committee, while commenting that 'domestic servants (where the family has such) seem to be always brought in to family worship',[95] remarked that this rarely or ever included out-of-door servants. It also observed that 'in the Lowlands some book (of prayers)[96] is a very general part of the furniture of the house'.[97] In the Highlands, however, such books were rarely used: they were, it was said, 'abhorred', since 'it would be offering other prayers than their own, which would make their worship formal, lifeless and unacceptable'.[98]

Returning to the subject in 1873, the committee, in its section on Family Life, again enquired into the state of family worship, commenting that

> statistical information on the subject is of course not to be expected, but the returns received from ministers, enable the committee to report with some confidence as to the

> impressions of those qualified to judge. In the upper and middle classes, family worship, with the aid of some book of prayers, may be said to be daily observed. The domestic servants and the children are gathered together for it. In the families of farmers it seems to be much less frequent than it used to be. In the families of labourers and mechanics, in both town and country, it seems to be far from usual . . .[99]

The reason for this, the committee had been told, was 'a prejudice against read prayers'. Yet many copies of the Assembly's manual were in fact selling, especially in churches where ministers preached special sermons on the subject. Perhaps the answer lay in simplifying the language of the manual;[100] and the committee recommended revisions with this in mind.[101]

The only other reference to this subject during the 'seventies has already been mentioned, in connection with the Licentiousness report of 1878, when the committee had commented on 'the lack of family religion and the decline of parental authority' as a fostering circumstance of the vice. The committee had found evidence of the latter in the fact that 'many parents' allowed their children to wander at late hours and that they seemed 'to think that the Sabbath-school and religious classes almost clear them of responsibility in regard to their children'[102] as far as family worship was concerned. A further discussion in the 1881 report dealt with family worship but added little to what had already been said. Standard criticisms and standard remedies of the kind already alluded to were brought up, together with recommendations on how families might be encouraged to read 'especially during the long nights of winter in country cottages'[103] and of how they might be encouraged to continue their education through evening classes or self-help, with the minister's assistance. The minister's role as an adviser on 'health and sanitary regulation'[104] either by direct teaching or by the promotion of schemes such as 'penny savings banks, cheap-clothing clubs, benefit societies, funeral societies, &c.'[105] was also stressed in this connection.

The Religious Condition of the People

The Church of Scotland's Commission on the Religious Condition of the People has been referred to above on a number of occasions. Under the convenership of J. Marshall Lang,[106] it reported to the Assembly between 1891 and 1898. It had been set up primarily as a means of dealing with non-churchgoing, and its task was to visit synods, presbyteries and 'necessitous parishes and districts' in order to assess and make recommendations about 'measures for supplying the religious wants of the people'.[107] This task it performed conscientiously, and while its more routine recommendations concerned such things as the building of church halls and the provision of ministers' assistants, it went so far in one or two cases as to advise the Assembly to retire unproductive ministers. Its motto might well have been the dictum of Howie, the Free Church statistician: 'Ministers must be efficient as well as evangelical.'[108]

The Commission's observations were not limited however to the domestic economy of the Church of Scotland; and its reports were full of information and opinions about the social and moral as well as the religious condition of the people. Its final report, in 1896,[109] included an extensive survey of the social condition of the country, focusing upon the problems of poverty, class distinction, labour and housing and, in addition, considering the bearing of intemperance, impurity and betting and gambling upon the wellbeing of the people. It was especially concerned, among the social problems, about the detrimental effects of class distinctions within the church, particularly in relation to seat rents, believed by many to be a serious obstacle to working-class church attendance. Its other special concerns included the church's ministry to children, and more particularly to adolescents, many of whom, it believed, were being lost to the church after leaving Sunday school.

In the present context however our main interest is in what the Commission had to say about sexual behaviour and its control, and about family religion. In what immediately follows we shall consider what it wrote about urban and rural aspects of the former.

Urban Sexual Behaviour

The Commission began its visitation of the synods with that of Glasgow and Ayr. This synod comprised an area whose rapid growth in population and industrialisation presented the Church with enormous problems, not least in terms of the large numbers — variously estimated at a fifth, a fourth or even half of the population — who were 'indifferent to Christian ordinances'. The reasons for this were 'too many and too subtle to be analysed';[110] and the commissioners found great difficulty in knowing how the church should deal with industrial society in general and Glasgow ('the sphinx-problem of civilization in its most sphinx-like aspect')[111] in particular. Its observations on the social morality of the people were accordingly pretty random, and although a certain amount was written about mixed marriages as a cause of non-churchgoing, the Commission was more concerned with the intemperance than with the sexual behaviour of the inhabitants of this part of Scotland. Its observations on these subjects confirm an impression that, during this period, the church believed — to speak very generally — that while sexual immorality was the vice peculiar to the rural working classes, drink was the curse of their urban contemporaries. (Domestic servants and Highlanders were, by and large, exceptions to this rule.)

The Commission however did not entirely ignore the great problem of urban prostitution, but like the Life and Work committee and the Housing committee of the Free Church it did not examine it in any depth. It received from the superintendent of the Glasgow City Mission what it termed 'interesting glimpses — some of them painfully interesting — of certain conditions of city life'.[112] These included references to the large number of brothels in the centre of Glasgow, as well as to other houses which 'cannot be designated as brothels' but to which 'young women go . . . in the evening for prostitution'.[113] It also noted the activities of an organisation which gave free breakfasts on Sundays to waifs and strays, including 'many girls of that class who are just between losing and winning', and commented that there was 'a sadder class still'.[114] It did not provide any further information about these or about any other features of prostitution in Glasgow or the towns of the West of Scotland however; and its observations on the Edinburgh scene were equally oriented to intemperance and away from sexual morality.[115] The Commission clearly was aware that prostitution existed on a large scale in the cities, and wrote that 'its victims are legion'.[116] But its intelligence was not good: it was not able 'to estimate the full extent of the social evil; it walks in the dark, and in the city its paths are not known'.[117]

This ignorance, as we have already seen, was a consequence of the enclosed congregationalism of the city churches — something which the Commission itself criticised,[118] and it is quite likely that a large number of the representatives of those congregations from whom it received its information were genuinely in the dark about the subject.[119] It had therefore to turn to missionary agencies for information. This in itself however does not entirely explain the Commission's reticence in dealing with the subject, since it could presumably have enquired further had it wished to do so. That it did not enquire further can of course be explained by saying that it was not part of its business to do so. And the explanation is satisfactory enough — until we discover the much greater extent to which the Commission, like other church committees before it, explored the parallel question of rural immorality.

The Ploughmen Answer Back

In view of all that had been written by church committees since 1858, it was perhaps inevitable that the Commission was fascinated by the question of farm servants. Its earlier reports (1891 and 1892), in dealing with them, spoke in terms similar to those of the Life and Work committee about the housing, migratory habits and hours of labour of farm servants in the West of Scotland, and of how these had a detrimental effect upon their churchgoing habits and character in general. But when, in 1892, its investigations took it to the Synod of Angus and Mearns — an area which, outside Dundee, had a considerable agricultural population — the Commission pushed some of its questions farther, and as a consequence found it harder to make general pronouncements on these subjects. Its informants, in addition to ministers, elders and farmers, now included farm servants themselves, and in October 1892 it met the secretary of the Ploughmen's Union.[120] This meeting involved the Commission even more deeply in such difficult questions as those of hours, wages, accommodation, half-holidays and the provision of small-holdings for farm servants; and since the union's secretary, Mr. Duncan, claimed to know every bothy in Forfarshire (in his fourteen years as a farm servant he had lived in a number of them), the Commission was forced to tread carefully. Although, six months later, it managed to arrange a meeting with about fifty ploughmen from the Coupar Angus area,[121] whose diffident response to its questions took the edge off some of Mr. Duncan's more radical claims, the Commission thereafter was more cautious in what it wrote on the subject. After a lengthy discussion of farm servants with the Presbytery of Deer in October 1893, its members were at pains to point out

> that in giving so much prominence to this class of the community it is very far from their intention to insinuate that farm servants are worse in any respect than other classes. It is only because they are a very numerous and important class in that part of the country now under consideration that this has been deemed necessary, and for the further reason that they have to encounter difficulties and temptations peculiar to their lot in life which demand the special help and sympathy of the Church. The Church of Scotland has no more loyal sons than are to be found among the farm-servants . . .[122]

This apologetic tone was adopted by the Commission partly, it seems, because so many of its informants (including ministers and elders) had told it that the real reason for the alienation of younger farm servants from the church was not their housing accommodation or even their hours of labour, but the fact that so many ministers did not bother to visit or even to get to know them.[123] All the complaints made about the migratory habit as an obstacle to this were, it was suggested, something of a smokescreen, since although in Forfarshire at least the average length of a younger farm servant's engagement was six months, 'they frequently re-engage in the same place';[124] and even if they moved, they did not move very far. The commissioners' tone was apologetic also, it may be assumed, because as a result of their enquiries they were beginning to think of farm servants less as some class of rural outcasts, and more in terms of the increasing number of members of this class whom they were meeting and who, because they could answer back, were not so easy to categorise. A fear that they might answer back by becoming even more alienated from the church no doubt also played its part in making the Commission apologetic.

Up to the point when this statement was made the Commission had not said much about rural sexual morality. It had, of course, hinted that all was not well, in its remarks about the half-yearly hiring markets: 'most people who have eyes to see, and who have any knowledge of country life,' it wrote, 'are aware of the degradation which follows in the rear of the feeing-fair'.[125] But of the 'many temptations to young men and women' which these events offered, it had preferred to concentrate upon intemperance, emphasising the point that farm servants' heavy drinking on these occasions[126] was in marked contrast to their usual commendable temperance.[127] Part of the reason for their reticence, at this particular time, about the subject of sexual behaviour was that although illegitimacy, running at a rate of 9.5 per cent., was a 'dark spot'[128] on the moral complexion of Forfarshire, this rate, worse indeed than that of any English county, was exceeded by those of eleven other counties in Scotland. Nor, at this time, could the Commission think of any remedy for illegitimacy, although it expressed the opinion that session discipline did nothing to help matters and might even be harmful. It did however record some advice on the subject given to it by Mr.

Duncan of the Ploughmen's Union. He, like Begg, blamed the bothies — places

> where the ploughman is ostracised from society. He is not allowed into his employer's house. It is, in nearly every case, instant dismissal for a man to be seen there. Hence you have what follows — night hawking, illegitimacy.[129]

Duncan also blamed illegitimacy on the place of the female farm servant in the rural economy:

> She has no chance of speaking for herself. She gives way to the first stout-tongued scoundrel that comes across her path if he makes fair promises;[130]

and he urged the Commission to persuade farmers' and ministers' wives 'and every lady that has any leisure in the country districts'[131] to visit and 'take an interest in . . . these females' and in widows who worked on farms.

The North-East

Apart from what was said about hiring markets and by Mr. Duncan, then, the Commission did not pay much attention to the question of rural sexual behaviour until its investigations brought it to the Synod of Aberdeen. But once it reached the North-East the question could not be avoided. At the meeting with the Presbytery of Deer, mentioned above, the question of housing was raised, with its effects on morality and family life specifically in mind. Here evidence was provided to show that there were still parts of Aberdeenshire where there were too few houses for married farm servants. The result of this, it was claimed, was that the wives and children were forced to live in towns and villages where they were only occasionally visited by their men. 'This system,' the Commission remarked, while stressing that it was not universal, 'obviously tends to break down family life and weaken parental authority.'[132] Perhaps it was also connected with whatever facts lay behind the opinion expressed at the same meeting that, while there was very little illegitimacy in small fishing villages, and while illegitimacy among farm servants was becoming less, it was most prevalent in the large villages.

Other presbyteries supported what was said here about the fishing population. At a meeting with the Presbytery of Fordyce a paper was presented by Dr. Cramond of Cullen, 'an accurate observer and statistician'.[133] In this it was argued that 'were it not for the modifying influence of a large fishing population, the character of Banffshire as a whole would be far blacker than it is'.[134] As it was, things were bad enough; and Dr. Cramond illustrated this point in a way which would have delighted Dr. Begg had he lived to see it. (He had in fact died ten years earlier.) Cramond produced

> a scale in inches showing the comparative state of the three kingdoms. Ireland was represented by a line 1⅔ inches long; England by one 5 inches long; Scotland by one 8 inches long; Banffshire by one 16 inches long.[135]

For this state of statistics, Dr. Cramond believed, 'the farm-servants, male and female, are alone responsible';[136] and he argued that the only possible remedy was that every farm should 'have upon it an amount of house accommodation for married servants, or servants inclined to marry, proportionate to the size of the farm'.[137] This too would have pleased Begg, although he would perhaps have been less happy that Cramond had to add that 'After the labours of the Churches for thirty years at least, they have not succeeded in effecting one iota of improvement.'[138]

A paper delivered to the same conference by W.S. Bruce, the minister of Banff,[139] also analysed the problem, dismissing, as causes: 'the bothy system, for it hardly exists . . . poverty or low wages, for none are better paid' and 'lack of education, for Banffshire has always been distinguished for the excellence of its parish schools'.[140] Mr. Bruce indicated his own list of causes, but the Commission in its report did not record what he said,[141] preferring to list the causes which had been mentioned in a report made thirty years earlier to the Synod of Aberdeen. Since things had not improved during the intervening period this report, the Commission believed, was still valid. (One of its two authors however had been Marshall Lang, the Commission's chairman, at that time minister of Fyvie.) This report had enumerated five main causes of North-Eastern immorality: first qualitatively and quantitatively inadequate houses for farm servants; second, 'the defectiveness of the early training of the young'; third, the indifference of employers to the moral character of their servants and their failure to supervise their conduct; fourth, the 'common practice' of employing males and females together in outdoor farm work; and fifth, the low moral standards of the rural population, especially their sexual 'uncleanness'.[142] Above all, remarked the Commission, the creation of 'a healthy public opinion' was required. But, they confessed,

> how to bring it about is a problem which has hitherto baffled and perplexed even the most faithful and devoted men who have striven honestly to overcome a state of matters which is scandalous in the extreme.[143]

A similar despairing note was sounded by the Commission when in 1894 it visited the Synod of Moray, the lowland areas of which shared Aberdeen's reputation for illegitimacy. In its remarks about the Presbytery of Strathbogie, the Commission again cited the 16 per cent. illegitimacy rate of Banffshire, but on this occasion pointed out that while some of those responsible for it were farm servants, 'others belonged to other sections of the labouring class', and 'some to classes in easier circumstances'.[144] This additional factor made it even more difficult for the Commission to unravel the problem, confronted as it was by so many conflicting opinions about nearly all aspects of rural social and religious life. Some hopes were expressed that the house-building activities of a number of landowners, the decline in the number of female outdoor farm servants,[145] and the success of schemes for registers of female servants[146] (as opposed to the feeing fair) in some districts, would promote self-respect and reduce the amount of immorality. But no real evidence of this consequence was, so far, forthcoming.

The South-West

The other notorious area, the South-West, in ecclesiastical terms the Synods of Galloway and Dumfries, was also visited in 1894 and the Commission discussed illegitimacy with most of the presbyteries in the area. In Galloway there was general agreement about what were not the causes of illegitimacy. Within the bounds of the Presbytery of Kirkcudbright the bothy system did not exist, housing was 'fair',[147] and there was 'nothing in the social conditions of the people to be adduced as an adequate explanation of this terrible evil'.[148] Similar comments were made by the presbytery clerk of Wigtown, who could attribute it ultimately only to the prevalent low tone of opinion, sinners being regarded at best with pity, but more usually with indifference. These two presbyteries also agreed that immorality was not confined to farm servants, domestic servants or even to the working classes. For although the latter were the most culpable there were, in Wigtown, 'one or two cases in the better class',[149] and in Galloway, 'in families whose education and social position would lead to the expectation of better things'.[150] A number of the members of both presbyteries believed that the sin was often hereditary, and an example was cited of a parish in which between 1880 and 1893 there were 488 births of which 42 were illegitimate, 28 or two-thirds of these being members of nine families.[151] Difference of opinion within the synod arose, however, over the question of whether matters were getting better or worse. In Kirkcudbright 'the general opinion was that there is an improvement',[152] and in Wigtown that 'the moral condition of the people as a whole has improved within the last twenty years'.[153] (The high illegitimacy rate was explained in terms of the hereditary theory, the parish just mentioned being cited as an example.) The presbytery clerk however disagreed, and producing the — by now almost canonical — Registrar General's Reports, pointed out that the illegitimacy rate within the presbytery's bounds in the six years preceding 1863 had been 14.7 per cent., compared with in the six years preceding 1876 and 1891, 15.8 per cent., and 16.9 per cent., respectively. In the ensuing gloom it was urged that the church, in order to remedy the situation, should 'take steps for the creation of new agencies, where the old ones have failed'.[154] In particular there should be 'a more frank and thorough recognition by the church of "the power of woman in social life," and a greater use made of that power by training and organising workers to grapple with this vice'.[155] This was not however an entirely new suggestion, although admittedly the untrained 'ladies' of a few decades earlier were here to be replaced.[156] The remedies proposed by the Presbytery of Kirkcudbright were even more well-worn, and as far as the Presbytery of Stranraer was concerned, its discussion of illegitimacy was so familiar to the Commission that nothing about it was recorded in the report, save its observation that 'a tendency' to employ mothers of illegitimate children on farms and in dairies 'indirectly encouraged immorality and illegitimacy'.[157]

The Synod of Dumfries was more sanguine in its analysis of immorality than its western neighbour. A minister from the Presbytery of Annan complained that 'we do not get justice in this matter . . . the immorality does not exist to the extent we are charged with'.[158] In recent years, he claimed, he had seen the growth of a much higher moral tone in the district, a claim similar to that which was to some extent substantiated in its own area by the Presbytery of Dumfries. It presented the Commission with statistics showing how the percentage of illegitimate births had fallen from 16.6 in 1882 to 12.7 in 1891.[159] Statistics, however, had power to craze as well as soothe the ministers of the South-West; and one, in the Presbytery of Penpont — a presbytery whose morals, its Moderator claimed, were generally improving — spoke of his own parish like a debtor compulsively counting up unpaid bills:

> I do not know if this parish is worse than the rest of Dumfries-shire, but the rate of illegitimacy has been very high: it has averaged 10 per cent. during the last forty years; during the ten years ending 1870 it was 9.3; during the ten years ending 1880 it was 6.5; during the ten years ending 1890 it rose to 10; for the last four years it went up to 12.5, being for those four years respectively 10.3, 18.9, 6.25 and 17.2. Things seem to be growing worse instead of better, and there is hardly any public opinion in the parish against the sin.[160]

Three further 'facts disclosed by statistics' — in this case the more widely based statistics of the Presbytery of Dumfries for 1882-91, were: first, that the percentage of illegitimate births was higher in 'purely rural parishes' (18.5 per cent.) than in 'parishes with town populations' (12.6 per cent.); second, that the percentage of illegitimate children baptised by parish ministers was higher in the rural parishes (51.3 per cent.) than in the town parishes (18.1 per cent.); and third, that the percentage of these (baptised) illegitimate children whose mothers were communicants was again higher in the rural parishes (23.9 per cent.) than in the town parishes (4.9 per cent.).[161] The Commission, commenting on these figures, took comfort from the fact 'that full membership of the Church appears to exert a restraining and elevating influence',[162] and suggested, in view of its supposition that many of the mothers of illegitimate children who were communicants fell before joining the church,

> that it might be well to try and induce our young women to become communicants at a rather earlier period than is common, and so fortify them, at the most critical period of their lives, to resist the temptation resulting from the low moral tone which prevails, by the grace which accompanies the faithful participation in the Sacrament, and the sense of comradeship with the pure and holy in the Church of Christ.[163]

The Commission also commented upon the small percentage of illegitimate children baptised by parish ministers. This was often due, it was told, to the unwillingness of mothers, especially in the towns, to become baptismal sponsors, since to do so they would first have to submit to session discipline.

As a result, the children were either baptised in churches which did not insist on discipline, or in what were probably the majority of cases, they were not baptised at all. Thus, it was said, 'they receive little Christian nurture, and accordingly grow up in carelessness, and perpetuate an evil which is so great a scandal to the Church and the country'.[164] The Commission believed that the church itself was partly to blame for this, because of the disciplinary system which ministers had to use. On its visit to Forfarshire it had already asked 'if the effect of the present modes of discipline is not in some ways hurtful';[165] and, as we shall see, this was a question to which it would later return.

The Lothians and Borders

On its visit to Forfarshire, the Commission had been told by Mr. Duncan of the Ploughmen's Union that in the Lothians fathers and the whole of their families were employed to work together as farm servants, and that this arrangement prevented the social divisiveness and consequent immorality of the bothy system.[166] When the Commission itself visited that area (in 1892 and 1893) it found evidence to support this contention. Within the bounds of the Presbytery of Dunbar it was said that farm servants' cottages were generally good, some of them 'having four fireplaces each';[167] and that all the members of a family often found work on the same farm. Thus, even when the family moved within the area, it could be kept together. But given these improved conditions the number of farm servants who in fact chose to move was diminishing. This applied as much to the unmarried, who normally lived in the house of a married servant or a cotter (there were very few bothies),[168] as to the married servants or hinds. In the Commission's view it was therefore not surprising that the illegitimacy rate in Haddingtonshire (East Lothian) was only 5 per cent., less than half that of Aberdeenshire and Banffshire (both of which were currently at 13.2 per cent.).[169] Even church attendance was better in this area, reports the Commission received being 'among the most favourable hitherto'; and although things were not so propitious farther west — the Presbytery of Dalkeith blamed Sunday visiting[170] for irregular churchgoing — even here farm workers were 'sober' and 'well-conducted'.

The Commission's approval of the religious and moral behaviour of farm servants in the Lothians extended to that of most of their fellows in those other areas south of the Forth and Clyde which have not so far been mentioned. In the Presbyteries of Peebles and Biggar non-attendance at church was said not to be widespread, and what there was could not be attributed either to bad housing or to poverty. Family life, the Presbytery of Peebles reported, was 'particularly satisfactory',[171] since married farm servants were preferred by the farmers and there was employment for all. From the Synod of Merse and Teviotdale (visited in 1895) there were reports of the absence of bothies in Berwickshire, from the Presbytery of Earlston of the 'relaxing'[172] of the bondager system, and from the Presbytery of Duns of the small numbers of unmarried servants. Even where these last were to be found, they usually worked alongside other members of their own family; and where the bondager system still existed, the bondager was also normally a member of the hind's family. Cases of female bondagers unrelated to the hind, being employed and invading 'the privacy of the home',[173] were rare. Where they were to be found they were 'a nuisance': but 'practically no immorality'[174] resulted from their presence. Indeed, in the Presbytery of Earlston, illegitimacy was not very prevalent: its 6½ to 7 per cent. rate, it was implied, was largely due to a few bad parishes. And the idea that immorality was not very prevalent was supported by reports of the rarity of cases of discipline (a doubtful method of arguing which, as we shall see, was more usually employed by the Free Church than by the Church of Scotland).

The one aspect of the agricultural economy in this area which the Commission did find disturbing was the number of 'led' farms. These, of which the Presbyteries of Dalkeith,[175] Earlston,[176] Selkirk,[177] and Jedburgh[178] all complained, were either owned or tenanted by farmers who did not live on them, and the presbyteries' criticism was that these farmers did not look after the welfare of their servants. The presbyteries alleged that led farms, besides being a cause of rural depopulation and 'a fruitful source of discontent', were responsible for 'painful cases of immorality . . . the circumstances of which might be traced to the system'.[179] Still, on balance, the general mood of Border presbyteries was optimistic. An old minister in the Presbytery of Hawick remarked that 'as regards impurity . . . a great improvement had taken place in the rural parishes within his recollection'.[180] And, visiting the Presbytery of Chirnside, the Commission found it 'gratifying to be assured that, at least in several of the parishes, there had been in late years a decrease of immorality and an improvement in all that relates to moral tone'.[181]

Fife, Perth and Stirling

North of the Forth, in the Synod of Fife[182] and in the Synod of Perth and Stirling[183] (visited by the Commission in 1894 and 1895 respectively), much less, indeed hardly anything, was heard about immorality. There were, of course, the usual complaints about migratory farm servants: the Presbytery of Cupar compared theirs unfavourably with those of Berwickshire and Haddingtonshire,[184] and in the Presbyteries of Dunblane,[185] Stirling and Auchterarder,[186] 'restlessness' among the younger servants was attributed in some degree to the fact that many of them came from nearby mining and manufacturing districts in search of temporary employment. But housing was said in general to be much improved, bothies were few and sanitary, and, in Fife, the Commission was warned against blaming the farm workers rather than their masters for their migratory habits.[187] Even where housing was not good, as in one parish in the Presbytery of Stirling, the Commission was told that 'the personal habits are, with very few exceptions, of a high character'.[188] It was pleased to hear this, especially 'in an age . . . when so much stress is laid on "the circumstances", and so little comparatively on the power of the man or woman to rise above the most adverse circumstances'.[189] An aspect of the age it must have found less pleasing, however, but one which it was advised (by a minister from the Presbytery of St. Andrews) that it must accept, bore almost the opposite testimony. Speaking of life 'in times of transition' and of the 'many new social forces at work' including 'the vastly increased diffusion of literature of many sorts . . . the altered relations between the working classes and their employers and the recent transference of nearly all political power into the hands of the former' (a singularly optimistic view of the democratic process), this minister commented upon

> the spirit of independence which is universal, and the consequent abolition of that authority which kirk-sessions and ministers used to possess, and which operated as a compulsory clause of the most stringent kind, both for church attendance and other things.[190]

The minister, whose views the Commission believed to be 'well-founded', pointed, as a further characteristic of the times,

> to that spirit of inquiry which is abroad, and which makes the age one of criticism more than of faith. Many things, with institutions and doctrines, handed down from past generations, and formerly accepted with blind acquiescence, are now on their trial, and what cannot render a satisfactory reason for its existence cannot hope to stand. Considering that there is such a searching and shaking of things going on all round, and united therewith the common feeling that to lose one thing is to lose all, I cannot help wondering that Churches and church-going are not suffering more than they do; and I incline to think that, in some quarters at any rate, non-church-going is not yet so common as it will be, and that the problem presented by it is not therefore fully before our view.[191]

The Highlands and Islands

Those parts of Scotland which, it might have been expected, were least affected by these aspects of late nineteenth-century culture, the Highlands and Islands, were visited by the Commission in 1891 and in 1896-1898. In the Highlands and Western Isles illegitimacy was said to be 'comparatively rare' by the Presbytery of Skye,[192] 'rare' by that of Lochcarron,[193] and 'extremely rare' by that of Tongue.[194] In some districts of Caithness, admittedly, it was reported, 'the standard of purity is not so high as in the neighbouring Presbyteries',[195] but farther south in the Easter Ross Presbytery of Tain, 'the moral life of the people' was 'said to be remarkably pure';[196] and in the nearby Presbytery of Chanonry, although illegitimacy, one minister remarked, was 'tending to increase', it prevailed to no great extent.[197] Other presbyteries in the North and West reported in similar terms while making some similar exceptions. In Lewis, although the population was said to be on the whole 'singularly free from vices',[198] two ministers thought that illegitimacy was increasing within their parishes; in Islay it was said to be 'considerable';[199] and while in the Presbytery of Mull it was generally low, on the island of Coll it was 'considerable and on the increase'.[200] These comments were made against the background of decreasing bitterness between the Free Church and the Church of Scotland in the Northern Highlands, and — or so it was believed — decreasing intemperance, notwithstanding the large quantities of whisky still consumed in Skye and the large number of distilleries in Kintyre. Not much was said about secularisation in general in the Highlands — except in the

Presbytery of Dunoon where, on a summer Sunday, the Kyles of Bute 'were more like a regatta than anything else, and the thing was growing'.[201]

The Northern Isles, in the Commission's view, shared many of the pleasing features of the Highlands. The inhabitants of Shetland were described as 'a hardy, industrious, sober, God-fearing, not over-wealthy race'[202] who, despite the fact that a considerable minority were Methodists, did not quarrel over ecclesiastical matters. The inhabitants of Orkney, where a substantial minority were United Presbyterians, shared the Commission's approval, although in their case there was an exception. The Presbytery of Cairston, which had conducted an 'exhaustive' study of the subject, reported on 'the prevalence of certain local customs connected with 'courtship' which tend to immorality'[203] There was not however a high illegitimacy rate,[204] and thanks to the efforts of ministers and sessions things were changing for the better.

Farm Servants, Purity and Discipline

In its lengthy final report,[205] the Commission included sections both on farm servants and on impurity. Its remarks on farm servants reiterated the point made in connection with its visits to the Presbytery of Deer. Farm servants were not exceptional men: they were, 'for the most part, manly, self-reliant, industrious and sober'.[206] They were prominent in the Commission's reports rather, because they had 'of late . . . bulked largely in the public view', because they formed 'one of the most important constituents of national prosperity', and because 'the desire to improve (their) condition proceeds on the assumption that (they are) worthy of such improvement'.[207] The Commission went on to note the improvements which had taken place, and the 'rising tide of feeling'[208] against bothies and in favour of larger cottages in which the unmarried servant could board with the married. It also noted some further improvements which could be made in connection with holidays and hiring markets, as well as the desire expressed by some for farm workers' crofts. And it mentioned the varying conditions of female farm workers. Finally, it wrote of the breakdown of 'the old ideal of the farm, with the kindly relations which existed between master and servant',[209] and criticised the led farm system. The breakdown was 'no doubt . . . only a sign of the revolution in social life',[210] the Commission commented, and warned its readers against blaming either the farmer or the farm worker exclusively for this new state of affairs.

Turning to impurity, the Commission reiterated a number of the comments made to it in the course of its visits. Of these it emphasised two points: the belief that 'the sin, though widely spread, is propagated largely from some families in which it has become almost hereditary';[211] and 'the laxity of tone as to sexual immorality in rural districts', especially of the North-East and the South-West. Improvement was impossible until 'a deeper reverence for the human person and a more potent fear of God pervade the younger people there'.[212] But how could the church achieve this? The Commission again suggested that churchwomen might do more to help, that guilds or leagues concerned with the promotion of purity might be formed, and that young people might be persuaded to become communicants at an earlier age.

The question of immorality was also clearly related to discipline:

> The end of all discipline is to mark the condemnation of the sin, and in so doing to arouse or intensify the conscience as to the sin, and to evoke 'the godly sorrow which worketh repentance repented of.' From the testimony borne, it is obvious that this end is not being adequately accomplished.[213]

The reason for this was that the more sensitive offenders had 'a natural repugnance' to appearing before the session with other offenders, while among the insensitive

> 'the standing of the session' is little regarded; the appearance and the rebuke are held to be 'a clearing' of them.[214]

Discipline, now 'practically narrowed to sins against one commandment', had become 'the remnant of a fact which was once powerful'.[215] The Commission thus considered that 'the concept and administration of ecclesiastical discipline by kirk-sessions needs revision',[216] and suggested that more emphasis should be placed on private interviews with the offender by the minister and perhaps a couple of elders. It also recommended some reconsideration of the procedure for the baptism of illegitimate children.

Urban Family Life: Dundee

Although, in its final report, the Commission had nothing to add to its previous brief comments on urban sexual behaviour, it did say a little about urban family life. Its visit to Dundee in 1892 had made this subject one which it could not ignore. Dundee's housing was so bad that compared with it 'the bothies in the country are palaces'.[217] Conditions of labour however were what the Commission found most 'painful'. Of the 5,000 children in Scotland of ten years and upward who worked 'half-time', 3,500 were employed in Dundee factories. Many of them said that they preferred the half-time they spent at work to the half-time in school. But the Commission believed that, despite this and despite benevolent employers, the half-time system was 'morally hurtful', destroying reverence for parents, making children difficult to control, and bringing 'all sorts of unrighteousness into play'.[218] In Dundee also, the Commission found, there were 17,000 more women than men: and it related this statistic to the men's extreme difficulty in finding employment after the stage of apprenticeship, and to the jute industry's preference for female labour. As a consequence of unemployment many of the men of Dundee were given to 'loafing' while very many married women worked in the mills. Even when the husband was employed and even when he was earning high wages, the idea that wives should work was still acceptable. This, the

Commission believed, 'means a large wreckage of family life'.[219] Issues of this kind would figure increasingly in church pronouncements after the turn of the century.

Family Religion

Family religion was not a subject into which the Commission enquired in any depth. Its 1892 report recorded some comments by the Presbytery of Lanark about the difficulties faced, by those farmers who wished for it, in persuading their servants to join in family worship. One farmer was told by his servants 'that he had nothing to do with their religion, and that if he insisted they would leave his service'.[220] Another found that whenever he invited them to attend family worship, his servants, 'especially the young men',[221] went out of the house. Little more than this was written on the subject by the Commission. But that this — or simply the absence of any corporate worship whatever on farms — was typical (except when those ministers who visited conducted it) may be assumed from the summary remark in the Commission's final report:

> Too seldom now is the worship of God maintained in the houses of its (Scotland's) people; too seldom is there found the gracious yet firm authority of the parent guiding the moral and religious education of his children; 'The Cottar's Saturday Night' is becoming more and more a bit of poetry.[222]

In making much the same comment about 'The Cottar's Saturday Night' however, a return to the Presbytery of Dunbar added that while such scenes were disappearing, 'the general moral and religious level of the people is perhaps higher'.[223]

But again there was no very obvious consensus, for complaints about the decline of parental authority were numerous. The Presbytery of St. Andrews was worried about lax parental control even among churchgoing families,[224] and even the Presbytery of Lochcarron was concerned about 'the relaxation of parental authority which is taking place'.[225] Both of these presbyteries feared that this would have a detrimental effect on churchgoing. Similar fears were expressed by the Presbytery of Dunfermline, in which complaints were made of the absence of religious instruction in day schools as well as in the homes of 'three-fourths of the population'[226] (the proportion there estimated to be 'virtually' non-churchgoing). The Sabbath school, it was claimed, could make no headway against this. Unlike 'the Roman Catholic Church, wise in their day and generation' who 'make this a vital point and spare no effort to secure it',[227] the Church of Scotland was making woefully inadequate provision for the religious education of the young.

In its final report the Commission came back to this question, expressing concern that while 'the vast majority of the children of Scotland are to be found in the Sunday-schools belonging to the different denominations',[228] many of these did not keep up their connection with the churches. Among the reasons for this was the fact that the Sunday school attended by children was often chosen on the ground of convenience, or because it was attended by the children's friends. It might well not be the Sunday school attached to the church with which the parents were connected. Children were also lost to the church because many children of church members or adherents joined some association such as the Glasgow Foundry Boys' Society, which met during the hours of worship. These associations were intended for the children of non-churchgoers, but their short addresses and 'catchy'[229] music attracted the others as well, even if the organisers tried to dissuade them; and the habit of churchgoing was lost. The Commission recommended closer co-operation between such bodies and the church, as well as some sort of 'continuation Sunday school',[230] to bridge the gap between Sunday school and church membership. It praised the work of the Boys' Brigade in this direction, but expressed regret that the guilds of the church had grown so slowly and sporadically. It also requested closer co-operation between churches when members moved from one district to another. None of this, of course, has much directly to do with family religion. The point being made in mentioning it here is to indicate how far the Church of Scotland was now emphasising church-organisation-oriented rather than family-oriented religion.

CHAPTER SEVEN

Religion and Morals: The Free Church View, 1870-1900

Themes and Regional Variations

HAVING now brought the Church of Scotland to the eve of the twentieth century, we must return to rescue the Free Church from the nineteenth, difficult though that may be. Between 1870 and 1900 the Free Church's Religion and Morals committee had a great deal to say about sexual morality and family religion, not simply in general, but also in terms of local conditions. To give some impression of this we can begin by considering the reports received by the committee from different districts of Scotland, dividing the sixteen synods of the Free Church into six groups, similar to those of the previous chapter: the North, the North-East, East-Central Scotland, West-Central Scotland, the South-East and the South-West. As has and will become apparent, these divisions do not always correspond to recognisable geographical or social divisions of, for example, a Highland/Lowland or agricultural/industrial nature; but they are perhaps sufficiently distinct to serve the present purpose. Since much of the information contained in the Religion and Morals reports was fragmentary, often vague and frequently repetitive, what is said here about each division concentrates upon the picture drawn by the committee in the early 'seventies, noting any significant changes recorded thereafter in the subsequent thirty years. The remainder of the chapter then deals with the vulture's-eye picture of the country as a whole, in the form of the committee's more general comments on Scottish sexuality and piety.

The North

In 1872 the Northern Isles[1] had the lowest illegitimacy rate in Scotland. This however did not deceive the committee on Religion and Morals, which complained that the islanders were too ready to tolerate ante-nuptial fornication and to assume that marriage put everything right.[2] In particular, the committee was concerned with the 'questionable' courtship system of the islanders, about which, in 1885, it had received numerous complaints from the majority of Free Church congregations in Orkney. Midnight courtship, its deputies reported, 'appears to have been an old and general custom in the islands', and they remarked — rather surprisingly for them — that 'in times of greater simplicity it was less objectionable than now'.[3] They were, however, convinced that it was now highly dangerous and although on prosecuting their enquiries they found elders very unwilling to discuss the subject, they had formed the impression that

> midnight-courtship is far from an uncommon practice — that in too many cases it is winked at by the parents — and that it is the fruitful source of immorality, which is often so far concealed from public notice, by subsequent marriage.[4]

It was the committee's hope, although it found the situation difficult to assess, that the 'many fine racial and Christian characteristics'[5] of the Orcadians would enable them to break free from these customs. But in 1886, two years after this statement was made, ministers in some districts were still reporting that the courtship system was 'looked upon more as an ineradicable custom than a grievous evil';[6] and although on this occasion the committee was told that public opinion against it was growing — so that midnight courtship perhaps might 'in a year or two be as much reprobated in Orkney as it would be in any part of the South'[7] — it was still being denounced by local presbyteries in 1888,[8] and in 1891 was referred to as what was 'too well known as "Orkney's running sore"'.[9] On this last occasion, however, one minister, following the committee's advice, had been 'forced to speak out on this subject both in public and private'; and more of his colleagues were now reporting that 'a higher tone is gradually showing itself in regard to this sin' and that 'things are improving decidedly'.[10] From Shetland too that year came reports that illegitimacy was decreasing[11] — for although on previous occasions the Shetlanders had been more reticent about the subject,[12] it had been made clear that midnight courtship there also was a custom 'of long standing', which 'almost universally prevails, and ... is not only connived at, but encouraged by professedly Christian parents'.[13] In Shetland, as in Orkney, better housing was considered to be a useful supplementary remedy to ecclesiastical means of dealing with the problem.[14] In Orkney particularly, defective housing and the 'great poverty' of many of the people made home life, in the committee's opinion, 'less favourable to pure ethical and spiritual life, than, in the Christian civilization of an enlightened age it should and might be'.[15] But the Free churchmen of the Northern Isles were also not above the tactic of blaming their problems on outsiders: a report of 1891 noted that there had been an 'increase of various vices, due chiefly, it is presumed, to the influx of strangers during the fishing season'.[16]

As far as family religion was concerned, however, problems began at home, and with the exodus of fathers rather than the influx of strangers. The majority of the young men in the islands, according to the 1872 report, spent most of the year at sea, and tended not to join the church. This they left to the women, who joined when they married, so that their children could be baptised. But one minister stated that heads of families were not admitted to Communion unless they held family worship. So perhaps this, and the men's absence at sea, accounted for the claim by another that family worship was far from universal and that parental authority was not respected. Complaints of this kind were still being made in 1884, when the committee was told about the situation in very gloomy — indeed apocalyptic — terms:

> The Family is a Divine institution, as well as the ministry or the magistracy; and the heads of families are called to be indeed ministers of the Lord — priests of God in their own house. A higher standard is needed — clamantly needed here. The excessive liberty allowed to the young, even to children, together with the cause of this — or both cause and effect of this — the signal absence of parental respect and authoritative control, is one of the evil features mentioned by the Apostle Paul as characterising the last times. These features are present now.[17]

One reason why the Northern Isles were viewed in this way by the Religion and Morals committee and by the local ministers may have been that they, unlike the Highlands, were by no means under the thumb of the Free Church. Free Church congregations in fact only accounted for 29 out of the 90 Presbyterian congregations in Orkney and Shetland.[18]

Across the Pentland Firth, reports from Caithness[19] and Sutherland[20] suggested that sexual morals were better in the country than in the towns — especially those of Caithness; and although a report of the 'eighties alluded to the bothies of Caithness, made infamous by the Revd. Charles Thomson, as places where 'immorality and licentiousness are sadly prevalent', it also pointed out that 'in other parts of the same county farm servants are spoken of as regular in their attendance at church and exemplary in their character and conduct'.[21] According to these reports, the bothy system was by no means universal in Caithness and the housing on a number of farms was considered to be quite good. Indeed, in 1892, after the Synod of Sutherland and Caithness had held a special conference on the subject of Purity, it blamed rural immorality not just on the bothy system, but also, albeit in veiled language, on 'immorality in high places'.[22] The Presbytery of Dornoch added to this the comment that 'dancing-balls accompanied with drink' were 'the cause of much sin'; and it remarked that 'since the introduction of railways, there have been more strangers and laxer morals'.[23] In general, however, both uncleanness, and discipline because of it, were rare in Sutherland and Caithness. The area was, after all, solid Free Church country. So too were the synods to the south, Ross on the east coast[24] and Glenelg in the west, both of which reported in similar terms about sexual sins and discipline. In the early 'seventies illegitimacy also was very rare in Glenelg[25] and Ross[26]. On those rare occasions when illegitimacy did occur, it was blamed, by Glenelg, upon young women who went into service in the less moral parts of the country (the same excuse was applied to male intemperance, which was decreasing but still 'far too common'[27]), and upon 'squads' of workmen employed on the larger farms, by Ross.[28] Reports from these synods in 1875, 1880 and 1884 continued to record that the people's sexual morality, usually measured by the infrequency of cases of discipline involving illegitimacy and ante-nuptial fornication, was high; and they continued to blame domestic service and other employment in the Lowlands for such sins as could be found. In 1890, however, the Presbytery of Lewis claimed that absence from home 'at the herring-fishing stations on the East Coast and in Shetland'[29] was responsible for lowering the tone of some of its men and women, and, in the following year, the Presbytery of Tain also expressed its belief that herring-fishing migrations 'exposed' its young women 'to great temptations'.[30]

As far as family religion was concerned, at least in the early 'seventies, such migrations were seen by the east coast presbyteries as beneficial to their people, for fishermen from the west coast and the Western Isles were said to be having a good effect upon the piety of the locals.[31] But even apart from this, the Free Church population of Caithness and Sutherland were almost devout enough to please even their own ministers: twice-daily family worship was said to be common in almost all homes, and catechising took place regularly. Children were taught the catechism on the Sabbath and sometimes on other nights as well. Reports throughout the 'seventies and 'eighties testified that much the same was true of Ross and Glenelg. In 1873 a report from Glenelg[32] stated that family worship was held twice daily, even where the head of the family was illiterate; and in 1884 the Presbytery of Tain reported that in one district within its bounds 'no family is known where worship is not maintained twice a day'.[33] Although, five years later, the minister of Tain had to inform the Assembly that farm servants — who left home early in the morning and whose children were at school when they came home at lunchtime — found it difficult to hold family worship at any other time than in the evening, the Religion and Morals committee remained on the whole very pleased with the Highlanders; and it remarked in 1884 that it wished that 'office-bearers in all parts of the country were as well acquainted with the religious life and habits of their brethren as their Northern brethren are'.[34] We shall see more of the reason for this remark in due course.

The North-East

But if the North-West Highland synods were pure and faithful to the Free Church, along the coast the Free Provincial Synod of Moray was uneasy about its religious and moral identity. Its western flank lay deep in Free Church territory, but in the east there was less devotion to Disruption principles; and throughout, in addition to the presence of congregations of the Established and United Presbyterian churches, there was 'a considerable admixture of native Popery'.[35] The geographical and religious divisions were also reflected in the people's morals. In the early 'seventies the illegitimacy rates, from west to east, were: Inverness and Nairn, 7 per cent; Elgin, 14 per cent; and Banff, 16 per cent. Morals were also categorised by occupation. Fishermen were pretty free of uncleanness, but unlike the rest of the population (except sailors who were bad on most counts), they drank too much. Domestic servants were on the whole very respectable.[36] And farm servants were very guilty of ante-nuptial fornication, although almost never, it was claimed, of adultery.[37]

The farm servants' fondness for fornication, the synod considered, although not increasing, was reinforced by the lack of parental discipline.[38] This in turn was attributed to the infrequency with which many married servants visited their wives and children, resident in distant towns or villages. Nor did the fact that these visits usually took place on Sundays, when they should have been in church anyway, do anything to help matters. For this state of affairs the synod blamed the farmers, who objected to 'children about their steadings',[39] and preferred the bothy system. One minister even went so far as to complain that 'while much is said about the immorality of farm-servants in this district, there is fully more drunkenness among middle-class farmers than there is among farm-servants'.[40] But although nothing was said directly about courtship customs, the synod's recommendation that 'opportunities for honourable courtship'[41] should be afforded suggests that it was not unaware of the existence of these customs within its bounds.

Despite all this, discipline was rarely exercised in the synod for cases of uncleanness. In the average congregation there were only one or two cases a year; a few of which, in the Presbytery of Inverness, were for illegitimacy. The synod made a point of indicating thereby how little discipline was needed when the Free Church's evangelical ministry was exercised. But that ministry could have had little effect on the agricultural population, since only a few farmers assembled their servants for religious instruction on Sabbath evenings. Among the fishermen, by contrast, family worship was said to be almost universal.

The Synod of Aberdeen,[42] to the south-east of Moray, and that of Angus and Mearns,[43] to the south again, each contained a city. Thus, it would seem, each had a larger number of social variables to be taken into account in evaluating its inhabitants' moral and religious behaviour. This was not, however, apparent in the reports, which read as if farm servants, fishermen and domestics were the only classes with sexual functions. In discussing these, the synods gave farm servants much the usual treatment, attributing their uncleanness to the bothy system and, in Angus and Mearns, to their migratory habits and loose attachment to the Established Church. This synod was, however, harsher on farm servants than Moray had been:

> To a large extent our farm-servants are ignorant, licentious, profane and rude, and the gulf between them and their masters is widening year by year to an alarming extent.[44]

This was a typically insulting and insolent comment. Fishermen too were treated as before, being given a good spiritual and sexual character; and so, in Angus and Mearns, were domestics. Aberdeen, however, rather more assiduous in its reporting, recorded the observation of an 'earnest labourer in the Lord's cause':

> The condition of many of the female servants in our city is very sad indeed. For a time last year hardly a week passed without the fall of some servant girl coming incidentally to our notice.[45]

This synod also ventured a more circumstantial account of the origins of rural uncleanness — which it applied to young people in general rather than to farm servants in particular. It reported:

> In the country young men and women, who have been to church in the (Sabbath) forenoon, often resort to the woods and fields, to the hills and river banks, where much frivolity and indecency takes place among them.[46]

One remarkable feature of this was the admission that these sinners actually had been to church; and a further comment by the Aberdeen synod, noting that uncleanness was not simply proved by the Registrar's statistics, but was also 'of frequent occurrence among our members',[47] showed that all of the responsibility could not be shifted to the Establishment.[48] This statement, a rare admission by a Free Church synod, was based on the number of discipline cases, and it may be that 'members' here included adherents. Cases, 'for obvious reasons',[49] were rarer in the towns.

Further reports from these synods during the remaining years of the nineteenth century made many of the same points. Very little was said about sexual behaviour in the cities — although in a rare reference to prostitution in Aberdeen it was reported, in 1880, that 'street walking has decreased, but illegitimacy has increased'.[50] On the whole, reports preferred to concentrate on the rural districts where, as for example in the Angus and Mearns parish of Glenbervie, 'uncleanness' was the great sin of the district, 'especially among the farm-servant class'.[51] It was also remarked on this occasion, however, that 'even the farmer class' was 'sadly tainted by it';[52] and a hint that some Free Church ministers were beginning to doubt the wisdom of their colleagues' onslaught upon farm servants was provided by a return from the Presbytery of Aberdeen's rural parish of Maryculter, in 1880, which stated that

> considerable agitation has been excited among (farm servants) through the action of church courts in picking them out, as if they were more degraded than labourers of the same class, while their employers, often as godless and profligate as they, are passed over. This is said to do much harm among the men.[53]

Opinions about the causes of uncleanness continued to range over the usual factors — bad or deficient housing, mobility, lack of parental discipline, and the lax discipline of the Established Church,[54] to which so many farm servants continued to adhere.

Reports on the subject of family worship in the Synods of Aberdeen and of Angus and Mearns were not very illuminating: in 1870, the former claimed that it was observed by most heads of families, but did not make clear whether this remark applied to the population as a whole or merely to the Free Church. In Angus and Mearns at any rate, it was only the latter, according to that synod's 1872 report. The usual form, this report stated, was either Bible reading and prayers once daily, or either or both on Sunday evenings only. But it believed that the practice, whatever the form, was increasing. Both synods complained, however, that religious instruction of the young and in families was neglected because parents left it to the Sabbath schools. This complaint was echoed, at the end of the 'seventies, in returns from Dundee congregations. In two of these, family worship was said to be common enough on Sundays, but not on weekdays; but in some others the elders found it difficult to give any account of the amount of family worship that went on.[55] One congregation stated that among its heads of families 'an inability to express themselves in prayer in the hearing of others was a hindrance to the practice of family worship', and it suggested 'that a manual of prayers, authorised by the Church, might be of great use'.[56] Aberdeen, it seemed, was more devout: even in what was described as a 'very low' district of that city, catechising was said to be general.[57]

In the rural areas of these synods during the 'eighties, returns spoke more hopefully than before about family worship. Even in the notorious areas around Banff and Turriff family worship was reported to be increasing, one parish in 1882 going so far as to claim that although there was not much catechising, it was exceptional for there to be no family worship in a home. Farther south, in 1883, there were reports from the Presbytery of Kincardine-O'Neil that family worship was 'pretty general' on the Sabbath, and held in 'a good many'[58] houses on weekday evenings. But farther south still, from the Angus presbyteries of Meigle and Fordoun, reports were less hopeful, the latter remarking that 'the evening service rather interferes with family catechising on the Sabbath evenings' — although, the presbytery admitted, 'the parents generally see that their children attend to their Sabbath-school lessons'.[59] Of course here again it is difficult to know how far all these remarks applied to the population at large or simply to the Free Church. That talk about family worship being general in these areas mostly was talk about the latter, is certainly suggested by a return in 1888 from the Presbytery of Deer, which referred to a Free Church congregation in which the minister could 'speak with certainty of at least thirty families, out of the seventy of which his flock is composed, as being regular observers of family worship'.[60] Or at least it would be, if we knew what on this occasion was meant by 'regular'. The subject is decidedly obscure.

East-Central Scotland

Obscurity also characterised the 1873 report of the Synod of Perth and Stirling,[61] which contained a great number of highly contradictory and inconclusive returns dealing with morality. Within the same presbytery and even within the same congregation, observers might claim that the immorality of farm servants was, variously, 'much the same', 'less', 'not more', 'increasing', 'decreasing' and 'not decreasing'. In general, the synod concluded 'that violations of the seventh commandment are less frequent than they were, and that the grosser forms of this sin are rare'.[62] What these grosser forms were is not specified: rape, incest, abortion, or simply adultery? The last seems most probable since the synod's disciplinary statistics recorded ninety-seven cases during the previous year, most of which were cases 'of fornication and ante-nuptial fornication',[63] and only two of which were cases of adultery. (In that year at least twenty sessions had no cases of discipline at all to deal with — and the synod believed that the disciplinary system was maintained fairly.) As far as fornication was concerned, one minister believed that there was 'a growing disinclination after guilt to make the reparation that marriage offers' and he regarded this 'as symptomatic of declension in the moral tone of the place'.[64] In favour of farmworkers, however, one return claimed that ploughmen and shepherds were spiritually as good as, if not better than those in other parts of the country, while other returns suggested that their moral character depended on that of their masters. But some were 'not in a good condition; many Irish Roman Catholics'.[65]

Irish Catholics were also blamed for 'evils' in the community, by the Presbytery of Stirling in 1879;[66] but this was a pretty standard complaint, as was that made in the same report of swearing children. The only relatively new factors mentioned were 'harmful theatres of a very low class';[67] and, in a report from Perth presbytery in 1884, 'elements of danger in church social meetings',[68] and 'the growing practice of exhibiting partially nude figures on bills on walls and in windows as advertisements of plays and other entertainments'.[69] The Presbytery of Perth set up a committee 'to deal with these evils', and in both presbyteries ministers preached special sermons on Purity in 1892.

Statements about family worship were, by the synod's own admission, 'vague and indefinite'.[70] One minister said that it was more general than he had once thought, another that it was increasing. But none could produce statistics nor perhaps wanted to. As one minister remarked, he had 'never *heard* of such statistics since the time of the *Searchers* during the covenanting period, — an institution that he would not like to see revived'.[71] And the synod concluded that 'family worship, though by no means as general as all testimony shows it must have been a century ago, has increased during the last few years'.[72] On the subject of parental authority there seems to have been a measure of agreement in the synod. It was 'not now reverenced as it once was'[73] — especially once children started to work,[74] when they often became disobedient.[75]

The Presbytery of Perth expressed much the same opinion, when in 1879 its members remarked upon 'the increase of insubordination and indocility in the youth of both sexes, indicating, as they fear, a change in household management and family discipline from what was wont to be all but universal in Scotland'.[76] (The presbytery made much the same point again in 1884, when it commented that 'there is not the attention given to family worship, nor the submission to parental authority that were formerly'.[77] And it recommended, to deal with this, special sermons, advice at baptisms, and 'elders conducting family worship in homes where it is neglected'.)[78] Its interest in youth did not however entirely dispel its concern with farm servants. 'Why,' asked the synod in 1891, 'should our Church lose hold of this large and interesting class?'[79] Many of its members seemed, quite genuinely, not to know.

The Synod of Fife gave the subject of illegitimacy very close consideration. It reiterated the charge that 'many of the children whose births are recorded as illegitimate are by the law of Scotland (be it a bad or a good law) perfectly legitimate'.[80] Nevertheless, it paid close attention to the published statistics of the Registrar General (for 1866-67), which showed, to its credit, that the illegitimacy rate in Fife (8.72 per cent.) was lower than that for the mainland rural districts of Scotland as a whole (10.82 per cent.). Within its own bounds, the synod found that illegitimacy was highest in the Presbytery of Cupar (11.31 per cent.), followed in turn by those of Kinross (9.81 per cent.), Kirkcaldy (8.37 per cent.), St. Andrews

(8.16 per cent.) and Dunfermline (7.64 per cent.). Comparing these statistics and those of individual parishes, the synod found it difficult to form exact conclusions, but was

> satisfied that the percentage is greatest among the agricultural population, though there are some rural parishes where the proportion is remarkably small; that it diminishes among the manufacturing and mining population, and is least of all among the fishermen.[81]

In discussing the agricultural population,[82] the synod distinguished between the mechanics and handloom weavers of the villages and small towns, and the farm servants. It was the latter class among whom unchastity, although not of course intemperance, was 'fearfully prevalent'.[83] Farm servants were 'very stolid and inaccessible' and 'sinking in regard to religious character'.[84] For this, migratory habits and a commercial rather than a paternal relationship between masters and servants were at least partly to blame. The synod said less about the morals of the manufacturing population, whose character in general (apart from their habit of walking five miles on a Sunday to buy a drink as *bona fide* travellers) was high and improving. Miners they divided into three classes: a fifth who were steady, kept their jobs, married young and except for occasional indulgence in ante-nuptial fornication rarely broke the seventh commandment; the majority, who were ready 'to flit on the prospect of the smallest gain', but among whom illegitimacy was 'almost unknown'; and a third and worst class, who were 'always on the move, and never entering a church', and whose wives were 'given to smoking and drinking' and getting 'credit on their husbands' wages before pay-day, that they may spend them in liquor'. Yet, said the synod,

> even among this class the marriage bond is respected, though there is a good deal of ante-nuptial fornication.[85]

The sexual morals of other sections of the Fife population were hardly discussed by the synod. It was highly reticent about the middle classes, vague about the urban population, and admitted to ignorance of the lives of sailors. It did however discuss fishermen, a class 'naturally reckless' because of the uncertainty and irregularity of their gains, 'but not vicious'.[86] 'Simple, affectionate and impressible', the fishermen worked hard and owned a little property.[87] Even among this class, however, ante-nuptial fornication was 'too common'. But there were few illegitimate births. The fishermen tended to intermarry, and 'in most cases the parties are married before the child is born; so that the birth is not recorded as illegitimate in the register'.[88]

If illegitimacy was rare among fishermen, it was rarer still in the congregations of the Free Church. On this subject also the synod had done its sums and reported that while, for example, within the bounds of the Presbytery of Dunfermline the Registrar General reported 109 illegitimate births in 1866, only 10 of these were at all connected with the Free Church. Although it had not calculated the proportions connected with other denominations or with no church at all, it was thus

> led to believe that a most material element in accounting for the very variable 'proportion of illegitimate births is the answer to the question, To what extent have the population attached themselves to the Free Church of Scotland?[89]

Further proof of Free Church purity was provided by the fact that, while discipline was faithfully administered, the number of cases was decreasing — so much so indeed that the synod found the absence of cases over a number of years in some congregations quite remarkable. But then it also found grounds for complaining about the number of fugitives from Free Church discipline who were received into the congregations of other denominations.

Returns from the Synod of Fife later in the century tended to confirm a number of these observations. But in 1888 fishermen came in for even sharper criticism from the Presbytery of St. Andrews: ante-nuptial fornication, it reported, was still 'very common' among them, even if 'the grosser forms' of this sin were 'hardly known'.[90] Their real offence, perhaps, was that they formed an exception to the presbytery's generalisation that immorality in Fife was 'not such a crying evil as in other parts of the country'.[91] Still, Fife was not going to be lulled into a false sense of security, as the synod observed in its report for the following year:

> Inside of congregations there have been but few indications of immorality. One Presbytery says 'There seems to be a general absence of any call for the exercise of discipline.' At the same time it is felt that this should not be taken too confidently as indicating a high moral tone in the district. The probability is that — as elsewhere — there is a good deal of latent immorality.[92]

How much family worship was latent in Fife was as difficult to tell. According to the synod's report of 1870, hardly any farmers held prayers for their servants, and returns left 'no room for doubt that there is room for great improvement'[93] in family religion in general. In 1875 the presbyteries of Kinross, Cupar and St. Andrews all complained that family worship was 'not as general as could be wished or expected';[94] and in 1888 St. Andrews remarked that 'in some places, even earnest Christian workers have worship only occasionally in their own families'.[95]

West-Central Scotland

Despite the existence of a large mining and manufacturing population within the bounds of the Synod of Glasgow and Ayr,[96] neither it nor the largely Highland Synod of Argyll[97] deviated very much from the established pattern of Religion and Morals reports. The former, noting that

> the agricultural districts seem to be the most notorious for uncleanness; while the towns and mining villages have a sad pre-eminence in profane swearing and drunkenness,

considered that these sins prevailed 'to an alarming extent in the general community'.[98] But it added nothing to the conventional Free Church descriptions and diagnoses,[99] except perhaps the information that in its area urban domestic servants were considered to be very respectable.[100] One reason why these reports tended to concentrate upon the working-class sins of uncleanness, swearing and drunkenness was of course that these were the sins or 'hindrances' about which the committee specifically requested information. Their presence in synod reports was thus as much a matter of the committee getting the answers it looked for, as of great synodical minds thinking alike. On the other hand the synods' replies are sufficiently varied to suggest that if they had discovered new categories of sin they would have said so, even if this did upset orthodox views.[101]

The Synod of Glasgow and Ayr had been quick to point out that those sins which prevailed so alarmingly in the general community were not to be found 'to any great extent among professing Christians';[102] and the Synod of Argyll, like its neighbours to the North, found little uncleanness within its bounds, except among a few young women who had gone into domestic service in other parts of the country. But in many Free Church congregations there were not even any of these to discipline, and some sessions had had no cases for years. Only drunkenness, designated by a number of returns as '*the* sin of their parishes',[103] disfigured some of these Highland areas.

Returns from these synods in the 'eighties continued to concentrate upon congregational morality, using the discipline cases as an index. Thus in 1881, for example, the Presbytery of Glasgow, while expressing concern both about drunkenness and about Sabbath-breaking Italian ice-cream shops, believed that sexual morality was higher than before. Thus also in Argyll, in the same year, the Presbyteries of Kintyre and Islay, which claimed that discipline within their bounds was strict, reported that there was little or no immorality. And in 1888, from South Ballachulish in the Presbytery of Abertarff, despite its being 'the stronghold of High Church Scotch Episcopalianism',[104] came the claim that morality was very high. There had been 'only two cases of discipline in 10 years, and these not of a glaring kind'.[105] This was 'characteristic of the whole district'.[106]

Something of a departure from the normal pattern of Religion and Morals reports, however, occurred in 1899 when the Presbytery of Glasgow presented the Assembly with a brief report from one of its committees, entitled 'Glasgow at Midnight'.[107] This committee had 'set themselves to investigate at first hand the State of the Streets from 9 P.M. to 3 A.M.', and its original report, according to the Religion and Morals committee, was 'detailed, precise and calm'.[108] Assembly commissioners were not given this report, however, and while the abbreviated version they received included a number of statistics on drunkenness,[109] the committee denied them the section on Prostitution: its 'detailed facts . . . could not, with wisdom, be reproduced here'.[110] The Commissioners however were advised of the success of the Magdalene Institution,[111] of the poor state of some of the common lodging houses,[112] and of nocturnal goings-on in Kelvingrove Park.[113]

Returns dealing with family worship were as conflicting as ever, although in

Glasgow and Ayr there seems to have been a general feeling that the practice was declining, except in the 'agricultural districts and wealthier congregations in towns',[114] and of course in Free Church congregations, where the instruction of children in biblical knowledge was also kept up. It is difficult to make much of these returns: where family worship was kept up, it seems to have been mostly on a Sunday evening and only occasionally on weekdays as well. The returns from Argyll were no clearer: in one parish it was 'very generally maintained', but the minister of another had 'fears that many of our adherents neglect it'.[115] In all cases however a connection seems to have been seen between the neglect of family worship, lack of respect for parents, and non-adherence to the Free Church. This, however, is not very surprising, especially since it too had its origin in the way the committee's questions were framed. Parents as much as young people, and especially the economic independence of the latter, were blamed for 'the practical abrogation of the fifth commandment'.[116]

Subsequent reports from these synods again showed no very clear pattern except that in the late 'seventies and 'eighties returns from the Synod of Argyll continued to bear witness to the relatively higher level of Highland piety. Reports from Kintyre and Islay in 1879, and Mull in 1888, also claimed that family worship was general — which it was, 'and on the increase'[117] in Fort William, while in South Ballachulish it was 'universal among communicants, but among others not certain, though the session bring them under promise to hold such when receiving baptism'.[118] Farther south, however, sessions were much less certain about the people's habits. In the Presbytery of Lanark in 1873, and Hamilton in 1880, many elders were unable to say anything about the extent to which family worship prevailed. But it was thought to be rare. The Hamilton elders in fact had not thought of asking people about it, but resolved to mend their ways. Only the parish of Blantyre in this presbytery reported that family worship was better maintained than hitherto. There had been a revival there — but even so, many people still neglected family worship, and there was far too little family catechising. In a report of 1879, the Presbytery of Paisley blamed the fact that things were not as they formerly had been in this respect on the state of modern social life in towns. But this, it added, did not necessarily mean that individuals neglected private prayer. Glasgow, for the most part, admitted either to family worship not being general, or not being so general as it once was, or to ignorant elders. In two of the city's congregations however it was general, in one it was even common, and in the Free Barony it was not extensively practised except on Sunday evenings, 'when the children are pretty generally gathered together for religious exercises, and more or less of catechising'.[119] Among the Glasgow congregations reporting at this time (1881), only the Gaelic church claimed almost universal family worship among its members and adherents. The Gaelic church in Greenock reported the same, but others in that presbytery were less sanguine. The Presbytery of Irvine, reporting in the following year, included returns from congregations in which it was more general, congregations in which it was declining, and congregations in which elders did not know what it was doing. In 1882 Dumbarton presbytery thought that family worship and catechising on

Sunday nights were both general. But back in the city, in 1891, a report from the North side of Glasgow 'feared that in many cases the exercise is reserved for Sabbaths'.[120] And in the following year, the Religion and Morals committee, presenting returns from the same area, remarked:

> Glasgow (North) ranges the whole scale from 'in all of them,[121] with comparatively few exceptions family worship is observed, and in these a promise was given that it will be begun,' to 'fairly well-observed;' thence to 'one half of the families', and thence to the depth of official nescience, if not family neglect, as shown by the words 'cannot tell'. We suspect that the last citation hits the mark in the centre. Did all ministers . . . make personal inquiry everywhere in the course of pastoral visitation, or such inquiry where he felt in uncertainty they might . . . meet with unexpected encouragement.[122]

The South-East

During the early 'seventies neither the Synod of Lothian and Tweeddale,[123] nor the Synod of Merse and Teviotdale,[124] was very forthcoming about the subject of sexual behaviour. In the former: the Presbytery of Biggar and Peebles reported that 'there has not been anything peculiar or deserving of special notice for the past few years';[125] that of Haddington and Dunbar that

> the ordinary forms of immorality in the shape of drunkenness, uncleanness and Sabbath desecration, though not materially diminished are not on the increase;[126]

and the Presbytery of Linlithgow blamed an increase in 'drunkenness and immorality (uncleanness)'[127] on social demoralisation in areas where there was Sunday work at public paraffin and oil works.

The Synod of Merse and Teviotdale however did make one rather surprising addition to the usual comments on this subject. The Presbyteries of Dunse and Chirnside, Kelso, Jedburgh and Selkirk had all alluded to the number of cases of discipline dealt with by Free Church congregations. But while the first of these claimed that the number was decreasing and expressed the hope that this was 'an indication of a higher tone of moral feeling',[128] Kelso admitted that the 'humiliating' practice of uncleanness was 'infecting even the congregations of the Church';[129] Jedburgh that, although church members were improving, one Hawick congregation was painfully afflicted with ante-nuptial fornication,[130] and Selkirk that cases were more frequent in Galashiels as a result of people coming to the congregation from country districts, some of them already under discipline. But perhaps the synod was able to extract a crumb of comfort from the observation of this last presbytery that people who attended no church were both less temperate and less moral than church people.

One of the reasons again given for the bad behaviour of non-churchgoers was the laxity of parental discipline among them. And this was contrasted, as usual, with Free Church behaviour. The optimistic presbyters of Dunse and Chirnside thought — although they could not be sure — that family worship was becoming more common. At any rate ministers questioned parents who brought their children for baptism about whether or not they held it; and they gave 'such reproof or encouragement as the case requires'.[131] The Presbytery of Selkirk also reported that family worship was general in Free Church congregations; and from Linlithgow returns stated that its observance was increasing in areas affected by revivals, although 'in general, it is to be feared that this ordinance is rarely or irregularly observed'.[132] Both synods were pleased with the spiritual state of domestic servants, who were described by the Presbytery of Selkirk as 'a very hopeful class',[133] and by the Presbytery of Edinburgh as 'in some cases . . . the liveliest and most self-denying Christians in congregations'.[134]

Further reports concerning the state of morality and family worship were mostly confined to what went on in Free Church congregations. The Presbytery of Edinburgh, in 1878, reported that 'the sin of uncleanness, as regards those connected with the churches, manifests itself chiefly in the form of ante-nuptial fornication, but the cases of this are few'.[135] And, two years later, the Presbytery of Jedburgh claimed that it had effectively employed a scheme for putting those guilty of fornication on a year's 'probation' in the shape of suspension from church membership. This presbytery had its troubles, however. It complained that young working people were too independent of parental control, and also that there was too much Sunday travel. The latter had been made possible by the railways, and farm servants were particularly guilty of it. Although there may have been some truth to their excuse that Sunday was the only day when they could visit old and sick relatives, the 'real reason' was their 'mere love of idle visiting and gossip'.[136] On the credit side however there was not only the conventional claim — made on this occasion by the Presbytery of Haddington and Dunbar in 1886 — that immorality within the bounds was outside the congregations, but also the claim — made in the same year by the Presbytery of Kelso — that uncleanness 'is not so prevalent as in the past, while the sentiments of the classes chiefly affected by it is undergoing a marked improvement'.[137] But no such improvement was seen in family worship. In 1873 and again in 1880 the Presbytery of Linlithgow reported that it was increasingly neglected, commenting on the latter occasion that young communicants needed to be taught the 'duty of cultivating the practice of *audible* prayer';[138] and in 1899 the Synod of Lothian and Tweeddale described family worship as 'the weakest point in the religious life of the Church'.[139]

The South-West

The Synods of Dumfries[140] and of Galloway[141] gave few hostages to history. The former, after complaining about the prevalence of urban intemperance, made clear that the subject of its loudest complaints was the prevalence of illegitimacy. It lost no time however in making the usual point about Free Church congregations, and it was quick to observe that, although its illegitimacy rate was high, that of the neighbouring Synod of Galloway was fully 6.9 per cent. higher. The latter, however, did not answer back and confined itself to observing that, within its bounds, the amount of uncleanness and the number of discipline cases, together with the amount of drunkenness and the number of public houses, were alike diminishing.

The Synod of Dumfries included, among its recommendations on what to do about illegitimacy, a plea for better control of the young and servants by parents and masters; and here, as in Moray, while nothing was said directly about the influence of courtship customs, the synod recommended that 'opportunities of honourable courtship' should be 'afforded, and stolen interviews discountenanced'.[142] It also ventured the observation however that 'the general testimony is that this evil is diminishing among us very considerably'.[143]

Whether or not any general improvement in sexual morality took place in Galloway during the 'eighties was not clear: in 1884 the Presbytery of Stranraer reported that illegitimacy in Wigtown was as bad as ever; although it did remark that it was 'hopeful', if also 'sad and almost startling', to hear 'in an upland parish, of the formation of a corps of the White Cross Army'.[144] This presbytery on the same occasion and the synod in 1899[145] were at pains to point out the contrast between the prevalent illegitimacy of the area and the declining numbers of sexual cases dealt with by Free Church sessions. But then, according to reports from the Presbyteries of Stranraer and Kirkcudbright in 1884,[146] the majority of the people within their bounds were connected with the Church of Scotland,[147] many of them being non-churchgoers. An ex-Provost of Kirkcudbright explained to the Assembly's deputies in 1883 that although Galloway was 'still redolent of covenanting memories . . . a sad declension from the evangelical teaching and religious fervour of earlier times had taken place'.[148] This had happened when 'the sore blight of Moderatism . . . during last century fell on that once favoured district of Scotland'. Thus,

> when the day of trial came, the never-to-be forgotten 18th of May 1843, we need not wonder that of the *sixteen ministers* in the Presbytery of Kirkcudbright, *three only* were faithful to the cause of the spiritual independence of the Church and the liberties of the people, and threw in their lot with the Free Church of Scotland.[149]

On the subject of family worship Dumfries was reticent, remarking that the practice, 'it is hoped, is on the increase'.[150] On the same subject, Galloway was even more reticent, and said nothing at all.

These regional reports, then, do not present a very clear or consistent picture of Scottish sexual behaviour or of Free Church discipline. Some features, however, recur more regularly than others, and these, together with some comments on them, and on some related themes, may be noted here.

Discipline and Morality

One of the most frequent claims made in the returns was that Free Church members and adherents were more moral than the rest of the population. Of course not all Free Church members were held to be blameless, as returns from Shetland, the Synod of Aberdeen, and some Border presbyteries had pointed out. But these were not typical, and even in these places nobody was supposed to believe that the mean of Free Church morality was as low as that outside it. Infrequency of discipline was the usual index of this, and any suggestion that it might not be a good index was countered by the assertion that the Free Church's discipline was strictly maintained. Thus, the committee wrote in 1887, if Free Church morals were higher, then

> such a fact as this ought to be stated, and generalised from too, if facts warrant, without any ground being afforded for a charge of denominational Pharisaism.[151]

Towards the end of the century, however, the committee began to have doubts about this.[152] It began to have doubts even more about whether or not discipline statistics could be used as an index of the moral tone of the wider community. Writing in 1894, it asked whether the declining number of cases throughout Scotland really reflected a higher moral tone among the people — or simply the fact that the people would no longer stand for the exercise of discipline. Returns in the previous year had included such comments as 'offenders are less disposed to submit to discipline',[153] and 'little penitence or shame is shown by those who come before the Session'.[154] These complaints, the committee considered, 'would be echoed pretty generally by the Church'.[155]

Farm Servants

A second feature of the regional reports was the Free Church's attitude to farm servants. This, as we have seen, was highly critical, and although some ministers defended them, and others criticised farmers even more, the majority clearly took a very dim view of this class, in particular of their mobility, immorality and Sunday visiting. To clear its mind on the subject, the committee made a number of enquiries among ministers, farmers, and even 'in some cases'[156] farm servants, in a selection of what were considered to be typical districts: Aberdeenshire, East Lothian, Forfarshire, Galloway and the Upper Ward of Lanarkshire; and it presented its findings to the 1897 Assembly in the form of a report 'On the Religious and Moral Condition of Farm Servants'.[157] This report did something to soften the committee's attitude, just as the investigations of the Commission on the Religious Condition of the People did that of the Church of Scotland during the same decade. The Religion and Morals committee reported, for example, that

> as a class farm servants are on the whole morally not worse than other classes of working people. The vices prevalent are such as might be expected among men and women placed in circumstances more favourable to the development of bodily than intellectual or spiritual strength. Their faults are those of youth placed amid strong temptations, while the checks to improper behaviour are fewer than in towns where people are more constantly under the public eye. When they settle down to married

life, a very fair proportion of them become highly exemplary in conduct, sober, steady, self-respecting, attentive to the welfare of their families and highly esteemed by their employers.[158]

In view of all that had been said by the Free Church since 1858 about farm servants, this was high praise indeed. Even what the committee said about their religious habits took on a more measured tone. It could not of course be denied that many of them claimed a connection with the Established church, nor could the increase in non-churchgoing which had recently taken place among them, especially in Aberdeenshire, Lanark and Galloway. But from East Lothian, the committee stated, reports were more favourable,[159] so all was not lost. Even the explanations given for non-churchgoing took on a different slant — for while the usual complaint about mobility was voiced, the committee, in accounting for the absence of farm servants from Free Church congregations, pointed out that this could to some extent be accounted for by the fact that the Free Church, in 1843, had been stronger in the towns than in the country, and that since then the population had been moving from the country into the towns. This, the committee implied, was scarcely something for which the Free Church could be blamed.

Turning to the question of rural morality, the committee was again rather less pessimistic than its predecessors had been. As usual it emphasised the sobriety of farm servants (except at feeing fairs)[160] and stated that 'the darkest blot on the moral character of farm servants is the prevalence of the sin of fornication'.[161] But it emphasised that this varied from area to area, and that while some districts were scandalous, in others the behaviour of farm servants was as good as that of any other class. And even in the notorious areas things were changing for the better. During the 'seventies, it had been alleged of many parts of Aberdeenshire, for example, that

the standard of morality among farm girls was terribly low; that it was so common a thing to be known as the mother of an illegitimate child that it scarcely involved any loss of character and was no bar to finding another situation or even to being married.[162]

But then in 1881 Lady Aberdeen had founded The Haddo House Association, later restyled The Onward and Upward Association which, aiming to improve the farm girls' morals, had met with success in many parts of the county. And even if there still were some areas where unchastity was taken lightly and where 'the better sort of girls'[163] would not work on farms, progress was being made.

The committee also found ameliorating factors in Galloway. It quoted 'one of the largest and most experienced farmers in Kirkcudbright' as saying:

Immorality certainly exists, as the illegitimacy returns indicate, but I do not think this is a true gauge of general impurity. My observations lead me to the conclusion that this is to a large extent a hereditary sin. It can be traced through certain families. Very often a woman may have three or four illegitimate children, and the average is consequently raised.[164]

This was of course a view also recorded in contemporary Church of Scotland investigations in this area, as was the same farmer's opinion that unmarried female farm workers, who had been let tied cottages after having had to leave domestic service because of pregnancy, had an 'abandoned attitude' and were 'too often a temptation to young men in the district'.[165]

Although the committee was more inclined to see improvement and some ameliorating and exculpating factors than its predecessors had been, it was no less anxious to find causes and dispense remedies for rural unchastity. But even in this the committee was adopting a softer approach to sinners, and was increasingly recognising the influence of environmental factors. In explaining the poor state of religion and morals in some districts, it pointed to 'the breaking up of old habits of church attendance'.[166] Churchgoing, it observed, 'like many other good things is largely a matter of habit and the habit once lost is not easily recovered'.[167] Thus in Wigtownshire, for example, the rapid expansion of dairy-farming connected with the local cheese-making industry had led to the employment of large numbers of farm servants on Sundays. But when, with improved methods, such employment was no longer needed, neither the farm servants nor their children (who had been allowed to play at home or in the fields on Sundays) resumed the churchgoing habit.

Factors more directly related to sexual behaviour were mentioned by the committee when it gave an account of how illegitimacy came about. It was described as a 'drift into evil' by young women, in bad circumstances on farms and among bothymen:

> They begin life at an early age with no knowledge of the temptations awaiting them. They are without a reverent and hallowed consciousness of all that is involved in the words 'love', 'betrothal', and 'marriage' and 'home', and are accustomed to hear such matters joked and chaffed about. And so, full of the high spirits of youth, with no definite aims, unaccustomed to self-control, they do as others do. They do not mean to do anything wrong, but simply to take what amusement they can, and courting is an amusement, and they go into it as into a dream, from which they awake too late, to find their lives forever overshadowed with a dark encumbrance.[168]

This more sympathetic (if no less paternalistic) view of the erring girl was paralleled by increasing ecclesiastical criticism of the middle classes and even of the churches themselves. The rigid social distinctions of rural life were criticised by the committee when it wrote that

> on many farms the ploughmen have become *pariahs* to the farmer. The farmer's family cannot associate with them without risk of moral injury and they, feeling themselves suspected and shunned, become reckless and indisposed to improvement. There is little hope of rising in the social scale to encourage aspiration and encourage self-control. More dreary even is the prospect for the women. Unless they are married, they must remain drudges to the end of their lives and so they are tempted to sink their modesty, and throw themselves to the ways of men.[169]

The nature of the farm servants' work, which was heavy and did not lend itself to the encouragement of 'mental pursuits', made them even less inclined to spiritual things. But even if they had been so inclined, observed the committee, 'no one church in the land bulks large enough to have a strongly attractive force'.[170] Being a Free Church committee, however, it could not resist a side-swipe at the Establishment, and blamed both Moderatism in the past and lax standards of discipline and of membership in the present Church of Scotland for the nation's moral ills.

The committee's remedies were almost too familiar to need reproduction here: farmers should do more for their servants. (One Kirkcudbrightshire farmer reported: 'I have found on more than one occasion, when I perceived young men tottering on the brink, that a solemn private warning produced a most extraordinary amendment.')[171] Ministers should visit farms more often and speak out about sin. (One minister commented: 'From my own experience, I can say that veiled hints are not sufficient. The people are accustomed from their youth with the plain unvarnished phraseology of sexual concerns.')[172] Special missionaries and Bible women should visit farm servants and the women; young men should be encouraged to form Mutual Improvement Societies; young women should be recruited to such bodies as the Girls' Friendly Society and 'The Upward and Onward Association';[173] the Established Church should improve its discipline. Given these things the committee was not totally pessimistic, since

> In our rural population we have splendid raw material, some of it very rough and rude, but the finished article, if the material could be rightly handled, would amply repay a large expenditure of money and labour.[174]

Other Sinners, Other Sins

Farm servants were not of course the only class which this committee criticised, nor was immorality the only sin. Other sections of the working-class (but rarely of the middle- or upper-class) population were taken to task by it. The committee was also concerned with other sins, especially drunkenness (the vice of the towns, fishermen and Highlanders), profane swearing (the schoolboy's vice) and 'promiscuous dancing' (a vice complained of by Northern presbyteries in particular — although in 1886 the committee told them that the 'mere prohibition of gaiety is no remedy').[175] Then, in the mid-'nineties, the committee began to take note of athletics, which it viewed with some ambivalence, since while they were not *per se* sinful, they could be accompanied by sin. As Professor George Adam Smith of Glasgow,[176] approving the committee's report in 1895 put it, not without some verbal gymnastics:

> the report told them that contemporaneously with a decrease of immorality there had been an increase in certain forms of athletics, especially of football and bicycling. For his own part, he should like to have had some evidence whether there was any connection between these two subjects. He had a strong impression that there was a distinct and arguable connection. (Slight applause.) These movements, no doubt,

> among the young men were attended, as they could not be but attended, with very great and singular temptations; but he felt that all movements which drew youth out for bodily exercise to the open air, and encroached upon and occupied the time that would otherwise be spent in mere loafing, might be heartily welcomed by religion as her allies in the reduction of the vice of the nation.[177]

Cheap Literature and Morality

Something which the Free Church did not see as an ally, and which the committee also dealt with during this period, was cheap literature. Reports from at least two synods[178] had expressed concern about this, and in 1899 the committee presented the Assembly with a special report on the subject. This report may be mentioned here since the committee believed that literature of this kind had some effect upon the morals, including the sexual morals, of young people. The Free Church had of course long been anxious about what the people read. It had in the early 'sixties attacked Norman Macleod for his attempt, in *Good Words*, to produce a popular periodical with a wide mixture of religious and secular topics.[179] But now it was concerned with what it viewed as a considerable change in the reading habits of the population — a change which had taken place, in its opinion, since about 1870, as a result of the abolition of the paper duty on the one hand, and the introduction of the School Board system on the other. Cheap light literature of the kind with which the committee's 1899 report was concerned was, in its opinion, 'at once an index to the tastes of a people, and the most powerful factor in the formation of these tastes'.[180]

It is clear from what the committee chose to include in this report that its concern was with what was read by the working classes. It specifically excluded books, intellectual and improving magazines and periodicals of the kind which might be read by the middle classes,[181] and concentrated upon 'the lighter papers, chiefly weeklies, which circulate among the masses'.[182] Of these, it wrote:

> Much of it is painfully vapid, foolish and inane, fitted to destroy the sense of the seriousness of life, and to prevent healthy development in those who make it the staple of their intellectual pabulum, but the great mass of it does not directly pander to the lower passions of human nature. There are exceptions to this rule; but, on the whole, there is reason for thankfulness that the censorship of public opinion prevents the inundation of the country with literature offensive to moral purity. To this remark it must, however, be added that it is a matter of regret and anxiety that in so many of the papers that exist chiefly for the amusement of their readers, love and matrimony are so frequently made the subject of witticisms, and that jokes and drawings are made piquant by allusions and suggestions which are hurtful to that reverence for womankind which is the strongest natural bulwark of morality.[183]

The committee's main criticism of these papers, then, was that although they sometimes contained 'an immense amount of interesting information', this was presented only in the form of 'isolated facts' and in such a way that it produced 'a distaste for more solid reading, and even a mental incapacity for continuous thought'.[184] On closer examination, it found four classes of such papers: Illustrated Papers, Comic Papers, Sporting and Athletic Papers, and Novelettes. The second and third of these classes were not associated with any corruption of sexual morals. Comic Papers ('Their name is legion. Their circulation is enormous') were, 'with very rare exceptions . . . free from anything morally offensive'.[185] Nor was it 'in itself an unhealthy sign that there should be a demand for literature whose primary purpose is to amuse'.[186] After all, 'God has given to some men wit, and to most an appreciation of humour, and it cannot be His will that these gifts should be either discredited or too severely repressed.'[187] But if God had given these gifts to the writers and readers of the Comic Papers, his action was not altogether to the committee's taste: 'Jokes and illustrations alike are often of a coarse and vulgar order, and humour trivial and sapless.'[188] It was of course this triviality, in the committee's opinion, which made these trashy comics so popular, especially among young people, many of whom, it alleged, read little else. And since triviality tended 'to destroy seriousness of thought, to check intellectual development, and generally to deteriorate the moral nature',[189] it would be better if ministers and others could wean young people from them by providing them with better papers such as *Chums* and the *Boys' Own Paper*. How they were to do this was not made entirely clear. In view of the committee's belief that young people who already were connected with the church avoided light literature,[190] it might have been difficult.

The committee's criticism of the Sporting and Athletic Papers was directly related to the amount of information these — of which there were a great number — gave to their readers about betting and gambling. They did not however compound their guilt like the daily newspapers, which, with a few exceptions, published hints and tips on the subject, and then 'in their leaders . . . from time to time, useful homilies on the folly and evil of gambling'.[191] The problem was a serious one:

> It is not only that amongst the wealthier classes large sums of money are passed in connection with events on the turf, and fortunes squandered in gambling; but people with moderate incomes, clerks in business houses, and thousands of youths, caught by the fascination and excitement of transactions in which there is an element of chance, are amongst the victims of this immoral and ruinous system.[192]

Gambling and betting had of course been a concern of this committee for some time, alongside its concern with sports and athletics, and in the consideration of Illustrated Papers the dangerous side of the latter was emphasised with special reference to boxing. Many of the Illustrated Papers reviewed by the committee were concerned with the heroes of 'the fistic ring' and dealt with the subject in such a wealth of technical detail as to imply 'an intimate familiarity with the mysteries of that debasing form of sport'[193] among their readers. No better, however, were those other Illustrated Papers which carried portraits of heroines of the music hall. These they 'referred to in terms of admiration and endearment, carefully framed to arouse the curiosity and foolish endearment of thoughtless youth'.[194] The Illustrated Papers were further criticised because

> Among the news, a large space is given to sensationally written accounts of all sorts of tragical events — assaults, murders, burglaries, suicides, *et hoc genus omne*. These are illustrated by pictures of the blood-curdling sort, often coarse in art, but always bold and graphic. Divorce cases are reported with a revolting minuteness of detail. A perusal of some of these papers, which bear the word 'Police' in their titles, is almost fitted to produce the impression that the law courts of this country are exclusively engaged with applications for divorce, with cases of assaults on women, and with the trial of murderers, whose violence is instigated by lust.[195]

But if these seemed bad, there was a worse class still. The committee had also uncovered a couple of papers, one claiming a weekly readership of 100,000, which were decidedly immoral. In these papers, the committee wrote:

> The illustrations are artistic in execution, but often grossly indelicate in suggestion. Advertisements which cover several pages are almost exclusively of a questionable nature — foreign books and pictures, whose titles at least suggest obscenities, and appliances which lend themselves to the protection of the immoral, the advertisement of which has been recently pronounced criminal in a court of law.[196]

Fortunately, the committee reported, such papers were few.

Novelettes or 'Penny Dreadfuls', the committee's fourth class, were more abundant and had 'a powerful attraction for the very young and the imperfectly educated'.[197] They were, however, pretty harmless. A member of the committee who, on its behalf, had read a number of them, commented that 'no moral lessons can be drawn from them, except that the villain is sure to be overtaken with punishment, and that iniquity does not prosper'.[198] Otherwise

> The subject-matter is highly sensational and exciting. There is a profusion of sentimentalism, and high-falutin, and of desperate blood-curdling incident; but there is a noticeable absence of immorality, in the usual sense of that word. The Society Novel, with its sickening and corrupting dissection of the grosser passions, and its detailed narratives of conduct subversive to the laws of purity, stands on a very much lower level than the most vapid of the penny stories.[199]

The absence of impurity was not enough to satisfy the committee, however. The sensationalism of the novelettes, it believed, tended 'to fill young minds with ideas of a falsely romantic order', and it went on to advise teachers and others to encourage young people to read 'the abundant issue of classical stories, and other standard works' which were available 'at prices almost nominal'.[200] It also commended healthier versions of the penny or halfpenny type of publications, which were produced specially to counteract the influence of the others.

But on the whole the committee was pleased to find 'in the ephemeral literature of the day so much that is clean and wholesome, and so little, comparatively, that is vicious and debasing'.[201] Looking back, in the following year, in its report to the last Free Church Assembly, the committee expressed satisfaction with this and its various other special and general reports since its inception in 1860. It noted also, without comment, its interest 'as far back as 1877' in the religious and moral condition of farm servants, 'a class, with exceptions in certain parts of the country

... represented as having become estranged from public worship, and as being specially guilty of breaches of the Seventh Commandment'.[202] But then it turned its face to the future, reporting from current returns 'that cases of discipline are infrequent and that impurity is not so common as it was',[203] and declaring that 'in its work amongst the Young, anxiety is balanced with encouragement'.[204] Among the synod reports for this year came one from Glasgow and Ayr, stating that 'what is needed more than anything is a revival of family religion':[205] and to this subject we must now return.

Parental Authority and Family Worship

It is clear from what was written in the regional reports that the Free Church found it extremely difficult to know how well or how badly family religion was maintained throughout Scotland. In considering immorality it was able to turn to the Registrar's statistics and even to session records for a yardstick, however unreliable these, and particularly the latter, may have been for its purpose. But as far as family religion was concerned, it was in the dark.

The Religion and Morals committee admitted as much. In its report to the 1883 Assembly it noted that

> as to family religion, while many families are in the habit of observing it, office bearers were often unable, when the question was put to them as to the regularity of its observance, to answer with any degree of certainty; their fear was that in too many cases it was neglected or only very partially observed by even the membership of the Church. This is a subject which calls for more earnest inquiry, and more faithful consideration on the part of the eldership of the Church.[206]

The eldership however was either unwilling or unable to fulfil this request, and the mood of uncertainty tinged with pessimism persisted. In its 1899 report the committee thought that it might have found a reason for the elders' difficulty. In the course of a discussion on 'The Family' ('the Church in miniature', whose worship and discipline determined those of the congregation as a whole) it made the following rather plausible observation:

> In former days, family worship, we are given to believe, was general, and its observance came to be an index of Christian respectability. This tradition has come down to us; and to question any church-going person whether he observes family worship is almost equivalent to asking him if he is a respectable man. We believe this lies at the root of the ignorance of our elders whether this duty is observed in the families of their districts or not.[207]

But whatever the truth of this assertion, it was not simply family worship which had declined, but the whole fabric of the religious upbringing of the young. The Sabbath schools, according to the 1883 report, were 'accepted as a substitute for the home training of children',[208] and even if some parents had substituted questions about what their children had learned in Sabbath school for the older tradition of family catechising, many other 'easy-minded' parents, the committee observed in 1885, left the whole matter entirely to the Sabbath schools. Otherwise, they might have been involved in 'effort, thought and, at times perhaps, a collision of wills'[209] — something which they obviously sought to avoid. Because of their 'growing mental and spiritual indolence', such parents

> seldom meet their own children on the platform of conscience, and deal less directly with them through the word of God. And where parental authority lacks the habitual support which the personal instructing of a child in the things of God gives it, then filial obedience comes to be more a thing of sentiment than of principle; the outcome of short-lived fear rather than of a lifelong reverence.[210]

Such relaxing of 'the bonds of family discipline and parental authority' was, the committee regretted to say, 'a feature of the age'.[211]

Or was it? The committee was after all not so sure that the past actually was better than the present in these respects. Were reports of a decline in parental authority 'based on actual knowledge', or were they 'impressions merely — impressions due a good deal, perhaps, to the changing standpoint which the years bring, placing us no longer among those under that authority, but among those who exercise it'?[212]

Questions of this kind however were rarely followed up by the Free Church; and in its reports of 1886, 1887 and 1888 the committee was again demanding more family worship and greater parental control, and blaming the better education and greater independence of young people for their lack of respect for parental authority. Yet once again, in 1889, the questioning note returned, when the committee stated apropos of a statement alleging declining parental control, that 'we have not the means of judging whether this state of things is very general, or on what the statement is based'.[213] On this occasion the committee even went so far as to venture the opinion 'that the control of former days is neither possible nor desirable in these'.[214] But, it added,

> while some relaxation may not be wholly evil, anything indicative of lawlessness, undutifulness, disobedience or disrespect, is only to be deplored. When the hearts of the children are turned against their fathers, the hearts of the country will be turned against God. The prosperity, the very life of the Church is bound up with the maintenance of the sacredness of all the family relations.[215]

Further complaints, in a similar vein, were recorded during the 'nineties. In 1890, 1895 and again in 1899 there were reports of declining parental authority, in the first case with special reference to fishermen, whose long absences from home were held responsible. In all except the Highland returns, wrote the committee in 1899, 'a very grave note runs through all the Reports as to home training'.[216] Youthful bad language, and parents' tendency to leave religious instruction to others, were specially mentioned. As far as family worship was concerned, things were no better. In 1893 the committee reported on the 'sad truth' that 'the observance of family worship is rapidly dying out'.[217] This was bound, 'by degrees', to produce 'a blighting effect on the spiritual life of the Church'.[218] But still, according to the reports of 1894, 1897, and 1899, it declined. Only the report of 1895 for some reason was more hopeful, remarking that it was general. One thing alone seemed certain amid the flux: family worship remained universal in the Highlands. This conviction was expressed by the 1895 and 1899 reports, the latter quoting the Synod of Ross which, although regretting that its adherents stoutly refused to become communicants, had expressed thanks to God 'that in the Highlands at least family worship is not a thing of the past'.[219]

Who really knew what was happening? In its final report the committee summed up visits to the Presbyteries of Alford, Brechin, Dunoon, Edinburgh, Forfar, Islay, Kincardine-O'Neil and Paisley — a fair cross-section — with a set of appropriately conflicting answers:

> The reports regarding religion in the family vary considerably. In some cases they are favourable: that 'family worship is still well observed', 'pretty general', 'regularly observed on Sabbaths', 'generally observed'. Other reports are not quite so favourable: 'Family worship very common, though probably falling off'; 'only in a part of the congregation is family worship observed'. A few reports refer to the exhausting and irregular hours of labour and the general conditions of city life as rendering the outlook for family worship not so hopeful: 'family worship not what it was long ago'.[220]

A Holy Willie Prayer Book

In an attempt to repair the bulwarks of the family, the Free Church eventually decided to issue a book of family prayers. This was done as the result of an overture to the Assembly of 1891 from the Presbytery of St. Andrews and on the recommendation of the Religion and Morals committee. It was not done, however, without misgiving, nor without heated debate in the Assembly. Even those, like the Reverend Duncan Macgregor of Elie, who believed that 'such a manual as was proposed would pave the way for many who felt difficulty in the matter', were forced to admit that

> when they thought of *The Cottar's Saturday Night*, they would feel it would have come as a strange thing if the head of the family had been represented as producing a prayerbook.[221]

And this Burnsian allusion was taken up by the Reverend John Telfer of Glasgow who declared, with more zeal than literary or grammatical accuracy, that the 'Church was considered by some to be a sort of "Holy Willie," and he thought the shade of Burns might suggest they should have a "Holy Willie prayer book"'.[222] With heavy irony, Mr. Telfer went on to suggest that any moment now there might be 'a request to a committee to give an opinion on the proper sort of praying mats to use, whether they should be plush or cotton'.[223] Indeed, he claimed, the Assembly 'would find it not very long before there would be a motion for a liturgy in the pulpit'.[224] The Assembly, however, did not seem to be over-anxious about this possibility, and its members, denying themselves the indulgence of continuing with this piece of provincial knockabout, smothered Mr. Telfer with cries of 'Order' and 'Shame'.[225] He was not, however, the only objector. Another speaker claimed that the Directions for Family Worship issued by the General Assembly in 1647 were quite adequate: 'cultured men would object to read prayers' and the proposed book would 'be an unworkable thing among working people'.[226] Further objectors claimed that read prayers could not possibly come from the heart, and that the real problem was that servants no longer shared in family worship.

Despite these misgivings and objections, the Assembly agreed to produce the prayer book. Clearly it believed that the situation was desperate enough to justify desperate remedies. As Sheriff Guthrie Smith, the last speaker in the debate put it:

> In Roman Catholic countries family virtue was preserved through the medium of the confessional; but in Scotland they had not that, and therefore it was all the more necessary that the Church should redouble its energy in this direction by the restoration of family religion.[227]

In his view, the proposed book would help towards this end. That it did not, seems from this distance pretty clear. In the short term, what had happened to family worship since 1850 is more obscure. The impression given by the Free Church at the end of this period, that it was now rather more willing to settle for family worship once a week rather than twice a day, suggests that some falling-off in the practice had in fact taken place in the meantime. But the Free Church's greater willingness to compromise was also in part the result of its greater sensitivity to the adverse pressure of conditions of life and labour on those whom it wished to see at prayer. These pressures had, in many cases, been in existence for a very long time.

CHAPTER EIGHT

Divorce, Impurity and The United Presbyterian Synod, 1850-1900

IN 1900 the Free Church and the United Presbyterians united, after a long and uncertain courtship. Up to this point the United Presbyterian Synod had not said a great deal about the questions we have been concerned with. But no Scottish church, perhaps, could entirely resist the temptation to talk about rural morality, or that of the young; and unlike the Free Church or the Establishment, the United Presbyterians had also discussed divorce, albeit on only two occasions.

Questions about Divorce

The first occasion on which the question of divorce was raised in the United Presbyterian Synod was in 1853, when the session of its Broughton Place congregation in Edinburgh brought to it an overture on the 'Separation of Christian Spouses'. The point at issue was whether, in the light of Scripture (Matthew, 5:31,32; Matthew, 19:4-6 and 1 Corinthians, 7:10,11) and in view of the Confession of Faith's statement that adultery and wilful desertion were the only grounds of divorce, it was possible — as some United Presbyterians appeared to think — for Christian spouses to be permanently separated when neither of these grounds was provided. The debate may have concerned the discrepancy between Scripture (Matthew, 5:32), in which divorce was allowed only for adultery, and the Confession (Chapter XXIV:VI), which allowed the additional ground; or it may have had to do with the possibility, under Scots law, of divorce *a mensa et thoro*. This latter was a form of legal separation which, although in practice it was largely replaced after the Reformation by divorce *a vinculo* (divorce proper), still remained a possible alternative. It could be awarded if the normal level of cruelty in a Scottish marriage (which was not a ground for divorce *a vinculo*) escalated to a degree which the court considered harmful to the life or health of one of the parties. Which of these points — if either — the Broughton Place session was concerned with in its overture is not clear from the Synod's records,[1] since no exact legal terms were used, and since the Synod in any case declined to enter upon the overture, 'on the ground that it craves legislation upon an abstract question'.[2] The Synod declined to enter on the overture despite a strong plea from the session for guidance, in connection with problems of the exercise of discipline, 'on those points, in which the interests of society and the peace and purity of the Church are deeply involved'.[3] Perhaps, given the infinite obscurity of Scots law, and the infinite capacity of ministers to get it wrong, the Synod was wise to decline.

The Synod's other allusion to divorce was made in 1891, when the committee on Public Morals, noting 'recent disclosures in the Divorce Court', expressed its conviction that

> any member of Parliament whose life is notoriously immoral, or who has been publicly convicted of offences against the moral law, is unfit to represent any constituency in this kingdom . . . and ought at once to retire into private life.[4]

This statement, which clearly referred to the Parnell-O'Shea divorce case, showed that there was one aspect of divorce at least on which the Synod did have a definite view. Its remarks had, however, rather more to do with conventional sexual morality than with divorce as such, and perhaps rather more to do with politics than sexual morals.[5]

Pastoral Advice on Impurity

Although the United Presbyterian Synod pronounced upon the sexual life of the lower orders much less frequently than either the Free Church or the Church of Scotland Assemblies, its pronouncements, when it made them, were not significantly different from theirs. A report of 1894, by its Church Life and Work committee, for example, was concerned with 'the saddening state of morality in many of our country districts, the low tone of opinion in regard to purity, and the high rate of illegitimate births'.[6] It blamed this — as the other churches had frequently blamed it — on 'the absence of the home and of family life' as a result of 'the reduction of the number of crofts and cottages which has taken place in this generation', together with the 'distinct encouragement'[7] given to immorality by the bothy and farm kitchen systems. In the same report the Synod followed the example of the Free Assembly by emphasising its own strict discipline,[8] and by calling for some ecumenical action to deal with fugitives.

One significant moment in the United Presbyterian Synod's progress through this period, however, was when its committee on Temperance and Public Morals decided that the Synod should address a Pastoral Letter on Social Purity to its own membership. The Synod of 1886, to which it made this suggestion, decided against a Pastoral Letter as such, but agreed that a statement on the subject should be prepared by the committee and published in the United Presbyterian *Missionary Record*.[9] In the event, the statement was written by the Reverend Andrew Thomson, minister of Broughton Place United Presbyterian church in Edinburgh, and was published in the *Missionary Record* in October 1887.[10] It was subsequently re-issued in a different form, widely circulated and referred to by the Synod of 1888 as 'the Pastoral Letter'.[11] It is worth examining critically here, since it shows, more clearly than most of the pronouncements of the period, the way in which the churches thought about the issues underlying their criticism of immorality.

The letter, entitled 'A Pure Life — An Address to Young Men', began by presenting its credentials. Paul had told Timothy to 'Flee youthful lusts',[12] and 'Keep thyself pure'.[13] If the apostle could say this to one who was such a faithful Christian, then the church to-day, 'painfully alive to the increasingly sensuous spirit of the age, and to its baneful influence even within our own churches',[14] should follow his example and address young men in its families and congregations on the same subject.

The letter was divided into two parts, the first devoted to showing why uncleanness was evil, the second to dispensing good advice. Four types of argument were advanced in the first part, relating to: first, scriptural condemnation of impurity; second, its effects on the body and personality; third, the body-temple argument; and fourth, the effect on the partner in sin. The scriptural condemnations were intended 'to produce a more adequate sense of the evil of this class of sins'[15] — something which, as we have frequently noted, the churches thought very necessary. In the author's view it should have been

> enough to note the fact that this sin stands distinct, as the subject of special divine condemnation and prohibition 'amid the eternal verities of the moral law' which 'Christ came not to destroy but to fulfill'.[16]

But in order to illustrate the point he cited four scriptural quotations — one from Proverbs and three from the Epistles.[17] These quotations, which no doubt seemed evidence enough for what he was writing to Dr. Thomson, do not however provide very certain foundations for saying that the sin of uncleanness, by which he presumably meant first and foremost fornication, was singled out for 'special divine condemnation'. The quotation from Proverbs is advice against adultery rather than simple fornication.[18] Nor do the quotations from the Epistles, although they make the Pauline attitude clear, substantiate the suggestion that this sin was specially sinful, or that this was the attitude of Scripture as a whole.

Dr. Thomson's arguments about the effect of impurity on the 'bodily and mental constitution' of offenders signalled the dangers of 'this class of sins' by stating that 'the recovery of those who have come under their dominion is rarer than in the case of most other forms of transgression', and that 'it is true of licentiousness more perhaps than of any other form of sin, that it exercises a peculiarly depraving and corrupting influence over the man's whole moral being'.[19] But here again the argument, although it may have seemed self-evident to the author and his readers, lacks firm foundations. Dr. Thomson made no reference to venereal diseases, which perhaps might have supported his case; and as an authority he cited not Scripture, but Burns: 'It hardens a' within, and petrifies the feeling'.[20] Burns of course *was* an authority on this subject. And no doubt there were many other men in nineteenth-century Scottish society, from farm servants to peers, of whom this was a just description. But no doubt there were many others again, who had indulged in ante-nuptial fornication, of whom such a description was far from fair. The weakness of Thomson's argument here — which is also the weakness of almost all that was said on the subject by nineteenth-century Scottish churchmen — lies in his failure to distinguish between different kinds of sexual behaviour and different kinds of persons. No doubt, in the climate of opinion created by the heavy moralising of ecclesiastics and others during this period, the fear that any form of sexual activity, other than that directed to reproduction within marriage, was infinitely dangerous, produced the desired deterrent effect in many minds. But in the light of the churches' continued complaints about the low tone of public opinion on the subject, it seems likely that such moralising was sufficiently overdone for those whose own experience, or whose knowledge of others' actual or mythological experience, did not substantiate such claims, to disregard them.

The third argument used to demonstrate the evil nature of 'these sins of the flesh'[21] was derived from 1 Corinthians, 6:15-20, a passage in which Paul argues that the Christian who has sexual intercourse with a prostitute becomes one flesh with her, thereby joining with her his body, which is a member of Christ and the temple of the Spirit. As used by Dr. Thomson, this argument is also problematic. Thomson's argument was, that since the bodies of Christians belong to God, and are thus sacred and to be used for God's purposes, the Christian who falls into sexual sin does not only 'degrade and defile himself and rob God of his rights, but he defiles His temple and perverts it to the basest uses'.[22] Thus, Thomson wrote, there 'is not only sin but sacrilege. "And if any man defile the temple of God, him will God destroy"'.[23] The major difficulty with this argument is that at each stage in its development from the Old Testament to the nineteenth century, meanings are subtly changed. The Old Testament idea of 'one flesh'[24] denoted the total union of two persons in a lifelong marriage relationship, and not simply the isolated act of sexual intercourse, as Paul seems to have thought. But even in Paul's teaching, the primary reference (especially in the Corinthian context) was to prostitution — although Paul would probably have included promiscuity also under the same head. By the nineteenth century the reference had changed yet again, this time to include all forms of pre- and extra-marital sexual intercourse, and possibly, as we shall see in a moment, even masturbation. Impurity at this point therefore comes to mean all forms of sexual activity, with the Calvinist implication that even sexual intercourse between husband and wife is only permitted to be enjoyable[25] (and, in the nineteenth century, perhaps only permitted) because God covers it with a veil to prevent Him seeing it. The crux of any criticism which may be made of the way in which the Christian tradition developed, then, lies in the shift of emphasis from ritual prostitution in the Old Testament, to prostitution and promiscuity in the New, to all forms of pre- and extra-marital sexual activity in the nineteenth century. The emphasis, in other words, has changed from the positive idea of faithfulness to God and loving marriage-companionship, to the negative idea of avoiding unregulated sexual activity at all costs. Purity is now defined primarily with reference to sexuality, and only secondarily with reference to religion. Or — if this point is contested — why was it that the body-temple argument was not adapted more frequently for use in connection with nineteenth-century conditions of life and labour?

Dr. Thomson's fourth illustration of the dangers of impurity was to the effect that even if both parties did not 'perish in their unrepented iniquity' and even if 'the tempter' (Thomson assumed that this would be the man) 'becomes penitent', nevertheless he 'has no assurance that his victim has not passed onward to final ruin'.[26] Young men should not, in other words, rely upon the possibility of repenting after they had sown their wild oats, because even if they did 'a perpetual cloud of sadness'[27] might darken their souls evermore. By remarking, in this connection, that there was 'always an accomplice', but only 'in the more aggravated forms of this sin',[28] Thomson must, by implication, have included masturbation in his wider, or less aggravated, category.

The writer thus was concerned not with any technical virginity, but with purity in thought, word and deed. His aim was to prevent the young man 'who has hitherto maintained his innocency' from falling into a career of sin, in which, 'by an irreversible law of heaven, written not only in the inspired word, but in your own physical and moral condition',[29] he would reap what he had sown — shame, sorrow, remorse and ultimately physical and spiritual destruction.

To avoid this fate young men must seek first 'true conversion to God', and then 'perfected salvation'.[30] With specific reference to the sexual dangers lying in their path, Dr. Thomson gave them five warnings. First they should flee youthful lusts by not allowing their minds 'so much as to look on the temptation' and by not allowing themselves 'to be placed in the midst of surroundings and circumstances, which, though not in themselves evil, are found, in practical experience, to be an inclined plane conducting to evil'.[31] Here, Dr. Thomson wrote, 'holy sensibility' was in order: in particular, young men should 'eschew the drunkard's haunts and the drunkard's cup'.[32] They should not, he said secondly, even think about subjects 'whose tendency is to inflame the passions and to pollute the soul'.[33] The 'hidden orgies' of the imagination were 'certain to quench the Spirit': for how could 'the holy dove consent to remain in a soul in which these obscene night birds are allowed to nestle'?[34] Dr. Thomson sympathised with those who had to struggle against such thoughts, but he emphasised the need to keep the struggle going and advised young men to keep such thoughts out by filling their minds 'with holy themes and with Christian maxims and motives'.[35]

'Sensuous novels' and 'pictures . . . suggestive of evil'[36] were, according to Dr. Thomson's third warning, particular dangers in this respect. The former 'flood our literature' and 'appear to be written as apologies for vice'.[37] Even if 'some of them contain passages of beauty which reveal the hand of genius', was it, Thomson asked, 'wise to wade through a cesspool in order to pluck a flower?'[38] If any of his readers owned such books they should burn them just as the converted magicians of Ephesus burned their books of witchcraft. They should, he solemnly warned, 'never have any book in your possession, which you could not read aloud to a mother or a sister'.[39] As for the pictures of those painters 'who employ their gift in pandering to vice and lowering the standard of moral living'[40] — they should be denounced, as they surely would have been by 'men like Michael Angelo and Fra Angelico, who were not ashamed to pray for divine help in producing their immortal works'.[41] Young men should avoid such paintings 'even though some should speak of you as a fanatic or a philistine'.[42]

Dr. Thomson warned the young men, fourthly, against 'indolence and brooding unsocial isolation' which were not only wrong in themselves, but which, because there were 'many points in our complex being in which the physical affects the moral, favourably or unfavourably', also tended 'to engender evils of a deeper hue'.[43] As an alternative, he commended 'manly exercises in the open air'.[44]

> Athletic exercises in the open air, and in the midst of fanning breezes, not only benefit the body, but the mind through the body, and no good moral education is complete without them.[45]

Fifthly, Dr. Thomson wrote, young men should seek not only to avoid the sins of the flesh, but also to 'love and practise the opposite good', in this case by thinking pure thoughts and by respecting women:

> Learn to respect woman by respecting and guarding her chastity and purity, 'putting honour upon her as the weaker vessel'; and feeling that man is her natural and divinely constituted protector, treat her with something of the chivalry of an earlier age. There is true manliness in this, and the noblest and bravest of our race, like our own hero-king, the Bruce of Bannockburn, have uniformly shown it most.[46]

Under the same head Dr. Thomson also urged early marriage 'when this would be prudent and practicable': it would surround the young man 'with the sanctities and safeguards of married life'.[47] Young men were also advised to 'frown upon' indecent speech, including coarse jokes and 'words with double meanings in which evil is insinuated under a garb of decency'.[48] These were 'base coinage from the mint of hell',[49] and to be avoided at all costs. On the positive side Dr. Thomson recommended the various purity guilds, whose formation he considered to be a hopeful sign. In a sixth and final point his readers were urged to 'ally' themselves 'with divine almightiness'[50] against temptation. Thus, they would be able 'to repel the moral sophistries of those in our day, who think they find an excuse for their sin in the force of their temptations, as if there were a necessity that they should fall'.[51]

The Pastoral Letter, then, was for the most part a statement of the conventional Victorian attitude to sex, with which its readers would probably have been familiar from other sources. In his analysis of 'The Victorian Frame of Mind', which deals with literary and other sources between 1830 and 1870,[52] W.E. Houghton has noted: that when, at puberty, children were told about sex (having hitherto been kept in ignorance, or so it was assumed), the parents 'spoke, vaguely but pointedly, about "uncleanness of body and mind"';[53] that premarital continence was taught to men and held to be absolutely necessary for women; that the Victorian youth was supposed to struggle against temptation and fight it down; that he 'was taught to view women as objects of the greatest respect and even awe';[54] that 'sexual irregularity' was 'the blackest of sins';[55] and that the Victorians were extremely prudish about literature, disapproved of 'levity', and banned 'any words which could conceivably carry a sexual suggestion'.[56] All of these features were, as we have seen, present in the Pastoral Letter,[57] together with that of muscular Christianity.[58] Other topics mentioned, such as the advocacy of early marriage and the avoidance of strong drink, were equally familiar elements in the conventional middle-class wisdom of the time, on which we have already commented. And the level of argument to scriptural principles was such as to suggest that these were brought in to support already developed attitudes.

The arguments and advice of the letter thus reflected the attitudes of the respectable. There was little in the letter that any respectable man would contradict upon a public platform. In private, many respectable men might have been less likely to insist on the same standard of sexual behaviour for men as for women, but then nothing very explicit was written about this in the letter. The letter in fact was explicit about very little. It was vague about sex, and its selective-fundamentalist approach to scripture obscured even the biblical testimony, exalting Paul at the expense of the whole. Whether or not the making of such pronouncements affected the behaviour of those who were not already predisposed to agree with them, is something we can only guess at. But perhaps the best that can be said for them is also the worst: that their doom-laden generalisations probably scared many church people off any form of unregulated sexual behaviour, thus persuading many Victorian Scots to do what may have been the right deed for what was probably the wrong reason.

But did writers like Thomson say the wrong thing for the right reason? This suggestion is unlikely to gain much sympathy in a post-Freudian society armed with penicillin and effective contraceptives; and seeing these ecclesiastics so often strain at the gnat of sexuality while swallowing the camel of economic injustice, it is tempting to leave them to the mercies of a Marxist critique, or to write them off as theological deviationists from the true prophetic spirit of John Knox and the Old Testament. Yet such a course oversimplifies matters just as seriously as the Victorians themselves did, and is as much an expression of the conventional wisdom of the late twentieth century as the church pronouncements we have been considering were of their own age's conventional wisdom. It may be understandable that the contemporary church, mesmerised by head-counting (in this respect things have not changed), seeks to politicise itself and hopes to gain the sympathies of the working classes and the intellectual Left, but that is not necessarily prophetic action. Nor is the adoption of more liberal views on sexuality. Nor for that matter is there much evidence either that contemporary church pronouncements make a greater contribution to the solution of problems of national and international social justice than did those of their predecessors, or that ecclesiastical politicisation does much to reconcile to the church those who have been alienated from it. These developments do not provide contemporary churchmen with any very substantial grounds for adopting a superior attitude to their predecessors.

A more fruitful course, perhaps, is to allow the Victorians, however unsympathetic twentieth-century minds may be to them, to be themselves; and thus to recognise the differences between the two eras. If this is allowed, there may be seen — behind the rhetoric of professional ecclesiastics and ecclesiastical bureaucrats who had made a remarkably successful adjustment to the interests of the dominant class of their period — the sincere and valid as well as the synthetic and imaginary hopes and fears of men to whom their own historical context was inescapable. It may still be impossible not to criticise them — not least on account of their thin theology — yet the theology of those who criticise is defective if it cannot see through the mystification and distortions of all ideologies to the human realities underlying them. As George Eliot wrote about an earlier generation of Evangelicals:

> Our subtlest analysis of schools and sects must miss the essential truth, unless it be lit up by the love that sees in all forms of human thought and work, the life and death struggles of separate human beings.[59]

CHAPTER NINE

Aftermath, 1900-1914

Discipline in the Church of Scotland

DISCIPLINE in the Church of Scotland clearly was in an unsatisfactory state, narrow, anachronistic and ineffective. The Commission on the Religious Condition of the People had said as much, and had recommended that the system be changed. As the nineteenth century ended, the Assembly was exploring the possibilities, in the first place through an enquiry conducted by its Life and Work committee.

In 1896 this committee sent out a series of questions to kirk sessions, and in the following year reported its findings. Each session was asked how many cases of discipline it had recently dealt with. Of those which replied, 196 could not say, since they kept no records; 118 had no cases to report; and the remaining 745 each reported a number of cases which, in the committee's opinion, were 'sufficiently large to demand the serious consideration of the Church'.[1] Of the offences dealt with in these cases, while a few were of 'drunkenness and, less frequently ... slander, theft (and) quarrelling', over 99 per cent. were 'connected with the sin of impurity'.[2] Cases of discipline normally involved only communicants or intending communicants, and nearly all of them were originated by voluntary confession. (Cases were very rarely originated by 'complaint or information',[3] although in 16 parishes, whose location was not recorded, all or most were originated by action by the minister or session.) The standard procedure involved nothing beyond 'submission to rebuke'; although in a few parishes the offenders were asked to attend worship, promise 'greater watchfulness',[4] or were put on probation either for three to eighteen months (in one case for two years) or till after the next communion. It was unusual for cases of scandal, apart from a few cases of drunkenness, to have taken place in a congregation and not to have been dealt with. In two-thirds of the cases reported as having been dealt with by rebuke, this had taken place in the presence of the session, while in the remainder it had taken place either privately in the presence of the minister, or — as was most usual in city parishes — in the presence of the minister and one or two elders. Many parishes used different methods in different cases, although in impurity cases it was normal for only the minister and one elder to be present — a practice which had been advocated by the Synod of Dumfries in 1891. In all kinds of cases contumacy was very rare, and when it took place the offender was either suspended or removed from the Communion Roll.

Not many returns specified any hindrances to discipline, but those which did remarked that ecclesiastical divisions were the most important. In a few, but not many cases, offenders had been received into the Free and United Presbyterian churches and in a larger number into the Scottish Episcopal Church, whose ministers were criticised for their 'readiness . . . to baptise and to receive into communion without any certificate'.[5] Other hindrances mentioned included the physical removal of offenders from the district, delays by other sessions involved, and

> shame, nervousness, &c., on the part of the women; reluctance, amounting to great unwillingness, on the part of the men, who refuse to be judged by those who are their daily companions (and who themselves are sometimes against them requiring to compear).[6]

More general hindrances included:

> 'religious indifference'; 'disregard of Church authority'; offenders will rather 'lapse' than 'stand the session'; a low moral tone prevailing in the community (ante-nuptial impurity not being regarded by many as a 'serious moral offence').[7]

The question of how far the administration of baptism was affected by the exercise of discipline — a question raised by the Commission — was also investigated. The majority of returns did not consider that it was affected very much one way or the other; but it was also reported that discipline was frequently submitted to 'in order "to get baptism" ',[8] and that baptism was frequently delayed on this count. When, as sometimes happened, submission was refused, the offender lapsed and the child remained unbaptised — although in a number of parishes illegitimate children were usually baptised to sponsors.

Suggestions about improving the system were received from 300 parishes, all of which recommended some 'uniformity of method'.[9] This was seen as a way to block the escape of offenders to more lenient parishes in the neighbourhood, and, by the same token, uniformity of practice among all Presbyterian churches was urged. Other suggestions pointed to the 'unfairness of summoning people for discipline only for the sin of impurity'.[10] (The committee pointed out here that the church's law did not restrict discipline to such cases.) There was also some pressure for giving up the keeping of records of discipline. As one return put it: ' "If the offence is blotted out before God, why keep a record of it here?" '[11] And another commented that many ministers would rather not know about such episodes in the past lives of their parishioners. There was, however, some disagreement about methods. One third of the returns wanted the abolition of discipline before the session, and especially for impurity cases where these were still dealt with in this way. These returns claimed, variously, that this method was ' "useless and worse", "effete", "utterly ineffective", "without salutary meaning".'[12] Others however wanted this method to be insisted upon, since the ' "Church gains nothing by laxity" ', and because abolition of it would be ' "detrimental to public morality" '.[13] One minister claimed that

> A private conversation would not suffice; the mind of the community, or congregation, would not be cleared; nor would it have the same end or value to the persons dealt with. The elders must share in the duty; to say that they are not suitable is for us to own our Church too little spiritual and tactful.[14]

Summing up, the committee, noting great diversity of practice and hearing of dissatisfaction on all sides, expressed a strong desire for some authoritative guidance from the Assembly. In too many, even if not in all cases, it believed, the way in which discipline was administered neither helped the offender, nor fulfilled the church's purpose. The matter, on its recommendation, was remitted for consideration to a special committee.

Changing the System

This committee, having considered the subject, proposed seven amendments to the existing system. These were: first, that in the case of an offender who delayed voluntary submission 'unduly'[15] long, the minister should make an initial pastoral approach, failing which the session-clerk should write and warn him that if he did not agree to submit to discipline within thirty days, he would be suspended from church privileges until he did submit; second, that in cases of fornication, if the session was satisfied that the accused woman was telling them the truth about the father, even if he denied paternity, the case could be proceeded with. (If they were not satisfied they could delay and do whatever they thought 'best for edification'.)[16] Third, that in cases where the accused was not willing to submit, the minister should meet him or her first, to 'ensure a correct and serious apprehension of his position',[17] and report to the session. The session would then discuss the case, and appoint the minister and one elder (in cases of fornication followed by marriage it could be the minister alone) to dispose of matters with the offender; fourth, that this last part of the procedure should take place somewhere other than in the offender's own house, and should comprise prayer followed by a statement of the minister and elder's authority, questions to satisfy them of his penitence, counselling and encouragement, further prayer and a statement of absolution; fifth, that a record of cases should be kept in a special book, the names of the offenders being obliterated after five years; sixth, that kirk sessions should afford one another facilities for transferring cases; and seventh, that in order 'to bring to an end the unauthorised and diverse methods that are practised in some parishes and parts of the Church',[18] kirk sessions should use only either the provisions of the original Form of Process or these amendments.

These recommendations were embodied in the law of the church by an Act (VIII) of the General Assembly of 1902. In practice this Act did nothing to satisfy those who wanted discipline to be made more effective. According to I.M. Clark, writing in 1929, minutes of discipline 'are now kept by very few Kirk Sessions';[19] kirk sessions very rarely transferred cases (in order, for example, to bring the father of an illegitimate child residing in another parish under the discipline of the woman's parish); and where discipline was operated, almost the whole procedure was in the hands of the minister. Commenting upon the effect of the Act, Clark pointed out: that both the Form of Process and the 1902 amendments were already 'almost a dead letter';[20] that the amendments were not very comprehensive and that the Act 'does look as if it were constructed for the one particular sin that so largely has engaged and still engages the anxious care of the Church';[21] and that by the 1902 Act almost all authority in cases of discipline was given to the minister — which was a departure from the primitive and Reformation model of public confession and almost a return to the pre-Reformation model of private confession. The danger of this, Clark thought, was not 'the rise of the confessional, though the way to it is more open than it once was, but the loss of the very idea of discipline'.[22] And, he commented, 'if discipline is, as the reformers held, one of the three true marks of a church, is its loss not to be regarded as a symptom of disintegration?'[23]

Clark's comments are very much to the point. The return to something like private confession signalled by the 1902 Act — although the Act was more a symptom than a cause of this — left the Church of Scotland in a curious limbo as far as its disciplinary and pastoral functions were concerned. For better or worse it remained a national church and could not adopt the disciplinary methods of sectarian bodies. At the same time however it was also a voluntary body and could not expect the state to enforce its disciplinary standards. Discipline therefore was a dead letter for all practical purposes. The higher courts of the church, of course, could still exercise discipline over ministers and elders. But this was not discipline as it had existed in the past. It was more like the activity of a professional body concerned with maintaining professional standards — something akin to an ecclesiastical General Medical Council. Against this background, then, it was very difficult for a minister to exercise discipline over church members, since with the virtual disappearance of elders from the disciplinary scene there was little to show that such discipline represented the mind of the community. What it could be represented as, of course, was an attempt by a religious professional to force his own standards upon laymen; and with that possible interpretation in mind, it was not surprising that ministers grew increasingly unwilling to exercise any discipline at all.

Discipline, however, was not the only form of pastoral care and with its decline others were to be tried. In the twentieth century some ministers were to draw inspiration from the Catholic priestly tradition and others from psychoanalysis, its secularised equivalent. But neither of these were quite to meet the case, and the folk-memories of session discipline and its concentration on sexual offences did not die easily. Pastoral care and counselling by ministers thus was suspected, not always without reason, as a highly judgemental activity, especially after the overtly non-judgemental professions of social work and secular counselling arrived on the scene. The Reformed ideal of the church as a body of mutually supporting individuals in a self-disciplining community — an ideal undermined by seventeenth-century zealotry, eighteenth-century formalism and nineteenth-century hypocrisy — had not yet been entirely abandoned: but by the middle of the twentieth century the problems of implementing it had yet to be resolved.

Irregular Marriages

The Christian Life and Work committee, in its report to the 1893 Assembly, announced that it had changed the name of its sub-committee on the 'Welfare of Farm Servants' to that of 'Deputations to Rural Parishes'. This was done, it remarked, because 'in some instances exception was taken to the apparent limitation of this work to one class of the community, as tending to draw an invidious distinction'.[24] Thereafter very much less was heard in the Assembly about the question of rural immorality.

Urban sexual morality — or at least one aspect of it which the church was able to observe — was not however neglected in the early years of the twentieth century. In 1905 an overture from the Presbytery of Glasgow expressed concern about the increasing number of irregular marriages in large cities, 'even between parties professing themselves Christians', and asked the Assembly to counteract this trend by making 'marriages *in facie ecclesiae* more easy to the people'.[25] The means suggested for this purpose included the preparation of a pastoral letter, more regular teaching on marriage from ministers, and better facilities for receiving applications for the proclamation of banns. A special committee set up to deal with the overture, reporting in 1906 and 1907, endorsed these suggestions, amending them only by the substitution of a memorandum to ministers and sessions in place of the proposed pastoral.

The memorandum noted that the number of registered irregular marriages had risen from 1 per cent. in 1875 to 6½ per cent. in 1902, and that they had declined in number only slightly thereafter. Overlooking the possibility that this rise might reflect an increasing number of registrations rather than an increasing number of irregular marriages as such, the authors of the memorandum expressed their concern that such an increase should have taken place in Scotland where, they claimed, such marriages were 'formerly rare'.[26] They were especially concerned about the high proportion of irregular marriages registered in the cities: in Edinburgh 20 per cent. of all marriages, in Glasgow 12 per cent., in Aberdeen 7¾ per cent., in Govan 6¾ per cent., in Perth 6¼ per cent., and in Dundee 5 per cent. They contrasted these figures with 'ten counties, chiefly rural in their character', in which 'there was not a single irregular marriage registered',[27] and some other rural counties in which there were almost none. The urban rate was high, they believed, partly because some couples came from the country to the towns to be married, in the belief that their marriages would thus be secret. This belief, they stated, was fostered by 'needy agents and others in the principal cities', who 'professed to carry through marriage "before the sheriff" ' or advertised their services in terms of ' "Marriages legally and privately completed: information free" '.[28] Such claims, the memorandum pointed out, were misleading, since no 'special licence' in fact existed in Scotland, and since those who underwent the process offered had to pay

> about £2 for fees of court, of registration and of agent; whereas in the case of regular marriage the only expense necessary is the proclamation fee — 2s.6d., which covers the cost of the proclamation of banns in the parish church, while the minister's certificate of a marriage, and the registration of that marriage, cost nothing.[29]

In order to encourage regular marriage the special committee accepted an addendum to its proposals which provided that 'one church in each town be open two hours in each week, and a minister in attendance, to marry those who apply for marriage after proclamation of banns'.[30]

The memorandum expressed a very high view of the church's part in regular marriage. It pointed out that 'in Scotland from the earliest times the Church has regulated not merely the religious ceremony, but also all the details necessary to the completion of the marriage union'.[31] This assertion was based upon Acts of Assembly and of the Scottish Parliament (1661 and 1698) — which, it seemed, were assumed by the committee to be evidence enough of what had happened 'from the earliest times'. The committee also asserted, without producing any evidence to prove the point, that 'everywhere in advanced society, and much more in Christian communities, marriage has been regarded as duly constituted only by religious recognition'.[32] It was at pains to point out that the alternative method of publishing notice, provided for by the Act of 1878 'IS OF NO VALUE UNLESS BOTH PARTIES RESIDE IN SCOTLAND',[33] and that a regular marriage always required a minister to perform it, whatever form the preliminaries took.

The state of the law, the memorandum observed, was based upon the fact that marriage, with its scriptural foundation and its analogy to the Christ-church relationship, could not be a 'mere civil contract'.[34] It was not, of course, a sacrament either, but 'common to all mankind' and 'of public interest to every community'.[35] Nevertheless, since Christians were told to marry 'only in the Lord',

> it is fitting and proper that their marriage be solemnised by a minister of religion, in order that he may suitably instruct and exhort those who are entering on a lifelong union so close and intimate, and pray for the blessing of God upon them. Such a marriage as this has always been recognised by the law of Scotland as a 'regular marriage', to distinguish it from 'irregular' and erratic unions entered into with a disregard of religious claims, sanctions or responsibilities.[36]

The authors of the memorandum thus continued to assume, perhaps unavoidably in a national church whose discipline rested upon such shaky foundations, that all who came to be married in church were Christians, and that the unrighteous should somehow be suppressed. The equation was one which many Scots were not disposed to question. But in view of the unrespectable and complicated alternatives to which others among their countrymen had to resort until 1939, they had, perhaps, little choice in the matter.

Other Issues

During this period the Church of Scotland's General Assembly discussed a number of other issues related in one way or another to sex, marriage and the family, but limitation of space precludes the consideration of these here. In any case such subjects as the development of the Church of Scotland's Women's Organisations, begun in the 'eighties under the aegis of the Life and Work committee, and the movement for the ordination of women, which came to a head in the nineteen-thirties,[37] deserve to be studied in their own right. The development of social work in the Church of Scotland, which created a special committee concerned with this subject in 1903, has been chronicled elsewhere,[38] and in the present context it may simply be noted that this committee's interests included 'rescue and redemptive' work among girls and women sexually at risk, especially in the cities, as well as the creation of a Women's Labour Bureau. Two other subjects which were discussed may also be noticed in passing: in 1911 the Assembly gave some consideration to technical matters relating to the celebration of marriage in the armed services (in connection with the report of its Army and Navy Chaplains committee); and in 1912 church representatives gave evidence to the Royal Commission on Divorce. This last, although it introduces a large subject upon which the nineteenth-century churches were largely silent, is of more relevance to developments in the post- rather than the pre-war period.

Social Problems and the United Free Church

For a number of years after the union in 1900 of the Free and United Presbyterian churches, the Assemblies of the new United Free Church were overshadowed by the much-publicised legal wrangle over the property of the former Free Church. The minority 'Wee Free' church which dissented to union regarded this controversy as one of principle. But since it so clearly concerned property, it can have done little to persuade outsiders that the churches were the poor man's friends. Yet this was what an increasing number of ministers and elders of the new church were anxious to prove. Reports of the Church Life and Work[39] and Social Problems[40] committees of the United Free Assembly, and debates concerned with these reports, suggest that the repentance they now expressed for their predecessors' alleged indifference to the problems of wealth and poverty was not entirely rhetorical. There were, of course, many churchmen who considered that ecclesiastical interest in social issues was 'a sort of red-herring trailed across the path to divert the Church's attention from her principal duty'.[41] But when the Church Life and Work committee announced in 1902 that the church had to take account of 'how social conditions bear upon the moral depression or elevation of the masses',[42] it was a sign that James Begg could rest more easily in his grave. (On this count at any rate: no doubt the Free Church case would have kept him agitated.) A new generation, forced by circumstances to regard an urban and industrial society as normative, and a lapsed proletariat as normal, was now, when it talked about 'the moral facts of life',[43] found to be talking about economics and politics as well as about sexual immorality and intemperance.

The United Free Assembly, on the advice of its Church Life and Work committee, however, was unwilling to 'hastily commit itself to great schemes of social work'.[44] It acknowledged the lead given in this direction by the Church of Scotland, and perhaps sensing that union with that church could not be postponed forever, limited its efforts in this field. It did, however, believe that 'the Church has a well-defined function in moulding public opinion and in holding forth higher ideals';[45] and during this period it discussed a wide range of social problems with this end in view.

Housing, Overcrowding and Immorality

In this discussion the problems of Scottish housing inevitably re-appeared. The Church Life and Work committee's report to the 1904 Assembly reviewed the social changes of the second half of the nineteenth century, comparing Guthrie's picture of the mid-Victorian *City, its Sins and Sorrows*,[46] with the 'public figures' for 1903. 'Nothing,' the committee declared, 'has been more striking in the period mentioned than the amelioration of the conditions of the working classes.'[47] But, after detailing improvements in wages, housing, education and public health, it still found 'many things to give us pause'.[48] Among these it included 'overcrowding', a phenomenon which more careful investigation and control by public authorities had revealed. 'Over-crowding is not allowed,'[49] the committee wrote. But it had to admit that 'the shiftlessness and moral defects of the people'[50] made it difficult to translate this principle into practice. The committee came down especially heavily upon 'those who will not trouble to gather a few sticks of furniture and take a home for themselves', but who instead 'pay a higher weekly rent for so-called furnished apartments, having as little stake in the country as a tramp by the roadside'.[51] (If the tone of these remarks was any guide, perhaps one might be forgiven for thinking that things had not changed so very much in the previous forty years after all.)

The Assembly's interest in overcrowding was stimulated by the report of the Glasgow Housing Commission, whose findings were communicated to it by the Church Life and Work committee in 1905. The committee's representatives made a great deal of the fact that the Commission had called attention to the superabundance of licensed premises in Glasgow, commenting that 'the wretched slums' were 'largely the product of this vice'.[52] The committee did not, however, seem too clear about the question of cause and effect: in the previous year it had quoted, apparently with approval, a remark by the Glasgow Chief Constable, describing 'an extraordinary outbreak of serious crime in the city in 1902' as ' "but the natural outcome of the wretched social conditions existing in the lowest stratum of city life" '.[53] In fairness to the committee, however, it should also be noted that it criticised not only the inhabitants of overcrowded slums but also the profiteers who sublet the furnished houses or rooms they lived in.[54] House-farming, as it was called — it seems as if rural metaphors were still indispensable — was to be discussed on a number of other occasions during this period; and clearly one of the aspects of this subject which disturbed the committee was, as its 1909 report put it, 'that a large proportion of these houses are hot-beds of immorality and disease':[55]

> The evils inseparable from overcrowding are too apparent to require indication. By the impossibility of securing privacy the bloom of modesty is easily removed, and the natural safeguards of purity are destroyed. The sanctities of home are violated and in the moral atmosphere generated it is scarcely possible for religion, even in its most elementary form, to thrive.[56]

Among the consequences of overcrowding mentioned by the committee was not only crime, especially murder, but also, according to the 1905 Report of the Royal Edinburgh Asylum, 'a rapid and alarming increase of general paralysis of the poorer classes'.[57] The committee connected this phenomenon with overcrowding and house-farming in particular, since so many such houses accommodated part- or full-time prostitutes. The Church Life and Work committee's report of 1904 had complained that although prostitution had been successfully contained by 'a policy of stern repression' in previous years, it was once again re-appearing in 'other and subtler forms' which were 'difficult to be brought within the reach of the law'.[58] And in 1908 a minister from Glasgow was to tell the Assembly that 'immorality was on the increase'.[59] This minister 'was informed that in Glasgow alone ten thousand women took gains for parting with their honour'.[60] Of these, he reported, only a few were saved: missionaries found that it was generally only those who had come from good homes that they could have any hope for, while 'the great majority never had a chance, physically, morally or spiritually'.[61]

The committee continued to discuss house-farming up to the outbreak of the Great War. In its opinion, local Acts were insufficient, and national legislation was required to give local authorities powers to regulate such houses. Its 1914 report quoted from a report received from Glasgow Corporation in which it was stated that the number of farmed-out houses in the city had almost doubled since 1901, and that of their inhabitants,

> 50 per cent. live under these degrading conditions as a consequence of their drunken habits; 10 per cent. are tramps and tinkers; 20 per cent. are idlers who do nothing but hang about these places, and 20 per cent. are women of ill-fame.[62]

Anxious about the urgency of the problem, and irritated by having to wait for the report of the Royal Commission on Housing, the committee remarked that it was 'amazing, in face of such a clamant case for reform, that the Department of State should maintain a policy of masterly inactivity'.[63]

Sweating and Family Life

The effect of labour conditions on family life was also discussed by United Free Assemblies of this period, especially in connection with 'sweated labour' and the employment of children. 'Sweating' mostly took the form of needlework (or sometimes matchbox making or shoemaking), done at home by women for extremely long hours and low wages. Parliament had been concerned about it for at least twenty years, but it was difficult to improve conditions, not least because the women were not easily organised in their own defence. The Church Life and Work committee, writing in 1908,[64] noted these points and, expressing its concern about the effect of sweating on home life, demanded the state regulation of wages (and possibly a minimum wage for workers), as well as the sanitary inspection of houses in which sweating was carried on. The committee would not commit itself on the controversial issue of whether home work should be totally abolished, but it tried to deal with one of the factors which gave rise to it by asking church members 'to moderate the demand for cheapness, so far as in their power'.[65]

The same report also included a survey of conditions in other industries. Here it was particularly critical of Sunday labour, especially since many of those who worked on Sundays were often free on Saturday afternoons, when their 'passion for sport interferes with work'.[66] There was a distinct echo here of what had been said in the 'nineties by the Commission of the Church of Scotland on the Religious Condition of the People: an echo heard again when the committee, commenting on the relation between industrial conditions and home life, focused its attention on Dundee, whose unenviable pre-eminence in infant mortality, the committee believed, was 'directly attributable' to the way in which domestic life was 'disorganised by the employment of married women in daily and all-day work'.[67] It is worth noting in this connection that the church's criticism of working mothers seems to have originated with what it saw in Dundee, and with the phenomenon of sweating. Mothers had of course worked for a long time. But it was the unquestionably bad conditions and effects of such labour in these sections of industrial society which finally provoked comment once the church admitted to becoming aware of them.[68] Criticism of working mothers as such was to remain a standard part of the church's repertoire long after these conditions had been abolished.

Social Conditions and Political Action

Despite its willingness to attack the problems of house-farming and sweating, there were some issues which the United Free Assembly found too hot to handle. The 1908 report of the Church Life and Work committee told of a meeting between the committee and a member of the Edinburgh Trades Council who 'in the course of an able and well-reasoned address presented the Socialistic view of existing conditions'.[69] The committee listened, told him that they were sympathetic, but concluded that 'the time has not arrived at which the Church is called to take a side on great economic questions'.[70]

In 1908, of course, not everybody in the U.F. Assembly agreed about this. While some believed that economic questions were too complex for the church to deal with in any detail, there were others, like Professor J.Y. Simpson, who held that it was up to the church 'to show that there is a will of God concerning questions relating to hours and wages, to the appropriation of land, to the enjoyment of luxury, the suffering of penury'.[71] Those who spoke in these terms were concerned lest Marxism in theory and Socialist Sunday schools in practice should replace Christianity and the church. They held that Socialism was good, but that Christianity — which included the good of Socialism — was better, and that the church should apply the light of the Gospel to the problems with which Socialism was concerned. Others again had doubts of a different kind. An elder from Glasgow (who was applauded simply for saying that 'he spoke as a working man and the son of a working man')[72] complained to the 1908 Assembly that the church's interest in social and economic questions gave the impression that it 'looked on the labouring portion of the people as being morally and spiritually in a more depraved condition than some other sections of the population'.[73] No doubt this was the impression it also gave to many other working people. Although it made a great show of goodwill towards the working classes (some of it no doubt genuine), its continuing unwillingness to translate its goodwill into political action limited its effectiveness. According to the Church Life and Work committee's 1909 report: 'for the church to become a partisan would be to hamper her mission in the spiritual domain with one or other of the parties involved'.[74] But the church had appeared too long to be on the side of the middle classes for things to be so simple. The report of a Church Life and Work sub-committee seemed to recognise this when in the same year it commented that 'the Church's partial neglect of (its social ideal) has had serious results in throwing the leadership of the masses of the poor into other hands'.[75]

The Morality of Young People

This sub-committee had been given the task of preparing a paper on 'the Social Teaching of our Lord', and this[76] showed the direction in which some churchmen were going. It emphasised that Christ was a poor man, that his example 'vindicates the claim of the poor to a life of happiness' and that he was peculiarly devoted 'to the Distressed and the Outcast Classes'.[77] Dealing with his teaching, it emphasised the teaching on the Kingdom, stressing that this was not only a spiritual reality but also a social ideal, with a bearing upon contemporary economic and industrial problems. Among the special problems 'looked at by Jesus in their connection with the Kingdom',[78] it singled out Wealth and The Family. Wealth, it commented, was 'a trust . . . often a moral danger . . . (and) a severe test'.[79] As far as The Familv was concerned:

> On this subject Christ's teaching is explicit. To Him the relation of man and woman in marriage is sacred and binding. His teaching made the marriage bond more stringent than it had ever been. His own example in His home life is equally instructive and significant. The basis of the Christian Institution of the family rests firmly on the authority of Christ.[80]

There was nothing very novel in these remarks about The Family. The context in which they appeared, however, was significant. The paper on Christ's social teaching reflects the influence of contemporary Ritschilian theology on the Scottish writers, particularly in its concentration upon the Jesus of History, the Kingdom of God, and the moral imperative. While it would be misleading to trace too direct an influence of German theology upon Scottish church pronouncements, it seems then that the church was beginning to awaken from its undogmatic slumbers of the nineteenth century to the task of correlating theology and culture.

Even this however can be overemphasised, and no doubt the fear of revolution, which had long influenced some churchmen and was now even more acute in certain quarters, played its part in the rediscovery of Christ's connection with the poor. Nor was the nineteenth century really dead. As far as comments on sexual behaviour were concerned, there were still a number of echoes of it. Only in the previous year the Presbytery of Blairgowrie had reported its anxieties about 'the thousands of girls engaged in the fruit industry in that district'.[81] Some of them, it wrote, were 'quartered in dormitories that are not suitably supervised. Crowded together in large numbers, or even sleeping in the open air, there is a great risk of serious scandal.'[82] But if complaints of this kind were all too familiar, some other traditional themes were being seen in a new and more optimistic light. The Assembly of 1902 had heard with some satisfaction that the amount of immorality in the South-West was decreasing and that the standard of behaviour was gradually rising.[83] And in the following year it was told of the progress made by the Onward and Upward movement in the Presbytery of Arbroath.[84] The subject of discipline also was being handled rather differently. The United Free Assembly, with its relatively more modern standards of congregational discipline, had fewer problems here than the Establishment. But its thoughts on the subject were going in much the same direction as those of the Church of Scotland. When it heard of four congregations in the ultimate north-western Presbytery of Tongue, which still insisted upon up to four public appearances in cases of discipline, it commented: 'This surely is a mode of procedure that might well be given up.'[85]

But if north-western righteousness and south-western immorality were now becoming matters of less moment to the United Free Assembly, this did not mean that the church had given up its interest in sexual behaviour. It meant rather, as we have already suggested, that this interest was now invested in the sexual behaviour of young people in general, and that most of these were now to be found in the towns rather than in the rural areas.

This point may be supported by reference to the 1912 Report of the committee on Church Life and Work and Public Morals, which included a special enquiry 'into questions affecting young people',[86] or adolescents, as they were now referred to. The enquiry dealt with three specific topics: the employment of children, street-trading by young people, and 'the prevention of girls and youths from immoral courses'.[87] As far as the first two of these topics were concerned, the church was on the side of reforming legislation, such as the Employment of Children Act of 1903, and further amendments which it believed were necessary.[88] It also saw 'a grand opportunity for social service'[89] by church members, in provision made for voluntary workers, under the supervision of the Children's Care committee, to keep in touch with and report on school-leavers for four or five years. This opportunity, the committee thought, would appeal to members of 'every congregation situated amid a working class population', who 'could organise a body of helpers, who could co-operate with the School and State authorities'.[90] Since 'the young people in a district are already known to Church workers through the Sabbath School, and kindred organisations . . . it would be simple to follow them up in this way'.[91] The great advantage possessed by the church in engaging upon this task, the committee suggested, was that it had 'the personal touch'.[92]

The sub-committee charged with discussing 'the Prevention of Girls and Youths from Immoral Courses' was convened by A. Herbert Gray, who was later to write a number of popular books and pamphlets on sex and marriage.[93] Its report began by noting that

> the attention of the public has of late been forcibly directed to the large amount of immorality in our large towns, and *even* in our country district. It is not necessary to discuss the question whether it has increased of late. Its present dimensions constitute a very grave national peril.[94]

The major cause of this, in the committee's opinion, was 'the lack of proper parental control, and the relaxation of the bonds of family life'.[95] This, it claimed, deprived young people of 'what ought to be their greatest moral safeguard'; and since 'the very fundamentals of Christian morality are at present being challenged in our country', the nation's 'greatest need just now is a firmer hold on the Christian conception of marriage . . . The call to the Church to make its testimony on these matters clear and unmistakeable is very loud.'[96] To do this, more should be said about the subject from the pulpit, 'difficult and delicate'[97] though this was. The committee pointed out that, compared with the church,

> no other institution in the country can possibly have such an opportunity, and therefore such a responsibility. We still have the majority of the children of the country in our Sunday Schools and if there those children were trained to hold true ideals of the sacredness of the family, we might hope to produce parents of a very different type for the next generation, and then this evil might shrink to very small dimensions.[98]

There were, in the committee's opinion, other considerations also involved in the problem. Specifically, it mentioned: first, 'the influence of unduly low wages';

second, 'the influence of evil housing conditions'; third, 'dangerous resorts'; and fourth, 'needed changes in the law'.[99] Its comments on the first two of these were standard: on the one hand, sweated wages tempted girls 'to augment their earnings in ways which involve the ruin of their life';[100] and on the other hand, inadequate housing forced both sexes in large families into the same beds — or at best the same rooms — thereby removing the 'barriers that ought to guard delicacy and chastity of feeling'.[101] The committee's criticism of such 'dangerous resorts' as public houses, ice-cream shops and public parks was not new either. Nor was its recommended alternative of ever more 'Lads' clubs and Girls' clubs'.[102] Among the reforms in the law for which it pressed were those relating to brothel-keeping, to keeping children in brothels, to farmed-out houses, to living on immoral earnings, to accosting, and to criminal assaults on children.[103] In each case the committee expressed a desire for heavier penalties or for more careful enforcement of the existing laws.

The committee continued to be concerned with the question of the low wages paid to girls, and the subject was discussed in the 1913 Assembly. But when the convener was in full flight, condemning these low wages, he was interrupted by a female voice from the gallery, shouting 'Votes for women'. The interrupter was quickly dealt with, but the same thing happened again in the following year, and one minister at least expressed anxiety lest 'some of these furies might in revenge add the Assembly Hall to their bonfires'.[104] The Great War, however, was now about to interrupt and recast the discussion in a more serious fashion, so that for better or worse the hall survived, although what was discussed in it thereafter was never to be quite the same, despite the valiant efforts of many later commissioners.

One issue which would continue to obsess subsequent Assemblies came into prominence during this period. This was the question of the promulgation, in 1908, of the decree 'Ne Temere' by the Roman Catholic Church in Britain. The decree stated that no marriage of a Roman Catholic was valid unless it had been celebrated by a Roman Catholic priest — even if the other partner was of a different faith. This rather aggressive move was soon met by a storm of criticism in the other churches; and protests, accompanied by appropriate horror stories of priestly activities, were made in the United Free Assemblies of 1911 and 1912.[105]

CHAPTER TEN

Theological and Other Factors

AT this point it may be worth pausing to ask what theological considerations informed the pronouncements we have considered so far. What the churches had to say, after 1858, about illegitimacy and sexual morality shows that they were in two minds. Unwilling to abandon the traditional view that immorality was attributable to sin and should be suppressed, they had also begun to ask if it was attributable to social circumstances. In asking this, the churches, partly as a result of their own social circumstances, lacked the courage of their Reforming fathers' convictions; and the hope of change through environmental improvement gained ground. But the older opinion was never wholly abandoned; and as what they said about the marriage law and ecclesiastical discipline showed, the churches were as unwilling to give up their formal authority as they were unable to exercise that authority in the spirit of the sixteenth century.

In making these pronouncements, the churches rarely raised or developed explicitly theological points. They did, of course, quote the Bible but often with as little relevance to its original context as to their own. As their Pastorals on family life showed, the language of the Authorised Version was interwoven with the everyday language of churchmen in ways which frequently distorted its meaning; and even when its original sense was discerned, little attempt was made to use this as a basis for theological reflection. Other pronouncements, whose lack of scriptural support is very obvious by comparison, demonstrate just how far the churches saw the contemporary scene through the spectacles of conventional middle-class morality and piety. This enabled them to make pronouncements which sounded confident, in language which sounded scriptural. But these pronouncements do not appear to have been the product of any very deep theological reflection.

It was not, of course, that these pronouncements had no theological basis. Many of the assumptions behind them, after all, could be traced back to the theology of Calvin and his successors. But time had interposed so many problems and raised so many questions about that theology — problems and questions which Scottish churchmen had lacked the opportunity or the desire to take seriously — that it is doubtful how far Calvin or even his Scottish followers can be held responsible for what their nineteenth-century successors were now saying. For the fact was that although theology was still done in Scotland, it was not much heeded by General Assemblies — at least not in the area of discussion which we have been considering.

Why was this? Robert Flint, the Church of Scotland's leading theologian, had suggested a reason. In an address to his students in 1881, Flint had criticised the view that 'the theologian ought to teach nothing but what is contained in the doctrinal statements of the creeds of the Church' and that he ought 'to propound no truths or ideas except those which the Church has already adopted'. Over against this 'false and degrading . . . theory of the theologian's duties' Flint had suggested that the theologian's relationship to the Confession of Faith was 'analogous to that of a professor of mathematics to the elements of Euclid'. The theologian, while 'content not to contradict the doctrine therein contained . . . would by no means be content to be confined to it and prevented from going on to the higher mathematics'. When a report of this speech reached James Begg, the comparison roused that champion of orthodoxy to deliver a verbal attack on the Establishment theologian. In reply, Flint, reminding Begg of his recent statement that he 'had no sooner entered the ministry than he fell into the stream of public discussion', commented:

> I do not like the stream into which he fell, and for this among other reasons, that it is a stream which has wasted and impoverished every field of theological science in Scotland, and into which whoever is completely drawn must be lost to theological science, and must lose to some extent a due interest in its progress. The fruit of science like the fruit of righteousness is sown in peace; it loves quiet places. For fifty years there has been no ecclesiastical peace in Scotland, and Scotland is fifty years behind some other countries of Europe in theological science. It is about time, in my opinion, that divines were thinking of coming out of a stream so unfertilising, and in some respects so unclean as that which has been flowing through Scotland, instead of plunging into it, as many of them are doing just now, more madly than ever, and trying to drag the whole country into it.[1]

Although these comments apply to theological science in general, they are equally applicable to the area which we have been considering since, as we have seen, the love of controversy displayed by Begg and many other churchmen does seem to have obstructed any mature theological reflection about Christian teaching on sex, marriage and the family.

This was not of course the only reason why the churches' pronouncements lacked theological depth. As we have seen, the churches' successful identification with the needs of the dominant new middle class required that they share its confidence in the sort of society it had established and hoped to improve. Thus, when that society appeared to be in danger, it was all the more necessary for the churches to rally to its support with pronouncements based on theological models which reflected its structures. These theological models, essentially those of the patriarchalism of love, but greatly modified to fit the nineteenth century, were however losing touch with everyday social reality. As they did so the churches clung to them all the closer, as if afraid seriously to question them. Thus, although as time went on the churches became more critical of the nineteenth-century social structure, their fear of what might happen should the associated theological models be questioned seems to have inhibited their theological thinking. In an age characterised by 'the common feeling that to lose one thing is to lose all',[2] this was a not unnatural response.

If theological reflection was almost absent, then, what — other than expediency — did inform the churches' pronouncements on sex, marriage and the family? In the figure of the farm servant, to whom the preceding chapters have repeatedly returned, we find a clue.

The central role assigned to farm servants in Assembly pronouncements was related to changes in the agricultural economy and to changes in the churches' relation to the working-class population. Various factors were involved in this. A great upheaval in the agricultural economy had disoriented much of the rural population, and may well also have disrupted the old-established courtship customs of at least some of the rural districts. Possibly this had produced an increase in illegitimacy. Or possibly illegitimacy had increased in rural districts as a result of the churches' loosening and less confident disciplinary grip. Or possibly it had not increased at all but had simply been brought into the light by the Registrar-General. Whatever the facts and whatever their causes, the churches, now solidly identified (at Assembly level at any rate) with the middle classes — who literally as well as metaphorically put a high price on female virginity — were particularly concerned about rural immorality. Now that so many of the urban and industrial workers were outside the church, the existence of such immorality seriously undermined any claim the churches might make about their influence over this remaining section of the working-class population. Such claims were further undermined by the churches' discovery that family worship among the lower orders, even in many rural districts, was not only 'by no means universally practised', but was also falling 'into more extensive neglect'[3] than had been thought earlier in the century — a development which the churches themselves, through the creation of church- (or church-hall-) oriented organisations, may well have helped to foster. This, together with widespread reports of declining parental authority, suggested that certain commonly held ideas about the rural population were ill-founded.

In Scotland, although they were to be found elsewhere,[4] these ideas were given a focus in the figure of the godly smallholder portrayed in Burns'[5] poem, 'The Cotter's Saturday Night'. This mythological figure, independent, 'moral' and pious, was not without historical substance. Reformed religion, although originally urban, had deeply influenced rural Scotland and, prior to industrial and agricultural change, men like the cotter had not been entirely atypical, while in the crofting counties, which were the last to feel the Reformation's effects, not a few of them still existed. For many of the middle classes (themselves often only a generation or two away from the croft and still returning for wet but idyllic Highland holidays) their way of life exercised a certain nostalgic attraction, especially when viewed through the romantic spectacles of Burns, Scott and their imitators. Seen — at a distance — the image of the Reformed pious peasant was merging with that of the romantic noble savage, making it possible for the middle classes, without too much difficulty, to keep up the fiction that outside the worst areas of Edinburgh, Glasgow and Dundee the cotter was still the real Scot, a sanctified MacRousseau.

Church leaders, as we have seen, also had reasons of their own for believing in the pious peasant. Thus, when that notion was contradicted by the realities of contemporary social life, underlined by surveys and statistics, the resulting conflict of romantic ideas and rural realities produced what might be called the cotter complex — a complex of irreconcilable and emotionally loaded ecclesiastical attitudes which the churches found difficult if not impossible to resolve without the loss either of face or integrity. Their repeated appeals to the memory of the cotter recall George Eliot's dictum: 'We all of us, grave or light, get our thoughts entangled in metaphors, and act fatally on the strength of them.'[6]

Many of the pronouncements considered in previous chapters seem to have owed less to mature theological reflection than to this cotter complex. The circumstances which produced it, of course, changed with time and as more and more people drifted from the land. And by the beginning of the twentieth century the churches had access to a greater store of information about urban life on which their pronouncements could be based. But although the specific reference to rural immorality was lost, the habits formed under the influence of the cotter complex were not. The churches were now beginning to turn their attention — as far as their critique of sexual behaviour was concerned — to another section of the population whose life was also often romanticised, namely 'youth'. This class, which even now could not answer back, was beginning to take up the burden which the farm servants had rejected.

PART TWO

Cleanliness or Godliness

IN May 1871 the General Assembly of the Free Church received a letter from certain Ladies' Associations in Glasgow and Edinburgh asking it to petition Parliament for repeal of the Contagious Diseases Acts.[1] These Acts, passed in 1864, 1866 and 1869, were designed to protect soldiers and sailors against venereal disease by providing for the compulsory medical examination of prostitutes in a number of English and Irish garrison and dockyard towns. To many military men, doctors and politicians these Acts seemed eminently sensible. Their opinion, however, was not shared by a considerable body of middle and artisan class opinion[2] which was disturbed by the emergence — despite much resistance to public discussion of the subject — of evidence suggesting that the Acts were as unjust in operation as they were in principle. Opposition to the Acts was soon channeled, by Josephine Butler and others, into what became known because of its desire to abolish the Acts as the Abolitionist movement. In appealing to the Free Assembly, the Ladies' Associations, who were part of this movement, were about to gain a significant adherent to their Great Crusade.

Before recounting the part which the Free Assembly and the United Presbyterian Synod played in that Crusade, however, something should be said about prostitution, venereal disease and the churches' attitude to these subjects prior to the passing of the Contagious Diseases Acts.

CHAPTER ELEVEN

Prostitution and Venereal Disease

Earlier Attitudes and Legislation

THE Contagious Diseases Acts were only the latest of many attempts to deal with prostitution, for although the more self-critical Victorians and their more censorious critics are at one in agreeing that there was an enormous amount of prostitution in the nineteenth century, that century can neither be blamed nor credited for inventing it. Who did, and how, and why, are complex questions, not least because prostitution itself is difficult to define.[1] But as far as European attitudes, and particularly church attitudes, are concerned, the experience of the Old Testament Jews clearly cannot be ignored.

The most significant aspect of prostitution in Israel before the Exile was its involvement with religion. In Canaan, as in many other agricultural societies, the idea of the fertility of the female was closely associated with the idea of the fertility of the field. This, together with the notion of the holiness of all forms of ecstasy, including sexual orgasm, gave rise to cults in which the sacred prostitute was a key figure. As such, the sacred prostitute embodied all that the less magical and more rational prophetic religion of formerly nomadic Israel was opposed to. In the consequent struggle the prophetic religion survived only with difficulty, and was often at a disadvantage. Not least to its disadvantage was the probability that pagan cults were partly maintained by the offerings of those Jews who visited sacred prostitutes, not because of any religious conviction, but simply because there was no readily available secular alternative.[2] (Many Jews of course were also potential converts. The Canaanite cults suited their new life-style and many were drawn into them as a result of intermarriage with the natives.) Perhaps for this reason there is, in the Old Testament Scriptures which relate to this period, little condemnation of secular prostitutes such as Rahab. Even after the Exile, when urban secular prostitution assumed much greater proportions, it was not criticised with the vehemence reserved for the sacred variety, but on more practical grounds, as a waste of young men's time and money. Later, however, the area of strong disapprobation expanded to include secular as well as sacred prostitution, and in the Christian tradition a clear distinction was not maintained.

The Christian tradition, however, was also influenced by other attitudes to prostitution, primarily those which had developed in Greek and Roman society. These societies, although each of them attempted at different times to suppress prostitution, were less concerned with its religious dangers, and on the whole were more tolerant of it. Indeed, at times, prostitutes in Greece and Rome were not only tolerated, but also licensed, registered and taxed. These tactics were carried over into the Middle Ages, despite opposition from the early church; and the efforts of later Christian emperors and kings, notably Charlemagne and Louis IX of France, who attempted to abolish prostitution by law, met with little success. Any attempt of this kind was no doubt complicated by the ambivalence of the church and its theologians. The most commonly quoted Christian observations on the subject of prostitution, prior to the Reformation, are those of Augustine and Aquinas, the church's most outstanding theologians. And both of them, while insisting upon the sinfulness of prostitution, and supporting the church's policy of keeping unrepentant prostitutes outside its pale, conceded that prostitution was a necessary social evil, which should be tolerated for fear of worse. If prostitution were abolished, they felt, other females might resort to promiscuity, and men to sodomy and other sins.[3]

Events in the fifteenth and sixteenth centuries, however, were to change this situation. The first of these was a major epidemic of syphilis, which invaded Europe in the 1490s, lasted for a hundred years, and killed tens of thousands. Whether Columbus and his crew brought it — as a new disease — back from America in 1493, or whether it was simply a new form of an old disease which somehow became much more virulent, is uncertain. But its deadly effect and the inability of contemporary doctors to treat it, are well documented.[4] It was not until the beginning of the seventeenth century that syphilis became a disease whose early stages were not commonly fatal. Thereafter it took on its more modern form, and while epidemics recurred, there were never again any so serious or on such an enormous scale.

The sixteenth-century epidemic was not, of course, the first European experience of venereal disease. Measures to deal with venereal infection were laid down in the Old Testament: in Leviticus 15: 1-18 and 25-30, where quarantine and washing were aspects of laws against ritual uncleanness; and in Numbers 25 and 31, where measures to check the disease included the slaughter of all the Midianite men and all of their women who were not virgins (some of whom had previously infected the Israelites) as well as the purification of the Israelite army by quarantine and washing, and of their baggage by fire and water.[5] In the subsequent history of Europe, quarantine continued to be the main form of treatment, and although mercury became a standard remedy for the early stages of syphilis, later stages (in the post-sixteenth century development of the disease) manifested themselves, if the earlier were not treated, in paralysis, syphilitic insanity, death and the infection of unborn children. No fully effective treatment for syphilis was found until 1943, when the use of penicillin was introduced, with dramatic results. (Penicillin also transformed the treatment of gonorrhoea, a less serious but much more common form of venereal disease).

The major problem in treatment, especially during an epidemic, was that of getting hold of infected persons. If a prostitute or a highly promiscuous woman was infected, the disease could spread rapidly. Literally as well as metaphorically, she could infect armies of men: and during the sixteenth-century epidemic, as in the Old Testament period, military campaigns had much to do with the progress of the disease. It came to Scotland with the supporters of Perkin Warbeck in 1496 and penetrated thereafter to most of the larger and smaller towns.[6]

The second event which was to influence the future course of public attitudes to prostitution was the Reformation. There seems to be no hard evidence to show that the epidemic of venereal disease was an important factor in forming the attitude of the Reformers towards sexuality. Any effect it might have had, however, would probably only have confirmed their insistence on a single standard of sexual morality. Yet the Reformers did not adopt a uniform policy in regard to prostitution. Luther, for example, was opposed to prostitution on principle and took the optimistic view that marriage was an adequate alternative. Nevertheless, when called upon to give practical advice, he was more ambivalent, suggesting in one case at least that the premature shutdown of brothels might do more harm than good.[7]

The Scottish Reformers seem on the whole to have been more single-minded. The Edinburgh Town Council, in 1560, gave 'whoremasters and harlots' two alternatives: either they could confess their conversion to a new way of life before the ministers and elders, or they could face a scale of penalties ascending, depending upon the number of their offences, from public rebuke and carting, through branding and banishment, to 'punishment to the death'.[8] These alternatives, save the last, were also offered by the Privy Council, when four years later it enacted legislation prohibiting brothels.[9] Such attempts to put down prostitution were of course part of the more far-reaching policy of the Reformers with regard to sex, and the keen-eyed council of Edinburgh were unwilling to leave any stone unturned. Aware of the close connection of drink and sex they ruled in 1560 that

> Because in past times the iniquity of women taverners in this burgh has been a great occasion of whoredom, insomuch that there appears to be a brothel in every tavern; therefore all vintners of wine who may engage women taverners before the next Martinmas hereafter were to be certified, that if their women committed any immoral fault they should have to pay forty pounds, except they deliver the offender into the hands of the bailie, to be banished, according to the laws, as soon as the offence comes to their knowledge.[10]

Such attention to detail suggests that the council's policy of repression was not only preached but also put into practice — or at least that there was a serious attempt to do so. But since a further 'most strict' proclamation against immoral women in taverns had to be issued in 1570, further efforts to banish harlots were made in 1587, and laws against streetwalking had to be repeated in 1585 and 1588,[11] it seems likely that success in this field of legislation was limited. Perhaps because of this, the councils, by the end of the century, were beginning to tire of such efforts, and certainly in one case a citizen was released from a charge simply by providing security that he would never again enter a brothel.[12] In the following century only two Acts[13] concerning prostitution were passed by the Edinburgh town council, one of 1650 prohibiting brothels and re-ordering the carting, scourging and banishing of whores, the other demoting an officer who was found guilty of maintaining a whore.[14]

Legislation relating to venereal disease in Scotland appears on the whole mostly to have had to do with the isolation of those who were infected. This was ordered by the authorities both before and after the Reformation. Town councils in the 1490s ordered harlots to give up their trade, and packed off infected citizens to islands or, alternatively, commanded them to stay inside their houses. Isolation was also ordered and in some cases forcibly imposed during later outbreaks of syphilis.[15]

But by the eighteenth century civic attitudes to prostitution were beginning to change. Prostitution had not been abolished, even in Scotland, and the Edinburgh councillors decided that if they could not beat prostitution they ought at least to recognise it. They declared therefore, in 1700, that

> notwithstanding the great care and pains taken by them to punish common whores and thieves and banish them from this city, yet they still are found within this city and suburbs, having no mark or distinction to make them known from other inhabitants; and therefore were of the opinion that, conform to the custom of other places abroad, those common thieves and whores should be marked upon the nose, by striking out a piece of the left side of the nose with ane iron made for that purpose.[16]

At first sight this pronouncement looks like yet another attempt to suppress or abolish prostitution. Certainly it was part of a larger package, containing threats to deprive unrepentant burgesses of their status, with which the council reinforced ecclesiastical attempts to put down adultery and fornication. But in fact it marked a significant change of direction: the reference to 'the custom of places abroad' was significant, since at about this time some continental countries were once again beginning to tolerate prostitution, regulating it through police and medical inspection of brothels and guarding against disease by suppressing the activities of unlicensed prostitutes.[17] Not all European countries were doing this,[18] and in Britain public opinion was still resistant to any regulating system.[19] Nevertheless, in this context, the council's admission of its failure to abolish prostitution, and its policy of branding common whores on the nose was recognition of a sort. Thereafter it took no further measures to abolish prostitution,[20] but concentrated instead on attempting to limit the amount of public disorder caused by it. Subsequently, the council issued a number of Acts forbidding respectable women from wearing plaids and other forms of clothing which might lead to their being taken for prostitutes.[21] This, recalling pre-Reformation legislation compelling harlots to wear clothing which would distinguish them from other women on the Edinburgh streets,[22] can be seen as further evidence of official toleration and recognition.

The Extent of Prostitution in the Early Nineteenth Century

What effect this return to toleration may have had upon the number of prostitutes in urban areas is a question to which no very satisfactory answer can be given. Prostitutes, as we have already noted, had been active in British towns and cities for many centuries, and even in Scotland the Reformers were unable to suppress them. What we do not know, however, is the scale on which prostitution existed during these centuries: we can only suppose, since the activities of the Reformers and their successors probably drove a certain amount of prostitution underground, that it is likely to have existed on a larger scale than was officially recognised. The problem of estimating if and by how much prostitution may have increased in the later eighteenth and in the nineteenth century is farther complicated by the consideration that greater toleration came at a period when the urban population, and with it the urban underworld, was increasing at a hitherto unprecedented rate.

This greatly enlarged urban underworld naturally enough provoked the interest and concern of a number of middle-class early Victorians. Increasingly cut off by economic progress from a common civic identity with the underworld's inhabitants, but energised in many cases by the spirit of Evangelicalism and in others by the desire for greater enlightenment, their enquiries included attempts to determine the 'nature, extent, effects, guilt, causes and remedy'[23] for and of prostitution. As far as the extent of prostitution is concerned, however, these enquiries were often as confusing as they were helpful. To illustrate this we can note a few of them in passing.

London's large underworld naturally attracted a good deal of attention. In his *Police of the Metropolis* the criminologist Colquhoun[24] estimated that between 20,000 and 25,000 women in London — the population of which at the time (1800) was about one million — made their living entirely by prostitution. There were in addition, he calculated, another 25,000 or so women who lived partly by prostitution, in other words a total of five per cent. of the London population making or eking out their living by it. Another authority, Dr. Ryan,[25] quoted in a magazine during 1840, thought that the total figure should be nearer 80,000, or eight per cent. of the total population. But then Sir Richard Mayne, the Chief Commissioner of the Metropolitan Police, stated in 1841[26] that the number of prostitutes in London was 9,409. This confusion was partly a matter of definition. Mayne was probably referring only to full-time prostitutes, while Colquhoun's estimate included part-timers — a class which in his terms included 'the multitude of low females who cohabit with labourers and others without matrimony'[27] — whose prostitute status was doubtful, to say the least. Even so, leaving part-timers aside, the difference between 25,000 and 9,409 was large enough. Here, however, contemporaries alleged, the problem lay with Colquhoun's methods: he was estimating 'the amount for the entire city from the numbers found in certain localities',[28] that is, the notorious ones. His estimate was thus far too high. Other authorities again, however, considered figures like those of Mayne to be far too low.[29] The debate about London prostitution was endless, and heavily coloured by comparisons to be drawn one way or the other with Paris, the regulationist's Utopia and the Evangelical's Gomorrah. 'The differences' in estimates, as Ralph Wardlaw, trying to make sense of them, remarked, 'are so very wide, as to be really marvellous'.[30]

Estimates were also forthcoming for Edinburgh and Glasgow. Here there were fewer experts, so less appearance of uncertainty. But even Tait, the Edinburgh authority, admitted that answers 'where information was expected . . . were so vague and unsatisfactory that no reliance can be placed upon them. One individual estimated the numbers of prostitutes at 6,000, and another as low as 300'.[31] Tait's own method of calculation[32] involved ascertaining the number of brothels in the city — the total of which in their various disguises was about 200 — multiplying this by the average number of girls living in each — which was three — and adding to the total the number of girls who lived in private lodgings or with friends, but who frequented these places. The number in this last category, the names of most of whom Tait claimed to have obtained, was 200. The total number of full-time prostitutes in Edinburgh around 1841 was thus, according to Tait, 800 — a figure corroborated by the Treasurer of the Magdalene Asylum. Since the total population of Edinburgh in 1841 was 137,899, this meant that full-time prostitutes accounted for around 0.6 per cent. of the population, a proportion similar to that in Glasgow, where the population was 280,682; and the number of full-timers, according to the city missionary Logan's account,[33] was put at 1,475 by police figures, at 1,600 by the Lock Hospital Surgeon, and at 1,800 by Logan himself. There was thus more unanimity about the extent of Scottish prostitution, but as we have noted, there were fewer authorities to contradict one another. On the other hand, since what authorities there were may well have been in close contact with one another, unanimity might simply have reflected mutual confirmation of one another's guesswork.

An added element of uncertainty in assessing the extent of early nineteenth-century prostitution was provided by the existence of part-time prostitutes, whose number in London alone Colquhoun had put at 25,000. Even if cohabitation without marriage accounted for some proportion of this supposed figure, there clearly was — and all of the accounts seem to agree upon this — a sizeable number of working-class women in towns and cities who were driven to prostitution, willingly or unwillingly, in order to help support themselves or their families. Some such women (what proportion it cannot be said) would no doubt have resorted to prostitution even if they had not needed the money. But in an age increasingly characterised by large-scale unemployment, inadequate provision for the poor, and the isolation of many individuals and families from the mutual support of rural community life, many women might have seen no alternative. There seem to have been many of them in Edinburgh. Tait calculated their number on the basis of investigation into the history of 300 girls employed in sewing and book-stitching, 130 of whom were 'known to deliver themselves up partially to a life of prostitution'.[34] From this he worked out that from 'the class of dress-makers, sewers, bonnet-makers, book-stitchers, shop-girls, house-servants and fishwives'[35] and from that of women either unemployed, widowed or deserted by their husbands, at least 1,160 and probably more were sly prostitutes.

The full impact of such figures — even if their authors and their contemporaries realised that they could not be proved — was brought home dramatically by Tait[36] when he estimated that in Edinburgh there was one full-time prostitute for every eighty adult males.[37] An estimate of this kind including the sly prostitutes would have made this figure one for about forty. Wardlaw,[38] noting Tait's calculations, was unwilling even to speculate upon whether there were proportionately as many sly prostitutes in Glasgow as in Edinburgh: if there were, over 2,000 would have to be added to the total. 'Distressing as it would be to believe this,' he commented, 'yet for aught I can tell, it may be true.'[39]

The Evangelical Approach

On even the most conservative reading of the late eighteenth and early nineteenth-century scene, then, it is clear that prostitution was a social phenomenon of considerable dimensions, and although greater toleration was extended to it for a time, dissatisfaction soon set in. In the interests of order and morality, of social justice and of public health, reformers sought for ways to deal with the problem.

Dissatisfaction with the toleration of prostitution was an inevitable concomitant of the influence exerted by Evangelicalism upon late eighteenth and early nineteenth-century British society. During those years, in which 'virtue was advancing on a broad invincible front',[40] at least three different ways of tackling the problem were advocated or adopted: the creation of asylums for female penitents, the enactment and enforcement of stricter laws, and the general reformation of social and sexual behaviour.

Penitentiaries

The first of these was not of course a new idea, since penitentiaries had existed in the past, but interest in them re-awakened during this period. In 1787 a Lock Asylum was opened in London to receive penitent prostitutes who had been discharged from the Lock Hospital (a hospital for treating venereal disease, opened in 1747), and other similar institutions were soon established: the Magdalene Hospital in 1758 (another venereal disease hospital) and the London Female Penitentiary in 1807. There were others outside London, including the Edinburgh Magdalene Asylum, founded in 1797 (Edinburgh already had a Lock Hospital), and the Glasgow Magdalene Asylum soon after.[41] Other institutions and societies with wider aims, but incorporating the penitentiary principle, were also set up: in London, the Guardian Society in 1812, the Maritime Female Penitentiary a few years later, and in 1835 the London Society for the Protection of Young Females and the Prevention of Juvenile Prostitution.

The last of these, parallel societies to which were set up in Edinburgh and Glasgow during the early 'forties, carried matters much farther than simply providing a place where prostitutes could repent and be retrained for a new profession. A major criticism of the penitentiaries, expressed by Tait[42] in the 'forties, and later by Acton,[43] was that they catered — with varying degrees of success — for only a very small proportion of the prostitute population. The Societies, by contrast, employed much more aggressive and missionary methods, attempting to search out and save the inhabitants of brothels, and especially their most recent recruits.

Laws

The London Society was also anxious to achieve changes in the law which would ensure easier convictions and more severe sentences in cases of procuring and brothel-keeping. This aim was in line with the policy of leading Evangelicals, such as Wilberforce, who (in setting up the Society dedicated to promoting the ends of the 1787 Royal Proclamation against Vice and Immorality) was concerned with the stricter enforcement of the law against Sabbath-breaking, drunkenness, pornography and other forms of immorality. The Evangelicals realised, as Wilberforce put it, 'that by regulating external conduct we do not change the hearts of men', but, hoping that their countrymen would be 'ultimately wrought upon by these means', decided that they 'should at least so far remove the obtrusiveness of temptation that it may not provoke the appetite which might otherwise be dormant and inactive'.[44]

It is difficult to measure the success of this second aspect of the Evangelical approach to prostitution, but for the present it can be noted that the police and magistrates were given greater powers to suppress brothels, to prosecute brothel-keepers, and to keep prostitutes from making too great a nuisance of themselves on the streets. These powers, granted by various local and national enactments, were not at first[45] fully employed, but by about 1870 the police and the courts seem to have become more enthusiastic about them. According to the statistics of the Metropolitan Police, the number of brothels proper (i.e. establishments lodging or boarding prostitutes only, as opposed to places where prostitutes, among others, lived) in their district had sunk from 933 in 1841, to 410 in 1857, to 2 in 1870.[46] A similar decline seems to have taken place in Scotland: in 1870 the Edinburgh police knew of 85 brothels in the city compared with over a hundred three years earlier;[47] and in the same year the Chief Constable of Glasgow expressed the opinion that neither prostitutes nor brothels had increased in number, during the previous twenty-one years, in proportion to the increased population; that the number of brothels had not increased at all, that large brothels no longer existed, and that prostitutes, thanks to policy activity, no longer made an obvious nuisance of themselves on the streets.[48] A similar decline in the amount of street-walking was reported by the Superintendent of the Greenock police after his force had been provided with powers to proceed against it when the town adopted the appropriate Act (of 1862).

Social Reformation

But beyond the penitentiary principle and beyond more rigorous enforcement of the law lay the larger vision of Evangelicalism. In attempting to deal with prostitution, the Evangelicals and those whom they influenced were working, in a particular case, towards the general goal of a new reformation. Tait, the Edinburgh surgeon (who, whatever his private convictions, had adopted the Evangelical tone), writing about remedies for prostitution, emphasised the importance of adopting 'a multiplicity of means, among which the removal of the causes will form the most important and successful'.[49] As enumerated by Tait, these removals added up to a programme for something little short of a total social and moral reformation.

This programme for a nineteenth-century reformation was in some respects strikingly reminiscent of the sixteenth century. Tait, although considering their methods too harsh, admired the determination of the Reforming magistrates of Edinburgh. He also laid great stress upon Education. Prostitution, he believed, was rooted in the poor religious and moral training of the lower orders. Through precept and example, masters, parents and peers could do much to minimise the effect of those 'natural'[50] traits — 'licentious inclination', 'irritability of temper', 'pride and love of dress', 'dishonesty and desire of property' and 'indolence' — which set a young girl's feet on the primrose path. Greater kindness at home, followed by more and better religious, moral and scientific education were also prescribed in order to counteract the social or 'accidental'[51] causes of prostitution. Other accidental causes would be dealt with by paying greater attention to the problems of poverty and Social Welfare, since female unemployment, low wages and destitution all contributed to the situation in which mothers took to the streets to support their children and daughters to support their parents. Like the Reformers, Tait was concerned about the poor, and advocated more generous poor-relief, but like them also he was unable to devise a lasting solution for regulating commerce in the poor's interest. He tentatively suggested the creation of a prices and incomes board which could penalise manufacturers and merchants who undercut their rivals and in so doing created unemployment. But then he drew back, afraid that this would 'infringe fatally on the freedom of trade', and expressed the hope that something might be done instead by 'voluntary benevolence'.[52]

The nineteenth-century reformation was also like the sixteenth in that the conventional socio-sexual system was questioned. In the nineteenth century, however, the pretensions not of celibacy but of marriage were condemned. Tait's criticism of the marriage system was the common one of 'bachelorism'[53] and delayed loveless marriages among the rich, of hasty marriages, desertion and destitution among the poor. This combination stood high among prostitution's 'accidental' causes. Reformation would not however be achieved by sweeping changes in the law, only by an elevation of moral standards. Professing Christians — especially those of the middle and upper classes — should therefore make every effort 'to give the tone to the manners of others, which', Tait believed, 'they might easily do with success'.[54] He particularly requested them to treat their servants with greater 'gentleness, patience and firmness', to ostracise seducers (whom the law ought to punish) and men who had any commerce with prostitutes, and to see that their household kept the Sabbath and stayed away from dancing parties and the theatre. If public opinion encouraged virtue and discountenanced vice, prostitution would 'wither and decay'.[55]

Prostitution, however, did not wither, nor did it decay. By 1840, when Tait was writing, the Evangelical reformation had gone about as far as it could go. It was still the Evangelicals' high noon, and they had succeeded in casting a long shadow over the rest of the nineteenth century, but already other men were aspiring to their place in the sun. Two movements in particular, which in the twentieth century would challenge Christianity's cultural leadership, were already beginning to devise alternative ways of dealing with prostitution. These, socialism on the one hand, and the therapeutic alternative on the other were, of course, still weak, and Marx and Freud, their major prophets, had yet to arise. But those who wittingly or unwittingly prepared the way for them regarded prostitution in a different light to that of the Evangelicals. It is difficult to say how far the Evangelicals realised the threat which these movements were to represent to their own ideas on the subject. But their vehemence in condemning what those who prepared the way had to say suggests that they sensed it.

A Socialist Alternative

By 1840, a Socialist view of prostitution, later endorsed and elaborated by Engels, had emerged in the writings of Robert Owen, the anti-clerical Utopian Socialist who had attempted to found a model community at New Lanark. Ralph Wardlaw, the leading Scottish Congregationalist minister of the time, was aware of Owen's existence and was unsympathetic to his ideas. Wardlaw, persuaded by eleven hundred and forty fellow-Glaswegians to lecture them on what, 'with unfeigned alarm and regret', they regarded as 'the vast amount and constant increase of female prostitution within the precincts of our own city',[56] lost no time in getting to work on those whose presuppositions threatened his own: 'the enemies of religion' who 'chuckled over'[57] the improper behaviour of some scriptural characters; and Robert Owen.

Owen took criticism of the kind expressed by Tait much farther. The conventional marriage system, in his eyes, was not a good thing gone wrong, but a confidence trick played upon his contemporaries' ignorant ancestors by power-hungry priests. Before this took place men had lived simple and innocent lives, unaware that they should be ashamed of their sexual feelings. The priests who persuaded them that they should had been responsible therefore for man's real fall, and now, in the West persuading them that monogamy, and in the East that polygamy, was God's will, they kept men slavish, superstitious and subservient to the church. Now, men and women had to promise to ' "love and cherish" what your organisation may compel you to dislike and loathe, even in a few hours'.[58] The marriage system, by concealing this conflict, was the cause 'of more than one half of all the vilest and most degrading crimes known to society' as well as 'the sole cause of all . . . prostitution'.[59]

Understandably, the author of these ideas was anathema to the Evangelical Wardlaw who, noting his ideas, confessed that 'my own loathing of the beastly system is so intense that I am unable to speak of it with patience'.[60] To him, the notion that 'religion, property and marriage are the real originators of all existing evils . . . and that no God no property and no marriage are the true panacea for the world's vices and the world's woes'[61] was 'drivelling folly', and Wardlaw was confident that there was 'a sufficiency of sound sense and of right feeling in the community'[62] to show this up for what it was. While not being willing to criticise Socialism in general, he believed that Owen's views on marriage 'deny the legitimate authority of any restriction, admit no rule but that of natural impulse, and would reduce us to the socialism of the brutes'.[63]

Owen's ideas, although often wild enough, did not deserve such strictures. His romantic naturalism was perhaps naive, but he could also be remarkably realistic. His proposals for new laws on marriage and divorce, which recognised the concept of marriage breakdown but also made provision for reconciliation,[64] included suggestions which orthodox Christians, a century or so later, were not to find unthinkable.[65] The later twentieth century also was to regard with greater sympathy Owen's opinions on chastity and the family.[66] The former, 'the chastity of Nature', he identified as 'real charity — that chastity, which alone is virtuous': it consisted, he believed, 'in the intercourse of the sexes when there is a pure and genuine sympathy or sincere affection between the sexes'.[67] The latter, he believed, was a school of selfishness: single families were 'dens of selfishness and hypocrisy' in which children were taught to say 'my' and 'our' and 'to seek, by . . . almost any means, except *direct* robbery'[68] to promote their own interests and those of close kin, instead of those of society as a whole.

In the long term, then, it seems as if Owen was justified when, on his deathbed, dismissing a hopeful clergyman, he remarked, 'I have been ahead of my time.'[69] But most of his contemporaries were far from admitting it.

The view of prostitution which Owen put forward was therefore not one which presented a live option for early Victorian society. Respectable men may have been willing — even eager — to admit that the marriage system was partly responsible for contemporary prostitution. But, as we have seen, it was the corruption of the system rather than marriage itself which they criticised. Marriage and the family were bulwarks of society, protecting Britain against sin and social chaos. Anyone who doubted this need only remember the depravity of the eighteenth century, or look across the Channel, to be convinced of the danger of disregarding or tampering with these divinely ordained institutions. There was still, undeniably, much sin in British society, and the threat of social chaos was never far from the minds of the bourgeoisie when they considered the ways of the rapidly multiplying lower orders. But sin might increase and social chaos threaten even more, if those who gave the lead to society faltered in their firm purpose and, beguiled by moral sophistries, confused those clear distinctions of right and wrong upon which their achievement had been built. Further moral improvement consisted not in asking what was right, but in ensuring that what was known to be right was done.

Owen's ideas, then, were not a live option. The alternative to them was greater godliness, which would check both the sexual passions which contributed directly to prostitution and the desire for greater affluence than was appropriate, which contributed indirectly to it. Not everyone however agreed that it was enough to desire and work for greater godliness. There was also greater cleanliness to be considered. The way in which the claims of this virtue, traditionally so closely associated with godliness, were argued was to prove very confusing to those who wished to maintain clear distinctions of right and wrong.

CHAPTER TWELVE

A Therapeutic Alternative

IF the well-scrubbed Christian was one consequence of the Evangelical movement, another was sanitary reform. Nineteenth-century efforts to improve the level of public health of course owed a great deal to the deterioration of the urban environment and to advances in medical science, which held out the possibility not only of halting this deterioration but of making the population as a whole healthier than ever before. But they also owed a great deal to the energy and earnestness of the Evangelical frame of mind; and while many of those who were concerned with public health eventually mislaid the doctrines of Evangelicalism, they held on to its moralising tone of voice. Even Freud, who offered their descendants a new therapeutic language, 'still clung' to 'something of the autocratic pose, the paternal strictness he distrusted'.[1] And even after that therapeutic language had been accepted by the majority of the lay public, the moralising tone of voice was not silenced. The guardians of public health still play on the guilt and fears of the public mind, offering to those who repent of cigarette-smoking, for example, the gospel, if not of eternal, then at least of longer life. The vacuum of meaning created by the downfall of Protestantism is unlikely to be filled simply by continual therapeutic readjustments to the changing configuration of social reality — if the recent resurgence of interest in the Occult, Eastern religions and even Evangelicalism is any guide — but the advocates of these continual therapeutic readjustments have had during the last hundred years just as much and probably more influence than the advocates of revolution, continual or otherwise.

For the present purpose, however, it is enough to note that this therapeutic[2] spirit was not accompanied by a new moral view of the world set up in conscious opposition to that of the churches, as was that of Owen,[3] but that it emerged within the context of Evangelical Christianity; and that while some of its exponents were to make an open break with the churches, many individuals within the churches, and ultimately even to some extent the churches themselves,[4] made use of it to free themselves from the sterner moral demands of Evangelicalism.

In the context of this discussion of prostitution we can see the stirring of the therapeutic spirit best expressed in the writing of William Acton, a London surgeon who specialised in diseases of the urinary and reproductive organs and who held strong views on the control of prostitution and venereal disease.[5]

Continence and the Individual

Acton was to come into conflict with the Evangelical approach to prostitution. He was not, however, either a sexual radical or a Freudian before his time. His views on the possibility and advisability of continence would have been perfectly acceptable to any Evangelical. Like Tait, he believed that male[6] sexual desire was a 'natural demand' whose force, although 'impossible to exaggerate',[7] was not so strong that it could not normally be contained by the floodgates of marriage. He did not go so far as to say, with Tait, that any man who was such an uncontrolled libertine as not to be satisfied by marriage 'cannot be in a sound condition of mind'[8] and ought to be sent to the madhouse; but he held that young men, until they were ready to marry, could have any 'morbid excitement . . . corrected by healthy bodily exercise and mental application'.[9] The theory of prostitution as 'the safety valve of society'[10] was, he held, false. There was no need to fear that 'any serious diminution in the number of prostitutes would be attended with an increase of clandestine immodesty',[11] since prostitution, although it had other causes, was also its own cause: its very existence made it a possibility, creating a want, and developing into a habit encouraged by prostitutes, who were, in Acton's terminology, 'the artificial supply'[12] of the natural demand. Here too he was very much at one with earlier writers of a more Evangelical cast: Tait had considered the argument that prostitution was 'absolutely necessary for preserving peace and good order in society' to be 'absurd':[13] this was demonstrated by other cases and places: murder and drunkenness were also crimes which no nation had ever been able to abolish — but this was never held to be an argument for tolerating them as socially necessary; nor, in practice, did the absence of prostitution in rural districts result in any public disorder there.[14]

At this point, however, Acton began to disagree with the viewpoint of his predecessors. The idea that prostitution was not 'inherent in the social system' but 'incidental to it only',[15] which Wardlaw, arguing on similar lines to Tait, had advanced, was not one which he could share. If the natural sexual instinct was one of the 'Universal causes'[16] of prostitution, whose influence could be resisted by religion, moral sanctions, or prudence, another was the sinful nature of man. 'The majority of the human race', who had not 'at any time submitted themselves to the following out of either a religious or a moral code',[17] were as ineradicably sinful as they were sexual. A hope of the kind expressed by Wardlaw — that although it was doubtful, on past experience, that prostitution could ever be totally abolished, nothing short of the 'annihilation'[18] of this and all other sins should be the aim of Christians — was an inappropriate basis for social policies to deal with prostitution. It might be a worthy ultimate goal; but, Acton held, it obscured the urgent need to provide penultimate remedies by refusing even to discuss the existence of prostitution as a system.

The Harlot's Progress

Acton's view of the nature of that system led him even farther away from that of his predecessors. Quite deliberately he set out to contradict the traditional picture of the harlot's progress on which much of their moralising and practical proposals had been based. Tait and Wardlaw had suggested that the great majority of prostitutes followed a career of inevitable degeneration through sufferings, mental and physical, to an early grave: few prostitutes, they emphasised, escaped venereal disease; and they illustrated their point by detailing the more hideous physical manifestations of syphilis, such as rotting of the flesh and exfoliation of the bones, implying that such cases were common. Only a very few, wrote Tait, escaped: if they were of the better class, ate well and kept off spirits, they might remain healthy enough to survive as brothel-keepers and kept mistresses. The great majority, however, aged rapidly and died prematurely,[19] either by their own hands or as a result of disease. Even reformation was no protection, since many of those who reformed or married soon succumbed to disease, venereal or otherwise, or to the various other after-effects of the prostitute's profession.

Acton challenged this view because, he held, it was out of date: ' "the dirty intoxicated slattern, in tawdry finery and an inch thick in paint" '[20] had been replaced by a 'pretty and elegant' young woman, fashionably dressed, 'whose predecessors cast away the custom of drunkenness when the gentlemen of England did the same'.[21] The idea that prostitutes degenerated socially was equally false, since today they had more self-respect. There was 'little promotion and less degradation'[22] between the three classes of kept women, common prostitutes and women to whom prostitution was 'a subsidiary calling';[23] and many of even the second class were in their own way highly respectable.[24] Those who died in utter misery and destitution among the empty bottles were 'the altogether rare exception': the typical prostitute 'succumbs at last, not to that calling, nor to venereal disease, but in due time, and to the various maladies common to respectable humanity'.[25]

Acton substantiated this point with 'a few stubborn figures . . . as to the causes of mortality among prostitutes',[26] which showed that syphilis, especially when properly treated, was now rarely fatal. Prostitutes indeed were on the whole more free from diseases of every kind than other classes of women. Compared 'at thirty-five with her sister, who perhaps is the married mother of a family, or has been a toiling slave for years in the over-heated laboratories of fashion, we shall seldom find', Acton claimed, 'that the constitutional ravages often thought to be necessary consequences of prostitution exceed those attributable to the cares of a family and the heart-wearing struggles of virtuous labour'.[27]

This alternative to the traditional picture of the harlot's progress was taken even farther by Acton when he went on to assert that 'by far the larger number . . . return sooner or later to a more or less regular course of life'.[28] He assumed that this was because the humiliation involved in all kinds of prostitution, and the poverty of the lowest, drove out all but the most hardened after about four years 'on the trade'.[29] With iron constitutions, youthful vigour and wordly wisdom greater than they could otherwise have gained, ex-prostitutes achieved respectability by marrying into 'every grade of society, from the peerage to the stable'.[30] These marriages were often to the women's advantage since 'as they are frequently barren, or have but a few children, there is reason to believe they often live in ease unknown to many women who have never strayed, or on whose unvitiated organisation matrimony has availed the burden of families'.[31] Others set themselves up as milliners, shopkeepers, lodging-house keepers or brothel-keepers, while a few passed through reformatories and others emigrated.

Acton's account of the way in which prostitutes survived and were received back into respectable society undermined not only the traditional picture of the harlot's progress but also the contrast drawn by many of his contemporaries between respectable society and the deviant minority who engaged in prostitution. The latter, in Acton's view, were far from being a minority: too many middle- and upper-class men visited prostitutes, kept mistresses or even married them, for this to be the case. And so far as the lower orders were concerned, the existence of prostitution in Britain was only one indication 'that vast masses from top to bottom of our people, have not the proper poetical or theoretical appreciation of female value, and are, at present, most indifferent to those laws of society and religion by which they are supposed to be swayed'.[32]

Thus, Acton argued, 'prostitution diffuses itself through the social fabric, though it is perceptible for a time only',[33] and any attempt to suppress it by force would not only be unacceptable in principle ('Virtue and vice, as we all know, are no subjects for enactment'),[34] but would also in practice be an endless and impossible task. Since prostitution was 'a transitory state, through which an untold number of British women are ever on their passage . . . it should be the business of us all, in the interests of the commonwealth, to see these women through that state, so as to save harmless as much as may be of the bodies and souls of them'.[35]

Inadequacy of the Evangelical Approach

These views about prostitution and its relation to society were highly controversial. In 1857, according to Acton, they were 'startling',[36] and in 1870 William Logan, the Glasgow City Missionary and writer on prostitution, described them as 'absurd'.[37] To those of an Evangelical disposition such ideas seemed subversive of the sort of moral standards they wished to promote, since whatever Acton might have written about the possibility of individual purity, in dealing with the problem in general he seemed prepared not only to accept a second-best morality, but also to suggest that the acceptance of a second-best morality would not lead to those individual and social disasters which the Evangelicals feared. The Evangelical strategy, grounded in the idea that the prostitute's 'end is bitter as wormwood'[38] and that as a class they were 'stamped with the indignation of Him whose laws they have violated',[39] was seriously threatened by the suggestion that there were other ways out of the trade than death or dramatic repentance. And it must have sounded like the devil quoting Scripture when Acton suggested 'that an all-wise, all-merciful God has provided these escapes' and that

> those are less impious and erring, than furthering God's will, who would widen the gates of the fold of penitence and rest, gather by all possible means yet another crop of Christian souls and claim the Christian's noble birthright of rejoicing over more and yet more repentant sinners.[40]

Evangelicals would have grown even more uneasy when Acton went on to discuss the practical implications of his view, since his criticism of penitentiaries, for example, went far beyond that of Tait: not only were they inadequate, he argued, but they would make the problem worse: a prostitute whose past was decently shrouded by marriage might well be accepted back into her own village, even if what she had been was suspected or known: a girl might have a 'misfortune', or even two, and it would be overlooked, but since 'these bucolic ways are very curious'[41] a woman who returned home as a repentant prostitute would not be forgiven. Evangelical Midnight Meetings for prostitutes were, by much the same token, Acton argued, 'about the worst . . . of all the useless expedients adopted for remedying by private measures public wrong'.[42]

Here Acton's alternative came most openly into conflict with the views of Evangelicals, since although they favoured some state intervention — to keep prostitutes off the streets and to suppress brothels — they did not favour intervention which could be construed as state recognition — or worse, state regulation — of prostitutes. Yet it was something of this kind, some form of state intervention based on the recognition that 'prostitution as a system'[43] existed on a large scale in contemporary Britain, which Acton saw as most imperative.

Local Causes and Venereal Disease

Two factors which may well have been significant in making Acton adopt a different approach to that of the Evangelicals were what he referred to as the 'local causes' of prostitution, and his own professional interest in venereal disease.

In describing the causes of prostitution, Acton, like Tait, had divided them into two broad categories, the Primary or Universal and the Secondary or Special, which roughly corresponded to Tait's categories of Natural and Accidental respectively. But the Secondary or Special causes of prostitution, in Acton's scheme, were subdivided into three further categories: the individual, the artificial and the local, the first of these being causes which brought individuals into the system, the other two being responsible for the system itself. Some of the individual causes, notably 'idleness, love of dress, love of pleasure',[44] were manifestations of the primary causes, in that they arose 'independently of the accidents of birth, fortune and education'[45] — but since they were not present in everyone, they demanded a separate category: other individual causes, such as 'seduction, poverty ... vicious training and associations, and evil habits'[46] were manifestations in the individual of the artificial and local causes. None of this differed significantly from Tait's scheme, nor did the artificial causes, which were similar to his accidental ones: the 'unnatural' marriage customs of the middle classes, based on a 'morbid'[47] fear of poverty, and leading to concubinage, contributed artificial causes on the side of demand; while, on the side of supply, seduction was not nearly so significant an artificial cause as 'cruel biting poverty' among 'actresses, milliners, shop girls, domestic servants, and women employed in factories or working in agricultural gangs'.[48] These artificial causes activated the primary, as did 'the promiscuous herding of the sexes' in 'low lodging-houses' and 'the miserable dwellings of the very poor':[49] under these circumstances decency was impossible and 'in the illicit intercourse to which such a position frequently gives rise, it is not always that the tie of blood is respected'. 'Certain it is,' Acton wrote, 'that when the relationship is even but one degree removed from that of brother and sister, that tie is frequently overlooked.'[50]

Much of this, then, was similar to Tait's inventory. Acton's third class of secondary causes of prostitution, the local, however, introduced a new emphasis. What Acton had in mind here were social circumstances particularly conducive to prostitution, notably those of garrison towns. In the army, except in India, 93 out of every 100 men were unmarried.[51] Prostitution was, therefore, in special demand in garrison towns, just as it was in seaports. Other places where it was specially likely to be found were factory towns, large cities, and agricultural areas where the gang system was in operation. Here, Acton admitted, the problem was less that of prostitution than of 'general immorality'.[52] This was, however, he added, 'immaterial'[53] to his present purpose.

Causes of prostitution such as fell within Acton's 'local' category had not of course been overlooked by previous writers. Wardlaw, for example, had pointed out that, as a Glasgow resident, he must add to Tait's list of causes 'the corrupting influence of extensive factories',[54] and Tait himself had emphasised that soldiers, especially Highland soldiers (because of their dress), were 'dangerous enemies to the female portion of the population'.[55] But Tait has put this down under the head of seduction (an accidental cause), whereas Acton (who, unlike Tait, was here concerned only with the men and not their officers), listing this as a local cause, argued that thus 'prostitution is by the state made a necessity'.[56]

Acton's use of 'necessity' here may seem inconsistent with his earlier criticism of the safety-valve theory and his remarks about the possibility of continence. He had not, however, spoken of continence as something to be expected of a man who had reached marriageable age; and here was arguing that the state, in practice, prevented certain men from marrying. It was therefore not entirely inconsistent to use the term 'necessity'. And it was certainly more humane than Tait's moralistic view which blamed the soldiers for 'the dissolute and idle life which they follow'[57] (although perhaps Tait was in his way more humane by including officers in his criticism).

This shift in emphasis, then, reflected the growth of a more therapeutic attitude (also, perhaps, growth in the size of the army, for Tait had been writing in the period following its post-war rundown). And the growth of this therapeutic attitude reflected developments in the treatment of venereal disease which had taken place during the intervening period. Acton himself certainly believed that improvement had taken place. In private practice, he wrote, patients were now more willing to present themselves when the disease was in its early stages; diagnosis and treatment were now much better; and medical science had 'been assisted by the almost complete abstinence of the upper classes generally from intoxication, though not from liquor, and the liberal ablutions now so much and so generally in fashion'.[58] Hospital treatment, as far as the other classes of the population were concerned, had also much improved: severe manifestations of syphilis were rare, gonorrhoea was now more common than syphilis, and it too was a milder form of disease than in the past.

These changes made for a better prognosis in all cases of venereal disease, and thus made its continued existence seem more intolerable than when much less could be done for sufferers from it. It was accordingly no longer appropriate to see those infected with it as under divine punishment;[59] and it was least of all appropriate for the state to take this view, when it was itself responsible for putting men at risk.

England and the Continent

The case for some form of state recognition of prostitution — as Acton argued it — thus rested upon a 'realistic' social and medical analysis of the nature of the existing problem. This analysis, he stated, was based not on 'fervid imagination, but hard memory and the experience of our profession'.[60] His case also rested, he argued, on Christian foundations: 'true religion' demanded that his findings and 'the real interests of the masses should not be ignored or set aside, only through fear of grating on the fanciful belief of poetical men and ladylike politicians, or breaking down their plaster-images of a perfectly genteel and virtuous polity'.[61]

To establish his case, however, it was essential to meet the objections which his predecessors and many of his contemporaries had raised simply by pointing across the Channel. Tait and Wardlaw, for example, had raised these objections, and had to their own satisfaction demolished the arguments put forward in favour of state regulation by the French authority, Parent-Duchatelet.[62] They had done this by attacking the safety-valve theory. But, as we have already noted, Acton also disagreed with this theory: he had 'only the most unmitigated abhorrence and contempt' for 'cold-blooded reasoners' who 'desire to obtain by legal enactments immunity from danger in the gratification of base desires' or who, 'regarding prostitution as the safety-valve of society, wish to preserve, at the expense of others, their own wives and daughters from contamination . . . Their maladies and pain deserve no sympathy,' he declared, 'and as for their wives and daughters, I can only join in the indignant remonstrance "who are they that they should be considered while others are left to perish?" '[63]

Holding such views, then, Acton was able to approach the question of

Continental state regulation as one who can touch pitch without being defiled. Having first-hand knowledge of France — he had trained at hospitals in Paris as well as in London — he would not deny that the French system of licensing prostitutes, so 'repugnant to English feelings',[64] could be very cruel and contained many evils. But such evils were not a necessary part of all systems of regulating prostitution: the 'terrible'[65] public brothels of Paris, and their keepers — 'a vicious and, as a general rule, ferocious mercenary band, tyrannising over the unfortunate helots who form their stock-in-trade, and abjectly crouching before the inspector, the surgeon and the mouchard'[66] — were not typical of all the Continental regulation systems; and even the French system had its softer aspects: the authorities made great efforts to dissuade young women from being licensed, often sending them back to their parents or placing them in reformatories 'at the public cost';[67] and French charity put the English to shame. It was true of course, Acton admitted, that the French system was not able totally to suppress clandestine prostitution, but the attempt kept many more clandestine prostitutes off the streets in Paris than in London. Thus the health risk they constituted was reduced, while the public prostitutes, being regularly examined — and if diseased, treated and cured — also presented a low health risk. Any argument against the practical usefulness of the licensing system in health terms had, therefore, more relevance to its operations than to the system in principle. England, moreover, came out very badly by comparison: the English, with their voluntary system, exhibited 'a perverse determination to ignore the presence of a vast mass of evil'; they allowed venereal disease to carry on 'its ravages unchecked, private charity being unequal to the task of combating an evil so gigantic'; and their streets were 'a standing disgrace, the police being unable, with the limited authority intrusted to them, to cope with the disorderly characters that throng them'.[68]

The reason for this contrast, wrote Acton, was that the French unlike the English had 'the merit of being logical'.[69] Confronted with a serious public health problem, they acted 'in accordance with common sense',[70] unlike the English, whose very arguments against a licensing system were self-contradictory. Some argued, for example, that the result of a licensing system was 'to lend to prostitution the appearance, at least, of a lawful calling, and to diminish sensibly both in men and women the sense of shame'.[71] Other opponents of licensing, however, argued that it was so degrading that no English prostitute would put up with it. These arguments, Acton observed, were contradictory, and critics of licensing, if they wished to prove their case must choose between them. He advised them to choose the first: if they did, he thought, 'probably . . . their position will prove impregnable'.[72]

Acton was able to offer this helpful piece of advice because, being English and not French, he was not in the end a defender of the licensing any more than of the 'voluntary system', but of a 'middle path that may be safely followed'.[73] This middle way, he believed, was provided by the Contagious Diseases Act, by which prostitution was 'checked and regulated without being licensed'.[74] Some of its provisions, he admitted, were 'open to criticism'.[75] But in principle it was 'utterly different'[76] from licensing, even if this was not always appreciated by its critics.

The Contagious Diseases Acts

This point was central to the debate into which both the Free and United Presbyterian churches were being drawn, and Acton's views have been examined at length here because they show that the moral problems involved were more complex than would always be apparent in the churches' debates. Before turning to examine these debates, however, we must first see what the provisions of the Contagious Diseases Acts were, noting what Acton found to criticise in them and how he defended them against the two major arguments of their opponents.

The Contagious Diseases Acts of 1864, 1866 and 1869 were passed because many people within and outside the army and navy were concerned about the large numbers of soldiers and sailors who suffered from venereal disease and were therefore unfit for active service. The general level of health in the services was poor enough at the best of times, but after the report of a Departmental Committee in 1862 had pointed out the large part venereal disease played in this, it seemed imperative to do something about it in particular. No doubt, as Acton observed, 'the loss sustained by the public purse' had 'touched . . . the cupidity of the legislature',[77] so that government action was not simply a matter of conscience, duty and obligation. But a good deal of medical, ecclesiastical and public opinion in general also supported the passage of the Acts[78] — although, as their opponents were always quick to point out, the relevant parliamentary business had been transacted with the minimum of publicity.

The Contagious Diseases Acts, then, were designed to protect soldiers and sailors from infection with venereal disease, by providing for the compulsory medical examination of prostitutes. The first Act of 1864 gave the police in eleven areas powers to report, to a justice of the peace, women whom they had reason to believe were infected common prostitutes. The justice could then compel the woman to be medically examined in a Lock hospital, where if she was diseased she could be kept for three months. This Act, which also included provisions for the prosecution of those who kept brothels without disclosing that the women in them were diseased, was a temporary measure, but after a favourable report from a Departmental Committee, the Act of 1866 was passed. Under its provisions the police need no longer believe the woman to be diseased: it was enough for them to have reason to believe that she was a common prostitute. The justice of the peace before whom she appeared could then order her to submit to periodical medical inspection for up to a year, and if she were diseased she could be detained in hospital for six months. Under this Act also a woman could voluntarily apply, in the presence of the police, to be regularly inspected; and once in hospital, either voluntarily or under compulsion, she could, if she thought that she was being detained too long, apply to a justice for release. In 1869, as the result of a further Act the maximum period of detention in hospital was increased to nine months.

Acton was on the whole satisfied with the medical consequences of the Acts. Visiting various hospitals where patients were detained, in 1868, he found that the women suffered little pain as a result of treatment, and although many of them were re-admitted with great frequency, they were cured very rapidly. Most of them, in fact, were cured, and at Aldershot, for example, nearly all submitted voluntarily to examination.[79] After some initial reluctance, prostitutes came to accept the system and, according to Acton's medical informants,[80] those who did not, and who protested most strenuously that they were neither prostitutes nor diseased, were usually found to be among the most badly infected. The police, his informants agreed, 'who have shown marvellous tact and judgement in carrying out their duties, have no real difficulty in applying the Act to all *known* prostitutes'.[81]

'The real difficulty', one of his medical informants remarked, lay in bringing clandestine prostitutes under the provisions of the Act; and here, Acton admitted, mistakes had been made. Acton was careful not to be too critical of the police, who 'are, as a rule, undoubtedly worthy men'.[82] But 'to guard against tyrannical and indiscreet behaviour in the performance of the difficult duties created by the Act',[83] the police (especially if the Acts were extended) should be responsible to persons 'of superior position and education'.[84] Without wanting to disparage the police, Acton advised that 'this duty should be entrusted to gentlemen and not left to mere police inspectors'.[85] At the same time he was anxious that prostitutes should not, as in France, be given a card when registered, since this would be too much like a licensing system and would in any case be unnecessary, given 'a little additional trouble'[86] on the part of the police.

Acton made some other criticisms of the operation of the Acts which were of a more specifically medical nature. His attitude to the police and to licensing is however the crucial issue here, since it illustrates the sort of opposition the Acts, and consequently any attempt to extend them, were running into.

The movement to have the Acts extended to the general population had in fact already begun. An association dedicated to achieving this purpose had been formed and a Bill to this end was to be presented to Parliament by the Home Secretary in 1872. It was therefore important for its defenders to establish their case. The efficacy of the Contagious Diseases Acts was not seriously in question at this stage: statistics seemed to show that the health of the services had improved as a result, and a Royal Commission of 1870-71, while it had come out against periodic medical examinations, had approved of the provisions of the 1864 Act. The two points at issue therefore were the fundamental ones of religion and civil liberty.

Religious Objections

The religious argument against regulation was that it licensed sin and even encouraged it by removing dangers from the sinner's path. Acton, as we have already noted, was at pains to repudiate the first part of this argument by pointing out that the Acts were not the same thing as a licensing system. Under both systems the state recognised prostitution and enforced examination and detention where necessary. The licensing system however did more: it 'licenses the plying of a shameful trade on certain conditions fixed by law'.[87] Whereas the Contagious

Diseases Acts, while based on the assumption that 'it is useless to deny or ignore the fact that prostitution exists' and that 'to strive to put it down is . . . worse than useless', were based on the further assumption that prostitution was 'a thing to be kept within certain bounds'.[88] The Acts were a recognition that the state could not prevent women from taking to prostitution, but by the Acts the state told the women that ' "we can, and will take care that your shameful lives shall no longer work injury to the health of others or outrage public decency" '.[89] The Acts were, Acton argued, analogous to the Divorce Courts which had recently been set up in England: the existence of these Courts recognised adultery, but could not be said to encourage it.

In dealing with the second part of the religious argument, Acton admitted that 'many worthy persons'[90] were of the opinion that ' "The present chances of contracting disease is the strongest means of deterring men from being unchaste" ' and that if the risk was removed ' "you put a premium on fornication, discourage matrimony and upset society" '.[91] But, he argued, however much this fear might deter 'a gentleman of education and refinement', for every thousand such there were 'ten thousand thoughtless, passionate habitually licentious men' who did not heed it, especially as they could usually point to 'some grey-haired offender, permitted by Providence to "go on still in the way of his wickedness", for every "frightful example" that can be adduced on the other side'.[92]

Civil Liberty

The other argument to be faced was that of civil liberty. The Acts were, their opponents held, 'invasions of private liberty, and therefore intolerable in the land which holds itself to be the peculiar home of freedom'.[93] This liberty, 'purchased by our fathers' blood' was, Acton agreed, 'a noble possession'.[94] It included, moreover, 'the right to sin as much as we please, so long only as we do not thereby commit any offence cognizable at law, against the property or person of our fellow subjects'.[95] Englishmen had a right to 'gamble, drink and whore', wrote Acton, but — and here was the rub — while 'the first must be done to a certain extent in private' and 'the second must not cause public commotion', the third 'may be done without any restriction whatever'.[96]

This, Acton believed, was taking liberty too far. Fishmongers had not the right to endanger public health by selling stale fish, nor butchers by selling tainted meat.[97] If they did they were punished, and so by the same token should diseased prostitutes be. It was true of course that this argument did not entirely cover the case, since the fishmonger was pursuing an honest calling unlawfully, while the prostitute's calling precluded honesty from the start. But the law on gambling provided a further analogy to complete it. Gambling was immoral, and was prohibited in public. Nevertheless someone who cheated at gambling could be punished for obtaining money by false pretence. 'The cases,' wrote Acton, 'are analogous . . . No man would willingly play with a cheat, neither would any man in possession of his senses knowingly go with a diseased woman.'[98] If it was argued, farther, that the case was still not covered, since the cheat was punished in retrospect, and was not under perpetual surveillance, then, Acton pointed out, the case of compulsory vaccination, where the law, in the interests of public health, interfered with private liberty in advance of possible danger, provided a suitable comparison. Farther legal analogies were provided: by the law for the suppression of betting houses, which established the principle 'that persons who will persist in doing an immoral thing must not do it in such a manner as to place temptation in the way of the thoughtless and ignorant';[99] by laws protecting minors and women in cases where property and contracts were concerned — the argument here being that the Contagious Diseases Acts protected prostitutes themselves from the consequences of a way of life almost as inevitable in their case as minority or femininity in the analogy; and by the Habitual Criminals Bill which in their case presumed guilt until innocence was shown.

By these analogies with what was mostly recent legislation Acton attempted to show that prostitutes and their customers, like other sections of the community, must accept a greater degree of official interference in the interests of public health. This was of course a highly debatable area, which had been referred to by J.S. Mill in *On Liberty* (1859) to illustrate the conflict between respect for individual liberty and the necessity of state interference with those whose activities were subversive of the public good. Mill had been uncertain how to resolve the question, and had written:

> Fornication, for example, must be tolerated, and so must gambling, but should a person be free to be a pimp, or to keep a gambling house? The case is one of those which lie on the exact boundary line between the two principles, and it is not apparent to which of the two it properly belongs. There are arguments on both sides.[100]

But Mill's uncertainty in the particular cases he mentioned had been overtaken by legislative events, and in the Contagious Diseases Acts, the principle of the necessity of state interference seemed to have been so strongly affirmed that Acton was able to suggest that 'the law that permits without restraining is in reality an accomplice, and chargeable with the evils which it refuses to remedy'.[101] A major difficulty, however, which those who wished to defend the Acts and extend them on such grounds would encounter, was that legislation of the kind mentioned by Acton in support of his position was based upon no clear philosophical foundations. As Burn has pointed out, the measures involved were 'the product of unco-ordinated decisions, responses provoked by anger or fear or pity or impatience':[102] ' "evils" . . . were dealt with . . . as they came to light';[103] and while 'on the whole these restrictions on individual liberty were moralistic and the morality which they tended to promote was, more or less, that of the religious, fairly well-educated middle class',[104] by no means all such measures were of this description.

The absence of any clear guiding principles behind such legislation created difficulties not simply for those who wished to endorse and extend the provisions of the Contagious Diseases Acts, but also for Scottish churchmen who wished to oppose and repeal them. Invasion of private liberty in the interest of godliness and morality was good Calvinism, but although Wardlaw, for example, had been able to sweep away arguments about 'encroachment on the liberties of the subject'[105] when he called for stricter penalties for those who seduced minors, he as much as Acton had felt the need to support his arguments by comparing penalties for seduction with the analogy of penalties for cheating at gaming. That he felt this need was an indication of how far social conditions and the cultural climate had changed since the time of the Reformation. Now that they were changing again, with the question of public health and the Contagious Diseases Acts introducing even more complex cross-currents of public opinion, it was far from obvious what attitude the Scottish churches ought to adopt, and on what grounds.

CHAPTER THIRTEEN

Repealing the Contagious Diseases Acts

Establishment Silence

THE problem of what attitude they should adopt to the Contagious Diseases Acts immediately divided the Scottish churches. The Church of Scotland Assembly said absolutely nothing, and maintained an enigmatic silence as to its motives.[1] The Free Assembly and the United Presbyterian Synod leapt on the abolitionist bandwagon almost without looking, and thereafter maintained a steady stream of arguments for having done so.

Since it chose not to explain its silence, we can only guess why the Establishment said nothing on the subject. Indifference to the serious social problem of prostitution was probably not the reason since, as we have seen,[2] the Christian Life and Work committee, although highly reticent, was aware of it, and of the debate surrounding the Acts. It is more likely that reticence about entering into possible conflict with Government over a matter which divided public opinion — and probably also opinion within the Church of Scotland — was the decisive factor which led the Scottish Establishment, like its English equivalent,[3] to keep silence.

Neither the United Presbyterian Synod nor the Free Assembly were constrained by such considerations, and there were those in the latter who took a dim view of the Establishment's position. 'I am not aware,' the Reverend Mr. Paton of Dalbeattie informed the Free Assembly in 1885, 'that the Established Church has denounced them (the Acts) or petitioned against them; and I regret this fact all the more, seeing that this Church claims to be the bulwark of national order.'[4] It was not a charge which could be laid against his own Assembly or the United Presbyterian Synod. Petitions from these bodies to Parliament, demanding immediate repeal of the Acts, were to be an annual event from 1871 until 1886, when their demands were finally met.

Free Church and United Presbyterian Objections

The Free Church's first petition for repeal of the Acts, which was sent to Parliament in 1871, rested on six objections to them: first, they had been passed with so little publicity that they could not be regarded as expressing the will of the people; second, they caused physical and mental suffering to the women involved;

third, they infringed these women's constitutional rights; fourth, they were unlikely to succeed in their aim; fifth, they were immoral, contrary to God's law, and likely to bring down divine judgement; and sixth, while venereal disease was a serious problem, the Acts hindered other 'more safe, scriptural and constitutional'[5] ways of dealing with it.[6] The United Presbyterian Synod's petition of the same year made much the same objections, emphasising that women were not the only sex responsible for spreading venereal disease, that not only 'gross cruelty' but considerable injustice was involved in the Acts' operations (since many innocent women were apprehended), and that the Acts had a 'hardening and debasing'[7] effect on the women subjected to them.[8]

Government Re-appraisal

In 1871, the churches which sent these petitions, and the various other bodies and individuals who were demanding immediate repeal, had some hope of success. A Royal Commission, set up on the advice of a parliamentary committee chaired by Lord Dalhousie (who had presented the Free Church's petition in the Lords), was reconsidering the whole question. But when it reported in July 1871, they were disappointed. Although the Royal Commission recommended raising the age of consent to fourteen, and wanted to do away with special plain-clothes policemen and fortnightly medical examinations, the majority of its members were not opposed to the Contagious Diseases Acts in principle. Prostitution, in their view, was inevitable, and something had to be done about venereal disease. Their proposals added up to a return to the provisions of the 1864 Act — which they considered less open to abuse than those of 1866 and 1869.

As frequently happens, however, the government did not implement the Royal Commission's proposals. Instead it attempted to solve the problem with a Bill for the Prevention of Certain Contagious Diseases and the Better Protection of Women. This Bill, presented in 1872, included provisions for raising the age of consent and for punishing brothel-keepers. It also provided for the conviction of women who were caught soliciting or importuning (not simply — as under the Acts — if they were known or suspected to be prostitutes) as common prostitutes, and for their detention for up to nine months in hospital if they were diseased. These provisions, unlike those of the Acts, were to apply throughout the whole country.

The immediate effect of this Bill was a serious division of opinion within the abolitionist camp. Many of those who wished to see the Acts repealed were also very anxious that the age of consent should be raised, since juvenile prostitution was an extremely serious matter. Others, however, including Josephine Butler, while sympathetic to this view, believed that the remaining provisions of the Bill were too high a price to pay for this, and saw it as a worse (because more all-embracing) version of the Acts. In the event the Bill was so controversial that Gladstone's unhappy Government was forced to withdraw it. But it had given the subsequently re-united abolitionists even more grounds to fear what the

Contagious Diseases Acts might lead to, and to struggle for their repeal.

Once involved in this struggle, the Free Assembly and the United Presbyterian Synod became increasingly committed to the cause, and although 'influential persons even with the (Free) Church'[9] supported the Acts, the majority which opposed them was large enough to sustain a campaign that lasted long after repeal of the Acts in 1886 had removed the original grievances. This campaign was conducted by the United Presbyterian Temperance and Morals committee, and in the Free Assembly by a committee known initially as that 'anent The Contagious Diseases (Women) Acts 1866-9'. The latter was set up in 1873: its convener (after 1874) was Dr. William Ferguson of Kinmundy, an elder; and its members included the inevitable and indefatigable James Begg, Francis Brown Douglas, an advocate and former Lord Provost of Edinburgh, and a Major Ross — who presumably was there to keep his colleagues right on military matters.

Cost and Ineffectiveness

Each year the reports of this committee had something to add to the battery of arguments for repeal. Its first report, in 1874, was concerned with the cost of the Acts: in financial terms this was almost three times what it had been a year earlier; in human terms it meant, despite two or three hundred women 'reclaimed' under the Acts' provisions, 1,605 'new recruits for this army of sin and shame', many of whom had been 'lured up from the country under false pretences' to be 'bought and sold by the dozen "like dumb driven cattle" '.[10] What happened to these women was described in the report of the following year — they were subjected to such physical and moral suffering under the Acts that many went mad or tried to kill themselves. These costly Acts threatened 'to land the country in the demoralised condition to which they have brought other nations'[11] — a proposition supported by the United Presbyterian Professor John Ker, quoted in the 1877 report, who implied that licensing had lost the Franco-Prussian war, the French army being 'powerless to break the line of the German *Landwehr*, nerved by the thought of wife and children'.[12] Above all, the Acts were ineffective as far as disease was concerned: up to December 1874 only 30,460 of the 276,187 examinations under the Acts proved to be of diseased women — which showed quite clearly that the examination procedure was not a sanitary measure at all, but 'a commission to sin'.[13] Anyone who might doubt the ineffectiveness of the Acts was referred, in the 1877 report, to the comments of M. Lecour, head of the Paris Medical Police, whose report of 1871 admitted not only that the licensing system, despite his own great powers and vigilant men, had failed to contain prostitution and disease, but also that 'the evil must be overcome not by legislative but by moral means'.[14] To the abolitionists Lecour was the demon king of French prostitution: this statement was almost equivalent to the Pope admitting the failure of the confessional.

Much the same line of argument was followed by the United Presbyterian Synod, whose annual petitions to Parliament, while resting upon the grounds stated in 1871, increasingly tended to emphasise the sanitary ineffectiveness of the Acts and of licensing systems in general.[15] Dr. Ker, in the paper already mentioned, claimed moreover that prior to the introduction of the Acts 'the health and morals of the army were improving, year by year',[16] but that now this improvement had ceased, and deterioration had set in. The difficulty with arguments of this kind of course was proof, since the other side could usually be relied upon to produce statistics to the contrary. The 1879 report of the Free Church committee thus had to go into great detail in explaining how statistics publicised by the Vicar of Portsmouth, showing a great decline between 1865 and 1876 in the number of prostitutes and in the amount of venereal disease, in fact were misleading — since they had originally come from one of the chief policemen involved in operating the Acts. Insofar as they were accurate, they could be attributed to legal action provided for outwith the Contagious Diseases Acts. On closer inspection, the committee reported, Portsmouth under the Acts had become 'a sort of Paradise for prostitutes' and its vicar's claims, as sixteen other ministers in the town had observed, obscured the fact that it was full of juvenile and clandestine prostitutes.[17]

How valid were arguments of this kind? Were the Acts as costly in human and financial terms and as ineffective in the control of prostitution and venereal disease as the Free and United Presbyterian churches claimed? On balance it now seems as if the Acts were both costly and a failure. The evidence which Josephine Butler and her colleagues were able to collect about their human cost and the interpretation they were able to put on British and foreign facts and statistics finally persuaded Parliament to repeal the Acts. The historian half a century later was thus able in tranquillity to recollect them as 'a bad system of vice-regulation'.[18] But just how bad were they? Were the stories of wrongful arrest, cruelty and suicide which the abolitionists collected a fair index of their value, or were these exceptions which could be learned from and avoided by better supervision, as Acton had suggested? Was the French example really a fair comparison, or would England, given time and appropriately amended legislation, have developed a uniquely humane method of dealing with the sanitary problem? These questions cannot easily be answered now, because so much that has been written about the Acts since their repeal has been selective, much of it biased in favour of the opinions of the dominant and courageous figure of Josephine Butler. Yet she and her colleagues were involved in a controversy which was deeply political and theirs was not a disinterested enquiry. For this reason it is difficult to avoid the suspicion that more might be said in favour of the Acts, in terms of their cost and effectiveness, than has hitherto been written.

Making Sin Safe

The fundamental principles on which the churches' opposition rested were not those of economics, however. The first and perhaps most important of their principles was that it was wrong for the state to attempt to make sin safe. The Acts, declared the Free Church committee in 1875, were 'essentially wrong and immoral in principle' because they made 'first legal and then safe' a form of sin which 'the law of nature visits with a signal retribution'.[19]

That this was the real purpose of the Acts was demonstrated by the judicious Principal Rainy in a paper reproduced in the committee's report of the following year. The problem, Rainy admitted, was extremely difficult: prostitution, though always immoral, could not be put down by law, and 'it was difficult for any but professional men to form an adequate idea' of 'the extent and malignity' of venereal disease: but his readers were not to be confused by claims that the Acts 'afforded an opportunity for dealing with the women, so as to induce them to give up their mode of life'.[20] In some cases that might happen incidentally, but the real object of the Acts, as its supporters would admit, was different. It could be summarised by the statement that, in the Acts,

> Government says to fallen women: 'We will induce you to leave your miserable way of life if we can; but those of you that will persist, we shall at all events take measures to examine, that we may know whether you are diseased, and if so to cleanse you from disease, that you may not spread it.[21]

In saying this, Rainy wrote, Government was primarily concerned not with the women but with the men who might be infected by them: the fortnightly inspections of the women would not have been provided simply for the women's sake, had that end not been in view. The Acts, in short, were the only example of Government making 'arrangements for the sole object of securing that immoral Acts may be committed in such circumstances as to guard against disadvantages that ordinarily attend them'.[22] In doing this, Government, and indeed the nation, sinned and became 'an accessory before the fact'.[23] Its action, moreover, had the serious consequence of creating the impression, among the women and many men, that although 'preachers and moralists may warn against it', prostitution was sanctioned by the state and 'regarded in high quarters as a recognised institution';[24] and the principle thereby established opened up a 'new and dark career'[25] for Government. However well intentioned the supporters of the Acts might be, they had chosen the wrong course, and must find other ways of dealing with the health problem, since 'arrangements which tend to give prostitution a more recognised and stable place in the social system, are absolutely certain in the long-run to prove injurious to all kinds of health, whatever effects may be ascribed to them in the meantime'.[26]

Other leading churchmen took much the same line. The United Presbyterian Professor, John Ker, in the paper already quoted, remarked that while the nation was 'struggling to advance in the path of freedom and moral progress' the Acts were 'a stride backward ... under cover of sanitary considerations'.[27] No one should be deceived by the appointment of chaplains and matrons and other 'very industrious measures' which were being made 'to show the reformatory effects of the system', because these were simply a 'superimposed patch': the 'original idea' had been quite clearly expressed by Sir Henry Storks, one of the Acts' best-known supporters, when he had said that 'very little benefit will result from the best-advised means of prevention until prostitution is recognised as a necessity'.[28] The real nature of the Acts was reflected by what happened in Bombay, Hong Kong and Yokohama, 'where the disguise is not so necessary' and brothels were 'registered and marked to all comers as certified by our Government'.[29]

Sir Henry Storks' remark was also quoted in a paper, included in the Free Church committee's report of 1878, which had been prepared by Professor Henry Calderwood and, before his death in 1873, by Thomas Guthrie. In this, Storks' remark was given as one of the 'alleged excuses' for the Acts, the other being to guard ' "innocent wives and children" from the fearful sufferings brought upon them in consequence of the immoral life of their natural protectors'.[30] The real purpose of the Acts, these writers held, was neither that of checking immorality, nor that of stamping out 'those diseases which are its natural results', but that of curing prostitutes quickly 'in order to enable them to continue their evil practices with safety to their guilty associates'.[31]

This argument about the real purpose of the Acts, which was advanced on numerous other occasions in the Free Assembly[32] and the United Presbyterian Synod, put an interpretation upon the intentions of their supporters which was difficult for them to deny. Sir Henry Storks was correctly identified as one of the leaders of the regulationists. He had been High Commissioner in Malta, where he had gained a rather misleading impression of the sanitary effectiveness of Regulation,[33] and thereafter became an enthusiastic supporter of such measures. Much of course turned upon what was meant by calling prostitution a necessity, especially if opponents of the Acts recognised that prostitution could not be put down by law. But substantially, the churchmen we have mentioned were correct in saying that what Rainy put into the mouth of Government was the position of the Acts' defenders. In this, Rainy was in fact writing in terms almost identical with those in which Acton had written.[34] Acton and those who thought as he did clearly were concerned primarily with protecting men from infection, and any attempt to persuade women to give up prostitution undoubtedly was given a much lower priority. Under these circumstances therefore it would have been difficult to deny that Government was an accessory before the fact, and that by its action prostitution was encouraged — for had not Acton himself argued that the existence of prostitution itself caused more prostitution to take place?

But then, as Acton had also observed, Government inaction as much as action made it an accessory before the fact, and prostitution already had an established place in the social system. This was something which the arguments of Rainy and the other churchmen tended to ignore, for while they admitted the existence of a health problem, they often wrote as if they, as critics, had no responsibility for solving it. Rainy, as we have seen, shifted the burden of responsibility on to the shoulders of medical and other experts. Guthrie's evasion was perhaps even worse, since a few years before the Acts were passed he had written to the *Daily Telegraph* in the following terms:

They talk, Sir, of the liberty of the subject. Let no man confound the liberty of the

> subject with licence and licentiousness, and I hold that the worst enemy of liberty is he who does so confound them. Why, the liberty is all on the side of evil-doers. I know many parents in Edinburgh who tremble to send their young men, even on lawful business, through the streets at night; I know of others who refuse to live in certain parts of the town, otherwise most desirable, on account of the temptation thrown in the way of the younger members of the family. Why should this be tolerated? Why should the liberty of the well-doing be encroached on and circumscribed by the licentiousness of evil-doers? Our magistrates should exercise the law — should clear the streets of every one of these infamous women, and make them at least decent if they cannot make them moral and virtuous. On the Continent no such offence to decency is seen.[35]

This outburst was not of course a demand for the Contagious Diseases Acts as such, but by referring to the Continent so approvingly and by demanding decency where morality might not be possible, Guthrie had been pointing in the direction of the Acts. His attack on them, and that of Rainy, insofar as they presented no positive alternative to the Acts, thus made it look as if they were exercising the harlot's prerogative, of using power over public opinion without accepting responsibility for what might happen were the Acts repealed.

In defence of these churchmen, however, it could be argued that they did suggest practical alternatives to the Acts. Professor Ker, for example, was aware of such criticism, and anxious to answer 'the wise men who fall back on their one argument in favour of the Acts — "But we must do something."'[36] In order to meet this, he cited the report of the Glasgow Chief Constable for the previous year, which showed that prosecutions had reduced the number of Glasgow brothels from 204 to 79, that police action had suppressed a great deal of soliciting on the streets, causing many prostitutes to leave the city, and that both the number of crimes in the city and the number of patients in the Lock Hospital had decreased. 'All this,' Ker stated, 'shows what can be done by wise and firm Magisterial action': and it was 'the direct reverse of the Government Acts, which legalise the vice . . . and naturally lead to the increase of vice, and by consequence, and ere very long, to an ever-enlarging circle of disease'.[37]

Claims of this kind, however, were not too difficult for the regulationists to answer, for even in the report cited by Ker it was admitted that many of the prostitutes driven out of Glasgow were 'possibly following their vicious calling elsewhere'.[38] The effectiveness of police measures of the kind described was extremely questionable; and there is some evidence to suggest that the policy of the Glasgow police may only have hardened the hard core of professional prostitutes (to whom frequent fines became in effect like licence-renewals) without removing (but perhaps intensifying) the causes of a vast amount of part-time prostitution in the urban underworld.[39] The reduction in venereal cases at the Lock Hospital, likewise, was no proof of a decline in the disease's incidence.

The churches did, however, suggest another alternative to the Contagious Diseases Acts, and this was more difficult for regulationists to answer on the grounds of principle. It appeared in the Free Church report of 1875, and in Guthrie and Calderwood's paper, and it referred to the fact, which Acton had assumed to be unalterable, that very few men in the army were married. The committee did not see this as unalterable, and 'urged the attention of all Christian patriots' to the 'anomaly in a Christian country of a great army prevented, with a few exceptions, from marrying'.[40] The army, the committee claimed, should be reorganised to 'permit the soldiers to form family ties'; and no doubt with its complaints about the expense of the Acts in mind, it remarked that 'all the statistics show that marriage means in military as in civil life steadiness, health, self respect, a longer life, freedom from invalidising (and) a superior and cheaper soldier'.[41]

This argument was difficult for regulationists to answer because the major argument against it was not one of principle but of expense. For what the Free Church wanted, more public money would presumably have had to be spent on soldiers' pay, married quarters and transport. No doubt this sounded extremely idealistic to many contemporaries, but it does in some measure save the churches' attack on the Acts from the charge of irresponsibility.

One further aspect of the churches' attack on the Acts as a way of 'making sin safe' remains open to serious questioning. What did they really believe about venereal disease? How far did they see it as a deterrent or as retribution? They certainly spoke of venereal diseases as 'the dreadful results of sin',[42] but they were vague about the nature of the causality involved. Prostitution was a sin 'which the law of nature visits with a signal retribution': the Acts, in making it safe, were thus held to 'traverse the moral law'.[43] Yet it was apparently quite different 'to endeavour to heal, and beseech the sufferer to "sin no more, lest a worse thing" befall her'.[44] The church did 'not oppose Lock Hospitals, or any approved means, including examination of the person of course, of alleviating and removing'[45] venereal disease. But it was 'quite a different thing to violate the sanctity of nature in a healthy woman, by such examination as these Acts enforce, before, and in order to, the commission of sin'.[46]

The notion of nature and of the moral law employed here was curiously confused. Leaving aside the question of compulsory examination — where they were on firmer ground and to which we shall return in a moment — the churches here seem to have been saying that treatment unaccompanied by moral teaching broke the moral law whereas treatment accompanied by it did not. Yet if venereal disease was nature's revenge, was it right under any circumstances to interfere? The probable reply to this was that mercy demanded treatment and so overruled the demands of natural law. But if that was the case, was preventive medicine of the kind employed under the Acts not also demanded by mercy? The distinction between these two kinds of medical treatment is a difficult one to sustain, since as Acton would probably have argued, the moral teaching which accompanied the former could represent little more than a pious hope, while its absence scarcely justified withholding treatment from those who almost certainly needed preventive treatment. What it meant, in this context, 'to violate the sanctity of nature in a healthy woman' — if that woman was willing to be examined — is difficult to locate on any moral map. The fact of the matter seems to have been that medical advance, and in particular the development of preventive medicine, had undermined the traditional, although sub-Christian, argument about venereal disease as a form of divine punishment.[47] The churches, however, were unwilling to give up this argument, presumably because they still believed that it was a deterrent to prostitution, despite what Acton had written to the contrary.

The Liberty of the Subject

A second fundamental objection to the Acts raised by the churches was that they violated not just the liberty of the subject, but that of the lower classes, and of women in particular. As the statements of Wardlaw and Guthrie, quoted above, have shown, this argument was not one which they had deployed against other methods of dealing with prostitutes. But once involved in the agitation for repeal, it was frequently on their lips.

This argument was popular with the abolitionists because their investigations had uncovered several cases of innocent women being arrested under the Acts as prostitutes.[48] It was also an argument which was likely to gain much popular support — for, since the Acts employed what were virtually secret police, who knew who would next be arrested, unless they were very obviously women of the middle and upper classes?

The argument that the Acts were biased against females and against the lower classes was used, as we have noted, from the beginning by both the Free and United Presbyterian committees. The former's report of 1882 summed the argument up by stating that the Acts 'are unequal laws, for one sex only — and that perhaps the least guilty. They ruthlessly degrade women, and bring many industrious and virtuous women under suspicion'.[49] The same report pointed up the class aspect by asking 'what classes of women are watched?' and letting one of the doctors involved reply, ' "dressmakers, married women, the wives of labourers and small tradesmen, and servants of course" '.[50] The Acts, in 'treating a woman as guilty until she can prove her innocence', were thus, the committee noted, 'a dangerous violation of the Constitution'.[51]

Insofar as the Acts were operated in this way, although it was not the way in which Acton had wanted them to be operated, arguments of this kind were unanswerable. Bearing in mind the sort of comments Wardlaw and Guthrie had expressed before the Acts came into being however, it is only fair to their supporters to point out that class distinction, disregard of female rights and indifference to prostitutes as persons were features which pervaded the middle and upper classes, and the churches of the time.

Repeal and After

By the end of the 'seventies the arguments of the abolitionists were gaining ground. The campaign no longer simply concerned the merits and demerits of the Contagious Diseases Acts but, especially after the creation in 1875 of The British and Continental Federation For The Abolition of Government Regulation of

Prostitution, the abolition of all and every system of regulation wherever it might be found. The Federation, again led by Josephine Butler and James Stansfield (whose total involvement in the campaign had already cost him his career in Government), attracted attention throughout Europe and beyond, held regular conferences and international congresses, and gained support for local activities, especially from women's and working men's associations.

None of this however was done without bitter opposition and often ridicule. Despite the presence in the abolitionist camp of such distinguished contemporaries as John Stuart Mill, Herbert Spencer, F.W. Newman and Florence Nightingale, influential sections of the press,[52] the medical profession and of course the services were hostile. H.A. Bruce, Home Secretary in Gladstone's first Cabinet, who had introduced the Bill of 1872, had described the abolitionists as 'hysterical and ignorant'.[53]

By 1879, however, Government was increasingly uncertain about what should be done with the Acts. Between 1870 and 1877, 8,046 petitions signed by 1,949,271 people had reached Parliament,[54] and the minority of M.P.s who voted for Bills demanding repeal was steadily growing. In 1877 a further 156 petitions signed by 20,880 people arrived.[55] Although the monster petition was something of a parliamentary commonplace,[56] and although the abolitionists remained in the minority, it was decided that the time was ripe for a Select Committee to reappraise the Acts. The possibility that repeal might save some public money was not least among the reasons why this committee was set up.

The Select Committee's work was interrupted in 1880 by the fall of Disraeli and the return of Gladstone. This helped the abolitionists, since although repeal was not strictly a party issue, the reconstituted committee now included abolitionist M.P.s, including Stansfield. This was noted with approval by the Free Church committee in 1880,[57] but the attack was kept up: Rainy and Begg both spoke against the Acts in the debate of that year,[58] and both the Assembly and the United Presbyterian Synod continued to send their annual petitions to Parliament.

The Select Committee eventually reported in 1882. Much to the disappointment of the abolitionists, the majority favoured retention of the Acts, on the grounds that they were effective, seemed not to encourage prostitution, and reduced the amount of child prostitution. The minority, however, produced another report, stating that soldiers in the areas under the Acts were no healthier or unhealthier than elsewhere, that prostitutes in those areas had greatly increased in number, and that if child prostitution had declined, it was because the police had been active in suppressing it of their own volition, and not because the Acts demanded this. This report was as effective as that of the majority, and in April 1883 Stansfield gained a parliamentary majority for a Bill to repeal the second of the Contagious Diseases Acts. This did away with the special police and the system of compulsory examination.

In May of that year the Free Church committee claimed, with some justification, that religious bodies had played a large part in the victory of the abolitionists. Their crusade, however, was far from over, and a new committee was appointed to watch over and assist further measures 'for the promotion of social purity, such as the proposed Act for the Protection of Young Women'.[59]

The White Slave Trade

Towards the end of the 'seventies some of the abolitionists became aware not only that there were child prostitutes in Britain, but that English girls were being abducted to the Continent and especially to Belgium, where they were enrolled as prostitutes. The reason for this trade was that while the age of consent[60] in most European countries was eighteen, in Britain it was only twelve: it was thus difficult to recruit children for prostitution on the Continent, where parents or others interested might find the children and bring a successful prosecution. English parents, however, had first to find the child and then to prove that she had gone unwillingly — a task made very difficult because the police (especially in Belgium) were often hand in glove with brothel-keepers and unlikely to help either in finding the girls or in proving an unwilling abduction.

That this trade was being carried on systematically was confirmed by an investigator sent to Belgium by the Home Secretary, on the prompting of Josephine Butler and others. The trade worried many people in Britain since all classes of girl were involved, some being kidnapped by apparently innocent and respectable governesses. Josephine Butler soon had a thousand ladies signing a petition to the Home Secretary demanding measures to rectify matters, including raising the age of consent. Petitions were also sent by the Free Church, as a result of an overture from the Presbytery of Ellon,[61] and by the United Presbyterian Synod. The latter demanded changes in Belgian as well as English[62] law to 'make it impossible for any woman, who is a subject of her Majesty the Queen, to be deprived of her liberty by fraud or force, and to be kept in bondage in that country for the vilest purposes'.[63]

Very soon after these petitions were sent, a Select Committee, whose members included Lord Dalhousie, was set up and reported a year later, in July 1882. Its conclusions, while doubting the unwillingness of some of the girls, in general substantiated the claims which had been made about the trade. It recommended raising the age of consent to sixteen and the age of unlawful abduction for immoral purposes from 16 to 21 (as well as some other measures designed to check the trade) and led in 1883 to a Criminal Law Amendment Bill, which incorporated these recommendations. It was to watch over this Bill that the Free Church had set up its new committee in that year.

This Bill passed through the Lords only to be shelved by the Commons in 1883 and again in 1884 on the grounds of pressure of other business. Part of the reason for this was that the Bill was concerned with abduction of juveniles into prostitution not only abroad but also at home, and while abolitionists did not underestimate the importance of this, they were still at this time preoccupied with what they considered to be the root evil, namely regulation — for attempts were still being made to reintroduce measures similar to those repealed by Parliament in 1883. On this point the Free Church for once did not see exactly eye to eye with

Josephine Butler, who had objected to certain aspects of the Bill directed against soliciting, on the ground that they were anti-woman. The Bill, said Dr. Ferguson, convener of the new as of the old committee, must be seen as an overall advance and so should be supported, especially now that Lord Shaftesbury had introduced an amendment making male as well as female 'loitering and importuning' punishable.[64]

The broadening interest of this committee in Social Purity[65] was illustrated at this time by its commendation of the Whitecross Union, founded by Ellice Hopkins, which now had an Edinburgh Council. Its aims for young men were very much in line with the church's general attitude at this time. These aims were:

> 1st. To treat all women with respect and to endeavour to protect them from wrong and degradation. 2nd. To endeavour to put down all indecent language and coarse jests. 3rd. To maintain the law of purity as equally binding upon men and women. 4th. To endeavour to spread these principles, and to help brothers and companions; and 5th. To use every possible means to fulfill the Command 'Keep thyself pure.'[66]

The third of these aims was perhaps the most important insofar as it represented a very pointed criticism of the double sexual standard of the time. 'The women of our land,' declared Dr. Ferguson, 'are awakening to the crisis that is upon us; let the men awake too, and join hand in hand that this body-and-soul-destroying vice may be driven from amongst us and purity and health restored and secured.'[67] In this demand for a single standard Josephine Butler and the Free Church were at one.

The wider interests of this committee, and its agreement with Mrs. Butler, were again reflected in the following year when its Report called for a '*Gospel Purity Crusade*', and for renewed efforts to keep up the campaign for repeal of the remaining Contagious Diseases Acts. In phraseology borrowed from Josephine Butler, it noted that ' "our real foes are the permanent officials of the great military and naval departments of the State" ',[68] who wanted to reintroduce the Acts' provisions in some form. The extent to which the patriarchs of the Free Church had been charmed by Mrs. Butler was remarkable. In the debate, Mr. Paton, the minister of Dalbeattie, declared:

> I do not know exactly the opinion of the members of this House regarding female franchise, but I most earnestly desire it; and one of my chief reasons for it is, that when the ladies have votes, they will be on the side of social legislation, and for sweeping away such obnoxious acts.[69]

Mr. Paton was roundly applauded for expressing these statements: the petition which followed, however, was for repeal of the remaining Acts and not for female suffrage.

It was the last of the Free Church's petitions against the Contagious Diseases Acts:[70] what was left of them was repealed before the Assembly met again in 1886. In the year between the Assemblies of 1885 and 1886 the Criminal Law Amendment Act also passed on to the statute book. Parliament, previously reluctant to proceed with Bills on this matter, had been precipitated into enactment by the publication of the journalist W.T. Stead's series of articles in the *Pall Mall Gazette* on 'The Maiden Tribute of Modern Babylon'. These articles confirmed the worst suspicions of many of Stead's contemporaries about the prevalence of juvenile prostitution in London, the trade in virgins for the domestic and foreign market, and the brutal atrocities which accompanied it. The low age of consent, Stead pointed out, made it impossible in most cases to proceed against those who procured, cheated, raped and half-murdered young girls. Particularly concerned to prove his allegations beyond any shadow of doubt, Stead, with the help of Josephine Butler and the Salvationist Bramwell Booth, forced a test case by himself buying a girl and then publicising what he had done. This resulted in a prison sentence of three months for Stead, but it helped to prove his case — although more substantial help was provided by his threat to name public figures, including members of the Government (from June 1885 to February 1886 the Tories were back in power), who were involved in the prostitution scene.

Stead's campaign was supported not only by Bramwell Booth, but also by other more orthodox ecclesiastical figures, including Bishop Temple of London and Cardinal Manning. The Free Assembly and the United Presbyterian Synod, meeting in 1886, also expressed their satisfaction at the passing of the Criminal Law Amendment Act as well as at the final repeal of the Contagious Diseases Acts. The former, declared Dr. Ferguson in the Free Assembly, had not been passed too soon, especially in view of revelations that 'in localities which seemed fair and pure and beautiful there had been an under-current of immorality which made one shudder to contemplate'.[71]

The deep disquiet aroused by the events of 1885-1886 obviously strengthened the Purity movement in the Free Assembly and the United Presbyterian Synod. It was in this year that the latter decided to issue its Pastoral Letter on Purity:[72] the Synod also, at this time, urged its Temperance and Public Morals committee 'to be watchful against any attempts to reintroduce the spirit of the (Contagious Diseases) Acts in the form of hospitals subsidized and controlled by Government'.[73] In the Free Assembly the Social Purity committee was discharged, but before it was, it took the question of the nation's sexual morals by the horns, declaring that while 'the attainments of the past year must be an encouragement to Christian people to persevere in seeking righteous legislation even in the face of the most formidable and persistent opposition',[74] it was now necessary to deal with the causes of prostitution rather than its effects:

> One of the most pressing needs of our time is a revolution in the morals of political life. Unless *principle* is put before *party*, and our legislators are men of Christian principles, whose views are sound on great moral questions, there is no security that our laws will be framed in accordance with the eternal laws of righteousness and truth.[75]

CHAPTER FOURTEEN

Regulation at Home and Abroad

Imperial, Colonial and Continental Vice

THE corpse of the Social Purity committee was barely cold before its convener, Dr. Ferguson,[1] was up on his feet again, informing the Assembly of 1887 that there was still in operation, in seventy stations in India and more than eleven in the Crown Colonies, a system of state-regulated prostitution similar to that which they thought had been abolished by the repeal of the Contagious Diseases Acts. The Great Crusade, far from having ended, was only entering a new phase, to which the Free Assembly responded by appointing a new Committee on the State-Regulation of Vice, under the convenership of the Rev. John Dymock of Kemnay in Aberdeenshire and with Dr. Ferguson among its members.

This committee and the United Presbyterian Committee on Temperance and Morals were if anything more active than their predecessors. A motive for this was provided by the churches' missionary interest, especially in India where, according to Dr. Ferguson, the system of state-regulated vice was 'seriously interfering with the work of the Christian church'.[2] The same point was made in the United Presbyterian Synod, which deprecated 'the setting before those under our rule in foreign lands of an example so lowering to the fair fame of our country, and so dishonouring to our Christian civilization'.[3]

To illustrate this point a member of the United Presbyterian committee had written an article for the church's *Missionary Record*, which appeared in November 1887. Under the title 'Britain's Mission of Vice to the World', the writer set out to show how 'both nationally by our Government, and individually by our actions, we are spreading evil, vice and death, among millions of our fellow creatures'.[4] He was concerned, in particular, with drunkenness and impurity. The former, 'our chief national vice', had 'degraded and destroyed . . . many native races' including 'the Red Indians of the Far West, the "Blacks" of Australia (and) the Maories of New Zealand'.[5] Currently it was most conspicuous in South and West Africa and in India. In South Africa, native customs discouraging or even forbidding drink and drunkenness had been disrupted by the arrival of the British, with 'the Bible in one hand and the brandy bottle in the other';[6] in West Africa, British firms, 'the members of which are most excellent men, many of them . . . sincere Christians', imported from Germany and sold, sometimes at a profit of 700 per cent., spirit 'so strong that the native painters use it instead of turpentine';[7] and in India, where although 'there have always been native intoxicating drinks, and, in consequence, native drunkards', the introduction of European habits and the custom of raising revenue by auctioning licences to the highest bidder had wrought havoc: 'the example of their rulers has led many native gentlemen to acquire intemperate habits, their comparatively feeble constitution, and the climate of the country, leading them quickly to ruin'.[8]

As far as impurity was concerned, however, there was little in this writer's view which the British could teach India. 'The natives, alas,' he declared, 'do not need to be encouraged in this direction. While their creed forbids drunkenness it panders to lust.'[9] Yet, he went on, 'if heathen religions thus approve of prostitution, is that any reason why we, with our enlightened Christianity should do the same?'[10] This, however, was just what Great Britain had done. Among its soldiers and sailors, 'the great proportion of which is celibate', he stated, 'sexual indulgence is regarded by the authorities as a necessary evil which, as it cannot be repressed, should be regulated and guarded'.[11] After the passing of the Contagious Diseases Acts the system had quickly been implemented overseas, with dire consequences. In Hong Kong 'men have been actually employed and paid by the representatives of the Queen of England to compass the fall of Chinese women, in order to lead them to enrol themselves in the ranks of registered unfortunates'; and Sir J. Pope-Hennessy, for protesting about this 'slavery ... under the flag of England',[12] had been forced to give up his governorship of the colony. The military authorities were 'so utterly indifferent ... to public opinion at home'[13] that whenever Egypt and Burmah were occupied (Egypt in 1882 and Upper Burmah in 1886), state-regulated prostitution was immediately introduced. Some progress, the writer was glad to say, had been made: repeal at home had led to the suspension or abolition of regulation in Jamaica, Trinidad, Barbadoes and Labuan, and it was expected soon to cease in Ceylon, Hong Kong, the Straits Settlement, Malta and Gibraltar. 'This is something to be thankful for. But much remains to be done.'[14] The list of places where regulation continued included India, Burmah, Egypt, Canada, Cape Colony, Queensland, Victoria, Tasmania, New Zealand and Fiji — 'that wonderful trophy of modern Missions'.[15]

The missionary motive for repeal, then, was prominent. This writer repeated the assertion that in India regulation was 'one of the most serious obstacles to the spread of the gospel'.[16] Missionaries and their wives protested against it, but their authority was undermined 'when the people turn to us and say "the Government allows it" '.[17] Together with drink and the opium trade, it made the missionary's task incalculably more difficult — 'Our work now in several parts of the globe is not merely to dispel heathen error, but to destroy the vices which we ourselves have introduced and fostered.'[18]

These complaints were re-echoed in the Free Assembly, whose committee had sent all of its ministers a copy of the Tract, 'Slavery under the British Flag', written by Josephine Butler's friend Alfred Dyer. Dyer was now in India gathering more information and learning appalling things, the Assembly was told. 'Some medical and military officers,' the committee stated, had even printed a document proposing 'a regular recruiting system, with a capitation fee of three rupees' to gather 'the greatest number of the most attractive women they can obtain to fill the barracks or camps in which the poor slaves of British lust are confined'.[19] Despite the evasive statements of the India Office and the 'painful and repulsive'[20] nature of the subject, the Church must continue to protest.

Protest followed. The committee and that of the United Presbyterian Synod joined with local Vigilance Associations to organise public meetings in Edinburgh, Glasgow, Dundee and Aberdeen. These, held in November 1887, were addressed 'by well-known speakers from the south, such as Mrs. Ormiston Chant,[21] H.J. Wilson, MP[22] and others, and also by local ministers and laymen of personal weight and representative character'.[23] The Free and United Presbyterian committees had hoped to involve the Church of Scotland as well, but 'it was found that there existed no established Church Committee within whose province it lay to take part in such a project'.[24]

The campaign thus launched was to be fought against regulation in three areas: in India, in the Colonies, and on the Continent. What the churches could do about the last of these, beyond sending representatives to meetings of the International Federation, was limited, but they kept their members informed of progress on that front year by year. They were also limited in what they could do about the self-governing colonies, although here they took more active measures to stimulate their Presbyterian and Protestant colleagues in those countries to set up their own repeal movements.[25] (They had been advised to do this in 1888 by the Colonial Secretary, Lord Knutsford, the first in a series of Colonial Secretaries, for whose abolitionist efforts in the other colonies they had, in general, only praise.[26]) The great problem however was India.

India

The problem, more precisely, was the Indian Army, in which disease was rife and the mortality rate had long been high.[27] Much of the disease could be attributed to tropical and insanitary conditions, but a good deal of it was venereal, and attempts to deal with venereal disease in the Indian Army dated at least from the early years of the nineteenth century. Various experiments had been made with the medical supervision of prostitutes: Lock Hospitals were opened 'in one Presidency or another because the state of things is so bad, closed because things only go on getting worse, and opened again because they have become worse still'.[28]

Things became worse than ever before, or at least seemed so to the authorities after the Mutiny, when large numbers of young soldiers were sent out to India and the proportion of married men, which under the East India Company had been between 20 and 30 per cent., sank to 12 and eventually to 4 per cent.[29] The tide of venereal disease seemed to be rising; and a Royal Commission on the health of the Indian Army, reporting in the early 'sixties, attempted to check it by recommending, on the one hand, greater opportunities for alternative forms of recreation and amusement for the soldiers and, on the other, regular medical inspection of prostitutes around the garrisons. As a result Lock Hospitals were again opened, in 1865 and 1867, but this had no sooner been done than the epidemic waned and, according to the official figures, the number of hospital admissions for venereal disease went down from 352 per 1000 in 1861 to 160 per 1000 in 1867. The figures then however proceeded to rise again, reaching 293 per 1000 in 1884.[30]

The military authorities were not sure what to make of these figures, even if it could be assumed that they were in any sense accurate.[31] The increase of the later years tended to be blamed upon the introduction of the Short Service System in 1873 (for what Acton would have called the demand), and the great famine of 1877 (for what he would have called the supply). During the years between 1867 and 1884, when the Regulation System was in operation, the Army Sanitary Commission (a medico-military body whose reports were based on local information) was at first optimistic about the success of the new measures, but it soon became uncertain as reports from different stations showed a great variety of results. Causes of this were sought, and suggestions included police inefficiency and bribery, as well as the soldiers' reluctance to identify infected women. Stronger measures were then called for, and attempts were made to round up more and more infected women: it was even suggested that informers should be paid. But by 1882 the causes of the diseases' fluctuations remained obscure, and the Government of India refused to extend the system to new stations, arguing that it had been a failure in the old ones.[32] Soon after this it went on, with the support of the Army Sanitary Commission, to recommend that the system should be totally abolished. This, however, was a highly controversial recommendation, not only because opinion on the subject was so divided (disease rates in Bombay had recently soared after an experiment in abolition), but also because the system was still in force (under the Contagious Diseases Acts) in England. The suggestion of abolition was thus amended to one of suspension, and this was implemented about 1885, when most of the Lock hospitals were closed. Disease, however, then increased more rapidly than before, and the hospitals were re-opened in 1887.[33]

The New Cantonment Act 1889

It was about this point that the British abolitionists got wind of what was happening. Hitherto they had not paid much attention to India, assuming perhaps that repeal of the Contagious Diseases Acts would apply there also. But if they did assume this they were mistaken, for the Acts had applied only to military stations at Madras, Bombay and Bassein. Elsewhere regulation was provided under the older, specifically Indian, Cantonment Act. This Act had not been repealed, but only suspended, and what this suspension meant in practice was far from clear, especially if reports of the kind being retailed to the Free Assembly were well-founded.

Such apparent indifference to the wishes of the Imperial Parliament outraged the abolitionists, and in 1888 Parliament itself was sufficiently indignant to resolve unanimously, on the motion of a leading abolitionist,[34] that 'any mere suspension of measures for the compulsory examination of women, and for licensing and regulating prostitution in India, is insufficient, and the legislation which enjoins, authorises or permits such measures ought to be repealed'. But this resolution was as far as the Commons could go. Any implementation had to lie with the Government of India.

The churches however wished to go farther, the Synod (and its presbyteries) sending memorials, and the Free Church a deputation, to Lord Cross, India Secretary in Lord Salisbury's administration. The Synod, afraid that 'the military authorities in India might do all in their power to evade'[35] the resolution, urged Lord Cross to give practical effect to it. But the Free Church deputation, although they 'felt that it was a great advantage to have made manifest the earnest and determined attitude of a body admitted, by Her Majesty's Secretary, to be so influential as the Free Church of Scotland', feared that no 'definite promise of decided action'[36] had been obtained from his Lordship. In an attempt to press matters farther they also sent a memorial to Lord Lansdowne, the newly appointed Viceroy, urging him to exercise his 'Viceregal authority on the side of purity and righteousness'.[37]

The Viceregal authority and the Government of India acknowledged the necessity of legislating in accordance with the 1888 Resolution of the Commons by repealing the Cantonment Act and introducing a new one. At the last moment however the New Cantonment Act was amended by the addition of a clause 'legalising "all orders, declarations, rules and regulations made" under the old Act'.[38] These orders and rules, the Free Church committee observed, 'included, strange to say, the disgraceful regulations unanimously condemned by the whole House of Commons'.[39] These might look innocent, but 'to practised eyes' they betrayed 'the cloven hoof', and any charitable interpretation of them was ruled out — for the Indian authorities had connived at regulation when the old Acts had theoretically been suspended, and already some of the Anglo-Indian papers were 'shamelessly' exulting that ' "the old order of things will be enforced under another name" '.[40]

Protest was apparently unavailing. A Missionary Conference at Calcutta had tried to dissuade the Government of India from passing the new Act, but without success. At home, various bodies including the Wesleyan Conference Social Purity Committee and the Free Church committee, sought interviews with Lord Cross, but were refused: there was, he claimed, no evidence for the construction they put upon matters, and 'any such action on his part might be interpreted as implying that he had reason to feel doubtful as to the good faith of the Government of India'.[41]

This was too much for the Free Church committee, and although they tactfully denied questioning the good faith of Lord Cross, they did declare their doubts about that of the Indian Government. Together with the other 'enemies of State-regulated Vice, in and out of Parliament', they warned, they had 'been and will be busy gathering their information and maturing their plans, with a view to striking an effective blow'.[42] The Indian officials, they declared, must 'pay honest and practical and thorough regard to the will of the British people, and the mind of the natives of India, as expressed in the unanimous Resolution of the House of Commons'.[43] The degree of bitterness which lay behind this came through more clearly in the debate on this report than in the report itself. Mr. Dymock, throwing tact to the winds, 'condemned the shuffling conduct of Lord Cross';[44] and Professor T.M. Lindsay, telling the Assembly of how in India an army doctor had advised him, ' "We are so arranging that we will do for you" ', declared, to applause from the fathers and brethren, that 'It was just for the Church to "do for them" '.[45]

To do for their opponents, however, the churches needed more information. Accordingly, in December 1890, Mr. Dymock wrote from his Aberdeenshire manse to 49 selected ministers and missionaries in India, asking them for news of the working of the new Cantonment Act. To his great disappointment — but perhaps by his own fault, since he had asked for this information by the end of January — only seven replied, none of them Free Church missionaries.[46]

From those who replied to Mr. Dymock, it was clear that current practice differed from cantonment to cantonment. In some, especially the smaller ones, the military authorities ordered their native subordinates to procure women for the troops; in some again these women were given special quarters — with, in one case, set hours when the men could visit them. Medical examination of the women took place weekly in at least two cantonments, and, in more than one, infected men were ordered to point out to a policeman the woman from whom they had contracted the disease. (The police were said to dislike having to attend to this.) The women thus pointed out had then to submit to a medical examination or leave the cantonment within 24 hours, or in some cases face imprisonment. Where regular or weekly examination took place, however, it was not strictly compulsory, nor were the women given licences, although some of them regarded examination as a form of licensing which, they felt, gave 'their profession a standing'.[47]

Two of Mr. Dymock's informants, an Indian Christian lawyer and William Huntly, a United Presbyterian medical missionary, were quoted extensively in the 1891 Report. The former remarked that 'our Hindu and Mohammedan fellow subjects . . . know the Government is determined by hook or by crook to drag prostitutes into Hospitals for the benefit of British lust', and commented that recourse to prostitution was 'almost universal'[48] among men of the Indian Army. The same point was made by Dr. Huntly, who issued a dire warning of what would happen when the 'young ignorant fools, both officers and privates', of the Indian Army were 'shipped home and let loose on England with their acquired lust thirsting to be satiated'.[49] The Indian authorities, in his view, did not fully realise 'the terrible evil and harm they are inflicting on the old country by encouraging the men to think they could escape disease — a medical lie, as they don't escape'.[50] Not 'merely India's women' were ruined by these regulations, but at the same time 'the virtue and honour of thousands of England's women are endangered'.[51] With something bordering on apparent indifference to the Indians, but with what was probably considerable insight into the motives of his readers, Dr. Huntly concluded: 'It is on behalf of England's women we must fight this out.'[52]

The Free Church was not alone in gathering information and, as its report in 1892 stated, there was 'now ample evidence, in other hands than ours, to support the most serious conclusions we came to'.[53] The most significant pieces of evidence in fact were now in the hands of the British Committee of the International Federation for the Abolition of State-Regulation of Vice. They had been carefully and painstakingly gathered by two American lady admirers of Josephine Butler, Dr. Kate Bushnell and Mrs. Wheeler Andrew who, visiting India for the American Women's Christian Temperance Union, were able to substantiate claims of the sort made by the missionaries, even to the extent of producing official tickets, given to women allocating them to particular groups of soldiers.[54] This information was widely publicised and presented to Lord Kimberley, Secretary for India in Gladstone's 1892-94 administration, by Stansfield and by Professor James Stuart, another leading abolitionist MP. Kimberley, the Free Church committee remarked, 'unhappily has a bad record in connection with this subject',[55] for when Colonial Secretary in an earlier Liberal administration, he had defended the system, including procuring, in Hong Kong, despite Governor Pope-Hennessy's condemnation of it. Their fears however were disappointed, for Kimberley not only set up a Departmental Committee to investigate the abolitionists' accusations, but included two abolitionists, Stansfield and Henry Wilson, in its membership. The Jubilee Assembly of the Free Church believed that victory was at hand. 'Surely the Fiftieth Anniversary of its own emancipation,' declared the committee, 'calls loudly on the Church to strike a specially vigorous blow, so far as words can do it, for freedom to those who are bound with the fetters of the vilest of slaveries.'[56]

These hopes were justified. The Departmental Committee, reporting later in 1893, confirmed what the abolitionists had said. Lord Roberts, the hero of the Afghan War and Commander-in-Chief in India, who had told Josephine Butler that the Free Church's claims were exaggerated[57] and the press that the American ladies were overstating what could only have been 'an occasional breach of the regulations',[58] had to climb down and was severely reprimanded. Dr. Bushnell and Mrs. Andrew were given over £800 by the British Government to cover their expenses, and Lord Kimberley sent a draft Bill for repeal legislation to the Government of India.[59]

The 1895 Act

In India the action of the home Government was deeply resented, and the authorities were not prepared to take it lying down. Interviewed in the summer of 1894, Sir George White, the new Indian Commander-in-Chief, indignantly spoke of 'the hideous evil that is done to our soldiers, morally and physically, by the non-enforcement of the Contagious Diseases Acts'.[60] During the previous two years, he claimed, 56,000 out of 70,000 men had been admitted to hospital 'suffering nameless horrors':[61]

> Picture to yourself the state of our army in such a condition, and its utter inability to endure the cold and wet and misery of a long campaign. And picture to yourself the no less miserable condition of the poor women for whose benefit the Acts work as completely as they do for the men. We are, I believe, the only nation so acting. Our neglect may be criminal; we shall in time poison and defile the whole world, and all for the sake of a certain feeling of sentiment. Don't think I exaggerate, for we who urge this matter know from painful experience the misery that is being wrought by evil-meaning fanatics.[62] There is not a general in the army or an admiral in the Navy, there is not a doctor in the service or a Catholic or Anglican chaplain who will not bear testimony to the truth of what I say.[63]

The other members of the India Council[64] also were unhappy, not least because the draft Bill included a clause threatening to penalise any public servant who enforced compulsory examination of women for venereal disease. But even when this penal clause was withdrawn by the Secretary of State, others, containing clauses forbidding regular or compulsory examination for venereal disease and any form of licensing, registering or legalising of prostitution in the cantonments, remained, and the Council was slow to enact them. Its Law Member complained 'that "the Bill had practically been drafted in England" and he "declined to express any opinion as to its necessity" '.[65] But the Council eventually passed it, in February 1895.

These events were reported to the United Presbyterian Synod and the Free Assembly by their respective committees. The United Presbyterian version was a fairly straightforward account of what had taken place. That of the Free Church, however, was highly polemical. The committee described Indian 'righteous indignation' over the penal clause as 'affected . . . considerably exaggerated, and . . . the work, to a large extent of wirepullers'.[66] It was natural for the Indian authorities to be angry about home Government interference, but they had only their own earlier devious conduct to blame: to the committee the fact that the India Office 'took fright' and withdrew the penal clause was really 'an occasion of great disappointment',[67] even though there was much to be thankful for in what remained.

The 'outcry, chiefly in medico-military quarters in India', which the committee thus dismissed, did not die down after the Act of 1895 was passed. A month later there appeared what the committee described as 'a very ominous symptom': a married officer had written to the *Times* of India proposing what the committee termed 'The Indian Army Encouragement-of-Fornication Association' — an organisation of married officers which would reinstate on a voluntary basis all the provisions of the Cantonment Act — to give 'our soldiers a fair chance of escaping the terrible consequences that are the natural result of sending young men under the present Army regulations to India'.[68] What happened to this proposal was not recorded by the committee, but his sentiments appear to have been shared by many of the officer's colleagues, for in 1896 Mr. Dymock was complaining loudly about recurrent articles in 'some medical paper, as *The Lancet*, or some military paper, as *The United Service Gazette*, clamouring for the revival of the C.D. Act system'.[69] This 'mania for regulation'[70] was intensified by letters to the British press, such as one from Lord Malmesbury, claiming that 'the absurd prudery and noisy shouting of a body of narrow-minded fanatics' was 'the real cause by which not only our young soldiers, but young England, is being demoralised — viz. the repeal of the Contagious Diseases Act'.[71]

Charges of this kind, in the committee's opinion, relied too heavily upon 'weak abuse' and, in Lord Malmesbury's case, upon a 'singular confusion of "demoralisation" with injury to health'.[72] In reply to them, however, it was only necessary to quote (and both the United Presbyterian and Free Church committees did quote, at length) recent reports of the Army Sanitary Commission. These had pointed out that despite all the care taken over the Lock Hospital system since 1864, venereal disease had actually increased during the period when the system was fully operative. It had therefore to be judged 'a failure'; and, the Commission had continued, 'the best practicable means of diminishing the prevalence of these diseases is to be found in establishing a system of voluntary lock hospitals and in providing the soldier, as far as possible, with healthy occupation and recreation'[73] — including 'all forms of athletic amusement, as physical fatigue acts as a deterrent to sexual indulgence'.[74] The Commission had also noted, for comparison, that venereal disease statistics in the home army had not been less under the Contagious Diseases Acts than after their repeal: for although during that period fear of the police may have deterred illicit prostitution, thereafter the rate of admissions for venereal disease had actually decreased.

These conclusions seemed pretty convincing to the United Presbyterian and Free Church committees, and in the House of Commons Campbell-Bannerman, the Liberal Secretary for War, had admitted their validity during the 1894 debate on the army estimates.[75] In June 1895 however the Conservatives returned to power, and the new War Secretary, the Marquess of Lansdowne,[76] did not share this view. After the 1895 Act came into force, most of the Lock hospitals had been closed and there were now disturbing rumours of a considerable rise in the venereal disease rate. Questioned about this, after Lord Malmesbury's and other letters had appeared in the press, Lord Lansdowne (Mr. Dymock informed the 1896 Assembly) 'cooly assumed that the increase of disease . . . was caused by the abolition of the C.D. Acts, and this cool assumption was received with loud cheers'.[77] Lord George Hamilton, the new India Secretary, in reply to another questioner, had made much the same assumption and had stated that the Indian Government were very concerned and 'were considering what instructions or regulations it might be possible for them to issue to mitigate the scourge without infringing the restriction imposed upon them by the Resolution passed by the House on the subject'.[78]

'Happily',[79] remarked the Free Church committee, this would be difficult, for the practices condemned in the Commons 1888 Resolution (compulsory examination, licensing and regulation) were not simply prohibited by an executive order in India, which the Indian Government could change, but had the force of law, and despite the abandonment of the penal clause in the 1895 Act, compulsory examination of a woman against her will now amounted to assault and was punishable as such under the Indian penal code.

The 1897 Panic

In discussing the concern of the home and Indian Governments over the rising venereal disease statistics, Mr. Dymock had remarked that his committee had no wish to challenge the figures, but only the implications drawn from them by regulationists and Government ministers. The committee felt confident that the findings of the Army Sanitary Commission had amply refuted the notion that removal of regulationist measures rather than an increase in vice was responsible for venereal disease.

It was just as well that the committee had not decided to challenge the statistics, for when the official figures for 1894 and 1895 were published, towards the end of 1896, they showed that the venereal disease rate in India was now higher than ever before.[80] This immediately provoked a great outcry and Lord George Hamilton set up a Departmental Committee under Lord Onslow (the Under-Secretary for India) to investigate the implications of the statistics. Reporting in February 1897, the Departmental Committee stated that the rising rate of disease, which 'seriously impaired' the military efficiency of the Indian Army, and which, as the soldiers returned home, was 'a growing danger to the health of the community', did not 'appear to be attributable to increased immorality in the army' since 'drunkenness and crime have greatly diminished'.[81] Nor were facilities for recreation at fault, since 'successive Commanders-in-Chief in India . . . none more than Lord Roberts' had done a great deal to provide and improve 'recreation rooms, libraries, regimental workshops, etc.' and to encourage 'cleanliness and, so far as the climate admits, . . . active exercise and sports'.[82]

These findings were a great blow to abolitionists and to the United Presbyterian and Free Church committees, for they undermined their claims that increased venereal disease reflected increased vice, and that recreation restricted copulation. But a greater blow was to fall a month later when the Army Sanitary Commission, until now the abolitionists' ally, had second thoughts about the matter. In a memorandum of March 1897 the Commission noted that since the withdrawal of Government control over prostitution in India there had been 'a progressive increase' in venereal disease among British troops and that there was 'no assurance that this increase had reached its limits'.[83] Although it had hitherto considered the former methods 'unquestionably a failure', it was now compelled 'to admit that, although they failed to bring about any marked reduction in the number of men affected, they nevertheless exercised a very sensible influence in checking increase'.[84] Treatment under these measures had also prevented venereal disease 'from assuming that virulent and destructive character'[85] it now exhibited. Therefore, the Commission concluded, 'control of prostitution in some form seems to be a reasonable method of dealing with the effects produced by prostitution'.[86]

As a result of these reports Lord George Hamilton had written to the Indian Government at the end of March 1897, requesting it to review its rules concerning venereal disease. His despatch excluded the possibility of re-introducing any measures which could 'be represented as an encouragement to vice': prostitutes were not to be registered, licensed or 'allowed to reside in regimental bazaars, or to accompany regiments on the march',[87] nor were women to be examined compulsorily or regularly. Instead, the rules of the 1889 Cantonment Act which applied to cholera, smallpox, diphtheria and typhoid were to be extended to cover all contagious and infectious diseases, including those of a venereal nature. Under these rules, women suffering from any of these diseases would not be compelled to attend hospital, but would be required to leave the cantonment if they did not. The British Government did 'not share the view'[88] that this amounted to compulsory examination.

The India Secretary left it to the Indian Government to draw up rules embodying these principles, and its reply was sent from Simla on the 18th of May, 1897. This was too late for comments upon it to be included in the United Presbyterian and Free Church committees' 1897 reports, but while the former reserved judgement until it saw the reply, the latter launched into a lengthy criticism not only of the reports of the Departmental Committee and the Sanitary Commission, but also of Lord George Hamilton's despatch.

In criticising the reports, the Free Church committee emphasised once again that it did not wish to question the awfulness of the Indian statistics. This, after all, was what the abolitionists — who were now 'charged with ignorance of the condition of the Indian Army'[89] — had for long been complaining about. The 'sudden panic that arose on the publication of the Report'[90] of the Departmental Committee was however not justified, for the rate of hospital admissions, which had been rising 'with fluctuations'[91] for the last twenty years, was at present[92] actually rising more slowly than at some times when the Contagious Diseases and Cantonment Acts had been fully operational. Admittedly it was not decreasing (as the rate at home had done after repeal of the Contagious Diseases Acts),[93] but the habits acquired by the soldiers during the regulationist period probably continued 'to bear fruit in increased vice and consequently in increased disease',[94] and the habits acquired by their superiors made the thoroughness of abolition uncertain even yet. A further reason for questioning the connection between abolition and the rising venereal disease rate was that after 1895 the rate had risen only on some stations. On others it had decreased and, as the Inspector General of Military Hospitals had remarked in 1879, when he was giving evidence in favour of the Contagious Diseases Acts, differences of this kind could only be explained in terms of differences 'in the character of the men, and in the traditional habits of the regiment'.[95] They could not in other words be attributed to regulation or to its abandonment. The cônversion to regulationism of the Army Sanitary Commission, whose own report contained statistics of this nature, was thus 'not easy to understand'.[96]

These reports, then, the Free Church committee considered, had added unnecessary fuel to the regulationists' fire, and press and public reaction to them had been greatly exaggerated. Newspapers 'repeatedly' ignored the fact that about a quarter of the 522 admissions to hospital were readmissions and — a particularly glaring example of 'ignorant exaggeration'[97] — the Inverness *Northern Chronicle* had even informed its readers that the 45 per 1000 constantly sick were 45 per 100. The press also tended far too readily to assume that venereal disease could be easily prevented, and it was frequently being suggested that

> but for Repeal, disease would have been almost, if not quite, extinguished, and disease has been laid at the door of Repealers just as if the soldier were not a voluntary and responsible agent. There has been nothing for him but pity, as for one to whom vice is necessary, and whom it is monstrous, not only not to try to cure (which no one objects to), but to allow to be sick, or even to fail to provide beforehand with the assurance of immunity. Floods of abuse have been discharged on Abolitionists; they have been accused, e.g., of utter heartlessness, of low motives, foul tastes, and in the chorus of execration that has arisen against them one voice has proclaimed that they deserve themselves to be inoculated with the virus.[98]

Fortunately, the committee noted, the India Secretary had so far resisted much of this regulationist pressure, and there was much in his despatch to the Indian Government 'to be satisfied with and to be grateful for'.[99] Nevertheless, the committee could hide neither from themselves nor the church 'that no small danger lurks beneath an innocent-looking surface', for the despatch was 'elastic enough to admit measures which shall amount practically to Vice-Regulation';[100] and it was difficult to see how examination could really be any more voluntary than it had been in the regulationist period, if now as then the only alternative was for the diseased woman to leave the cantonment. In the despatch the committee saw 'the door opened for the oppression of women, and men too',[101] for nothing was said about judicial procedures, and thus all the old dangers arose. Their fear that it might eventually lead to a reintroduction of all the old evils was intensified by the fact that regulationists were now either complaining that the Indian Government should be given more of a free hand than the despatch allowed them, or were congratulating themselves that this had already been given, if one read between the lines of the despatch.

The Free Church committee concluded its report (which even it admitted was 'too long')[102] by remarking that the Government would have been wiser to appoint a Select Committee than a Departmental one, for the latter had not gone into the question in sufficient detail. Its suggestion, for example, that there was no evidence of 'an increase of vice to account for an increase of disease' was ill-founded, for 'diminution of drunkenness and crime is not incompatible with increased immorality'.[103] A more substantial enquiry would also have suggested more thorough improvements in conditions for men in the Indian Army, especially in relation to 'facilities for marriage'.[104] The fact that the disease rate among the native troops (in 1895) was less than a seventeenth of what it was among

British soldiers was clearly related to the fact that just over 4 per cent. of the British were married.[105] This was 'nothing short of scandalous':

> The cost of *married* soldiers is made an objection: but what of the cost of *diseased* soldiers, and what of the eternal difference between right and wrong? It is *wrong* to have an army of young men in India under the conditions to which the British troops are subject, and it is surely very disappointing that the first utterance and proposals of Government, in the face of a state of things that has spread consternation through the land, should not as much as hint at a remedy which is at once obvious, natural and God-appointed.[106]

Dissension in the Free Assembly

On the afternoon of Monday May 31st, 1897 the Free Assembly was not in a particularly serious mood. It was debating whether to license a candidate for the ministry who had been studying for sixteen years, but always had a serious illness when due to be examined. On the advice of Principal Rainy, and amid no little laughter, it agreed to waive all but the final examinations in this 'thoroughly exceptional'[107] case. It then called for the lengthy report which we have just been considering. This was introduced by Mr. Dymock, and the Assembly quickly sobered up.

As was customary, the convener's speech summarised the main points of his committee's report for the benefit of those present who either had not read or had forgotten its contents. In view of the number and length of the reports which members of the Assembly were now given to digest, this practice was not only necessary but also provided conveners with an opportunity to comment on any relevant developments which had taken place in their field since their report had been printed.

In Mr. Dymock's case two relevant developments had taken place: the Viceroy Lord Elgin[108] and the India Council had replied to Lord George Hamilton's despatch, and the report of the Departmental Committee (which had provoked the despatch) had been debated in the House of Lords. Each of these events had taken place a fortnight earlier, but so far Mr. Dymock was aware only of the second, which clearly had made a deep impression on him. It had, for one thing, confirmed some of his worst fears about the British ruling classes: in the course of the peers' debate 'one so-called noble Lord', the Earl of Clarina, he informed the fathers and brethren, 'had not been ashamed to describe himself as "a bachelor who occasionally obeyed the strongest instincts of human nature" '.[109]

Perhaps this was all that could be expected of some regulationists. More disturbing, was a 'singular change' which Mr. Dymock observed coming over others among them:

> Religion was now invoked. They had Lord Dunraven[110] 'thanking God' that public opinion was coming more and more to that side; and they had Lord Lister saying that the Government was 'entering on a Christian course' — a course that, according to his

> lordship, was to end in the C.D. Acts. Christianity was repeatedly appealed to, and repeal spoken of as 'iniquity' and 'sin'. But . . . they knew that a thing might be called Christian which was the reverse of that, and that God might be thanked . . . when thanks were due in an opposite quarter altogether.[111]

Despite these brave words the conjunction of religion, respectability and regulationism was not new,[112] nor — to many contemporaries — was it as incongruous as it seemed to Mr. Dymock. The emergence of Lister as a regulationist represented a particularly serious threat to abolitionists, especially if, as Godlee (Lister's nephew, and himself a surgeon) asserted, his regulationist opinions reflected 'the general view of the medical profession in this country at that time'.[113] Nor was there any doubt that Lister was a regulationist. He chose this, his maiden speech, to criticise the India Secretary's despatch for unduly hampering the Indian Government in dealing with venereal diseases. All contagious diseases including venereal diseases, he stated, should be treated in the same way, and in principle he had no objection to the Contagious Diseases Act. It was, he considered 'a most beneficient act' which, 'he hoped, at no distant time to see . . . re-enforced in this country'.[114]

The spectre of regulationism in high places clearly agitated Mr. Dymock considerably, and led him, in his speech, to express much more extreme opinions than were contained in his committee's report. Lord Lister's remarks, he claimed, 'had let the cat out of the bag' by showing that for Lord George Hamilton's despatch to be 'of any use'[115] there must be periodical examination; and that, he suspected, was just what it was going to lead to. No doubt some people 'were quite delighted and disarmed' by the good things in the despatch, and no doubt they were 'honestly meant'.[116] But they had all been heard before — from Lord Cross. The Assembly therefore ought to object to the despatch as 'a step backwards' and 'part of a policy of despair' which 'opened the door to all the evil practices' of the past, leading ultimately to an 'out-and-out C.D.A. system'.[117] Mr. Dymock's anger was intensified by the fact that General Chapman,[118] who under Lord Roberts had sent out the 'notorious circular' calling for 'a larger supply of younger and more attractive women' for the troops, had now had 'the effrontery' to write to the Moderator asking him 'to use his influence with ministers in the Highlands to get them to be practically recruiting sergeants for the army'.[119] The only course open to the Government, declared Mr. Dymock, recovering his main theme, was a return to the conditions, of 'long service and greater facilities for marriage',[120] which had existed before the Mutiny. This was 'God's way' and 'even her Majesty's Government . . . would find that it was vain to fight against God'.[121]

This was also strong language. But Mr. Dymock's speech was applauded by the Assembly only at its conclusion, which suggests that its reception was not over-enthusiastic. Principal Rainy, who was a member of the committee and now rose to move the deliverance, thus had the difficult tasks of speaking for the report without identifying himself too closely with his convener. He did this by emphasising that it was important for the Assembly to 'make clear what they objected to' and to 'take care to take up grounds that they could clearly understand

and clearly define'.[122] Thus, 'for instance', Rainy went on, 'when Mr. Dymock said that one of his objections was that these operations tended to protect men from the consequences of vice, he had to say that he would go a long way to deliver men from the consequences of their own vice if he were not required in so doing to connive at their vice, and make himself responsible for it'.[123]

This judicious, if convoluted, piece of reasoning was applauded by the Assembly, which again applauded the Principal when he went on to state that only if the Government was under 'strong pressure' from regulationists was it right for the Assembly to exert 'counter-pressure'.[124] This, he believed, was 'the proper way of supporting the Government'.[125] Under the present circumstances, since many of the officials who would have to carry out the provisions of the despatch wanted to go back to the old system, and since support for this view had been expressed in the House of Lords, it clearly was right for the Assembly to state that it had, in the words of the deliverance, 'reasonable ground for apprehension as to the effects of this despatch'.[126] But this was as far as it should go, and the Assembly should 'be duly cautious in taking up any ground in the way of condemning this despatch'.[127]

Rainy had good reason to take a more moderate line than his convener, for an Edinburgh[128] elder, Mr. McCandlish, had already intimated his intention to move that the committee should be discharged. Dr. Ferguson of Kinmundy, seconding the adoption of the deliverance, remarked that this would be 'a sore discouragement' and 'a highly undesirable step', since the Free Church 'was regarded as the outstanding exponent of public opinion on this subject'.[129] Dr. Ferguson, however, was an old opponent of Mr. McCandlish, for the latter, when he rose to speak, declared that he had protested against the establishment of the committee twenty-two years earlier, and the Assembly 'had allowed the thing to go on too long'.[130]

Mr. McCandlish objected to the committee's existence because, as he put it, 'it dealt with a subject with which, as a Church, they had nothing to do'.[131] Greeted with 'cries of "Oh" ' for saying this, Mr. McCandlish quickly added that members were entitled to express their opinions on such subjects 'as individual Christians': but 'when from Church Courts and pulpits views were expressed upon social, moral or political subjects upon which the members of the Church were divided', he argued, it 'told seriously against religion'.[132] He doubted moreover if there was in the Assembly 'one man in twenty who had mastered this subject so as to be justified in taking a serious responsibility in connection with it', and so although they all condemned vice, it was wrong for the Assembly to be committed to the 'extreme views'[133] of the committee.

This was not however the only ground of criticism of this committee advanced by Mr. McCandlish, for he had 'strong views' upon the question of regulation as well as that of the church's involvement in politics. The Government and the Indian army, he stated, were well aware of the serious nature of the problem and were doing their best to deal with it in a way which would reduce disease, raise morality, and undo some of the harmful effects of the 1888 resolution, which 'had acted as a stimulant to vice'.[134] The committee however seemed to be interested only in preventing the authorities from interfering with an 'army of professional prostitutes, native women who made a trade of vice, and who were brought up to this trade':[135] they seemed unconcerned to 'deliver the lads who sinned from . . . suffering all their lives from a loathsome and often fatal disease, and transmitting it to the wives they might afterwards marry on their return home, and to their children'. The committee indeed seemed determined to ensure that these young men should suffer. 'Were the members of Assembly,' he asked, 'prepared to take this responsibility on themselves?'[136]

This view, as extreme in its own way as that of Mr. Dymock, did not commend itself to the members of Assembly, who refrained from applauding even at the end of Mr. McCandlish's speech. Nor were they very enthusiastic when two other and very distinguished elders rose to express their dissent.

Colonel Cadell, V.C.,[137] 'one of the few military men' in the Assembly and recently retired after thirty-eight years in India, informed the Assembly that he agreed with 'the practically unanimous opinion of the officers of the army in India' that it was 'the duty of the Government of India to regulate, not vice, but the prevention of disease'.[138] There were, he said, 'as good men in the army as there are in the Church' and the Indian authorities wanted to keep the men away from temptation, but thanks to the new regulations, following 'a recommendation passed by chance in the House of Commons on a Wednesday afternoon'[139] (the 1888 Resolution), they no longer had any powers to keep prostitutes out of cantonments. Simply warning the soldiers against disease was useless, for they did not give the fear of disease 'a second thought'.[140] It was his opinion therefore that 'no man of common-sense, if he knew the circumstances as I do, would object to the rules proposed by the Government of India'.[141] These rules were 'based on the principle of general registration of all civil inhabitants of the Cantonment'[142] and medical examination was 'entirely voluntary', for the women could choose to leave the cantonment if they did not wish to be examined. Colonel Cadell concluded by pointing out that although many great and good ladies had signed memorials protesting against these rules, another memorial supporting the measures proposed in the India Secretary's despatch, and declaring that it was 'the duty of the state' to protect unmarried soldiers 'from the consequences of evils which are unavoidable' under the conditions imposed on them by the State, had been signed by many other 'equally revered'[143] ladies, including Florence Nightingale.

The colonel's reference to the famous nurse was swiftly followed by the speech of a distinguished doctor, Professor Sir Thomas Grainger Stewart, Physician in Ordinary to the Queen for Scotland, who remarked that he could not support Dr. Rainy, for 'he knew what the results of these diseases were, not only in the victims themselves . . . in many a poor hospital patient, and in many a patient of good social position . . . but in the individuals contaminated, and their children and even their grandchildren . . . and he knew also that it was possible to prevent such things'.[144] It was the Assembly's duty 'where they could, to prevent disease with the utmost earnestness'.[145]

These formidable allies did not however win the day for Mr. McCandlish, and Rainy's motion was carried by a majority.

Compromise in the Free Assembly

The motion which was carried was not, however, exactly the same as that originally proposed, for Rainy had agreed to add the words 'contrary to the intentions of the Secretary of State as expressed in the Despatch'[146] to the Assembly's expression of apprehension about what might follow the implementation of the despatch. Rainy had suggested these words after a short speech from an elder with some experience of India, who was unwilling to support Mr. McCandlish; the elder believed that 'it was the duty of the Church to inform the State upon moral questions' (which, as well as being a 'medical and military' question, this was), but he was unwilling to support the deliverance, because he believed that the Secretary for India, after listening to what the churches had to say, had issued 'a despatch with which no reasonable fault could be found'.[147]

The elder, whose speech was punctuated with as many bursts of applause and cries of 'Hear, hear' as all the other speeches put together, was Andrew H.L. Fraser, C.S.I., who had just completed seven years as a civil servant in the Central Provinces. Now at home on leave, prior to taking up his appointment as Officiating Secretary to the Indian Government's Home Department, Fraser was poised, at the age of 49, on the brink of promotion which would bring him in two years to the Chief Commissionership of the Central Provinces and in six to a knighthood and the Lieutenant-Governorship of Bengal. Whatever reasons his superiors may have had for promoting him, Fraser's own expression of his attitudes[148] suggests that he was a remarkably conscientious and compassionate civilian, who not only believed it his duty but also enjoyed meeting Indians of all classes. Very critical of colleagues who did not trouble to learn the local customs and languages, and who failed to keep 'in mind that an Indian gentleman ought to be treated as a European gentleman should be treated',[149] he was himself criticised for being too soft with the natives when he insisted that peasants should be treated with respect. He was not, of course, immune from the contemporary European's sense of superiority, believing that 'British rule is necessary for the maintenance of peace and for the progress of the country',[150] and he was unsympathetic to Congress, whose members were, he believed, a minority of disaffected intellectuals. There was, in his view, 'no Indian nation'[151] and he thought that it would be 'a long time before the races of India can be left to manage their own affairs'; but he recognised that 'intellectual unrest' in India was only to be expected after the introduction of 'Western civilisation, our industrial methods, our education and even our political ideas',[152] and he argued that Indians should be given an increasing part to play in Government.

On matters of religion Fraser, as a good civil servant, believed in the principle of religious neutrality and had 'never conscientiously favoured Christian or Hindu or Muhammadan for his creed' nor used his 'official influence in any way to undermine or change the faith of any man'.[153] But he had 'never regarded the principle of neutrality as involving indifference or opposition to religion'.[154] Early in his service he had attended a mission church, together with Europeans, Eurasians, a few Indian Christians and some non-Christian Indians, and when the missionary — the only one in the district — had to be absent, Fraser had conducted the service. His superior, 'an upright English gentleman', consequently told him 'that, as Indians attended the service, it was incompatible with my duty to Government to conduct it, especially as some of these were Hindus'.[155] Fraser however refused to accept this view of his duty and asked to have the matter referred to the Local Government. His superior 'very courteously and kindly' agreed to this, and the reply came back that 'so long as I merely took part in a Christian service in a place to which no one was compelled to come',[156] the Government had no objection. He 'never had any trouble again in this connection',[157] and during his time in Nagpur (which presbytery he was representing in the 1897 Assembly) he was one of only two European elders (the other was a missionary) on the session of the native church. His attitude to missionaries was mixed: some, he thought, were 'unsympathetic towards the natives . . . jealous, suspicious and even hostile to their fellow-countrymen . . . narrow, ill-educated, and wanting in tact and judgement'.[158] Such missionaries, he said, 'probably do more harm than good'; and although he stressed that these were 'exceedingly exceptional',[159] his vivid characterisation of their faults suggests that he must have had a few in mind. He also may have had in mind some situation such as that under discussion in the 1897 Assembly when he remarked that 'to them, as a body, we owe the awakening of the conscience of the Government to some of the abuses of Indian administration',[160] as well as when he noted that some missionaries 'although no doubt well-meaning, forget that not all the information that reaches them is accurate': he would

> like to see all missionaries willing to enter fully and with kindly confidence into friendly relations with the officers of the Government. They ought not readily to take up an unfavourable impression of the character and conduct of officers of Government, and least of all when they are their own fellow-countrymen. Officers of Government, whether European or Indian, are for the most part animated by a strong sense of duty.[161]

It was not surprising then that this realistic, compassionate and high-minded Scottish civilian was able to make common cause with Rainy, nor that the Nomination committee immediately added his name to the membership of the Committee on the State Regulation of Vice.[162]

It is not clear, either from Fraser's autobiography or from the Assembly records, whether he was able to attend any meetings of the committee between his appointment in May 1897 and the subsequent Assembly, or whether he had to return to India in the meantime. What is clear, however, is that he was present at the 1898 Assembly and that he had not attended the crucial committee meeting which adopted the report to that Assembly — for he told the Assembly as much when he submitted the report to it.

The report which Mr. Fraser submitted contained none of the committee's usual allusions to Continental and Colonial Vice. Instead, it quoted in full the Indian Government's reply to Lord George Hamilton's despatch, plus his response thereto, and made some comments of its own on this exchange.

In reply to the despatch, the Indian Government had framed rules enabling cantonment authorities to prohibit brothel-keeping, soliciting, and the residence of prostitutes in cantonments. The military authorities had agreed, further, to make deductions from soldiers' pay for days spent in hospital with venereal disease (unless the soldier could prove that the disease was 'contracted under circumstances, not the result of his own immorality')[163] and to warn 'young soldiers on their arrival in India of the dangers to which they are exposed, and of the terrible consequences attending the contraction of venereal disease in a tropical climate'.[164] These were provisions to which it might seem that no abolitionist could take exception.[165] The Free Church committee, however, while expressing some satisfaction with them, was concerned that 'the mere *permission* given to the Cantonment authority to prohibit brothel-keeping or the residence of prostitutes in the Cantonment, or in any specified part thereof'[166] might lead soldiers and the women to think that those houses and women not prohibited were for practical purposes licensed.

The committee's main objection, however, was to the Indian Government's recommendation (which Lord George Hamilton agreed to) that, for the rules applying to other infectious and contagious diseases to be extended to venereal disease, it would be necessary to repeal the Act of 1895 and to amend a section of the Act of 1889. This was necessary because any medical officer examining a woman under the new rules could be penalised under the 1895 Act. (The amendment to the 1889 Act was proposed in order to give more explicit protection to an officer doing this.) The Free Church's objection to this (made 'without in the least imputing sinister motives to the Viceroy and his Council') was that 'this Repeal, with the free hand it gives to medical and other officers, will operate towards the admission of those evil practices which the Act repealed peremptorily excluded'.[167] Examination would not be voluntary, and 'the door will be opened for the oppression even of innocent women by unscrupulous men'.[168] The committee 'carefully abstaining from all over-statements, from undue suspicions, and from ill-advised denunciations', was bound to record its conviction 'that the *status quo* is one of great peril'.[169]

The defensive way in which this conviction was registered suggests that Mr. Dymock, who presumably drafted the report, was licking his wounds. Further evidence of his feelings however is lacking, for he was unable to attend the Assembly, and Mr. Fraser's submission of the report, although made at Mr. Dymock's request, was very different from that which he would have made had he been present.

Although Mr. Fraser asserted that he 'had no hand in drafting the Report', was 'not, therefore, responsible for it' and wished that 'some parts of it' had been 'at least expressed differently', he nevertheless expressed his general approval of 'the views contained in the Report and the spirit in which it has been drawn up'.[170] He then went on to outline the history of the controversy in a manner appropriate to someone trying to be loyal both to the Indian Government and the Free Church. Venereal disease, he emphasised, was a more serious disease in India than at home, so it was not surprising that the Indian Government followed the example of the

Home Government when the Contagious Diseases Acts were passed.[171] Nor was it surprising that when there were abuses under the Acts at home, abuses also took place in India. But the Indian Government issued orders to put these down, and did not realise that these orders were being disobeyed by some local authorities until the ladies from the World's Women's Christian Temperance Union[172] reported upon them, and the Government of India itself discovered General Chapman's circular. 'These awful discoveries,' Mr. Fraser noted, 'filled the Government of India with horror and shame';[173] and as a result it passed the 1895 Act, since, as the Military Member of the India Council remarked, ' "in face of the Quartermaster-General's[174] circular of 1886, they had not a sufficiently clear conscience" to make a stand for protective measures'.[175] The difficulty with the 1895 Act however was that it was legally binding and because of the danger of prosecution put a stop to all treatment of venereal disease among women. Despite the India Secretary's opinion that the regulations proposed in his despatch would not amount to compulsory examination under the 1895 Act (which might 'morally' be the case), lawyers were uncertain about this and the medical men were afraid — especially 'in India, where malicious charges are more rife'[176] — to treat women while the 1895 Act remained in force. For whether compulsory or not, the Act forbade periodical examination, which might well be necessary in the course of treatment. The Indian Government and the India Secretary were therefore right, in Mr. Fraser's opinion, to repeal the 1895 Act.

As far as the new rules were concerned, Mr. Fraser emphasised the absence of registration and compulsion and the fact that the choice of examination or leaving the cantonment could only be offered to a woman if the medical officer and the commanding officer were agreed that it was necessary. He also emphasised the positive aspects of the new system which discouraged vice and warned soldiers against the dangers facing them. The new system, he observed, was completely different from the old one, and he believed that the church had 'no cause whatever to be ashamed to have had a share in the efforts of Christian people which have led to this . . . clear recognition of moral principle'.[177] The only danger now was that 'even fairly good men, looking at a subject like this from only one point of view', might repeat the 'awful blunders'[178] of the past. Repeal of the 'rightly repealed 1895 Act' thus called 'for careful watchfulness against local abuse'.[179]

By stating his case in this way Mr. Fraser had managed to support the deliverance, which expressed 'grave apprehension' as to the 'local working out'[180] of the system following repeal of the 1895 Act, without endorsing the 'great regret'[181] at repeal expressed by the report. Thus, although an Edinburgh elder[182] attacked 'the biassed and hostile tone of much of this Report' and persuaded Rainy on behalf of the committee to accept an amendment converting the 'grave apprehension lest' local evils would ensue to 'the earnest hope'[183] that they would not, the deliverance was adopted, and the committee and convener re-appointed, without any further controversy.

The absence of any further controversy, which was carefully managed by Rainy, may well have been, as much as anything else, an attempt to protect Mr. Dymock. For after his long labours the absent convener was dying.[184] With his death, the committee entered its own terminal stages, which were, appropriately, less stormy. Mr. Fraser returned to India, but remained a member of the committee and later went on to become 'one of the most prominent and highly respected members of the church', playing an important part in the negotiations for Union with the Establishment and wielding, as before, 'great influence in an unobtrusive way on every occasion when his advice was sought'.[185]

The new convener of the committee, Dr. J.G. Cunningham of Edinburgh, produced shorter and more optimistic reports. That of 1899 had in fact nothing but praise for the Indian authorities. A member of the committee (perhaps Mr. Fraser, but he was not mentioned by name) had written from India to Dr. Cunningham with 'reassuring statements as to the manner in which the Cantonment regulations were being carried out',[186] and the committee quoted 'as one of the hopeful signs of the times' a memorandum from the Commander-in-Chief, Lord Wolseley, which matched his exalted situation with appropriately exalted sentiments:

> It will be the duty of the Company officers to point out to the men under their control, and particularly to young soldiers, the disastrous effects of giving way to habits of intemperance and immorality; the excessive use of intoxicating liquors unfits the soldier for active work, blunts his intelligence, and is a fruitful source of crime. The man who leads a vicious life, enfeebles his constitution and exposes himself to the risk of contracting disease of a kind which has, of late, made terrible ravages in the British Army. Men tainted with this disease are useless to the State while in the Army, and a burden to their friends when they leave it.[187]

United Presbyterian Hostility, United Free Compromise and the Establishment

The United Presbyterian Synod's reaction to the repeal of the 1895 Act was similar to that of Mr. Dymock, and if anything more hostile. Repeal, it considered, had removed any legal means whereby a return to the old system might be prevented and, the Synod observed, 'in view of the way in which the Indian authorities have acted in the past there is grave cause to fear that the 'new rules will be used to reintroduce the old system'.[188] The Synod admitted, however, that the Army was now aware of the need to attack vice as well as disease. Even Sir George White was strongly urging the application of moral pressure on the grounds that 'soldiers listen with attention to the teaching of those they respect and who can speak to them from the standpoint of higher education, of a blameless life, or of technical knowledge'.[189] But these measures, the committee believed, would 'never be used in adequate measure, so long as any system of regulation is in force';[190] and it petitioned Parliament for re-enactment of the 1895 Act, together with greater facilities for marriage and moral training. (Not even the United Presbyterian Synod, however, could resist the high moral tone of Lord Wolseley's memorandum, which it quoted at length, remarking that it could not 'fail to produce good moral results among the officers and men of the army'.[191])

The United Presbyterian analysis of the Indian situation now directly contradicted that which the Free Church committee had adopted. There were, it held, 'strong reasons to fear that the governmental regulation of vice has been restored to India in the Cantonments, with all its repulsive practices', and the regulationist lobby at home was so strongly in favour of re-enacting the Contagious Diseases Acts for the whole of Britain that it seemed as if 'the battle against the State Regulation of Vice will require to be fought all over again'.[192] The same fears were again expressed by this committee in its report to the United Presbyterian Synod in 1900. A petition had been sent to the Commons, it noted, from 'most of the Protestant Missionary Societies of India'[193] requesting repeal of the 1899 Act and Rules, and 'the abandonment of the proposal to employ 'female hospital assistants' in an occupation which is immoral, and which must necessarily ruin the reputation of any young woman entering upon it'.[194] The committee was at the same time, however, more optimistic about 'the question of social purity in military circles':[195] Lord Wolseley's memorandum had, it believed, helped to improve the tone there, and 'with such men as at present occupying the chief military posts, who discountenance vice in all its forms, the outlook is hopeful',[196] it commented.

This was the last report of the Temperance and Morals committee before the Synod united with the Free Assembly. After the Union, Temperance became a separate committee, Morals were incorporated in Church Life and Work, and the United Presbyterians' concern with regulation was channeled into the new United Free Assembly Committee on the State Regulation of Vice. The last Free Church Report under that title[197] had said nothing about India, but the United Presbyterians reintroduced the subject, and the new committee remarked that the 1899 Act caused it 'serious misgiving'.[198] The Assembly approved this report, but not entirely happily: the former Free Church elder who seconded it[199] thought that there was really no need for the misgiving.

The following Assembly in fact was the last to receive a report from this committee. Despite the need, expressed in the 1902 report, for the church to 'maintain with boldness and with hope new testimony on the side of national purity and righteousness, as in former years',[200] the general feeling seems to have been, as the 1901 report put it, that there was now 'a lull in the agitation . . . in favour of re-introduction into this country of legislation on the lines of the Contagious Diseases Act';[201] and although 'the spirit of militarism which is fostered by the long continuance of the South African War'[202] temporarily strengthened regulationist feeling, it seems likely that the majority of the new Assembly were glad to lay the vexed question of Indian vice to rest.[203]

Before leaving the Indian question, it may be noted that the Church of Scotland was not unaware of what was going on in India. Its committees on Foreign Missions[204] did not mention the subject of prostitution, but there were hints in reports from colonial chaplains about 'the danger that meets young men in Indian life',[205] and the section of the Colonial committee concerned with army and navy chaplaincies was 'urging the General Assembly to take steps to remedy a state of things which is not creditable, and is fraught with danger to the spiritual interests of our soldiers — so many of whom are young soldiers — placed amidst the temptations of Indian life'.[206] This was not however a reference to prostitution or venereal disease, but to the fact that only a few of the nine Scottish regiments in India had a Presbyterian chaplain paid for by the Government.[207]

India unquestionably was the main interest of the Free Church and United Presbyterian committees during this period, but events in the other parts of the British Empire did not go unnoticed. When Mr. McCandlish attacked the Free Church committee in 1897, he complained of it continually taking the Assembly 'to New Zealand, the Transvaal, to Geneva and Guernsey with none of which places this Church has any special connection'.[208]

Self-governing Colonies

This was not strictly accurate. The committee, as we have noted, had been told in 1898 by Lord Knutsford that while his Colonial Office could not interfere with New Zealand, Cape Colony and other self-governing colonies, the Free Church might very effectively stimulate abolitionist movements in these countries, most of which had at that time some form of Contagious Diseases Act on their statute books.[209] It had accordingly written to all Protestant ministers in Canada, enclosing Rainy's pamphlet,[210] in 1889, and in December 1895 it had sent an appeal to all of the five or six hundred Presbyterian ministers in New Zealand. The effect of the Canadian correspondence was not recorded by the committee,[211] but the abolitionist movement in New Zealand, it noted, had 'got a great impetus recently, due in large measure to influence brought to bear from the mother country'.[212] The New Zealand press had been reporting the Free Church of Scotland's activities in this sphere, and the Dunedin Presbytery had made a firm stand against regulation. So far, this had not amounted to repeal: a Bill had been defeated in the Upper House and some of the women of this country where female franchise had first been gained had organised a regulationist association. But this association, the committee noted, was neither large nor representative and had 'called forth indignant protests from the women of New Zealand'.[213] The Premier of New Zealand had also come out publicly against regulation, and had received a letter from the Free Church committee 'expressing great gratification at his utterance'.[214]

The only other self-governing Colonial area which the Free Church committee mentioned at any length was South Africa.[215] Regulation had been introduced in five towns in Cape Colony in 1885,[216] and was extended to Kimberley in 1892.[217] By 1896, however, a Contagious Diseases Act Amendment Bill which, according to the committee, 'recommended changes which were in part for the better, but in part for the worse',[218] was under consideration by the Legislative Council: the Lord Chief Justice and the General-in-Command at the Cape had come out in favour of repeal; and a minister's wife was writing to tell the committee that the Dutch MPs were increasingly opposed to the Act and likely to bring about its repeal in the next year. An attempt shortly afterwards to introduce Contagious

Diseases Acts into the Transvaal, Mr. Dymock told the 1897 Assembly, 'had been firmly resisted by the President, who was reported to have said that he would rather have his right hand burned than sign such an Act'.[219] Efforts were also being made to introduce regulation to Rhodesia, but 'how our Government would deal with it, remained to be seen'.[220]

In the event, however, neither Mr. Dymock nor his committee was able to follow these developments through to their conclusion. As early as 1896 the committee was noting the 'distracting effect' of 'recent events in South Africa',[221] and in 1900 it was able to attribute decline in the regulationist movement at least partly to the fact that 'the military authorities have had their whole attention engrossed by the stern necessities and cares of actual war'.[222] What happened in the meantime was not something which the Free Church committee, which supported the war,[223] or the Synod's committee, which attacked it,[224] cared to look at too closely. After their churches united, the statements of the new committee were ambiguous as far as the army was concerned: 'the moral quality of our soldiers in the field has been to some extent tested by the experiences of incessant and harassing warfare',[225] it remarked, and while it was afraid that 'the spirit of militarism fostered by the protracted war'[226] might reinforce regulationist pressures, it let the matter rest in the hope that the question of regulation in South Africa could be reviewed in the period of post-war reconstruction, when it would 'be necessary to use every effort to protect our African fellow-subjects from the imposition of the yoke of a demoralising legislation'.[227]

Crown Colonies

The Colonial Office, Lord Knutsford had told the Free Church committee in 1888, would not interfere with self-governing colonies. It was however responsible for Crown Colonies, and the committee was anxious to see this responsibility exercised in the matter of abolition. At first, under Knutsford, things seemed to be going well: the Contagious Diseases Acts, the committee informed the 1889 Assembly, had been repealed in Ceylon, Hong Kong and the Straits Settlements; and although inspection of brothels had not been discontinued in the latter two, such was the faith of the committee in Lord Knutsford that it told the Assembly that this was 'done in the interest of women and children'.[228] The 'special circumstances' which led to its continuance there, and to the delay of repeal in Fiji,[229] did not mean that the committee approved of this situation, simply that they felt 'assured that Lord Knutsford is acting conscientiously in the matter, and that he is eager to see his way to discontinue what is so like an official sanction of vice'.[230] The progress made so far in colonial repeal was, after all, 'due, under God, to the Colonial Secretary'.[231]

But progress was slow, and when the United Presbyterian committee wrote to Knutsford in the same year, he explained that registration in Hong Kong and the Straits Settlements was a 'necessity' because 'the circumstances' there were 'very peculiar'.[232] The Free Church committee however was to hear in 1890 that new regulations had been promised by the Colonial Secretary, and that while 'no advance in the right direction' had been made in the colonies, neither had 'any ground . . . been lost'.[233] Nothing further could be done until some definite step was taken, although in the meantime there was 'much need for watchfulness'.[234]

Nothing further had been done however by 1893, and the Free Church committee took the opportunity provided by a change of Government to write to Lord Ripon, the new Liberal Colonial Secretary, asking what was happening in the Straits Settlements, Fiji and Hong Kong. It was difficult to get information, they noted, and they expressed the hope that Ripon's previous statements as Viceroy of India (1880-84) were a sign of his good intentions at the Colonial Office. Ripon's reply gave the committee another opportunity to express its 'gratitude to God, and under Him, to the Secretary of State for the Colonies':[235] he had 'formed an opinion adverse to (the) system of brothel registration' which continued in Hong Kong and the Straits Settlements and had asked the Governor of these colonies to bring their law 'more into harmony with the recognised policy of Parliament on such questions'.[236] He had also written to the Governor of Fiji, expressing his view that 'the special consideration affecting the health of the natives',[237] which had persuaded his predecessor to leave the Contagious Diseases Ordinances in operation there, were no longer valid, and he was waiting for the Governor's reply.

Thus, declared the committee in 1895, 'the Marquess of Ripon . . . steadfastly carried out, to its full issues, the work which Lord Knutsford nobly forwarded, but hesitated to perfect'.[238] Its admiration for noble Colonial Secretaries was equal only to its denunciation of regulationist colonial officers: 'It is only from a perusal of the official correspondence,' the report went on, 'that one can learn what difficulties have to be overcome, and what unflinching determination must be exercised, before the Colonial Secretary can give effect to his convictions, and bear down the persistent and sometimes plausible pleading of functionaries who *will* not be divorced from the Regulation System.'[239] Magnanimity in victory was not a characteristic of the committee.

Victory however was elusive,[240] and in 1896 Mr. Dymock had to inform the Assembly that the Governor of Mauritius had set up a committee to look into the desirability of introducing a Contagious Diseases Act there.[241] The committee did not refer to this subject again, nor to the question of regulation in Malta, where around 1889 Lord Knutsford had introduced a Repeal Bill which, under the colony's new constitution, had been 'thrown out' because 'the native members had a majority against it'.[242] The Contagious Diseases Acts 'by a deplorable inconsistency'[243] were still in force in Malta in 1895, the committee noted. No more was said about this however, nor, apart from the passing notice in 1901 of 'a recent Sanitary Ordinance for Gibraltar',[244] about that colony, and this was strange, because Malta and Gibraltar were places where the Free Church was the only Presbyterian body responsible for the spiritual oversight of soldiers and sailors. Perhaps the near-Establishment status of the Free Church in these places made its representatives adopt Establishment reticence on this subject.

Nearer home a more serious situation had arisen, which the committee did strongly protest about. In Guernsey, its 1895 Report stated, 'a regulation scheme of a very shameless character has been recently propounded, and is, in part at least, in temporary operation'.[245] This scheme was however being resisted by residents, aided by helpers from England,[246] and Mr. Dymock informed the 1896 Assembly that he expected the Privy Council, to which the local authorities were subject, to veto it.[247] The committee and other bodies (including the United Presbyterian committee)[248] had memorialised the Privy Council to this end. To their 'deep regret',[249] however, the Privy Council, after sitting on the matter for a year and without hearing representatives of the abolitionists, had sanctioned the scheme. In the committee's opinion it was especially deplorable that such a 'retrograde measure' should have been passed by 'the Queen in Council . . . in this year of national rejoicing'.[250] The Privy Council's decision was however final, and no more was heard from the committee on the subject.

Before concluding this review of the Free Church and United Presbyterian committees' concerns with a brief notice of their continental interests, it may be remarked that the Synod's and the Assembly's colonial concerns were not confined to vice. The Synod's committee, throughout this period, kept a critical eye on opium, drink, slavery and war throughout the world, and both churches were committed to global mission. Even so, said Mr. Hugh Black of Edinburgh, moving the adoption of the Colonial Committee's report in the Free Assembly of 1898:

> He did feel that their Church, as a Church, did not pay as much attention to the Colonies as they deserved. When they thought of it, they belonged after all to an imperial race, and at a time when, as never before, all the instincts of our imperial politics appealed to us, and national bonds were being shattered and burst asunder, we were having larger conceptions of the future of our race, and they ought to remember they belonged to an imperial race. They also had an imperial faith — a religion which adapted itself to every need and to every situation. We dared not let ourselves be narrowed down to small, petty provincial views of religion. They dared not, for their own sake, and for the sake of the world. They belonged, further, to an imperial Church. Their organisation was suited to every free people, and alone suited to every free people with free Parliamentary institutions. (Applause.) It would be well for them to remember — it would keep them from having a small view of their Church — that they belonged to the largest Protestant Church in the world, a Church in comparison with which many other sects, such as bulked largely in certain parts of the Empire, like the Episcopalians, dwindled into their proper position as being provincial and local. Scotland was the mother country of Presbyterianism. The future was with them and with their Presbyterianism as a system. He did not mean that the whole race must become Presbyterians, but he said that whatever Church would lay hold of the Anglo-Saxon race must adapt itself to the free political and Parliamentary institutions in their midst, and become somewhat like them. He was willing to confess that he was a jingo in foreign politics, though not in the ordinary sense, but in the sense of believing that God had a work and a purpose for this great world power of the British Empire, and in the sense of believing that, in spite of all the faults of our race and institutions, the British settlers and colonists all over the world sought after righteousness, and sought, more perhaps than the other races that were in competition with them, to deal justly and truly and righteously with all subject races. 'Keep ye the law' had ever been the secret of Britain's success.[251]

To those with such a high view of the mission of Empire it was clearly essential that the Empire's law should not 'make provision for the flesh to fulfill the lusts thereof'.[252]

The Continent

The White Slave Trade had aroused United Presbyterian and Free Church interest in Continental Vice and this interest was maintained through the churches' connections with the British, Continental and General Federation for the Abolition of the State Regulation of Vice. The Federation, founded by Stansfield and Josephine Butler, had branches in most European countries, and each year its congress was attended by delegates from Europe and beyond. Free Church representatives were often to be found among these, but rarely United Presbyterians, unless the Congress met in Britain.[253] The United Presbyterians, however, usually sent a message of support, which the Free Church also did when no delegate could be present.[254]

For those who attended them, these Congresses clearly were very influential, and no doubt they helped to reinforce their sense of membership in a worldwide movement. Those who attended were, naturally enough, the leading Free Church abolitionists. Mr. Dymock attended the Congress of 1889 in Geneva,[255] Mr. Cunningham (Dymock's successor as convener) and the current Moderator, Dr. Thomas Smith, that of 1891 in Brussels[256] (to which they carried the 'fraternal greetings' of the United Presbyterian Synod[257]), Mr. Dymock, the Revd. Dr. Scott of Saltcoats and Gilbert Beith MP, that of 1894 in London,[258] Mr. Dymock and (now) Dr. Cunningham that of 1895 in Colmar,[259] and Dr. Cunningham that of 1898 in London.[260] Mr. Dymock in particular was very much impressed by his international travels. At the Geneva Congress of 1889 he had seen all the eminent abolitionists of Europe and took especial note of the presence of a Dutch professor of medicine recently converted from regulationism. He also had addressed the Congress, speaking 'of the position taken up by the Free Church of Scotland on this question, and of the duty of other churches to make a similar stand'.[261] This address, he informed the Free Assembly, had then been 'translated into Dutch, and inserted in the organ of the Dutch National Church, with friendly remarks on the part of the Editor'.[262]

Mr. Dymock, although unable to attend the Brussels Congress, enjoyed a prominent position again in 1891, for that year he took part 'by request' in the annual meeting of the Ladies' National Association in London, where 'the Free Church's support of the movement was much appreciated'.[263] Still, he was no doubt disappointed at not being able to go to Brussels (where the delegates' 'representation of the mind of the Free Church of Scotland was held to be a valuable contribution to the weight of the Congress'),[264] for he had asked to go,[265] and the abolitionists considered it one of their most significant demonstrations: the Belgian Government lent them a palace to meet in, the Prime Minister gave them a reception, other Ministers attended their meetings, and the Belgian newspapers ('unlike those of this country, which mainly boycott the subject')[266] gave them extensive and for the most part favourable coverage.

Mr. Dymock may, however, have been compensated by the fact that the Assembly allowed him to attend the London Congress in 1894, and to mingle with delegates 'from the four continents' who included ('a thing which never occurred before') a 'Romish priest from Belgium'.[267] An even greater compensation to Mr. Dymock may have been the fact that in this, the first year after the sphere of his committee's action had been enlarged by the Assembly 'so as to embrace State-Regulation of Vice anywhere and everywhere',[268] he had been appointed to the executive committee of the International Federation.

The last abolitionist conference attended by Mr. Dymock recorded in his committee's report was called by the British Committee of the Federation to protest against what it considered to be the growing threat of a reintroduction of regulation in India and at home. It was held in Birmingham in November 1896 (two months after the Berne Congress, which was held as usual in September), and there Mr. Dymock was supported by Dr. Cunningham and the Earl of Moray. At about the same time the committee and the Commission of Assembly sent memorials to the Government, protesting against a possible reintroduction of the Contagious Diseases Acts. 'There is no saying,' the 1897 report remarked, 'how far these and similar demonstrations may have contributed to the emphatic repudiation of the old system, which has since then proceeded from Government and other quarters.'[269]

But how effective were these demonstrations in continental Europe itself? At first, the Free Church committee was optimistic about Europe, for in 1888 the Italian Parliament had agreed to abolish its regulation system, and the fact that Lord Knutsford had been able to use this as an argument for abolition in Malta seemed in the committee's eyes to justify British and Free Church involvement in the Federation: 'the thorough effacement of the foul stain from the escutcheon of the British Empire,' it stated, 'will be promoted by its removal elsewhere.'[270] At this stage it seemed possible that abolition might come as quickly in Europe as it had done in Britain. At the 1889 Congress Professor James Stuart, the abolitionist MP, told the Genevese that their regulationist government was 'behind the times',[271] and he informed the Stockholm Congress a year later that 'in Paris the system of regulated vice is in ruins. In Holland we gain every year.'[272] (At this time large towns in Holland were abolishing regulation at the rate of about two each year.) There were also 'prospects of improvement in Italy',[273] the Congress was informed, and of abolition in Amiens.

The fact that the Congress was told to look for improvement in Italy however was a sign that matters were not as cheerful as some abolitionists had hoped. Italy, apparently the largest catch so far outside Britain, had not in fact totally abolished regulation in 1888, and even its limited repeal measure, the Free Church committee recorded, 'was not fairly put in force, owing to the determined opposition of corrupt officials, and of the many whose foul interests are bound up with the flourishing of vice'.[274] By 1892, indeed, it seemed as if Italy was destined for the full reintroduction of regulation, Morals Police and all, and the abolitionists had to call a special conference in Rome to protest. The Free Church ministers of Rome and Florence were promised as delegates by the committee, but the Italian abolitionists' desire for support from the British press was, the committee considered, 'hopeless'.[275] They were, however, supported by the majority of delegates at an Italian medical congress held in Milan in 1894, who were 'entirely against regulation from a sanitary point of view'. But then, although 'when a motion for its entire abolition was brought before Parliament, not a voice was raised to the contrary', the system was 'not actually abolished'.[276] Despite these various abolitionist demonstrations and despite the goodwill shown by the Belgian Government to the 1891 Congress (at the time, it had seemed that even in Belgium, 'a country in which regulation has long prevailed and been carried far . . . the downfall of the system is not far off'),[277] the committee had to record in 1895 the 'deplorable fact that in Europe there are only two countries free from the demoralising abomination of State Regulation, viz., Great Britain and Switzerland, and in Switzerland, alas! Geneva has to be excepted'.[278]

The exception of 'Calvin's City', understandably enough, was a thorn in the side of the Free Church committee: 'it was painful to mention that great name in connection with such a thing,'[279] said Mr. Dymock. Particularly painful was what the 1896 report described as 'the event of the year'[280] — the decision by two thirds of the Council and two thirds of the people of Geneva to maintain the century-old system of Government-controlled brothels. This decision, the result of organised and sometimes violent opposition to the abolitionists by the brothel keepers and their patrons, was celebrated 'by orgies of mingled profanity and obscenity such as perhaps never before were enacted'.[281]

Although this seemed like a crushing blow (the United Presbyterians were particularly distressed that this should have been the result 'the first time a moral question of this kind has been submitted to the vote of the people'),[282] the abolitionists did not admit defeat and actually gained support from some of their fellow-citizens who were aroused by the violence of the event. But when a new Grand Council was elected in the autumn of 1896, the regulationist majority was doubled. This gave rise to a further 'hideous Saturnalia'[283] in which even the previous year's orgies were exceeded. The only grim comfort the Free Church committee could draw from these events, was that after three successive nights on which the brothel keepers opened their doors without charge, 'ghastly results were visible in the victims' which 'showed the delusive nature of the protection promised to the patrons of State-Regulated Vice'.[284]

Apart from the fragmentary comments already cited about Italy, Belgium, Holland and Geneva, the Free Church committee in fact had very little to say about continental vice.[285] Although after 1894 it was supposed to be concerned with regulation 'anywhere and everywhere', this made little difference to the amount of information it provided for the Assembly to consider. Its Indian and colonial concerns were presumably more than enough for it to be going on with.

Those sections of the committee's reports which dealt with Europe were thus not the most cheerful ones. Indeed at times Mr. Dymock had sounded very depressed about the Continent: 'The black flag of regulation,' he had informed the

1896 Assembly, 'hung its voluminous folds, to a greater or lesser extent, over every country in Europe, with the exception of Norway (where a relic of the system might be said to remain), and Great Britain (which as regarded its colonies, was not all it ought to be).'[286] But neither he nor his colleagues had ever really been tempted to throw in the sponge, and by the end of the century their reports began again to sound more optimistic. Regulation in Europe, even if not abolished, was not making much progress, and medical opinion was coming round to the abolitionist position. This had been foreshadowed when at the August 1891 meeting of the International Society of Hygiene and Demography, abolitionists had prevented regulationists from moving a regulationist resolution.[287] But the great medical conference held in Brussels in September 1899 was the really decisive event.

The Brussels conference had been convened[288] to examine the effectiveness of regulation systems and to consider ways in which prostitution and venereal diseases might be diminished. Delegates were appointed by the government of most major nations[289] and included 'nearly all the great Regulation leaders of the world'.[290] The medical directors of the Paris, Tokyo[291] and Berlin regulation systems were there, together with many of their subordinates. So were representatives of the War Offices of most of the participant nations, including Britain, which also sent delegates from the India and Colonial Offices. Also present were the 'most noted specialists' of 'practically all the great medical bodies of the world', including the English Royal College of Surgeons, which was represented by Dr. Jonathan Hutchinson, 'one of the greatest specialists in Europe'.[292]

In the course of the conference regulation was, of course, discussed at length. Eventually a Russian professor moved that the conference should adopt a resolution describing 'the sanitary surveillance of prostitution' as 'one of the most important means for diminishing the propagation of syphilis and venereal maladies'.[293] The subsequent debate was summed up by the correspondent of the *British Medical Journal*, whose account was quoted by the Free Church committee:

> The failure of the statistical argument in favour of regulation was emphasised by Professor Fournier,[294] the very able leader of the French Regulationists, who said he rejected it altogether and preferred to rely upon 'common sense'. Professor Fournier's 'common sense' reasoning amounted to this — that if you shut up an infected prostitute you thereby protect society against the danger she constitutes, but if you do not she becomes necessarily a focus for the dissemination of the disease. To this the opponents of regulation replied that it is impossible to shut up every infected prostitute until she ceases to be a source of danger; that only a small proportion of women engaged in prostitution come under medical inspection; that inspection itself, as usually practised, is inefficient, and probably must always be more or less so, for gonorrhoea; and, finally, that it is absurd to say that a prostitute with syphilis may safely return to her trade after a few weeks or months of treatment. The only reply to this was that a partial remedy is at least better than none at all. The medical line of argument being exhausted, the reserve of Abolitionists marched up with their battery of moral and political objections. The end of the fight was that the question was not put.

The fact that this conference could not make up its mind about regulation was taken by the Free Church committee as 'an extraordinary and epoch-making confession of the failure, from the medical point of view, of the whole system of State Regulation of Vice'.[295] Although 'these experts had before them the results of an experiment which has been made in France and some other countries for a hundred years . . . yet when they came together to frame an answer to the question concerning this system — "Is it from heaven or of men?" they answered, "We cannot tell" '.[296]

This of course was not quite the question the conference was attempting to answer,[297] and in the last resort the Free Church committee had always claimed that its position rested on moral rather than sanitary grounds,[298] but the impression that abolitionist leaders were 'now listened to with a new interest and respect'[299] seemed to vindicate the long struggle of the United Presbyterian and Free Church committees and their now United Free[300] hope that the abolitionists' 'confident predictions of the overthrow of this legislation, even in the lands in which it has held longest sway, may perhaps be ere long fulfilled'.[301]

Venereal Disease, the Birth-Rate and the War

Despite the confident predictions of abolitionists at the turn of the century, regulation was far from being overthrown. At the beginning of the Second World War some form of it still existed in 50 countries. In Europe, Britain, Scandinavia and Yugoslavia were about the only places where officially approved brothels or registered prostitutes were not to be found, and while Holland and Germany had given up the system officially, tolerated areas existed in some of their cities. France and Italy did not get rid of their brothel systems until after the Second World War, and although the rates of abolitionist to regulationist countries had risen by this time from 50 to 29, to 119 to 19, many of the 119 had informal regulation and inspection schemes. The White Slave Trade also continued, and although the subject of League of Nations investigation and activity in the 'thirties, it was still to be found in a lesser and less open fashion during the 'fifties.[302]

Investigation of this extremely obscure subject is not part of our present purpose, however, for although the United Free Church's Committee on the State Regulation of Vice remained in existence for the first few years of the new century,[303] it made no further reports after 1902. One of two Assembly reports during the pre-war years recalled the committee's heyday, however.

The first of these was the report of the Church Life and Work and Public Morals Committee to the 1913 Assembly. Two items in this are relevant. The first referred to the 1912 Criminal Law Amendment Act which had extended the provisions of the 1885 Act of the same name by giving the courts discretionary powers to whip as well as imprison men convicted of procuring. 'Horrible disclosures', the committee stated, had created a 'wave of moral indignation' which 'carried the Act triumphantly through both Houses of Parliament'.[304] This had been 'in every way satisfactory' and the Act was already having a 'beneficial' and 'deterrent'[305] effect. As a result of this, the committee went on, 'the public conscience has been so shocked, that not only has there been greater freedom in the discussion of such matters, but there is a more enlightened determination to seek public social purity'.[306] The committee's own determination to 'take definite action' in this area had manifested itself in enquiries made to the police, parish councils and voluntary 'preventive and rescue' organisations — which furnished it with 'reliable evidence' that immorality was increasing and that the age of erring girls was decreasing — and in advocating that the church, which had 'too long maintained silence', should adopt 'a policy of clear and pointed teaching on the subject of purity'.[307] The present 'dangerous' situation, which was 'not confined to one class', pointed to 'a breakdown of parental concern and control' and to the need for parents to 'exercise a firm control over their children' and to 'inform them as to the dangers that beset them'.[308] In schools, lectures should be given 'to senior girls by medical women on health and hygiene',[309] and the committee was writing to sessions appealing to them 'to encourage and strengthen the home influence': it also was preparing a series of pamphlets to be 'circulated among the youth'.[310] Subsequent reports of the committee recorded that a circular letter and copies of a 'leaflet on "Parental Responsibility" ' had been sent to all sessions in the hope that the leaflet would 'be sent into every home'.[311] Two further leaflets, a 'Letter to Boys' and a 'Letter to Girls', were also sent, but were not for 'indiscriminate circulation': the committee, 'aware that there are differences of opinion on this matter', was relying on the discretion of sessions to distribute them 'with the greatest care wherever their need is felt'.[312] Sessions must, however, have been either indiscreet or pessimistic, for the committee noted a year later that the letters to boys and girls had been 'in considerable demand'.[313]

The other matter discussed by the Life and Work committee in its 1913 report recalled the later stages of the Vice committee's activities. The British committee of the International Federation had been in correspondence with the India Office from 1909 to 1912 about 'certain of the former abuses' which had 'crept in at some of the military stations' in India, and they had ' "now elicited at last from the Indian authorities an admission that in many cantonments the periodical examination of women has been regularly permitted" '.[314] Nor was it denied that ' "brothels known to be for the use of soldiers are not only permitted in the cantonments, but are placed under some sort of medical supervision or control" '.[315] The Life and Work committee, however, with quite un-Dymock-like reticence, decided that it was 'not fitting to go into the details' and, praising Lord Kitchener (and his successor as Indian Commander-in-Chief) for trying 'to dissuade his men from vice', expressed gratification 'that quite recently the military authorities have expelled all European women from some of the cantonments'.[316] The old spirit flared up momentarily when it declared that 'the Christian sense of this nation cannot be satisfied until all evasion of the expressed will of Parliament shall cease',[317] and when it asked for permission for representatives to attend an abolitionist conference on the subject in London. But all this, while generally approved, was not debated in the Assembly, and no more was heard of it. Perhaps Sir Andrew Fraser — who was present at the Assembly but did not speak on this subject — had a quiet word with someone about it.[318]

But although the Assembly had finally loosened its grip on the thorny problem of vice in the Indian Army, it had not lost interest in vice as such, or in venereal disease. A year later, in 1914, the Church Life and Work and Public Morals Committee noted that 'a Royal Commission has been inquiring to the prevalence of diseases caused by immorality, and which have assumed the proportion of a grave menace to the national health and well-being'.[319] When this Commission reported, in 1916, an Edinburgh elder, Dr. J.W. Ballantyne, was to describe its report as 'one of the great historical disillusioning documents of these times' — 'a destructive bomb' which had 'torn down the curtain which we had continued to suffer to hang over a most disagreeable subject', revealing 'the skeleton in our national cupboard'.[320]

Two of the United Free Assembly's committees — that on Church Life and Work and Public Morals and that on Social Problems — were to be especially concerned with the Royal Commission's report. The Life and Work committee, investigating a decrease in the number of baptisms,[321] had attributed it, for the most part, to the declining birth-rate[322] and had passed the subject on to the Social Problems committee for further investigation, since that committee was already concerned with problems such as housing and the welfare of mothers and children. Both committees were alarmed by the fact that the birth-rate was declining among the middle and well-to-do artisan classes — from which the Protestant churches mainly drew their members[323] — but not among 'the least competent class of the population'.[324] The Social Problems committee attributed the decline among the middle and artisan classes not 'to natural causes' but to voluntary limitation which was in turn due to 'the desire for social comfort, the dread of the future for children, and the increased cost of maintaining a family': to this however it added as further causes of decline ('in the opinion of eminent medical men') 'certain racial poisons, due to alcohol, lead poisoning and venereal diseases'.[325]

The subject of venereal diseases was thus to some extent already associated with that of the declining birth-rate in the mind of the Social Problems committee when in 1917 its report dealt not only with the Royal Commission on Venereal Disease but also with the National Council of Public Morals' Commission on the Birth Rate.[326] The latter, which confirmed that the decline was greatest among Protestants and the better-off,[327] declared that 'all interference with nature by the destruction of the unborn babe, except to save the life of the mother, is criminal in the highest degree',[328] a view shared by witnesses from all the churches who 'were almost without exception opposed, on moral and religious grounds, not only to the practice of abortion, which had no defender among those who have given evidence before the Commission, but to the use of mechanical and chemical means to prevent conception'.[329] The churches were not however unanimous about 'the morality of restricting the family in other ways'.[330] Among the Commission's recommendations (which also included a minimum wage, unemployment insurance, state family bonuses, cheap education and lower rents) were: 'censure of the poor for recklessness in undertaking unlimited parental responsibility, and of the selfish luxury of the rich who shirk it' and 'a stimulation of the popular sentiment regarding the value and sacredness of family life'.[331]

The need to stimulate this sentiment was echoed in the Social Problems committee's treatment of the Royal Commission's report. The latter had stated 'that the number of persons infected with syphilis, acquired or congenital, cannot fall below ten per cent. of the whole population of large cities, and the percentage affected with gonorrhoea must greatly exceed this proportion'.[332] Venereal disease led to 'an enormous amount of disease and suffering' including an estimated 25 per cent. of blindness among the population and 30 to 50 per cent. of sterility among women. This, together with infant mortality cases associated with venereal disease, was related to the Social Problems committee's interest in promoting family life, and led it to urge the church 'to be up and doing', since a 'policy of masterly inactivity will not serve in the present crisis'.[333] Although 'the minister need not proclaim his views from the pulpit[334] and the elder is not required to talk about the subject unless he is consulted', they ought to have an opinion about it, distinguishing between 'self-control without indulgence' and 'sexual gratification with artificial prevention'.[335] The minister ought to get to the bottom of people's motives, 'for he cannot be ignorant that prudence is often given as the reason, whereas, lack of faith in God, or no higher motive than the selfish desire to enjoy some luxury, ought to be confessed'.[336]

The committee, thus set upon a course of denunciation which was not to run out of steam for half a century, passed the task of dealing with other implications of the Royal Commission's report back to the Life and Work committee — although not before noting with satisfaction that the Commission, whose remit included the understanding ' "that no return to the policy or provisions of the Contagious Diseases Acts of 1864, 1866 or 1869 is to be regarded as falling within the scope of the inquiry" ', had also placed ' "on record their view that the evidence they have received, which includes that of several Continental experts, points to the conclusion that no advantage would accrue from a return to the system of these Acts" '.[337]

The Life and Work committee, however, preoccupied with Systematic Giving, Cinematograph Censorship, Housing, Romanism and Ritualism, and Betting and Gambling,[338] must have lost its cue, for it was not until a year later that it took up the subject, and only then as a result of its discovery of Regulation 40D of the Defence of the Realm Act. Under this regulation no woman infected with venereal disease was allowed to have intercourse with any member of His Majesty's Forces. If she did, she could be charged and remanded for not less than a week for medical inspection, with the right of choosing her own doctor. To the Life and Work committee this was a 'virtual re-enactment of the Contagious Diseases Acts' and it wrote to the Home and War Secretaries urging them 'at once to rescind the offensive Regulation'.[339] The fact that the Royal Commission had decided that such enactments did no good hardened the committee's opposition, as did 'reliable information' it had received, that in some military units and in the navy men were issued with 'so-called preventives' and told that these would protect them. 'We are now,' it stated, 'in the hands of the generation of (often well-meaning) men who not only do not realise the nature of what they are doing, but are quite unaware that where medical examination has been introduced, it has been quite inefficacious as a check against the spread of disease.'[340]

A year later, however, the Social Problems committee, re-assuming responsibility for purity, was able to report that D.O.R.A. 40D had been withdrawn by the Government, although 'in a spirit of very bad temper, with an indication that it might be restored under another form'.[341] Access to licensed brothels in France for British troops, against which the Social Problems committee had also protested as, among other things, an 'offence . . . to the French people', had also been withdrawn 'in face of a storm of moral indignation'.[342] But the United Free Assembly had obviously been severely shaken by these and other revelations of wartime military morality; and the demand for 'a uniform standard for men and women with regard to purity',[343] which had always been a major element in the abolitionist programme and had been emphasised by feminists and purity societies in the pre-war period, was re-asserted. Along with this now, however, went a great emphasis on sex education and the recognition of social factors in the development of attitudes to marriage and the family. In terms strikingly reminiscent of James Begg, the convener of the Social Problems committee, Dr. R.J. Drummond, told the 1919 Assembly that there 'was a close relation between morality and religion and the houses in which men and women had to live. If they gave people houses where there was no privacy, no opportunity for the maintenance of modesty and no opportunity of secret devotion, they were taking away from them great factors in the building-up of character.'[344]

The Church of Scotland View

The Church of Scotland's attitude to such matters continued to be characterised by greater reticence, but wartime developments precluded total silence. The 'gravity' of the findings of the Royal Commission on Venereal Disease was noted by its Social Work committee in 1917, but mainly in connection with 'the stream of broken lives pouring through our Rescue Homes'.[345] The church's committee on Army and Navy Chaplains also was concerned with wartime sexual morality and was co-operating with the United Free and other churches in making representations to the Army Council about 'several matters affecting the wellbeing of our soldiers in France' with an eye on protecting 'the interest of morality'.[346] The interdenominational committee which did this also conducted a purity campaign among servicemen in France and the U.K. during 1917 and 1918. This took the form of lectures by selected chaplains to which 'officers and men were paraded'.[347] Later, the same committee took the army medical authorities to task 'in regard to the wording of the specimen lecture to troops on the prevention of disease, and also on the indiscriminate distribution of prophylactics'.[348] Parts of the lecture, it pointed out, could be taken 'as likely to encourage immorality, to create a false security and as condoning immorality if the consequences could be escaped'.[349] Changes in the lecture were promised, but nothing was said about the prophylactics.

The Church of Scotland's Commission on the War[350] also dealt with the problem of Impurity. A paper by Professor W.A. Curtis examined the whole spectrum of what could be subsumed under the title of 'Impurity and . . .',[351] including sections on 'Impurity and Prostitution' and 'Impurity and Disease'. The first of these betrayed considerable ambivalence on the writer's part toward the prostitute. In the Old Testament, he admitted, 'her foul trade . . . is so familiar in the town life of Israel as almost to evade censure when she appears in the unaffected narrative': yet 'her occupation is so wicked' that the prophets used her as 'a symbol of idolatry'.[352] In the New Testament again, she is 'the outcaste, but the object of Divine compassion': yet 'in the Epistles her fatal work is not concealed'.[353] To some extent Curtis was able to avoid the difficulty of choosing whether to condemn or be compassionate by echoing the 'apostolic censure' of 'the men who live upon her earnings or defile themselves with her flesh',[354] and when he went on to condemn brothel-keepers and clients, he described their crime as worse than that of the 'besotted women and tender girls'[355] whose bodies they exploited. Of one thing however he seemed certain: prostitution 'may have its phase of pleasure and idleness and luxury and dissipation, but it sinks to a condition which is almost too repulsive for human compassion — filth, poverty, shame, starvation, insanity'.[356]

That Curtis wrote this was curious, for two paragraphs later, reviewing Flexner's recent study of European prostitution,[357] he remarked that a 'surprising discovery is the extent to which women of their own accord succeed in extricating themselves from the morass and returning to respectability, disillusioned by their experience, not seldom financially enriched by their shame'.[358] Apart from the fact that Acton had made this 'surprising discovery' half a century earlier, it was odd that these two statements did not seem incongruous to Curtis, and was some indication of the ecclesiastical mind's need for moralistic overkill.

Despite this, however, Flexner's other 'discovery', that most prostitutes came from the lower reaches of the working classes, supported the compassionate side of Curtis' attitude to them. For many, he recognised, prostitution seemed the only way out, and illustrating his point with some Glasgow statistics, he argued that 'fines and imprisonment fail utterly to cope with the evil' and that 'no remedy that fails to reach them in their early homes, and to raise them above the level of casual unskilled and underpaid workers, can deal effectually with the problem'.[359]

The section of Professor Curtis' paper which dealt with 'Impurity and Disease' was little more than a brief account of the findings of the Royal Commission, emphasis being laid upon similar aspects to those emphasised by the United Free committees, at least insofar as the civilian population were concerned. On the question of venereal disease in the armed services, however, Curtis was somewhat ambiguous. Although he emphasised the enormity of the problem, he merely noted, without comment, that 'so hopeless has it appeared to the authorities to induce men to refrain from the evil in the Navy and the Army, that a medical preparation is served out to protect them as far as possible from the contagion they incur';[360] and although he asked, 'What would a prophet say to these things?' and 'What shall it advantage a great empire to gain a military victory and lose its own soul?' he also remarked, ambiguously, 'Much has been done to appeal to our men to resist temptation. Practically nothing has been done in France and Britain to remove the temptation. In Germany stern measures were promptly taken to protect the soldiery from a disease-spreading camp-following, for our enemy, if he is not devoted to chivalry, at least bows down to efficiency.'[361]

Whether or not Curtis was advocating regulationist measures here is not entirely clear. But he may well have been, for the official figures put the number of British soldiers hospitalised as a result of venereal disease at 4.3 per cent.,[362] and the numbers infected were, it was later alleged, 17.4 per cent., as opposed to 2.5 per cent. in the German army[363] — where prostitutes visited by soldiers were regularly inspected.[364] Britain, at least officially, was the only combatant nation which did not enforce regulation of some kind.[365] It is possible that the Church of Scotland as a whole was much less abolitionist than were its representatives sitting on the Interdenominational Purity Committee with the United Free churchmen.[366]

It may be noted, in conclusion, that after these two churches had united and when the country was once more at war, the Church and Nation committee, alarmed at the rising venereal disease rate especially in the vicinity of ports and military areas, and concerned 'that many infected persons are not coming to clinics', unanimously urged, in 1944, 'that strong efforts should be made to secure compulsory notification and complete treatment of Venereal Disease in the interests of the individual, the future family and the community'.[367] Since the country already had, in the form of Regulation 33B of the Defence of the Realm Act, a new wartime measure providing for compulsory examination of infected persons of both sexes, the church's late conversion to this aspect of 'the system' was perhaps rather gratuitous.

Conversion, however, was not total: a year later the Church and Nation committee, under the coy subtitle 'anent a certain allegation',[368] recorded how it had been pursuing the military authorities about the issue of contraceptives to servicemen going on leave. But even here the fires of indignation were burning low. When the committee was informed, by the services' medical departments and by their chaplains, that contraceptives were 'available' rather than 'offered' to the men, and that the chaplains had 'every opportunity, and the first opportunity when men enter the Services, to stress the obligation of sexual purity on moral and spiritual grounds', it judged that 'before the Church could insist on the cessation of the availability practice, it would require to be convinced that its abolition, if secured, would not result in greater evils than those it sought to remedy'.[369] In saying this, the committee tacitly accepted the official view that the social and financial cost of venereal disease among men who 'despite moral and spiritual persuasion . . . will go their own way'[370] was a greater evil than the moral cost of making contraceptives available. 'Account,' they considered, 'had to be taken of the actual conditions in time of war' — not least significant among which now was the fact that contraceptives were 'obtainable by civilians in every city and town and even in the country'.[371]

CHAPTER FIFTEEN

Theological and Other Factors

BEFORE leaving the subject of church attitudes to regulation, it may again be worth asking how far the arguments used were influenced by theological reflection. The arguments used by the United Presbyterian and Free Churches, as we have already noted, were of three kinds, concerning cost and effectiveness, civil liberty, and making sin safe.

Cost and Effectiveness

Arguments of the first kind were frequently introduced into the controversy about regulation. Those concerning effectiveness were probably more important than those concerning cost, for there was little point in regulation being cheap if it did no good. Cost arguments, however, were useful, for accusations about Government extravagance always make good debating points. But neither arguments about cost nor arguments about effectiveness ever rose far above the level of political expediency, for regulationists and abolitionists alike were able to use them with great confidence when current statistics proved the point they wished to make, only to reject them with equally great confidence (and comments on the unreliability of 'mere' statistics) when they went against them. Such arguments may therefore be seen as confirming rather than creating the views of either side. Principal Rainy frequently advised the Free Church that their fundamental objections to regulation were moral and religious: Professor Fournier agreed that the statistical argument had failed and preferred to rely upon 'common sense'.

Civil Liberty

How far fundamental moral and religious arguments on the one side and common sense on the other were in fact responsible for making some people abolitionist and others regulationist is of course difficult to tell, for the reasons why the protagonists of public controversy espouse their respective causes are usually much more mixed than they allow. It seems likely that in the early years of this particular controversy arguments of the second kind — about civil liberty — came closest to representing the deeper feelings of those who wanted to repeal the Contagious Diseases Acts. The thought that Englishwomen might be arrested on mere suspicion and perhaps out of malice, by a secret police force, represented a threat to individual liberty the more severe because it had been documented with graphic and gory examples. It was understandable that working men, whose wives and daughters were in most danger, were among those who signed the numerous repeal petitions.

When such petitions were framed by the Free and United Presbyterian churches they included arguments about civil liberty and constitutional rights, but the theological presuppositions which informed them were rarely if ever articulated. Perhaps it was difficult for the descendants of Calvinists to know where they stood over against those who used Calvinist coercion for ungodly ends. Or perhaps it simply was that the rights of an Englishman[1] to the churches, like the rights of Roman citizenship to St. Paul, were too self-evident to require justification. Even so, the espousal by the churches in this context of arguments in defence of the constitutional rights of women of the lower classes at least implied a theological presupposition. Directly or indirectly, the idea expressed in Christian teaching by the dictum that there is 'neither bond nor free . . . neither male nor female' in Christ underlay this aspect of the churches' pronouncements. So far as it went, this idea contrasted markedly with the note of social and sexual superiority in the voices of many medical and military professionals.

It did not go very far, however: for the churches were rather less expressive of their own time's variant on 'neither Jew nor Gentile' — neither British nor lesser breed — than of the other two distinctions. When the controversy entered its later stages there was little to substantiate Mr. McCandlish's assertion that the Free Church committee was only concerned about protecting Indian prostitutes.[2] Scarcely any mention was made of these women except as ciphers of vice, and even Dr. Huntly, one of the few people involved who had actually spoken with some of them, clearly was more concerned about the women of England.[3] Insofar as the churches were now concerned about protecting anyone (apart from the women of England — and everyone, including the regulationists, was concerned about protecting them), the most likely candidates were the British soldiers, who required protection from sin (but not from its fruits) by being given facilities for marriage. But then soldiers too were being converted into ciphers as the controversy dragged on: and even the benighted Hindus and Mohammedans, whose conversion had been hindered by Britain's Mission of Vice, sank almost out of sight as abolitionists and regulationists fired off familiar-sounding salvoes from familiar-looking positions. It would probably be a mistake therefore to imagine that much theological reflection relating to the second kind of argument informed the churches' later pronouncements.

Making Sin Safe

The third argument — that regulation encouraged vice by appearing to make sin safe — was, however, a fairly constant feature in the churches' pronouncements from beginning to end; and it seems likely that this argument represented, as Rainy wanted it to, the churches' central objection to regulation. It correctly identified the main purpose of regulation as the protection of soldiers from venereal disease — rather than their or the prostitutes' reformation. But the implications it drew from this, notably that regulation encouraged prostitution and hence venereal disease, were more difficult to substantiate; and the alternatives to regulation suggested by the churches were frequently impractical, the only exception being the expensive suggestion of a married army.

The great difficulty about this argument, however, was the churches' ambivalent attitude towards the notion that venereal disease was a deterrent to and a punishment for illicit intercourse. That it was not a deterrent to the men most at risk must surely have been clear from the numbers involved; and this argument, like subsequent ecclesiastical arguments against contraception, rested upon a somewhat naive analysis of the psychology of their fellow-countrymen, in which churchmen took their own attitudes as normative. Such an analysis was not of course totally misguided, since it was based upon a desire to appeal to the men's higher nature. But it was not particularly realistic either.

More serious was the churches' refusal to come to terms with the idea that venereal disease was a punishment. As we have seen, this idea was expressed in vague references to the law of nature, which suggest that the churches were as reluctant to deny as to affirm that God caused venereal disease. The opportunity for a theological reappraisal of this notion was certainly not taken up by the churches in this connection, and one is left with the suspicion that they preferred to keep their thinking on the subject vague, perhaps because they were afraid of the consequences of any theological conclusion which might demythologise venereal disease.

The churches' use of this third argument therefore suggests that the introduction of therapeutic and prophylactic considerations into what had hitherto been a much more straightforward argument about sin, caught the churches off balance and left them unable to offer any very convincing theological critique of the new situation.

Political and Historical Perspectives

The churches' reaction to regulation, then, seems to have owed less to theological reflection than to the exigencies of their own historical situation. The situation of the two churches which protested against regulation was a complex one. In theory, the Free Church stood for the Establishment principle and the United Presbyterians for the Voluntary principle: but in practice neither church was established. In practice too, the opinions expressed by their members did not always reflect the principles for which their churches stood. Matters were further complicated by the fact that even if all of the Presbyterian churches had been united and together established, their influence on Government for righteousness would have been severely limited by the provincial character of their sphere of influence.

Under these circumstances the Free Assembly and the United Presbyterian Synod had little hope of exercising much diplomatic influence on the Imperial Government — even though Rainy was a distant cousin of Gladstone. If the Government was encouraging unrighteousness (a far cry from the days when it had complied with their fathers' demand to suppress unrighteousness), the most they could do was to ally themselves with others, including regiments of women, to rouse public opinion, and hence the electorate, against its unwisdom. Unlike the Church of Scotland, which provided the services with their Presbyterian chaplains, and therefore was on the whole more likely to understand, to sympathise with, and even to hope to influence the motives of the military leadership, the Free and United Presbyterian churches had no lines of communication to those who had decided that regulation was necessary. Consequently they tended to view them in caricature, and lacked any very effective desire to understand their position, or for that matter the position of medical men and officials once it had been ascertained that they were regulationists.

The fact that the Free and United Presbyterian churches protested against regulation must therefore, to some extent, be accounted for by the position they occupied in contemporary society. This contention is supported by the observation that the Free Church's anti-Government polemic slowed down and eventually ground to a halt at about the time when some of its ministers were added to the Government chaplaincy payroll, and when some of its elders who were also prominent members of the medical, military and Indian establishments undertook to interpret the motives of their colleagues to their fathers and brethren.

Since this also took place at a time when the evils abolitionists wished to abolish were becoming too distant and too complicated for the average British citizen to wish to understand, especially as the Contagious Diseases Acts which might have affected him or his sister had long since been repealed, abolition was no longer the popular cause it once had been. Without such popular support and the resources of a great movement, the United Free Church could do little for the cause, even if it had wanted to.

The abolitionist tradition of the Free and United Presbyterian churches more or less died out therefore long before the Union of 1929. What survived was a compromise between the anti-establishmentarian Free Church policy of denunciation and the establishmentarian Church of Scotland policy of silent influence; but when the former flared up, as in the 1940's case of the 'available' contraceptives, it was soon smothered by the smooth words of the latter. The genuine abolitionist tradition had long since run out of steam.

Despite this, it would be a mistake to suppose that the abolitionists had laboured in vain, however much the Church and Nation committee's demand for compulsory notification and examination might suggest this.[4] Consideration of what had happened to regulation in Britain shows that this was not the case.

To Acton the Contagious Diseases Acts had seemed an excellent public health measure, abuses of which could be corrected by ensuring that the medical profession was firmly in control of its operations. If he and many members of his profession — perhaps the majority[5] — regarded abolitionists as religious fanatics and obscurantists, intent on impeding the beneficent progress of medical science, this would have been highly understandable, for medicine had frequently been in this position before. The fact that the abolitionist movement received vocal support from Scotch Nonconformists would have done little to undermine this view.

Regulation was not supported only by doctors, however, but also by the military authorities, who had more pressing concerns to attend to than that of devising safeguards to mollify the abolitionists. Even if General Chapman was not typical, it is likely that many and perhaps the majority of his colleagues were in favour of some form of state regulation of prostitution in order to keep venereal disease in check as simply and efficiently as possible.[6] They had, after all, wars to fight and an Empire to defend.

But in the end the decision about regulation had to be taken not by the military or medical authorities, but by Parliament, and Parliament could not afford to ignore public opinion. This was where the abolitionists, and with them the churches, played an important and perhaps decisive part in preventing the totalitarian elements in the medical and military professions from extending regulation at home and from making it work as completely as they wished abroad.

It remains of course an open question whether or not much human suffering would have been spared had the regulationists had their way. But the relative ineffectiveness of the medical methods at their disposal suggests that regulation was not at that time an adequate way of dealing with venereal disease and that consequently the abolitionists prevented the authorities from pre-empting a problem to which a more adequate response, both medical and social, had yet to be found. Whether or not in medical terms penicillin, and in social terms the de-professionalising of prostitution, are that response, is of course another question.

PART THREE

Scripture and Common Sense

IN October 1871 a letter to the ministers of the nonconformist churches of England was signed by 'the most eminent theological and leading Ministers of the Church of Scotland, the Free Church of Scotland, the United Presbyterian Church, the Reformed Presbyterian Church and the Original Secession Church'.[1] Not everyone in Scotland would have agreed that the Church of Scotland signatories really were the most eminent: of Lord Sand's catalogue of her greatest preachers of the period — 'Norman Macleod, Caird, Tulloch, Flint, Macgregor, Boyd, Burns and Milligan'[2] — only the last[3] was represented, and other great names, not least Charteris, were absent. The credentials of the Free Church signatories however could not be questioned: R.S. Candlish[4] and Patrick Fairbairn, principals of the Free Church Edinburgh and Glasgow colleges, Duff, the first Scottish missionary to India, the inevitable James Begg and Thomas Guthrie and Rainy (a late signatory) were all included, as were John Cairns and Andrew Thomson from the United Presbyterians, together with others from the smaller churches. It was an impressive exhibition of unanimity by churches which often appeared bound to one another only by their common investment in Scottish Presbyterianism and mutual suspicion. Alongside their lack of public agreement about banns and about repeal of the Contagious Diseases Acts it was perhaps even more remarkable, since the subject of their letter also concerned legislation relating to sex and marriage.

The subject of the letter was marriage affinity, or more exactly the proposal to legalise marriage with a deceased wife's sister (hereinafter referred to as MDWS). Of this proposal, the signatories reminded their readers, the Lord Chancellor Sir William Page Wood had remarked, 'I would rather hear of the landing of 300,000 French at Dover than of the passing of this Bill.'[5] Attempts to pass it had been made year after year in Parliament since 1847, and the question would not finally be settled until 1907. Year after year, Assemblies too were to pronounce on it, and for once not without having to do some theological rethinking. The results of that rethinking will be difficult to follow, however, unless we begin by saying something about the historical and legislative background to the controversy.

CHAPTER SIXTEEN

The Development of The Affinity Law

Before the Reformation

EARLY Christian teaching on consanguinity and affinity as impediments to marriage was unsystematic and largely a matter of practical and pastoral concern. The civil marriage law of the Roman Empire prohibited marriage with any direct ascendants or descendants and with relations in the collateral line to the third degree;[1] and Christians obeyed this, as their apologists were quick to point out, since misunderstanding of their talk about 'brothers', 'sisters' and 'love feasts' had led to accusations of immorality and even of incest.

Christians were also subject however to the church's own understanding of marriage. This was based upon the fragmentary teaching of the New Testament on the subject and upon Jewish law. The latter held that the impediments of consanguinity and affinity actually mentioned in the Mosaic law made a marriage incestuous and void from the beginning: but consanguinity and affinity impediments added later and collected in the Talmud were not regarded so seriously, although they could be grounds for the cancellation of a betrothal or for divorce. These laws were not of course taken over *in toto* by the early Christians, for their attitude to Judaism — not least on the subject of divorce[2] — was far from uncritical. Their ambivalence however did not lead them to reject the Levitical roots of Jewish teaching on consanguinity and affinity.

For several centuries the Western church, whose discipline remained distinct from Roman marriage law even after the latter came under its influence, had no very clear marriage law of its own. During these centuries its teaching on consanguinity and affinity was somewhat haphazard and subject to a variety of authorities and local customs. Gregory the Great,[3] for example, informed Augustine of Canterbury that the church could not approve of certain marriages allowed under Roman law, because they were prohibited by Leviticus, condemned by John the Baptist, and infertile in practice. At the same time however he advised Augustine to deal gently with Englishmen who had already contracted such marriages, and not to deny them baptism or to separate them from their women; and on another occasion he told Augustine that two brothers might marry two sisters since Scripture did not condemn it.[4]

But although Christian teaching on marriage was haphazard, it was making headway. As one commentator has put it: 'The divine law was crudely conceived in terms of the Levitical books, but even so it conquered men's imagination. Of those sacred books the spiritual chiefs of the Church were the guardians and interpreters.'[5] Thus in the eleventh and twelfth century the church was assuming control over the constitution of marriage, codifying its canon law, and attempting, with a varying measure of success and failure, to impose that law on a chaotic variety of local folk-laws and customs.

In codifying its teaching on consanguinity and affinity, the church relied for the most part on the Old Testament book of Leviticus. There had, however, been two schools of thought on how it should be interpreted. Some authorities held that only the impediments of consanguinity and affinity actually mentioned in Leviticus were of importance, others that these were part of a more general law prohibiting intercourse or marriage with near kin. The second view predominated and, by analogy with the recognised limits of kinship in the civil law of succession, marriage was forbidden with kin up to the seventh degree of the Roman computation. But matters had been complicated when in the ninth century the Western church had adopted the German method of computation,[6] without abandoning the notion that prohibitions should extend to the seventh degree.

This change in computation widened the range of kin with whom marriage was prohibited to an extent which made the system virtually unworkable, and in 1215 the Fourth Lateran Council limited the prohibition to the fourth degree, at the same time making it a diriment impediment (that is, an impediment which prevented such a marriage from coming into being at all), and ruling that sexual intercourse whether inside or outside marriage created consanguinity.

The Pauline 'one flesh' argument[7] which lay behind this last point was also the basis of the church's rules on the impediment of affinity. By the eighth century these prevented a man from marrying not only his own blood-relations up to the seventh degree, but also any kin, up to the seventh degree, of his wife or any woman with whom he had sexual intercourse. The husbands and wives of these women's kin were also prohibited, as were any wives or husbands whom they as widowers or widows might subsequently marry. In such cases the number of prohibited degrees was soon reduced, as it was in the case of affinity between the children of a widow's second marriage and the kin of her first husband. But even so, such notions of affinity went well beyond the provisions of Roman or Mosaic law, and created a situation in which not only was the system virtually unworkable, but in which it was virtually impossible to determine whether or not it could work. The fact that spiritual kinship, which was a form of affinity established by participation in the baptism of a child by parents, sponsors and the priest, also had to be taken into consideration, only compounded this difficulty, and it was a singularly wise child who knew all his affines. The fourth Lateran Council consequently thought it best to restrict affinity as well as consanguinity prohibitions to the fourth degree.

The Lateran Council's action thus removed some practical difficulties, but by removing obstructions which had been viewed as part of the Divine law it again raised doubts about the principle underlying the system. These doubts were compounded by the fifteenth-century practice of granting papal dispensations in cases where impediments had hitherto been regarded as of Divine origin. This practice provided many opportunities for the satisfaction of doubtful motives and for corruption. The case of Henry VIII of England illustrates both the complexity and the corruption of the system.

Calvin and Leviticus

Subsequent developments in the law of England provided the occasion for the nineteenth-century controversy about MDWS. But the tradition which Scottish churchmen fell heir to had developed rather differently. It stemmed, of course, from the Reformers, who rejected the complexities of ecclesiastical law[8] and turned for advice to Scripture, and particularly, as their predecessors also had done, to the book of Leviticus.

The subject was dealt with by Calvin in *The Harmony of the Four Last Books of the Pentateuch*, which he wrote towards the end of his life. In it, he divided the four books — Exodus, Leviticus, Numbers and Deuteronomy — into two principal parts, the 'Historical Narrative' and the 'Doctrine'. He subdivided the latter by taking each of the ten commandments in turn, and adding to each the remaining chapters as 'Supplements' — 'by which word', he wrote, 'I mean with respect to the First Table,[9] the Ceremonies and the outward Exercises of Worship; with respect to the Second Table, the Political Laws, for the object of both these parts is merely to aid in the observance of the Moral Law'.[10] Calvin believed that the Law had not been abrogated except insofar as it no longer condemned Christians: its function now was 'to pinch them awake to their imperfection'.[11] The ceremonial law however had been abrogated 'in use', but not 'in effect', by Christ, who provided release from the sin of which the ceremonies were confessions, and thereby 'terminated them, but has not deprived them of anything of their sanctity; rather, he has approved and honoured it'.[12] Similarly, wrote Calvin,

> the form of their judicial laws, although it had no other intent than how best to preserve that very love which is enjoined in God's eternal law, had something distinct from that precept of love. Therefore, as ceremonial laws could be abrogated while piety remained safe and unharmed, so too, when these judicial laws were taken away, the perpetual duties and precepts of love could still remain.[13]

In this context the chapters of Leviticus (18 and 20) which deal with consanguinity and affinity were included by Calvin under the Seventh Commandment, as one of the Supplements dealing with the Political Laws. Before noting his comments, it will be useful to quote the passage around which controversy was later to rage. It is Leviticus: chapter 18, verses 6 to 18, quoted here in the Revised Standard Version:

> 6None of you shall approach any one near of kin to him to uncover nakedness. I am the Lord. 7You shall not uncover the nakedness of your father, which is the nakedness of your mother; she is your mother, you shall not uncover her nakedness. 8You shall not uncover the nakedness of your father's wife; it is your father's nakedness. 9You shall not uncover the nakedness of your sister, the daughter of your father or the daughter of

your mother, whether born at home or born abroad. [10]You shall not uncover the nakedness of your son's daughter or of your daughter's daughter, for their nakedness is your own nakedness. [11]You shall not uncover the nakedness of your father's wife's daughter, begotten by your father, since she is your sister. [12]You shall not uncover the nakedness of your father's sister; she is your father's near kinswoman. [13]You shall not uncover the nakedness of your mother's sister, for she is your mother's near kinswoman. [14]You shall not uncover the nakedness of your father's brother, that is, you shall not approach his wife; she is your aunt. [15]You shall not uncover the nakedness of your daughter-in-law; she is your son's wife, you shall not uncover her nakedness. [16]You shall not uncover the nakedness of your brother's wife; she is your brother's nakedness. [17]You shall not uncover the nakedness of a woman and of her daughter, and you shall not take her son's daughter or her daughter's daughter to uncover her nakedness; they are your near kinswomen; it is wickedness. [18]And you shall not take a woman as a rival wife to her sister, uncovering her nakedness while her sister is yet alive.

These verses were prefaced by a warning from God that the Israelites should not follow the customs of the Egyptians and the Canaanites. The existence of such customs, Calvin observed, was what made it necessary for God to list here 'the kinds of incest of which the mention would else have been superfluous': for 'since all the Orientals are libidinous, they never had any scruple in polluting themselves by incestuous marriages'.[14] Not every kind of incest however was mentioned in this passage. But, Calvin argued, the 'monstrous indecency in the connexion of father and daughter, or mother and son'[15] was sufficient indication (verses 7 and 10) of a ban on intercourse with all ascendants and descendants. In the case of the collateral line, intercourse with uncles (in the case of females) and aunts on both sides (verses 12 and 13) was 'a somewhat similar impropriety'[16] to intercourse with one's parents, as was connection with a step-mother (verse 8) or a mother-in-law, and with a paternal (verse 14) or maternal uncle's wife; similarly intercourse with a step-daughter (verse 17) or daughter-in-law (verse 15) was like that with a daughter; in all of these cases 'the same rule affects affinity'[17] as consanguinity. The list, Calvin admitted, did not prohibit a maternal or paternal uncle from marrying his niece. Here, he said, 'we must form our judgment by analogy as to what is prohibited'.[18] Thus, 'since the nephew is interdicted from marrying his paternal or maternal aunt the mutual relation of the inferior to the superior degree must prevail', especially since 'the reason added by Moses' in the former case (verses 12 and 13) — ' "She is thy father's or thy mother's near kinswoman" '[19] — could refute any objection to this. Intercourse or marriage with sisters or half-sisters (verses 9 and 11) was also prohibited, he added.

Calvin emphasised that this list applied to marriage as well as to illicit intercourse, pointing out that although such marriage regulations were 'a part of the political constitution which God established for his ancient people', they were not 'merely political'[20] nor were they dissolved because of the abrogation of the law. 'Whatever is prescribed here,' he stated, 'is deduced from the source of rectitude itself, and from the natural feelings implanted in us by Him.'[21] The non-observance of these prohibitions by certain nations at certain times did not detract from the fact that 'the prohibition of incests here set forth ... flows from the fountain of nature itself, and is founded on the general principle of all laws, which is perpetual and inviolable'.[22] God was displeased with the heathen customs against which this chapter was directed 'because nature itself repudiates and abhors filthiness': the incests prohibited here were thus 'absolute prohibitions'.[23] Although the New Testament said little on the subject, it was clear that when Paul condemned incest of a stepson and his father's wife as falling short even of Gentile standards, he endorsed the general prohibition which even the secular Roman laws accorded with — 'as if their authors had learnt from Moses what was decorous and agreeable to nature'.[24]

Calvin recognised however that three cases might be seen as problems. The first of these concerned first cousins, who were permitted by Scripture to marry. Calvin was rather uneasy about this. 'Since from long custom,' he wrote, 'it is established that cousins-german should not marry, we must beware of giving scandal lest too unbridled a liberty should expose the Gospel to much reproach; and we must bear in mind Paul's admonition, to abstain even from things lawful when they are not expedient.'[25]

The second problem lay in the interpretation of verse 16 of Leviticus chapter 18, which concerned marriage with a brother's wife. 'Bad interpreters',[26] he wrote, tried to make this verse into a prohibition of illicit intercourse with a brother's wife or marriage with her after divorce from, but during the lifetime of, the brother. But they were wrong: for it was 'incongruous to twist into different senses declarations which are made in the same place, and in the same words'.[27] Calvin was 'not, however, ignorant of the source from whence those, who think otherwise, have derived their mistake' — which was Deuteronomy chapter 25 verse 5, where 'God gives a command . . . that if a man shall have died without issue, his surviving brother shall take his widow to wife, in order that he may raise up of her seed to the departed'.[28] What the 'bad interpreters' overlooked, observed Calvin, was the 'well-known Hebrew idiom' which embraced 'under the name of brother all near kinsmen in general', a usage also employed by the Latins to designate first cousins.[29] The Deuteronomic command thus only applied to relations not barred by the consanguinity and affinity prohibitions mentioned above. The case of Ruth and Boaz[30] illustrated the point, said Calvin, while

> if any object that Er, Onan, and Shelah, the sons of Judah, were own-brothers, and still that Tamar married two of them, the difficulty is easily solved, viz., that Judah, following the common and received practice of the Gentiles acted improperly in permitting it. By evil communications then, as is ever the case, Judah was led into giving the same wife to his second son as had before been married to his eldest.[31]

This case therefore did not constitute any objection or exception to the rule.

The third problem noted by Calvin was that of the meaning of verse 18. 'Certain froward persons',[32] he wrote, were arguing that this allowed MDWS, since it forbade (polygamous) marriage with a wife's sister only during the wife's lifetime. Had this simply been a prohibition of uncovering her 'turpitude',[33] then 'there would have been some colour to their pretext'.[34] It was necessary however 'to consider the intention of the legislator from his own express words', which 'expressly stated' that 'she, who was legally married should (not) be troubled by quarrels and contentions'.[35] It was therefore, wrote Calvin, 'plain that the licence for polygamy is restricted by this exception, in order that the Israelites should be contented with one evil, and, at least, should not expose two sisters to hostile competition with each other'.[36] Polygamy, in other words, was bad enough for Israelite women to put up with — they were to be spared the additional burden of having to put up with rival wives among their own near kinswomen — here again Calvin interprets sister in a very broad sense. Finally, wrote Calvin, the prohibition of a brother marrying his brother's widow shows that MDWS was not meant here. 'But hence,' he added, 'we see the diabolical arrogance of the Pope, who by inventing new degrees of kindred, would be wiser than God; whilst he also betrays his cunning, because from this kind of sport he made himself a fat game-bag.'[37]

Having noted how Calvin dealt with these three possible problems, and at the same time with his antinomian and papal opponents, it is worth repeating that the two main points made in his commentary on Leviticus 18 were: first, that the prohibitions, while part of the law given by God for the political government of Israel, and as such merely aids to the observance of the moral law, were also absolute, since they had been deduced from the natural feelings implanted in men's hearts by God, and thus should be part of the law under contemporary civil government also — a law to which Christians as much as others should, in Calvin's view,[38] be subject; and second, that while not all the prohibited degrees were mentioned in Leviticus 18, the general outline was given and should be reasonably clear by analogy to those who used their judgement.

One further point to be made about Calvin's interpretation of the question concerns his handling of Leviticus chapter 20, verses 11, 12, 14, 17, 19 and 20 — 24 of which list penalties, mostly capital punishment, for sexual intercourse within some of the degrees mentioned in chapter 18. Although Calvin does not explicitly say that these penalties ought to form part of contemporary law, and although he perhaps takes something from the importance of the passage by adding (in some editions) the qualifying sub-title 'These Supplements as Judicial',[39] he does not seem to dispute the appropriateness of the penalties.

The Law of Scotland and the Confession of Faith

Calvin's commentary on Leviticus was written in 1563 and published in 1564, the year of his death. But before this, the question of consanguinity and affinity had already been considered by the Reformed Church of Scotland. At its first meeting, the General Assembly declared:

> The question being proponed anent marriage in second and other degrees of consanguinity forbidden by the Pope to be solemnized betwixt parties being of second, third, and fourth degrees of affinity and consanguinity and others such as are not prohibited expressly by the Word of God, and therefore to desire the Lords and Estates to interpone their authority and approve the same and make laws thereupon.[40]

This declaration, by omitting any mention of the first degree of consanguinity and affinity, suggests that the General Assembly, like Calvin, wished to imply that the Levitical prohibitions (as verse 6 of chapter 18 might be taken to mean) were intended as prohibitions of marriage of a male or female with a female or male related to him or her by consanguinity or affinity both in the direct line and in the collateral line up to the first (German) degree.

In making this declaration the Assembly was requesting Parliament to replace the existing ecclesiastical law with a new civil statute. The existing ecclesiastical law had been enacted in Canon 65 of the Scottish Provincial Council at Perth in 1242, which embodied the teaching of the fourth Lateran Council of 1215. It recognised, in respect of the prohibited degrees, a distinction between those prohibited by the divine law, and those which could be sanctioned (but only by dispensation) by the church which had forbidden them. MDWS and marriage between an uncle and niece were among the latter.

The Scottish Parliament did not respond to the Assembly's request until 1567, when in an Act of that year 'Anent thame that committis incest' it provided the death penalty for those

> that abusis their body with sic personis in degree as Goddis Word has expresslie forbidden in ony time cummin as is contenit in the 18th chapter of Leviticus.[41]

The following section (c.15) enacted that it was lawful for all related in the second and further degrees to marry, provided the marriage was not otherwise repugnant to God's Word. Until the nineteenth century this was the basis of the statute law of Scotland on the subject. Whether or not those who drew it up intended MDWS to be included is not certain, but since there is on record one case in which the court exacted the death penalty for intercourse between a deceased wife's sister and her deceased sister's husband,[42] it seems likely that Calvin's interpretation of Leviticus 18.18 was commonly accepted.

The next development took place a century later, in 1690, when the Scots Parliament ratified the Westminster Confession of Faith, voting upon each article. Article 24, section 4 of this read:

> Marriage ought not to be within the degrees of consanguinity and affinity forbidden in the Word; nor can such incestuous marriages ever be made lawful by any law of man, or consent of parties, so as those persons may live together as man and wife. The man may not marry any of his wife's kindred nearer in blood than he may of his own, nor the woman of her husband's kindred nearer than in blood of her own.[43]

This interpretation of Leviticus was based upon parity of reasoning of the kind employed by Calvin (as in the uncle/niece, nephew/aunt cases). The prohibition thus applied to all persons related by consanguinity and affinity in the first degree, the relationship being determined by counting either from the female or from the male.

Having approved this interpretation as the law of the church, the Scottish legislature did not go on to alter the civil law. But subsequent practice and the opinion of legal authorities on the subject agreed that although the penal Act 1567 c.14 might not justify capital punishment in MDWS cases (because the wording of that Act made everything hinge on the ambiguous verses 6 and 18 of Leviticus 18), the Act 1567 c.15 clearly prohibited MDWS (because the parity of reasoning employed in the Confession of Faith, and endorsed by Parliament, brought MDWS within the scope of the first degree of affinity). This was finally established by the court in the case of *Fenton v Livingstone*, 1861,[44] which confirmed that MDWS was illegal in the civil law of Scotland. The controversy which we are concerned with here, however, also involved English law, which had developed somewhat differently.

The Law of England

Sixteenth-century English law[45] on the subject of consanguinity and affinity tended to follow Lutheran practice, by keeping close to the letter of Leviticus. At the same time however it was beginning to move in the direction of Calvinist parity of reasoning. It was also much affected by the domestic entanglements of Henry VIII and by Elizabeth's need to secure her succession. By the end of the century — whose second half had seen 'one of the most sordid chapters of English legislation'[46] — there were thus several different laws on the subject in the statute book.

The church as well as the state was making laws, however. In 1603 a canon enacted by the Provincial Synod of Canterbury endorsed a table of sixty prohibited degrees of consanguinity and affinity which had been issued on his own authority in 1563 by Matthew Parker, the Archbishop of Canterbury. Parker's Table was based on Leviticus 18, interpreted by the process of parity of reasoning discussed above. When the canon endorsing it received the Royal Assent, this became the church's official list of prohibited degrees.

The canon of 1603 required marriages within the prohibited degrees to be dissolved, after being declared incestuous and unlawful by the ecclesiastical courts. (These retained their jurisdiction over marriage, whereas in Scotland jurisdiction had passed, in 1560, to the crown.) The civil authorities, however, were to execute this, and were consequently in some difficulty, since it was far from clear that the civil law prohibited all the unions listed by Parker. In an attempt to resolve this difficulty, efforts were made to establish the legality of MDWS. These were unsuccessful. The civil courts however were successful when they prohibited the ecclesiastical courts from declaring — after the death of either or both parties to MDWS — that the union was void and the children were illegitimate.

This was an important move, because it affected the question of inheritance. Jealous relatives could and did bring actions before the ecclesiastical courts, in order to bastardise and thus disinherit children of such unions after their parents' deaths. The civil courts' prohibitions made such unions voidable rather than void. They were thus relatively safe unless or until an action was raised in the ecclesiastical courts, and absolutely safe after the death of one of the parties. So matters stood until the nineteenth century.

During this period it was sometimes assumed that MDWS was legal. One reason for this was that some of those whose marriages were thought to be voidable arranged for friends to bring to court against them an unsuccessful but indefinitely prolonged suit which effectively prevented any other and potentially successful suit being brought. Practices of this kind, and in other cases the cost of proceedings, meant that many illegal and voidable unions were unchallenged. Parker's Table was thus not always adhered to in practice, and the future of children involved was uncertain. To remedy this situation Parliament, in 1835, passed Lord Lyndhurst's Act, which adopted Parker's Table into the civil law and ruled that any marriage thereafter contracted within the prohibited degrees should be no longer voidable, but simply and without the need of any legal process void from the beginning.

To some people this remedy seemed worse than the disease — especially as some assumed that MDWS had hitherto been legal. Although Lyndhurst's Act left voidable marriages contracted before 1835 as they were and applied only to new ones, it created considerable opposition and controversy. By 1847 petitions were being presented to Parliament, signed by Anglican and Dissenting clergymen among others, asking for the law to be made more liberal. As a result the Government set up a Royal Commission to investigate the whole question of consanguinity and affinity. In the course of its enquiries the Commission discovered that, even since 1835, the number of cases of MDWS contracted in England had been considerable, and that such marriages had been contracted by people of all classes, including five mayors and several clergymen.[47] Its report, after it had heard this and a great deal of argument on either side, recommended that the law of consanguinity and affinity should be made more liberal, and specifically, following the example of a number of European countries and American states, that MDWS should be made legal.

This report strengthened the movement to legalise MDWS, and a Bill to that end was introduced into Parliament and given a second reading by the House of Commons in 1849, only to founder at the committee stage. A second attempt was made in 1850, when the Bill got as far as the House of Lords, but was then withdrawn. Brought there a year later, it was defeated by a large majority, only to reappear in the Commons in 1855, where it again foundered in committee. In 1859, after some further attempts, it was once again passed by the Commons, only to be defeated yet again in the Upper House. The margin by which the MDWS Bill, now and for the rest of the century firmly established as an annual parliamentary event, either passed or failed in either the Lords or the Commons was generally small.[48] The nation, if Parliament reflected its views, was unable to make up its mind. But what was the mind of the Scottish churches?

CHAPTER SEVENTEEN

Manning the Floodgates

WHEN the first MDWS Bill was introduced into Parliament in 1849, neither the Established nor the Free Assembly were in any doubt of their opposition to what it proposed. Their position on MDWS had been clearly re-stated only ten years earlier, when the General Assembly had ruled that marriage between a man and the sister of his deceased wife was prohibited by the Word of God and contrary to the Confession of Faith.[1] On this subject at least, the Disruption had not divided them, and when Bills began to appear in Parliament, so too did petitions against them from both Assemblies.

Scriptural, Scottish and Social Arguments: 1849-1871

The reasons for the Free Church's opposition were stated in its 1849 Assembly by William Cunningham, the orthodox and influential New College professor. MDWS, said Cunningham, was prohibited by the Confession of Faith, which was based (although 'the mass of business before the house precluded'[2] him from proving this) on Scripture; and the Confession was built into the law of Scotland, which was in turn protected by the Treaty of Union. The Confession's view moreover was 'in accordance with sound reason and calculated to contribute to the welfare and comfort of the community'.[3] Two Members of Parliament present, Fox Maule and Charles Cowan, agreed. The former accepted the Confession, 'which had been framed by wiser heads than his',[4] and was of the opinion that MDWS 'was abhorrent to . . . the people of Scotland'.[5] In the unlikely event of the Bill getting as far as the committee stage in the Commons, he would introduce a clause exempting Scotland and the property of Scots from its provisions. Charles Cowan was equally opposed. To illustrate his concern he read a letter from a Scotswoman resident in England, expressing 'her alarm' at 'this anti-scriptural, unhinging and domestic-peace-destroying Bill, which would bring them back to the days before the Flood, when men took wives wherever they chose'.[6] It was Cowan's intention to do what he could in Parliament, 'in behalf', as his lady correspondent put it, 'of the weaker vessels, alas! unrepresented in your Honourable House!'[7]

The thought of women in Parliament was greeted with 'loud laughter'[8] in the Assembly, but did not detract from the earnestness of their efforts 'in behalf of the weaker vessels' and against MDWS. The subject was taken up again at the following Assembly,[9] the church's objections restated, a further petition despatched, and the inferior courts urged (as they had been in 1849) to send up their own petitions also. A committee was set up 'to take all competent steps for opposing'[10] the Bill.

The pattern of Free Church opposition to MDWS was now set. The principal reasons continued to be those stated in 1849: Scripture, and hence the Confession of Faith, and hence again the law and constitution of Scotland, were against MDWS: so too were the Scottish people. MDWS was socially harmful, and if it were allowed, worse would follow. Much the same points were to be made by the Church of Scotland Assembly. Summing up its objections, already voiced in previous petitions,[11] the Assembly of 1869 stated that it opposed MDWS:

> Because it is one of the relations in affinity prohibited by the law which is in accordance with the Standards of the Church of Scotland, which declare that in the Divine institution of marriage the relations of the one, whether by consanguinity or affinity, become the relations of the other.
>
> Because the observance of the existing law secures the sanctity of home, and the comfort of domestic relations, and many social and family advantages which the proposed relaxation would tend to disturb and overthrow.
>
> Because the relaxation sought would pave the way for others of a kindred nature prejudicial to the peace and purity of family life.
>
> Because your petitioners are convinced that the proposed measure is against the sentiments and feelings of the people of Scotland.[12]

The churches' opposition was grounded, then, in scriptural, Scottish and social arguments. As one Bill followed another during the 'fifties and 'sixties, much more was to be heard from the Assemblies on these subjects than had perhaps been anticipated in 1849. Before turning to see what happened to the churches' opposition after 1870, we can look a little more closely at some of the ways in which these objects were elaborated in the Free Assembly.

A good deal of the Free Assembly's time was spent on the scriptural argument against MDWS.[13] One reason for this was the admitted ambiguity of Leviticus 18:18, which allowed English Nonconformists and Evangelical Anglicans to support the movement in favour of MDWS. R. S. Candlish, the leading Free Church minister of the time, accused the former of 'not asking the question — What saith the Lord?', and the latter of showing 'a strong tendency to evade the conclusions of the Word of God, by some wretched considerations of expediency'.[14] Another speaker, Mr. Montgomery of Innerleithen, explained that the curious attitude of both English groups arose because they associated MDWS with the pre-Reformation canon law, and failed to realise that the Reformers — even in England — had opposed MDWS on scriptural grounds, just as the Free Church now did.[15] Neither threats nor explanations from the Free Church were enough to convince the non-Calvinist Evangelicals of England of the error of their ways — for as we saw earlier, Scottish churchmen were still trying to win them over in 1871. Their contrary attitude did however make it important for the Free Church to make sure of the scriptural foundations of its own position.

The challenge of undertaking this task was accepted, at his own invitation and with his own characteristic zeal for orthodoxy, by James Gibson, a Free Church minister who at the beginning of this period was Presbytery Clerk of Glasgow, and by its end was Professor of Church History and Systematic Theology in the Glasgow Free Church College. In the early 'fifties, fresh from his labours as policeman, prosecutor and judge of the unfortunate Mr. Macbeth,[16] Gibson sat down to write the definitive Free Church book on MDWS.[17] The resulting concatenation of quotations, refutations and speculations was described by James Begg as a 'masterly volume . . . which exhausted the whole subject';[18] and the Free Assembly of 1869 was treated by its author to a lengthy résumé of its arguments.[19]

MDWS, according to Gibson, had been prohibited by the Jews, the church, and all of Protestant Europe until 'Rationalist and French principles began to prevail'[20] at the end of the eighteenth century. Up to this point everyone who acknowledged the Word of God had agreed that, in Leviticus 18, what applied to men also applied to women; and that the general principle of nearness of kin applied to affinity as well as consanguinity. But then, turning from this more or less orthodox exposition of Leviticus 18 to the special case of its 18th verse, Gibson branched out on an ingenious sideline of his own. He had, 'after reading and re-reading, and reading again and again the Hebrew',[21] come to the conclusion that this verse, far from being a prohibition of polygamous marriage with a living wife's sister (which could by implication allow MDWS), was in fact a prohibition of polygamy as such. It should be read simply as 'thou shalt not take a wife (or woman) to her sister in her life':[22] the last 'her', Gibson argued, could apply to either the first or second woman, either of whom might or might not be actual sisters. It was quite clear, Gibson stated, that polygamy had been unlawful from the Creation to the time of Moses, 'that is for the space of 2,500 years'[23] (the 'one flesh' argument of Genesis 2: 23 and 24 proved this); that Christ prohibited it (Matthew 19); and that there was 'nothing in the Mosaic period, or in the character and conduct of the men of that period'[24] that made it more lawful than at any other time — as God's displeasure, voiced by the prophet Malachi (Malachi 2: 14 and 17), had shown.

Among the reasons for Gibson's vehemence on this point was the fact that the protagonists of MDWS had quoted in their support no less a figure than Chalmers. In his *Daily Scripture Readings*, Chalmers had noted not only how 'remarkable' it was that Leviticus 18:18 'implies a liberty to marry' a deceased wife's sister, but also that it implied 'a connivance at polygamy';[25] and James Wortley, the Buteshire M.P. who led the parliamentary campaign to legalise MDWS, had written, in no less a place than the *Free Church Magazine*, that 'by the whole Church of Scotland, notwithstanding recent differences, the judgement and opinion of Dr. Chalmers will command respect'.[26] Gibson, staunch Free churchman though he was, was thus forced to contradict this with the views stated above, and with the comment that Chalmers, although eminent in many fields, was 'not remarkable for biblical scholarship'[27] nor had he studied the passage in any detail.

On this as on other points, however, Gibson was eccentric, even in the Free Church; and it was a pamphlet by one of his colleagues, Dr. Douglas, the Professor of Hebrew and Old Testament Exegesis, rather than Gibson's book, which the 1858 Assembly chose to send to Members of Parliament. When Rainy — by 1871 convener of the committee dealing with the subject — outlined the Free Church's objections, he emphasised the dangers of being misled by the view that 'on very minute processes of biblical criticism the whole issue of the case depended',[28] and stressed that the Confession of Faith was the ground on which their stand should be taken. (The same point had been made by Cunningham in 1853.)[29] Polygamy, Rainy went on to observe, was contrary to 'the permanent principles obligatory on men with respect to marriage'; but God had 'claimed and exercised the right of varying the application of them (the principles) in particular circumstances'.[30] God had thus 'exercised ... forbearance ... for wise reasons and in certain circumstances'[31] in the case of polygamy and in the case of the Levirate marriage. But this forbearance on God's part was now at an end and did not constitute a precedent. God expected 'superior strictness' among Christians than among 'His people of old'.[32]

But Rainy was also concerned with the present; and here too he was more willing than Gibson to admit that there might be problems. He conceded, for example, that some of the forbidden degrees were 'more shocking, more manifestly objectionable and demoralising when permitted than others'.[33] But this, he argued, with the passion for clear distinctions so characteristic of his century, made it all the more 'important to draw the line at those points with more care, because those are the very points at which laxity begins; and when it begins it will be found pervading the whole subject and relaxing the sense of the obligation in connection with this matter'.[34] Even without 'the Divine Rule' it was clear 'in the light of nature' alone that legislators had 'to draw a line somewhere'.[35] The problem was, where?

To Rainy, developing his metaphor, it seemed clear that the circle described by the line drawn round consanguinity and affinity by the Confession of Faith was so small 'that if you break it at any point it is impossible after that to establish a principle which will maintain the line you draw'.[36] When the Dutch Jews,[37] for example, had once allowed MDWS, uncle-niece marriages soon followed. The Confession's unbroken circle was based on the simple 'one flesh' principle, covering affinity as well as consanguinity. A break in this circle, he believed, would undermine the public's attitude to marriage, and would lead to further laxity even in matters such as divorce. It would also present the church with the 'pretty'[38] problem of having to maintain its discipline against marriages which the civil law did not prohibit.[39]

Social and constitutional considerations such as these were noted by other speakers in the Assembly debates of this period, although not always in Rainy's reasoned tones. The fact that there were 20,000 divorces in France in 1793, a year after MDWS had been legalised, was seen by one speaker[40] as a clear case of cause and effect; and similar allegations were made about German and American states which had legalised MDWS. Mr. Montgomery of Innlerleithen used the inevitable metaphor: the MDWS Bill was 'nothing else than the opening of a floodgate, through which a torrent of vice and immorality would pour in';[41] and Mr. Matheson of Kilmuir Easter declared that 'it would have the effect of separating the unmarried sister from the married sister, preventing that close intercourse and family interest which has hitherto existed in such relations'.[42]

Any suggestions moreover that the libertarians, as Gibson called them, might have altruistic motives, was ruled out of court — or at least out of the supreme court of the Free Church. The libertarians frequently argued that MDWS would help the many poor families in which a deceased wife's sister often took charge of the children, by allowing the widower and the woman, if they wished, to marry. This argument however was swept aside by Lord Dalhousie (formerly Fox Maule) as an 'argument for the multitude, which did not consider the scriptural relations of the matter'.[43] In fact, the Free Church peer believed, such arguments were misleading, obscuring the fact that 'this agitation originated in a breach of the law on the part of a few who now wanted the law altered, so as to sanction their breach of it'.[44] The protagonists of MDWS also got a bad character from Candlish, who described them in 1855 as 'a small number of interested individuals, whose purses are very full'[45] and, in 1869, as 'millionaires . . . moneyed people in London who had an interest in the question'.[46] This meant, Candlish rather optimistically believed, that the MDWS agitation 'must become weaker and weaker in proportion as those who wish to contract that kind of marriage became older and older, and pass away'.[47] It was not, however, any reason why the Free Church should relax its vigilance.

This vigilance was certainly not relaxed on the specifically Scottish grounds of opposition to MDWS: no doubt, remarked Mr. Montgomery of Innerleithen, it was 'to get quit of the dreaded opposition of Scotland'[48] that the proposers in that year (1855) had introduced an MDWS Bill the provisions of which did not apply north of the Border. But 'who could imagine that if the promoters of this Bill were to gain their object for England, Scotland could long remain exempt from its operation'?[49] This view was widely held in the Free Assembly, and in 1861 Cunningham took issue with the five Scottish MPs who had voted for the current Bill. After naming them, he remarked:

> I would rather shrink from making any one question the turning point of an election, for I think that might be carried too far . . . but . . . the Presbyterian people of Scotland . . . are at least entitled, nay bound, to see to it that no one of their representatives shall vote for the change.[50]

The least the MPs could do, Cunningham said, was to abstain; and turning to the case of Mr. Adam Black, a pro-MDWS Edinburgh MP, he added ominously: 'I hope that the people of Edinburgh will take care that no man shall again represent them in the House of Commons unless he is prepared to pledge himself at least to that extent.'[51] Mr. Wortley, the Buteshire MP and leader of the MDWS party, had also been reminded (by Candlish) that the pleasure of his constituents tended'[52] to his giving the whole business up.

Colonial MDWS, Scripture and Unanimity: 1871-1900

In the 1869 Free Assembly, Sir Henry Moncrieff, the retiring Moderator, had remarked that he 'took it for granted that the General Assembly will petition both houses of Parliament against the Bill'.[53] He was not disappointed. The pattern established in 1849 was repeated not only on its twentieth anniversary, but also for the next thirty years. Some changes in the pattern did take place, however, and three of these can be mentioned here. They had to do with MDWS in the colonies, the scriptural arguments against MDWS, and the unanimity of the Free Assembly on the subject.

The committee on the Marriage Affinity Bill, still under the convenership of Rainy, informed the Free Assembly of 1872 that the South Australian legislature had passed a Bill legalising MDWS. The committee had accordingly written to Gladstone urging the Government to advise the Queen against giving her assent. The colonies, the committee believed, should manage their own affairs, but this case introduced 'dangerous and perplexing anomalies' into the law of the Empire: the MDWS party, 'anxious to unsettle the existing law throughout the Empire',[54] had chosen to begin where they would meet the least opposition, rather than in the Imperial Parliament, where the matter would be much more fully discussed. It was therefore 'imperative' for the British Government to use 'the suspensive power of the Crown'.[55] In reply to this request Gladstone, himself an opponent of MDWS,[56] had been sympathetic but unhelpful. The colony, he observed, had passed an MDWS Bill five times since 1857, and the British Government was no longer in a position to advise against the royal assent: the majority in the South Australian legislature favouring MDWS was overwhelming.[57]

Victoria (the state, not the Queen) soon followed South Australia — despite an attempt by its Presbyterian church to persuade the British Government to refuse the royal assent and despite that church's threat to enjoin its own ministers not to solemnise MDWS but to discipline the parties.[58] Thus, even before Canada followed suit some years later,[59] the Free Assembly's fears were realised when a Bill was introduced in the House of Commons, designed to legalise colonial MDWS for inheritance purposes in the United Kingdom.[60] Neither this Bill, nor a similar one introduced to the Lords in 1879,[61] was successful, but they showed the way in which MDWS might get a foot in the British door.

A restatement of the Free Church's position in the committee's report to 1879 Assembly showed very little movement in its position. The committee, whose convener was now James Candlish (son of the Candlish already mentioned), argued against MDWS on the usual grounds that it was unscriptural, that it was harmful to social morality and wellbeing, and that it would lead to greater laxity, especially in connection with divorce. This last point was established by the usual references to countries where MDWS and divorce were both to be found, and by the statement that 'laxity in regard to the contraction of marriage is naturally connected with laxity in regard to its dissolution'.[62] There were, however, some signs that the committee's views on the scriptural arguments against MDWS had shifted very slightly, for it now spoke rather more respectfully of the 'highly esteemed and learned men'[63] who took the view that Leviticus 18 forbade only the cases mentioned therein.

This change was more clearly seen in the committee's 1883 report,[64] which had to deal with a pamphlet published by the Marriage Law Reform Association — the pro-MDWS body. This pamphlet listed the replies of the Hebrew and Greek Professors of the European universities to the question of whether Leviticus 18 and Ephesians 5:31 ('and they two shall be one flesh') prohibited MDWS. The enquiry, to make matters worse, had been conducted by Lord Dalhousie, heir of Fox Maule mentioned above. (In the debate on this, James Begg 'regretted that a young nobleman, who held a name of great repute in the past, was making himself so very officious in an attempt to break down the Scotch law of marriage'.[65])

The committee dealt with the pamphlet by denying that the New Testament case against MDWS was ever seriously based on Ephesians 5:31, and by stating that the question of whether Leviticus 18:18 prohibited MDWS was the only one 'on which Hebrew scholarship has any bearing'.[66] It conceded that Hebrew scholarship had somewhat changed its view on this, and admitted the possibility of verse 18 being a prohibition of marriage with a wife's sister during the wife's lifetime. But, it argued, the subject was not to be decided on verse 18, but on verses 6-17. This being so, the prohibition was either only of the cases mentioned, or was based on a principle of which the cases were illustrative. The first alternative was not possible — since it would allow marriages with a daughter, grandmother or niece, which was 'unthinkable'.[67] A principle must therefore be involved, and since the principle of consanguinity alone failed to cover all of the cases, the principle of affinity must also be involved.

All the cases involved would be covered, the committee observed, by the principle of consanguinity plus the principle of affinity if these principles forbade marriage with the wives of blood-relations but not marriage with the blood-relations of wives (except in the ascending or descending line). This complicated principle would prohibit marriage with a deceased brother's wife, while permitting MDWS. The possibility that this principle lay behind the Levitical prohibitions was one which the committee was prepared to concede.

The committee was prepared to concede this however only if it was understood in its proper relation to Scripture as a whole:

> The law contained in the Pentateuch was given to the ancient people of Israel, and it is recorded in the Bible, not because it is as such directly binding on us, but because it forms an important part of God's special training of his people, and gradual revelation of truth and duty ... In many respects, we know from the teaching of Christ, the legislation of the Old Testament was imperfect, adapted to the necessities of a rude and hard age and people. It was the best possible for them, at the stage of moral progress which they had reached; but it was not absolutely the best, or the best fitted for the higher advancement of those who received Christ's teaching, and followed him as their

> Lord. But the elevation of Christian morality was not indicated by Christ or His apostles giving a new code of laws, or a detailed revision of the Old Testament legislation, but by laying down some general principles, and showing the spirit by which men ought to be guided.[68]

In this context the committee considered that the church should be guided by 'two general principles that seem to be mentioned very emphatically in the New Testament: the . . . inviolability of the marriage union, and . . . the equality of the sexes in the eye of Christian precept'.[69] The first of these principles was 'asserted by Jesus in his teaching about divorce', the second was 'implied in that teaching when our Lord founds it on the creation record that God made them male and female; and (was) brought out by Paul when he declares that in Christ there is no distinction of male or female any more than of Jew and Gentile'.[70] It was, the committee considered, 'an undoubted fact of history that the spirit of Christianity, as it had tended to abolish slavery, has elevated woman to be the equal and help-meet of man'.[71] This being the case, the preferred modern interpretation of Leviticus 18, which allowed MDWS, had to be qualified by the knowledge that the society to which it applied also allowed polygamy and arbitrary divorce to the men, the women not being protected. But this was not a law 'which God's regulation in Christ teaches to be proper for the state of enlightenment and humanity that we have now reached'.[72] The committee thus preferred the 'symmetry'[73] of the position it had hitherto upheld — as, it noted, did a number of the professors of Hebrew consulted by Dalhousie, including Wellhausen.

Modern scholarship, then, had not destroyed the scriptural foundations of the church's position. Nor, in 1883, did its other foundations seem insecure. To its own satisfaction, the committee effectively dealt with what it believed was the principle by which the marriage law reformers were guided. This was the notion that a man should not marry his own blood-relations or their wives, but could marry the blood-relations of his wife, since his own blood really was in the former but not in the latter. This idea, the committee conceded, might have some physical basis, but those who held it overlooked the fact that the law had been established for social rather than physical reasons. The additional confusion caused by bringing in 'the law of nature'[74] was also criticised by the committee, which held that 'incest' was an unscriptural and imprecise term. Its use led people to suppose that matters could be settled by asking if a union was incestuous and then allowing it, if the idea of it did not 'arouse immediate horror'.[75] But in the committee's eyes it was enough 'to warrant a law of prohibited degrees, that the preservation of chastity among near relations having close and familiar ties absolutely requires that all conjugal union between them be forbidden'.[76] Such close and familiar ties, it considered, were formed by both husband and wife on marriage, and the prohibition was sufficient 'to prevent the rise of unlawful passion among those who have free and affectionate intercourse with each other'.[77] Thus, in the case at issue, the law against MDWS allowed the deceased wife's sister to 'live with him as a sister, take care of his children, as their aunt, have the freest possible intercourse with him and be joined in the warmest sisterly love'.[78] The only reason for MDWS was thus no 'higher motive' than 'the gratification of sensual passion in one particular way'.[79] The committee then summed up its argument in these words:

> The morality of the marriage law in general consists in this, that the sexual instinct that belongs to human nature is to be never separated from, but always, as it were, wrapped up and veiled in personal and faithful love; and the ground on which marriage between near kindred is essentially immoral is that between such a moral and personal love already exists, so that a desire for marriage could only be an animal passion. Thus the matter comes to this, that if marriage with a deceased wife's sister is to be morally pure there must be no affection between them during the wife's life-time. This might indeed be possible in oriental society, where a wife's unmarried sister would be secluded from all intercourse with men, even her brother-in-law; but in other circumstances it could hardly be. Nor would it be desirable, even if it were possible, to put a check on the diffusion of family affection among those who are related by marriage. It is to be feared that the legitimising of marriages within the near degrees of affinity will tend to lower the idea of marriage, and to increase temptation to immorality. A man who after his wife's death receives his sister to live with him and take charge of his family, will presumably already feel for her all the affection of soul of which he is capable; and the desire for marriage in such a case cannot be a truly moral one, and, being merely or predominantly animal passion, may but too readily seek its gratification outside marriage.[80]

In the much-advertised case of the very poor's need for MDWS, the committee added, why were the marriage law reformers not arguing for brother-sister marriage also? For the aunt called in to help with the children, and for whom there was only room enough to live as the widower's wife, might equally be a paternal as a maternal aunt. And even if she were the latter, 'a man could not marry his sister-in-law immediately after his wife's death, nor could he safely have living with him one whom he loved with a view to marriage'.[81] In any case, if people really were — 'to the shame of this Christian land'[82] — so poor that they had not enough room, the answer was to improve their circumstances rather than to change the law.

Despite this return, at the end of the 1883 report, to Begg's universal remedy, it is not surprising that one member of the Free Assembly, after a few more years of hearing such arguments, remarked that the apprehension of moral chaos entertained by some of his brethren in connection with MDWS was 'merely the figment of a brain accustomed to deal with such matters in a theoretical way in the quietness of the study instead of working them out in the exigencies of practical life'.[83] This speaker, Mr. R. H. Falconer of Carnbee, was not the first to break the unanimity of the Free Church's opposition to MDWS. This third change in the pattern was already discernible in 1879, when the MP Charles Cowan, although still opposed to MDWS, quoted Brougham's remark that 'he had just told his wife's sister that nothing on earth would persuade him to marry her'[84] and urged the Free Church to stop agitating the question. This appeal had been totally unsuccessful. More open opposition, however, emerged in response to the report of 1883. In the Assembly of that year, Mr. Watson, an Edinburgh advocate, challenged the view that the present law either prevented cases of MDWS or was supported by public opinion: the 1847 Royal Commission had disproved the former, and the statement, recently made in the Lords, that there were at least

5,000 couples living in this way in London 'not condemned by public opinion'[85] disproved the latter. He proposed that the Free Church should leave the question alone, and was seconded by Charles Cowan. One or two other elders supported this, but then Rainy got up and said that 'it was good that the difference had come out'[86] but someone had to draw a line somewhere and the church ought to make its own views on the subject clear. These smooth words, followed by alarmist talk about everyone going to the Establishment to get married if MDWS was legalised and the Free Church was true to its principles, ensured that the traditional position was held by a vote of 194 to 52.

The argument about the Free Church holding to its principles after MDWS became legal was raised again a year later, but to the opposite purpose, when Brown Douglas, the Edinburgh advocate and sometime Lord Provost, suggested that in view of the difficulties this would involve, the Free Church should drop its opposition. He had also found the scriptural arguments unconvincing, especially as Leviticus was so full of other regulations, about 'the manner of worship, social duties, dress, food, etc.',[87] which nobody now wanted to enforce. Again, however, Rainy smoothed matters over with the observation that the church had to have a clear position on the subject; and the report and an anti-MDWS petition were again approved by a vote of 118 to 18.

In that speech Rainy had remarked that he had been 'unable to observe an intelligible theological position' in what those who argued for MDWS or for dropping the church's opposition said. Judging by the speeches of the minority who supported MDWS in the Free Assembly, this was fair comment. Their commonest argument was that it was all very confusing: and in 1883, one elder, Mr. Tod of Edinburgh, had even remarked that since 'the biblical question was practically given up', the whole thing now 'therefore turned on a question of expediency'.[88] This was not strictly accurate: but it was understandable that the change in the church's method of presenting the scriptural argument should have seemed — however logical its new arguments were — to have been something of a backtracking exercise, which undermined the church's position.

Despite this, the minority remained a minority: only 46 voted for a do-nothing policy in 1888;[89] in 1890 Mr. Falconer of Carnbee, amid laughter, did not even press a division;[90] and in 1895, after a few years of silence from the committee, only ten members supported a motion to discharge it. The majority decision was taken, as so often, on Rainy's advice. But the house was far from full, and it seems as if interest on all sides was flagging.[91] A year later, indeed, only three members voted to discharge the committee.[92] Thus it remained, silent[93] but secure, to the end of the Free Church's separate existence.

By the end of the century the Church of Scotland Assembly also was silent on the subject of MDWS. The silence here, however, had fallen much earlier. Perhaps this was because the Establishment's unanimity on the subject had been broken earlier than that of the Free Church. The anti-MDWS petition of 1869, mentioned above, had been opposed by a small but apparently determined minority of ten members; and although it was sent, and further petitions were sent by the 1872 Assembly and its March Commission,[94] these appear to have been the last. (The terms in which they were couched were strongly constitutional, mentioning the protection of the Confession by the Union, and only adding a brief sentence about the 'mischievous consequences'[95] of the current Bill.) A committee to watch over an MDWS Bill was set up in 1876,[96] and its convener, Dr. Phin, an opponent of MDWS, gave a brief verbal report in 1880,[97] but the committee was not heard of thereafter.

Law and Liberty in the United Presbyterian Synod: 1847-1900

The United Presbyterian Synod was much more openly divided on the subject of MDWS than was either the Free or the Church of Scotland Assembly. The matter was first brought to its attention in 1853 when an overture from a member of a Glasgow congregation asked it to modify the relevant section of the Confession of Faith, on the ground that MDWS 'does not seem to be forbidden by the Word of God, and the civil law of Scotland'.[98] This request was turned down; and when a year later it was repeated, and memorials on the subject were received from two Glasgow congregations, the Synod again declined — but by a narrow majority — to pass any judgement on the matter, refusing even to set up a committee of investigation.[99] The reason given in the overture and the memorials for raising the subject was that since the church was divided on the question, and since sessions were dealing with it in different ways, some United Presbyterian members were under discipline for having done something in which many other United Presbyterian members could see no wrong.

The Synod did not discuss MDWS again until over twenty years later, but when it did, in 1878, the question was raised in the same terms. On this occasion however the Synod was faced with a concrete problem. Mr. Steele, a member of the Sir Michael Street congregation in Greenock, had married his deceased wife's sister (quite legally, for the marriage had taken place while they were abroad) and was consequently suspended from church membership. His minister and session now wanted to know from the Synod whether they should excommunicate him, or whether he could be restored to full membership. The problem was one which the Synod found difficult to solve. It regretted that Mr. Steele had married his deceased wife's sister, especially 'as he contracted said marriage after he had been warned of the consequences'.[100] At the same time, however, Mr. Steele had professed and promised 'to regard its claims as sacred',[101] and at least some members of the Synod believed that 'the peace and edification' of the congregation would be 'furthered rather than hindered'[102] by restoring him to membership.

This was not the view of the majority of members, however, and the Synod ruled that the law of the church made Mr. Steele's restoration 'inadmissible'.[103] But it did not order his excommunication, and sent down to presbyteries and sessions an overture which it had received from his minister, asking it 'no longer to base the discipline of the Church on higher grounds than the consciences of many of the members and office-bearers of the Church will warrant'.[104] When returns were collected in the following year, it was found that a majority of the office-bearers were in fact unsympathetic to retaining MDWS as a bar to church membership.[105]

This however was not decisive, for the Synod now rejected by a narrow majority a motion suggesting that MDWS cases should be left to the discretion of sessions, and set up instead 'a large Committee'[106] to consider the related questions of the civil law, and of liberty and diversity of opinion in the church. As a result of this committee's report, the 1880 Synod decided 'that no change be meanwhile made in the law and practice of the Church in this matter'.[107] But again the vote was close, and the case of those who voted that the question should be left to sessions' discretion had now been strengthened by the Synod's adoption of its Declaratory Act in 1879.[108] This had extended to United Presbyterians greater freedom of opinion on questions dealt with by the Confession of Faith, and those who wished to leave matters to the sessions argued that it had been 'authoritatively declared that' MDWS 'was a subject on which liberty of opinion is allowed'.[109] The weak point in this argument however was the continuing illegality of MDWS.

Thus matters stood for another seventeen years, during which time the Synod did not discuss the question. But then in 1897 the Presbytery of Greenock brought an overture, advancing the same arguments as before, and observing that the 1880 decision had been 'to the effect "that no change be *meanwhile* made in the law and practice of the Church in this matter"'.[110] In reply to this overture and to another, from the session of Carron, the Synod by its customary narrow majority agreed that the overture's proposal — that sessions should use their discretion — should be sent down to presbyteries and sessions for their opinion.[111] The returns, reported to the 1898 Synod, were strongly in favour of the proposals: twenty-nine were fully in favour, five approved with qualifications, and only six disapproved. Of those which approved with qualifications, two (Lanark and Kelso) wanted the Synod to go further and alter the church's law so as to ensure uniformity among sessions, and one (Kelso) decided by a majority 'that every effort should be made to get the law of the land relating to such marriages altered'.[112] Very few of the presbyteries voting either way were unanimous in their decision, and two of those which fully approved, and one which disapproved, did so by their moderator's casting vote. But 122 of the 173 sessions which replied fully approved, so that the majority undoubtedly favoured the proposal.

Despite this clear majority the Synod was still not ready to settle the matter. An overturist put forward the argument that it was 'the obligation of Church members to obey the law of the land as a religious duty, except only where such obedience is, in the judgement of conscience, contrary to the law of God',[113] and after the customary motions — to leave the question as it was, and to leave it to sessions — had been proposed, the decision was shelved for a further year. When it was then reconsidered, the two motions were again put. But the Synod adhered to its former position, deciding in this penultimate year of its existence that it was not 'expedient to proceed further meanwhile in the matter'.[114] The subject was not raised at its meeting in 1900, and thus the Synod left it, avoiding what no doubt could have provided the anti-unionists in the Free Church with further grounds for complaint.

The Flood

For the first few years of the twentieth century the Church of Scotland and United Free Assemblies remained silent on the MDWS question. But in 1906 a Bill to approve colonial marriages with a deceased wife's sister was passed by Parliament. The Bill was supported by the Government and not even debated in the Commons. Winston Churchill, then Under-Secretary for the Colonies, attempted to reassure the Bill's opponents that the question of legalising any such marriages other than those of returned colonials was not involved. But they had good reason to be apprehensive, for only a year later the Government introduced an MDWS Bill for Britain. Hitherto such Bills had been brought forward by private members. Now Government support was decisive, and the Bill was passed.[115]

The Peace of the United Free Church

What were the Assemblies to do? That of the United Free Church, meeting in 1908, was presented with overtures asking advice, and after some discussion which exposed the conflicting opinions and traditions represented in it, decided to set up a committee to look into the church's position. One member of the Assembly, the minister from Carron who had brought an overture on the subject to the 1897 Synod, remarked that 'this came rather late in the day for many people. In his own Presbytery there had been at least two cases in which such marriages had been celebrated, and the Presbytery had taken the wisest course of dealing with the subject when they left the matter alone.'[116]

The committee's report, presented to the 1909 Assembly, was not a long one. Noting the recent legislation, in which 'a difference has for the first time been created between the law of the Church and of the land',[117] it briefly summarised the position of the Reformers and the Confession. In practice, it suggested, all Protestant churches accepted that Leviticus Chapters 18 and 20 referred to marriage within certain degrees rather than to 'breaches of the Seventh Commandment'. These churches accepted, it continued, that 'strictly parallel cases' were implied (or else marriages 'revolting to morality'[118] would be permitted) and that in the light of New Testament teaching, what applied to men must apply to women. The only point at issue, then, was verse 18, which 'many in this and other Churches, whose loyalty to Scripture cannot be questioned',[119] understood as a prohibition not of MDWS but of marriage with a wife's sister during the wife's lifetime. Many others did not take this view: but the point was clearly disputed within, as well as outside, the church.

Given that the law had now been changed, the church, the committee observed, had certain precedents provided by other Presbyterian churches in countries where MDWS had previously been legalised. Of these, the strictest was the Church of Victoria, which had ordered its ministers 'to adhere to the Confession of Faith'.[120] Secondly, there was the position of the Presbyterian Church in the

United States, which had struck out from the Confession the words: 'The man may not marry any of his wife's kindred nearer in blood than he may of his own, nor the woman of her husband's kindred nearer in blood than of her own.' A third position was that of the Canadian Presbyterian Church, which had struck out only the first half of that sentence; and a fourth was that of the United Church of New Zealand, whose Presbyterian predecessors in 1885, 'without committing the Church to an approval of such marriages, left it to the individual ministers and members to determine what course they shall pursue in celebrating or entering upon any such marriage, as they have to give account to God'.[121]

Of these precedents, the first did not appeal to the committee, because of the number of United Free members who did not believe that MDWS was contrary to the word of God. Nor did it like the second, related as it was to the laws of the several states which 'greatly vary and are in many cases extremely lax'.[122] And the third, by making a distinction between the sexes, was not only contrary to New Testament teaching, but also failed to provide 'definite guidance as to what degrees of consanguinity and affinity forbid marriage to the man'. The New Zealand example however did commend itself, being compatible with the statement of the Declaratory Acts, by which MDWS could be interpreted as 'one of thc "points which do not enter into the substance of the Reformed Faith"'.[123]

Recommending this procedure to the Assembly, Dr. Archibald Henderson — convener of the committee, one of the Assembly clerks, and a former Free churchman married to a sister of J. S. Candlish — remarked 'that the line we have taken is in the interests of the peace of the Church'.[124] Most members of the Assembly, he believed, would 'agree it would be an undesirable thing to have this sent down to the Presbyteries to be debated as an alteration on the *Confession of Faith*'.[125] But the proposed deliverance — which declared 'that those entering into such regular marriages are not to be regarded as having thereby forfeited their standing and privileges as Church members, and that while every minister is entitled to refuse to solemnise such marriages, those taking part in solemnising such marriages shall be regarded as at liberty to do so'[126] — obviated this difficulty by treating it as a matter of discipline, stating, as it were in advance, the position the Assembly would take were a case brought to it.

Personally, said Dr. Henderson, he was 'one of the old-fashioned people who stand by the *Confession of Faith*', but he was 'satisfied that others, studying the Word of God with more intelligence perhaps, hold a different position'.[127] Under the circumstances, he believed that the report and the motion 'will satisfy all parties in regard to our position and leave us all quite clear'.[128] Strangely enough, after so many years of argument, Dr. Henderson was right. His motion was agreed to without even being debated.

The Church of Scotland: Scriptural, Philosophical and Constitutional Considerations

The question of the recent MDWS legislation was raised in the 1908 Church of

Scotland Assembly by Lord Balfour of Burleigh on behalf of the Church Interests committee. Balfour, a former Conservative Scottish Secretary, was convener of this committee, which had been created in 1882 as the spearhead of Church of Scotland resistance to the Liberals' Disestablishment policy. Now another issue which threatened to disturb the church's relation with the state had arisen, and a special committee, with Balfour as one of its members, was appointed to examine the problem.[129]

The committee, under the convenership of Christopher Johnston, the Assembly's Procurator (later Lord Sands, and one of the architects of the 1929 Union), began its work by examining 'the question whether marriage with a deceased wife's sister is to be condemned as contrary to divine law revealed in the Scriptures'.[130] Four Hebrew and four New Testament professors from the universities were asked for and produced memoranda on this carefully phrased question. None of the Old Testament scholars was willing to condemn MDWS on the evidence of Leviticus 18, although each dealt with the question in different ways. Professor D. M. Kay of St. Andrews argued that verse 18 was the prohibition of a special case of bigamy in a system permitting polygamy, and presenting evidence for and against the idea that the prohibition extended beyond the death of the married sister,[131] he left the question open. Professor W. B. Stevenson of Glasgow attempted to find some principle or principles according to which the list had been constructed, but admitted that the special phrasing of verse 18 meant that 'it cannot well be understood except as leaving the way clear for marriage with a deceased wife's sister'.[132] Professor James Gilroy of Aberdeen rejected the idea that the cases mentioned in Chapter 18 were 'illustrations of a principle, for no principle is laid down, and none is suggested — except it may be expediency or experience';[133] and in any case verse 18 was clearly a prohibition valid only during the wife's lifetime. And Professor A.R.S. Kennedy of Edinburgh, repeating this argument about verse 18, pointed out that since the wife became a member of her husband's family at marriage, but not *vice versa* ('according to the view widely prevalent in antiquity'),[134] the argument from analogy with the prohibition on marriage with a deceased brother's wife (verse 16) was invalid. Nor, he noted, was MDWS explicitly prohibited in mainstream Judaism (Professors Kay and Gilroy had also remarked on this, noting the exception of the ninth-century Karaites' school).

Nor did the New Testament scholars condemn MDWS. Each of them — Allan Menzies of Aberdeen, William Stewart of Glasgow, Thomas Nicol of Aberdeen[135] and John Patrick of Edinburgh — failed to find anything relevant to MDWS in the New Testament. The only New Testament reference they took up was the 'one flesh' phrase (Mark 10: 8, Matthew 19: 5ff., 1 Corinthians 6: 16 and Ephesians 5: 31). But this quotation from Genesis 2: 24 had, they argued, nothing to do with the case. As Professor Stewart put it:

> Those who find in the words an utterance germane to the question of affinity must go back to the passage in Genesis, and find in it, if they can, a recondite, physiological doctrine. Whether Genesis in this passage does teach physiology I leave to the Old Testament exegetes to say.[136]

This however was not a subject on which the Old Testament exegetes had chosen to say anything.

At this stage the way seemed clear for the committee to find that MDWS was not to be condemned on scriptural grounds. But it was not going to be so easy. One of the committee's members was James Cooper, the high-church Professor of Ecclesiastical History from Glasgow, who had long been a violent opponent of MDWS;[137] and who now presented the committee with a memorandum setting out the scriptural and other arguments against allowing ministers liberty to celebrate such marriages.

In this memorandum, Cooper argued that the Church of Scotland, which did not make out a table but laid down a principle of consanguinity and affinity, was in accord with Scripture. The advice of the Hebrew experts — that MDWS was allowed under the Mosaic law — might be taken, but it should be understood that MDWS was only allowed in Leviticus as an exception which, it might be expected, would disappear (as it did in some Jewish quarters and in the church) with the further 'education of Israel' and when the principle was set forth in its 'logical completeness'[138] by Jesus. Jesus' teaching in Mark 10 and Matthew 19 did not explicitly deal with MDWS, Cooper admitted (adding that 'we did not require to learn . . . that'[139] from the New Testament experts). It was reasonable however to infer that his teaching on 'one flesh' dealt with the establishing of a relationship which had not simply one consequence — greater limitations on divorce — but many, including the prohibition of polygamy and 'a stricter and more consistent rule as to affinity'.[140] In addition to these texts, however, Cooper went on, the consistent New Testament teaching on marriage was to the effect that the husband should 'restrain his passion',[141] and Christendom had strengthened this check on the husband's desire, already present in the Mosaic legislation, by extending the prohibition to the deceased wife's sister.

Cooper's argument was in many ways similar to the revised scriptural argument of the Free Church in the 1880s. He added to it by observing that MDWS was 'hardly consistent with the Golden Rule (S. Matt. 7: 12)',[142] since he doubted whether the husband would be willing 'to extend a parallel encouragement to his wife', and remarked that the church should also consider 'the law of Christian Chivalry'.[143] This law, whose scriptural basis was found in Romans 15:1 ('We that are strong ought to bear the infirmities of the weak'), and whose practical application was found in 1 Peter 3: 7 ('Giving honour to the wife, as unto the weaker vessel') was endangered, Cooper believed, by MDWS.

> If (he wrote) Marriage with a deceased wife's sister is to receive the Church's sanction, a man may bring his brothers quite freely to his house, because his wife can never be their wife. But she (if she have any reason to dread his 'passion of desire') must not invite her sisters! *He* can have the pleasure of his relatives' company; she, who, by the very fact of her sex, is likely to be *more dependent on* the society of her kindred, is to be debarred, in many cases, from their dear company! The weaker, in short, is to go to the wall. The man is to please himself, instead of giving himself up for his wife. And this, again, in the teeth of Scripture, which enjoins, not that the wife shall forgo her family, but 'the man shall leave his father and mother and shall cleave unto his wife'.[144]

How seriously Cooper's colleagues on the committee viewed the social and moral dangers he described here is not recorded. Many churchmen in the previous century had taken them seriously, and some still did. But was Cooper the best authority on the subject? At sixty-three he was still a bachelor, who 'throughout life . . . cultivated . . . old ladies . . . with ungrudged attention', and whose 'other main affection was for youth and especially for boys and young men';[145] since 1895 and until her death in 1909, he had lived with his aging mother; 'and never were mother and son more to each other,'[146] remarked his biographer. Only in 1912 did he marry, and begin 'a union of unbroken happiness'[147] which lasted until his death in 1922. Such biographical details probably did not raise for Cooper's colleagues the suspicions they would have raised in a more cynical post-Freudian generation. At the same time, however, even they were unlikely to have considered him the best guide to the social implication of MDWS.

For guidance on the social and moral aspects of the question the committee had in fact turned elsewhere, and alongside Cooper's memorandum they had two others: from W.R. Sorley, the Cambridge Professor of Moral Philosophy, and from the Reverend William Davidson, the Aberdeen Professor of Logic and Metaphysics. Sorley, after comparing the near-universal horror of incest with the widespread aversion to inter-racial marriages ('one might ask the question, is it worse for an Englishman to marry his deceased wife's sister than for him to marry a Hottentot?'),[148] pointed out that what constituted incest varied from one society to another. In the case of exogamous societies, he argued, 'a reflective member of an exogamous tribe' might 'anticipate McLennan[149] and the rest' and understand that the 'curious prohibition' on his 'marrying a girl within the tribe' derived from the tribe having been 'originally constituted "maternally"'.[150] If he did this 'he would or might see', wrote Sorley, 'that, whatever its original justification, that justification no longer held'.[151] This, however, did not help to provide a universal rule of incest, since other kinship systems were different. Sorley therefore left this problem and made 'a jump to the modern question'.[152]

The problem here, he wrote, was threefold: 'the criterion of the morality of the act in question is to be found in the ideal of marriage as moralising the individual, promoting social order and securing the education and welfare of the race'.[153] If MDWS was neither illegal nor believed to be sinful, Sorley observed, it could not hurt individuals' morals, nor was there any ground for supposing that it affected offspring. Social order was the only real question. Marriage made a man to some extent a member of his wife's family, it was true: but her death, he held, altered 'the household (or rather "visiting") relations';[154] and in any case cousins, with whom marriage was allowed, were as much involved in these social relations as sisters-in-law. The only other point was the notion that 'one flesh' made the wife's sister her husband's sister also — but while this satisfied 'some people's desire for a principle' it was 'arguing from a metaphor', and those who held the principle did not 'carry it out to its logical conclusion'[155] which would extend indefinitely and perhaps even prohibit marriage with all (equally metaphorical) Christian brothers and sisters in the land. MDWS, Sorley therefore concluded, was 'not to be condemned on these grounds'.[156]

Professor Davidson reached the same conclusion by a similar route. Beginning with roughly the same argument Sorley concluded with, he went on to ask what would be the social effect of legalising MDWS after it had been so long forbidden. Only good, he concluded. For a prohibition 'that is found not to rest on a *rational* basis cannot, in the long run, be favourable to character'.[157] People would begin to resent it. 'Nor,' he added, 'need the peace of a household be disturbed by the possibility of the sister of a wife becoming her successor, any more than it need be disturbed by the possibility of any other unmarried lady, who is a frequent guest in the house, becoming her hostess's successor'[158]: the sister was if anything less likely to be feared.

To these philosophical arguments, Davidson added some considerations of Christian ethics, which brought a breath of fresh air into the foetid drawing-rooms of the ecclesiastical imagination:

> The whole tendency of Christianity, as taught by Christ and as formulated by St. Paul, is to remove unnecessary burdens and enactments that have become burdens, and therefore hindrances, in the interests of morality and the higher life (see, for instance, Christ's treatment of divorce). Nor must the 'authority' of the Church be allowed to interfere with this. Surely the Spirit is constantly revealing truth and adjusting it to circumstances, — to wider knowledge and deeper experience on our part, and progress is possible in religion as in other spheres. Christianity is not a closed system, but is still a living and progressive thing; and that makes all the difference.[159]

With the philosophers as well as the biblical scholars finding no reason to condemn MDWS, the committee had now only the constitutional hurdle to get over. This was not a subject on which Professor Cooper had been able to put up much of a case. His only arguments had been, that since the 1907 Act confined itself to marriage as a civil contract, and since it provided clauses protecting Church of England clergymen from being compelled to celebrate MDWS[160] (but not protecting them from ecclesiastical censure if they themselves contracted MDWS), there was no reason why the Church of Scotland should set the 'very dangerous precedent'[161] of changing her law or doctrine on the subject. This, he held, would be abandoning the church's hard-won position, and would 'make Parliament, and not the Church, the authority according to whose findings ministers were to discharge their sacred functions'.[162]

But Cooper had only three supporters on the committee, D.M.M. Milligan, an Aberdeen elder, the Reverend Dr. T.W.B. Niven of Pollockshields, and Lord Balfour of Burleigh. The remaining twenty-two members seem to have been convinced — if they were not convinced before — by the biblical scholars and the philosophers that there was no real reason for the church to disagree with the state. All that they needed now was a smart lawyer, and with the Procurator as their convener and Mr. James Crabb Watt K.C. among their number, that difficulty was easily overcome. In a memorandum on the legal aspects of the subject Mr. Watt enabled them to argue that although the church, under the 1707 Act of Security, had 'a constitutional obligation to the state, as regards fidelity to her doctrine as ratified by law',[163] the state could not now make a constitutional complaint against the church if it changed its law on MDWS, because the 1907 Act had withdrawn the state's endorsement of MDWS as an incestuous marriage. (Although the Scots Parliament in endorsing the Westminster Confession had declared that its interpretation could not 'ever be made lawful by any law of man' Parliament, having unlimited powers, had been in a position to make MDWS lawful.) In any case, it could also be argued that MDWS was not a matter of doctrine, and, further, that the clause added to the Churches (Scotland) Act of 1905,[164] giving the Church of Scotland power to amend her ministers' formula of subscription to the Westminster Confession, made change even easier. The church, after the 1907 Act, was thus in a position where it could change its law, and was thus certainly, in the committee's view, in a position where it ought at least to reconsider its attitude now that it was free to do so. If it still believed that MDWS was contrary to divine law it could maintain the prohibition. But, if not, it was faced — as the committee believed it was — with the consideration that 'all the arguments of social expediency' against the church legalising MDWS did not outweigh 'the inexpediency of attempting to maintain in the Church, on such grounds, the prohibition of a marriage regarded as valid by the civil law'.[165] Such a prohibition would not work, would alienate people from the church, and could not 'preserve to the sister-in-law any position of privilege which she has hitherto enjoyed in virtue of the prohibition'.[166]

Thus, protesting that their examination of the issue had 'been in no way influenced by the action of the State'[167] and promising that any future changes would have to be considered afresh and not with this as a precedent, the committee recommended that an overture, declaring any ministers celebrating or parties contracting MDWS free from ecclesiastical censure, should be sent down to the presbyteries. Cooper, Balfour and their two allies lodged their dissent, on the grounds: that the proposal attacked the principle of affinity laid down in the Confession and reasonably inferred from Scripture; that the church would now have to find a new principle, thus disturbing 'the whole doctrine of marriage' and giving 'currency to loose and degraded views of this fundamental ordinance of Christian Society'; that many ministers would 'certainly refuse to obey';[168] that further prohibitions would be relaxed; that the church was not required to change; that 'for the Church slavishly to follow the State is to inflict a blow on its independence'; and that the desirability of keeping church and state laws in step could 'not justify a change of front so sudden and so complete'.[169]

Despite all this, the Assembly agreed to the committee's request; and the overture was sent to the presbyteries,[170] who approved it by 81 to 3. After this had been reported to the next Assembly,[171] the Act XII 1910 was passed in terms of the committee's overture.[172]

Subsequent Developments

Professor Cooper, defiant to the last, had along with five others recorded his dissent to the Assembly's MDWS Act.[173] Eleven years later, in September 1921, he noted in his diary:

> Today (I think — anyhow this week,) Mrs. — — 'married' her deceased husband's brother — the first to avail themselves of the new Act of Parliament legalising it . . . The 'Headship of Christ' does not seem to require obedience to the Divine Law of Marriage: this comes apparently of denying that Marriage is a Sacrament, and feeling it needful to make it as much of a civil matter as possible. It is a sad feature of our Scottish Church History since the Reformation. Our standards are all right, but there is scant respect paid to them. The Chancellor, Lord Selborne, was right when he said the Deceased Wife's Sister Bill meant the destruction of a code.[174]

Cooper had lived to see his fears further realised in the 1921 Deceased Brother's Widow's Marriage Act. According to the traditional interpretation of Leviticus 18, this Act relaxed a prohibition clearly laid down in verse 16 of that chapter. None of the special arguments used in connection with verse 18 and MDWS applied here, although a case might perhaps have been made out in connection with the levirate law of Deuteronomy, Chapter 25. In the event, however, the subject was not pronounced upon by the now re-united Church of Scotland. Nor did the Assembly say anything about the 1931 Marriage (Prohibited Degrees of Relationship) Act. This Act permitted marriage between a man and his father's brother's widow, his mother's brother's widow, his deceased wife's father's sister, his deceased wife's mother's sister, his brother's son's widow, his sister's son's widow, his deceased wife's brother's daughter and his deceased wife's sister's daughter. All of these relationships were prohibited by the parity of reasoning argument of the Confession, and the first was explicitly mentioned in Leviticus 18: 14, such a union (according to the traditional interpretation) being threatened with childlessness in Leviticus 20:20.

Although the Assembly said nothing about the 1921 and 1931 Acts at the time when they were passed, its Committee on General Administration did touch upon them in a 'Memorandum on Marriage Questions and Problems' which appeared as an appendix to its report to the 1933 Assembly.[175] The memorandum noted that the Assemblies of 1921 and 1922 had not pronounced, and commented: 'it may be assumed that the liberty given by the Acts mentioned (U.F. 1909 and C. of S. 1910) would be extended to cover this relationship'.[176] It then went on to say, in relation to the 1931 Act: 'It may probably be assumed, with regard to the marriages of persons' mentioned in that Act 'that the attitude of the Church will be the same as that adopted in 1909 and 1910 by the two sections of the Church now united'.[177] These assumptions were perhaps fair enough in the light of the United Free Assembly's earlier judgement. But in the case of the Church of Scotland they appear to have broken the promise given by the 1909 Committee: 'if any proposal should hereafter be made to alter the civil law in regard to any such marriage' (i.e. any other marriage involving the remaining prohibited degrees of affinity as well as consanguinity) 'it will be the duty of the Church carefully to consider her position in relation to any such proposal, and to resist and to refuse to recognise legislation sanctioning any marriage which she holds to be contrary to divine law'.[178] No such consideration of the matter by the church as a whole appears to have taken place.

Nor was this the end of the story. The question of the Consanguinity and Affinity prohibitions was considered by the 1951-1956 Royal Commission on Marriage and Divorce,[179] which recommended that a man or woman, after divorce, might 'marry during the lifetime of his or her former spouse any person whom he or she could lawfully marry at the present time if that former spouse were dead'.[180] This proposal was opposed by the Archbishop of Canterbury. Giving evidence to the Royal Commission, he stated: 'It is supremely important for the stability of the family and for the protection of its members from indulging in unlicensed thoughts or desires that there should be the strongest possible barrier against any thought or possibility of marriage with the brothers or sisters of a partner.'[181] The possibility of marriage with an affine after death did not threaten the stability of the family and was in accordance with canon law,[182] but divorce which could 'be planned for and brought about'[183] did. It is interesting to see how the form of the nineteenth-century social argument was still being used although the point at issue had changed.

The Church of Scotland witnesses were also opposed to the Commission's proposal, but it passed into law under the 1960 Marriage (Enabling) Act. This further liberalisation of the law was in many respects a different issue to the 1907-1931 legislation, since it involved divorce, and it was the question of the remarriage of divorced persons as such rather than the marriage of a divorced wife's kin which concerned the Church of Scotland Assemblies during the late 1950's. As far as the Church of Scotland's attitude to the 1960 Act is concerned, Cox's *Practice and Procedure in the Church of Scotland* (1964 revision) uses much the same formula as did the General Administration Committee in 1933, stating that 'it may be assumed that the Church will take no disciplinary action against persons contracting, or ministers officiating at'[184] such marriages.

Those who believed, in 1909, that the legalising of MDWS would shatter a logical system and lead to further relaxation of the law have thus been proved right by subsequent legislation. Any attempt to find the application of a consistent principle in the Scots law of consanguinity and affinity is virtually impossible, and the 1969 Secretary of State's Committee on The Marriage Law of Scotland remarked of this branch of the law that 'its form is undoubtedly deplorable. It is the despair of the student and a labyrinth to the qualified practitioner.'[185]

CHAPTER EIGHTEEN

Theological and Other Factors

THEOLOGICAL considerations seem to have played a much greater part in the MDWS controversy than in the others which we have discussed. But what kind of theological considerations were involved in the constitutional, social and scriptural arguments, and how decisive were they?

The Constitutional Argument

The constitutional argument was obviously an important determinant of Established and Free Church attitudes to MDWS. The Free Church until 1892 and the Church of Scotland until 1905 were tied to the letter of the Westminster Confession, which clearly disallowed MDWS; and in the 1840s, when the controversy had begun, churchmen might privately ignore the Confession, but in public they did not criticise it. Criticism of one part, it seems to have been felt, might lead to criticism of others, perhaps even of the Establishment principle itself; and that was not something which Established, or even at this stage Free churchmen wanted. Those most sympathetic to MDWS, significantly, seem to have been found among the United Presbyterians, who also opposed Establishment and were the first to grow restive under the Confession, achieving a measure of freedom from it in 1879. The United Presbyterians' general constitutional position, in other words, allowed them to sympathise with the non-Calvinist fundamentalist interpretation of those English Dissenters and Evangelical Anglicans who supported MDWS; while the fact that some of the pressure for change came from these non-Calvinist English quarters was useful to the Free and Established Assemblies in defending the specifically Scottish character of their opposition to MDWS.

In this respect, then, it looks as if the relevant theological considerations had more to do with church-state relations than with the merits of MDWS. The Free Church certainly represented MDWS as a constitutional crisis. The vital question, it suggested, was whether the law of the land was to rest on Christian foundations; and when the social and scriptural arguments were also brought into play, MDWS began to look like a battle, perhaps a decisive one, in the war over Christianity's authority in society. Not unnaturally, therefore, the churches' eventual response to the 1907 Act looked like a defeat for religion. In the Church of Scotland, Cooper certainly saw it as such. The Act, he said, was

> a reversal to the Naturalism (which at this moment is so strong and dangerous an element in popular literature), and to purely animal conceptions of the sexes . . . a return to pagan ethics — to lax Hellenic standards, even lower than those of pagan Rome.[1]

And he went on to describe the Church of Scotland's position as

> slavish Erastianism, an uncalled-for abandonment of the Church's whole tradition of spiritual independence, and the way to public contempt . . . a surrender of the claim to educate the general conscience.[2]

Cooper's interpretation had a certain plausibility. To impartial observers it may well have seemed that the churches were now accepting, for the sake of a quiet life, an innovation which one of their authorities had once attributed to 'the spirit of levity, latitudinarianism and German rationalism';[3] and in an age accustomed to singing about Christian soldiers, it might well have looked as if they had once again lost the battle. But if it did, it was largely because some churchmen had chosen a battleground on which many others were not prepared to fight; and there was an alternative interpretation. Professor Davidson had advised the church that 'the Spirit is constantly revealing truth and adjusting it to circumstances', that 'the "authority" of the Church' should not 'be allowed to interfere with this', and that 'progress is possible in religion as in other spheres'.[4]

The Social Argument

The trouble with the constitutional argument, then, may have been that the churches did not think deeply enough about its theological implications until it was too late. But presumably this could not be said of their social argument. The social argument might be summed up by saying that, in the divine economy, the combination of original sin and sexual desire could not be held in check, nor affection between members of the larger family allowed to develop, unless a carefully maintained system of consanguinity and affinity prohibitions were maintained by law in every traditional detail. If the legal circle was broken at any point, original sin and sexual desire were so strong that no end could be seen to the number of further prohibitions which would be dispensed with.

The trouble with this argument however is that if you take away the words 'in the divine economy' and replace 'original sin' with 'human nature', you are left with a view so fully congruent with the conventional nineteenth-century conservative middle-class view of the family that it is difficult to know what significance to give to theology in determining it. No doubt the theology of previous centuries had helped to create the conceptual framework of nineteenth-century conservative middle-class thinking, and no doubt Evangelicalism had helped to create the mood which produced that thinking. But the form which it took and the intensity with which it was defended do seem to have owed a great deal to factors of a social rather than a theological character.

Among these social factors was the Victorian middle-class family itself, by mid-century a ubiquitous and moralising institution which shared some characteristics with the earlier Puritan family, but was now enjoyed by many who had only recently risen to wealth and respectability. Despite a degree of social equilibrium around 1850, the middle classes and their family life were far from secure. For the time being the threat of a violent revolution in Britain had passed, but it had not been forgotten; and the security of the middle-class home depended on fluctuations of trade and industry which, if things went wrong, could spell disaster and disgrace. There were certainly still plenty of servants, on whose presence the smooth running of the home depended, and to some extent the habits of deference engendered by centuries of feudalism had been transferred to the master-servant relationship. But deference was far from universal (it is difficult to see how it could have been, for example, in houses where the mistress' mother had herself once been in service, especially when other forms of female employment began to become available), and the precarious order created by wealth had to be reinforced by a firm insistence upon the proprieties.

For the new middle-class family to survive, therefore, it was important for the principles which governed it to be clearly established and carefully observed. But since some of these principles were arbitrary, and since they lacked the inborn authority of long tradition, the new middle classes were not sufficiently confident of their way of life to tolerate anything which threatened to upset any part of it, since that might well threaten the whole.[5] Exactly what constituted a threat, however, was not always clear. Some thought that prostitution was a threat to the family, others that it reinforced it. Divorce, by contrast, seems to have been very commonly seen as a threat, which is understandable, since unlike prostitution it inevitably undermined the principles which were being established. In this context some, but not others perceived a threat in MDWS.

The threat perceived in MDWS was twofold: it was a threat in itself and a threat as the first of many other relaxations. The immediate dangers of MDWS, one suspects, were sometimes exaggerated. Opponents hinted that legalising MDWS would probably lead some husbands and their sisters-in-law to poison the unfortunate wife;[6] and Gibson, putting the case in more general terms remarked:

> It is a well-known fact, exhibited in many frightful instances in the Bible, recognised even as a principle of law in modern times, verified in the history of mankind, and awfully demonstrated in the records of criminal courts, that cruelty and lust, impurity and bloodshed, are fearfully allied. Everything that tends to break down the just and reasonable barriers which God has raised to restrain the gratification of impure passions, is not only a restraint and check upon impurity, but upon cruelty and violence. Every one who can read and observe, knows what multitudes of murders and acts of violence are the fruit of impure passions, and the danger, consequently, of diminishing the horror of their indulgence. To go no farther, look at the cases of Rush and the Mannings in England, Kirwan in Ireland, and the late Glasgow murders in Scotland.[7]

Even if it could not be proved that MDWS would lead to murder being committed or contemplated, the reality in Gibson's eyes was bad enough. 'I believe,' he wrote, 'that it could be made out, could we get access to the actual facts, that in almost every one of the cases where marriage has ensued between a man and the sister of his deceased wife, the attachment has been formed, and the arrangement contemplated, before the first wife was removed from the stage of time.'[8]

Gibson's views, of course, were extreme even by Free Church standards; but some of his fears seem to have been shared by other opponents of MDWS, and social crises can be perceived on the slimmest evidence (or even, as with the Scottish illegitimacy statistics, on mistaken evidence). Once perceived, however, social crises take time to evaporate, especially when influential groups have an interest in keeping them plausible; and in the nineteenth-century middle-class context it was not too difficult to do this with MDWS. Not all members of the middle classes, of course, were convinced that there was fire behind the verbal smokescreen, and for some, further evidence was needed. For members of the Assemblies, further evidence of a crisis was provided, not only by the constitutional aspect of MDWS, but also by the scriptural.

The Scriptural Argument

By the 1880's, a scriptural crisis was also in evidence, and the modifications which the Free Church arguments against MDWS underwent reflected this. Two years before the 1883 report, in which these modifications became evident, the Free Assembly had deposed William Robertson Smith from the chair of Old Testament in its Aberdeen college. Smith, too advanced for the conservative wing of the Free Church, was an outstanding Semitic scholar, much admired by J.G. Frazer, and both Durkheim and Freud were to make use of his work.[9] Despite his deposition, he had many supporters in the Free Church, and among the most outstanding of these was the Glasgow Professor J.S. Candlish, who was also convener of the MDWS committee.

The committee's 1883 report, as we have seen, modified the scriptural arguments against MDWS in at least four ways: it abandoned arguments based on the Old and New Testament use of 'one flesh'; it accepted that Leviticus 18: 18 might be a prohibition of polygamous marriage with a wife's sister during the wife's lifetime; it accepted that the underlying principle of the whole chapter (as far as affinity outside the direct line was concerned) might be a ban on marriage with the wives of blood-relations, but not the blood relations of wives; and it declined to argue on grounds which had anything to do with the natural horror of incest.

The significance of these modifications was twofold: they represented not only a more open attitude to the kind of biblical criticism in which Robertson Smith had been engaged, but also an endorsement of the general philosophy which lay behind it. A major aim of this was to disentangle the positive ethical religion of Hebrew monotheism from what were seen as the savage and primitive taboos of magic and superstition.[10] In his *Religion of the Semites*, Smith was to conclude that Leviticus marked an earlier stage in the development of those 'rules of conduct for the regulation of man's contact' with a 'friendly' God, which were part of 'religion proper'[11] and would be fully revealed in the Christian era. As Candlish's committee had put it, the Christian 'general principles' of 'the inviolability of marriage' and 'the equality of the sexes' enabled the church to draw out from Leviticus a social and moral code appropriate to 'the state of enlightenment and humanity that we have now reached'.[12] With the help of biblical criticism it was now possible to distinguish this rational code from superstitious and irrational survivals of primitive and magical views about incest.

While this revised version of the scriptural argument against MDWS adapted rather than abandoned Calvin's approach to the subject, it also had more radical implications. Two key ideas, for example — that of a rational code and that of progressive revelation — were present in both versions: but the new version was markedly different from the old.

The rationality of the consanguinity and affinity code had always been a strong plank in the churches' defence of the system, but this had become, increasingly, a popular rather than an intellectually defensible argument. Calvin himself, despite his reliance on Scripture, had argued that God had written his law on this subject so deeply in men's hearts that they were able to sense it in the light of nature alone. But Calvin had also undermined natural law arguments by his general emphasis on the effect of sin on human understanding and by his many hidden assumptions about the 'clear' meaning of Scripture as an index to the natural. Reformed theologians and legal theorists thus distrusted arguments based on natural law and the theologians relied even more heavily upon Scripture. Gibson, for example, discussed the bearing of natural law on MDWS only very briefly, concluding that since so little could be learned from it, 'we must therefore have recourse to the word of God'.[13]

Calvin himself, then, had been a precursor of the Humean scepticism which in due course had forced religion to turn 'for support from speculative argument to Scripture and experience', and had forced Calvinism, despite its intellectual tradition, 'to begin over again as a scriptural piety'.[14] But in the nineteenth century, although biblical and anthropological studies were further discrediting the old natural law arguments, many were still unwilling to abandon the convictions which these arguments had sought to justify. Thus by the 1880's the rationality of interpreting Leviticus 18 by some sort of parity of reasoning had become the commonsense of so doing. The difficulty with commonsense, however, not only was that it depended on changing notions of scriptural interpretation and social utility, but also that it was no longer sufficiently common to be enforced by law. Calvin's position — that the prohibition of incest was not simply a political law but one which God had implanted in human nature — might have been sufficiently plausible in the sixteenth century for affinity laws based upon it to be generally accepted. But the nineteenth-century version of this — that the same laws were a code which God wished men to decipher but also distinguish from their Levitical foundations in the general light of Scripture — was much less plausible, especially as Christians themselves were so divided on the reasoning involved.

In the event, this adaptation of Calvin's idea of a rational code tended to create the impression that the scriptural argument against MDWS had been discredited; and eventually the attempt to establish a more rational and modern approach to consanguinity and affinity prohibitions was carried much farther than Candlish and his committee had intended. Nor was their reinterpretation of the idea of progressive revelation in the end any more successful in stabilising the situation.

That the idea of progressive revelation was part of Calvin's teaching may not be immediately obvious from his handling of Leviticus 18, but there is evidence elsewhere in his writings that he held it.[15] For Calvin, of course, it was a progressive revelation which culminated in Christ and was thereafter embodied in Scripture; and this view was shared by the 1883 report, with its emphasis on New Testament principles. The 1883 report however seems also to go farther, not perhaps so much in what it said as in how it said it. Phrases like 'the stage of moral progress which they had reached', referring to Leviticus for example, and particularly 'the state of moral enlightenment and humanity which we have now reached',[16] seem to owe at least as much to the doctrine of Progress as to any doctrine of Calvin's; and although this doctrine may have had antecedents in Christian notions of providence, its use in the 1883 report bears an unmistakable nineteenth-century appearance.

This appearance of nineteenth-century progress in the guise of progressive revelation raised, of course, the possibility that further progress might imply change rather than stability in the consanguinity and affinity code. Once the argument had reached the stage of interpreting Leviticus in terms of general principles of New Testament teaching such as the inviolability of marriage and the equality of the sexes, it was equally possible to interpret it, as Professor Davidson did, in terms of other general New Testament principles, such as those aimed 'to remove unnecessary burdens and enactments which have become burdens, and therefore hindrances, in the interests of the higher life'.[17] This possibility however was not seriously taken up by the churches either in 1883 or during the following quarter of a century; and when it was taken up it was seized not at all enthusiastically, but simply as a way of getting out of difficulties over MDWS, rather than of reappraising the whole consanguinity and affinity question.

Why was this option not taken up? Several reasons can be suggested for what happened around 1883. At that time the Free and Established churches were still tied to the Confession; and in the Free Assembly at any rate, the social arguments against MDWS still seem to have carried a good deal of conviction. But of at least equal importance was the vexed question of biblical criticism. Robertson Smith's removal in 1881 had not removed the problem, and had revealed a deep division of opinion. Those, like J.S. Candlish, who supported him were not going to abandon their critical studies. But if it were to be shown that these critical studies might have practical consequences in the realm of morality — consequences which might, moreover, by overturning the church's position in the MDWS case, undermine her authority — then perhaps neither the church nor criticism would gain anything. Nor for that matter did the prospect of further public wrangling over criticism appeal to many of those who had defended or sympathised with Robertson Smith.

If these considerations go some way to explain why the Free Church did not develop its thinking on MDWS in 1883 along the lines of a more positive approach to the whole subject, it is more difficult to explain the United Free and Church of Scotland Assemblies' action in these terms. In the United Free case many of those who had opposed the development of criticism had either died or cast their lot with the small Free and Free Presbyterian churches; the United Free Assembly moreover contained a substantial proportion of former United Presbyterians, many of whom had been in favour of legalising MDWS. Nor, after its long silence, can it be easily assumed that anti-MDWS opinion in the Church of Scotland was strongly represented outside the small group of Scoto-Catholics led by Cooper. It may of course have been that the constitutional issue was still in the Assemblies' minds, particularly after the prolonged legal contest in which the United Free Church had almost lost its patrimony on account of its deviation from Calvinist orthodoxy. Or perhaps the social arguments, even yet, carried considerable weight. Or perhaps again those, like Dr. Henderson, who held to the Confession's interpretation in the teeth of biblical criticism, were too influential to ignore. Whether such considerations were responsible for the churches' silence on later occasions when further prohibitions were relaxed is, in the absence of debate, even more difficult to determine. By 1921 and 1931 the issue may have been considered too unimportant to debate, and certainly to risk stirring up the old hornet's nest.

The major twentieth-century reason for letting these sleeping dogmas lie thus probably was fear of disturbing the peace of the church — fear not so much of internal conflict as of a forced battle in defence of a lost cause, on which neither Scripture nor the church had anything very authoritative to say. To avoid further damage to the church's authority, therefore, the practical question was left to the lawyers on the General Administration committee, and the theoretical one abandoned to anthropologists, no doubt with Robertson Smith on their bookshelves.

Postscript

THE nineteenth-century Scottish churches said a great deal about topics related to sex, marriage and the family, but little theological thinking seems to have lain behind it. Most of the theological points the churches made were already summed up in the Westminster Confession's chapter on marriage and divorce[1] and in the Westminster Catechisms' answers to their questions on the fifth and seventh commandments.[2] Two centuries after the General Assembly had adopted these statements, its successors saw little need to change them; and although towards the end of the century they were questioning their relationship to the Westminster standards, it was not, with the exception of marriage affinity, in terms of this aspect of their teaching. Was this because the Reformed churches, on divorce and sexual equality[3] for example, had been ahead of their time? Or was it because, as in the case of marriage affinity, their logic seemed too perfect? Certainly, as that case showed, the churches were not ready for theological reappraisal until they had no other option; and many churchmen, no doubt, had hoped that the moment for reappraisal could be postponed *sine die*, when the question perhaps could be remitted to a special committee. In June 1882, for example, Principal Tulloch had written to his wife:

> We have had an evening meeting of the Assembly again. Lord —— is a bother; I have told him, of course, that it is nonsense saying that marrying a deceased wife's sister is against the law of God. But on one hand I have no particular sympathy with people who, with so many women in the world, marry their deceased wife's sister; while on the other hand I do not wish to punish them. Can not they marry some one else? Speaking of marriage, get Trollope's new novel 'Marion Fay'. It is very Trollopy here and there, but also in parts very touching.[4]

Tulloch was too much of an academic to be taken for the average churchman, and too advanced a theologian for many, particularly in the Free Church, to identify with. But his impatience with those who agitated a question like marriage affinity was probably shared by not a few ministers and elders in all the churches, as they turned away from theology, if not to Trollope, then at least to Burns' *Cotter*.

Neither the Assemblies and Synods, nor the churches they represented, then, seem to have been in any mood to reappraise their traditional teaching on sex, marriage and the family. As far as the Assemblies and Synods were concerned, part of the reason may have been that they were no longer a suitable place in which to do this. The Church of Scotland Assembly at least, according to Professor Cooper's biographer, had become during the later nineteenth century 'less of a Court and more of a popular gathering, less of a deliberative body and more of an audience. Its lay members had become more fluctuating in composition and the proportion of members strange to its forms and unfamiliar with its topics was larger.'[5] Under these circumstances, and in 'the stream of public discussion', there was little opportunity for the fruit of theological science, as Flint had put it, 'to be sown in peace'.[6]

But there was not much sign of its being sown anywhere else in the Scottish churches. In this respect, the churches' thinking about sex, marriage and the family reflected the state of Scottish theology in general. According to J.R. Fleming, Scottish theology, until the mid-1870's,

> was more alive as an inspiring principle of Church life than as a regulative force in religious thought. The humblest Scottish peasant regarded himself as an authority on 'The Headship of Christ,' but no one attempted a worthy theological treatment of the theme. The oracles were still sought among the divines of the sixteenth and seventeenth centuries; the application had to be found in actual experience.[7]

Fleming (whose view of the Scottish peasant we have reason to doubt) believed that Scottish theology did not really revive until Flint, since the creative thinkers of an earlier generation, such as Erskine of Linlathen and Macleod Campbell, had been either condemned or ignored. But although Flint and other theologians of the last quarter of the century may have revived academic theology, their efforts seem to have had little effect upon the pronouncements we have been considering. Flint, as we have seen, was aware of the lost ground, attributing the poor state of Scottish theology to the discordant ecclesiastical controversies of the time. But although he himself conducted a spirited defence of 'the bourgeois family' in his volume on *Socialism*,[8] most of what was written on the subject was on a level with the popular writings of W.G. Blaikie who, by his own confession, had left himself 'little time for the deeper studies of the systematic theologian . . ., had no great turn for the philosophy of theology', and considered that it 'was solely as a practical man that I had any fitness'[9] for the New College chair of Apologetical and Pastoral Theology. Even in the early twentieth century, when W.S. Bruce of Banff wrote his *Social Aspects of Christian Morality*,[10] his chapters on 'Marriage' and 'Family Life and Relationships', although replete with references to sociology, and critical of eugenicists, socialists and neo-Malthusians, were for the most part a reiteration of traditional ideas.

Except in the very limited terms in which the Free Church discussed marriage affinity, then, the theological presuppositions of the sixteenth century were not subjected to any serious theological criticism during the period we have been concerned with. The churches pronounced, it almost seems, by instinct and supported their pronouncements with an appeal on the one hand to selected passages of Scripture and, on the other, to selected aspects of their own experience. What was said, how it was said, and the fact that it was said at all seem attributable, largely, to a variety of more or less contingent cultural, political and personal factors. The middle classes were interested in social stability, and saw lower-class sexual and spiritual disorder as a threat to this. Middle-class Scotsmen were seeking a cultural identity to deliver them from the loss of their political independence and of the real or imagined certainties of pre-industrial society. Middle-class Scottish church leaders were interested in recovering, particularly for their own denomination, something of the authority their predecessors had enjoyed; and a few of them were able to promote particular causes they believed in, as long as the silent majority of their fathers and brethren were prepared to let them.

Such factors seem to have influenced what the churches said about Scottish sexuality and piety, and things were not very different in their discussion of state-regulated prostitution and marriage affinity. On both of these subjects, of course, the churches were divided, but so too were the middle classes whose more pious opinions they so faithfully reflected. The fact that the churches and the middle classes agreed upon so much may indeed be one reason for their lack of critical theological thinking: where consensus reigns, after all, there is little incentive to ask radical questions; and since it still was, to so many appearances, a Christian consensus, the churches' incentive was even less.

Thus, despite their divisions, their failure to reach the lapsed masses, and their fear of fractured floodgates, the nineteenth-century Scottish churches still spoke with that confidence, part-aristocratic, part-parochial, which brooks no contradiction; and which, to avoid embarrassing confusion, drops the subject when it is presented in a new and unfamiliar light. Norman Macleod, probably the greatest nineteenth-century Scottish churchman, had observed this confidence in action. In January 1870, he wrote in his journal:

> The power of mere traditional views of so-called Christianity is to me utterly astounding. I heard an excellent young man preach last night. He logically carried out the assumption that our Lord endured the very punishment our sins deserved. Hence, he said, the damned in hell alone could understand his sufferings! Yet such monstrous — shall I call it blasphemy? — never struck him. God forgive us clergy, who have made men infidels by all the 'hard speeches' we have in our ignorance uttered against Thee.[11]

Two years later, in the last entry in his journal, written within a fortnight of his death, Macleod asked:

> Where is the germ of the Church of the future? In what Church? In what creed? In what forms of government? It may come from India, as the first came from the East. But all our old forms are effete, as old oaks, although young ones may grow out of them. Neither Calvinism, nor Presbyterianism, nor Thirty-nine Articles, nor High Churchism, nor Low Churchism, nor any existing organisation can be the Church of the future! May God give us patience to wait! It may be a

> thousand, or three thousand years yet, ere it comes, but come it will! I do not think any Broad Church can be *the* Church yet; it wants definiteness to meet the common mind of rough humanity. But in a Church it can modify and liberalise extremes, witness for individuality against any extreme views of the body, and so help to an ultimate solution of the problem between the individual and the Church. I shall see it from the other side; but not from this.[12]

Still on this side, but only just, Macleod had written, above this strangely prescient vision of the future:

> As for Scotland! The Church of the future is not here! We ignore great world-questions. We squabble like fisherwomen over skate and turbot.[13]

Thus appeared, to a prophetic and compassionate contemporary churchman, both the darker and the more ridiculous aspect of Victorian Scottish religion. This aspect was much in evidence in what the churches said about sex, marriage and the family. Clearly it is not the whole story: the regulationist and affinity controversies, after all, are only minor footnotes to Scottish church history, and the former at least is not an entirely discreditable one. But the significance of the churches' attitude, not only to the sexual behaviour of farm workers, but also to sexuality in general, cannot be so easily dismissed. If any single negative feature other than sectarianism discredited their contribution to Macleod's 'Church of the future', it was their suspicion of human sexuality. In the nineteenth century, indeed, these two features were brought into such prominence that the Scottish churches' opposition to sex and to one another became, for many, almost their most familiar characteristics.

It was not, however, entirely the nineteenth-century churches' fault. Parents since time immemorial have worried about the sexual behaviour of their young, particularly their female young, and particularly if they owned any property; and there is little reprehensible in the desire to avoid unwanted pregnancies. In an age before the development of effective contraception, an age familiar, recently enough, with the ravages of syphilis, it was entirely natural to be apprehensive about sex; and as far as the churches were concerned, this apprehension had been justified by a theological tradition stretching back beyond Calvin to Augustine and Paul. The tradition represented, perhaps, little more than the sanctified instinct of the herd,[14] an instinct which also found expression in the marriage rituals of the Victorian middle classes and the courtship customs of their social inferiors. It was a tradition which doubted the wisdom of this aspect of creation, and also the possibility of its redemption, a tradition largely deficient in faith, hope and charity, and hence, in the light of the wider Christian tradition, one which would need revision. But it is doubtful if the nineteenth century was the time or the place for such revision. Perhaps it needed, in the end, that *reductio ad absurdum* of the tradition, which the nineteenth-century churches so willingly provided, for its bathos and pathos to be seen in perspective, and for sex to be seen as only human. The nineteenth-century Scottish churches may thus have been wise in their generation, when they declined to examine their theological presuppositions on the subject too closely.

Appendix

The Case of Mr. Macbeth

IN January 1842 the Reverend James Macbeth was translated from a parish in Arbroath to the new church extension district of Laurieston in Glasgow. The church had been completed only a year earlier, and Mr. Macbeth was its first minister. At thirty-two, he was a popular and able Evangelical preacher who soon attracted a large congregation, a high proportion of whose members were serious-minded and enthusiastic young men. Together, Macbeth and his congregation vigorously evangelised the neighbourhood, and for a time Laurieston seemed to be a highly successful example of Chalmerian ideals. Although the minister and most of the congregation were led, again at Chalmers' inspiration, to 'come out at the Disruption', their exodus was purely metaphorical, for their building, which had been erected by the Glasgow Church Building Society, remained in their possession. Mr. Macbeth even seemed to be launching into a literary, or at least a pamphleteering, career — for by 1846 he had published tracts in defence of Free Church Principles and against Morisonianism and slavery in America.

In 1848 the congregation's progress and their minister's career were rudely interrupted. On the 8th of November the Presbytery of Glasgow charged Macbeth with having attempted to have sexual intercourse with one of his domestic servants and with having behaved immodestly to two others. From the beginning of December to the end of the following March evidence was heard and witnesses examined and cross-examined by the presbytery and Mr. Macbeth. During this period between twelve and thirty ministers and six and a dozen elders met most weekdays, often twice daily and sometimes late into the night to hear all the horrible details. In the midst of this, in February 1849, the House of Lords awarded all the buildings erected by the Glasgow Church Building Society to the Church of Scotland, and Macbeth's congregation had to move into a store-room above a railway goods-station.

Much of the evidence brought against Mr. Macbeth was hearsay, some of it malicious: the neighbour's servant who had provided members of the presbytery with grounds for their first charge against him — that he had behaved immodestly towards her — confessed at the trial that her story was a fabrication of what had been an innocent incident: she had persisted in it largely at the encouragement of her mistress, who seemed ready to believe any tale about the sexual activities of the minister upstairs. Even the presbytery could not make this charge stick, and found it not proven. The second charge was simply that Macbeth had remained alone for a few moments in a bedroom on the morning of his wife's confinement while another maid had made up the bed. Macbeth and the maid both claimed that he had simply gone on reading a book during this period. The presbytery, however, despite this and other evidence to the contrary, claimed that the mere fact of being alone in a bedroom with a maid 'without any ostensible cause therefor' was — in the case of a Free Church minister — an offence 'of a scandalous and heinous nature', probably committed 'for some lewd and improper purpose' (F.C.G.A. Papers: 1849: Case of the Rev. James Macbeth: pp. 1, 2). On this second charge the presbytery found Macbeth guilty.

The third charge however was more serious, since it was the only one which the servant involved persisted in before the court. Other servants to whom she had previously retailed the story suggested to the court that she had several not very consistent versions of it. In one, she had claimed that Macbeth 'gied me as good a toosling as ever I got' (*ibid*: p.87), but in others, including that told to the presbytery, she had repelled his advances. These, she claimed, included night visits, on one of which he spoke to her in 'filthy obscene language that I could not come over in public' (*ibid*: p.66). Her husband, however, a clerk whom she had married sometime after leaving Macbeth and his wife's service and before the trial, had written it down at her dictation, and it was 'shewn to every member of the Court present before being recorded', although they all refused to read it. Couched in the rudimentary sexual slang of the nineteenth-century lower classes, it offered, besides intercourse, the promise to 'take care of' the possibility of her falling 'in the family way' (*ibid.*).

Macbeth attempted to counter this servant's evidence by citing several witnesses, who told the court that she had denied the whole story to Mrs. Macbeth and a friend who had gone to see her, and that she had signed a paper to that effect at the request of Macbeth's beadle and one of his elders. Further, one of the two young men who lodged in the Macbeths' house — which never seems to have been empty except at the time of the first unproven charge — informed the court, under pressure, that the servant (he had overheard this) had told Mrs. Macbeth that she was afraid of being left alone in the house with the young male lodgers overnight. This could have damaged the servant's case, but on any occasion when Macbeth's questions were in danger of doing so they were ruled out of order by the presbytery. Macbeth's own case was further damaged by the fact that the signed confession by the servant (which the elder and beadle asserted they had taken) had been burned by Mr. Macbeth, and by the fact that she had received an anonymous letter during the trial warning her to give up her story or she would be exposed as a liar: this letter, the presbytery charged, was in Macbeth's disguised hand. It produced handwriting experts to prove this. But Macbeth produced another who denied it.

After hearing all this and much more, but not very incriminating, evidence, the presbytery, by thirty votes to one, found Macbeth guilty on the third charge. Mr. Macbeth immediately appealed to the Synod of Glasgow and Ayr, protesting about the way the trial had been conducted, and especially about his being prevented from questioning the credibility of the third servant. The synod, meeting in April, sustained most of Mr. Macbeth's appeals, found him not guilty on the first and second charges, and found that the third was not proven. Both Mr. Macbeth and the presbytery then appealed to the Free Assembly, the former to have himself completely cleared (as 'not guilty') on the third charge, the latter to have its own judgement on this and the second point sustained. The Assembly, meeting soon after, sustained the synod's judgement, but only after a day-long hearing and by a narrow (109 to 103) majority.

Although Mr. Macbeth had not persuaded the Assembly to find him not guilty, he had perhaps won his point, and was received back by his congregation with open arms. Throughout the trial most of them had taken his part — so much so indeed that when the presbytery reproved his session for holding a congregational meeting which gave him a vote of confidence, eight out of ten of them had offered their resignation. Macbeth and his congregation immediately set about finding a site for a new church to replace the building awarded to the Church of Scotland. By December of the same year (1849) they had found one, and, on April the 22nd following, Mr. Macbeth was presiding with great aplomb at the foundation-stone-laying ceremony. The minister, office-bearers and other men connected with the congregation then adjourned to the Eagle Tavern where, over supper, 'their meeting was very happily constituted, and the greatest harmony and cordial feeling prevailed' (D. Elder: *Union Free Church*: 1894: p.58).

Within the month Mr. Macbeth had again 'been accused of certain acts of immorality, which were investigated by two of the office-bearers of his congregation and reported to him. He neither admitted or denied the accusation, but on 29th May he sent a letter to the presbytery demitting his charge and his status as a minister of the Free Church, and subsequently left for America' (F.C.G.A. P. & D: 1850: p.254). For technical reasons the presbytery could not accept Mr. Macbeth's resignation and had to refer it to the Assembly, which gave it permission to hold a further examination and bring the results to the next Commission of Assembly for approval, and in case of appeal.

The presbytery, meeting on June 12th and 24th, July 1st and August 6th and 7th, conducted an investigation, whose findings were then forwarded to the Commission, which on August 14th found him guilty of fornication, deposed him and declared the charge of Laurieston vacant. (*Vide*: *Acts of the General Assembly of the Free Church of Scotland*: 1848-1852: p.354). Mr. Macbeth did not re-appear or appeal at any point.

This further blow was hard for the congregation to take. They had the greatest difficulty in finding a new minister, and in the end the candidate they settled on — like Mr. Macbeth in different circumstances — refused either to accept or to decline. He would, he said, abide by his own presbytery's (Fordoun) ruling. It told him not to go and in the end the Presbytery of Glasgow had to bring the matter to the Assembly of 1851 — which told him he must. To make matters easier the congregation, who apart from anything else were disturbed by the notoriety Laurieston Church now suffered from, had in the meantime changed its name to Union Free Church.

During Mr. Macbeth's suspension, Rainy, at that time a probationer, had occupied the Laurieston pulpit. He later remembered (Elder: *op.cit.* p.60) 'how strongly the most of the office-bearers and congregation adhered to the minister, being persuaded that the accusations could not possibly be true; and added that when 'after his acquittal, new evidence which was conclusive came to light, there was no hesitation at all in taking the proper course; and the congregation at once set itself to face its new duties in the best spirit'. The chronicler of Laurieston/Union Church, although (*ibid*: p.10) he had consulted the presbytery records, decided to leave it at that. Others were less convinced of Macbeth's guilt. One member of Macbeth's congregation was the father of Robert Flint, the Church of Scotland theologian. Flint's father 'always maintained that Macbeth was innocent' and that the Rev. Dr. Gibson, minister of the neighbouring Kingston Free Church and Presbytery Clerk of Glasgow had 'been a bitter persecutor of Mr. Macbeth' (D. MacMillan: *Life of Robert Flint*: 1914: p.67). The Flint family's hostility to Gibson was one of the factors which made Flint decide in 1856 not to go to the Free Church College in Glasgow, where Gibson, now a Free Church professor, was soon to get up a heresy hunt — fortunately for the Free Church it was unsuccessful — against his own students, including Robert Howie who later was to become the Free Church's statistician. (Flint, who was treated unsympathetically by Candlish when making enquiries about the Edinburgh Free Church College, eventually entered the Church of Scotland and its Divinity Hall, whence he was thereafter able to make a more creative contribution to theology than would have been possible had he remained in the Free Church.)

Gibson's part as presbytery clerk in the trials of Mr. Macbeth is also mentioned by the Laurieston chronicler, who while not judging the merits of the case observes the large part Gibson played in it, and notes that when Macbeth returned after his first acquittal by the Assembly 'a large number of Mr. Gibson's congregation were present' on the first Sunday Macbeth preached, 'out of curiosity to see the man, as one old lady put it "that our minister has such ill-will at" '. The reason for Gibson's ill-will may be left to conjecture, for at this distance it is difficult to say how much Gibson, by his own confession a far from popular preacher (*vide* J. Wylie: *Disruption Worthies*: 1881: p.264), was motivated by jealousy of his highly successful neighbour.

Notes

Part one

1. Robert Wallace: 'Church Tendencies in Scotland', in *Recess Studies*, ed. A. Grant, 1870, p.223.

2. D. MacMillan: *The Life of Robert Flint,* 1914, p.127.

3. *Ibid.*, pp.127ff.

Chapter one

1. W. Aiton: *General View of Agriculture in the County of Ayr*, 1811, p.xiv.

2. *Ibid.*, p.159.

3. *Ibid.*, p.158.

4. *Vide* G.D. Henderson: *The Scottish Ruling Elder,* n.d., p.241.

5. Aiton: *op.cit.*, p.xiv.

6. Around 1825 there were many parishes in which the kirk session scarcely existed and never met. Vide Henderson: *op.cit.*, p.229.

7. *Ibid.*, p.242.

8. *Vide* A. Ross: 'Reformation and Repression', *passim* in *Essays on the Scottish Reformation*, ed. McRoberts, 1962.

9. *Vide* chapter four, below.

10. J. Calvin: *Institutes of the Christian Religion*, Book IV, Ch. XII, 26 and 23.

11. *Vide* J. MacIntosh: *The History of Civilization in Scotland*, 1893, vol.2, pp.249ff.

12. J. Calvin: *The Harmony of the Four Last Books of the Pentateuch*, 1854 translation, vol.III, p.69.

13. *Ibid.*, p.70.

14. *Vide* J. Knox: *History of the Reformation*, (1949 edition) II, p.306.

15. J. Calvin: *Commentaries on Genesis*, 1850 translation, vol.II, pp.286ff. (Calvin was commenting here on the story of Judah and Tamar in Genesis 38, and on verses 24 and 25 in particular.)

16. *Ibid.*

17. *Vide* G.D. Henderson: *op.cit.*, Ch. IV and I.M. Clark: *A History of Church Discipline in Scotland*, 1929, Chs. V and VI.

18. E. Troeltsch: *The Social Teaching of the Christian Churches*, 1911, (English edition 1931), p.653.

19. J. MacIntosh: *op.cit.*, vol.2, p.248.

20. This and the Disruption of 1843 are two outstanding examples in the history of the Scottish church of struggles in which the establishment of an ecclesiastical ideal in principle ultimately resulted in a diminution of the church's real power and influence. From the point of view of the nineteenth and twentieth centuries the opportunities for serving the welfare of the community, on the basis of a flexible set of shared values, which could have been presented to a genuinely popular and adaptive church with less grandiose ideas of its own significance, are very great. Instead, the essential initiative in this field passed at the end of the seventeenth century to the state, when the ruling classes finally got the upper hand over the representatives of the church; and while the part which the state was to play

in making provision for community welfare was to lie dormant for over two hundred years, the church's part was to become smaller as society became increasingly differentiated. The end of this process, which just conceivably might be the evolution of a society able to locate its social policies in the context of a common but flexible structure of self-understanding, rather than in the context of an ideologically pluralist society serviced by professionals whose function is dependent upon the distinction drawn between them and those whom they help, is not yet in sight. But its origins, in Scotland at any rate, are clearly related to the dissociation of religion and politics which took place in the early eighteenth century; and for which, in view of the totalitarian claims of the custodians of the national religious tradition, the politicians can scarcely be held responsible.

21. *Vide* G.D. Henderson: *op.cit.*, Ch. IV, and I.M. Clark: *op.cit.*, pp.163ff.

22. According to I.M. Clark: *op.cit.*, p.143.

23. *Ibid.*, p.144, quoting *The Form of Process*, Ch. IV.

24. *Ibid.*, p.144.

25. H.G. Graham: *Social Life in Scotland in the Eighteenth Century*, 1906, p.323.

26. *Vide* G.D. Henderson: *op.cit.*, pp.118ff. Cf. W. Ferguson: *Scotland: 1896 to the Present*, 1968, p.164. N.B. Infanticide may be distinguished from the accidental death of infants as a result of being overlain by parents. Among poorer people when, as was common, several persons slept in the same bed, this had 'often' happened, according to pre-Reformation Statutes warning against it. (*Vide* I.M. Clark: *op.cit.*, p.99.) This was not something which Scottish ecclesiastical or civil laws mentioned after the Reformation (*ibid.*), although sleeping arrangements had not significantly improved, and presumably it was not less common.

27. *Vide* G.P. Murdock on 'The Universality of the Nuclear Family' in *A Modern Introduction to the Family*, ed. N.W. Bell & E.F. Vogel, 1968, p.43.

28. G.D. Henderson: *op.cit.*, p.138.

29. *Ibid.*, p.116, quoting Burt's *Letters from a Gentleman in the North of Scotland*, 1754 (written c.1730).

30. *Ibid.*, pp.116ff.

31. *Ibid.*, p.144.

32. *Ibid.*, p.106.

33. *Vide* I.D.L. Clark: 'From Protest to Reaction: The Moderate Regime in the Church of Scotland, 1752-1805' in *Scotland in the Age of Improvement*, ed. N. Phillipson and R. Mitchison, 1970, pp.200ff.

34. Population estimates from T.C. Smout: *A History of the Scottish People 1560-1830*, 1969, Ch. XI; and R.H. Campbell and J.B.A. Dow: *Source Book of Scottish Economic and Social History*, 1968, p.8. Ecclesiastical estimates from R. Wallace: 'Church Tendencies in Scotland' in *Recess Studies*, ed. A. Grant, 1870, pp.187ff; J. Barr: *The United Free Church of Scotland*, 1934, p.303 (chart); J.R. Fleming: *A History of the Church in Scotland*, 1933, vol.2, p.146.

35. *Vide* D. Fraser: *The Story of Invergordon Church*, 1946, p.9.

36. W. Aiton: *op.cit.*, p.117.

37. *Ibid.*

38. Metaphors of this kind were frequently used by W.G. Blaikie, the Free Church Professor of Pastoral Theology who was born in 1820, 'a few months after the Queen', as he put it (*Autobiography: Recollections of a Busy Life*, 1901, p.1), and died in 1899. See his bestseller: *Better Days for Working People*, 1867, *passim.*

39. C. of S.G.A.R., 1881, p.480.

Chapter two

1. William Collins, quoted in W. Ferguson: *op cit.*, p.313.

2. Although there were also 'two or three as bad, immoral fellows as were to be found in the whole country' who 'were never out of church'. *Autobiography and Memoir of Thomas*

Guthrie, ed. Guthrie & Guthrie, 1877, p.105.

3. Guthrie: *op.cit.*, p.323.
4. R. Wallace: *op.cit.*, p.187.
5. *Ibid.*, p.188.
6. David Nasmith, quoted in D. MacColl: *Among the Masses; or, Work in the Wynds*, 1867, p.59.
7. C. of S.G.A.R., 1896 (R.C. of P.), p.808.
8. *Ibid.* The Commission found it difficult to know what to do about the situation. It supported the idea of University Settlements, of which Oxford had one in London, and approved of the Salvation Army's Slum Sisters. Tentatively, and perhaps foreseeing opposition, it suggested that a 'beginning might be made by the planting of houses for the clergy and Christian workers in the denser parts of city parishes'. But then Guthrie had written sixty years earlier, (Guthrie: *op.cit.*, p.309) 'if a man won't live among the scum of the Cowgate, I would say at once to him "You can't be its minister"'.
9. *Vide* J.R. Fleming: *op.cit.*, vol. i, p.80.
10. *Vide* W. Logan: *The Great Social Evil*, 1871, p.179.
11. *Vide* Guthrie: *op.cit.*, Ch. VII.
12. Blaikie: (Autobiography), *op.cit.*, p.329.
13. *Ibid.*
14. *Ibid*, p.328.
15. *Ibid*, p.316.
16. *Ibid.*
17. C. of S.G.A.R., 1893. (R.C. of P.), pp.1087ff.
18. Guthrie: *op.cit.*, p.313. He is credited by his biographers (*ibid.*, p.441) with the invention of the term 'City Arabs'.
19. D. MacColl: *op.cit.*, p.196.
20. *Ibid.*, p.81.
21. D. MacColl: *op.cit.*, p.327.
22. F.C.G.A.P. & D. 1881, R. & M.R. Appendix.
23. But *cf.* A.A. Maclaren: 'Presbyterianism and the working class in a mid-nineteenth century city', *Scottish Historical Review*, vol. 46 (1967), pp.115ff. — a study of Aberdeen which suggests that working-class elders were uncommon there. Scattered references in Assembly Reports, throughout the second half of the century, to the difficulty of finding suitable elders seem to support this.
24. E.g. F.C.G.A.P. & D., 1871, R. & M.R., p.30.
25. R. Howie: *The Churches and the Churchless in Scotland*, 1893, pp.118-119.
26. F.C.G.A.P. & D., 1870. R. & M.R., pp.12ff.
27. *Vide* Howie: *op.cit.*, p.38.
28. *Ibid.*, pp. 36 and 37.
29. C. of S.G.A.R., 1896 (R.C. of P.) pp.819ff.
30. C. of S.G.A.R., 1896 (R.C. of P.) p.823.
31. *Ibid.*, p.821.
32. *Ibid.*, p.823.
33. *Ibid.*, p.827.
34. *Ibid.*
35. *The Army & Religion*, ed. D.S. Cairns, 1919.
36. *Ibid.*, p.189.
37. *Ibid.*
38. *Ibid.*, p.191. The enquiry provided no statistics about the relative proportions of male and female members and adherents. Territorial ('largely middle class') battalions had not as high a proportion of men outside vital relationship.
39. *Ibid.*, p.187 and Ch. X, *passim.*
40. *Ibid.*, p.213.

41. *Ibid.*, p.187.
42. *Ibid.*, p.229.
43. R. Wallace: *Life and Last Leaves*, (ed. Smith & Wallace), 1903, p.44.
44. *Recess Studies*, p.188.
45. *Ibid.*, p.204.
46. Here Begg came across traces of an earlier and more celebrated practitioner of immorality: he paid frequent pastoral visits to Mrs. Armour, the aged widow of Robert Burns. Although she could no longer be called 'bonnie' Jean, he observed, 'I can quite well imagine that when young she may have been very engaging to an intellectual man.' She was now 'an excellent Christian woman'. *Vide* T. Smith: *Memoir of James Begg*, 1885, vol. i, pp.101ff.
47. *Ibid.*, p.98.
48. *New Statistical Account*, 1845, vol. xiv, Ross & Cromarty, p.27.
49. *Ibid.*, p.279.
50. *Ibid.*, p.331.
51. This number was not dramatically larger than that of other Easter Ross parishes for which a figure was recorded in the *New Statistical Account*. Only one parish — Tain — had more than ten in the three-year period recorded. The minister of Tain explained that its 15 included 'several cases that were afterwards followed by marriage' (*ibid.* p.292). In those parishes which recorded them, the average number of illegitimate births *per annum* compared with the total population of each of these parishes was: Tain, 1 for 589; Nigg, 1 for 1,400; Kiltearn 1.3 for 1,605 (this represented 3 per cent. of the Kiltearn annual birth rate); and Fearn, 1 for 1,695. Similar figures were given for some parishes in the Black Isle, nearby: Cromarty, 1 for 1,450; Rosemarkie, 1 for 1,800 (about 2 per cent. of the annual birth rate); and Avoch, about 0.7 for 1,936 (1.4 per cent. of the annual birth rate) (*Ibid: passim*).
52. J. Noble: *Religious Life in Ross*, 1909, p.186. The absence of illegitimacy was the only example given here by Noble of improved morals. The only other 'good result' he mentioned was 'an eager desire to learn to read' (*ibid*).
53. *New Statistical Account*, *op.cit.*, p.331.
54. *Ibid.*, p.224. (The account of Dingwall was not drawn up by its minister but by a layman with the same surname as the minister.)
55. *Ibid.*, p.31.
56. *Ibid.*, p.32.
57. *New Statistical Account*, 1845, vol xiii, Banff, p.166. The number of illegitimate births in this parish was small compared with some Banffshire parishes. Of those which recorded figures, Gamrie had 1 illegitimate birth for every 150 members of its population; Forglen, 1 for 200 and Banff 1 for between 250 and 300. (The Banff figures also represented between 20 and 23 per cent. of the annual birth rate of that parish.) Gartly had 1 for 300 (about 19 per cent. of the annual birth rate); Cabrach and Botrophnie each, 1 for about 350; Deskford, Cullen and Inverkeithney each, about 1 for 500. (In Deskford this was 7 per cent. of the annual birth rate, in Cullen 3.5 per cent.) Given that the annual average in Alvah was 2.5, with a population of 1,407, this makes it 1 for 563, near to Kirkmichael at 1 for 550, and greater only than Rothiemay at 1 for 600. There is nothing very obvious to account for the differences between these parishes. Coastal parishes with fishing populations, like Banff and Cullen, could be either high or low. Kirkmichael was a Highland parish to the west of the county, but Rothiemay was well to the east and in an area where some parishes had a high proportion of illegitimate births. (*Vide ibid.*, *passim*.)
58. *Ibid.*, p.232.
59. *Ibid.*
60. *Ibid.*, p.233.
61. *Ibid.*

Chapter three

1. *New Statistical Account*, 1845, vol.xiii, Banff, p.166.

2. The number of persons to every 100 houses were, in 1801: 546, and in 1851: 780. In 1861 one third of the Scottish population was living in one-roomed houses. (R.H. Campbell: *Scotland Since 1707,* 1965, p.193.)

3. In the overcrowded Old Town of Edinburgh (c.1858) there were 33 deaths per 1,000 of the population in one district annually, compared with 12 per 1,000 in a comparable district of the more spacious New Town. (F.C.G.A.P. & D. 1859, p.58.)

4. This act also affected families insofar as it refused relief to the wives and children of unemployed men unless they had been deserted by them.

5. F.C.G.A.P. & D., 1858, pp.238ff. This speaker (Dr. Grierson) had twenty bothies in his parish, each containing two to eight unmarried men.

6. *The Witness,* January 23, 1858.

7. *Vide The Witness,* May 5, 1858.

8. The Forbes Mackenzie Act had come into force in 1854 and the Temperance Movement was now in full swing.

9. *Vide* T. Ferguson: *The Dawn of Scottish Social Welfare,* 1948, p.286.

10. *Vide The Witness,* March 27, 1858.

11. F.C.G.A.P. & D., 1859, p.68. The speaker, Alex Earle Monteith, was Sheriff of Fife, which had its fair share of illegitimacy. But how far was his attitude an example of the mannered naivety sometimes displayed by the members of his profession?

12. When a fuller picture was available in 1859 the South-Western as well as the North-Eastern counties of Scotland were seen to have the highest illegitimacy rates. The counties of Edinburgh and Lanark, for example, had rates of 8.3 per cent. and 7 per cent. respectively, whereas the respective rates for Wigton and Banff were 15.5 per cent. and 16.6 per cent.

13. The term 'illegitimacy rate' was widely used at this time to refer to the percentage of illegitimate births to total births. Today, a distinction is made between 'the illegitimacy ratio . . . i.e. the proportion of illegitimate births to total births' and 'the illegitimacy fertility *rate,* the number of illegitimate births per 1,000 unmarried women of childbearing age' which 'was not calculated by the early Scottish Registrar Generals'. T.C. Smout, 'Aspects of Sexual Behaviour' in A.A. MacLaren (ed): *Social Class in Scotland,* 1976, p.62.

14. F.C.G.A.P. & D., 1859, p.67.

15. *The Witness,* March 27, 1858.

16. The Assembly had another committee in 1860 and 1861 on 'The Causes and Remedies of Social Evils'. This, however, added nothing significant to the findings of the Housing committee.

17. These reports were much more concerned with the rural situation than that of the towns, and contain very little about sexual behaviour or family life in the latter. There is however in the 1862 report some reference to, on the one hand, prostitution and, on the other, slum conditions affecting family life in the Edinburgh Canongate. (F.C.G.A.P. & D., 1862 Housing Report, Appendix II.) And in the debate on this report Begg remarked, apropos of the famous collapsing tenement of 1861: 'He would rejoice, though it seemed strange matter for rejoicing, if that dreadful event which hurried so many away into a premature eternity recently in the High Street were followed by practical measures' (*ibid.,* p.187).

18. Although Begg was a member of this committee also. He was, in fact, in 1861 a member of 25 of the Assembly's 40 committees. Only Candlish, who was a member of 27 Assembly committees, beat this record.

19. In England there was 1 illegitimate birth for every 35 unmarried women between 15 and 45, in Scotland 1 for every 41.1 (figures for 1861). (F.C.G.A.P. & D., 1864, Housing Report, Appendix IX, p.25.) These conclusions however were questioned by the Royal Commission on the Marriage Laws (see chapter four below).

20. F.C.G.A.P. & D., 1864, p.325.

21. F.C.G.A.P. & D., 1867, Housing Report, p.7.

22. F.C.G.A.P. & D., 1862, Housing Report, p.12.
23. F.C.G.A.P. & D., 1867, p.485.
24. *Vide* R.H. Campbell, *op.cit.*, pp.301-310.
25. *Vide* W.S. Bruce: *Social Aspects of Christian Morality*, 1905, p.85 fn.
26. Never a man to put all his rhetoric in one basket, Begg was also attacking Sabbath desecration, organs and Romanism. Against the last in particular he could summon the power of unparalleled invective. In 1861 he informed the Assembly, which had just approved his Housing Report, of the thirty agents, 'almost all perverts from the Church of England' of Brompton Oratory, where 'there was a billiard-room . . . employed for the purpose of carrying young men from Protestantism to Rome'. F.C.G.A.P. & D., 1861, p.324.
27. T. Smith: *Memoir of James Begg*, 1885, 2 vols; S. Mechie: *The Church and Scottish Social Development, 1780-1870,* 1960; D.H. Bishop: *Church & Society* (Unpublished Edinburgh Ph.D. Thesis, 1952) and D.C. Smith: *The Failure and Recovery of Social Criticism in the Scottish Church* (Unpublished Edinburgh Ph.D. Thesis, 1964).
28. Begg's general point about there being a connection between overcrowding and slum conditions (whether rural or urban) on the one hand and morals on the other was however taken by many of his colleagues and reference to it thereafter, as we shall see, became obligatory. For example, Blaikie wrote (c.1867):

> The late census has brought out the appalling fact, that no fewer than a million of the people of Scotland have dwellings of but one apartment, where, obviously, in the case of families, no attempt can be made at the separation of the sexes. Like Mrs. Bayly, we instinctively exclaim, when this fact is brought before us, It is of the Lord's mercies we are not consumed; it is amazing, when we consider the influence for evil of this one arrangement, that virtue and chastity survive at all.

Blaikie: *Better Days for Working People*, p.176. (The reference is to the census of 1861. The churches were, as will be seen in part three below, also concerned with incest, which has some bearing on this.)
29. F.C.G.A.P. & D., 1860, Housing Report, p.4.
30. *Ibid.* The Superintendent of Poor in Scotland had written in his report for 1858 that a very large and increasing number of women were receiving relief for their illegitimate children. (T. Ferguson: *op.cit.*, p.299.)
31. F.C.G.A.P. & D., 1860, pp.235ff.
32. F.C.G.A.P. & D., 1859, p.65. Begg was considered a dangerous radical by some of his contemporaries and what seems today to be his paternalism was mixed with some appreciation of the feelings of the workers. Obvious though it seems, he had to tell the Assembly that 'it was a thorough mistake to treat working men as if they were a kind of grown-up children'. (*Cf.* the Religion & Morals Report, F.C.G.A.P. & D., 1870, p.14, which described Fife miners as 'peculiar in their habits, in many ways resembling overgrown children'. This judgement seems to have been based on the miners' enjoyment of a weekly dance on the evening of pay-day.) But Begg disliked revolutionaries. He had perhaps inherited this from his father, who had described the local Lanarkshire Radicals in the early nineteenth century as 'the scum of the earth'. (T. Smith: *op.cit.*, vol.i, p.7.)
33. F.C.G.A.P. & D., 1860, Housing Report, p.10. But Begg was not the only Free Churchman able to make his fellow countrymen's flesh creep with stories of French horrors: Blaikie was at it as well (*Better Days for Working People*, 1867, pp.193ff.):

> It is a remarkable fact that the countries in Europe in which there is most disorder, are those in which the family constitution is least attended to. We refer to such countries as France, Ireland and Spain. Home is a word hardly understood in Paris. It is not improbable that the cold-blooded atrocities that make one shudder in reading the accounts of the first French Revolution were largely due to the early loosening of family ties, to the violence done to nature's method of making men 'kindly affectionate one to another'. If there be one symptom more than another

fitted to create alarm for the destinies of our own country, it is the wide-spread evil of parental neglect. Whether it is right to represent it as an increasing evil, we do not know; men are very apt to think that certain evils are increasing when it is that they are bestowing increased attention upon them. Perhaps it is the increased density of the population that makes the evil bulk more largely now than formerly. But whether it be increasing or not, there is enough of it to create much anxiety. In that awful state of darkness and corruption into which the world had sunk before the coming of Christ, the 'turning of the hearts of the fathers to the children and of the children to the fathers' is declared to be necessary else God would come and 'smite the earth with a curse'. To remove the curse and to bring a blessing, let us work and pray for — Home-Sunshine.

34. F.C.G.A.P. & D., 1860, Housing Report, p.11.

35. F.C.G.A.P. & D., 1860, Housing Report, p.1.

36. F.C.G.A.P. & D., 1858, p.65. Begg cited no authorities to substantiate this claim, which he no doubt believed to be self-evident. In the same Assembly, however, Professor I.M. Hetherington of Glasgow, comparing contemporary moral degradation with the high morals of the mid-seventeenth century, cited as his authority the historian Kirkton. (According to a recent historian, Kirkton, 'not a particularly truthful man anyhow, was writing (his) happy picture of a police state a good while later'. R. Mitchison: *A History of Scotland*, 1970, p.228.)

37. F.C.G.A.P. & D., 1859, Housing Report, and 1860, Housing Report, *passim.*

38. Begg believed that the 'great mass of the ministers of the South of Scotland . . . from Berwick to Portpatrick were at that time (1830) decidedly Moderate' (T. Smith: *op.cit.*, p.97). This was a popular, if mistaken, view. (*Vide* I.D.M. Clark: *op.cit.*, pp.213ff.)

39. Begg claimed that the influence of Popery as well as Moderatism had been strong in the North-East. He was on rather more firm ground here, especially if, as seems likely, he thought of Episcopalians as much the same as Catholics.

40. Begg had the grace to include this in the Housing Report of 1860 (p.21).

41. F.C.G.A.P. & D., 1862, p.353 (Guthrie's Moderatorial Address). Others in the Free Church Assemblies who questioned Begg's criticisms of bothies included a tenant farmer who said in 1862 that bothies were necessary because there was no alternative way of accommodating young men on farms and although he admitted failure on his own and other farmers' parts to exercise 'moral control' over them, he believed that the church was equally at fault since, while it was 'an imperative condition' of employment on his farm that the men attend 'a place of worship on the Sabbath-day', yet 'in the course of thirty years experience he could not state above three or four, or almost half-a-dozen visits from a clergyman' to his workers. The Earl of Dalhousie supported this farmer, praised his courage and said that bothies were not the real problem. (He had a bothy for his gardeners and was 'blessed with a pious head gardener who held classes with the young men'.) Some of the people living in the bothies might not be 'quite so cleanly as people ought to be, but in his eyes it was perhaps a verification of the old Scotch saying 'The clartier the cosier'. (F.C.G.A.P. & D., 1862, pp.195ff.)

42. The National Association for the Promotion of Social Science was one of his enthusiasms.

43. F.C.G.A.P. & D., 1860, Housing Report, p.9.

44. P.C. Simpson: *The Life of Principal Rainy*, 1909, vol.ii, p.50. (This was not, of course, the immediate context of Rainy's remark.)

45. F.C.G.A.P. & D., 1861, p.323 (Begg's 'mere').

46. *Ibid.* These statistics, Begg thought, would keep the respective denominations on their toes. (F.C.G.A.P. & D., 1863, p.314.)

47. F.C.G.A.P. & D., 1864, Housing Report, Appendix XII.

48. F.C.G.A.P. & D., 1863, Housing Report, Appendix II, pp.13ff. (Gerrard's remarks were contained in full in the 1863 report and referred to again in that of 1864.) Gerrard also

described his method of acquiring this information:

> Anxious to know the feelings and sentiments of the rural labourers themselves on this matter of illegitimacy, I have, while professionally attending their families, and from peculiar circumstances possessing a fair share of their confidence, talked the subject over with some of the more intelligent men, taking care to select those only of fair common sense, of steady habits, men, too, valued by their employers and respected by their fellows, but all placed in the unfortunate circumstance of having a double family to be provided for, the earlier portion being illegitimate. The great regret of these men had been that, when the first offence occurred, they had not the means of making the proper amends by marrying and sheltering mother and child in a dwelling of their own; nay more, they needed no hint to assure me that, if houses could have been readily had, they would in every probability have married early, and their children would have been born in wedlock. (*Ibid.*)

49. It probably sounded even more plausible when he compared agricultural workers with fishermen in the North-East. The latter, although heavy drinkers and 'remarkably prolific', produced very few illegitimate children, and if illegitimacy occurred it excited the 'displeasure and scorn of the whole village': but by comparison with the farm workers, the fishermen enjoyed adequate housing. As far as Gerrard's picture of the farm workers is concerned, recent research suggests that he was describing a real, but also a restricted problem:

> The plight of the servant with his wife in lodgings at a distance was an evident scandal which received some attention in reports of the second half of the nineteenth century. Some villages appear to have been notorious in providing for this form of existence, and clusters of families in this condition are to be found in the records . . . But when, in a diverse collection of parishes, the numbers are averaged, this is found to be a relatively infrequent arrangement; the majority of servants on marrying would find other ways of earning a living. Certainly, more would find cottages than would continue to live on the farm as married men. (M. Gray, 'North-East Agriculture and the Labour Force', in A.A. MacLaren (ed): *Social Class in Scotland*, 1976, p.99.)

50. The question of the causes of rural illegitimacy is conflated in the Housing Reports, and elsewhere in church pronouncements of the time, with that of sexual immorality or licentiousness in general. Gerrard, for example, seems to be specifically concerned with illegitimacy, whereas Thomson of Wick and others are discussing a much wider range of sexual (and marginally sexual) behaviour. The question of whether illegitimacy was really the same thing as immorality was in fact raised by Begg in the 1860 debate (F.C.G.A.P. & D., 1860, p.236.):

> I know that it has been hinted that illegitimacy is not to be regarded as a criterion of profligacy. I don't enter into the grounds on which that statement is made. There may be some truth in the general theory considered physiologically. At the same time, the inference from that truth is a most fallacious one, because the spread of profligacy soon leads to universal corruption.

The inference here seems to be that illegitimate children might not be the result of what we would now call promiscuity. Although Begg gives this argument short shrift, it would find support in Gerrard's account, and a high illegitimacy rate, far from being an indication of promiscuity, and all the attendant evils described and imagined by Begg, could well have indicated either the absence of suitable housing or traditional indifference to the timing of marriage, or both, preventing legitimation of the children of stable relationships.

51. Presbytery of Dunkeld F.C.G.A.P. & D., 1860, Housing Report, p.21.

52. These arrangements were also cited in the 1859 report, in a quotation from a recent report of the Board of Supervision of the Poor, which spoke of 'young and old of both sexes sleeping in the same beds' (in this case in cottages, as an example of the evils of the bondager system) and in Begg's speech in support of the same report, providing the emotive example of a bothy with Highland girls upstairs and Irishmen downstairs. (It is difficult to tell

whether concern for Highland virtue or Irish vice was uppermost — the Assembly was told more than once about what happened to Highland girls abroad.) (F.C.G.A.P. & D., 1859, Housing Report, p.2, and Proceedings, p.60.) The inundation of Irishmen caused the Housing committee further concern in 1866: 'If the Irish element continues to augment, they will not only not maintain . . . the high moral position (of) the peasantry of Scotland, but all the evils which have made Ireland the problem of statesmen and the dread of landlords may soon be expected to develop themselves in our rural districts.' (F.C.G.A.P. & D., 1866, Housing Report, Appendix I, p.7.)

53. F.C.G.A.P. & D., 1862, Housing Report, pp.40ff. Mr. Thomson was a member of the Housing committee.

54. There were various attempts at this time to collect evidence, other than that of Begg, the Registrar and the United Presbyterians (see below). The Society for the Promotion of Social Morality 'widely circulated' a set of questions to 'influential persons in all parts of the country', and found 'in regard to certain points a remarkable concurrence of opinion'. There was general agreement that 'the social immorality of Scotland must be largely traced — to hindrances in the way of marriage, arising from a variety of causes, but especially from the want of suitable houses for the people in many districts.' The bothy and large farm-kitchen systems were singled out, for particular criticism, and the comparison with the fishing population, made also by Gerrard, was mentioned. Were these 'influential persons' 'gentlemen amateurs'? (*Vide* F.C.G.A.P. & D., 1864, Housing Report, Appendix XI, p.27.)

55. F.C.G.A.P. & D., 1862, p.198.

56. F.C.G.A.P. & D., 1859, p.68.

57. F.C.G.A.P. & D., 1861, Housing Report, p.17.

58. F.C.G.A.P. & D., 1862, p.192.

59. F.C.G.A.P. & D., 1862, Housing Report, p.18. The farmers were here, of course, advised to imitate patriarchs in general rather than to imitate the marital behaviour of Abraham and Boaz. That the latter had been subject to 'night courtship' by Ruth was not a point Begg mentioned.

60. E.g. F.C. G.A.P. & D., 1862, p.187.

61. Begg also considered that the 167, 287 'excess of females' in Scotland (attributed to emigration and the greater male mortality rate) was 'a prominent cause of moral evil, as it is evidently a violation of the Divine arrangement in regard to the sexes'. (F.C.G.A.P. & D., 1862, Housing Report, p.1.) 'Interference' with 'God's ordinance of marriage', Begg believed, resulted in a 'crop of vice'. This, together with the 'close affinity' between 'moral and physical degradation' was 'a fixed law of nature'. (F.C.G.A.P. & D., 1864, Housing Report, Appendix XII, p.26.)

62. Begg was active in mid-nineteenth century Scottish Nationalist movements as well as in campaigns such as that for the forty-shilling freeholder franchise.

63. F.C.G.A.P. & D., 1867, Housing Report, p.7.

64. F.C.G.A.P. & D., 1862, Housing Report, p.19.

65. Mechie: *op.cit.*, p.134.

66. F.C.G.A.P. & D., 1862, Housing Report, p.19.

67. F.C.G.A.P. & D., 1860, pp.242ff.

68. F.C.G.A.P. & D., 1861, Housing Report, Appendix II.

69. F.C.G.A.P. & D., 1859, Housing Report, p.8.

70. *Social Evils and Problems*, ed. W.P. Paterson and D. Watson, 1918, pp.72ff.

71. *Ibid.*

72. *Vide* F.C.G.A.P. & D., 1864, Appendix XV, Housing Report.

73. U.P.S.P., (1864) pp.27ff.

74. Set up in 1863, not reappointed in 1867.

75. Cf. J.R. Fleming: *op.cit.*, vol. i, p.154.

76. C. of S. Acts and Proceedings, 1861, pp.79ff.

77. The Established Church also had critics of bothies, notably the Revd. Harry Stewart of Oathlaw.

78. A further prophylactic against sin which the Assembly commended was the establishment of female schools which, in its opinion, checked 'that coarseness of manners which often results from the teaching of the young of both sexes promiscuously'. Family religion was seen as another way of preventing unchastity, and landowners and farmers, together with parents, were urged to supervise the recreations of workers and young people in general, in order to keep them occupied, and at a distance from 'opportunities for loose conversation and other temptations to sin', as well as from 'meetings under night and other practices'. (*Ibid.*)

79. *Ibid.*

80. F.C.G.A.P. & D., 1863, R. & M.R., question 2.

81. *Ibid.*

82. F.C.G.A.P. & D., 1866, R. & M.R., p.3.

83. F.C.G.A.P. & D., 1863, R. & M.R., p.6.

84. F.C.G.A.P. & D., 1865, p.17.

85. F.C.G.A.P. & D., 1863, R. & M.R., p.6. The committee nevertheless went on to urge 'the parents of the working classes' to exercise such supervision, especially over night-courtship. Masters and mistresses however were also called in to help.

86. *Ibid.*, p.7. Here again a contrast was drawn by the committee between the agricultural and fishing populations. It was customary in the Free Church Assembly also to contrast lowland rural immorality with the high morality of the Highlands, where the Free Church was very strong. In May 1865, however, the minister of Tain in Easter Ross informed the Assembly that 'in the northern counties where illegitimacy was scarce known before, it had increased to an alarming extent'. He must have forgotten what his predecessor had written twenty years earlier if he thought it had not existed before, at least in his own parish (*vide* chapter two above); but then in June of the previous year the Highland Railway had opened a section of line between Invergordon and Meikle Ferry (*vide* The Stephenson Locomotive Society: *The Highland Railway Company*, 1953, p.20), and this line ran through, and the constructors of it would have resided in, his parish. This would have been enough to allege an increase of illegitimacy, whether or not the navvies were responsible, and indeed probably whether or not there had been any increase.

87. F.C.G.A.P. & D., 1863, R. & M. R., pp.7ff.

88. F.C.G.A.P. & D., 1866, R. & M. R., p.3.

89. F.C.G.A.P. & D., 1861, pp.352ff.

90. F.C.G.A.P. & D., R. & M. R., 1861, Appendix III.

91. *Ibid.*

92. *Ibid.*

93. *Ibid.*

94. *Ibid.*

95. *Ibid.*

96. *Ibid.*

97. P. Fairbairn: *Pastoral Theology*, 1875.

98. *Ibid.*, p.330. Fairbairn also noted that 'public professions of repentance and rebukes are no longer practicable as in the olden time, and in the few cases where I have known a return to them attempted, under a zealous pastorate, the attempt has always failed, and it was found necessary, in the interests of righteousness themselves, to have them abandoned'. (*Ibid.*, p.345).

99. W.G. Blaikie: *For the Work of the Ministry*, 1885.

100. *Ibid.*, p.156. Blaikie commended daily exercises in controlling the voice, 'taken in moderation'. 'The time most favourable for these exercises is an hour or two after a meal; the stomach ought to be neither too full nor too empty.' *Ibid.*, p.248.

Chapter four

1. *The Witness*, March 27, 1858.

2. Parliamentary Papers, 1868: *Royal Commission on the Law of Marriage*, Appendix p.43, (evidence of the Free Church).

3. This development took place at an earlier date in the East than in the West. There is however some evidence to suggest that moves in this direction in the West had been made at an earlier date. About 780 Charlemagne had promulgated an edict to the effect 'that no marriage should be celebrated any other way than by blessing, with sacerdotal prayers and oblations; and whatever marriages were performed otherwise should not be accounted true marriages'. This rule (according to A. Edgar: *The Church and the Marriage Notice Act*, 1878, p.17) either was 'inefficient from the first, or fell into disuse, or was never widely adopted'.

4. *Vide* E. Schillebeeckx: *Marriage: Secular Reality and Saving Mystery*, 1965, vol.ii, pp.205ff.

5. T. Johnston (*History of the Working Classes in Scotland*, 1921, p.12) discusses the evidence for the existence of a *Jus Primae Noctis* in Scotland. It seems likely from what Johnston says, taken alongside the conflicting evidence on this subject in E. Westermarck (*The History of Human Marriage*, 1921, vol.i, pp.176ff.) that the *merchet*, a fine paid by a vassal to his superior on the vassal's daughter's marriage, was paid in recompense for the loss of working livestock, rather than in place of the exercise of the *droit du seigneur*.

6. Thus in the 19th century the Scottish Roman Catholic authorities regarded irregular marriages of Catholics, provided no impediments intervened, as valid and indissoluble, although also sinful and unlawful from the Roman Catholic Church's point of view. (Royal Commission: *op.cit.*, p.12.)

7. Handfasting at any rate is said to have died out about twenty years after the Reformation: *vide* C. Rogers: *Social Life in Scotland*, 1884, vol.i, p.104.

8. The terms 'irregular marriage' and 'clandestine marriage' are sometimes used interchangeably, but irregular marriage usually means any valid form of marriage other than before a clergyman and witnesses (*in facie ecclesiae*) whether or not any attempt was made to do this in secret, whereas clandestine marriage implies secrecy and in many cases the presence of a dissenting priest or minister or a celebrant who was disqualified for some reason.

9. This practice was said to have continued until the beginning of the eighteenth century (Royal Commission: *op.cit.*, p.138).

10. For some relevant parochial statistics and a full discussion of irregular marriage in eighteenth-century Leith, *vide* J.S. Marshall, 'Irregular Marriage in Scotland as Reflected in Kirk Session Records', *Records of the Scottish Church History Society*, 1972, Vol.XVIII Part 1.

11. Royal Commission: *op.cit.*, p.83.

12. The Free Church Assembly happened to be meeting in Edinburgh in May 1849 while the Bill was being debated in Westminster. Part of the Free Church's opposition to it was sectarian, in that it was critical of the Bill's proposal to make session clerks of the Established Church the local registrars of marriage. But nationalism was also involved: 'It were better for England, as she had taken her king from Scotland, to take also sometimes a leaf out of the book of Scots law instead of trying to assimilate it to her own,' said Mr. Mackgill Crichton, and roundly abused Fox Maule and the Lord Advocate, hoping that, in view of the latter's conduct, 'not a lawyer, and especially not an overburdened lawyer, would in future be appointed to superintend the business of Scotland'. Charles Cowan, the Edinburgh M.P. and Free Church elder, warned the Assembly, however, that it should not sit 'as a court of review on political matters at a time when political excitement was particularly intense'. (F.C.G.A.P. & D., 1849, pp.48ff.)

13. Royal Commission: *op.cit.*, p.xxi.

14. *Ibid.*

15. Much uncertainty existed about the extent of this practice. Some said that it had only

existed in Annan, Dumfries, Rutherglen and the Canongate in Edinburgh. Others held that it had been much more common. It certainly existed in some places as late as 1853.

16. Royal Commission: *op.cit.*, *passim.*

17. Royal Commission: *op.cit.*, p.43. (Free Church evidence — the United Presbyterian evidence was very similar.)

18. *Ibid.*

19. *Ibid.*

20. Strahan subsequently studied a wider range of Highland and Lowland parishes: his findings, which confirmed many of his earlier impressions, were published in a series of articles in *The Scotsman* in 1870. *Vide* T.C. Smout, 'Aspects of Sexual Behaviour' in A.A. MacLaren (ed.): *Social Class in Scotland*, 1976, pp.67ff.

21. Royal Commission *op.cit.*, p.172.

22. *Ibid.*

23. *Ibid.*

24. *Ibid.*

25. *Ibid.*

26. *Ibid.* Strahan was asked by a Commissioner, 'Are the dwellings of the classes of which you have spoken such that the young women have separate bedrooms?' and replied that although things were improving, 'grown-up sons and daughters' amongst the labouring classes shared a bedroom. But presumably the sons were out courting themselves.

27. *Ibid.*

28. *Ibid.*

29. *Ibid.*, p.173.

30. *Ibid.*, p.175.

31. *Ibid.*, p.172.

32. *Ibid.*, p.173.

33. *Ibid.*, p.174.

34. *Ibid.*, p.172.

35. *Ibid.*, p.175.

36. *Ibid.*, p.174.

37. *Ibid.*, p.173.

38. *Ibid.*

39. *Ibid.*, p.123. (The witness was Norman MacPherson, Professor of Scotch Law in Edinburgh University.)

40. The lawyers did not necessarily paint a different, only a less detailed, picture. According to the Lord Advocate (J. Moncrieff): 'In many of the counties it is an understood thing among the lower orders that if a girl has a child she is married, and if she has not a child she is not married' (*Ibid.*, p.69).

41. *Ibid.*, p.174.

42. This was particularly true of the Church of Scotland representatives. 'How long is it since you ceased to be a parish minister?' a Commissioner testily asked Dr. Barclay, the Principal of Glasgow University, who had claimed 38 years' experience as a parish minister. It was in fact eight years since. Another Church of Scotland witness was Dr. Cook, the Principal Clerk, who was known as a Moderate. On the legal ability of Presbyterian ministers, Robert Wallace was to comment (*Recess Studies*, p.198), apropos of the need for all the business of the church to be conducted by ministers:

> In this way men of ability, who, under a different stimulus might have ripened into erudite divines, instructors and liberalisers of their fellow-beings in matters about which they have very great need to have their minds enlightened and opened up, have yielded to the temptation of growing into what are called church lawyers — that is amateurs and dabblers in legal principles and cases — of nearly equal capability with third-rate solicitors.

43. Royal Commission: *op.cit.*, p.174.
44. *Ibid.*
45. *Ibid.*, p.173.
46. *Ibid.*, p.174.
47. Strahan may or may not have been right about the infrequency of written promises: it was not something which could be easily ascertained. But his view that it required a good deal of 'coolness' on the part of the woman makes his account seem plausible, and it was supported by the evidence of other witnesses, notably Patrick Fraser, the Sheriff of Renfrew. On the basis of his judicial experience in filiation cases, Fraser gave the following example (*ibid.*, p.143): 'Take the ordinary case of a ploughman, which is a very ordinary case; the girl is sitting by the kitchen fire along with the man, *et pares aetate et viribus coeunt*. The ploughman and the servant girl have connexion according to the impulses of human passion, stimulated by temptation and opportunity, and without any reference to marriage. That is my notion of illegitimacy in Scotland . . .' Fraser saw this as normal, except in 'one or two counties in the north' where 'it is very common amongst the lower orders, and also the middle classes, where they have taken each other as lovers, to have connexion before marriage, and if the woman becomes *enceinte*, the man marries her, but very often does not.' Further doubts about the frequency of written promises, of course, are raised by the illiteracy of a substantial minority (but perhaps those most at risk) of the population. In 1872, among those married regularly, ten per cent. of men and twenty per cent. of women signed the marriage register by a mark. *Vide* Drummond, A.L. and Bulloch, J., *The Church in Late Victorian Scotland*, 1978, p.138.
48. Royal Commission, *op.cit.*, p.174.
49. English law, unlike that of Scotland, France, Spain, Portugal, Germany and most other European countries did not receive legitimation *per subsequens matrimonium*. An attempt to introduce it in 1235 was supported by the bishops but rejected by the temporal lords '*quod nolunt leges Angliae mutari*'. (*Ibid.*, p.81.) This reasoning was now operative in the Scotch law.
50. John Inglis.
51. *Ibid.*, p.lv.
52. *Ibid.*, p.xxix.
53. *Ibid.*, p.12. Irregular marriages among Scottish Roman Catholics were in the eyes of that church valid, since the Tridentine Decree *Tametsi* had not been promulgated in Protestant Scotland. Catholics were, however, instructed to regard irregular marriage, or any marriage not celebrated according to Roman rites, as sinful and unlawful; and these could be invalidated if there were impediments, of which Rome still retained more than the Reformed churches.
54. Although this could have been proved or disproved in cases of subsequent legitimation, by reference to the Registrars, if those who made the claim had cared to enquire.
55. A fatal weakness of much that nineteenth-century Scots said about English habits: in the famous debate of 1863 in the Free Church on the Sunday opening of the Edinburgh Botanical Gardens, Charles Cowan, the M.P., was making a mild defence of the case for Sunday opening, and was interrupted by the Edinburgh Baillie, Blackadder, who said, damningly, 'Mr. Cowan has been . . . for a time in the south, where the seventh day is not only a day of work, but a day of amusement. The theatres are all open.' 'That,' cried Cowan, no doubt in despair, 'is not the case in England.' To which the invincible Baillie replied: 'I am afraid that it will be the case in Scotland.' It clinched the case against Cowan. (F.C.G.A. P. & D., 1863, pp.325ff.)
56. Royal Commission: *op.cit.*, p.xxxi.
57. *Ibid.*, p.46.
58. In connection with Brougham's Act.
59. *Vide* G.F.A. Best: *Mid-Victorian Britain*, 1971, p.98.

60. Especially since the registration of irregular marriage cost only 5/-.

61. Royal Commission: *op.cit.*, p.146. He pointed out that these fees were 'the source of emolument of the Session Clerk in most parishes'.

62. *Ibid.*, p.150.

63. *Ibid.*, p.xii.

64. *Ibid.*

65. C. of S.G.A.R., 1878, pp.717ff.

66. *Ibid.*, p.718.

67. U.P.S.P., 1876, p.735.

68. *Ibid.*, 1877, pp.102ff.

69. A. Edgar: *The Church and the Marriage Notice Act*, 1878, p.10.

70. *Ibid.*

71. F.C.G.A.P. & D., 1878, pp.40ff. The speaker was Mr. McMicking of Glasgow and Helensburgh.

72. F.C.G.A.P. & D., 1879, p.37. The speaker was Mr. William Balfour, whose remarks were related to a fear that if marriage with a deceased wife's sister became legal the registrar could issue a certificate for such a marriage, whereas the church would be unable to proclaim banns for it. (See part three below.)

73. F.C.G.A.P. & D., 1881, p.47.

74. *Ibid.*

75. By A. Ashley in *The Honourable Estate*, 1950, p.38.

76. *Ibid.*

77. *Ibid.*

78. *Vide* T.C. Smout, 'Aspects of Sexual Behaviour', *op.cit.*, p.79:

> in the towns, working class morality was probably more heterogeneous than anywhere else. Some were heavily influenced by 'middle-class morality' — either those who were most firmly controlled by the middle classes, like domestic servants, or who aspired in this and other respects to resemble the middle classes, like shop-workers and craftsmen. Some took the tone of their behaviour from the rural areas from which they had immigrated — and in the case of the Irish this could place a high premium on female chastity, in the case of the north-eastern Lowlanders, rather a low one. Others lived, or partly lived, on the receiving end of prostitution. It seems impossible to discover any proletarian norm of urban society: this is probably because there was not one, but many.

79. *Ibid.*

80. M.O.W. Oliphant: *A Memoir of the Life of John Tulloch*, 1888, p.72.

81. *Vide* E. Shorter: *The Making of the Modern Family*, 1976, chapter three.

82. W.J. Goode: *The Family*, 1964, p.27.

83. For a more detailed analysis of the Scottish scene and its local variations *vide* T.C. Smout, *op.cit.*, and the further account by the same author in M. Flinn *et al*: *Scottish Population History*, 1977, pp.349-369. The subject is also discussed in A.L. Drummond and J. Bulloch: *The Church in Victorian Scotland*, 1975, pp.125-138.

84. It was of course only partially so. However, the membership figures for 1879 (Howie: *op.cit.*, p.38) gave these proportions: Synods of Dumfries and Galloway: C. of S. 33, F.C. 12, U.P. 5; Synods of Ross, Sutherland and Caithness: C. of S. 19, F.C. 30, U.P. 2. The corresponding figures for Scotland were: C. of S. 52, F.C. 30, U.P. 17. (These figures all include the Gaelic adherents.)

85. Or, perhaps, in distorting the illegitimacy statistics, since there is always the *outside* possibility that, in the early days of registration, local registrars in the Highlands, being themselves members of communities in which illegitimacy was frowned upon more than elsewhere, may have accepted at face value the custom of regarding some illegitimate children as the late offspring of their grandparents.

86. C. of S. Acts and Proceedings, 1861, p.79.

87. There was, or soon would be, criticism of this practice from within the Church of

Scotland. Andrew Edgar (*vide* A. Edgar: *op.cit.*, pp.36ff.) pointed out that marriage in private houses was a departure from what was commanded in the First Book of Discipline. The same point was made by the Reverend John Mackie of Dalbeattie in an article in *Life and Work* in 1884. (*Vide Life and Work* (August) 1884, pp.124ff.) He argued for marriage in church 'on the ground of antiquity, solemnity, economy and morality' (economy, because of the heavy cost to young couples of the home marriage feast, fear of which 'oftentimes . . . helps the postponement of marriage'; morality, because 'the drinking and dancing through the midnight hours that sometimes — we do not say often — accompany the household celebration of marriage are not calculated to promote what is pure and lovely and of good report' (*ibid.*, p.125)). Mackie claimed that 'only within very recent years' had a trend towards marriage in church reappeared, and he was writing to defend this against the charge of 'Anglicising'.

Chapter five

1. Family prayers were integral to pre-Reformation English Catholic piety and in Scotland were enjoined by Hamilton's Catechism (1552). *Vide* L.L. Schücking: *The Puritan Family*, (English edition, 1969), pp.61ff.
2. G.D. Henderson: *op.cit.*, p.126; and *Acts of the General Assembly of the Church of Scotland*, 1638-1843 (1843), 1649, xiii (p.241), and 1697, vii (pp.259ff.).
3. G.D. Henderson: *op.cit.*, p.127.
4. *Ibid.*, p.126.
5. Aiton: *op.cit.*, pp.166ff. Aiton also criticised the Ayrshire custom of praying over sick persons by elders and 'all who were fond of performing worship': 'Devotion is highly becoming in its proper time and place, and sickness and death ought to excite every one to such exercises; but when any person is very ill, noisy worship is apt to prove fatal to them.' (*Ibid.*, p.167.)
6. *Vide* J.H.S. Burleigh: *A Church History of Scotland*, 1960, p.372.
7. Church of Scotland Committee on Aids to Devotion: *Family Prayers*, 1871, p.2.
8. *Ibid.*, p.1.
9. *Ibid.*, p.3. This passage is a composite of Isaiah 28:10 and 13, and Jeremiah 10:25. As scriptural authority it is dubious — even for fundamentalists — especially since the original of the latter part was not a divine promise but a prayer by the prophet (or perhaps a later addition) to God to 'Pour out thy fury on the heathen that know thee not, and upon the families (i.e. peoples) that call not on thy name; for they have eaten up Jacob . . . and have laid his habitation desolate'.
10. *Ibid.*
11. *Ibid.*
12. *Ibid.*, p.4.
13. *Ibid.*
14. *Ibid.*, p.5.
15. *Ibid.*, p.6.
16. *Ibid.*, p.7.
17. *Ibid.*, p.8.
18. *Ibid.*, p.9.
19. *Ibid.*, p.x.
20. *Ibid.*, p.vi. Previous volumes had been designed for 'Soldiers, Sailors, Colonists and other persons who are deprived of the ordinary services of a Christian ministry' (*ibid.*, p.v).
21. *Ibid.*, p.xiii.
22. *Ibid.*, p.xiv.
23. 'Address by Committee of Synod to parents and families of the United Presbyterian Church, on the Subject of Family Worship': *United Presbyterian Monthly Record*, Jan. 1, 1858, pp.3-6. (The hopefully auspicious date of publication was deliberately chosen.)
24. *Ibid.*, p.4.

25. *Ibid.*

26. G.D. Henderson (*op.cit.*, p.254) suggests that there was a general decline in the observance of family worship in the early nineteenth century, but that 'probably it was better observed in the Secession Church'.

27. *U.P. Monthly Record*, op.cit., p.4.

28. *Ibid.*, p.5.

29. *Ibid.*, p.6.

30. The commercial crisis referred to (F.C.G.A.P. & D., 1858, p.262) was that of 1857, which brought about the dramatic failure of the Western Bank, whose policy had been more adventurous than that of the longer established and more conservative Edinburgh banks. (*Vide* R.H. Campbell: *op.cit.*, pp.142-147.) The Western was a very large institution and many influential men in Glasgow and the West of Scotland were among its backers and customers. The church's criticism, expressed in the Pastoral Address issued by the Commission of Assembly in October 1858, did not mention by name either the Western Bank or the four firms whose failure had precipitated its collapse, nor apparently could the bank itself be charged with fraud — which was one of the major criticisms made, in the address, of what were termed 'the conventional immoralities of worldly business'. (*Acts of the General Assembly of the Free Church*, 1858-1863, p.181.) The nub of the church's criticism, insofar as it can be disentangled from the Address's thundering rhetoric, was an attack on 'the determination to be rich, to be speedily rich, — and if that may not be, to have the name and appearance of wealth, and live in splendour and luxury' (*ibid.*), and it looks as if this was a reflection of the view of the Edinburgh bankers, that stability was more important than the commercial and industrial progress which might have come from the more (although probably too) liberal policy of the Western. It was not of course the case that the Free Church was opposed to making money as such (its own prosperity was not after all founded entirely upon widows' mites); and it believed that there was 'something truly valuable in real, solid prosperity, honestly reached, with God's blessing thereon' (*ibid.*). But it did object to 'those great and gross frauds, such as have of of late come to light' (*ibid.*) and also to the 'great variety of little dishonesties (pardon the expression) in the form of adulterations and untruths' (*ibid.*) which were examples of the same evil on a smaller scale. The Church was particularly distressed that some of these had been 'practised by men professing godliness' (*ibid.*), who ought, it believed, to have known better. 'Reverses and losses,' it wrote, 'may overtake a man in business, but he never need be fraudulent or dishonest . . . And when all is correct and honest, even if adversity should befall, God's blessing may still be there, and the heart be calm and happy' (*ibid.*).

The Free Church, then, criticised any departure from conservative and correct commercial practice, and condemned anyone who took too great risks in the pursuit of prosperity. It was not altogether a contradiction of the parable of the talents, more a commendation of the man who gained an extra two. It was also however an attack on 'the spirit of worldliness and selfishness in the eager race for riches which men are running' (*ibid.*) and a warning to those involved — Free churchmen included — of the danger to their souls.

> What a rebuke the late commercial distresses gave to this eager engrossing spirit of worldliness! To how many hundreds have worldly losses and difficulties and anxieties shewn the unsatisfactoriness and uncertainty of merely worldly possessions and pursuits! Will you who have thus felt and suffered learn the lesson, and henceforth make it your chief business to lay up for yourselves treasure in heaven? (*Ibid.*)

Statements of this kind no doubt pleased the solid Edinburgh bankers (who perhaps did not see the contradiction between what was said and the Free Church's own earthly treasures), and no doubt the 'little dishonesties' were fairly extensive, but the Free Church's criticism did not go much beyond the conventional commercial pieties of the period, and can hardly be regarded as in any sense a form of social criticism which might have contributed to the general prosperity and wellbeing of the community. But in the jumpy financial atmosphere of the time there was perhaps little which the church could say that might help; and it may have been that some unfortunate members of the middle classes who had lost money, found, in such talk, a way of orientating themselves to their reduced circumstances.

James Begg, incidentally, was behind this episode also. It was on his motion that the Presbytery of Edinburgh overtured the General Assembly for this Pastoral. The aspects of commercial immorality which he chose to single out included Sunday trading, and the punishment of small-time swindlers while 'great culprits, gigantic culprits who swindled on an immense scale' (Begg is the grand argument against those who claim that the English language is being devalued by the late twentieth-century addiction to superlatives) 'were to a large extent allowed to pass with impunity'. (T. Smith: *op.cit.*, vol. ii. p.245.) Part of the reason for this, according to Robert Wallace, writing fifteen years later, was that the churches were afraid to tackle openly the speculative activities of those who, while they remained within the law, were in moral terms just as guilty. Speculation, he claimed, was 'in no respect a productive industry': it was 'simply gambling'. If the church were to say this, however, 'a good many of the Church's best subscribers might be offended'. (Wallace: *Life and Last Leaves*, pp.203-204.) Wallace's contention that success was the yardstick by which commercial morality was measured helps to explain why the Pastoral made no direct condemnation of speculation as such. The Protestant churches' attitude to usury was of course a much older and more tangled story. For Rainy's reaction to another bank crash, that of the City of Glasgow Bank in 1878, and his comments on the moral issues involved, *vide* A.L. Drummond and J. Bulloch: *The Church in Late Victorian Scotland*, 1978, p.129.

31. *Acts of the General Assembly of the Free Church*, 1858-1863, p.182.
32. That of 1860, *ibid.*, p.290.
33. *Ibid.*, p.183.
34. *Ibid.*
35. *Ibid.*
36. Galatians 5:19 and Ephesians 5:4.
37. *Acts of the General Assembly of the Free Church*, 1858-1863, p.183.
38. *Ibid.*, p.181.
39. *Ibid.*
40. *Ibid.*, p.182.
41. *Ibid.*
42. *Ibid.*
43. *Ibid.*
44. *Ibid.*
45. The language of the Pastoral is so like that used by Begg in the overture requesting it as to suggest that he had no small part in drafting it.
46. *Ibid.*
47. *Ibid.*
48. *Vide* G.F.A. Best: *op.cit.*, p.274.
49. F.C.G.A. P. & D., 1859, p.211.
50. *Ibid.*, p.210.
51. *Ibid.*, p.211.
52. *Ibid.*, p.210. The speaker was a Mr. Brodie.
53. *Ibid.*
54. *Ibid.*
55. *Acts of the General Assembly of the Free Church*, 1858-1863, p.289.
56. *Ibid.*
57. *Ibid.*, p.290.
58. *Ibid.*
59. *Ibid.*, p.292.
60. *Ibid.*

61. *Ibid.*
62. *Ibid.*
63. *Ibid.*, p.293.
64. *Ibid.*
65. *Ibid.*, p.294.
66. The 1862 Pastorals were drafted by Mr. Charles Brown (presumably the Edinburgh minister C.J. Brown) and revised by the Religion and Morals committee, on which Begg and Blaikie still served.
67. *Acts of the General Assembly of the Free Church*, 1858-1863, p.489.
68. *Ibid.*
69. *Ibid.*
70. *Ibid.*
71. *Ibid.*, p.490. In support of their view of the 'vital and central' place of the family the authors listed 'a somewhat carefully formed selection' (*ibid.*) of scriptural passages mentioning the family, 'to which we affectionately invite your attention at leisure' (there were nearly fifty passages listed) (*ibid.*). These and what had been written in the Pastoral so far should not only convince their readers of their parental responsibilities, but indeed 'might well overwhelm you with anxiety and fear, but for the Divine promises scattered up and down these same passages'. (*Ibid.*)
72. *Ibid.*, p.491.
73. *Ibid.*
74. *Ibid.*
75. *Ibid.*
76. *Ibid.*, p.491. The main O.T. reference was Deuteronomy 11:18-21.
77. *Ibid.*
78. *Ibid.*, p.492.
79. *Ibid.*
80. *Ibid.*
81. *Ibid.*
82. *Ibid.*
83. *Ibid.*
84. *Ibid.*, p.493.
85. *Ibid.*
86. *Ibid.*
87. *Ibid.*
88. *Ibid.*
89. *Ibid.*
90. *Ibid.*
91. *Ibid.*
92. *Ibid.*
93. *Ibid.*, p.494.
94. *Ibid.*
95. *Ibid.*
96. *Ibid.* 'It is worthy to be noted that in both these passages' (Ephesians 6:4 and Colossians 3:21), the authors commented, 'Paul says "fathers" — probably because the fathers are more prone in this matter to err.' (*Ibid.*)
97. *Ibid.*
98. *Ibid.*, p.495. The authors also expressed the hope that their readers would not now put the Pastoral aside, but read it again 'from time to time', to remind them of 'things too apt even when known, to be lost sight of and forgotten' (*ibid.*). Evidently these pastorals were designed to be read not simply from pulpits but also at home.
99. 'A meeting of several hundred Ministers and Elders gathered together from all parts of Scotland in the name of Jesus to consult about the advancing of his cause and kingdom in our beloved country and throughout the world'. (*Ibid.*).

100. *Ibid.*
101. *Ibid.*, p.496.
102. *Ibid.*
103. *Ibid.*
104. Such as, 'Behold, I stand at the door and knock'. The hymn was 'Just as I am — and waiting not/To rid my soul of one dark blot'.
105. *Acts of the General Assembly of the Free Church*, 1858-1863, p.497.
106. *Ibid.*
107. *Ibid.*
108. *Ibid.* Thomas Guthrie, who as Moderator of the 1862 Assembly signed this Address, expressed concern about recruitment to the ministry in his Moderator's Address (F.C.G.A.P. & D., 1862, p.353). He believed that ministers should have better pay and more incentives. (Before becoming a parish minister he had been a banker.) There was, he thought, too much dread of debt, or at least of genteel poverty, among ministers; and he claimed that 'the result of the inadequate livings of our ministers is, or, as sure as the tide will make Leith tomorrow, will be, unless the Christian people under God prevent it, that the rising talent, genius and energy of our country will go away to other professions, leaving the pulpit to weakness and fanaticism'.
109. *Acts of the General Assembly of the Free Church*, 1858-1863, p.497.
110. *Ibid.*
111. *Ibid.*
112. In particular about her 'noble sons', Knox, Melville, Henderson, Chalmers and 'her martyrs . . . her Patrick Hamiltons and George Wisharts and Argyles and John Browns and Margaret Wilsons'. The authors also hoped that the children's parents would 'try to explain to you how it comes that we, in these later days, have taken to ourselves the name of the *Free* Church of Scotland'. (*Ibid.*, p.498.)
113. *Ibid.*
114. *Ibid.*
115. *Ibid.*
116. This was an age group for which, during the second half of the nineteenth century, the Free Church was to develop a great variety of competitions and examinations concerned with knowledge of Scripture and of the church's history. The names of those who succeeded in these were listed at great length, down to the humblest certificate holder, in the Assembly Reports.
117. G.F.A. Best: *op.cit.*, p.79.
118. *Ibid.*
119. *Ibid.*, p.104.
120. *Ibid.*, p.102.
121. W. Tait: *Magdalenism*, 1842, p.15.
122. *Ibid.*, p.11.
123. *Ibid.*, p.15.
124. *Vide* T.C. Smout: 'Aspects of Sexual Behaviour', *op.cit.*, p.58: 'four-fifths of the applications to the Edinburgh Magdalene Institute between 1855 and 1860 had once been domestic servants'; citing A.C.C. List: *The Two Phases of the Social Evil*, 1861. *Vide* also I.A. Muirhead: 'Churchmen and the Problems of Prostitution in Nineteenth-Century Scotland', *Records of the Scottish Church History Society*, 1974, Vol.XVIII, Part 3, p.237.
125. H. Ellis: *Studies in the Psychology of Sex*, 1919, vol.vi., p.265.
126. *Ibid.*, pp.291ff.
127. But *vide* Smout, *op.cit.*, p.59, which casts doubt on this as far as middle-class Edinburgh households were concerned.
128. T. Smith: *op.cit.*, vol.i, pp.245ff.
129. *Acts of the General Assembly of the Free Church*, 1858-1863, p.498.
130. *Ibid.*

131. *Ibid.*, p.499.
132. *Ibid.*
133. *Ibid.*, p.501.
134. *Ibid.*, p.502.
135. *Ibid.*, p.501.
136. *Ibid.*, p.500.
137. *Ibid.*
138. *Ibid.*
139. *Ibid.*, p.502.
140. *Ibid.*, p.503. (Titus: 2:10.)
141. *Ibid.*, p.500.
142. *Ibid.*, p.499.
143. *Ibid.*
144. *Ibid.*
145. *Ibid.*, p.501.
146. *Ibid.*
147. *Ibid.*
148. *Ibid.*, p.500.
149. *Ibid.*
150. Norman Macleod, one of the Church of Scotland's most outstanding ministers, came into conflict with it at this time when he attacked Sabbatarian views. Macleod believed that those who attacked working men for 'walking on the Sabbath' were 'less liberal than God' (D. MacLeod: *Memoir of Norman Macleod*, 1877, p.289), and endangered the Church's interests. He also perceived however that Sabbatarianism was not an isolated phenomenon, but part of a more comprehensive 'Judaizing' of Christianity; and he wrote that 'the awful conviction is deeply pressing itself upon me, that the gospel is not preached generally in Scotland; that so-called "Evangelicalism" is Judaism . . . that it is not a gospel of glad-tidings but of lamentation and woe' (*ibid.*, p.368). As Macleod saw clearly, the future of the Church in Scotland would depend, among other things, on whether or not it could get beyond the Mosaic '"Thou shalt" and "shalt not"' (*ibid.*, p.371) of those who regarded 'the finding of the Westminster Assembly as perfect and incapable of improvement' (*ibid.*, p.372), 'to the gospel "Believe and live"' (*ibid.*, p.371).
151. Tait: *op.cit.*, p.14.
152. *Ibid.*, p.282. 'Leisure in the evenings is decidedly objectionable, as it is attended with the same bad consequences as leisure on the Sabbath' (*ibid.*).
153. *Ibid.*
154. *Ibid.*
155. *Ibid.*, p.291.
156. *Ibid.*, p.292. He did not care whether this was done by a Voluntary or by an Established agency, by 'the old parochial system' or by 'town missionaries and tract distributors': what was clear, however, was that 'the means at present employed are vastly disproportioned to the exigencies of the community' (*ibid.*).
157. *Ibid.*, p.293.
158. G.F.A. Best: *op.cit.*, p.278.
159. *Acts of the General Assembly of the Free Church*, 1858-1869, p.502.
160. The authors of the Pastoral cautioned servants 'against *a style of dress* unsuitable to your station, too gay and showy, which can add nothing to your real respectability, and which, arising out of an unbecoming state of mind, powerfully tends to feed and aggravate the evil from which it flows' (*ibid.*, p.502). Tait had listed 'pride and love of dress' among the causes ('natural' as opposed to 'accidental') of prostitution, and had remarked, with effortless male superiority, that the 'desire to appear more gay than her companions is a prominent feeling in the breast of every female child' (Tait: *op.cit.*, p.119). These views seem to have had the character of received opinion among some Scottish clergymen and

doctors. James Miller, Professor of Surgery in Edinburgh University, and Convener of the Free Church Committee on Temperance, in a pamphlet published in 1859, had pressed the need for a 'great and general reform ... as regards the arrangement and construction of female attire', a subject, in his opinion, to which the commercial crisis had drawn attention, 'the scandal having become great, through pecuniary extravagance' (quoted in W. Logan: *The Great Social Evil*, 1871, p.226). Miller, concerned lest the 'innate love of dress ... of young persons in the positions of servants and operatives ... continue to be fanned into a passion' (*ibid.*, p.227), asked ladies to 'use the pruning-hook' for their sakes. Tripping over his metaphors, he advised them against such fashionable 'exposure of the person, in evening costume, as is otherwise inconsistent with the fine sense of true delicacy innate to the virtuous female' (*ibid.*). If ladies were to avoid such exposure, a source of danger would be removed, 'enhancing ... the gracefulness of the form, as well as conserving the characteristic modesty of the wearer' (*ibid.*).

161. *Acts of the General Assembly of the Free Church*, 1858-1869, p.500.

162. Genesis, Ch. 24. The use of this story again illustrates the nature of Free Church fundamentalism. The aged Hebrew servant, sent to find a wife for his master's son, was a figure very far removed from the average nineteenth-century domestic servant. The latter, to make sense of this allusion, must have required considerable powers of 'spiritualising' the story with its strange and foreign incidents.

163. *Acts of the General Assembly of the Free Church*, 1858-1869, p.499.

164. *Ibid.*

165. *Ibid.*

166. *Ibid.*, p.502.

167. F.C.G.A.P. & D., 1865, R. & M. Report, p.7.

168. F.C.G.A.P. & D., 1866, R. & M. Report, p.3.

169. G.F.A. Best: *op.cit.*, p.278.

170. *Vide* chapter three, n.60.

171. In the chapter: 'Houses versus Hovels': *op.cit.*, pp.164ff.

172. *Ibid.*, p.181.

173. Blaikie's credentials as a philanthropist who was fully awake to the extent of urban poverty and degradation were as good as those of most other middle-class observers of this scene (and perhaps better than many), as the description of his case-book in his autobiography shows. (*Vide Recollections of a Busy Life*, pp.318ff.)

174. *Better Days for Working People*, p.199.

175. *Ibid.*

176. *Ibid.*, p.200.

177. *Ibid.*, p.211.

178. *Ibid.*, p.200.

179. *Ibid.*, pp.177ff. (a case cited from Edwin Chadwick).

180. Blaikie recognised the influence of health as well as of housing. *Better Days* included a chapter (pp.137ff.) on 'Health without Drugs', in which the working classes were advised of the need for proper ventilation and fresh-air — 'Nature herself is a great ventilator, and if men would but take lessons from her, they would be great ventilators too' (*ibid.*, p.146), exercise, cleanliness (including the water-cure), and neither too much nor too little food, not to mention not too much drink. This included not too much tea or coffee, as well as alcohol: Blaikie could not commend those females 'who take little exercise' and live 'chiefly upon bread and tea: Broken sleep and trembling limbs are likely to result' (*ibid.*, p.160).

181. There were a number of prominent laymen and ministers during this period who came from lowly homes. Hugh Miller was a favourite example used by Blaikie. Blaikie was also the biographer of David Livingstone. Duncan McLaren, the Edinburgh M.P., was another very prominent Scot who rose from a humble home. But men of this kind were, unlike William Logan, the author of *The Great Social Evil*, very rarely born into the rootless

urban proletariat. Very often they came from families which on closer examination turn out to have been marginal cases. John Cairns, the U.P. leader, is a good example of the type.

Cairns was born in 1818 in rural Berwickshire, not far from where Alexander Somerville was brought up. His father and grandfather were farm servants. Both parents were able to read, and his father had taught himself to write as well as learning arithmetic at evening classes. Their religious background was in the Burgher sect, and although this was not the strictest version of Presbyterianism, the children attended church from about the age of seven. This involved a walk of about two miles each way from home. On Sundays the children also attended the Sabbath-school (during which the pupils had to relate 'the dimensions and illustrations' of the sermon). In addition to these religious exercises in church, family worship was held earlier on the Sunday morning and again in the evening, preceded by repetition of the Shorter Catechism. Evening but not morning family worship took place on weekdays. John Cairns' formal education at the local school included English, Arithmetic and repetition of the Bible, the Shorter Catechism and the metrical Psalms and Paraphrases. To this, later, were added Latin, Greek, Euclid and Algebra. This had to be paid for (the fees were 3/- or 4/- a quarter, rising to 7/6 when Latin was added) by Cairns' father. Since his wages were small, and paid for the most part in kind, this could be done only by very careful management (especially on the part of his thrifty mother). Cairns' education, after the age of twelve, had to be continued in evening-classes, and by day in intervals of his work as a shepherd. With what he earned he borrowed books from the subscription library, reading history and theology, as well as the *Waverley Novels*. (His parents, although they enjoyed reading, were suspicious of novels: Cairns' father had a small library of his own, which included a variety of religious works such as Boston's *Fourfold State* and Jonathan Edwards' *History of Redemption*, as well as *The Pilgrim's Progress*, a 'fragmentary' (presumably expurgated) Burns and even *The Wealth of Nations*.) Newspapers were read by the family, being bought by a consortium of eight men including Cairns' father, and passed round from house to house. Out of this background Cairns progressed to Edinburgh University at the age of sixteen, and became a famous minister. This was surely a vindication of the humble home theory.

But some other features may be marked: 1) Cairns' father, although a farm servant and the son of one, was descended from farmers; and of Cairns' maternal uncles, two were large farmers and two were self-employed carriers. When he went to Edinburgh University Cairns was able to board with an uncle and aunt in the town. These better-off relations may not have given his parents financial assistance, but the family was socially mobile, and the possibility of upward mobility was visibly present. 2) Besides the interest in his education shown by his parents, Cairns benefited from the interest taken in him and in his education by the local minister and schoolteacher. The latter offered to waive the extra 3/6 for Latin, although Cairns' independent parents declined his offer. 3) Cairns' father was a shepherd, in relatively stable employment. Within limits he would have been reasonably free to organise his own time. So too could the young Cairns, able to continue his education sitting in the ruins of an old church within sight of his flock — a practice which perhaps laid him less open to the charge of misusing his employer's time (against which we saw the Free Church warning domestics) than, for example, that of David Livingstone, reading at his loom. 4) Cairns' formal education was, and not without much parental heart-searching, purchased at the expense of that of most of his siblings. (His brothers became a shepherd, a tailor, a mason (who later became a schoolteacher), and another minister: one of his sisters went into domestic service, another married a minister, a third lived with Cairns' family as housekeeper.) 5) The family had strong ties with a dissenting religious body and were part of a religious rural community in the early nineteenth century.

None of these features is recorded in order to detract in any way from the achievements of Cairns and his parents, which, even allowing for them, were considerable. But without them, how much would have been possible? (*Vide* A.R. MacEwan: *Life and Letters of John Cairns*, 1898, chs. I-IV, *passim*.)

On the specific subject of family worship, what has been said about the Cairns and Somerville families may be compared with what Robert Wallace recorded about his own family in the 1830s and '40s. Wallace's father, the Fife gardener (he was something between a head-gardener and a market-gardener, perhaps both), was accustomed 'to pronounce a very long grace at all meals, Sundays and other days as well' (*Life and Last Leaves*, p.59), only longer on Sundays. This, according to Wallace, 'was the traditional way of keeping up family worship among people whose work did not allow time for separate reading, singing and prayer' (*ibid.*). Wallace clearly associated family religion chiefly with the lower classes, since he wrote that it was not just 'the poorer class of the people that was specially distinguished for loyalty to the Puritan tradition in this matter. The middle class had it in much the same proportion as regards quantity, though, perhaps, somewhat diluted in point of intensity. It was when you came to the aristocracy that the heart of the devout Puritan failed within him — or her' (*ibid.*, p.46). The aristocracy were 'nearly all' Episcopalians, were regarded as 'semi-Papists', and attended church only once on Sundays.

182. There were of course other reasons why the crushed spirit of the Highlanders was ready, in the eighteenth century, for a new form of religion which would enable them to keep their self-respect by feeling morally and spiritually superior to their Southern neighbours. (There are some interesting comparisons — and differences — here with the nineteenth-century experience of the North American Indians.)

183. Taking two years at random: in the General Assembly of the Free Church in 1867, the largest class, apart from ministers and those listed only by their place of residence, were merchants, followed by farmers, members of the various professions, notably lawyers and teachers, those employed in commerce and public administration, and manufacturers. There was one earl and one labourer, two Members of Parliament and two gardeners. Were the calico printer, seedsman, housepainter and plumber working men? Or, to take another example, were the two cabinetmakers and the carpenter attending the 1871 Free Assembly employers or employed? There was no labourer that year, but there was a gardener and a cashier, a night watchman, a mason, a calico printer, a warehouseman and a carver and gilder. It is difficult to be sure if all of these designations implied working-class status, but the fact that the number of elders who might have been working men is so small, itself makes the point. (F.C.G.A.P. & D., 1867 and 1871, Roll of Members.)

184. *Vide* R. Fletcher: *The Family and Marriage in Britain*, 1966 edition, *passim.* The evidence on which Professor Fletcher bases what he writes about Religious Functions (*ibid.*, pp.192ff.) does not however go farther back than the eighteenth century and is mainly concerned with England. It is, moreover, set in a highly polemical context which equates Christian teaching with the more grandiose claims of Roman Catholicism (*ibid.*, pp.22ff.)

185. E.g. Matthew 10:35-36; Luke 14:26.

186. W.E. Houghton: *The Victorian Frame of Mind: 1830-1870*, 1957, p.343.

187. W.G. Blaikie: *op.cit.*, p.190.

188. 'More wife-beating,' wrote Robert Wallace in 1876, (*Life and Last Leaves*, pp.212ff.) 'is coming to take so regular a place as a news paragraph that it will require to be classified with other kindred items in the department of the sheet set aside for them. Probably the Manly Exercises column is its most natural receptacle.' Wallace (at this point Editor of *The Scotsman*) thought that wives were as much to blame as their husbands, but reserved his most caustic comments for the churches:

> Mr. Chadaband, the missionary, and Mrs Stiggins, the Bible woman, who are employed to visit Mrs Collier and friends at a low salary by the wealthy congregation of St. Shoddies, with the view of enabling them to state in their congregational report that they are doing their duty in turning sinners from the error of their ways, occasionally call upon Mrs Collier, but it cannot be said that their operations are pre-eminently calculated to effect either a substantial or an immediate improvement. Their form of procedure usually is to pull out a volume whose history and authority

> are very much disputed between Professor Smith and the Rev. George Macaulay, and to read to her some extracts about the burden of Damascus, or about the four-and-twenty elders and the beast, thereafter reciting a prayer whose meaning, if it has any, is wholly beyond Mrs Collier's comprehension . . . It would have done much more good to have told Mrs Collier that she was a wicked old sinner for being dirty and ragged and unprovided with a bit of ham or cheese. There is no saying how much verberation she might have saved herself and Collier had she only learnt in time how to keep a trim house, and provided that . . . husband with a Saturday's supper, hot and full, flanked perhaps by a little beer, and crowned even with a modicum of whisky . . . (*ibid.*, pp.214-215).

Wallace returned to the subject two years later (*ibid.*, pp. 260ff.), this time rather more seriously, but still making the point that although the husbands' behaviour was inexcusable, fines or imprisonment did not help, and that some responsibility lay with working-class wives to humour rather than antagonise their drunken husbands. He criticised temperance reformers for not being practical enough, and churchmen for not explaining to people the effects of alcohol on the body. But then, he wrote, perhaps clergymen 'are not altogether to blame, as their system keeps them hard at work trying to reconcile their audiences to schemes of mediaeval metaphysics, of which the more intelligent among them seem to have great difficulty in persuading themselves' (*ibid.*, p.264.).

Chapter six

1. It was in fact the only report of this committee to be included in the relevant Assembly records. Earlier reports seem to have been verbal ones. The committee was continued until 1874, when it was discharged, at its own request (*vide* C. of S.G.A. Acts (1870-75), 1874, p.77).

2. Perhaps this was why the Church of Scotland affected as its symbol at this time (*vide* volumes of *Life and Work* from 1879 onwards) the plough and anchor — as opposed to Moses' burning bush (the Free Church symbol, appropriate to those who considered the Disruption a new Exodus) and the dove returning to Noah's compact ark (the symbol of the United Presbyterians, themselves a compact body).

3. C. of S.G.A.R., 1870, p.419.

4. *Ibid.*

5. *Ibid.*

6. *Vide* Part Two, below.

7. C. of S.G.A.R., 1871, p.403.

8. *Ibid*: 'Even married servants, who have cottages to live in do not stay more than a year in one place. One minister of a rural parish says that 25 per cent. of his congregation leave for other parishes every Whitsunday.'

9. *Ibid.*

10. The committee claimed that 'the comforts which the labourer can command are incomparably greater than they were at the beginning of this century, and much better than they were even a quarter of a century ago' (*ibid.*, p.404).

11. *Ibid.*

12. Lord Kinnaird and his bothy schools were singled out for praise (*ibid.*, p.406). Both George, ninth Baron Kinnaird and lord-lieutenant of Perthshire (died 1878), and his brother Arthur who succeeded him were active philanthropists. Arthur's wife had edited a book of 'Servants' Prayers' in 1848 and was among the founders of the Young Women's Christian Association.

13. *Ibid.*, p.408. A footnote to this referred to a speech made by Lord Shaftesbury in 1870, referring to the rapidly multiplying 'masses' who, 'now a prey to every agitator, political and religious', would, unless 'brought within the fold of order, discipline and the Gospel, . . . break out . . . at no distant day, in a scene of violence and revolution, which will lay low all the honours of this country and its prosperity for many generations' (*ibid.*).

14. *Ibid.*, p.409.
15. *Ibid.*
16. C. of S.G.A.R., 1872, p.436.
17. *Ibid.*
18. *Ibid.*
19. *Ibid.*, p.437.
20. *Ibid.*
21. C. of S.G.A.R., 1878, p.539.
22. C. of S.G.A.R., 1872, p.439: the committee considering Sabbath Observance reported in the following year that 'the "going home" to their parents' houses with their clothes for washing is often only the name for a general visiting and even junketting, while churchgoing is entirely left out of consideration' (C. of S.G.A.R., 1873, p.427).
23. C. of S.G.A.R., 1872, p.439.
24. *Ibid.*, p.437.
25. *Ibid.*, p.438.
26. *Ibid.*
27. *Ibid.*
28. *Ibid.*
29. *Ibid.*
30. *Ibid.*
31. *Ibid.*
32. *Ibid.* The simile was perhaps too apt.
33. *Ibid.*, p.440.
34. Especially in Forfar, Perth and Aberdeen counties.
35. *Ibid.*, p.441.
36. *Ibid.*
37. *Ibid.*
38. *Ibid.*, p.499.
39. *Ibid.*, p.500.
40. The report repeated the opinion, questioned by the 1865 Royal Commission, that the explanation for the illegitimacy rate of Scotland being higher than that of England arose 'partly from the greater strictness with which the law as to registration of births is enforced in Scotland' (*ibid.*, p.499, *vide* Chapter Four above). It also commented that the law of 'legitimation for *subsequens matrimonium*' might be partly to blame, although its benefits made repeal of it unwise.
41. *Ibid.*
42. *Ibid.*, p.501. (The doctor's name was spelt in different ways. The Royal Commission of 1865 at one point (*op.cit.*, p.xxix) even referred to him as 'the Right Rev. Dr. Strahan'.)
43. C. of S.G.A.R., 1878, p.537.
44. *Ibid.*, p.538.
45. *Ibid.*, p.537. Further evidence of confusion about just what phenomena the committee was investigating is provided by the fact that some returns also dealt with 'the prevalence of foul speech' (*ibid.*, p.538), which was described as a 'form of licentiousness'. Not everyone was sure that this was so, however: some perceptive ministers remarked that 'the standard which educated people adopt in judging as to the coarseness of language used by the labouring classes is to a certain extent misleading; since the use of coarse expressions by them does not involve the same degree of coarseness of idea as in the case of persons of a higher social class' (*ibid.*).
46. *Ibid.*
47. *Ibid.*, p.538.
48. *Ibid.*
49. *Ibid.*
50. *Ibid.*

51. *Ibid.*
52. *Ibid.*, p.539.
53. *Ibid.*
54. *Ibid.*
55. *Ibid.*, p.540.
56. *Ibid.*, p.543.
57. These were a favourite idea of Charteris, the committee's convener: in his training scheme for his New College students he had created one. (*Vide* A. Gordon: *The Life of A.H. Charteris*, 1912, p.165.) This was about 1872-3. The idea later became quite popular (*ibid.*).
58. C. of S.G.A.R., 1878, p.543.
59. *Ibid.*
60. *Ibid.*
61. *Ibid.*, p.540.
62. *Vide* J.A. Banks: *Prosperity and Parenthood*, 1954, Ch. III.
63. Advice was not in short supply, however. Blaikie, in *Better Days for Working People*, devoted a chapter to the subject 'Make the Most of your Money'. In this, young men of the working classes were advised to lay aside 3/- a week between the ages of 18 and 30, on the assumption that while during this time their incomes would be much the same as later, their expenditure would be less. The £100 saved thereby would, wisely invested in Savings Banks, Friendly Societies, Annuities, or Life Assurance, Co-operative or Building Societies, provide him with resources for the rest of his life. 'Practically,' wrote Blaikie, 'the difference between having nothing and having a hundred pounds, is the difference between slavery and freedom' (*op.cit.*, p.117). Similar advice was given in an article on 'The Finance of Young Men' by 'a country minister' in the first issue of *Life and Work*, the church magazine for which the committee was responsible. The country minister (*Life and Work*, January 1879, pp.13ff.) warned his readers of the dangers of early marriage without financial resources; and from what both he and Blaikie wrote, it looks as if the best time for marriage, in their opinion, was between 25 and 30, at least for men. James Miller, the Professor of Surgery, seems to have held a similar view. But his remarks on the subject (quoted in W. Logan: *op.cit.*, pp.230ff.) point up the fact that the advice proffered by churchmen on this subject differed according to which class was being addressed; the upper classes were urged to avoid delay, despising fashion and luxury, while 'the operative class' was urged to avoid 'hasty premature unions'. The 'marriageable age' for operatives mentioned by Miller was 20 to 25. At about this age 'and when, by honest industry, they can secure a home for themselves and family — humble it may be, but sufficient for that maintenance of both body and mind to which their station entitles them — let them marry too, expecting, not in vain, like blessings with their betters'. In Miller's opinion, then, while the 'best time' might be much the same for both classes, the rich were marrying too late and the poor too early.
64. C. of S.G.A.R., 1878, p.540.
65. *Ibid.*, p.538.
66. *Ibid.*, p.541.
67. *Ibid.*
68. *Ibid.*
69. *Ibid.*
70. C. of S.G.A.R., 1881, p.478.
71. *Ibid.*
72. *Ibid.*, p.479.
73. *Ibid.*, p.478.
74. *Ibid.*
75. *Ibid.*
76. C. of S.G.A.R., 1885, Christian Life and Work report, *passim*. This report came to the definite conclusion that 'it does not appear that bothies are more dangerous than farm

kitchens' (*Life and Work*, (August) 1885, p.116), and placed much of the onus for the conditions which produced licentiousness and careless behaviour among farm servants on farmers.

77. C. of S.G.A.R., 1886, p.436. (The White Cross League, a sexual purity movement, had been founded by Ellice Hopkins in 1883.) *Vide* also *Life and Work* (November) 1885, p.163, where Charteris reported on a meeting at Alford in Aberdeenshire, at which 'it was said that every lad employed on a farm in Alford was there, and many from other parishes'; and after which 300 waited to hear Charteris speak about the White Cross movement.

78. *Life and Work* was still full of good advice on the subject, however. During the 'seventies it had included articles such as the series 'Occasional Homely Papers for the Working Classes', with titles like 'The True "Gentleman" and the True "Lady"' (*Life and Work*, (June) 1879, p.82); and the series 'Short Papers on Family Life' by the Revd. George Wilson of Cramond (*ibid.*, (February) 1880, p.19, and (February) 1881, p.25) instilled the virtues of loving patriarchalism into its readers, in terms similar to those used by the Free Church Pastorals of the 'sixties. Articles dispensing advice to sections of the working classes also often appeared under such pseudonyms as 'an old Collier', and 'an old Farm Servant'. The latter was the Revd. Alexander Gray of Auchterless, who was highly thought of by his peers. A recent Church of Scotland publication (L.L.L. Cameron: *The Challenge of Need*, 1971, p.15) still considers him 'one of the ablest spokesmen to farm servants'. Gray had certainly been a farm servant in his time, but his advice does not seem to be very different from or more distinguished than that of other ministers — although admittedly he managed to avoid commenting at the outset of his piece on 'Courtship and Marriage' (*ibid.*, (May) 1881, pp.70ff.) that the subject was 'difficult and delicate': he called it 'ticklish' instead. Gray warned farm servants in that article against being deceived by the outward appearance of courtship partners, advising them to think what it would be like to be married to them. He also warned against marrying too soon, and told the farm servants that their courtship should be 'rational' and 'godly'. But, he wrote, (*ibid.*, p.71)

> as a general rule your courtship and marriage are not of this rational, pure and godly sort. How do I know? I see it in our Birth Registers — in the deplorable amount of illegitimate children recorded. What are these Records? They are little else but sad and sickening revelations of courtships and marriages defiled and darkened by sensuality. I know also, from having been for years among you as one of yourselves, seeing and hearing how you feel, think, speak and behave, as lads and lasses. Oh, right well do I know, and the knowledge grieves me to the heart, and makes me very earnestly pray and strive to get your courtship and marriage, and all your intercourse as men and women elevated, purified, lifted up out of the pollution in which it is degraded, into the chaste, pure, bright and blessed thing that God who made you male and female desires and intends it to be.

In advising farm servants not to marry until the proper time, Gray (*Life and Work*, (June) 1881, pp.89ff.) carefully detailed how much they could spend, out of their wages, on clothing, pocket money (he even allowed them £1 per annum for tobacco, although he considered this a waste of money), and donations to charity. This, after they had also paid £2 p.a. for insurance (returning as £100 at age 55) came to £12, or half of their wages, which Gray estimated as £24 p.a. (i.e. for 'a good servant', which, wrote Gray, 'you *ought* to be' (*ibid.*, p.90). £12 could thus be put in the bank each year. At this rate a young man aged 28 could have saved £130 in ten years. A young woman aged 22 could have saved £30, at the current rate of wages. When they each had this amount, they could marry. But, wrote Gray, 'Is this usually *your* time and way of marrying? I am sorry to say *it is not* . . . You marry at haste and repent at leisure' (*ibid.*). He warned them again therefore against delusions of love and against wasting money by not taking care of their clothes, by 'buying, selling and exchanging watches', by buying whisky and 'fanciful harness and ornaments for your master's horses'. Such 'foolish and sinful waste' led to sickness, an early grave and a widow thrown on the Parochial Board:

There was no Poor Law or Parochial Board in my farm-servant days. And I, for one, think it a great pity that such a law should ever have been made. I believe it has done a great deal to degrade our peasantry . . . God's own poor — those who were poor through no fault of theirs — were and would be better off without this law. They were and would be more satisfactorily supplied in God's own way — viz. from the love and charity which He hath put into the hearts of His own rich and well-to-do. The devil's poor — those who are poor from their own carelessness and thriftlessness and sin — would not be so well off without this law. It has done a great deal to make them comfortable and to encourage them in their sin' (*ibid.*, pp.90-91).

These articles were the seventh and eighth in a series of which six appeared in 1879 — *ibid.*, 1879, pp.19ff., 35ff., 59ff., 77ff., 99ff; and 187ff. — these dealt with aspects of rural living conditions similar to those which Assembly reports were concerned with. Further advice, on happy homes and on old age and death appeared in 1882 — *ibid.*, 1882, pp.36ff., and 86ff.

If Gray, then, was one of the church's ablest spokesmen to farm servants, what were the less able like? The church's good name however was to some degree rescued for posterity by another pseudonymous writer, an Aberdeenshire minister who wrote in *Life and Work* subsequently, on 'Farm Servants and how to help them' (*ibid.*, 1882, pp.166ff. and 1883, pp.167ff.). This writer, himself a farmer's son from the North-East, took up cudgels in defence of agricultural labourers:

I would protest as strongly as I can against the sweeping charges brought, sometimes in Church Courts even, against farm servants as a class. They have been called drunken; they are no such thing, they are as temperate a class as we have in the community. They have been called immoral and, alas, for that charge there is but too much ground; but if some of their accusers had been placed in their circumstances, they might not have had the right to cast a stone. They have been stigmatised as heathens who never go to Church, and there is too much non-church-going among them; but on the other hand I have found the great majority of them my most regular attenders (*ibid.*, (November) 1882, p.167).

This minister stressed the importance of tactful ministerial visitation of farm servants, announced in advance, and conducted in their own quarters where they might feel at ease. A further article in his series (*ibid.*, (February) 1884, p.29) dealt with Bible Classes, Recreation and Farm Servants' Accommodation, the last of which the writer believed to have recently improved.

79. C. of S.G.A.R., 1887, p.448.
80. *Ibid.*
81. *Ibid.*
82. *Life and Work* (August) 1885, p.116.
83. C. of S.G.A.R., 1871, p.402.
84. *Ibid.*, p.405.
85. *Ibid.*
86. *Ibid.*
87. *Ibid.*, p.407.
88. C. of S.G.A.R., 1872, p.435.
89. *Ibid.*, p.435.
90. *Ibid.*
91. *Ibid.*
92. *Ibid.*
93. *Ibid.*
94. *Ibid.*
95. *Ibid.*
96. The book was often the Assembly's own book, if the minister had publicised it, but more often its 1841 volume, or that of Dr. Dewar or of Fletcher. The last of these was presumably the

Guide for Family Devotions compiled by the Revd. Alexander Fletcher of the Finsbury Chapel in London in 1835. This large volume of 762 pages was certainly bulky enough to be classified as furniture. It comprised a Discourse on Prayer, Advice on Family Worship and morning and evening services for every day of the year. The latter each comprised a hymn, 20-30 verses of Scripture and a prayer. (A few sentences of 'reflections' on the Scripture readings were added: these were mostly those of John Brown of Haddington.) In his introductory Discourse Fletcher pointed out that petition was the most important part of prayer (i.e. more important than adoration, confession and thanksgiving, although these were important in their own way); but the petition must only be for things which were agreeable to God's will, through Christ, and in the assurance of the Spirit. Among the things to be prayed for (Fletcher stressed that his work was 'not sectarian') were the unity of the church and the destruction of 'all foolish distinctions' (*ibid.*, p.iii). He distinguished four kinds of prayer: 'Secret, Ejaculatory, Private and Public' (*ibid.*, p.vii). Family Prayer (together with 'social prayer' — i.e. prayer in religious groups short of the congregation) was a form of Private Prayer, and was made up of the parts provided in his book: praise, Scripture reading and prayer. Fletcher drew arguments in support of Family Worship from Natural Religion (since man depends on God, God deserves man's homage; since God continues his blessings he is to be thanked; even the 'enlightened heathens' (*ibid.*, p.xi), such as Cicero and Hesiod, understood man's spiritual needs: Hesiod (a great favourite of Fletcher's) 'earnestly enforced the propriety of the morning and evening sacrifice') and Revealed Religion. He also pointed out that God was the Founder of Families. ('The relation of husband and wife is God's invention and appointment: Genesis ii.24. On this divine appointment depends all the comfort of social life and civilized society. Without this, the world would exhibit a picture too frightful to be described, or even conceived' (*ibid.*, p.xi).) God was also the Owner, Governor and Benefactor of Families; his aim in establishing them was 'that he might be known, loved, served and adored'. Among the benefits of Family Worship, Fletcher wrote, was that 'it restrains from vice, and maintains order and decency, which are of the greatest use' (*ibid.*, p.xiii). His argument for daily worship was that God's mercies came daily, as did sins, wants, employments, temptations, dangers and afflictions. Hesiod was again quoted in support of this argument. Advice on the manner of observing family worship included counsel to avoid indifference, unintelligibility of language and tedium: 'neither should we be so personal as intentionally to wound the feelings of any individual present' (*ibid.*, p.xv).

Among the objections which might be offered to the practice of Family Prayer neither the claim that it was uncommon, nor that it was difficult, were seen by Fletcher as insuperable obstacles. 'There is,' he wrote, 'sufficient time for the objects of the present life and for the life which is to come. Pious heads of well regulated families, who have the management of extensive and important business, find time to serve God and to call their families around the domestic altar . . . O follow the example of those holy characters . . . "Prayer and provender hinder no man" ' (*ibid.*, p.xvii). He also made much of the dangers of neglecting family worship and then regretting it when a member of the family died without its benefits. The 'nation's interest' was something else which family prayer benefited. Where there was none 'the land becomes a moral desert, exhibiting a spectacle too dreadful to be conceived' (*ibid.*, xix). Like the sources mentioned above (Ch. 5, note 9) Fletcher cited the quotation from Jeremiah about God pouring out his fury on families which did not call on his name. And to this he added the cautionary tale: 'This threatening (by the mouth of an inspired prophet) is the curse of God: and who can tell what that curse is? In the year 1584 an earthquake destroyed a town consisting of ninety houses; all were destroyed except the *half* of one house, and in that half a praying family resided' (*ibid.*).

An Appendix to Fletcher's daily prayers included prayers for special occasions and particular purposes (*ibid.*, pp.733ff.). These included Christmas, Good Friday, Easter, Pentecost, the Fast-Day and the Thanksgiving Day; Spring, Summer, Harvest and Winter; Before and After the Lord's Supper; for the King and Royal Family; for the British

Churches, for Bible, Missionary and other Sacred Institutions, for the Jews, for a friend or member of the family in affliction, and for after his recovery, for after the death of a parent, for an afflicted infant and for after its recovery or for after its death, for before and after the interment of a friend, for an afflicted minister and for after his recovery, for after the death and interment of a useful minister, an orphan's prayer, a widow's prayer ('... I confess, O my God, that my sins deserve this heavy calamity! ... Say unto my afflicted soul, I will betroth thee unto me for ever ...'); prayer for a mother and new born babe, for a son leaving home with a view of going into business ('... Grant him grace readily and meekly to submit to the restraints connected with the acquirement of that knowledge in business which is necessary for his future support, usefulness and happiness. Make him dutiful, obedient and kind to his employers. Give him grace to manage his temper, and most wisely to govern and regulate his speech ... Make him a praying youth ...'); for a rebellious son who has left his father's house ('... in this most distressing family calamity ... We acknowledge that it is a just punishment for any carelessness or neglect we, as parents, are chargeable with, in the tuition of our son ... Stop him, O Lord, in his career of sin, and let him not plunge headlong into the lake of woe! ...'); for before and after a journey; for rain and thanksgiving for rain; for fair weather in a time of threatening rain, and thanksgiving for fair weather; in a thunder storm ('... We now hear the thunder which is thy voice. Who can thunder with a voice like thine? ... The help of men is vain; even the rocks of the mountains could afford us no defence ... We lay ourselves at thy feet and cry, Lord save us, or we perish ...'), and for after a thunder storm ('We adore thee, O Lord, in all the suffering, or injury, sustained by the late tempest of lightning and thunder; and we praise thee that we are not numbered with the dead ...'); thanks for an abundant harvest, in time of pestilence or of an infectious disease, and thanks for the removal of pestilence, or an infectious disease; in time of war and for its destruction ('... We would mourn, O Lord, over the pride, and haughtiness, and envy, and revenge, which agitate the bosoms of earthly rulers, and make them rush into unnecessary wars, and thus sport with the property, the comfort, the blood and the lives of the children of men. In thy righteousness, O Lord, remove from the thrones of kingdoms such scourges of mankind ...'), thanksgiving for peace; for during a storm at sea and thanksgiving after a storm at sea; for setting out on a voyage, or outward bound, for on reaching a foreign port (any foreign port, apparently: '... While we remain in this foreign port, suffer us not to be corrupted by the sinful manners of those around us. May we mourn over prevailing depravity, and long for the day when all nations should be sprinkled with the blood of Jesus ... Preserve us from every sin and every excess, which may bring a reproach on our country or the religion of Christ ...'); for homeward bound, and for on reaching home.

The Assembly's own books of prayers, beginning with the 1841 edition mentioned here, were revised and recast on a number of occasions during the second half of the century (including the occasion on which the 1859 edition was produced). An edition of 1889 (*Prayers for Social and Family Worship for the use of soldiers, sailors, colonists, sojourners in India, and other persons, at home or abroad, who are deprived of the ordinary services of a Christian ministry*) came nearest to rivalling the comprehensiveness of Fletcher's eye for a crisis. (Travellers in a foreign country were to pray: 'Preserve us from all sinful conformity to manners and customs opposed to Thy holy will.' But in time of war the people were to be more submissive: 'Endue our statesmen and councillors, we beseech Thee, with wisdom to devise, and energy to execute, such measures as are most expedient at this time.') It will, however, take us too far from the present purpose if we pursue this farther.

97. C. of S.G.A.R., 1872, p.436.

98. *Ibid.* The 1873 report also mentioned problems relating to Highland prayer. In that report a Highland minister told how on coming to his parish forty years earlier he had found, after directly questioning the people, that family worship was 'in a rather unsatisfactory state' (C. of S.G.A.R., 1873, p.427). Now he was more reluctant about asking so directly and was not prepared to say how general the practice was at present. But,

he ventured, 'in many of the houses I visit I find the Bible and *a*, not *the* Prayer Book on their tables'. He did not know however how much these were used. Probably family worship was 'not altogether neglected' among 'the more intelligent families'. But others had real difficulties. Many were 'in a sort of transition state — a passing over from Gaelic to English. The consequence is that the Highlander is not able to read with ease and edification prayers in English before his family, and prayers written in his own language or mother tongue he could not read at all — at least not many of the heads of families in this parish could do so' (*ibid.*). This evidence is interesting since it seems to go against much that has been said about Highland education. Unfortunately the report gives no clue to what part of the Highlands it referred to.

99. C. of S.G.A.R., 1873, pp.426ff.

100. In this connection the committee argued (*ibid.*, p.427) that 'the amazing spread of periodical literature, with its simple colloquial forms of expression, is so changing men's habits both of speech and thought, that it has become necessary to have prayers for common use composed in a very simple and direct style. The last ten years have made great changes in the language in which an earnest man naturally seeks to express his thoughts and desires when he prays.'

101. Other improvements suggested included the proposal that something like the Quaker practice of a Scripture reading followed by silent prayer might be helpful (*ibid.*). And why, asked the Highland minister mentioned above, was there no prayer in the Assembly's manual for the Assembly itself? (*ibid.*)

102. C. of S.G.A.R., 1878, p.539.

103. C. of S.G.A.R., 1881, p.479.

104. *Ibid.*

105. *Ibid.*, p.480.

106. Lang (1834-1909), the first minister to introduce an organ into Church of Scotland worship (in Anderston church, Glasgow), was at this time minister of the Barony of Glasgow and later became Principal of Aberdeen University. He was the father of Cosmo Lang, Archbishop of Canterbury (1928-1942). The previous Archbishop, Randall Davidson (1903-1928) and the influential Archbishop A.C. Tait (1869-1882) were also originally Scottish Presbyterians.

107. C. of S.G.A.R., 1819, p.979.

108. Howie: *op.cit.*, p.xxxviii.

109. The reports of 1897 and 1898 were supplementary ones, dealing with Highland synods which the Commission had not previously been able to visit.

110. C. of S.G.A.R., 1891, p.1014.

111. C. of S.G.A.R., 1892, p.953.

112. *Ibid.*, p.957.

113. *Ibid.*, p.958.

114. *Ibid.*

115. The only comment about sexual morality in Edinburgh was made by a working-class elder who remarked, apropos of the Commission's interest in church-going, that churchmen might be better employed if they were concerned about young men at 11 p.m. rather than at 11 a.m. He complained that his attempt to conduct a White-Cross movement in his congregation 'did not meet with the support which he desired' (C. of S.G.A.R., 1893, p.1094). The Commission had also received a letter (it was not said from whom) asking why the subject of 'personal purity' was dealt with by the Church of Scotland in so 'remiss a fashion'. Why had it no societies like the Church of England Purity Society? (*ibid.*, p.1090).

116. C. of S.G.A.R., 1896, p.815. The President of the Sabbath-School Association informed the Commission, on its visit to Paisley (the town with 'the highest percentage of increase of population in the list of large towns of Scotland in the last decade') that sins of impurity were 'slaying their thousands and . . . ravaging where they might least be expected' (C. of S.G.A.R., 1892, p.945).

117. C. of S.G.A.R., 1896, p.815.

118. C. of S.G.A.R., 1892, p.994: referring to Dundee, the Commission stated: 'The congregation, not the parish, is the *terminus ad quem*. If the parish is attended to at all, it is relegated to a missionary and a mission.'

119. It is very difficult to form an opinion about the relation of middle-class churchgoers to prostitution during the second half of the nineteenth century. It is tempting to see in the church's reticence a hint that some proportion of its members did visit brothels; and since prostitution flourished during this period, it seems inevitable that some did. (Tait's observations on the religious affiliation of prostitutes (Tait: *op.cit.*, p.41) date from too early a period to be helpful.) But given the middle-class lapsing alleged by the Commission, it is also possible that most middle-class clients of prostitutes were not among the churchgoers. The desire to debunk Victorian hypocrisy is as suspect a motive in trying to uncover what actually went on, as the Victorians' own desire to cover things up.

120. C. of S.G.A.R., 1893, pp.1068ff. Farm servants' organisation in the nineteenth century began as early as 1805, mostly as local unions. About 1866 a national Farm Servants' Protection Society brought some of these together. But this fell apart in the '70s. The Union referred to here was the Scottish Ploughmen's Federal Union, which was strong in Perthshire, had branches in Paisley and Ross-shire, and, from what the Commission found, also in Forfar. There was at roughly the same time another Union in Aberdeenshire with which this eventually merged in 1895. Both of these unions seem to have been founded in the '80s. The joint union which at one time had up to 60,000 members was dissolved in 1900. Farm servants were not fully organised again until the creation of the Scottish Farm Servants Union in 1913. For the fragmentary history of this, *vide* T. Johnston: *The History of the Working Classes in Scotland*, 1920, pp.355ff., and W. H. Marwick: *A Short History of Labour in Scotland*, 1967, p.36, p.66 and p.80. According to the latter, the Scottish Ploughmen's Federal Union was 'mainly a benefit society, but sought a weekly half-holiday and abolition of long-term engagements' (*ibid.*, p.66). These were ends which Mr. Duncan, the union secretary, pressed on the Commission.

121. C. of S.G.A.R., 1893, pp.1075ff.

122. C. of S.G.A.R., 1894, p.728.

123. Reasons for this were not very forthcoming at the time, other than that ministers were preoccupied with congregational work at the expense of their parishes. This, however, could hardly have applied to country ministers to any extent comparable with their colleagues in the towns. A clue to the problem was given in the Commission's discussion of the latter, and in particular in relation to inner-city parishes when it remarked that many of the lapsed masses 'regard ministers with aversion'. This view, it believed, was 'grievously mistaken'. But it admitted that 'ministers have not always the knack of speaking to their heart, of getting beneath the shell of the life that is lived by the submerged tenths', and that the 'younger men, fresh from the Universities, want the kind of experience that establishes a complete *rapport*' (C. of S.G.A.R., 1896, p.831). Psychological factors of this kind may well have accounted for some country ministers' unwillingness to visit bothymen. A. Herbert Gray, writing (in *About People*, 1934, Ch. XVI) a generation or so later, indicated three points which may be relevant: 1) the minister's professional status, he believed, was 'a very serious hindrance' to his availability: 'We are supposed to be constantly disapproving of so many things that ordinary people do,' he wrote (*ibid.*, p.147).2) Ministers, he thought, took themselves too seriously, and partly because of the licence given to them in the pulpit 'we come to expect that anything we say shall be listened to with respect' (*ibid.*, p.148). (A minister's wife had told him that the ministers of her acquaintance all considered themselves 'the great I am' — *ibid.*) 3) Very many ministers, he believed, were shy and 'feel awkward in the society of ordinary men, and still more so in the society of ordinary women' (*ibid.*, p.150). No doubt all of these factors (and awareness of some of them) played a part even in the earlier generation with which we are concerned here. Even though the minister's role in society was then rather more clearly defined than when Gray wrote, their

anxiety about the lapsed masses and their awareness that society and their place in it was changing, must have reinforced a tendency to take refuge in congregationalism, and to avoid situations where their authority might be challenged.

124. C. of S.G.A.R., 1892, p.991.

125. *Ibid.*

126. Aiton had written (*op.cit.*, pp.571ff.) in such detail about the heavy drinking and uninhibited sexual behaviour of farm servants on the evening after the hiring market, as to make the reader suspect either that he had himself been an active participant or that his criticism of ministers for prying could have been reciprocated by them. Logan mentioned the fairs as places (along with railway stations) where girls were trapped into prostitution, under the guise of being engaged as domestics (Logan: *op.cit.*, p.115). But the Commission, visiting Brechin, were informed of what fairs had been like in the past, and told that 'some of the worst features of that previous time have disappeared' (C. of S.G.A.R., 1893, p.1052). (It was, according to one report, not the quantity but the quality of the whisky sold which was responsible: 'the stuff prepared for the feeing-fairs is so bad that it will not keep over the night' (C. of S.G.A.R., 1892, p.950); and in Aberdeenshire the problem was said to be that of immature rather than adulterated drink (C. of S.G.A.R., 1894, p.753).) The Commission was also told of 'a free registry for girls' in Glasgow, which had 'almost banished the deplorable evils which formerly resulted from the market' (C. of S.G.A.R., 1892, p.992).

127. How far this was because of the absence of public houses outside villages in rural areas was not questioned, but concern was expressed to the Commission about the vans being sent round rural Forfarshire by licensed grocers. 'The mission of the licensed grocer' may not have been the only danger to rural temperance: ministers in the Presbytery of Aberdeen were very anxious about the growth of bicycling among farm servants. (C. of S.G.A.R., 1893, p.1061; 1894, p.727.)

128. C. of S.G.A.R., 1892, p.981.

129. C. of S.G.A.R., 1893, p.1069.

130. *Ibid.*, p.1071: women farm-servants, according to an elder from Kirriemuir (*ibid.*, p.1065), often worked longer hours than men.

131. *Ibid.*

132. C. of S.G.A.R., 1894, p.726.

133. *Ibid.*, p.734.

134. *Ibid.*

135. *Ibid.*, p.735.

136. *Ibid.*, p.734.

137. *Ibid.*, p.735.

138. *Ibid.*

139. The author of a variety of books including *Social Aspects of Christian Morality* (1905), the Croall Lectures for 1903-04, an early Scottish attempt to write social ethics in a systematic way.

140. C. of S.G.A.R., 1894, p.735.

141. Bruce's views were however recorded in *Social Aspects of Christian Morality*, which included chapters on 'The Family', 'Marriage' and 'Family Life and Relationships'. In the second of these Bruce wrote of marriage being endangered by 'the absence in rural districts of fit dwellings for labourers' (*ibid.* p.85fn.), as well as by delayed marriage among the middle and upper classes, and 'the existence of an unwillingness to submit to the irksome restraints of married life' (*ibid.*, p.88fn.).

142. C. of S.G.A.R., 1894, p.735.

143. *Ibid.*, p.736.

144. C. of S.G.A.R., 1895, p.776.

145. *Ibid.*, p.756.

146. *Ibid.*, p.765.

147. *Ibid.*, p.746. (Although there were no bothies, unmarried farm servants slept in 'a distinct room, in most places plastered and made comfortable' above the stables. As in the case of the 'chambers' of Aberdeenshire and the outhouses in Moray, the distinction between these and bothies may have been largely a matter of terminology.)
148. *Ibid.*
149. *Ibid.*, p.749.
150. *Ibid.*, p.747.
151. *Ibid.*, p.750 (the Parish of Monigaff.)
152. *Ibid.*, p.747.
153. *Ibid.*, p.749.
154. *Ibid.*, p.751.
155. *Ibid.*
156. The 'great influence' of 'ladies of leisure' running clubs and other activities, and thereby 'elevating the working girls' was, however, commended in the Commission's comments on Dumfries (*ibid.*, p.790).
157. *Ibid.*, p.754.
158. *Ibid.*, p.794.
159. *Ibid.*, p.788.
160. *Ibid.*, p.786.
161. *Ibid.*, p.788.
162. *Ibid.*, p.789.
163. *Ibid.*
164. *Ibid.*
165. C. of S.G.A.R., 1892, p.981.
166. C. of S.G.A.R., 1893, p.1069.
167. C. of S.G.A.R., 1894, p.761.
168. The Presbytery of Haddington however did express some misgivings about many 'little parties of four or five . . . girls brought from the Highlands to labour in the fields', who lived in bothies. It was suggested that 'some Gaelic-speaking lady might be obtained from Edinburgh to visit and converse with them' (*ibid.*, p.769).
169. *Ibid.*, pp.762ff. Even the hiring markets of Haddington were more respectable than those in other towns.
170. C. of S.G.A.R., 1893, p.1111. The fact that Sunday was their only holiday was blamed for the visiting. The Commission also heard criticism here of temporarily employed, occasional farm workers, who were 'frequently rough and coarse' (*ibid.*).
171. C. of S.G.A.R., 1894, p.759. But in Biggar, as in Forfarshire, churchmen were worried about 'the daily perambulation of the country districts by (licensed) grocers' vans' (*ibid.*, p.773). They were also concerned about the public house, five hotels and seven licensed grocers in Biggar — 'a very extraordinary number' for a town with a population of 1356, 'even though there was no licensed house in any of the other ten parishes of the Presbytery' (*ibid.*). But here, as elsewhere, rural temperance was praised, even if room remained for improvement. In order to achieve improvement in their area 'the minister with three other Earlston gentlemen, joined at pecuniary loss in buying up an inn' (C. of S.G.A.R., 1896, p.751). But Kelso Presbytery reported that in areas without public houses there was 'a certain amount of shebeening' (*ibid.*, p.770).
172. C. of S.G.A.R., 1896, p.754.
173. *Ibid.*
174. *Ibid.*
175. C. of S.G.A.R., 1893, p.1111.
176. C. of S.G.A.R., 1896, p.754.
177. *Ibid.*, p.766.
178. *Ibid.*, p.772.
179. *Ibid.*, p.766.

180. *Ibid.*, p.776.
181. *Ibid.*, p.763.
182. C. of S.G.A.R., 1894, pp.773ff.
183. C. of S.G.A.R., 1895, pp.799ff.
184. C. of S.G.A.R., 1894, p.786.
185. C. of S.G.A.R., 1895, p.819.
186. *Ibid.*, p.823. Auchterarder, by contrast with some Border presbyteries, had 337 married and 680 unmarried farm servants within its bounds. Of the total, 338 were church members, and 200 unmarried servants were adherents (*ibid.*, pp.822ff.).
187. C. of S.G.A.R., 1894, p.786.
188. C. of S.G.A.R., 1895, p.813.
189. *Ibid.*
190. C. of S.G.A.R., 1894, pp.784ff.
191. *Ibid.*, p.785.
192. C. of S.G.A.R., 1897, p.951.
193. *Ibid.*, p.946. There had been no illegitimate births in the last seven years, and only seven in the last twenty.
194. *Ibid.*, p.942. Farr, a typical parish, had illegitimacy rates for 1893: 0%; 1894, 0%; 1895 5%; 1896 0%. Given its population of 1081, even the 1895 figure (i.e. 5% of births, not of the population) could not have been high.
195. C. of S.G.A.R., 1896, p.779.
196. *Ibid.*, p.783.
197. C. of S.G.A.R., 1897, p.955.
198. C. of S.G.A.R., 1898, p.877.
199. *Ibid.*, p.887.
200. *Ibid.*, p.893.
201. C. of S.G.A.R., 1896, p.790. What was perhaps worse was that on Sundays, during their 'residence of two or three months at the coast . . . well-known city elders and members of the Assembly' worshipped either in the Episcopal church, or in no church at all (*ibid.*).
202. C. of S.G.A.R., 1894, p.719.
203. *Ibid.*, p.716.
204. Perhaps the apparent ability of Orcadians to maintain the old courtship customs without producing a high illegitimacy rate had something to do with the size of the population and the limited opportunities for a false lover to escape, except by going to sea.
205. C. of S.G.A.R., 1896, pp.797ff.
206. *Ibid.*, p.802.
207. *Ibid.*
208. *Ibid.*, p.803.
209. *Ibid.*, p.804.
210. *Ibid.*, p.805.
211. One group whom the Commission may have had in mind were the tinkers or vagrants. Few of these, it wrote, were married, 'except in some way of their own' (C. of S.G.A.R., 1896, p.812). Their children were registered as illegitimate and grew up uneducated and ignorant of religion. What to do with them was a problem, but some means of civilising them should be found.
212. C. of S.G.A.R., 1896, p.816.
213. *Ibid.*, p.817.
214. *Ibid.*
215. *Ibid.*
216. *Ibid.*
217. C. of S.G.A.R., 1892, p.982.
218. *Ibid.*, p.984.
219. C. of S.G.A.R., 1896, p.811.

220. C. of S.G.A.R., 1892, p.949.
221. *Ibid.*
222. C. of S.G.A.R., 1896, p.827.
223. C. of S.G.A.R., 1894, p.763.
224. *Ibid.*, p.777.
225. C. of S.G.A.R., 1897, p.946. *Vide* also the Presbytery of Jedburgh (C. of S.G.A.R., 1896, p.776).
226. C. of S.G.A.R., 1894, p.805.
227. *Ibid.*
228. C. of S.G.A.R., 1896, p.846.
229. *Ibid.*, p.848.
230. *Ibid.*, p.849.

Chapter seven

1. *Vide* F.C.G.A.P. & D., 1872, R. & M.R., pp.20ff. This information came from the Assembly's deputies, sent to confer with and report on the islanders. The reports dealt with in this chapter came either from these deputies (mostly ministers and elders from other parts of the church than that visited) or directly from the synods, presbyteries, sessions and ministers of the areas concerned.
2. Nor, incidentally, did they see any harm in smuggling. Their ministers, however, thought that, to deter them, this should be made an ecclesiastical as well as a civil offence.
3. F.C.G.A.P. & D., 1885, R. & M.R., p.27.
4. F.C.G.A.P. & D., 1886, R. & M.R., p.33.
5. F.C.G.A.P. & D., 1884, R. & M.R., p.33.
6. F.C.G.A.P. & D., 1886, R. & M.R., p.34.
7. *Ibid.*, p.33.
8. F.C.G.A.P. & D., 1888, R. & M.R., p.16.
9. F.C.G.A.P. & D., 1891, R. & M.R., p.13.
10. *Ibid.*
11. *Ibid.*, p.12.
12. The Report of 1885 (F.C.G.A.P. & D., 1885, R. & M.R., p.2) had mentioned 'difficulties of a kind which the careful language of Shetland prudently leaves under the veil'.
13. F.C.G.A.P. & D., 1890, R. & M.R., p.12.
14. *Vide ibid.* (Shetland) and F.C.G.A.P. & D., 1884, R. & M.R., p.57 (Orkney). There were however few bothies in Orkney — according to F.C.G.A.P. & D., 1886, R. & M.R., p.33.
15. F.C.G.A.P. & D., 1884, R. & M.R., p.57.
16. F.C.G.A.P. & D., 1891, R. & M.R., p.12.
17. F.C.G.A.P. & D., 1884, R. & M.R., p.57.
18. *Vide* Howie: *op.cit.*, p.38. These figures are for 1879. Membership figures were: C. of S., 11,649; F.C., 6,043; U.P., 4,805. There were also 21 congregations of non-Presbyterian denominations.
19. F.C.G.A.P. & D., 1872, R. & M.R., p.13.
20. F.C.G.A.P. & D., 1873, R. & M.R., pp.49ff.
21. F.C.G.A.P. & D., 1884, R. & M.R., p.19. This report also complained about pluralist farmers whose grieves were uninterested in the conduct of farm servants.
22. F.C.G.A.P. & D., 1893, R. & M.R., p.13.
23. *Ibid.* At this conference the synod was also concerned with swearing and graffiti. It wrote (*ibid.*) that 'considering the stringency of our laws against obscene publications of all sorts, it is scandalous that so much moral filth should be allowed to flaunt itself and force itself on the eye, and the mind, and that public conveyances and even one's own doors should be defaced by the abominations of foul-minded schoolboys and others'.

24. The total population of Ross — the synod, not the county (the former comprised presbyteries situated in Easter Ross and the Black Isle) was 41,654, of which 29,432 persons were connected with the Free Church. The total average F.C. (Free Church) attendance in the synod was 15,960 and there were 2,155 F.C. communicants (F.C.G.A.P. & D., 1871, R. & M.R., p.40). In the two Sutherland presbyteries, Tongue and Dornoch, the total population was 23,186 and the total average F.C. attendance was 8,209. As in Ross, the number of communicant F.C. members (836) was very small (F.C.G.A.P. & D., 1870, R. & M.R., p.21). If, as in Ross, the total average F.C. attendance was roughly half the total number of those connected with the F.C., then roughly 16,000 or well over half of the population would have been connected with the F.C. These must have included children, since Howie's figures (*op.cit.*, p.38) for 1879 (allowing for depopulation in the meantime) of F.C. members and Gaelic adherents over 18, were roughly similar to the total average church attendance. Howie (*ibid.*) showed that the F.C. was only slightly less dominant in Caithness than it was in Sutherland.

25. F.C.G.A.P. & D., 1873, R. & M.R., pp.45ff. Glenelg comprised the west of the counties of Ross and Inverness, together with Skye, Lewis and Uist.

26. F.C.G.A.P. & D., 1870, R. & M.R., pp.19ff.

27. F.C.G.A.P. & D., 1873, R. & M.R., p.48. These reports were supported by a report from the Free Presbytery of Cupar (F.C.G.A.P. & D., 1875, R. & M.R., p.13), which complained about the 'evil influence of the bothy system, especially in the case of Gaelic speaking women, who came in numbers from the Highlands for farm work, and who attend no church'.

28. But in the Presbytery of Tain at least, the bothy system was said to be 'almost unknown' (F.C.G.A.P. & D., 1884, R. & M.R., p.23).

29. F.C.G.A.P. & D., 1890, R. & M.R., p.13.

30. F.C.G.A.P. & D., 1891, R. & M.R., p.14.

31. East coast fishermen in Sutherland, although irregular, were not non-church-attenders.

32. F.C.G.A.P. & D., 1873, R. & M.R., pp.45ff.

33. F.C.G.A.P. & D., 1884, R. & M.R., p.6.

34. *Ibid.*, p.5. In 1890 the Presbytery of Tain was still prayerful. It reported that 'in two districts all the people assemble together on Sabbath evenings for worship and all the heads of families, without exception, lead the meetings in turn in public prayer' (F.C.G.A.P. & D., 1890, R. & M.R., p.14). The religiosity of Easter Ross was also illustrated by the Presbytery's observation that 'some of the young men seem very anxious about their souls, so anxious, indeed, that they come to their ministers with the all-important inquiry, "What must we do to be saved?"' (*ibid.*).

35. F.C.G.A.P. & D., 1871, R. & M.R., pp.11ff. The west of this synod included the county of Nairn, and parts of the counties of Inverness and Elgin (Morayshire). The east included the rest of Elgin and the county of Banff. A proportion of the Roman Catholics in the county of Nairn had been driven there by famine, from Barra, in 1846. In the town of Inverness, according to the synod, there was too much Episcopacy. But congregations of the smaller denominations, it noted happily, were 'weak and struggling', throughout the synod (*ibid.*, p.12).

36. But there was 'alas, frequent occasion to deplore the thoughtlessness with which many of them expose themselves to temptation' (*ibid.*, p.14). 'Alas', particularly perhaps, because according to the synod many of those who were at risk came from its Highland parishes.

37. Not even, it was claimed, in the areas with the highest illegitimacy rates. But then, if those who might have been guilty were never married in the first place, the risk of adultery may have been reduced.

38. Things did not improve with time. In 1899 the synod reported that it had to bewail 'the laxity of home discipline and the inadequate appreciation of parental responsibility'

(F.C.G.A.P. & D., 1899, R. & M.R., p.9).

39. F.C.G.A.P. & D., 1871, R. & M.R., p.13.

40. *Ibid.*, p.14.

41. *Ibid.*, p.18.

42. *Vide* F.C.G.A.P. & D., 1870, R. & M.R., pp.3ff.

43. *Vide* F.C.G.A.P. & D., 1872, R. & M.R., pp.5ff.

44. *Ibid.*, p.9. It is perhaps no surprise therefore to read the statement made by one Free Church minister (*ibid.*, p.11): 'When I reprove any on the street for swearing, they either speak rudely or silently look in astonishment.'

45. F.C.G.A.P. & D., 1870, R. & M.R., p.8.

46. *Ibid.*

47. *Ibid.*, p.7.

48. The Free Church was in a minority in both synods' areas. The membership (including Gaelic adherent) figures for 1879 (Howie: *op.cit.*, p.38) were: Aberdeen: C. of S: 74,022; F.C: 28,717; U.P: 5,103. Angus & Mearns: C. of S: 58,226; F.C: 25,221; U.P: 10,944. The number of congregations gave a rather different proportion: Aberdeen: C. of S: 137; F.C: 105; U.P: 29; Other: 96. Angus & Mearns: C. of S: 110; F.C: 81; U.P: 34; Other: 81. (The 'Other' figures are for 1885.)

49. F.C.G.A.P. & D., 1870, R. & M.R., p.8.

50. F.C.G.A.P. & D., 1880, R. & M.R., p.46. In the previous year's report it was stated by some Free Church congregations that ante-nuptial fornication was not increasing in Dundee (F.C.G.A.P. & D., 1879, R. & M.R., p.18), and that while there were not many farm servants in Free Church congregations in the area, those who were to be found were 'highly respectable' (*ibid.*, p.20).

51. F.C.G.A.P. & D., 1883, R. & M.R., p.22.

52. *Ibid.*

53. F.C.G.A.P. & D., 1880, R. & M.R., p.48.

54. E.g. Glenbervie: F.C.G.A.P. & D., 1883, R. & M.R., p.22.

55. The minister of one congregation reported that he always urged the duty on couples whom he married (F.C.G.A.P. & D., 1879, R. & D., 1879, R. & M.R., p.20.)

56. *Ibid.*, p.19.

57. F.C.G.A.P. & D., 1880, R. & M.R., p.47.

58. F.C.G.A.P. & D., 1883, R. & M.R., p.29. (Parish of Lumphanan.)

59. *Ibid.*, p.21.

60. F.C.G.A.P. & D., 1888, R. & M.R., p.61.

61. *Vide* F.C.G.A.P. & D., 1873, R. & M.R., pp.29ff.

62. *Ibid.*, p.39.

63. *Ibid.*, p.31.

64. *Ibid.*, p.33. On discipline, the comment was also made that 'in the case of parents who have been under discipline, the baptism of their first child is not seldom in private or before the session, and the same may be said in reference to illegitimate children' (*ibid.*, p.30).

65. *Ibid.*, p.37. The synod was also concerned about the behaviour and influence of navvies working on the railways (*ibid.*, p.31).

66. F.C.G.A.P. & D., 1880, R. & M.R., *passim.*

67. *Ibid.*

68. F.C.G.A.P. & D., 1884, R. & M.R., p.59. Some sessions 'suggested that a stand should be taken against young people appearing in character when singing songs'. Were the sessions trying to enact new sumptuary legislation? They also considered 'that ministers should revise the programme as a condition of attendance' (*ibid.*), and were very concerned about 'the existence of dancing saloons that are demoralising the youth of both sexes in large towns' (*ibid.*).

69. *Ibid.*

70. *Ibid.*, p.37.

71. *Ibid.*
72. *Ibid.*, p.38.
73. *Ibid.*, p.31.
74. In the case of boy and girl weavers this could be at the age of thirteen or fourteen.
75. In common with some other synods, Perth and Stirling was curious about demoralising and immoral publications. Apart from some Tractarian tracts, whose purveyors were said not to be very successful, they found little of either kind of publication. In Free Church congregations, by contrast, the *Missionary Record* sold well, the *Children's Missionary Record* even better. Moray (F.C.G.A.P. & D., 1871, R. & M.R., p.23) had complained about the distribution of 'cheap sensational novels' and that books of the type of Renan's *Life of Jesus*, *Ecce Homo*, etc., are read to a considerable extent, and although the views which these works advocate may be rejected, they often leave behind them a seed of scepticism and cavilling'.
76. F.C.G.A.P. & D., 1879, R. & M.R., p.2.
77. F.C.G.A.P. & D., 1884, R. & M.R., p.58.
78. *Ibid.*
79. F.C.G.A.P. & D., 1891, R. & M.R., p.18.
80. *Vide* F.C.G.A.P. & D., 1870, R. & M.R., p.15. This was presumably a reference to the children of unregistered irregular marriages.
81. *Ibid.*, p.17.
82. On the synod's discussion of the churchgoing habits of all these classes *vide* chapter two above.
83. F.C.G.A.P. & D., 1870, R. & M.R., p.13.
84. *Ibid.*
85. *Ibid.*, p.14.
86. *Ibid.*
87. The synod implied that they could have owned more. 'They trust to the anticipated success of the morrow, instead of providing for to-day' (*ibid.*, p.15) — a comment which sounds like a desperate attempt to square the Sermon on the Mount with the spirit of Capitalism.
88. *Ibid.*
89. *Ibid.*, p.17.
90. F.C.G.A.P. & D., 1888, R. & M.R., p.52.
91. *Ibid.*
92. F.C.G.A.P. & D., 1889, R. & M.R., p.46.
93. F.C.G.A.P. & D., 1870, R. & M.R., p.15.
94. F.C.G.A.P. & D., 1875, R. & M.R., p.13.
95. F.C.G.A.P. & D., 1888, R. & M.R., p.10. This led one of the deputies to raise again the question of the church producing 'a small cheap manual of family prayers' (*ibid.*), which he believed would be useful.
96. *Vide* F.C.G.A.P. & D., 1871, R. & M.R., pp.26ff.
97. *Ibid.*, pp.24ff.
98. *Ibid.*, p.33.
99. I.e. farm-servants were too attached to the migratory habit; large farms deprived them of the opportunity of looking forward to owning a farm, and thus of 'a great motive to industry and good morals' (*ibid.*, p.30); they did not keep the Sabbath but spent it visiting friends and relations; the morals of the women were as bad as those of the men; shepherds were a more respectable class; farmers did not supervise their servants properly; Irish Catholics introduced a demoralising factor; Free Church ministers could not 'get at' nine-tenths of farm servants because they claimed to be connected with the Church of Scotland; etc. (*ibid.*, *passim*).
100. But then the synod may well have had Free Church servants in mind.
101. The Synod of Glasgow and Ayr did in fact take the middle classes to task when it

complained

> that large numbers of the wealthier classes change their residence during several months in the summer, and that the effect, morally and spiritually considered, both on themselves and on those who live in the locality thus visited is bad. Too many of those who go to the coast throw aside their wonted respect for the Sabbath, become irregular in their attendance on the means of grace, and remiss in other religious duties. They scruple not to do things at the sea-side that they would abstain from at home, and their example is very injurious (*ibid.*, p.32).

The Synod of Argyll also complained about what went on at the sea-side, but it was more concerned with the lower orders and (*ibid.*, p.25) 'the crowds that flock to watering places, for a few days, or merely from Saturday to Monday'. The Sunday steamer was 'a great curse' to Rothesay. But the 'Free Church families that settle down for months at the coast' were, in its opinion, 'as regular and strict as our own people'. *Vide* chapter six above for the Church of Scotland's comment on the same subject twenty years later.

102. F.C.G.A.P. & D., 1871, R. & M.R., p.33.

103. *Ibid.*, p.24.

104. F.C.G.A.P. & D., 1888, R. & M.R., p.41. According to Howie's figures for 1891 (*op.cit.*, p.19), the comparative figures for the Established, Free and Episcopal churches, each of which had two congregations in the district (although the Church of Scotland congregations were linked) were C. of S: 69; F.C: 329 (266 of whom were Gaelic adherents over 18) and Episcopal: 203.

105. F.C.G.A.P. & D., 1888, R. & M.R., p.41.

106. *Ibid.*

107. F.C.G.A.P. & D., 1899, R. & M.R., p.12.

108. *Ibid.*

109. E.g. that although there were up to 250,000 people 'on the main streets on a Saturday night', the record number of arrests for drunkenness was only 486. The majority were 'well-behaved and apparently sedate people' (*ibid.*).

110. *Ibid.*

111. 'Two out of every three women passing through their hands,' it was reported, were 'restored to well-doing ways' (*ibid.*).

112. There were 81 of these, accommodating 9,351 people. Among the worst were the 17 for women, which were overcrowded (some small rooms had 5 beds in each, some with two to a bed) and paid their owners well (one room could yield 17/6 a night). In one of these, all the girls interviewed were prostitutes; and the committee recommended the creation of a better kind of lodging house, for girls up from the country seeking work, where they would not so easily gravitate to prostitution (*ibid.*, p.13).

113. This was the only park which did not shut at sunset.

114. F.C.G.A.P. & D., 1871, R. & M.R., p.29.

115. *Ibid.*, p.24.

116. *Ibid.*, p.28.

117. F.C.G.A.P. & D., 1888, R. & M.R., p.40.

118. *Ibid.*, p.41.

119. F.C.G.A.P. & D., 1881, R. & M.R., p.28.

120. F.C.G.A.P. & D., 1891, R. & M.R., p.47.

121. I.e. the households of the congregation being quoted.

122. F.C.G.A.P. & D., 1892, R. & M.R., p.7.

123. *Vide* F.C.G.A.P. & D., 1870, R. & M.R., pp.10ff.

124. *Vide* F.C.G.A.P. & D., 1873, R. & M.R., pp.39ff.

125. F.C.G.A.P. & D., 1870, R. & M.R., p.10.

126. *Ibid.*, p.11. In this presbytery concern was also expressed about the Yeomanry Races which, being held on a Saturday, led to 'much dissipation and the consequent desecration of the following day' (*ibid.*). Here, as elsewhere, the working classes were still

too apt to go visiting on a Sunday: a practice which the middle classes were giving up, it was said.

127. *Ibid.*, p.12.

128. F.C.G.A.P. & D., 1873, R. & M.R., p.40.

129. *Ibid.*, p.41. This presbytery said much the same of intemperance. It too was also worried about Sunday visiting among farm servants.

130. Intemperance was also a problem within this synod's bounds, but less so in country districts than in Hawick.

131. *Ibid.*, p.40.

132. F.C.G.A.P. & D., 1870, R. & M.R., p.11. Even, according to the deputies writing in another report (F.C.G.A.P. & D., 1873, R. & M.R., p.18), by many communicant members of the Free Church.

133. F.C.G.A.P. & D., 1873, R. & M.R., p.43.

134. F.C.G.A.P. & D., 1870, R. & M.R., p.10.

135. F.C.G.A.P. & D., 1878, R. & M.R., p.16, i.e. cases of discipline.

136. F.C.G.A.P. & D., 1880, R. & M.R., p.4.

137. F.C.G.A.P. & D., 1886, R. & M.R., p.48.

138. F.C.G.A.P. & D., 1880, R. & M.R., p.3.

139. F.C.G.A.P. & D., 1899, R. & M.R., p.8.

140. *Vide* F.C.G.A.P. & D., 1871, R. & M.R., pp.7ff.

141. *Vide* F.C.G.A.P. & D., 1873, R. & M.R., p.45.

142. F.C.G.A.P. & D., 1871, R. & M.R., p.8.

143. *Ibid.*

144. F.C.G.A.P. & D., 1884, R. & M.R., p.45.

145. F.C.G.A.P. & D., 1899, R. & M.R., p.8.

146. F.C.G.A.P. & D., 1884, R. & M.R., pp.44 and 48.

147. According to Howie (*op.cit.*, p.36), within the bounds of the Synod of Galloway the population (in 1881) was 66,738, of which (in 1879) members of the C. of S. were 14,618; F.C. (including Gaelic adherents) 5,339 and U.P. 1,963. By 1891, when the population of the area was down by 4,000, the C. of S. had gained about 700, the U.P.s 26 and the F.C. had lost nearly 300. The number of congregations were: in 1879: C. of S. 45; F.C. 31; U.P. 13; others (in 1885) 20; in 1891: C. of S. 45; F.C. 31; U.P. 14; others 22.

148. F.C.G.A.P. & D., 1884, R. & M.R., p.49 (the deputies visited in 1883).

149. *Ibid.*

150. F.C.G.A.P. & D., 1871, R. & M.R., p.7.

151. F.C.G.A.P. & D., 1887, R. & M.R., p.7.

152. Perhaps earlier, since in addition to what had been written by some synods the convener of the Religion and Morals committee, in the debate on its report in 1876 (F.C.G.A.P. & D., 1876, Proceedings, p.14), 'did not further allude to the subject of illegitimacy than by expressing doubt as to the advisableness of holding evening services on Sundays in country districts'.

153. F.C.G.A.P. & D., 1893, R. & M.R., p.12.

154. *Ibid.*

155. *Ibid.*

156. F.C.G.A.P. & D., 1897, R. & M.R., p.26.

157. *Ibid.*, pp.26ff.

158. *Ibid.*

159. Reports from 17 farms suggested that each one was different. On four, church attendance was as high as 80 to 100 per cent., even if this did not imply total regularity of attendance. On the remaining 13, it was either irregular or non-existent. But on at least one of these all the families were Roman Catholics, while on another one in five attended the Free Church.

160. Like the Commission on the Religious Condition of the People, it was also

concerned about the licensed grocers' vans.

161. F.C.G.A.P. & D., 1897, R. & M.R., p.27.

162. *Ibid.*

163. *Ibid.*

164. *Ibid.*

165. *Ibid.*

166. *Ibid.*, p.28.

167. *Ibid.*

168. *Ibid.*

169. *Ibid.*

170. *Ibid.*, p.29. The committee based this assertion on the assumption 'that bodies attract in proportion to their size'.

171. *Ibid.*

172. *Ibid.*

173. *Ibid.*, p.30. The committee seems to have been uncertain about which direction had priority.

174. *Ibid.*

175. F.C.G.A.P. & D., 1886, R. & M.R., p.16.

176. Smith (1856-1942) was to succeed Marshall Lang as Principal of Aberdeen University in 1909, and was knighted in 1916. A noted Hebrew scholar, his *Historical Atlas of the Holy Land* was presented, in 1917, to General Allenby by Lloyd George, who considered the book 'a better guide to a military leader whose task was to reach Jerusalem than any survey to be found in the pigeon-holes of the War Office'. (James Morris: *Farewell the Trumpets*, 1978, p.173.)

177. F.C.G.A.P. & D., 1895, Proceedings, p.79.

178. Moray, and Perth and Stirling.

179. *Vide* D. Macleod: *op.cit.*, pp.292, 301 and 320ff.

180. F.C.G.A.P. & D., 1899, R. & M.R., p.27.

181. The committee specifically excluded 'such well-known and high-class papers as *The Graphic, The Illustrated London News, Black and White, The Navy and Army, The Gentlewoman, The Ladies' Pictorial, The Ladies' Field* and others of that class; as well as 'the various illustrated penny newspapers, after the model of *The Daily Graphic*' (*ibid.*, p.28). *Punch*, which had 'taken and maintained so high a standard on all questions of morals and social ethics' (*ibid.*), was also excluded. (The compliment was not returned, however. 'According to Punch' — 'an incorrigible Erastian', as critical of Evangelicals and Nonconformists as Papists and Puseyites — 'the doughtiest supporters of the Free Kirk were elderly females with an inveterate suspicion of organs.' A.L. Drummond: *The Churches Pictured By 'Punch'*, 1947, pp.10, 46.)

182. F.C.G.A.P. & D., 1899, R. & M.R., p.28. These 'lighter papers' were not mentioned by name.

183. *Ibid.*

184. *Ibid.*

185. *Ibid.*, p.29.

186. *Ibid.*

187. *Ibid.*

188. *Ibid.*

189. *Ibid.*

190. *Ibid.*, p.27.

191. *Ibid.*, p.30.

192. *Ibid.*

193. *Ibid.*, p.28.

194. *Ibid.*, p.29.

195. *Ibid.*

196. *Ibid.* There were a number of trials relating to the publication and advertising of books and pamphlets giving advice on contraception in the second half of the nineteenth century. The most famous was the Bradlaugh-Besant trial of 1877 (*vide* J.A. and O. Banks: *Feminism and Family Planning in Victorian England*, 1964, pp.87ff.). Other trials took place in 1891 and 1892 (*vide* P. Fryer: *The Birth Controllers*, 1965, p.191). This is the only reference I have found to contraception in nineteenth-century Assembly reports.
197. F.C.G.A.P. & D., 1899, R. & M.R., p.31.
198. *Ibid.*
199. *Ibid.*
200. *Ibid.*
201. *Ibid.*
202. F.C.G.A.P. & D., 1900, R. & M.R., p.3.
203. *Ibid.*, supplementary report, p.1.
204. *Ibid.*, p.2.
205. *Ibid.*
206. F.C.G.A.P. & D., 1883, R. & M.R., p.5.
207. F.C.G.A.P. & D., 1899, R. & M.R., p.9.
208. F.C.G.A.P. & D., 1883, R. & M.R., p.5.
209. F.C.G.A.P. & D., 1885, R. & M.R., p.9.
210. *Ibid.*
211. *Ibid.*
212. *Ibid.*
213. F.C.G.A.P. & D., 1889, R. & M.R., p.9.
214. *Ibid.*
215. *Ibid.*
216. F.C.G.A.P. & D., 1899, R. & M.R., p.8.
217. F.C.G.A.P. & D., 1893, R. & M.R., p.6.
218. *Ibid.*
219. F.C.G.A.P. & D., 1899, R. & M.R., p.8.
220. F.C.G.A.P. & D., 1900, R. & M.R., p.6.
221. F.C.G.A.P. & D., 1891, Proceedings, p.259.
222. *Ibid.*, p.261.
223. *Ibid.*
224. *Ibid.*
225. Mr. Telfer had already antagonised some members of the Assembly by declaring his fears that this 'wretched prayer book' would be used by men like captains of steamers. Having 'seen a good deal of life on board steamers', he did not favour the idea of such people 'reading prayers from a prayer book on Sunday' when they had been 'employed in cursing during the week' (*ibid.*). This produced an immediate response from an ex-Lord Provost (of Glasgow, I think), who was applauded for interjecting with the remark, 'I wish to say that there are no such commanders on our steamers' (*ibid.*).
226. *Ibid.*
227. *Ibid.*, p.262.

Chapter eight
1. U.P.S.P. (1853) pp.433ff.
2. *Ibid.*, p.445.
3. *Ibid.*, p.444.
4. U.P.S.P. (1891) p.231.
5. Charles Parnell, the Nationalist Irish M.P., was cited as having committed adultery with Mrs. O'Shea, when her husband divorced her in November 1890. Parnell had in fact lived with her for the previous nine years, while he was at the peak of his political career, and the relationship was a stable one. The facts could not however emerge because Parnell and

Mrs. O'Shea wanted the divorce and could not therefore contradict her husband's accusations. Coming four or five years after the divorce case in which Dilke, the Liberal politician, had been involved, there was much public indignation and the Irish party were forced by Gladstone and others to depose Parnell. In June 1891 Parnell married Mrs. O'Shea, and four months later he died. The U.P. Synod 'expressed its approval of the position Mr. Gladstone had taken' (*ibid.*). It took much the same line on this as the English Nonconformists and the Roman Catholic leaders. (*Vide* R. Ensor: *England: 1870-1914*, 1936, pp.183ff. and 564ff.)

6. U.P.S.P. (1894) p.156.

7. *Ibid.*

8. *Ibid.*, p.156: 'Indeed, in some districts our congregations stand out prominently as maintaining a high standard of discipline at the expense of comparatively small membership.'

9. U.P.S.P. (1886) p.60.

10. U.P. *Missionary Record*, Vol.VIII, No. X. (October 1 1887) pp.321-324.

11. U.P.S.P. (1888) p.1167.

12. 2 Timothy, 2:22.

13. 1 Timothy, 5:22.

14. U.P. *Missionary Record*: *op.cit.*, p.321. The reference to 'churches' could have been a let-out for U.P.s.

15. *Ibid.*

16. *Ibid.*

17. Proverbs, 7:27: 'Here is the road which leadeth down to the chambers of death'; Ephesians, 5:5: 'No unclean person hath any inheritance in the kingdom of Christ and God'; Galatians, 5:19: 'Now the works of the flesh are manifest, which are these, adultery, fornication, uncleanness, lasciviousness; of the which I tell you, as I have told you in times past, that they which do such things shall not inherit the kingdom of God'; and Colossians, 3:5: 'Mortify, therefore, your members which are upon the earth: fornication, uncleanness, inordinate affections; for which things' sake, the wrath of God cometh upon the children of disobedience'.

18. W.G. Cole (*Sex and Love in the Bible*, 1960, p.315) argues that the chapter is directed 'not against sexuality as such, but against squandering one's substance'. There is also a suggestion in verse 14 of criticism of, if not ritual prostitution, then at least religious hypocrisy.

19. U.P. *Missionary Record*, *ibid.*

20. *Ibid.*

21. *Ibid.*, p.322.

22. *Ibid.*

23. *Ibid.*

24. Genesis, 2:24, *vide* W.G. Cole: *op.cit.*, pp.252ff.

25. *Vide* J. Calvin: *Harmony of the Pentateuch*, 1854 translation, vol.III, p.84.

26. U.P. *Missionary Record*: *op.cit.*, p.322.

27. *Ibid.*

28. *Ibid.*

29. *Ibid.*

30. *Ibid.*

31. *Ibid.*

32. *Ibid.*

33. *Ibid.*

34. *Ibid.*, p.323.

35. *Ibid.* This, wrote Thomson, was Pauline advice (Colossians, 3:16).

36. *Ibid.*

37. *Ibid.* He did not say which books he was talking about.

38. *Ibid.*
39. *Ibid.*
40. *Ibid.* Again unspecified.
41. *Ibid.*
42. *Ibid.*
43. *Ibid.*
44. *Ibid.*
45. *Ibid.* This advice, he wrote, also was Pauline (1 Corinthians, 9:27).
46. *Ibid.*
47. *Ibid.*
48. *Ibid.*
49. *Ibid.*
50. *Ibid.*, p.324.
51. *Ibid.*
52. A slightly earlier period, but there is often a cultural lag in relation to Scotland.
53. Houghton: *op.cit.*, p.354.
54. *Ibid.*
55. *Ibid.*
56. *Ibid.*, p.356.
57. There was even an appeal to the chivalrous past. Houghton mentions Arthurian legends and Tennyson. Thomson had Bruce.
58. *Vide* Houghton: *op.cit.*, pp.202ff.
59. George Eliot: *Scenes of Clerical Life*, (Janet's Repentance, Ch. X).

Chapter nine

1. C. of S.G.A.R., 1897, p.720. (Howie estimated (*op.cit.*, p.38) that there were 1409 congregations in all of the Established Church in 1891, so the 1059 which reported would have been the majority.)
2. C. of S.G.A.R., 1897, p.720.
3. *Ibid.*, p.721.
4. *Ibid.*
5. *Ibid.*, p.723.
6. *Ibid.*
7. *Ibid.*
8. *Ibid.*
9. *Ibid.*, p.724.
10. *Ibid.*
11. *Ibid.*
12. *Ibid.*
13. *Ibid.*, p.725.
14. *Ibid.*
15. C. of S.G.A.R., 1899, p.11.
16. *Ibid.*, p.12.
17. *Ibid.*
18. *Ibid.*, p.13.
19. I.M. Clark: *op.cit.*, p.168.
20. *Ibid.*
21. *Ibid.*
22. *Ibid.*, p.169.
23. *Ibid.* The possible causes discussed by Clark 'making for the decline of discipline in the Church of Scotland' (*ibid.*, pp.171ff.) were: I The Reaction against Puritanism; II Dependence upon the Civil Magistrate; III The Legalistic Nature of the Discipline of the Form of Process; IV Dissent; V The Industrial Revolution; VI Publicity and the Press; VII

The Discipline of Preaching Emphasised. Most of these have been discussed above, some of them being described rather differently. VI corresponds somewhat to what has been said about the role of public opinion.

24. C. of S.G.A.R., 1898, p.652.
25. C. of S.G.A.R., 1906, p.5.
26. C. of S.G.A.R., 1907, p.1218.
27. *Ibid.*
28. *Ibid.*
29. *Ibid.*
30. *Ibid.*, p.1219.
31. *Ibid.*, p.1216.
32. *Ibid.*
33. *Ibid.*, p.1217.
34. *Ibid.*
35. *Ibid.*
36. *Ibid.*
37. *Vide* C. of S.G.A. Proceedings, 1931, pp.144ff.
38. *Vide* L.L.L. Cameron: *op.cit.*, pp.23ff.
39. The Church Life and Work committee of the U.F. Assembly replaced the U.P. committee of the same name and the Free Church Religion and Morals committee.
40. This committee was created in 1910.
41. G.M. Reith: *Reminiscences of the United Free Church General Assembly*, 1934, p.94. Reith remarked that reservations of this kind were most likely to be heard at the Assembly 'in the freer environment of intercourse in the corridors and the smoking-room' (*ibid.*).
42. U.F.C.G.A., 1902, Report XVIII, p.3.
43. U.F.C.G.A., 1904, Report XVIII, p.3.
44. U.F.C.G.A., 1906, Report XVIII, p.6.
45. *Ibid.*
46. Published in 1857.
47. U.F.C.G.A., 1904, Report XVIII, p.4.
48. *Ibid.*, p.5.
49. *Ibid.*, p.6.
50. *Ibid.*
51. *Ibid.*
52. U.F.C.G.A., 1905, Proceedings, p.164.
53. U.F.C.G.A., 1904, Report XVIII, p.6.
54. The 1906 Report of the Church Life and Work committee included an appendix (U.F.C.G.A., 1906, Report XVIII, pp.9ff.) dealing with housing and other social problems in the four Scottish cities. This appendix included the following relevant observations:

(i) In *Glasgow*, according to the report of this city's Housing Commission of 1904, in the old city 15.89% of the population lived in 1-roomed houses, 49.95% in 2-roomed, 20.49% in 3-roomed and 13.67% only in houses with more than 3 rooms. Some of these 1-roomed houses, in the view of the Life and Work committee, were found to be 'ample and suitable' by 'single women, aged couples, young couples entering on married life, or two young women keeping house together' (*ibid.*). But of the 19,919 'ticketed' houses in Glasgow (i.e. houses of no more than 2,000 cubic feet, each of which had a metal ticket on the door stating the permitted number of inhabitants), the Glasgow sanitary inspectors, after visiting 3,970 of them, found that while 64% of the inhabitants were 'respectable' (the criterion of respectability being self-support and the payment of rent), 24% were 'addicted to drink', and 12% were 'vicious and criminal' (*ibid.*). House-farming involved the sub-letting of insanitary slum property, subdivided into single rooms, scantily furnished, and badly ventilated and lighted, at an average rent of 4/6½ per week. The house-farmers were in many cases making enormous profits: in one of the worst cases, a farmer was receiving an income of £2 a week for property which cost him only 8/- a month to rent. Those who lived in these houses must have been desperately in need of accommodation, however, since great efforts were made by them to avoid detection of overcrowding by the sanitary inspectors: 'In one case seven persons were found skulking on an adjoining roof and in several cases persons were found hidden between the boards and mattress of the bed' (*ibid.*). While the Housing Commission was disposed to blame overcrowding for such social evils as 'the superabounding drinking and immorality', the usual confusion between cause and effect was evident. Some of their informants blamed drink for the bad accommodation, and 59% of those who lived in farmed-out houses themselves blamed their bad accommodation on their addiction to drink. (Perhaps this, in turn, was an example of their addiction to the dictates of the collective Calvinist conscience.) Inhabitants of the model lodging houses (7 of which were run by the Corporation and 60 of which were privately run) were described in similar terms, although the Commission spoke in generally favourable terms about conditions in the lodging houses themselves. In view of the part played by drink, the Commission recommended that the number of licences in working-class districts of the city should be reduced. But it also pointed out, the drink question aside, that although wages in general had improved and although tradesmen could afford to live in good accommodation, common labourers, often paid under 20/- a week, and women workers, often paid between 4/- and 15/- a week, could not afford good accommodation and often had to resort to bad.

(ii) Information about *Edinburgh* was provided for the Church Life and Work committee by one of its members. This information was not comprehensive, but many examples of house-farming were produced, including houses as bad as any in Glasgow, and condemned by the sanitary authorities. According to this source, an Edinburgh house-farmer would pay the proprietor about 2/- per week for each room and rent each out to tenants at 5/-, 6/- and in some cases even 7/- a week. If the tenant could not pay weekly, he was often charged 1/1 nightly, and, the writer noted, 'inability to pay in advance means summary ejectment' (*ibid.*, p.10). Farmers of large blocks often made profits of from 200 to 300 per cent. In the farmed houses the condition of family life varied considerably, even on the same stair. But there was a very great deal of poverty, and 'a considerable number are rented by young girls who live by prostitution' (*ibid.*), the writer commented, adding that 'In one room visited there were two young women, between 20 and 25 years of age. A man lived there also. There was but one bed.' He suggested that some landlords encouraged prostitution by preferring to let at the higher nightly rate to single girls than at the weekly rate to married women or widows. And indeed 'to pay the rent and get drink' (*ibid.*), he claimed, many married women living in such accommodation also resorted to prostitution. The same reporter also visited a large lodging-house for women. Beds here cost 4d. per night before 11 p.m. and 6d. thereafter, but the majority chose the latter. Few of the younger girls in the lodging-house had work. When they were 'in luck, as they say' (*ibid.*, p.11), they took to furnished rooms and prostitution. The older women were mostly hawkers.

Leith, where an official register of farmed-out houses was kept and where there were 'numerous day and midnight inspections', had 130 farmed-out houses. None of these was permitted to be of less than 400 cubic feet in size for each adult inhabitant; and the same sleeping apartment was not allowed to contain persons of the different sexes over 10 years of age, except husbands and wives. Rents varied, the average being 4/7½ per room per week, or 9d. per night. Leith house-farmers were making not less than 100%, but at least they did not rigidly enforce ejection for non-payment — a mixed blessing, since arrears could be high. The majority of these houses were occupied by married couples among whom were a good number of dock labourers.

Of these, the committee remarked, 'generally speaking, the tenants may be described as drinking when there is work, and living on charitable organisations when there is none' (*ibid.*). There were 9 lodging-houses in Leith accommodating a total of 957 persons.

(iii) Information about *Dundee* was provided by a report compiled by the Social Union in 1904, with the co-operation of the Medical Officer of Health. It concentrated on 'four specially selected blocks' in the poorer parts of the city. (Most of the 'merchants and professional men', it noted, lived outside the city.) In the areas selected, 49.9% of the houses were of less than 5 rooms with more than 2 persons in each room. This compared adversely with the other cities: Edinburgh: 32.7%; Aberdeen: 37.7%; and Glasgow: 47.8%. The only compensation perhaps was that Dundee rents seem to have been lower.

Dundee, however, had other problems than housing (cf. Chapter Six above). Because of the peculiar nature of the jute industry there were, according to this report, of all persons aged between 20 and 45, 3 women for every 2 men in employment. Among those employed in the jute industry, 73% were women, 11% were males under 20 years of age and only 16% were adult males. These men had, in addition, little hope of promotion. Of the females in employment, a large proportion were married, and were often the only wage-earners in their families. Dundee had the highest rate of infant mortality in Scotland (17.4% compared with 13% in Edinburgh: 59% of the children of a sample of working mothers in Dundee died in infancy compared with 42% of those whose mothers had ceased working). The average male wage in Dundee was between 15/- and 20/-, the average female wage between 12/- and 18/-. Investigations conducted in Dundee schools found that the children were 'under the standard' (what constituted the standard was not stated) 'in respect to height and weight' (*ibid.*, p.12): 'No fewer than 17.5% were classified as bad in respect of cleanliness of clothing, and 16.7% in respect of bodily cleanliness, as against 3.17 and 8.5 for Edinburgh and .8 and 2.5 for Aberdeen respectively' (*ibid.*). There was a licence for every 376 of Dundee's population, 1.2% of the total having been arrested for drunkenness in 1902; and the death-rate on account of alcoholism was much above the average.

(iv) The Synod of *Aberdeen's* special report of 1903, also quoted in this appendix, did not present a very clear comparative picture of housing in that city. It did state, however, that in one district 60% of the population lived in 1-roomed houses with 3 to 6 persons per room; and that rents, without closets, varied from £1.10/- to £2.10/- per annum. With a closet they were £5.4/-, and about half of the houses had them. Rents quoted for other districts of the city in which the poorer working classes lived were comparable. (By comparison with the other cities rents seem to have been high: but some wages also seem to have been higher: dock labourers were reported to earn up to 30/- per week.) As in the case of the other cities the condition of family life was reported to vary considerably in these districts: there were some prostitutes and a good deal of drinking in the houses visited. The inhabitants regarded the church (for the most part only a few attended) in a way which was 'essentially superstitious'. They looked upon it 'as an institution which lives in a higher social scale, and many of them believe that even if they were to come to church they would not be welcome' (*ibid.*, p.13). Some who still had a connection but had lapsed from churchgoing defended themselves 'on the ground that the minister and office-bearers did not attend to them' (*ibid.*).

55. U.F.C.G.A., 1909, Report XVIII, p.3.

56. U.F.C.G.A., 1906, Report XVIII, p.5.

57. *Ibid.* Dealing with general paralysis of the insane (i.e. syphilitic insanity — one of the later manifestations of this disease), the Asylum's report stated that 'In 1872 there were no admissions of this class of insane; in 1905 there were thirty-eight — all, with one exception,

from the poorer class. For the first time the number of female general paralytics exceeds that of men' (*ibid.*). It found 'the explanation of this sad fact in the bad moral status and mode of life of the class from which these patients come' (*ibid.*). (I do not know how far these comments reflected a real increase in G.P.I. or simply better diagnoses. The connection between the earlier forms of syphilis and G.P.I. was confirmed during the nineteenth century: *vide* R.S. Morton: *Venereal Diseases*, 1966, p.28.) The church's committee complicated the cause-effect question here again when, dealing with more general subjects a few lines later, it gave way to alliterative rhetoric, and declared (U.F.C.G.A. 1906, *ibid.*): 'The homes are dirty because the tenants are drunken, and filthy because the tenants are foul.'

58. U.F.C.G.A., 1904, Report XVIII, p.5.
59. U.F.C.G.A., 1908, Proceedings, p.265.
60. *Ibid.*
61. *Ibid.*
62. U.F.C.G.A., 1914, Report VI (The Church Life and Work and Public Morals committee's report), p.5.
63. *Ibid.*
64. U.F.C.G.A., 1908, Report XVIII, pp.3ff.
65. *Ibid.*, p.5.
66. *Ibid.*, p.6.
67. *Ibid.*, p.8. At this time, according to the 1908 report, 55% of the female population, aged over 15, of Dundee were employed. In the jute trade 51% of the employees were women over 20 years, 22% girls under 20, and only 16% adult men. These figures were much the same as those given in 1906, and housing conditions were also much the same — although the Town Council, it was said, were planning 'the extension of the city on "Garden City" lines' (*ibid.*, p.7). The committee also investigated the condition of textile workers in Dunfermline. These were better on the whole than in Dundee — partly, it was claimed, thanks to Carnegie money. An interesting sidelight on the committee's assumptions was provided when they discussed the condition of members of miners' families who came from the surrounding countryside and found work in Dunfermline. It stated that 'through the influence of town-life, "a gradual elevation is visible among them"' (*ibid.*, p.8).
68. Individual ministers had of course much earlier criticised the industrial conditions under which 'the females who should be in the house, and the children who should be in the school, have been sent to the factory': *Lectures on the Social and Physical Condition of the People, especially in Large Towns, by Various Ministers of Glasgow*, 1843, p.106.
69. U.F.C.G.A., 1908, Report XVIII, p.9.
70. *Ibid.* The Commission on the Religious Condition of the People had held a similar meeting in 1892 with a deputation of the Arbroath and District Trades Council, who had complained that 'ministers take no interest in the social welfare of the poor' (C. of S.G.A.R., 1892, p.976). The Commission had expressed sympathy, but declined to enter into 'the consideration and adjustment of economic questions' (*ibid.*, p.977).
71. U.F.C.G.A., 1908, Proceedings, p.269. Simpson compared the present state of society with that in which 'the great industrial deliverance' of the Exodus had taken place. Another speaker, the left-wing Glasgow minister Colin Gibb, spoke eloquently about 'the system' which separated 'the manual worker from the sources of wealth and from the use of the means of production'. This 'with the elimination of the humanising relationship between masters and men' tempted managers 'to increase dividends and raise their own salary by cutting expenditure and grinding the face of the workers' (*ibid.*, p.264).
72. *Ibid.*, p.273.
73. *Ibid.*
74. U.F.C.G.A., 1909, Report XVIII, p.9.
75. *Ibid.*, p.16.

76. *Ibid.*, pp.14ff.
77. *Ibid.*, p.13.
78. *Ibid.*
79. *Ibid.*
80. *Ibid.*
81. U.F.C.G.A., 1908, Report XVIII, p.2.
82. *Ibid.*
83. U.F.C.G.A., 1902, Report XVIII, p.5.
84. U.F.C.G.A., 1903, Report XVIII, p.6.
85. U.F.C.G.A., 1910, Report XVIII, p.18. This Assembly was also concerned with the Royal Navy's practice of giving 24-hour leave to sailors 'at places where suitable lodgings do not exist, or cannot readily be found' (*ibid.*, p.7). This presumably referred specially to such Scottish anchorages as Scapa Flow and the Cromarty Firth (around whose shores Free Church virtue had so singularly flourished in the past). This practice, the Church Life and Work committee claimed (in a letter to the First Lord, who promised 'that it would receive attention'), was 'attended by grave perils to the morals of the men themselves and of the general community' (*ibid.*). The committee, hyper-tactful, pointed out that this was not intended as a reflection on the morals of the men themselves. There were more complaints in 1913 about streetwalking in Edinburgh when the fleet was in the Forth (U.F.C.G.A., 1913, Report V, p.16).
86. U.F.C.G.A., 1912, Report V, pp.13ff.
87. *Ibid.*, p.24. The subject was also described as that of 'the protection of young persons from immoral courses' (*ibid.*, p.14).
88. *Vide* also U.F.C.G.A., 1909, p.3 and U.F.C.G.A., 1913, p.19.
89. U.F.C.G.A., 1912, Report V, p.15.
90. *Ibid.*
91. *Ibid.*
92. *Ibid.*
93. E.g. *Men, Women and God*, 1923.
94. U.F.C.G.A., 1912, Report V, p.24. (My italics.)
95. *Ibid.*
96. *Ibid.*
97. *Ibid.* This phrase was identical with that used by Wardlaw when he took up his pen to write about prostitution, in the 1840s (*vide* R. Wardlaw: *op.cit.*, p.2).
98. U.F.C.G.A., 1912, Report V, p.24.
99. *Ibid.*
100. *Ibid.*, p.25.
101. *Ibid.*
102. *Ibid.*
103. In some cases, according to the committee, men convicted of this had 'escaped with sentences of a few months' (*ibid.*, p.26). The committee was inclined to think that life-imprisonment would be a more appropriate penalty.
104. *Vide* G. Reith: *op.cit.*, p.153. Reith, commenting on 'these lawless women' who 'had deliberately adopted the policy of the mosquito', remarked that 'it is an interesting and perhaps relevant zoological fact that all stinging insects are unsexed females' (*ibid.*).
105. U.F.C.G.A., 1911, Report V, pp.17ff. and 1912, Report V, pp.9ff. The Church of Scotland had also taken this subject up at about the same time. *Vide* C. of S.G.A.R., 1912, pp.820ff.

Chapter ten

1. D. MacMillan: *op.cit.*, pp.364ff. When Flint was being urged to accept the Chair of Divinity in Edinburgh University (in 1875) he observed: 'so long as the salaries of our theological Chairs are only a half, or less than half, of many of our city churches, I do not see that the Church can expect men to make great sacrifices in regard to work to fill them . . . the

Church will only have to blame her own parsimony for leaving her theological Chairs in the state of miserable poverty in which they at present are' (*ibid.*, p.248). Flint however did eventually apply for and was appointed to the Chair — after the salary had been increased.

2. C. of S.G.A.R., 1894, p.785.

3. Church of Scotland Committee on Aids to Devotion, *Family Prayers*, 1871, p.2.

4. *Vide* Max Weber: *The Sociology of Religion*, (1922), English ed. 1956, p.83. and D. Craig: *Scottish Literature and the Scottish People*, 1961, *passim.*

5. Without a separate study of the part played by Burns in the consciousness of Scottish churchmen of the nineteenth century it is not possible to evaluate the influence of his life and writings on church pronouncements with any degree of accuracy. But on the evidence of what some church leaders wrote and said, the signs are that these were important in the formation of a number of their attitudes and presuppositions. It was, after all, difficult to avoid Burns in mid-nineteenth century Scotland. By 1888 lives of Burns and articles about him had been written by Lockhart, J.S. Blackie, Carlyle, Robert Chambers, Jeffrey, Andrew Lang, George Gilfillan, Charles Rogers, Christopher North and many other lesser-known authors, including a number of clergymen. (*Vide* J.S. Blackie: *Life of Robert Burns*, 1888, Bibliography V.) Much of what was written laureated the poet, but attacks on Burns-idolatry had been launched by the Free churchman Hugh Miller in 1844, (Hugh Miller: *Essays*, 1869, pp.132ff. — a reprint of an article in *The Witness*, 24/8/1844.) Miller, although critical, in a phrenological note compared the head of Burns with that of Robert the Bruce. Even more complimentary to both was his remark that the heads of both men were 'of about the same bulk as the head of Dr. Chalmers' (*ibid.*).) and by the U.P. minister Fergus Ferguson in the 'sixties (*vide* J.R. Fleming: *op.cit.*, vol.i, p.225). Such attacks were usually keenly contested by admirers of the poet. R.S. Wallace, in an address to the Leeds Caledonian Society in 1899 (*vide* Wallace: *Life and Last Leaves*, pp.610ff.), was highly critical of R.L. Stevenson for having suggested, about ten years earlier, that Burns had feet of clay. (Wallace held a low opinion of Stevenson in any case, and described him (*ibid.*, p.486) as a 'middle-class prig'. He also attacked Stevenson, on this occasion as 'the Samoan Scotsman', for telling the Thistle Club of Honolulu that Scotland's history was 'a long brawl'. Perhaps this was too near the bone.) Wallace went on to deliver a vitriolic attack upon a London journalist who had dared to enlarge upon the now deceased Stevenson's criticism. The journalist had called admirers of the poet 'Common Burnsites'. Wallace was proud to be one. Even in his earlier Edinburgh days Wallace had been a devotee and perhaps conveyed something of his enthusiasm to Dr. Stanley, the Dean of Westminster, who had preached for him in Greyfriars before delivering his controversial lectures on Scottish Church History in January 1872 (*vide* P.C. Simpson: *Life of Principal Rainy*, vol.i, p.222). Stanley's lectures provoked an immediate response from Robert Rainy, the Free Church leader, who took particular exception to his description of Burns as 'a wise religious teacher'. Rainy complained bitterly of the 'crowds of rhetorical men' who went about 'in never ending floods of eloquence to prove his life a great moral victory', and asked if Burns could ever conceivably have foreseen 'that every after-dinner orator who wished to show what a flexible thing advanced Christianity can be, would harp upon the passages that saddened his own thoughtful hours, as proofs of what may comport with high moral and Christian excellency' (*ibid.*, p.239). Rainy's attack thus demonstrated the other side of the coin — that it could be as controversial to overpraise as to overcriticise the national poet. The subject was clearly a highly emotional one, on which public figures, especially ministers, had to tread warily.

This was particularly true of the middle of the century. At an earlier stage it may have been easier for ministers to criticise, or at least to avoid joining publicly in the hero-worship. Norman Macleod, for example, had refused to take the chair at a Burns festival in 1839 because, despite his admiration of the poems, he could not 'as a Christian minister . . . but in the strongest manner disapprove of any dinner to his memory' (D. Macleod: *Memoir of N. Macleod*, 1877, p.102). Twenty years later, Macleod's attitude had changed. 1859 was the year of Burns' centenary and, according to Macleod's brother (*ibid.*, pp.279ff.), 'the signal for the outbreak of bitter war between the pulpit and the press. There were fanatics on both sides. Admirers of the poet would not brook exception being taken to their hero-worship; this provoked, on the other side, unmeasured abuse of his character and influence. The sacred name of religion was so constantly invoked in the quarrel that no clergyman could take part in the festival without risk to his reputation.' This was not strictly true, for A.H. Charteris certainly took part in an Ayrshire Burns Dinner this year, and, replying to the toast of 'The Clergy', praised Burns as a man who had 'purified the sentiments of those songs which the peasantry of Scotland hear on the harvest field, in the rustic merry-making and by their own fire-side'. But, he added, 'if along with this there be errors of careless life and thoughtless word we do not soil our admiration of genius with approval of the erring man' (A. Gordon: *Life of A.H. Charteris*, 1912, p.63). Like Charteris, then, Norman Macleod, who was an honest man, and by this time a well-known parish minister in Glasgow, risked his reputation and accepted an invitation to speak at the Glasgow Burns Centenary celebration. He was the only minister on the platform. In his speech he praised the poet for 'his noble protest for the independence and dignity of humanity', and was greeted with loud cheering; he praised the poet again for making 'our Doric for ever poetical' and welding 'the hearts of Scotchmen throughout the world', and was loudly applauded; he then stopped praising Burns, and said that he wished some of his poems 'were never written, never printed and never read', and was greeted with a 'storm of hissing, mingled with cheers' (Macleod: *ibid.*). Macleod's address concluded with an appeal for the centenary to be marked by a new edition of the poems 'from which everything would be excluded which a Christian father could not read aloud in his family circle, or the Christian cottar on his 'Saturday night' to his sons and daughters (*ibid.*). This appeal was applauded by Dr. Duncan, the Hebrew Grammarian, in a letter to Macleod. It seems likely that it was the implied approval of extramarital sex in some of Burns' poems (not, it is likely, in the more explicit ones, whose circulation was limited) rather than the poet's criticism of Holy Willies to which Macleod took exception.

Many of Macleod's middle-class contemporaries shared his views on Burns. They could not perhaps carry the political implications of his ideas as far as radicals and socialists did. (Both Alexander Somerville and Keir Hardie claimed to have been inspired by Burns.) But neither could they resist the Burns cult, which had something for everybody. Yet like Macleod they could not embrace the cult totally. Robert Chambers, the Edinburgh publisher, who was not a particularly prudish man, remarked that it was 'to the lasting grief of all the friends of our Poet' that his collection of bawdy folksongs — 'these facetiae' — had ever been printed. (*Vide The Merry Muses of Caledonia*, 1966 ed., p.14.) Burns' life as well as his art was also criticised by J.S. Blackie, the patriotic Professor of Greek, who tempered his praise with an appropriately classical remark to the effect that the great mistake of the poet's life was that, scorning 'the safety which nature and Aristotle have combined to indicate as the golden mean', he 'did not know where to stop' (Blackie: *op.cit.*, p.163). And, equally in character, Thomas Guthrie remarked that 'if he had had the happiness at a certain point of his career to meet with an evangelist of the right sort . . . he would not have started off the rails of moral rectitude so grossly as he sometimes did' (*ibid.*, p.169).

Nineteenth-century Scottish attitudes to Burns, and particularly those of clergymen, thus seem to have been formed out of an inability to refrain either from praising him or criticising him. Churchmen's attitudes to Burns were thus rather like the advice to hate the sin and love the sinner, only, as it were, put in reverse: to criticise the poet and, with some exceptions, to praise the poems. Above all it was advice to praise one poem in particular. 'The Cotter's Saturday Night', declared the Reverend James Robertson of Whittinghame, writing in *Life and Work* in 1880 (*Life and Work*, Vol.II, (December 1880) p.187), made you feel proud to be descended from Scottish peasants. But here was the rub. The poem also made you humble. As Mr. Robertson wrote (*Life and Work*, Vol.II (April 1881), p.60), 'It is, I fear, the fact that family worship in cottage homes, like this described in the poem, once was general and now is rare . . . It is common . . . to hear people of middle age tell with pride how constant family worship was in their parents' house. But what if the children of the next generation will be unable to bear this witness of us? . . . Is that form of life passing away . . . which gave to the world men of letters like Burns and Carlyle; men of science like Hugh Miller; missionaries like Duff and Moffat; and last, not least, the heroic Livingstone, who counted it one of the privileges of his life that he was born of "poor and pious parents"?' A footnote to this, although it does not directly concern the cotter, may be added. In October 1866, Norman Macleod, writing to his wife from Balmoral to explain a longer-than-expected stay there ('the Queen is pleased to command me to remain here till Tuesday'), told her: 'After dinner, the Queen invited me to her room, where I found the Princess Helena and the Marchioness of Ely. The Queen sat down to spin, at a nice Scotch wheel, while I read Robert Burns to her: "Tam o' Shanter" and "A man's a man for a' that," her favourite.' (D. Macleod: *op.cit.*, pp.377ff.)

6. George Eliot: *Middlemarch* (1871-72), Book I, Ch.X.

Part two

1. F.C.G.A.P. & D., 1871, p.263.
2. A petition against the Acts was sent to Parliament at this time by 7,200 Edinburgh working men: *vide* J.B. Mackie: *The Life and Work of Duncan McLaren*, 1888, Vol.ii, p.96.

Chapter eleven

1. While it is possible to achieve a large measure of agreement on what might be called the hardcore of prostitution, its borderlands are obscure. Two characteristics often regarded as distinguishing prostitution are its indiscriminate or promiscuous nature and the involvement of payment in cash or kind. There are, however, a variety of sexual activities involving payment or reward which may not be particularly promiscuous or entirely indiscriminate, for example the activities of Greek hetairae, Renaissance courtesans, Victorian kept women and modern callgirls. These inhabit some ill-defined no-woman's land between prostitution and concubinage. Even more difficult to classify are the women who sleep with selected men in order to advance their own or their husband's career or social position. And on the other hand there are those whose sexual activities may be indiscriminate or promiscuous, but who neither ask for nor expect payment. In the context of European rural courtship, discussed above, there were no doubt some women, more sought after than others, who demanded neither payment nor promise of marriage — at least for the time being. Such women cannot be regarded as prostitutes if hire or reward are seen as necessary elements in prostitution. Yet if their willingness to be sexually promiscuous was widely known, it is hard to draw a distinction between their activities and those of a prostitute — *vide* H. Benjamin and R.E.L. Masters: *Prostitution and Morality*, 1965, pp.21ff.
2. *Vide* Max Weber: *The Sociology of Religion* (English ed., 1965), p.237.
3. *Vide* D.S. Bailey: *Sexual Offenders and Social Punishment*, 1956, pp.42ff.
4. *Vide* R.S. Morton: *Venereal Diseases*, 1966, pp.22ff.
5. Not all commentators are convinced that these are references to venereal disease. *Vide* D.R. Mace: *Hebrew Marriage*, 1953, p.239.
6. It was known on this occasion variously as the Spanish sickness, the sickness of Naples, the French sickness or Grandgore (large sore). The normal custom throughout Europe was to designate the disease by the name of some other country: in a later epidemic introduced to Scotland by Cromwellian troops in the mid-seventeenth century the terminology was reversed, the troops calling it the Scotch pox. *Vide British Journal of Venereal Diseases* (1962), 38, 175: 'Some Aspects of the Early History of Syphilis in Scotland', R.S. Morton.
7. *Vide* D.S. Bailey: *The Man-Woman Relation in Christian Thought*, 1959, p.182.
8. *Vide* J. MacIntosh: *A History of Civilization in Scotland*, 1893, vol.II, p.247.
9. *Ibid.*, p.250.

10. *Ibid.*, p.248.
11. *Vide* W. Tait: *Magdalenism*, 1842, pp.296, 297, 307.
12. *Ibid.*, p.308.
13. These Acts were in fact passed in the same year in which Cromwell's soldiers brought a new epidemic of syphilis to Scotland. They were passed, however, in April and May of that year, whereas Cromwell's soldiers did not cross the border until July. It seems likely therefore that they had more to do with the politico-religious attitudes of the Covenanters than with the fear of infection by venereal disease.
14. *Ibid.*, p.309.
15. *Vide* T. Ferguson: *The Dawn of Scottish Social Welfare*, 1948, p.110.
16. *Vide* Tait: *op.cit.*, p.309.
17. *Vide* Havelock Ellis: *Studies in the Psychology of Sex*, vol.VI, p.249.
18. In Austria, for example, the Empress Maria Theresa's Chastity Commission was trying to put down prostitution and all forms of fornication with as much zeal as the Scottish Reformers two hundred years earlier (*ibid.*, p.241).
19. Bernard Mandeville's *Modest Defence of Public Stews*, an attempt to argue for regulation in England, was greeted with hostility (*ibid.*, p.249).
20. Tait (*op.cit.*, p.311) suggested that perhaps this was because they were afraid of being caught up in their own legislative net.
21. *Ibid.*
22. J. MacIntosh: *op.cit.*, Vol.II, p.233.
23. Subtitle of R. Wardlaw: *Lectures on Female Prostitution*, 1842.
24. *Vide* R. Wardlaw: *op.cit.*, p.21 and *cf.* F. Henriques: *op.cit.*, pp.49ff.
25. *Vide* Wardlaw: *op.cit.*, p.23.
26. *Vide* W. Logan: *The Great Social Evil*, 1871, p.88.
27. *Vide* Henriques: *op.cit.*, p.49.
28. *Vide* Wardlaw: *op.cit.*, p.22.
29. *Vide ibid.*, pp.24ff. Mayne's estimate was questioned by Wardlaw on the ground that this figure of 8,000 to 9,000 prostitutes was too low by comparison with his report of 3,335 brothels. (The respective figures appear in Logan: *op.cit.*, p.88, as prostitutes: 9,409, brothels: 3,325 — but Wardlaw was writing quickly: the lectures were first delivered at the end of May, the book appeared in August.)
30. *Ibid.*, p.24.
31. Tait: *op.cit.*, p.5.
32. *Ibid.*
33. Logan: *op.cit.*, pp.72ff.
34. Tait: *op.cit.*, p.10.
35. *Ibid.*, p.2.
36. *Ibid.*, p.7.
37. This was not as bad, however, noted Tait, as the proportions for London, Paris and New York, which were 1 to 60, 1 to 15 and 1 to 6 or 7 respectively. New York's figures in particular distressed Tait: it was a city whose inhabitants were supposed to be 'independent, liberal, religious and enlightened', yet a city whose depravity 'was not surpassed even by the metropolis of France during the heat and fervour of the Revolution, when libertinism reigned triumphant, and the laws of God and man were alike set at defiance' (*ibid.*, pp.6ff.). Wardlaw (*op.cit.*, pp.28ff.) found the New York figures equally distressing and 'would fain discredit' them. Yet Tait's calculations, he noted, had been based on figures provided by a 'much respected minister of the gospel' (the Revd. Dr. McDowall, Chaplain to the New York Magdalene Asylum) who was 'one of themselves, (i.e. New Yorkers) and therefore, we may presume, one who would be the less likely to deal in exaggeration'. Tait (*op.cit.*, p.7), incidentally, was careful here to defend Edinburgh's reputation from the charge that Edinburgh citizens were religious hypocrites — which might be made on the ground that the majority of prostitutes in Edinburgh were of the

secret rather than the public variety. No doubt religion did influence public opinion and keep much prostitution secret. But there was as much secret prostitution in Paris and New York — and the large amount of public prostitution (even if secret prostitution there was disavowed) was surely no proof of superior morality. The canard against Edinburgh attacked by Tait is repeated by Henriques (*op.cit.*, p.94), who claims that 'in Latin countries a less rigorous interpretation of Christianity in relation to the flesh and the devil, has sponsored less hypocrisy'.

38. Wardlaw: *op.cit.*, p.32.

39. *Ibid.*, p.35.

40. G.M. Young: *Portrait of an Age*, 1936, p.4.

41. *Vide* Muirhead, *op.cit.*

42. *Vide* Tait: *op.cit.*, pp.333ff. In Edinburgh, between 1797 and 1837, only 814 penitents entered the Asylum, and only about 36 per cent. of these were sent on to their friends or to fresh employment, a much lower success rate than in comparable London establishments. Tait laid much of the blame for this on the respectable citizens of Edinburgh, who failed to provide financial support for this, or indeed any other charity ('on glancing over the reports of the different charities in Edinburgh, it is observed that they are supported by a few individuals and that these invariably subscribe to them all, while thousands of respectable citizens do not contribute to any of them' — *ibid.*, p.336). He also criticised respectable Edinburgh families for not being willing to employ the reformed and retrained women as domestic servants. But this, he noted, was not surprising, since very few of the Asylum's directors had enough confidence in their work to employ the women either. The system of solitary confinement for the first two or three months in the Asylum was also criticised by Tait.

43. W. Acton: *Prostitution*, 2nd edition (1870), pp.263ff.

44. From a letter to a friend, quoted in M. Jaeger: *Before Victoria*, 1956, p.26.

45. *Vide* Tait: *op.cit.*, pp.298ff. and *Lectures on the Social and Physical Condition of the People especially in Larger Towns: By Various Ministers of Glasgow*, 1843, p.104.

46. *Vide* Acton: *op.cit.*, p.4, and Logan: *op.cit.*, p.87. The number of prostitutes accommodated in these brothels declined from 2,071 in 1841, to 921 in 1857, to 11 in 1870. Overall numbers of prostitutes known to the Metropolitan Police during this period were, however, 9,409 in 1841, 8,600 in 1857, and 6,515 in 1870.

47. Logan: *op.cit.*, pp.91ff.

48. *Ibid.*, pp.92ff.

49. Tait: *op.cit.*, p.360.

50. *Vide ibid.*, pp.113ff. and 273ff. for the 'natural causes' of prostitution and their remedy.

51. *Vide ibid.*, pp.129ff. and 277ff. for the 'accidental causes' of prostitution and their remedy.

52. *Ibid.*, p.280.

53. 'The bane of the female population; for while it disappoints the one half, it ruins the other.' *Ibid.*, p.136.

54. *Ibid.*, p.293.

55. *Ibid.*, p.294.

56. Wardlaw: *op.cit.*, p.v.

57. *Ibid.*, p.3.

58. A.L. Morton: *The Life and Ideas of Robert Owen*, 1969, p.207. (The quotation is from Owen: *Lectures on the Marriages of the Priesthood of the Old Immoral World*, 4th ed., 1841.)

59. *Ibid.*, p.206.

60. Wardlaw: *op.cit.*, p.11.

61. *Ibid.*, p.10.

62. *Ibid.*, p.13.

63. *Ibid.*, p.10.

64. Marriage was to be constituted after two public declarations, separated by three months, and made by both parties. It could be terminated, but not sooner than twelve months after its constitution, and if both parties wished it, by a public declaration, followed by a further six months together, and then, if both still wished it, by a second and final declaration. If by the end of the six months one party objected to the separation, a second six months together was prescribed; and at the end of these, if the two parties remained in disagreement, the separation would be final. (Owen: *Lectures on the Marriages of the Priesthood of the Old Immoral World*, 1835, Appendix to 1841 edition.) *Vide* Morton: *op.cit.*, pp.213ff.

65. E.g. R.C. Mortimer *et al*: *Putting Asunder*, 1966.

66. *Cf.* the Reith Lectures of G.M. Carstairs (1962) and E. Leach (1967).

67. *Vide* Morton: *op.cit.*, p.208.

68. *Ibid.*, pp.209ff.

69. *Ibid.*, p.63.

Chapter twelve

1. W.H. Auden: *Collected Shorter Poems 1930-1944*, 1950, p.174.

2. For the use of this word which, for reasons which I hope will become apparent, is more apt than, for example, Utilitarian, *vide* P. Rieff: *The Triumph of the Therapeutic*, 1966, *passim*.

3. Although not, of course, of all Socialists.

4. In the churches' case this has been, in so far as it has taken place, a relatively recent development.

5. For evidence that Acton was regarded as one of the leading advocates of Regulation, *vide* Josephine E. Butler: *Personal Reminiscences of a Great Crusade*, 1910, p.63.

6. Acton's views on female sexual desire were expressed in his volume on *The Functions and Disorders of the Reproductive Organs*, in which (6th ed., 1875, p.213) he wrote: 'A modest woman seldom desires any sexual satisfaction for herself. She submits to her husband's embraces, but principally to gratify him: and were it not for the desire of maternity, would rather be relieved of his attentions.'

7. W. Acton: *Prostitution*, 1870 edition, p.162.

8. Tait: *op.cit.*, p.269.

9. Acton: *op.cit.*, p.163. He illustrated this point by referring to the healthy habits of the ancient Germans (as opposed to the decadent Romans), stallions and short-horn bulls. In making this point he also took a sideswipe at the population theories of Malthus and Mill. The proper remedy for over-population, he noted (p.165), was emigration; and 'preventives' — 'which whatever may be thought of them in other countries are thoroughly repugnant to Englishmen'.

10. *Ibid.*, p.166.

11. *Ibid.*, p.166.

12. *Ibid.*, p.162.

13. Tait: *op.cit.*, p.266.

14. 'A robust and healthy country population have full control over their sexual propensities' (*ibid.*, p.270).

15. Wardlaw: *op.cit.*, p.120.

16. Acton: *op.cit.*, p.167.

17. *Ibid.*, p.168.

18. Wardlaw: *op.cit.*, p.119.

19. Tait was not certain exactly how high the early mortality rate among prostitutes was. But he thought that some indication of it was given by the fact that most prostitutes were under twenty-five, and that perhaps a fifth or sixth of these died each year. A third or a quarter of prostitutes in this age-range had at least attempted suicide at some time in their career. Tait: *op.cit.*, p.227.

20. Acton: *op.cit.*, p.27.

21. *Ibid.*, p.28.

22. *Ibid.*, p.29.

23. *Ibid.*

24. In this class you might find a loud and lively tavern bar prostitute 'looked on as "first rate company" by aspiring gents' (*ibid.*, p.30). But you might equally well find a quiet sober girl, who preferred 'the respect and counsel of well-bred men of settled character' from whom she would 'get lessons, rarely thrown away, on the value of repose and thrift' (*ibid.*, p.31). The first of these girls was 'a mercenary human tigress' (p.30), the second, a female 'in whose hands . . . the sick man is safe . . . and the fool's money also' (p.31).

25. *Ibid.*, p.33. Acton (*ibid.*, p.38) found no evidence of a high suicide rate among prostitutes.

26. *Ibid.*, p.33.

27. *Ibid.*, p.39.

28. *Ibid.*

29. *Ibid.*

30. *Ibid.*, p.40. In his first edition of 1857, Acton wrote, he had not had any statistical evidence to confirm this, but since the passing of the Contagious Diseases Acts the reports of medical officers concerning the Acts' operation corroborated his claims. The medical officer at Devonport, for example, stated that of 1,175 sometime prostitutes there, 250 had married, many of them respectably. Given that the Acts had not been long in operation, and thus that the time had not yet arrived for many of these prostitutes to return to respectable society, this does seem to confirm Acton's view — at least in an area where the Acts were in operation (*vide ibid.*, p.49). The point, however, is somewhat weakened by his observation, elsewhere (*ibid.*, p.198), that soldiers' wives who had been prostitutes often went back to the trade after marriage, because their husbands were so badly paid.

31. *Ibid.*, p.40.

32. *Ibid.*, p.48. Acton illustrated this point anecdotally, and by referring to a set of illegitimacy statistics, a popular proverb ("'if thou houd'st, I wed thee; if thou doesn't, thou'rt none the waur", is a north country proverb, familiar enough to many southerners, and acted upon to an immense extent, as I have been repeatedly and seriously informed by reliable authorities' — *ibid.*, p.47), Mayhew's findings and (*ibid.*) 'the experience of the clergy, who are the best authorities upon the social condition of both urban and manufacturing communities'.

33. *Ibid.*, p.48.

34. *Ibid.*

35. *Ibid.*, p.49.

36. *Ibid.*

37. Logan: *op.cit.*, p.104. Logan did not however substantiate this remark with any contemporary evidence, statistical or otherwise, although he claimed (p.96) to have read everything written about the subject in Britain since the 'forties. Instead, he quoted his own experiences from that earlier period, some of Wardlaw's gorier flights of rhetoric and a touching, if Tupperish, poem found 'among the papers of a poor penitent prostitute who died of want in a garret in Glasgow' (p.107). The sincerity of all this was beyond question. What was questionable was how far Logan's criticism had been vitiated by the passage of time, and by the fact that even in the 'forties his experience — as a city missionary — was more likely to have been of destitute than of successful prostitutes.

38. *Proverbs*: Ch. 5. v.4, quoted by Tait: *op.cit.*, p.206.

39. Wardlaw: *op.cit.*, p.49.

40. Acton: *op.cit.*, p.33.

41. *Ibid.*, p.265.

42. *Ibid.*, p.260.

43. *Ibid.*, p.77.

44. *Ibid.*, p.168.
45. *Ibid.*
46. *Ibid.*
47. *Ibid.*, p.171.
48. *Ibid.*, p.180.
49. *Ibid.*, p.181.
50. *Ibid.*, p.182.
51. *Ibid.*, p.176.
52. *Ibid.*
53. *Ibid.*, p.177.
54. Wardlaw: *op.cit.*, p.103.
55. Tait: *op.cit.*, p.133.
56. Acton: *op.cit.*, p.188.
57. Tait: *op.cit.*, p.133.
58. Acton: *op.cit.*, p.70.
59. Tait had recognised that venereal disease affected the innocent as well as the guilty, as, for example, when children of healthy parents were infected by diseased wet-nurses, or wives infected by husbands. (*Vide* Tait: *op.cit.*, pp.250ff.)
60. Acton: *op.cit.*, p.47.
61. *Ibid.*, p.48.
62. *Vide* Tait: *op.cit.*, pp.265ff., and Wardlaw: *op.cit.*, pp.18ff.
63. Acton: *op.cit.*, p.203.
64. *Ibid.*, p.160.
65. *Ibid.*
66. *Ibid.*, p.108. (The mouchard was the police informer.)
67. *Ibid.*, p.104.
68. *Ibid.*, p.205.
69. *Ibid.*, p.160.
70. *Ibid.*
71. *Ibid.*, p.204.
72. *Ibid.*, p.205.
73. *Ibid.*
74. *Ibid.*
75. *Ibid.*
76. *Ibid.*
77. *Ibid.*, p.83.
78. *Vide* W.L. Burn: *The Age of Equipoise*, 1964, p.159.
79. Acton: *op.cit.*, p.90.
80. In this case Dr. Barr of the Aldershot Lock Hospital (*ibid.*, p.92).
81. *Ibid.*, p.95.
82. *Ibid.*, p.216.
83. *Ibid.*
84. *Ibid.*
85. *Ibid.*, fn.
86. *Ibid.*, p.217.
87. *Ibid.*, p.206.
88. *Ibid.*
89. *Ibid.*
90. *Ibid.*, p.207.
91. *Ibid.*, p.208.
92. *Ibid.*
93. *Ibid.*, p.217.
94. *Ibid.*, p.218.

95. *Ibid.*
96. *Ibid.*
97. *Vide* Burn: *op.cit.*, p.158.
98. Acton: *op.cit.*, p.219. This argument did not sit very easily alongside what he had written about venereal disease being no deterrent to many men.
99. *Ibid.*, p.220.
100. J.S. Mill: *On Liberty*, 1859, Everyman (1910) Edition, p.154. Mill later became an opponent of the Contagious Diseases Acts.
101. Acton: *op.cit.*, p.221.
102. Burn: *op.cit.*, p.194.
103. *Ibid.*, p.160.
104. *Ibid.*, p.220.
105. Wardlaw: *op.cit.*, p.153.

Chapter thirteen

1. An overture to the 1875 Assembly, from an individual asking the Assembly to petition Parliament for repeal of the C.D. Acts, was withdrawn after it failed to gain support (*vide* C. of S.G.A. Acts (1870-75), 1875, p.70.) The 1884 Assembly did agree, however, to petition Parliament in favour of the Criminal Law Amendment Bill. (*Vide* C. of S.G.A., Acts (1882-87) 1884, p.84.)
2. *Vide* C. of S.G.A.R., 1870, p.419.
3. At least at first.
4. F.C.G.A.P. & D., 1885, Debates, p.56.
5. F.C.G.A.P. & D., 1871, Debates, p.263.
6. This petition for the most part reproduced the arguments of Josephine Butler's Women's Protest of 1870 — *vide* J.E. Butler: *op.cit.*, p.9.
7. U.P.S.P., 1870-73, p.304.
8. John Cairns, the U.P. leader, was an early recruit to the Abolitionist cause. Josephine Butler (*op.cit.*, p.22) wrote of her visit to Berwick-on-Tweed in 1870: 'The United Presbyterians and other Scottish ministers were my best friends here. The Rev. Dr. Cairns was timid about holding a meeting although he was wholly in sympathy with us, and he did not at first like the advocacy of ladies. He is a man of much influence in the Scotch Church, and is said to be one of Sir William Hamilton's most distinguished pupils. On reaching the platform he offered up a fervent prayer. It was a full and excellent meeting, and, towards the close, unanimous.' Cairns' biographer does not record this incident. He does however include (MacEwan: *op.cit.*, pp.582-3) an extract from one of Cairns' sermons, warning individuals against prostitution and denouncing the argument that it is socially necessary as 'only worthy of hell and the father of lies'. The sermon, preached in Berwick, was an exposition of Proverbs, Chapter 7.
9. P.C. Simpson: *Life of Principal Rainy*, 1909, vol.ii, p.176. Rainy, addressing the 1880 Assembly (F.C.G.A.P. & D., 1880, Debates, p.284) was careful not to condemn totally those who 'sincerely argued themselves into the conviction that these Acts were right'.
10. F.C.G.A.P. & D., 1874, Debates, p.840.
11. F.C.G.A.P. & D., 1875, Report XXX, p.2.
12. F.C.G.A.P. & D., 1877, Report XXXIII, p.4.
13. F.C.G.A.P. & D., 1876, Report XXX, p.4.
14. F.C.G.A.P. & D., 1877, Report XXXIII, p.2.
15. *Vide* U.P.S.P.' 1870-73, p.451 (1872), pp.655 and 741 (1873).
    U.P.S.P., 1874-76, pp.56, 99 (1874); pp.406, 435 (1875); pp.684, 734 (1876).
    U.P.S.P., 1877-79, pp.50, 100 (1877); pp.379, 419 (1878).
16. F.C.G.A.P. & D., 1877, Report XXXIII, p.3.
17. F.C.G.A.P. & D., 1879, Report XXI, *passim*.
18. R.C.K. Ensor: *England 1870-1914*, 1936, p.171.

19. F.C.G.A.P. & D., 1875, Report XXX, p.2.
20. *Ibid.*
21. *Ibid.*
22. *Ibid.*
23. *Ibid.*, p.3.
24. *Ibid.*
25. *Ibid.*
26. *Ibid.*, p.4.
27. F.C.G.A.P. & D., 1877, Report XXXIII, p.3.
28. *Ibid.*
29. *Ibid.*
30. F.C.G.A.P. & D., 1878, Report XXXI, p.3.
31. *Ibid.*
32. In the debate in 1882, for example, Dr. Ferguson, the Convener of the Free Church's committee, noted that nine-tenths of the examinations under the Acts (up to 1880) had been of healthy women and were thus really just to find out if the woman was fit to work as a prostitute (F.C.G.A.P. & D., 1882, Debates, p.48).
33. *Vide* Acton: *op.cit.*, pp.189ff., and G. Petrie: *A Singular Iniquity*, 1971, pp.99ff.
34. *Vide* Acton: *op.cit.*, p.206.
35. *Daily Telegraph*, July 1 1862, quoted in Acton: *op.cit.*, p.221.
36. F.C.G.A.P. & D., 1877, Report XXXIII, p.4.
37. *Ibid.*
38. F.C.G.A.P. & D., 1877, Report XXXIII, p.5.
39. *Vide* A. Flexner: *Prostitution in Europe*, 1919, pp.244ff. for the account of an acrid controversy between the Chief Constable of Glasgow and the Inspector of the Parish, which supports this contention.
40. F.C.G.A.P. & D., 1875, Report XXX, p.3.
41. *Ibid.*
42. F.C.G.A.P. & D., 1876, Report XXX, p.4.
43. F.C.G.A.P. & D., 1875, Report XXX, p.2.
44. F.C.G.A.P. & D., 1876, Report XXX, p.4.
45. *Ibid.*
46. *Ibid.*
47. On the history of the relation between this argument and medical treatment, *vide* O. Temkin: *The Double Face of Janus and other Essays in the History of Medicine*, 1977, Chs. 32 and 37.
48. *Vide* F.C.G.A.P. & D., 1882, Report XXXI, pp.1ff.
49. F.C.G.A.P. & D., 1882, Report XXXI, p.4.
50. *Ibid.* This was taken from the evidence of Dr. Barr of Aldershot to the Commons Select Committee of 1869. Evidence of the class bias of regulation systems outside Britain was provided in the Free Church committee's 1877 report. This (F.C.G.A.P. & D., 1877, Report XXXIII, pp.5ff.) cited an account by Josephine Butler of M. Lecour's failure to prove the impartiality of his system by prosecuting an upper-class male. The issue was somewhat confused however by Josephine Butler's intense dislike of Lecour and her desire to prove that (*ibid.*) 'Regulation . . . opens wide the floodgates of fiendish passion'.
51. F.C.G.A.P. & D., 1882, Report XXXI, p.4.
52. The Free Church committee complained indignantly (F.C.G.A.P. & D., 1877, Report XXXIII, p.7) that the British press totally ignored the activities of the Federation.
53. *Vide* F.C.G.A.P. & D., 1877, Report XXXIII, p.4., for Dr. Ker's defence against this charge. In relation to Mill and Spencer's opposition to the Acts he declared (*ibid.*), 'though every bishop and presbyter in the Christian Church were on the other side, I should say, "let my soul be with the philosophers." I honour in my heart their noble stand for constitutional right and the dignity of the moral law'.

54. *Vide ibid.*, p.2.
55. *Vide* F.C.G.A.P. & D., 1878, Report XXXI, p.1.
56. By 1882 the Free Church committee was sending out instructions about the proper way to frame petitions to Parliament (*vide* F.C.G.A.P. & D., 1882, Report XXXI, p.4).
57. F.C.G.A.P. & D., 1880, Report XXXI, p.1.
58. *Ibid.*, Debates, pp.284ff.
59. F.C.G.A.P. & D., 1883, Debates, p.189.
60. I.e. the minimum age at which marriage was legal.
61. F.C.G.A.P. & D., 1881, Debates, p.248.
62. The age of consent for females in Scots law was also twelve years.
63. U.P.S.P., 1880-82, p.385 (1881). *Vide* also *ibid.*, p.681 (1882).
64. *Vide* F.C.G.A.P. & D., 1884, Report XXXI, and Debates, pp.190-192.
65. The committee's name was changed this year to 'The Committee on Legislation concerning Social Purity' (*ibid.*).
66. *Ibid.*, p.192.
67. *Ibid.*
68. F.C.G.A.P. & D., 1885, Report XXXI, p.3.
69. *Ibid.*, Debates, p.56.
70. The U.P. Synod also kept on petitioning to the end. *Vide* e.g. U.P.S.P., 1883-85, p.594 (1885).
71. F.C.G.A.P. & D., 1886, Debates, p.60.
72. U.P.S.P., 1886-88, p.60 (1886).
73. U.P.S.P., 1886-88, pp.60 and 272ff. (1886).
74. F.C.G.A.P. & D., 1886, Report XXXI, p.3.
75. *Ibid.*

Chapter fourteen

1. Dr. Ferguson, although 'a staunch Conservative in politics' according to Rainy's biographer (P.C. Simpson: *op.cit.*, Vol.2, p.202), was not afraid of embarrassing his party, now back in office after a six months' break in 1886.
2. F.C.G.A.P. & D., 1887, Debates, p.188.
3. U.P.S.P., 1886-88, p.487 (1887).
4. *The Missionary Record of the United Presbyterian Church*, Nov. 1 1887, p.346.
5. *Ibid.*
6. *Ibid.*, p.348 (a popular phrase: *vide* F.C.G.A.P. & D., 1888, Report XXXII, p.3: 'What can the natives of India think of Christianity, when a nation calling itself Christian brings Bibles in the one hand and Vice-licences in the other, and provides for its troops prostitutes as well as preachers?').
7. *U.P. Missionary Record*: op.cit., p.347.
8. *Ibid.*
9. *Ibid.*, p.348.
10. *Ibid.*
11. *Ibid.*
12. *Ibid.*
13. *Ibid.*
14. *Ibid.*
15. *Ibid.*
16. *Ibid.*
17. *Ibid.*
18. *Ibid.*, p.349. The U.P. writer, not insignificantly, failed to touch upon one aspect of this question. Although, during the nineteenth century, syphilis was not, in general, as dangerous or fatal a disease as at earlier periods in Europe, European expansion brought it to all but the remotest areas of Central Africa and Central America, and often with

devastating effects, since the native population lacked European immunity. According to Havelock Ellis (*op.cit.*, vol.VI, p.327), 90 per cent. of the Baganda people of Uganda were found to be suffering from it in 1907, and it accounted for 50 to 60 per cent. of infant mortality among them. This people, wrote Ellis (*ibid.*) 'were a highly intelligent, powerful and well-organised tribe before they received, in the gift of syphilis, the full benefit of civilization and Christianity, which . . . has been largely the cause of the spread of the disease by breaking down social customs and emancipating the women. Christianity is powerful enough to break down the old morality, but not powerful enough to build up a new morality.'

19. F.C.G.A.P. & D., 1888, Report XXXII, p.2.

20. *Ibid.*, p.3.

21. Mrs. Chant figured in numerous protest movements of the period, concerned with the subject under discussion, with temperance and with women's suffrage. She seems to have been the late nineteenth-century equivalent of a cross between Mrs. Mary Whitehouse and Miss Vanessa Redgrave.

22. M.P. for Sheffield. Mrs. Butler should also have spoken, but was ill.

23. U.P.S.P., 1886-88, p.1167 (1888). Meetings were later held in Inverness, Perth, Hawick and Greenock.

24. F.C.G.A.P. & D., 1888, Report XXXII, p.2.

25. To the Free Church committee's delight, when they asked an experienced English repealer what was the most suitable piece of literature to send to these ministers, he replied that 'there was nothing equal to a statement prepared sixteen years ago by Principal Rainy' (F.C.G.A.P. & D., 1889, Report XXXII, p.3).

26. F.C.G.A.P. & D., 1889, Report XXXII, p.2.

27. 'Statistics (c.1862) showed that for years the death-rate of the British Army in India had been 69 per 1,000': C. Woodham-Smith: *Florence Nightingale*, 1952 Reprint Society Edtn., p.320.

28. Blanche Leppington: 'Public Morals and the Public Health' in *Public Morals*, ed. James Marchant, n.d. (c.1902), p.186.

29. *Vide* F.C.G.A.P. & D., 1897, Report XXIX, p.10.

30. *Vide* Leppington: *op.cit.*, p.188.

31. The methods of calculation were not always known, and may have included re-admissions of the same patient after a relapse.

32. *Vide* Leppington: *op.cit.*, pp.188ff.

33. *Ibid.*

34. Walter McLaren, 'worthy son of a worthy sire' (Duncan McLaren), as the Free Church Committee put it. *Vide* F.C.G.A.P. & D., 1889, Report XXXII, p.1.

35. U.P.S.P., 1889-90, p.340 (1889).

36. F.C.G.A.P. & D., 1889, Report XXXII, p.2.

37. *Ibid.*

38. F.C.G.A.P. & D., 1890, Report XXXVII, p.2.

39. *Ibid.*

40. *Ibid.*

41. *Ibid.*, p.3.

42. *Ibid.*

43. *Ibid.*

44. *Ibid.*, Debates, p.256.

45. *Ibid.*, p.257.

46. Help had been offered however by the Revd. Henry Rice, an established Church missionary in Madras (*vide* F.C.G.A.P. & D., 1891, Report XXXVII, p.3).

47. F.C.G.A.P. & D., 1891, Report XXXVII, p.5.

48. *Ibid.*

49. *Ibid.*

50. *Ibid.*
51. *Ibid.*
52. Dr. Huntly's report was commended by the U.P. Synod in 1892 (U.P.S.P., 1892, p.143) and again quoted by the Free Church committee in 1893 (F.C.G.A.P. & D., 1893, Report XXXIII, p.3.), the latter adding 'Yes! and England's *sons* too, and Scotland's and Ireland's are being ruined, and working men's homes are known of, where there is mourning over the soldier-boy that has gone out to India to be corrupted.' The same report (*ibid.*, p.4) included a further letter from Dr. Huntly, which helped to explain his passionate attack. There had been three hospitals in Nusseerabad, one beside the native infantry's quarters, Huntly's mission hospital, and a government hospital directly opposite Huntly's. The first of these dealt with the native soldiers, with cases of assault in the bazaar involving legal action and with sanitary notification and cases of cholera and smallpox. The mission hospital dealt with sick natives from the bazaar and the surrounding villages. The third hospital was visited every Friday by the surgeon of the British regiment, and at this time Huntly saw 'a number of women who were well known to be prostitutes' (*ibid.*) going in and coming out again. They told Huntly that they went for examination, and the natives referred to the place as the Lock Hospital. It had never more than one or two in-patients, and these were prostitutes being treated for venereal disease. Huntly's complaints about this were known in Nusseerabad, and the surgeon who visited the Lock Hospital had 'chaffed' him for his views. By November 1892, when Huntly was writing to Dymock again, he had left Nusseerabad, but had returned to check up on the Lock Hospital. Things were going on as before, only the surgeon of the British regiment now visited the Lock Hospital on a Thursday. The only way to deal with this was to stop the special allowance given to the surgeon and to close the Lock Hospital. The women's attendance only appeared to be voluntary because (as Huntly had been told on very high authority, but unnamed, because he was told in private), although no direct pressure was put on the women, their only alternative if found diseased was to leave the cantonment directly. Huntly had also watched the soldiers regularly visiting the quarters of prostitutes, which were well known. Other Nusseerabad missionaries and 'many natives' (*ibid.*) would substantiate all this, he wrote.
53. F.C.G.A.P. & D., 1892, Report XXXIV, p.1. Although regulation was 'not in the least a party question', this report urged church members to question candidates in the forthcoming parliamentary election about their views on it (*ibid.*).
54. *Vide* G. Petrie: *op.cit.*, pp.266ff. and F.C.G.A.P. & D., 1893, Report XXXIII, pp.5ff.
55. F.C.G.A.P. & D., 1893, Report XXXIII, p.5.
56. *Ibid.*, p.9.
57. *Vide* G. Petrie: *op.cit.*, p.267.
58. U.P.S.P., 1894, p.193.
59. In the midst of all this, controversy had blown up over the Decennial Conference of Missionaries, which had met in Bombay in 1892-93. This body, to the dismay of abolitionists at home, had withdrawn its resolution condemning licensed vice in India. It seemed inexplicable. It was however explained to the U.P. Synod (U.P.S.P., 1893, p.189) in a letter from one of their medical missionaries, the Rev. Dr. J. Husband, which showed that the missionaries were not all like Dr. Huntly. Dr. Husband gave four reasons for withdrawal of the resolution: firstly, that the Conference was 'a consultative and not a deliberative body' (*ibid.*) and the Steering committee had decided against any resolutions; secondly, that 'half of the members were ladies, and many of them young ladies'; thirdly, that many of the missionaries had never lived in a cantonment and so to be asked 'to vote in a matter of which (they were) profoundly ignorant was neither fair nor Christian' (*ibid.*); and fourthly, that the medical missionaries were divided on the subject. Dr. Husband added that he believed that this last meant division on the medical rather than the moral aspects of it. He was sure that they all must agree on the latter. The 'official silence of the Conference'

still troubled the U.P. Committee, however, and, they added, opened the views of missionaries to 'misconstruction'.
They were, however, cheered to report that the South Indian Missionary Conference and the Bombay Conference of the Methodist Episcopal Church had subsequently resolved to condemn state-regulated vice.

60. U.P.S.P., 1895, p.204. (Interview in *Black and White*, September 1 1894.)

61. *Ibid.*, p.205.

62. The general had remarked, earlier in the interview (*ibid.*, p.204): ' . . . I greatly respect the motives of those who are diametrically opposed to me in this matter.'

63. *Ibid.*, p.205.

64. After the Mutiny the India Council, under the Viceroy, was made up of a (British) Executive Council, and about twelve other members, half of whom were British officials, the other half being Indian princes, nobles or administrators. The Council could consider only matters set before it. *Vide* P. Spear: *A History of India* vol.2, 1965, p.149.

65. U.P.S.P., 1895, p.204.

66. F.C.G.A.P. & D., 1895, Report XXXI, p.2.

67. *Ibid.*

68. *Ibid.*, p.3.

69. F.C.G.A.P.&D., 1896, Debates, p.52.

70. *Ibid.*

71. *Ibid.*, Report XXIX, p.2.

72. *Ibid.*, p.3.

73. *Ibid.*, p.2. The committee was quoting from a Memorandum of 1895. But similar sentiments had been expressed for some time by the Army Sanitary Commission.

74. *Ibid.*, p.4.

75. *Vide* U.P.S.P., 1895, p.206. Campbell-Bannerman had been referring to the 1892-93 report of the Army Sanitary Commission.

76. The former Viceroy of India.

77. F.C.G.A.P. & D., 1896, Debates, p.52.

78. *Ibid.*, Report XXIX, p.3.

79. *Ibid.*

80. In 1895, 522 in every 1,000 British soldiers in India had venereal disease, half of whom had syphilis. 3,200 of the total force of 71,000 were always totally disabled and many more partially disabled by venereal disease. Venereal disease represented about a third of the total amount of sickness at any one time in the Indian Army. *Vide* U.P.S.P., 1897, p.180.

81. *Ibid.*

82. *Ibid.*

83. *Ibid.*

84. *Ibid.*

85. *Ibid.*

86. *Ibid.*

87. *Ibid.*, p.181.

88. *Ibid.* The despatch also endorsed the suggestion of the Army Sanitary Commission that female hospital attendants should assist in examination of the women.

89. F.C.G.A.P. & D., 1897, Report XXIX, p.4.

90. *Ibid.*

91. *Ibid.*

92. The rate of rise in admissions in 1895 was only 11 per 1,000 compared with 45 per 1,000 in 1894 (*ibid.*).

93. The rate of admissions had decreased from 285 per 1,000 in 1885 to 173 per 1,000 in 1895 (*ibid.*, p.5).

94. *Ibid.*

95. *Ibid.*
96. *Ibid.*, p.4.
97. *Ibid.*, p.3. (More probably a misprint.)
98. *Ibid.*
99. *Ibid.*, p.8.
100. *Ibid.*
101. *Ibid.*
102. *Ibid.*, p.9.
103. *Ibid.*
104. *Ibid.*, p.10.
105. The committee stated that the proportion of married native troops was 'altogether otherwise' but gave no figure (*ibid.*).
106. *Ibid.* An Appendix to the report listed some alternative ways of dealing with the situation. These, taken from a memorandum of the British Committee of the International Abolitionist Federation, included recommendations that moral character should be made 'an important element in promotion' (*ibid.*, p.11) in the Army (as things were, 'habitual profligacy' was 'no impediment' (*ibid.*)); that venereal disease should be mentioned when a soldier was discharged (as things were, he could have had it and be discharged with an 'exemplary' character); and that the officers and regiment involved should be disciplined if they had a bad record in this respect.
107. F.C.G.A.P. & D., 1897, Debates, p.212.
108. Lord Elgin was later to be a member of the Royal Commission which reported on the Free Church case in 1905.
109. F.C.G.A.P. & D., 1897, Debates, p.213.
110. Lord Dunraven had raised the matter in terms of a motion for a more general enquiry into the effect of venereal disease on the Army and the civil and native population.
111. F.C.G.A.P. & D., Debates, p.213.
112. Mr. Dymock, apparently, was not acquainted with the religious opinions of Mr. Acton.
113. R.J. Godlee: *Lord Lister*, 1917, p.545.
114. *Ibid.* The seventy-year old surgeon to the Queen and founder of antiseptic surgery had been raised to the peerage in January of that year and did not speak in the Lords unless he felt deeply about the matter in hand. (His only other important speech there was made a year later, in support of the Vaccination Bill). Nor, with his Quaker background, did he talk lightly about Christianity. His earlier involvement in the stormy Scottish medical scene (where Simpson, who had had to battle with biblical texts against the opponents of painless childbirth, had been still active) and in other controversies of the period, had forced him to think deeply about the conflict between religion and science, leading him to the conclusion that there was 'no antagonism between the religion of Jesus Christ and any fact scientifically established' (R. Truax: *Joseph Lister*, 1947, p.114). He had, moreover, demonstrated the courage of his convictions when he refused Queen Victoria's request to make a public statement condemning vivisection. Neither his significance nor his sincerity could easily be questioned — nor for that matter his information, if as Godlee (*op.cit.*, p.545) claimed, Lister, 'impatient of inaccurate statements and loose arguments such as were often put forward by sentimentalists or enthusiasts', preparing for this speech, 'confirmed the opinion he had long held, by reference to documents and statistics and by a considerable correspondence'. His convictions were firm, and on this subject he 'continued to exercise his influence upon members of the Government in private' (*ibid.*).
115. F.C.G.A.P. & D., Debates, p.214.
116. *Ibid.*
117. *Ibid.*, p.215.
118. Chapman was intensely disliked by Josephine Butler, who described him as 'a dark evil-looking man, lean, dried up like a piece of old tree-trunk'. He also was 'a Plymouth

Brother and holds prayer-meetings' — *vide* G. Petrie: *op.cit.*, p.269.

119. F.C.G.A.P. & D., 1897, Debates, p.216. Only that morning, said Mr. Dymock, he had received a letter from a Highland minister, stating 'that he would rather do what he would to prevent young men from entering the Army when vice was treated as a necessity' (*ibid.*).

120. *Ibid.*

121. *Ibid.*, p.217.

122. *Ibid.* — such as had been outlined in Rainy's pamphlet on the subject, 'which he believed was still in circulation' (*ibid.*).

123. *Ibid.*

124. *Ibid.*, p.218.

125. *Ibid.*, p.217.

126. *Ibid.*, p.218.

127. *Ibid.*

128. He was one of the representatives of the Presbytery of Italy.

129. *Ibid.*, p.219.

130. *Ibid.*

131. *Ibid.*

132. *Ibid.*, p.220.

133. *Ibid.*

134. *Ibid.*

135. *Ibid.*

136. *Ibid.*

137. Colonel Thomas Cadell (b.1835) won his V.C. for 'bringing in wounded men under severe fire' in Delhi during the Mutiny. He subsequently entered the Political Department and served in Central India and Rajputana until he retired in 1892. *Vide* C.E. Buckland: *Dictionary of Indian Biography*, 1906, p.65. He was a member of the Free Church Committee on Presbyterian Chaplains in the Army and, from 1899, its convener.

138. F.C.G.A.P. & D., 1897, Debates, p.221.

139. *Ibid.*

140. *Ibid.*

141. *Ibid.*, p.222. Colonel Cadell may have known what the Indian Government had by now proposed, or he may simply have been referring to the older practices.

142. *Ibid.*

143. *Ibid.*

144. *Ibid.*

145. *Ibid.*

146. *Ibid.*, p.221.

147. *Ibid.*

148. *Vide* his autobiographical reflections: *Among Indian Rajahs and Ryots*, 1912, *passim.*

149. *Ibid.*, p.36. 'There is no one that is more sensitive, nor more observant, in regard to courtesy than the Indian gentleman' (*ibid.*).

150. *Ibid.*, p.91.

151. *Ibid.*

152. *Ibid.*, p.300.

153. *Ibid.*, p.277.

154. *Ibid.*

155. *Ibid.*

156. *Ibid.*

157. *Ibid.*

158. *Ibid.*, p.268.

159. *Ibid.*

160. He might of course have been thinking of some other example such as the part

played by missionaries in protecting the peasants from the indigo planters: *vide* M. Edwardes: *Bound to Exile*, 1969, pp.133ff.

161. Fraser: *op.cit.*, p.269.

162. *Acts of the General Assembly of the Free Church*, 1894-1898, p.538.

163. F.C.G.A.P. & D., 1898, Report XXVII, p.8. With some ingenuity this might just have been possible.

164. *Ibid.*, p.3. Lord George Hamilton, in his reply, was insistent upon this last point. He wished to see a copy of the warning and urged that it should be given to all troops on embarkation for India. He also insisted that the Indian Government should give 'a trial wherever possible' (*ibid.*, p.9) to the Army Sanitary Commission's recommendation that female hospital assistants should help with the examination of women for venereal disease. He disagreed with their contention that 'for the class of common prostitutes in India, with which we have mainly to do, it is an entirely unnecessary and in many respects unsuitable, provision' (*ibid.*, p.2).

165. Abolitionists might of course argue that pay-stoppage could lead to concealment of disease. B. Leppington (*op.cit.*, p.183) argued that this happened under the C.D. Acts when the admissions rate in the home army (1873-79) fell, during the period when pay-stoppage for V.D. hospitalisation was in force.

166. F.C.G.A.P. & D., 1898, Report XXVII, p.11.

167. *Ibid.*

168. *Ibid.* Such fears, it claimed, had also been expressed by a number of British missionaries in India, led by their own Mr. Campbell of Toondee; and the Directors of the London Missionary Society, as well as 'many societies and public meetings' (*ibid.*), had condemned the new Act and Rules.

169. *Ibid.*

170. *Ibid.*, Debates, p.222.

171. He made no mention of any earlier measures by the Indian Government.

172. 'Their reports,' Fraser remarked, 'contained some matter which may easily enough be turned to ridicule.' (*Ibid.*)

173. *Ibid.*

174. General Chapman.

175. *Ibid.*, p.223.

176. *Ibid.*

177. *Ibid.*, p.224.

178. *Ibid.*

179. *Ibid.*

180. *Ibid.*

181. *Ibid.*, Report XXVII, p.9.

182. Mr. Robert Simpson, a builder.

183. *Ibid.*, Debates, p.224.

184. He died the following February (1899). The generation which had fought the C.D. Acts was going: Stansfield died in 1898, and Josephine Butler, although she lingered on until 1906, was now less active.

185. A. Muir: *John White*, 1958, p.164.

186. F.C.G.A.P. & D., 1899, Debates, p.239.

187. *Ibid.*, Report XXVII, p.2.

188. U.P.S.P., 1898, p.201. Disturbing evidence had again been furnished by Dr. William Huntly, the U.P. medical missionary. Dr. Huntly had been running a lazar hospital in buildings leased from the Government for 25 years (following the closure of Government lock hospitals) for a nominal rent. When the new rules were issued he was asked if he would carry them out:

> I asked (he wrote) how they were to be construed, and received, to me, no satisfactory reply. I also pointed out that since the lock hospital had been closed, the mission

hospital had been treating any poor woman with the disease, who came, and would continue to treat them, but that any examination of the woman because she was a prostitute, with a view to discovering disease, was out of the question. A short time after this a notice was served on the mission that the Government would take over the building in which was our mission after six months ... The old lock hospital had been cleaned up, servants, etc., put in, and a British surgeon attached to the Army (appointed) (*ibid.*).

189. *Ibid.*

190. *Ibid.*, p.202.

191. U.P.S.P., 1899, p.185.

192. *Ibid.*

193. U.P.S.P., 1900, p.156.

194. *Ibid.* It was curious that this should be opposed, since its introduction had apparently been designed as a measure to reassure abolitionists. On the subject of 'vice at home' (*ibid.*) the committee found it 'difficult to speak with certainty' but found 'evidence of the prevalence of immorality' in 'the increase in the number of divorce cases, and the amount of organised profligacy of the streets' (*ibid.*).

195. *Ibid.*

196. *Ibid.*

197. F.C.G.A.P. & D., 1900, Report XXVII, *passim.*

198. U.F.C.G.A.P. & D., 1901, Report XXV, p.3. The report also noted further opposition in India to the employment of female hospital assistants in examining women for V.D. Any employee of the Lady Dufferin Fund who engaged in it faced immediate dismissal.

199. Mr. D.M. Traill, an ex-Indian member unsympathetic to the Dymock line.

200. U.F.C.G.A.P. & D., 1902, Report XXIV, p.2.

201. U.F.C.G.A.P. & D., 1901, Report XXIV, p.1.

202. *Ibid.*

203. The committee's last report (U.F.C.G.A.P. & D., 1902, Report XXIV, p.1) recorded the death of the Earl of Moray, an 'uncompromising' opponent of State Regulation, who was 'one of the committee's most valued members'. His death, following Dymock's, may have weakened the committee's position.

204. *Vide* C. of S.G.A. Reports, 1891-99, Committee on Foreign Missions, and Women's Association for Foreign Missions, *passim.*

205. C. of S.G.A.Reports, 1891, p.268 (Colonial Committee).

206. C. of S.G.A.Reports, 1896, p.325 (Colonial Committee).

207. Some concessions were made: *vide* C. of S.G.A. Reports, 1899, pp.372ff. (Colonial Committee). In 1891 the Free Church protested to the War Office that Presbyterian chaplains to the Army and Navy were always either Church of Scotland or Irish Presbyterian ministers. The War Office asked the Church of Scotland Assembly for advice and the latter, pointing out that the Free Church was not excluded (its ministers in various places such as Malta and Gibraltar were the only, albeit part-time chaplains), and that the system was not, as the Free Church claimed, breaking down, recommended that, if as was advisable the number of full-time Government-paid chaplains was increased, a proportion of the additional chaplains might be Free churchmen. *Vide* C. of S.G.A.R., 1892, pp.353ff. (Special Report on Army and Navy Chaplains). Here also some concessions were made by the Government. *Vide* C. of S.G.A.R., 1896, p.314 (Colonial committee).

208. F.C.G.A.P. & D., 1897, Debates, p.220.

209. F.C.G.A.P. & D., 1889, Report XXXII, p.2, which mentions some such Act in Victoria, Queensland, New Zealand, Tasmania and Cape Colony. Canada (*ibid.*, p.3) had just reintroduced regulation.

210. Assisted by grants from the Gospel Purity Association and others (*ibid.*).

211. Canada was not included among the list of regulationist self-governing Colonies in

the 1895 Report. *Vide* F.C.G.A.P. & D., 1895, Report XXXI, p.5.

212. F.C.G.A.P. & D., 1896, Report XXIX, p.4.

213. *Ibid.*

214. *Ibid.*

215. Little progress, from the abolitionist point of view, was made in Australia, where C.D. type Acts were on the Statute Book, although sometimes kept in abeyance: *vide* F.C.G.A.P. & D., 1896, Report XXIX, p.5. An Act for South Australia was proposed around 1897: *vide* U.P.S.P., 1897, p.181. (Victoria was the only other regulationist Australian state mentioned in this report.)

216. *Vide* U.F.C.G.A.P. & D., 1901, Report XXV, p.2.

217. *Vide* F.C.G.A.P. & D., 1892, Report XXXIV, p.2.

218. F.C.G.A.P. & D., 1896, Report XXIX, p.5.

219. F.C.G.A.P. & D., 1897, Debates, p.213.

220. *Ibid.*

221. F.C.G.A.P. & D., 1896, Report XXIX, p.5.

222. F.C.G.A.P. & D., 1900, Report XXVII, p.1.

223. *Vide ibid*: 'The events of the Transvaal War have tested in the eyes of all the nations the quality of the soldiers now gathered from all parts of the British Empire to serve their Queen and country; and it is not too much to say that the heroism, endurance and loyalty of all the officers and men rallied round our national flag have earned not only the gratitude of their countrymen, but the admiration of the world.'

224. *Vide* U.P.S.P., 1900, p.156: 'This is a war which all must deplore, since it is waged between two peoples having so much in common . . . To all appearance the war must be waged to the bitter end; but with the triumph of our arms let us hope and pray that an honourable peace may be established, and that with its establishment the two peoples may come to entertain for each other mutual respect, and live together in the enjoyment of equal rights.' (But Rainy, for one, had initially been against the war — *vide* P.C. Simpson: *op.cit.*, vol.ii, p.281.)

225. U.F.C.G.A.P. & D., 1902, Report XXIV, p.1.

226. *Ibid.*

227. U.F.C.G.A.P. & D., 1901, Report XXV, p.2.

228. F.C.G.A.P. & D., 1888, Report XXXII, p.3.

229. There (*ibid.*) 'the regulations seem free from some of the objectionable features found elsewhere'.

230. *Ibid.*

231. *Ibid.*

232. U.P.S.P., 1889, p.340.

233. F.C.G.A.P. & D., 1890, Report XXXVII, p.2.

234. *Ibid.*

235. F.C.G.A.P. & D., 1893, Report XXXIII, p.10.

236. *Ibid.*

237. *Ibid.*

238. F.C.G.A.P. & D., 1895, Report XXXI, p.1.

239. *Ibid.* This was illustrated by remarks in a letter of 1891, from the Resident of Perak to Lord Knutsford, which had described prostitutes as 'a necessary evil' whose 'calling supplies a public want' (*ibid.*).

240. In an addendum to its 1895 report the committee noted (*ibid.*, p.7) that 'information has come to hand which seems to show, beyond question, that, in the Straits Settlements, the directions of the Colonial Secretary are being grossly set at nought'. It promised investigation by the British Committee of the International Abolitionist Federation.

241. F.C.G.A.P. & D., 1896, Debates, p.52 and Report XXIX, p.7.

242. F.C.G.A.P. & D., 1889, Report XXXII, p.3.

243. F.C.G.A.P. & D., 1895, Report XXXI, p.5.
244. U.F.C.G.A.P. & D., 1901, Debates, p.271.
245. F.C.G.A.P. & D., 1895, Report XXXI, p.6.
246. *Ibid.*
247. F.C.G.A.P. & D., 1896, Debates, p.52.
248. *Vide* U.P.S.P., 1896, p.189.
249. F.C.G.A.P. & D., 1897, Report XXIX, p.2.
250. *Ibid.* (1897 was the year of Queen Victoria's Diamond Jubilee.)
251. F.C.G.A.P. & D., 1898, Debates, p.227.
252. Romans, Ch.13, v.14. Almost the only scriptural text quoted by the Assembly and Synod committees in the C.D.A. debate: *vide*, e.g., F.C.G.A.P. & D., 1895, Report XXXI, p.3.
253. The Synod sent representatives, for example, to the 1898 Congress which was held in London. *Vide* U.P.S.P., 1899, p.185.
254. For example, to the 1888 and 1890 Congresses which were held in Copenhagen and Stockholm respectively. *Vide* F.C.G.A.P. & D., 1889, Report XXXII, p.4., and 1890, Report XXXVII, p.2.
255. *Vide* F.C.G.A.P. & D., 1890, Report XXXVII, p.1.
256. *Vide* F.C.G.A.P. & D., 1892, Report XXXIV, p.2.
257. *Vide* U.P.S.P., 1892, p.142.
258. *Vide* F.C.G.A.P. & D., 1895, Report XXXI, p.6.
259. *Vide* F.C.G.A.P. & D., 1896, Report XXIX, p.6.
260. *Vide* F.C.G.A.P. & D., 1899, Report XXVII, p.1.
261. F.C.G.A.P. & D., 1891, Report XXXVII, p.1.
262. *Ibid.*
263. F.C.G.A.P. & D., 1892, Report XXXIV, p.2.
264. *Ibid.*
265. F.C.G.A.P. & D., 1891, Report XXXVII, p.1.
266. F.C.G.A.P. & D., 1892, Report XXXIV, p.3.
267. F.C.G.A.P. & D., 1895, Report XXXI, p.6. 'The voice of that Church,' the Committee prophesied, 'may soon be heard in the most emphatic way' (*ibid.*).
268. *Ibid.*, p.1.
269. F.C.G.A.P. & D., 1897, Report XXIX, p.2.
270. F.C.G.A.P. & D., 1889, Report XXXII, p.4.
271. F.C.G.A.P. & D., 1890, Report XXXVII, p.1.
272. F.C.G.A.P. & D., 1891, Report XXXVII, p.1.
273. *Ibid.*, p.2.
274. F.C.G.A.P. & D., 1892, Report XXXIV, p.3.
275. *Ibid.*
276. F.C.G.A.P. & D., 1895, Report XXXI, p.5.
277. F.C.G.A.P. & D., 1891, Report XXXVII, p.2.
278. F.C.G.A.P. & D., 1895, Report XXXI, p.6.
279. F.C.G.A.P. & D., 1896, Debates, p.53.
280. *Ibid.*, Report XXIX, p.6.
281. *Ibid.*, p.7.
282. U.P.S.P., 1896, p.189.
283. F.C.G.A.P. & D., 1897, Report XXIX, p.1.
284. *Ibid.*
285. Reference was also made: in 1892, to Germany, France, Belgium and other countries where 'there are very hopeful appearances, yet of actual achievement there is little to record' (F.C.G.A.P. & D., 1892, Report XXXIV, p.3); in 1893, to new legislation in preparation in Norway, Finland, and Denmark, providing 'for the better protection of the young, and for the repression of vice' — but not doing away with compulsory examination

and thus unacceptable to 'genuine abolitionists'. In Holland on the other hand the Minister of the Interior was expected to propose repeal of compulsory examination — and while this would not amount to complete abolition, it was acceptable, since the regulation system 'could hardly survive such a loss' (F.C.G.A.P. & D., 1893, Report XXXIII, p.2); in 1895, to 'the suppression of every trace of the regulation of prostitution in the Swiss Canton of Zürich, to withdrawal of a proposal for regulation in the Canton of Vaud ('owing in large measure to the splendid stand made by the women of the Canton') and to proposed legislation in Norway, brought forward in the interests of morality, but in which 'intelligent friends of our cause' detected 'a surrender of anti-regulation principles, and hence opposed' (F.C.G.A.P. & D., 1895, Report XXXI, pp.5ff). Norway also disgraced itself in the Committee's eyes by having 'a purity society, composed entirely of women, pleading "for the compulsory examination of their poor sisters," etc!' (*ibid.*, p.6); in 1896, to Colmar (where that year's Congress was being held), which was the only town in Germany without regulation, even though it was a military centre; and to New York, where an 'Anti-Vice Society' had proposed regulationist legislation (F.C.G.A.P. & D., 1896, Report XXIX, pp.6ff.).

286. F.C.G.A.P. & D., 1896, Debates, p.52.

287. *Vide* F.C.G.A.P. & D., 1892, Report XXXIV, p.2.

288. By 'a Committee of Belgian officials, acting under the sanction of the Belgian Government' — according to B. Leppington: *op.cit.*, p.171.

289. The list comprised (F.C.G.A.P. & D., 1900, Report XXVII, p.2) Germany, Austria, Bosnia, Brazil, Bulgaria, Chile, Denmark, Spain, the U.S.A., France, Great Britain, Honduras, Hungary, Italy, Japan, Mexico, Norway, Paraguay, Persia, Peru, Holland, the Argentine Republic, Roumania, Russia, Servia, Sweden, Switzerland and Belgium.

290. *Ibid.*

291. In Tokyo, a newcomer to the Free Church's repertoire, there were (*ibid.*) '7,000 women segregated to a life of vice' under Government control.

292. *Ibid.* Sir Jonathan Hutchinson (1828-1913), Surgeon to the London Hospital, was well known for his research on syphilis and leprosy (*vide* D. Guthrie: *A History of Medicine*, 1958 ed., p.329). According to B. Leppington (*op.cit.*, p.180), Hutchinson, in his speech,

> deprecated panic and exaggeration; and pointed out that the disease was not increasing but diminishing in England, and that hereditary syphilis in particular was becoming rare among the educated classes, as men were warned by their doctors not to marry till completely cured. The same ideas would gradually permeate all classes. He agreed as to the importance of warning young men in schools and colleges. He thought a better tone was already asserting itself among medical students and other young men of that class. Dissolute habits were no longer considered inseparable from Army life. Men enlisted young and left the Army early, and they might reasonably be expected to keep straight from eighteen to twenty-seven. The effect would develop character, temperance and industry. If the matter were put before them in a reasonable way, he was certain the men would respond, and that would do more to reduce disease in the Army than all the regulations that could be devised.

293. *British Medical Journal*, September 16, 1899. Quoted in F.C.G.A.P. & D., 1900, Report XXVII, p.3.

294. Jean-Alfred Fournier (1832-1914) was director of the Saint-Louis Hospital in Paris, and 'wrote extensively on the clinical and social aspects of his subject' (syphilis) (*vide* D. Guthrie: *op.cit.*, p.384).

295. F.C.G.A.P. & D., 1900, Report XXVII, p.3.

296. *Ibid.* The reference is to Mark, Chapter 11, verses 30-33.

297. Not even the evangelical Acton had suggested that regulation was comparable to the baptism of John.

298. This was reaffirmed by Professor Alexander Hislop, Joint-Convener of the U.P.

committee when commenting on the conference and on the marked decrease in the Army's venereal disease rate (in Britain) since repeal of the C.D. Acts: (U.F.C.G.A.P. & D., 1901, Debates, p.201) 'the legalising of vice is always wrong. It is a crime against women. It breaks down in immoral men the checks of self-restraint and conscience. If the state cannot repress profligacy, it should not go to the opposite extreme, and provide securities beforehand against the consequences of immorality. Rather should it so adjust the theatre of life as to make virtue easy and vice difficult.' *Vide* also *ibid.*, Report XXV, p.2.

299. U.F.C.G.A.P. & D., 1901, Report XXV, p.3.

300. The U.P. and Free Church committees each already had a sub-committee working with the other. (*Vide* F.C.G.A.P. & D., 1897, Report XXIX, p.2.)

301. U.F.C.G.A.P. & D., 1901, Report XXV, p.3.

302. *Vide* Henriques: *op.cit.*, pp.284ff.

303. *Vide* Acts of the General Assembly of the United Free Church of Scotland, 1900-1904, pp.560 and 709.

304. U.F.C.G.A.P. & D., 1913, Report V, p.15.

305. *Ibid.*

306. *Ibid.*, p.16.

307. *Ibid.*

308. *Ibid.* According to a report from the Edinburgh Chief Constable, this was particularly necessary in the case of 'girls, many of them scarcely out of their teens', who, when the Fleet was in the Forth, could 'be seen, some of them to all appearance the worse of drink, going arm in arm with the sailors, singing and dancing as they go along, and conducting themselves in such a manner as to suggest to the onlooker that they have lost all sense of maidenhood' (*ibid.*). He complained that 'the police have no remedy, and all they can do is to see that the peace is not disturbed, and arrest any who may become obstreperous' (*ibid.*).

309. *Ibid.*, p.17. The Glasgow School Board had recently decided to do this, and the United States, Canada, Australia, Germany and France had set a good example.

310. *Ibid.*

311. U.F.C.G.A.P. & D., 1914, Report VI, p.3.

312. *Ibid.*

313. U.F.C.G.A.P. & D., 1915, Report VI, p.11. The committee had however received 'gratifying testimony to their usefulness . . . from many quarters, including Old Calabar'.

314. U.F.C.G.A.P. & D., 1913, Report V, p.17.

315. *Ibid.*

316. *Ibid.*, p.18. This was the first occasion on which a church committee mentioned the existence of *European* prostitutes in India.

317. *Ibid.*

318. He spoke, however, in the debate on the report of the Temperance committee (*ibid.*, Debates, pp.174ff.), where once again he asked for a more sympathetic attitude to the Government of India (here in connection with the opium trade); in support of giving more money for Foreign Missions (*ibid.*, pp.210ff.); and in favour of trusting the church's leaders in negotiating with the Church of Scotland (*ibid.*, pp.260ff.).

319. U.F.C.G.A., 1914, Reports, VI, p.4.

320. U.F.C.G.A., 1917, Debates, p.236.

321. *Vide* U.F.C.G.A., 1915, Reports, VI, p.7. The number of baptisms had been decreasing since 1897 in all of the Scottish Churches except the Roman Catholic Church — whose baptisms had risen by nearly 15 per cent.

322. In the event, the committee later discovered, baptisms had been decreasing at more than twice the rate of births. *Vide* U.F.C.G.A., 1916, Reports, VI, p.1.

323. *Vide* U.F.C.G.A., 1915, Reports, VI, p.8.

324. U.F.C.G.A., 1916, Report XXXII, p.4 — 'for the saving of infant life has been much more common in such circles through the operation of maternity and child welfare

schemes'. (*Ibid.*).

325. *Ibid.*, p.5.

326. The Commission (U.F.C.G.A., 1917, Reports, XXVIII, p.8) 'was representative of the Clergy, the Medical Profession (including Women Doctors), Statisticians, Publicists and others'. Although 'privately appointed', some Government officers served on it, and this, and a promise by the Prime Minister 'to regard its work as of value', gave it 'semi-official recognition'.

327. Fertility was rising in Ireland, except in Ulster. Over the 'last few years' it had risen from 36.1 to 37.0 (per 1,000 of the population), whereas in England and Wales it had decreased from 28.4 to 24.7 and in Scotland from 33.4 to 29.7. The birth-rate among miners was twice that among doctors. (*Vide ibid.*, p.9.)

328. *Ibid.*

329. *Ibid.*, p.10.

330. *Ibid.*

331. *Ibid.* The Commission also recommended 'a fairer distribution of the burden of parenthood between the mother and the father' (*ibid.*).

332. *Ibid.*, p.11.

333. *Ibid.*, p.12.

334. This remark suggests a growth rather than a decline in reticence in the church's attitude since the nineteenth century, when committees used to urge forthright pulpit proclamations on purity. Perhaps birth control was regarded as a more delicate subject.

335. *Ibid.*, p.13.

336. *Ibid.* '"Be fruitful and multiply and replenish the earth",' the committee declared, 'is one of the Creator's oldest commands to his creatures, and while it is old it is not antiquated, nor has it been abrogated.' (*Ibid.*, p.14.) The committee was to some extent concerned with replenishing the earth after the loss of life in the war. The next section of its report (*ibid.*, pp.15ff.), dealing with infant mortality and the welfare of mothers and children, was entitled 'Saving the Infants' and began (*ibid.*, p.15): 'Under impetus of the appalling loss of manhood by the war, the certainty of a further diminution in the rate of births, and the necessity for the maintenance of the British race for the homeland and our far-flung dominions, there has been an increasing interest in the subject of Infantile Mortality and the Welfare of Mothers and Children.'

337. *Ibid.*, p.11.

338. U.F.C.G.A., 1917, Reports, VI, *passim.*

339. U.F.C.G.A., 1918, Reports, VI, p.6.

340. *Ibid.*, p.7. (This was a quotation from 'a recent article on the question' of which the committee approved.)

341. U.F.C.G.A., 1919, Debates, p.244.

342. U.F.C.G.A., 1918, Reports, XXIII, p.9.

343. U.F.C.G.A., 1919, Debates, p.244.

344. *Ibid.*

345. C. of S.G.A., 1917, Reports, p.535.

346. C. of S.G.A., 1918, Reports, p.292.

347. C. of S.G.A., 1920, Reports, p.339.

348. *Ibid.*

349. *Ibid.*

350. *Social Evils and Problems*, ed. W.P. Paterson and D. Watson, 1918.

351. *Ibid.*, pp.65ff. The paper began with the customary reference to the difficulty and urgency of the problem. ('While we are clearing our throats and casting about for language of sufficient delicacy and reserve the cradle and the grave are being flooded with corruption' — *ibid.*, p.66.) It then discussed historical aspects of impurity. (Although the Reformers and their successors had some successes, 'the baptismal and session records of the Church down to the present day show how lax and depressing a view our people have

taken of the sacred duty of sexual purity' — *ibid.*) It turned to self-abuse (i.e. masturbation, citing Mark 7:21 and Matthew 7:28 and declaring that the church had to 'persuade our youth to honour their own bodily members, and remember that even these are not their own to do with as they please' — *ibid*, p.68); and to the idea that continence was harmful to health. ('To science it is absurd. To religion it is blasphemous. To innocent youth it brings a shameful temptation. To the sexually guilty it supplies a moral anaesthetic. And from married life it withdraws restraint and chivalry, defrauding it even of that secondary motive and sanction . . . "It is better to marry than to burn" (1 Cor. vii.9)' — The church had to 'denounce and discredit' the 'sinister plausibility of this idea' — *ibid.*) The paper then dealt with *Impurity and Marriage* ('Health and happiness' could 'be wrecked by excess, by parental evasion, by recourse to unnatural methods of preventing conception and by abortion however early induced' — *ibid.*, p.69); *Impurity and Pre-Nuptial Relations* (the latter, although in some districts 'the survival of an ancient rural instinct to make sure of fertility before entering marriage' could no longer be explained so charitably — *ibid.*, p.70); *Impurity and Divorce or Separation* (records of divorce and separation showed that adultery was 'only too evident' — *ibid.* — and 'the publicity given by the press to the sordid evidence adduced, and the shameless illustrations of adultery and free love which form the stock-in-trade of "problem" novelists and playwrights, deserve the sternest condemnation' — *ibid.*, p.71); and *Impurity and Illegitimacy* (where a falling illegitimacy rate at last cheered Professor Curtis up, but only momentarily — in view of the tendency of illegitimacy 'to perpetuate itself' it was a 'wonder . . . that a percentage so serious in each generation does not increase' — *ibid.*, p.75). The paper then dealt with *Impurity and Prostitution* and *Impurity and Disease*. These were followed by *Impurity and its Crimes* (a set of statistics showing statistics of proceedings against and convictions for various crimes from rape to bigamy from 1898 to 1915); *Impurity and Economic Loss* (the cost of hospital and other services, mainly in connection with V.D.); *Impurity and Alcohol* ('Wine or beer may, indeed, be more dangerous than spirits as a stimulus to this form of sin, for it preserves longer the illusion of self-control, and gives longer opportunity for the cumulative influence of sensual temptation' — *ibid.*, p.86. This presumably was why the Scots were not even worse than they were.); *Impurity and Housing* (mainly overcrowding, shared beds, etc.); and *Impurity and the Church's Duty* (to 'look at the facts, and listen to their appeal, and let her voice be heard' — *ibid.*, p.89).

352. *Ibid.*, p.76.

353. *Ibid.*

354. *Ibid.*

355. *Ibid.*, p.77.

356. *Ibid.*, p.76.

357. Abraham Flexner: *Prostitution in Europe*, 1914 (references above to the same author and title are to the abridged 1919 edition).

358. *Social Evils and Problems*, p.77.

359. *Ibid.*, p.79. In the course of his paper Curtis had of course noted the connection between prostitution and alcohol, commenting that 'at their lowest their (prostitutes') condition is so physically revolting that it is inconceivable that without the blinding influence of drink they can be attractive to any man' (*ibid.*).

360. *Ibid.*, p.83.

361. *Ibid.*, p.84.

362. *Ibid.*, p.83.

363. At least according to Professor Blaschko, the German venereologist. *Vide* H.C. Fischer and E.X. Dubois: *Sexual Life during the World War*, 1937, p.373.

364. *Ibid.*, Chs. XII and XIII.

365. *Ibid.*

366. *Social Evils and Problems* also contained a paper, by the Revd. Dr. Norman Maclean, on *The Decreasing Birthrate* (*op. cit.*, pp.93ff). It made much the same points as

U.F. reports, emphasising the decrease among the middle classes and those on whom the churches depended for membership and finance. It blamed 'the withering blight' of 'neo-Malthusianism' (*ibid.*, p.98), venereal disease, landlords, and, fundamentally, loss of 'the sense of the sacredness of life' (*ibid.*, p.102). As a result of the war, it argued, 'the Wastage of the War has to be Replaced', 'the Wastage of Disease will be Increased' (*ibid.*, p.103), and 'the Empire must be Peopled' (*ibid.*, p.104 — 'If Australia and New Zealand are not occupied by the British, the yellow man cannot be shut out'). Possible remedies by the state included a ban on the manufacture and sale of contraceptives, improved health and housing measures, and tax relief for larger families. For its part the church should give more 'definite teaching' on contraception — otherwise 'the future of the race must lie with the Roman Catholic Church'. It should also pronounce God's judgement on sin, and teach the sacredness of life. The alternative, as in Greece, Rome and France, was racial suicide.

367. C. of S.G.A., 1944, Reports, p.281.
368. C. of S.G.A., 1945, Reports, p.279.
369. C. of S.G.A., 1946, Reports, p.326.
370. *Ibid.*
371. *Ibid.*

Chapter fifteen

1. 'English' was so frequently used as a synonym for 'British', especially by U.P.s, but also by Free churchmen, that it would be pedantic not to use it here.
2. *Vide* F.C.G.A.P. & D., 1897, Debates, p.220.
3. *Vide* F.C.G.A.P. & D., 1891, Report XXXVII, p.5.
4. Regulation 33B was in fact used sparingly, and of those notified under it only half were compelled to attend for examination and very few indeed were prosecuted. The great majority of those notified were women, but some men were also notified (in 1944 at least, *Vide* R.S. Morton: *op.cit.*, p.31).
5. I.e., if Godlee (*op.cit.*) is to be believed. A. Comfort (in *The Anxiety Makers,* 1968 ed., p.148) suggests that prior to 1914 'advocacy of licensing on the one hand and of prophylaxis on the other was limited to eccentrics', and that the profession as a whole was silent, preferring to leave things as they were. But unless Lister and Grainger Stewart *were* regarded as eccentrics, or unless it is stretching the meaning of licensing too far, the fact that they were willing to express the opinions they did, in the House of Lords, and more, in the Free Assembly, suggests that they probably were conscious of considerable support for their views among their colleagues. There were of course also, as Josephine Butler observed (*op.cit.*, p.12), 'among the men who gradually rallied around us . . . from all ranks and all professions, pure hearted physicians . . . among the foremost, both in action and in indignant denunciation of the theories and practices which we abhorred'.
6. Some comments recorded in *The Army and Religion* (*op.cit.*, pp.143ff.) support this impression and suggest that military behaviour had not changed very much since Tait had condemned it nearly a century earlier. An 'officer in an East of Scotland regiment': '"Impurity . . . is the rule in the Army; purity the exception. The opinion of Society on these matters, judging from my experience in the Army, I should say is frankly pagan, and not Christian at all"' (*ibid.*, p.144). A 'minister, a hut worker at a base in France': '"It is to be regretted that in so many cases there is a distinct laxity in this connection among the higher authorities, due to the notion that immorality is natural and inevitable, and the only thing to do is to try to minimise the ill effects on the military efficiency of the men"' (*ibid.*, p.145). A 'chaplain of wide experience': some of his colleagues '"were very distressed by the callous matter of coarseness of public opinion among the officers as to pre-marital continence"'; this view was '"accompanied, I think, increasingly by the opinion that a State licensed system is the best practical and public solution of the problem"'. This chaplain added that '"There is very little knowledge of the cruelty of the prostitution system. Men who would not seduce a girl will accept the fact of prostitutes being *there* for

their use"' (*ibid.*, p.153). *Sexual Life During the World War* (*op.cit.*, pp.345ff.) records the view of the British General Crozier:

> My job was to provide food for cannon and good food at that. Far better to eradicate the cause — war itself — than to build up false hopes that it can be waged in any other way than by brute force and brutal means. I go so far as to say that free love in discretion for many of the celibates of both sexes, engaged in war work between 1914 and 1918, was as inevitable as the rising and setting of the sun.

Following the Armistice Crozier addressed his colonels:

> The men have evidently gone woman-mad . . . The venereal sick rate is mounting. Many women must be diseased. I hear the Germans let the diseased women out of prison the day we arrived. It was an offence for a French woman to give a German venereal, for which she was locked up, for the protection of the soldiers, of course! As the Army is now returning to England by degrees it is essential that, so far as is possible, we protect the women at home by returning the men clean. You must lecture your men on the subject and provide every convenient and reliable means of protection and sterilization. I will see the mayor about the detention of the women and their treatment and segregation (*ibid.*).

Part three

1. The Marriage Law Defence Union: *Tracts*, 1884, Tract VIII, 'What the Presbyterians say'.
2. *Vide* J.R. Fleming: *op.cit.* vol i, p.257.
3. Milligan was Professor of Divinity and Biblical Criticism at Aberdeen. The other Church of Scotland signatories were T.J. Crawford (Professor of Divinity, Edinburgh), W. Stevenson (Divinity and Church History, Edinburgh), A.F. Mitchell (Ecclesiastical History, St. Andrews), N. Christie (Divinity and Church History, Aberdeen), W. Lee (Church History, Glasgow), J. Macrae (minister of Hawick), Robert Nisbet (minister of West St. Giles' parish, Edinburgh), and K.M. Phin (an influential ecclesiastical bureaucrat).
4. R.S. Candlish, who was also minister of Free St. George's, Edinburgh, had led the Free Church Assembly since Chalmers' death in 1847. He died in 1873, handing on the leadership to Rainy. His son, J.S. Candlish, was a professor in the Glasgow Free Church college from 1872 to 1897.
5. Marriage Law Defence Union: *op.cit.*, Tract VIII, p.26.

Chapter sixteen

1. The collateral line, i.e. descended from a common ancestor by a different line. The Roman computation of degrees of relationship involved counting from one of the parties back to the common ancestor and thence to the other party. A man was thus related to his female first cousin, for example, in the fourth degree, and to his female second cousin in the sixth degree.
2. *Vide* Matthew, 19:3-9, etc.
3. *Circa* 540-604 A.D.
4. *Vide* T.A. Lacey (ed. R.C. Mortimer): *Marriage in Church and State*, 1947, pp.113ff.
5. *Ibid.*, p.117.
6. The German method of computation differed from the Roman in that it did not count back from one party to the common ancestor and thence to the other party, but only back to the common ancestor, from whichever of the parties was the farther removed therefrom. A man was thus related to his female first cousin, for example, in the second degree, and to his female second cousin in the third degree. (Under Roman Law these were the fourth and sixth degrees.)
7. 1 Corinthians, 6:16.
8. In the *Institutes*: IV, XIX, 37, Calvin alluded scornfully to the 'mire' which the

church had got into in its handling of matrimonial cases.

9. In Calvin's view the First Table comprised the 1st. to 4th. commandments, and the Second, the 5th. to 10th. Augustine's opinion, that the First Table comprised only the 1st. to 3rd. commandments, so 'that believers might learn to worship God in the Trinity, and thus adore God in three persons' was 'frivolous' (Calvin: *Harmony*, (1854 Translation), vol.III, p.6.). It also enabled Calvin to include Sabbath Observance (the fourth commandment) among the vertical rather than the horizontal ones, and thus to reinforce its importance over against those who argued that Sabbath Observance was Judaistic — *vide*: *Institutes*, II, VIII, 33.

10. *Harmony*, Vol.I, p.xvii (Calvin's Preface.) According to Calvin, the moral law 'is contained under two heads, one of which simply commands us to worship God with pure faith and piety; the other, to embrace men with sincere affection' (*ibid.*).

11. *Institutes*, II, VII, 14.

12. *Ibid.*, II, VII, 16.

13. *Ibid.*, IV, XX, 15.

14. *Harmony*, Vol.III, p.97. Calvin instanced brother-sister marriages among the Egyptians, who were (*ibid.*) 'so dead to shame, that they were carried away by their lusts to trample upon all the laws of nature'.

15. *Ibid.* p.102.

16. *Ibid.*

17. *Ibid.*

18. *Ibid.*

19. *Ibid.*

20. *Ibid*, p.99.

21. *Ibid.*

22. *Ibid.*, p.100.

23. *Ibid.*

24. *Ibid.*, p.99.

25. *Ibid.*, p.105.

26. *Ibid.*, p.103.

27. *Ibid.*

28. *Ibid.*

29. Calvin makes much the same points when dealing with this passage at another point in the same commentary (*ibid*, pp.177ff.). In defence of his argument about the meaning of 'brother', he adds here that (*ibid.*, p.178)

> if any should object that it is not probable that other kinsmen should dwell together, I reply that this passage is improperly supposed to refer to actual living together, as if they dwelt in the same house, but that the precept is merely addressed to relations, whose near residence rendered it convenient to take the widows to their own homes; for if any lived far away, liberty was accorded to both to seek the fulfillment of the provision elsewhere. Surely it is not probable that God would have authorised an incestuous marriage, which he had before expressed His abomination of.

30. Ruth, 1-4.

31. Calvin: *Harmony*, III, p.104. It is interesting to compare this comment with Calvin's treatment of this story (Genesis, Chapter 38) in his *Commentaries on Genesis*. In the latter (1850 translation, Vol.II, pp.275ff.) Calvin is highly critical of the whole episode and especially of Judah's part in it. However, he remarks on verse 8 (*ibid.*, p.281):

> Although no law had hitherto been prescribed concerning brothers' marriages, that the surviving brother should raise up seed to one who was dead; it is nevertheless, not wonderful that, by the mere instinct of nature, men should have been inclined to this course. For since each man is born for the preservation of the whole race, if any one dies without children, there seems to be here some defect of nature. It was deemed therefore an act of humanity to acquire some name for the dead, from which it might

appear that they had lived.

This act, wrote Calvin, 'does not proceed from any rule of piety, yet the Lord had impressed it on the hearts of man as a duty of humanity; as he afterwards commanded it to the Jews in their polity'. With this last phrase Calvin inserted a reservation about the universal application of this 'duty of humanity' in the particular form mentioned, yet there is some inconsistency in all this, which is compounded by Calvin's criticism of Onan for his 'outrageous act of barbarity in denying seed to his brother'.

32. Calvin: *Harmony*, Vol.III, p.104.

33. Calvin prefers this to 'nakedness' because it showed the filthiness and shamefulness of the act (*vide: ibid.*, p.99).

34. *Ibid.*, p.104.

35. *Ibid.*, p.105.

36. *Ibid.*

37. *Ibid.*, p.105.

38. *Vide*, e.g., *Institutes*, III, XIX, 15; and IV, XX, 14,15.

39. *Harmony*, vol.III, p.106.

40. *Vide*: C. of S.G.A.R., 1909, p.1271, citing the *Book of the Universal Kirk*.

41. *Ibid.*

42. *Ibid.*

43. *The Confession of Faith*, 1647.

44. C. of S.G.A.R., 1909, pp.1272, 1273.

45. On this and subsequent legislation mentioned in this section, *vide* Lacey (ed. Mortimer): *Marriage in Church and State*, 1947, *passim*; R. Haw: *The State of Matrimony*, 1952, *passim*; and C.F. Behrman: 'The Annual Blister', in *Victorian Studies*, Vol.XI, No.4, June 1968, pp.483ff.

46. Lacey, *op.cit.*, p.157.

47. *Vide* Behrman: *op.cit.*, p.492.

48. *Marriage Law Defence Tracts: 1884*, pp. viff.

Chapter seventeen

1. *Vide* C. of S.G.A. Commission, May 28 1839. The reference was to a case in which Robert Lauder, who had married his deceased wife's sister Margaret Farlane, appealed from his kirk session to the Presbytery of Stirling for admission to church privileges. The presbytery referred the matter to the Assembly, whose Commission for the reasons given, stated that it was 'not at liberty, under present circumstances', to allow Lauder to be admitted. It instructed the session involved to proceed in discipline against both parties.

2. F.C.G.A.P. & D., 1849, Debates, p.87.

3. *Ibid.*

4. *Ibid.*

5. *Ibid.*, p.88.

6. *Ibid.*, p.89.

7. *Ibid.*

8. *Ibid.* MDWS was not, according to Behrman (*op.cit.*, p.494), a subject which feminists were very interested in. They were, Behrman suggests, more concerned with the subject of married women's property. That, needless to say, was a matter never even mentioned in the Free Assembly.

9. F.C.G.A.P. & D: 1850: Debates: pp.195ff. and p.289.

10. *Ibid.*, p.195.

11. *Vide* C. of S.G.A., Acts, (1844-50), 1849, pp.51 and 59;
1850, pp.69ff.
C. of S.G.A., Acts, (1851-58), 1855, p.56.
C. of S.G.A., Acts, (1859-65), 1859, p.82.

12. C. of S. Acts, (1866-72), 1869, p.69.

13. It should be noted however, so as not to get the subject even more out of proportion than the Free Church itself did, that its debates on MDWS occupied only a few hours during the 12 days on which it met each year.

14. F.C.G.A.P. & D., 1850, Debates, p.195. The MDWS controversy incidentally made bedfellows of the Free Church and High Anglicans, since, as Cunningham defensively explained to the 1861 Assembly (F.C.G.A.P. & D., 1861, Debates, p.349), their views were 'generally very sound upon questions of this kind'.

15. F.C.G.A.P. & D., 1855, Debates, Tuesday June 5.

16. *Vide* Appendix.

17. James Gibson: *Marriage Affinity Question: Or, Marriage With The Sister of A Deceased Wife Fully Discussed, In The Light Of History, Ecclesiastical and Civil Law, Scripture, Reason, And Expediency*: 1854. There were in fact many definitive books on MDWS. E.S. Turner (*Roads to Ruin*, Penguin 1966 Edition, p.112) notes that 'it would take a man more than a year, reading the equivalent of a book a day, to toil through the vast morass of literature inspired by the theme of marrying a deceased wife's sister'. Mr. Turner does not however provide a comprehensive bibliography: but then if the rest of this literature is like Gibson's book, or the *Marriage Law Defence Tracts*, one can hardly blame him.

18. F.C.G.A.P. & D., 1869, Debates, p.275. The irony is doubtless unintended.

19. *Ibid.*, pp.273ff.

20. *Ibid.*, p.274.

21. Gibson: *op.cit.*, p.82.

22. F.C.G.A.P. & D., 1869, Debates, p.274.

23. *Ibid.*

24. *Ibid.*

25. T. Chalmers (ed. Hannah): *Daily Scripture Readings*, 1848, p.225.

26. Gibson: *op.cit.*, p.158.

27. *Ibid.*

28. F.C.G.A.P. & D., 1871, Debates, p.273.

29. F.C.G.A.P. & D., 1853, Debates, p.186.

30. F.C.G.A.P. & D., 1871, Debates, p.273.

31. *Ibid.*, pp.273-4. Rainy did however later claim that the interpretation of Leviticus 18:18 as a reference to polygamy was 'dubious' (*ibid.*, p.276) and not fully established.

32. F.C.G.A.P. & D., 1871, Debates, p.274.

33. *Ibid.*

34. *Ibid.*

35. *Ibid.*, p.275.

36. *Ibid.*

37. Jewish advocates of MDWS were usually given short shrift in the Free Assembly. Dr. Adler, the Chief Rabbi in London, had given evidence in favour of MDWS to the Royal Commission. In his book Gibson roundly contradicted Dr. Adler (Gibson: *op.cit.*, pp.12ff.); and Mr. Montgomery of Innerleithen asked the 1855 Assembly (F.C.G.A.P. & D., 1855, Debates, June 5) why they should regard as an authority on Jewish Law and the Old Testament one who was 'the living representative of the very men of whom our Saviour said, that they made the law of God void through their tradition'.

38. *Ibid.*, p.277.

39. Similar views to Rainy's were expressed by Begg, who addressed the Assembly of 1870 (among others) on the subject. (*Vide* F.C.G.A.P. & D., 1870, Debates, p.329.) Begg wanted 'simple and clear' principles, such as the Confession, he believed, gave, and appealed 'to the God of holiness and order'.

40. F.C.G.A.P. & D., 1855, Debates, June 5.

41. *Ibid.*

42. *Ibid.*

43. F.C.G.A.P. & D., 1871, Debates, p.276.
44. *Ibid.*
45. F.C.G.A.P. & D., 1855, Debates, June 5.
46. F.C.G.A.P. & D., 1869, Debates, p.276.
47. *Ibid.*
48. F.C.G.A.P. & D., 1855, Debates, June 5.
49. *Ibid.*
50. F.C.G.A.P. & D., 1861, Debates, p.350.
51. *Ibid.*
52. F.C.G.A.P. & D., 1855, Debates, June 5.
53. F.C.G.A.P. & D., 1869, Debates, p.8.
54. F.C.G.A.P. & D., 1872, Report XXV, p.1.
55. *Ibid.*
56. Gladstone's own views on MDWS were quoted by Candlish in the 1879 Assembly. (F.C.G.A.P. & D., 1879, Debates, p.227.) He had remarked, in his characteristic prose:

> The culmination and perfection of the Christian morality was found in that high and severe doctrine of marriage, against which we may confidently anticipate, and almost venture to predict, that the anti-Christian spirit will direct its first attack, encouraged by those preliminary operations in the legislative reaction of divorce, which have already, through a variety of ill-omened causes, found a place upon our own as well as upon other statute books.

Gladstone had also said (*ibid.*) that the existing law

> with its restraint of kin of unity and of perpetuity, is perhaps the subtlest as well as the most powerful of all the social instruments which the Almighty has put into use for the education of the race, and it is one, I am firmly persuaded, which no self-acting force, or any considerations of policy, will ever be able to uphold in modern societies when it shall have been severed from its authoritative source.

57. *Vide* F.C.G.A.P. & D., 1872, Report XXV, p.1.
58. *Vide* F.C.G.A.P. & D., 1873, Report XXVIII, p.1.
59. *Vide* F.C.G.A.P. & D., 1877, Report XXVIII, p.1.
60. *Vide* F.C.G.A.P. & D., 1876, Report XXVIII, p.1.
61. *Vide* F.C.G.A.P. & D., 1879, Report XXVII, p.1.
62. F.C.G.A.P. & D., 1879, Report XXVII, p.4.
63. *Ibid.*, p.1.
64. F.C.G.A.P. & D., 1883, Report XXIV, pp.1-8.
65. *Ibid.*, Debate, p.167. Begg also 'regretted to see princes of the blood busying themselves in connection with this foul proposed change'. The Prince of Wales (later Edward VII) was in favour of MDWS. Dalhousie, at this time representing the Home Office in the Lords in Gladstone's administration, went on to introduce an MDWS Bill soon after. He was not however able to lead the marriage law reformers for long, for he died, in 1887, of apoplexy, within twenty-four hours of his wife's death. He was only forty. Local (Brechin) Free Church as well as U.P. and Church of Scotland ministers joined in paying memorial tributes to him. (*Vide*: S. Hay: *Biographical Sketch of the Life of the Earl and Countess of Dalhousie*, 1888, *passim.*).
66. F.C.G.A.P. & D., 1883, Report XXIV, p.2.
67. *Ibid.*, p.3.
68. *Ibid.*, pp.4ff.
69. *Ibid.*, p.5.
70. *Ibid.*
71. *Ibid.*
72. *Ibid.*
73. *Ibid.*
74. *Ibid.*, p.7.

75. *Ibid.*
76. *Ibid.*
77. *Ibid.*
78. *Ibid.*
79. *Ibid.*
80. *Ibid.*, pp.7ff.
81. *Ibid.*
82. *Ibid.*
83. F.C.G.A.P. & D., 1888, Debates, p.67.
84. F.C.G.A.P. & D., 1879, Debates, p.228.
85. F.C.G.A.P. & D., 1883, Debates, p.168.
86. *Ibid.*, p.169.
87. F.C.G.A.P. & D., 1884, Debates, p.199.
88. F.C.G.A.P. & D., 1883, Debates, p.168.
89. *Vide* F.C.G.A.P. & D., 1888, Debates, p.68.
90. *Vide* F.C.G.A.P. & D., 1890, Debates, p.253. Opposition to MDWS may have hardened at this point, since a Bill to legalise it in Scotland was before Parliament in 1889 and 1890. (*Vide ibid.*, p.252, and F.C.G.A.P. & D., 1889, Report XXVIII, p.1.)
91. *Vide* F.C.G.A.P. & D., 1895, Debates, p.195.
92. *Vide* F.C.G.A.P. & D., 1896, Debates, p.187.
93. The committee's silence may in part have had to do with the fact that J.S. Candlish, its dedicated convener during the last two decades of the century, died in 1897.
94. *Vide* C. of S.G.A. Acts (1866-72), 1872, pp.75 and 81.
95. *Ibid.*, p.81.
96. *Vide* C. of S.G.A. Acts (1876-81), 1876, p.100.
97. *Vide* C. of S.G.A. Acts (1876-81), 1880, p.82.
98. U.P.S.P. (1847-1856), 1853, p.436. This request was made prior to the decisive case of *Fenton* v. *Livingstone* of 1861. It was also made by the same Synod which declined to pass judgement on the 'separation of Christian Spouses' question: *vide* chapter eight above.
99. U.P.S.P. (1847-1856), 1854, pp.527ff., and p.530.
100. U.P.S.P. (1877-1879), 1878, p.384.
101. *Ibid.*
102. *Ibid.*
103. *Ibid.*, p.385.
104. *Ibid.*, p.597.
105. U.P.S.P. (1877-1879), 1879, p.651.
106. *Ibid.*
107. U.P.S.P. (1880-1882), 1880, p.43.
108. The Free Church did not pass its Declaratory Act on the subject until 1892.
109. U.P.S.P. (1880-1882), 1880, p.43. MDWS was not of course specifically mentioned in the Act, but it could easily be argued by analogy that it was a case of the type with which the Act could deal.
110. U.P.S.P. 1897, p.436.
111. *Ibid.*, p.49.
112. U.P.S.P. 1898, p.213.
113. *Ibid.*, p.51.
114. U.P.S.P., 1899, p.23. It may be added here that some individual U.P.s were notable opponents of MDWS. Duncan McLaren, for example (although his brother-in-law, John Bright, was an advocate of MDWS), took Free Church petitions against it to Parliament (*vide* e.g. F.C.G.A.P. & D., 1880, Debates, p.55); and William Lindsay, the U.P. Professor of Sacred Languages and Biblical Criticism published, in 1871, his *Inquiry into the Christian Law as to the Relationships which Bar Marriage*, a more readable anti-MDWS volume than that of Gibson. The opposition to MDWS of John Cairns and Andrew Thomson has

already been mentioned.

115. *Vide* Behrman: *op.cit.* pp.495ff.

116. U.F.C.G.A.P. & D., 1908, Debates, p.370.

117. U.F.C.G.A.P. & D., 1909, Report XXXVI, p.1.

118. *Ibid.*, p.2.

119. *Ibid.*, p.3.

120. *Ibid.*, p.3. The Federated Church of Australia had given no judgement on the subject.

121. *Ibid.*

122. *Ibid.*

123. *Ibid.*, p.4.

124. *Ibid.*, Debates, p.353.

125. *Ibid.*

126. *Ibid.*

127. *Ibid.*

128. *Ibid.* Dr. Henderson added that the committee had thought about making a statement on marriage with a deceased brother's wife, since there had 'been cases of that kind within our Church' (*ibid.*). In the end, however, they decided not to raise this question.

129. C. of S.G.A. Acts (1903-1910), 1908, p.59.

130. C. of S.G.A. Reports, 1909, p.1260.

131. In the course of which he touched, not very conclusively, on the examples of Adam, Abram, Jacob and others. These cases, which were mentioned from time to time during the controversy, were ones which anti-MDWS churchmen had never been very sure how to deal with.

132. *Ibid.*, p.1280.

133. *Ibid.*, p.1281.

134. *Ibid.*, p.1282.

135. Professor Nicol remarked that he 'deplored' the MDWS Act, but on social and not scriptural grounds. *Ibid.*, p.1285.

136. *Ibid.*, p.1284.

137. *Vide* H.J. Wotherspoon: *James Cooper*, 1926, pp.128, 219, 239ff., 261 and 330. Cooper was later to be an active opponent of what he considered to be doctrinal watering-down in the discussions about union with the U.F. Church.

138. C. of S.G.A. Reports, 1909, p.1293.

139. *Ibid.*

140. *Ibid.*, p.1294.

141. *Ibid.*, p.1295.

142. C. of S.G.A. Reports, 1909, p.1295.

143. *Ibid.*

144. *Ibid.*, pp.1295ff.

145. H.J. Wotherspoon, *op.cit.*, pp.342ff.

146. *Ibid.*, p.55.

147. *Ibid.*, p.266.

148. C. of S.G.A. Reports, 1909, p.1287.

149. I.e. J.F. McLennan (1827-81), the Scottish lawyer whose *Primitive Marriage* (1865) had put forward the view that marriage and kinship customs went through the stages of 1, promiscuity, 2, kinship traced through females only, 3, kinship traced through males only, and 4, monogamy with kinship traced through males and females. This idea of universal evolution was discarded by later anthropologists, because, among other reasons, the data on which it was based were insufficient and contradicted by later fieldwork. (*Vide* R. Fox: *Kinship and Marriage*, 1967, pp.17ff.) Sorley seems to accept this.

150. C. of S.G.A. Reports, 1909, p.1287.

151. *Ibid.*

152. *Ibid.*
153. *Ibid.*, p.1288.
154. *Ibid.*
155. *Ibid.*
156. *Ibid.*
157. *Ibid.*, p.1289.
158. *Ibid.*
159. *Ibid.*, p.1290.
160. A form of protection unnecessary in Scotland where clergymen were not compelled to marry anyone.
161. *Ibid.*, p.1292.
162. *Ibid.*
163. *Ibid.*, p.1262.
164. The Act which had been necessary to sort out the Free Church case. The new formula gave Church of Scotland ministers some of the freedom granted by the U.P. and Free Church Declaratory Acts.
165. *Ibid.*, p.1263.
166. *Ibid.*, pp.1263ff.
167. *Ibid.*, p.1263.
168. *Ibid.*, p.1267.
169. *Ibid.*, p.1268.
170. C. of S.G.A. *Acts*, (1903-1910), 1909, p.47.
171. *Ibid.*, 1910, p.55.
172. *Ibid.*, p.29:

> Whereas marriage between a man and the sister of his deceased wife has hitherto been prohibited by the law both of the Church and of the State: Whereas Parliament has now enacted that this marriage shall be lawful and valid as regards civil relations, and whereas this marriage is not contrary to any rule expressly declared in or plainly deducible from the Holy Scriptures, and the matter is one of interpretation which does not enter into the substance of the faith, the General Assembly, with consent of the majority of the Presbyteries of the Church, hereby enact and declare that marriage between a man and the sister of his deceased wife shall not be visited by any ecclesiastical censure or disability either upon the minister proclaiming the banns for this marriage or celebrating it, or upon the parties contracting it.

173. *Vide ibid.*, p.82.
174. H.J. Wotherspoon: *op.cit.*, p.330.
175. C. of S.G.A. Reports, 1933, pp.41ff.
176. *Ibid.*, p.46.
177. *Ibid.*
178. C. of S.G.A. Reports, 1909, p.1261.
179. Cmd. 9678, pp.298ff.
180. *Ibid.*, p.302.
181. *Ibid.*, p.300.
182. The Church of England initially (Lambeth Conference 1908) decided to regard MDWS as 'a marriage ecclesiastically irregular while not constituting the parties "open and notorious evil livers" ', but there had been some difficult cases involving church-state dissension, and a revised Table of Consanguinity and Affinity, excluding the degrees relaxed by the 1907-1931 legislation, was adopted in Canon 99 of 1946. (*vide* Haw: *op.cit.*, pp.122ff.)
183. Cmd. 9678, p.300.
184. Cox p.56.
185. Cmd. 4011, p.16.

Chapter eighteen

1. C. of S.G.A. Reports, 1909, p.1296.
2. *Ibid.*
3. Gibson: *op.cit.*, p.41.
4. C. of S.G.A. Reports, 1909, p.1290.
5. *Vide* F. Steiner: *Taboo*, 1967 Pelican edition, p.51.
6. Turner: *op.cit.*, p.122. The suggestion was made at a Glasgow meeting and (*ibid.*) 'received with cries of "hear, hear"'.
7. Gibson: *op.cit.*, p.143. As an afterthought he added, in a footnote (*ibid.*), 'The history of Nunneries furnishes an illustration of the same terrible truth.'
8. *Ibid.* This conviction gave him the incidental bonus of an extra scriptural argument against MDWS: if true, it was also adultery, according to Matthew 5:27, 28.
9. *Vide* A.L. Drummond and J. Bulloch: *The Church in Late Victorian Scotland*, 1978, p.74.
10. *Vide* F. Steiner: *op.cit.*, Chapters IV-VI.
11. *Ibid.*, pp.74ff. The phrases are from Robertson Smith's *Religion of the Semites* (1889 and 1894).
12. F.C.G.A.P. & D., 1883, Report XXIV, p.5.
13. Gibson: *op.cit.*, p.53.
14. J.T. McNeill: *The History and Character of Calvinism*, 1967 edition, p.396.
15. *Vide*, e.g. *Institutes* II, 10, 20: 'The Lord held to this orderly plan in administering the covenant of his mercy: as the day of full revelation approached with the passing of time the more he increased each day the brightness of its manifestation.'
16. F.C.G.A.P. & D., 183, Report XXIV,p.5.
17. C. of S.G.A. Reports, 1909, p.1290.

Postscript

1. *The Confession of Faith*, 1647, Chapter XXIV.
2. *The Larger Catechism*, 1648, Questions 123-133 and 137-139; *The Shorter Catechism*, 1648, Questions 64-66 and 70-72.
3. The Calvinist tradition, it can be argued, acknowledged the equality of male and female. Commenting on Genesis 2:18, Calvin prefers to read, 'I will make him a help "which may be like him"', since, as he put it, 'Moses intended to note some equality' (Calvin: *Harmony*, Vol.I, p.131.), and in general Calvin emphasises the element of companionship, which implies some idea of equality. But how far Calvin intended the idea of equality to go is not clear, for the woman's role is defined only in relation to the man ('woman is given as a companion and an associate to the man' (*ibid.*, p.129.)); and when he comments on I Corinthians, 14:34, Calvin argues that the reason for women being commanded to keep silent in church is obvious: 'how unsuitable it would be for a woman, who is in subjection to one of the members, to be in an authoritative position over the whole body' (Calvin: *Commentary on I Corinthians* (1960 translation), p.306.). Admittedly, Calvin allows that 'a situation can arise where there is a need of such a kind as calls for a woman to speak'; but the note of male chauvinism keeps on breaking through: 'there is no doubt that wherever natural propriety has its effect, women in all ages have been excluded from the control of public affairs. And common sense tells us that the rule of women is improper and defective' (*ibid.*). The Calvinist view on sexual equality is thus rather ambivalent, and this is reflected in the churches' pronouncements, or rather in the lack of them: for whatever importance they may have attached to female equality in the regulationist and affinity controversies, they do not seem to have considered it sufficiently important to make equally vehement pronouncements about female equality in relation to the then controversial issues of women's entry into the professions, their civil enfranchisement, or, if they were married, their property rights.

To be scrupulously fair, however, it must be admitted that in the United Presbyterian and Free churches, women were allowed to take part when congregations called a new minister. This voting right was conferred on women by the Burghers in 1747, and was continued in the United Secession and, later, the United Presbyterian church. By an extension of the Veto Act in 1843 they were given the same right in the Free Church, with the warm approval of James Begg and in the teeth of opposition from James Gibson, who argued 'that the Word of God made it plain that this was "not a right which females should exercise" and . . . desired "to protect them from the habits of public debate and collision"'. (J.R. Fleming: *op.cit.*, vol.i, pp.44ff; *cf.* R. Small: *History of the Congregations of the United Presbyterian Church*, 1904, vol.i, pp.711ff.) Women were also able, in the Church of Scotland, to exercise the rights of patronage (*vide* A.L. Drummond and J. Bulloch: *The Church in Victorian Scotland*, 1975, p.115.)

4. M.O.W. Oliphant: *op.cit.*, p.397.
5. H.J. Wotherspoon: *op.cit.*, p.239.
6. D. MacMillan: *op.cit.*, p.364.
7. J.R. Fleming: *op.cit.*, vol.i, p.94.
8. R. Flint: *Socialism*, 1895, pp.282ff. Flint argued that Socialist criticism of 'modern domestic life' was not without foundation, but that the Socialist alternative, 'absorption of the family into the community, free love, the separation of spouses at will, transference of children from the charge of their parents to that of the State', would 'introduce evils far worse'. He did not produce any evidence to prove this, however. He then went on to state that 'the autonomy of the family' must be protected from 'the encroachment of the community', and to argue in favour of extending women's rights and opportunities. This would 'favour the formation of a better class of women' and would 'increase the number of women who are not necessitated to enter upon loveless marriages'. As such, it was a superior alternative to the 'slavery' women, forced to work by being freed from their families, would have to undergo under Socialism.
9. W.G. Blaikie: *Recollections of a Busy Life*, 1901, p.196.
10. W.S. Bruce: *Social Aspects of Christian Morality*, 1905, Chapters III and IV.
11. D. Macleod: *op.cit.*, p.455.
12. *Ibid.*, p.507.
13. *Ibid.*
14. *Vide* N. Berdyaev: *The Destiny of Man*, 1937, pp.232ff.

Bibliography

(The place of publication is Edinburgh unless otherwise stated.)

I. *Assembly and Synod Records*

Acts of the General Assembly of the Church of Scotland, 1538-1843, I Vol., 1843.

Acts of the General Assembly of the Church of Scotland, 1843-1914.

Reports of the General Assembly of the Church of Scotland, 1843-1918, 1920, 1933, 1944-1946.

Acts of the General Assembly of the Free Church of Scotland, 1843-1900.

Proceedings and Debates of the General Assembly of the Free Church of Scotland (including Reports), 1843-1900.

United Presbyterian Synod Papers, 1847-1900.

Acts of the General Assembly of the United Free Church of Scotland, 1900-1914.

Proceedings and Debates of the General Assembly of the United Free Church of Scotland, 1900-1919.

General Assembly of the Free Church of Scotland, Papers, 1849.

J. Wilson: *Index to the Acts and Proceedings of the General Assembly of the Church of Scotland from the Revolution to the Present Time,* 1843.

J.A. McClymont: *Index to the Acts and Proceedings of the General Assembly of the Church of Scotland,* 1871-1923.

II. *General*

W. Acton: *The Functions and Disorders of the Reproductive Organs*, 6th Edtn., London 1875.

W. Acton: *Prostitution*, 2nd. Edtn., London 1870.

W. Aiton: *General View of Agriculture in the County of Ayr*, London 1811.

A. Ashley: *The Honourable Estate*, London 1950.

W.H. Auden: *Collected Shorter Poems, 1930-1944*, London 1950.

D.S. Bailey: *Sexual Offenders and Social Punishment*, London 1956.

D.S. Bailey: *The Man-Woman Relation in Christian Thought*, London 1959.

J.A. and O. Banks: *Feminism and Family Planning in Victorian England*, Liverpool 1964.

J.A. Banks: *Prosperity and Parenthood*, London 1954.

J. Barr: *The United Free Church of Scotland*, London 1934.

C.F. Behrman: 'The Annual Blister', in *Victorian Studies*, Vol.XI, No.4, June 1963, pp.483ff.

N.W. Bell and E.F. Vogel: *A Modern Introduction to the Family*, New York and London 1968.

H. Benjamin and R.E.L. Masters: *Prostitution and Morality*, London 1965.

N. Berdyaev: *The Destiny of Man*, London 1937.

G.F.A. Best: *Mid-Victorian Britain*, London 1971.

D.H. Bishop: *Church and Society*, Unpublished Edinburgh Thesis, 1952.

J.S. Blackie: *The Life of Robert Burns*, London 1888.

W.G. Blaikie: *Better Days for Working People*, London 1867.

W.G. Blaikie: *For the Work of the Ministry*, London 1885.

W.G. Blaikie: *Recollections of a Busy Life*, London 1901.

W.S. Bruce: *Social Aspects of Christian Morality*, London 1905.

C.E. Buckland: *Dictionary of Indian Biography*, London 1906.

J.H.S. Burleigh: *A Church History of Scotland*, London 1960.

W.L. Burn: *The Age of Equipoise*, London 1964.

J.E. Butler: *Personal Reminiscences of a Great Crusade*, London 1910.

D.S. Cairns (ed.): *The Army and Religion*, London 1919.

J. Calvin: *Commentary on I Corinthians*, 1960 Translation.

J. Calvin: *Commentaries on Genesis*, 1850 Translation, 2 Vols.

J. Calvin: *The Harmony of the Four Last Books of the Pentateuch*, 1854 Translation, 4 Vols.

J. Calvin: *The Institutes of the Christian Religion*, London 1961 Translation, 2 Vols.

L.L.L. Cameron: *The Challenge of Need*, 1971.

R.H. Campbell: *Scotland Since 1707*, Oxford 1965.

R.H. Campbell and J.B.A. Dow: *Source Book of Scottish Economic and Social History*, Oxford 1968.

T. Chalmers (ed. Hannah), *Daily Scripture Readings*, 1848.

Church of Scotland Committee on Aids to Devotion: *Family Prayers*, 1871.

Church of Scotland Committee on Aids to Devotion: *Prayers for Social and Family Worship for the use of soldiers, sailors, colonists, sojourners in India, and other persons at home or abroad, who are deprived of the ordinary services of a Christian Ministry*, 1889.

Church of Scotland: *Life and Work*, 1879-1885.

Church of Scotland (ed. W.P. Paterson and D. Watson): *Social Evils and Problems*, 1918.

Church of Scotland (ed. J. Baillie): *God's Will for Church and Nation*, London 1946.

I.M. Clark: *A History of Church Discipline in Scotland*, Aberdeen 1929.

W.G. Cole: *Sex and Love in the Bible*, London 1960 Edtn.

W.G. Cole: *Sex in Christianity and Psychoanalysis*, New York 1966.

A. Comfort: *The Anxiety Makers*, London 1968.

The Concise Dictionary of National Biography, Parts I and II, London 1953 and 1961.

J. Cox (ed. J.B. Longmuir): *Practice and Procedure in the Church of Scotland*, 1964.

D. Craig: *Scottish Literature and the Scottish People*, London 1961.

A.L. Drummond: *The Churches Pictured by 'Punch'*, London 1947.

A.L. Drummond and J. Bulloch: *The Church in Victorian Scotland, 1843-1874*, 1975.

A.L. Drummond and J. Bulloch: *The Church in Late Victorian Scotland, 1874-1900*, 1978.

A. Edgar: *The Church and the Marriage Notice Act*, Paisley 1878.

M. Edwardes: *Bound to Exile*, Newton Abbot 1969.

D. Elder: *Union Free Church*, London and Glasgow 1894.

G. Eliot: *Middlemarch*, 1871-72.

G. Eliot: *Scenes of Clerical Life*, 1857.

H. Ellis: *Studies in the Psychology of Sex*, Vol.VI, Philadelphia 1919.

R. Ensor: *England, 1870-1914*, Oxford 1936.

P. Fairbairn: *Pastoral Theology*, 1875.

T. Ferguson: *The Dawn of Scottish Social Welfare*, 1948.

W. Ferguson: *Scotland, 1689 to the Present*, 1968.

H.C. Fischer and E.X. Dubois: *Sexual Life During the World War*, London 1937.

J.R. Fleming: *A History of the Church in Scotland*, Vol.I, 1927. Vol.II, 1933.

A. Fletcher: *Guide for Family Devotions*, London 1835.

R. Fletcher: *The Family and Marriage in Britain*, Harmondsworth 1966 Edtn.

A. Flexner: *Prostitution in Europe*, London 1919 Edtn.

M. Flinn et al: *Scottish Population History from the seventeenth century to the 1930s*, Cambridge 1977.

R. Flint: *Socialism*, London 1895.

A.H.L. Fraser: *Among Indian Rajahs and Ryots*, London 1912.

D. Fraser: *The Story of Invergordon Church*, Inverness 1946.

P. Fryer: *The Birth Controllers*, London 1965.

R. Fox: *Kinship and Marriage*, Harmondsworth 1967.

J. Gibson: *Marriage Affinity Question: Or, Marriage with the Sister Of A Deceased Wife Fully Discussed, In The Light of History, Ecclesiastical And Civil Law, Scripture, Reason, And Expediency*, Glasgow 1854.

R.J. Godlee: *Lord Lister*, London 1917.

W.J. Goode: *The Family*, Englewood Cliffs, New Jersey 1964.

A. Gordon: *The Life of Archibald Hamilton Charteris*, London 1912.

H.G. Graham: *Social Life in Scotland in the Eighteenth Century*, London 1906.

A. Gray: *Talks With Our Farm Servants*, 1906.

A.H. Gray: *About People*, London 1934.

A.H. Gray: *Men, Women and God*, London 1923.

D. Guthrie: *A History of Medicine*, London, 1958 Edtn.

T. Guthrie (ed. Guthrie and Guthrie): *Autobiography and Memoir of Thomas Guthrie*, London 1877.

T. Guthrie: *The City, Its Sins and Sorrows*, 1858.

R. Haw: *The State of Matrimony*, London 1952.

S. Hay: *Biographical Sketch of the Life of the Earl and Countess of Dalhousie*, Dunoon 1888.

G.D. Henderson: *The Scottish Ruling Elder*, London n.d.

F. Henriques: *Modern Sexuality*, London 1968.

W.E. Houghton: *The Victorian Frame of Mind, 1830-1870*, New Haven and London 1957.
R. Howie: *The Churches and the Churchless in Scotland*, Glasgow 1893.
M. Jaeger: *Before Victoria*, Harmondsworth 1956.
T. Johnston: *History of the Working Classes in Scotland*, Glasgow 1921.
J. Knox: *History of the Reformation*, London 1644.
T.A. Lacey (ed. R.C. Mortimer): *Marriage in Church and State*, London 1947.
B. Leppington: 'Public Morals and the Public Health', in J. Marchant (ed.), *Public Morals,* London n.d. (circa 1902).
W. Lindsay: *Enquiry into the Christian Law as to the Relationships which Bar Marriage*, London 1871.
W. Logan: *The Great Social Evil*, London 1871.
D. MacColl: *Among the Masses; or, Work in the Wynds,* London 1867.
D.R. Mace: *Hebrew Marriage*, London 1953.
A.R. MacEwan: *Life and Letters of John Cairns*, London 1898.
J.B. Mackie: *The Life and Work of Duncan McLaren*, London 1888, 2 Vols.
J. MacIntosh: *The History of Civilization in Scotland*, Paisley 1893, 4 Vols.
A.A. MacLaren: 'Presbyterianism and the working class in a mid-nineteenth century city', *Scottish Historical Review*, Vol.46 (1967), pp.115ff.
A.A. MacLaren: *Religion and Social Class*, London 1974.
A.A. MacLaren (ed.): *Social Class in Scotland*, 1976.
D. Macleod: *Memoir of Norman Macleod*, London 1877.
D. MacMillan: *The Life of Robert Flint*, London 1914.
J. MacMurray: *Reason and Emotion*, London 1936.
J.T. McNeill: *The History and Character of Calvinism*, London 1967 Edtn.
S. Marcus: *The Other Victorians*, London 1966.
Marriage Law Defence Union: *Tracts*, London 1884.
J.S. Marshall: 'Irregular Marriage in Scotland as Reflected in Kirk Session Records', *Records of the Scottish Church History Society*, 1972, Vol.XVIII, Part 1.
W.H. Marwick: *A Short History of Labour in Scotland*, 1967.
S. Mechie: *The Church and Scottish Social Development, 1780-1870*, London 1960.
J.S. Mill: *On Liberty*, 1859. (London 1910, Everyman Edtn.)
Hugh Miller: *Essays*, 1869.
R. Mitchison: *A History of Scotland*, London 1970.
J. Morris: *Farewell the Trumpets*, London 1978.
R.C. Mortimer et al: *Putting Asunder*, London 1966.
A.L. Morton: *The Life and Ideas of Robert Owen*, London 1969.
R.S. Morton: 'Some Aspects of the Early History of Syphilis in Scotland', in *British Journal of Venereal Diseases*, 1962, 38, 175.
R.S. Morton: *Venereal Diseases*, Harmondsworth 1966.
A. Muir: *John White*, London 1958.
I.A. Muirhead: 'Churchmen and the Problems of Prostitution in Nineteenth-Century Scotland', *Records of the Scottish Church History Society*, 1974, Vol.XVIII, Part 3.
New Statistical Account, Vol.XIV, (Ross and Cromarty), 1845.

New Statistical Account, Vol.XIII, (Banff), 1845.
D.E. Nineham: *St. Mark*, Harmondsworth 1963.
J. Noble: *Religious Life in Ross*, Inverness 1909.
M.O.W. Oliphant: *A Memoir of the Life of John Tulloch*, 1888.
Parliamentary Papers, London 1868, *Royal Commision on the Law of Marriage.*
Parliamentary Papers, London 1956, *Royal Commission on Marriage and Divorce, 1951-1956*, 1956 Cmnd. 9678.
G. Petrie: *A Singular Iniquity*, London 1971.
N. Phillipson and R. Mitchison (eds.): *Scotland in the Age of Improvement*, 1970.
G.M. Reith: *Reminiscences of the United Free Church General Assembly*, 1934.
P. Rieff: *The Triumph of the Therapeutic*, London 1966.
C. Rogers: *Social Life in Scotland*, 1884, 3 Vols.
A. Ross: 'Reformation and Repression', in D. McRoberts (ed.): *Essays on the Scottish Reformation*, Glasgow 1962.
E. Schillebeeckx: *Marriage, Secular Reality and Saving Mystery*, London 1965 Translation, 2 Vols.
L.L. Schücking: *The Puritan Family*, London 1969 Translation.
Scottish Home and Health Department: *The Marriage Law of Scotland*, 1969, Cmnd. 4011.
E. Shorter: *The Making of the Modern Family*, London 1976.
P.C. Simpson: *The Life of Principal Rainy*, London 1909, 2 Vols.
R. Small: *History of the Congregations of the United Presbyterian Church*, 1904, 2 Vols.
D.C. Smith: *The Failure and Recovery of Social Criticism in the Scottish Church*, Unpublished Edinburgh Thesis, 1964.
S.G. Smith (ed.): *The Merry Muses of Caledonia*, London 1966 Edtn.
T. Smith: *Memoir of James Begg*, 1885, 2 Vols.
T.C. Smout: *A History of the Scottish People, 1560-1830*, London 1969.
P. Spear: *A History of India*, Vol. 2, Harmondsworth 1965.
F. Steiner: *Taboo*, Harmondsworth 1967 Edtn.
Stephenson Locomotive Society: *The Highland Railway Company*, London 1953.
W. Tait: *Magdalenism*, 1842.
O. Temkin: *The Double Face of Janus and other Essays in the History of Medicine*, Baltimore 1977.
E. Troeltsch: *The Social Teaching of the Christian Churches*, New York 1931 Translation.
R. Truax: *Joseph Lister*, London 1947.
E.S. Turner: *Roads to Ruin*, Harmondsworth 1966 Edtn.
United Presbyterian Church: *United Presbyterian Monthly Record*, 1858.
United Presbyterian Church: *United Presbyterian Missionary Record*, 1887.
Various Ministers of Glasgow: *Lectures on the Social and Physical Condition of the People, especially in Large Towns*, Glasgow 1843.
R. Wallace: 'Church Tendencies in Scotland', in A. Grant (ed.): *Recess Studies*, 1870.
R. Wallace (ed. Smith and Wallace): *Life and Last Leaves*, London 1903.

R. Wardlaw: *Lectures on Female Prostitution*, Glasgow 1842.
M. Weber: *The Sociology of Religion*, London 1956 Translation.
E. Westermarck: *The History of Human Marriage*, London 1931, 3 Vols.
The Witness, Jan-May 1858.
C. Woodham-Smith: *Florence Nightingale*, London 1952 Edtn.
H.J. Wotherspoon: *James Cooper*, London 1926.
J. Wylie: *Disruption Worthies*, 1881.
G.M. Young: *Portrait of an Age*, London 1936.

Index